R. Gupta's®

Popular Master Guide

BA Hons. ENGLISH

Entrance Test

For **Jamia Millia Islamia** and
Guru Gobind Singh Indraprastha University

2027
EDITION

RAMESH PUBLISHING HOUSE, NEW DELHI

Published by

O.P. Gupta *for* Ramesh Publishing House

Admin. Office

12-H, New Daryaganj Road, Opp. Officers' Mess,
New Delhi-110002 ✆ 23275224, 23245124

E-mail: info@rameshpublishinghouse.com
For Online Shopping: www.rameshpublishinghouse.com

Showroom

• Balaji Market, Nai Sarak, Delhi-110006 ✆ 23282525 📱 9354373464
• 4457, Nai Sarak, Delhi-110006

Book Code: R-1962

ISBN: 978-93-87604-51-3

Price: ₹ 390

Printed at: Deepak Offset, Delhi

Contents

SCHEME OF EXAMINATION

Jamia Millia Islamia, B.A. Honours (English)

Part A – 40 Objective Type Questions

Maximum Marks : 40 [1 mark each]

40 Multiple Choice Questions on authors, books, current literary scene in India and abroad

Part B

Maximum Marks : 60

Unseen Passage for Comprehension: 20 marks

Grammar and Vocabulary : 10 marks

Essay : 30 marks

Previous Years' Paper

JAMIA MILLIA ISLAMIA

B.A. (HONS.) ENGLISH

Entrance Exam-2025

(Exam held on 24-04-2025)

PART-A

1. Which writer won the 2024 Nobel Prize in Literature for their poetic prose dealing with historical trauma?
   A. Han Kang
   B. Olga Tokarczuk
   C. Annie Ernaux
   D. Orhan Pamuk

2. What is the pen name of Mary Ann Evans, author of *Middlemarch*?
   A. Emily Brontë
   B. Elizabeth Gaskell
   C. Charlotte Perkins
   D. George Eliot

3. What is the literary term for a story within a story?
   A. Allegory
   B. Frame narrative
   C. Irony
   D. Parable

4. *The Divine Comedy* was originally written in which language?
   A. French
   B. Old English
   C. Italian
   D. Latin

5. Which Shakespeare play features the characters Rosencrantz and Guildenstern?
   A. Othello
   B. Macbeth
   C. The Tempest
   D. Hamlet

6. Who is the author of the bestselling self-help book *Atomic Habits*?
   A. Cal Newport
   B. James Clear
   C. Mark Manson
   D. Charles Duhigg

7. The Italian or Petrarchan sonnet is divided into:
   A. Three quatrains and a couplet
   B. An octave and a sestet
   C. Four couplets and a refrain
   D. Two sestets

8. Which ancient Indian text is known as the world's longest epic poem?
   A. Ramayana
   B. Bhagavad Gita
   C. Arthashastra
   D. Mahabharata

1. A	2. D	3. B	4. C	5. D	6. B	7. B	8. D

9. Who was awarded the 2025 Holberg Prize?

A. Homi K. Bhabha
B. Judith Butler
C. Arundhati Roy
D. Gayatri Chakravorty Spivak

10. What is the primary genre of Gabriel García Márquez's *One Hundred Years of Solitude*?

A. Fantasy
B. Historical Fiction
C. Magical Realism
D. Realism

11. Who is the author of the epic poem *Paradise Lost*?

A. Geoffrey Chaucer
B. William Blake
C. Edmund Spenser
D. John Milton

12. Which Indian author won the Booker Prize for *The God of Small Things*?

A. Kiran Desai
B. Arundhati Roy
C. Anita Desai
D. Jhumpa Lahiri

13. Who wrote *The Trial*, a novel published posthumously?

A. Albert Camus
B. Franz Kafka
C. Jean-Paul Sartre
D. Thomas Mann

14. Which author created the dystopian world of *The Handmaid's Tale*?

A. Margaret Atwood
B. Sylvia Plath
C. Octavia E. Butler
D. Ursula K. Le Guin

15. Identify the figure of speech in: "Tim a thief."

A. Simile
B. Metaphor
C. Allusion
D. Irony

16. Who is the protagonist of *Crime Punishment*?

A. Raskolnikov
B. Pierre Bezukhov
C. Gregor Samsa
D. Ivan Karamazov

17. Which Nobel laureate is also known her powerful exploration of Black iden and history in *Beloved*?

A. Alice Walker
B. Toni Morrison
C. Maya Angelou
D. Zadie Smith

18. The poem *'Kubla Khan'* was written b

A. William Blake
B. William Wordsworth
C. Percy Bysshe Shelley
D. Samuel Taylor Coleridge

19. The literary term "epiphany" refers to

A. A symbol representing death
B. A sudden moment of realization
C. A climactic battle
D. A divine prophecy

20. What is the name of the fictional sch in the Harry Potter series?

A. Middle Earth Academy
B. Narnia High
C. Avalon Institute
D. Hogwarts

9. D	**10.** C	**11.** D	**12.** B	**13.** B	**14.** A
15. B	**16.** A	**17.** B	**18.** D	**19.** B	**20.** D

. "The wind whispered through the trees" is an example of which figure of speech?

A. Metaphor
B. Alliteration
C. Personification
D. Irony

. Who created the detective character Hercule Poirot?

A. Agatha Christie
B. Dorothy L. Sayers
C. P.D. James
D. Arthur Conan Doyle

3. Who is the narrator of *The Great Gatsby*?

A. Jay Gatsby
B. Nick Carraway
C. Daisy Buchanan
D. Tom Buchanan

4. "Parting is such sweet sorrow" from Romeo and Juliet is an example of:

A. Oxymoron B. Metaphor
C. Synecdoche D. Irony

5. Who is the author of *Midnight's Children*?

A. Salman Rushdie
B. Vikram Chandra
C. Kiran Nagarkar
D. Arundhati Roy

6. Who was the first African writer to win the Nobel Prize in Literature?

A. NgügiwaThiong'o
B. Wole Soyinka
C. ChimamandaNgoziAdichie
D. Chinua Achebe

7. Who wrote the poem *"The Waste Land"*?

A. W.H. Auden
B. Robert Frost
C. Ezra Pound
D. T.S. Eliot

28. The phrase "stream of consciousness" is closely associated with which author?

A. James Joyce
B. T.S. Eliot
C. F. Scott Fitzgerald
D. George Orwell

29. What is the central theme of Orwell's *Animal Farm*?

A. Capitalism and class struggle
B. Totalitarianism and revolution
C. Industrialization
D. Colonialism in Asia

30. Who wrote the novel *Sea of Poppies*, the first in the Ibis Trilogy?

A. Salman Rushdie
B. Vikram Chandra
C. Shashi Tharoor
D. Amitav Ghosh

31. What is the term for a novel that focuses on the psychological and moral growth of the protagonist from youth to adulthood?

A. Bildungsroman
B. Epistolary
C. Allegory
D. Picaresque

32. *The Diary of a Young Girl* was written by:

A. Anne Brontë
B. Anne Frank
C. Louisa May Alcott
D. Sylvia Plath

33. The Harlem Renaissance is associated with which country?

A. South Africa
B. United States
C. Jamaica
D. France

21. C	**22.** A	**23.** B	**24.** A	**25.** A	**26.** B	**27.** D
28. A	**29.** B	**30.** D	**31.** A	**32.** B	**33.** B	

34. The novel *The Guide* by R.K. Narayan is set in which fictional town?

A. Palanpu
B. Kanthapura
C. Kasauli
D. Malgudi

35. Which Indian epic is reimagined in Chitra Banerjee Divakaruni's novel *The Palace of Illusions*?

A. Ramayana
B. Mahabharata
C. Bhagavata Purana
D. Silappatikaram

36. The novel *Kim* by Rudyard Kipling is set in:

A. Afghanistan
B. Burma
C. Tibet
D. India

37. In literature, "elegy" refers to:

A. A romantic song
B. A poem mourning a death
C. A dramatic monologue
D. A humorous poem

38. Devdutt Pattanaik has written extensi on which Indian epic in his books *J* and *The Boys of Karna*?

A. Ramayana
B. ShivPurana
C. Bhagavata
D. Mahabharata

39. In which Shakespearean play does character Iago appear?

A. Macbeth
B. Othello
C. The Tempest
D. King Lear

40. Which of the following best define traditional Haiku?

A. A four-line Chinese quatrain regulated tonal patterns
B. A three-line Japanese poetic form a 5-7-5 syllabic structure, often evo nature
C. A five-line humorous poem with AABBA rhyme scheme and anap meter
D. A three-line Sanskrit verse usec classical Indian devotional poetry

EXPLANATORY ANSWERS

1. The 2024 Nobel Prize in Literature was awarded to Han Kang for her poetic prose that explores historical trauma and human fragility. Her works, such as *The Vegetarian,* deeply examine memory, violence, and identity through intense and lyrical storytelling.

2. Mary Ann Evans wrote under the pen name George Eliot to ensure her works were taken seriously in a male-dominated literary world. Her novel *Middlemarch* is considered one of the greatest English novels fo psychological depth and social realism

3. A frame narrative is a literary techn where a main story encloses one or r smaller stories within it. Classic exam include *The Canterbury Tales* and *Thousand and One Nights,* where the c story provides context for inner tales.

4. Dante Alighieri originally wrote *The D Comedy* in Italian (Tuscan dialect), not L

34. D	**35.** B	**36.** D	**37.** B	**38.** D	**39.** B	**40.**

This made the work accessible to common people and helped establish Italian as a literary language.

5. The characters Rosencrantz and Guildenstern appear in William Shakespeare's play *Hamlet*. They are childhood friends of Hamlet, later used by King Claudius to spy on him, adding to the play's themes of betrayal and intrigue.

6. James Clear wrote *Atomic Habits,* a bestselling self-help book that focuses on small behavioral changes and habit-building strategies to achieve long-term success.

7. The Petrarchan (Italian) sonnet consists of 14 lines divided into an 8-line octave and a 6-line sestet. The octave presents a problem or theme, while the sestet provides resolution or reflection.

8. The Mahabharata is the world's longest epic poem, containing over 100,000 verses. It narrates the Kurukshetra war and includes philosophical texts like the Bhagavad Gita.

9. The 2025 Holberg Prize was awarded to Gayatri Chakravorty Spivak, a distinguished Indian scholar and University Professor in the Humanities at Columbia University. She was honored for her groundbreaking interdisciplinary contributions across comparative literature, postcolonial studies, translation, political philosophy, and feminist theory. Her influential 1988 essay *"Can the Subaltern Speak?"* reshaped postcolonial discourse by examining the voice and agency of marginalized groups. She is also widely recognized for translating Jacques Derrida's *Of Grammatology,* which introduced deconstruction to the English-speaking world.

   The Holberg Prize, often regarded as the Nobel equivalent for humanities and social sciences, was awarded to her in June 2025 in Bergen, Norway.

10. Gabriel García Márquez's *One Hundred Years of Solitude* is a landmark work of magical realism, blending realistic narrative with fantastical elements presented as ordinary aspects of life.

11. *Paradise Lost* was written by John Milton, a 17th-century English poet. This epic poem explores the Biblical story of the Fall of Man, focusing on Satan's rebellion, Adam and Eve's temptation, and themes of free will, obedience, and redemption.

12. Arundhati Roy won the Booker Prize in 1997 for *The God of Small Things.* The novel deals with social discrimination, caste system, and forbidden love in Kerala, combining political insight with lyrical storytelling.

13. *The Trial* was written by Franz Kafka and published posthumously in 1925. It tells the story of Josef K., who is arrested and prosecuted by a mysterious authority, symbolizing absurdity and alienation in modern society.

14. Margaret Atwood created *The Handmaid's Tale,* a dystopian novel depicting a totalitarian regime where women's rights are severely restricted. It explores themes of power, gender, and control.

15. The statement "Time is a thief" is a metaphor because it directly compares time to a thief without using words like "as" or "like," suggesting that time steals moments from our lives.

16. The protagonist of *Crime and Punishment* by Fyodor Dostoevsky is Rodion Raskolnikov. The novel explores his psychological turmoil after committing a crime and his journey toward guilt and redemption.

17. Toni Morrison, a Nobel laureate in Literature (1993), wrote *Beloved.* Her work powerfully explores Black identity, slavery, memory, and trauma in American history.

18. Samuel Taylor Coleridge wrote the poem *Kubla Khan.* It is a Romantic poem inspired by a dream, known for its vivid imagery and exploration of imagination.

19. In literature, an epiphany refers to a sudden insight or realization experienced by a character, often leading to a deeper understanding of themselves or their situation.

20. The fictional school in the Harry Potter series is Hogwarts School of Witchcraft and Wizardry, where young wizards and witches are trained in magic.

21. The sentence "The wind whispered through the trees" gives a human action (whispering) to wind, which is a non-living entity. This attribution of human qualities to non-human things is called personification, commonly used to create vivid imagery.

22. Agatha Christie created the famous Belgian detective Hercule Poirot. He appears in numerous novels like *Murder on the Orient Express,* known for his sharp intellect and methodical reasoning.

23. F. Scott Fitzgerald's *The Great Gatsby* is narrated by Nick Carraway. He serves as both a participant and observer, providing insight into Gatsby's life and the moral decay of society.

24. The phrase "Parting is such sweet sorrow" combines two contradictory terms—"sweet" and "sorrow"—to express the bittersweet feeling of separation, making it an example of an oxymoron.

25. Salman Rushdie wrote *Midnight's Children,* which won the Booker Prize in 1981. The novel blends history and fantasy to narrate India's transition from colonialism to independence.

26. Wole Soyinka became the first African Nobel laureate in Literature in 1986. His works focus on African culture, politics, and human rights.

27. T.S. Eliot wrote *The Waste Land,* a landmark modernist poem published in 1922, reflecting post-World War I disillusionment and cultural fragmentation.

28. James Joyce is closely associated with the "stream of consciousness" technique, especially in *Ulysses,* where characters' inner thoughts are presented in a continuous flow.

29. George Orwell's *Animal Farm* is an allegorical novella criticizing totalitarian regimes, especially Stalinist Russia, and shows how revolutions can lead to new forms of oppression.

30. Amitav Ghosh wrote *Sea of Poppies,* the first novel in the Ibis Trilogy, which explores colonial trade, opium production, and migration in the 19th century.

31. A Bildungsroman is a novel that traces the psychological and moral development of a protagonist from youth to adulthood. It focuses on personal growth, self-discovery, and the shaping of character through experiences, as seen in works like *David Copperfield.*

32. Anne Frank wrote *The Diary of a Young Girl,* documenting her life in hiding during World War II. The diary provides a powerful personal account of fear, hope, and resilience under Nazi persecution.

33. The Harlem Renaissance was a cultural and literary movement that took place in the United States during the 1920s. It centered in Harlem, New York, and celebrated African American art, literature, and identity.

34. R. K. Narayan set *The Guide* in the fictional South Indian town of Malgudi. This town appears in many of his works and represents a microcosm of Indian society.

35. Chitra Banerjee Divakaruni's *The Palace of Illusions* retells the Mahabharata from Draupadi's perspective, offering a feminist reinterpretation of the epic.

36. Rudyard Kipling's novel *Kim* is set in colonial India and explores themes of identity, espionage, and cultural diversity during the British Raj.

37. An elegy is a poetic form that expresses sorrow, especially for someone who has died. It often reflects on loss, grief, and remembrance.

38. Devdutt Pattanaik has extensively written about the Mahabharata in books like *Jaya* and *The Boys of Karna,* interpreting its myths and characters in a modern context.

39. The character Iago appears in William Shakespeare's play *Othello.* He is the main antagonist, known for his manipulation and deceit that lead to tragedy.

40. A traditional Haiku is a concise Japanese poem of three lines with a 5-7-5 syllable pattern. It typically captures a moment in nature and conveys deep meaning through simplicity.

YOUR SPACE

Previous Years' Paper

JAMIA MILLIA ISLAMIA

B.A. (HONS.) ENGLISH

Entrance Exam-2024

(Exam held on 06-05-2024)

PART-A

1. The writer known for writing about Indian mythology is:

A. Agha Shahid Ali
B. Amitav Ghosh
C. Chetan Bhagat
D. Devdutt Pattanaik

2. Identify the odd one:

A. Spondee B. Villanelle
C. Sonnet D. Canzone

3. An 'Aside' is a dramatic device in which:

A. A character speaks to the audience unheard by other characters
B. A character speaks to himself unheard by other characters
C. A character speaks to another character in the corner of stage unheard by other characters
D. It is synonymous with monologue.

4. *The Bourne* films are based on novels by:

A. Robert Ludlum B. Margret Mitchell
C. Dan Brown D. Ian Fleming

5. The phrase "From what I've tasted of desire" (Robert Frost) is an example of:

A. Imagery B. Synaesthesia
C. Allusion D. Metaphor

6. Arrange the following *Harry Potter* novels in the order of their publication:

1. Harry Potter and the Half Blood Prince
2. Harry Potter and the Prisoner of Azkaban
3. Harry Potter and the Philosopher's Stone
4. Harry Potter and the Goblet of Fire

A. 3, 1, 4, 2 B. 2, 3, 4, 1
C. 3, 2, 4, 1 D. 1, 2, 3, 4

7. *The Second Sex* was written by:

A. Kate Millett
B. Donna J. Haraway
C. Simone de Beauvoir
D. Judith Butler

8. "An Ode to a Grecian Urn" is a famous poem by:

A. Wordsworth B. Lord Byron
C. Mary Shelley D. John Keats

9. *Frankestein* is a famous work by:

A. Richardson B. Daniel Defoe
C. Mary Shelley D. Sir Walter Scott

10. In Shakespeare's play *The Tempest* Miranda is the daughter of:

A. Caliban B. Prospero
C. Ferdinand D. Alonso

1. D **2.** A **3.** A **4.** A **5.** D **6.** C **7.** C **8.** D **9.** C **10.** B

11. The author of the story "The Last Leaf" is:

A. O. Henry
B. Helen Cixous
C. Charlotte Perkins Gilman
D. Anton Chekhov

12. A poem of mourning is called:

A. A Sonnet B. An Epic
C. An Elegy D. An Epistle

13. The poem which has fourteen lines is called:

A. A Sonnet B. An Epic
C. An Elegy D. An Epistle

14. A poem T.S. Eliot did not write is:

A. "Gerontion"
B. "The Journey of the Magi"
C. "Among School Children"
D. "Four Quartets"

15. The Nobel Prize in Literature in 2022 was awarded to:

A. Ngugi Wa Thiong'O
B. Annie Ernaux
C. Zadie Smith
D. Louise Gluck

16. Ahmad Ali is the author of:

A. *Twilight in Delhi*
B. *Phoenix Fled*
C. *In Custody*
D. *A Bend in the Ganges*

17. Girish Karnad wrote plays in English and:

A. Telugu B. Kannada
C. Malayalam D. Hindi

18. Mark Antony is an important character in Shakespeare's play:

A. *A Midsummer Night's Dream*
B. *Julius Caesar*
C. *Hamlet*
D. *Twelfth Night*

19. The word that best describes the following is:
"Open to more than one interpretation"

A. Obsolete B. Alchemy
C. Obvious D. Ambiguous

20. A novel that does not deal with Delhi is:

A. *City of Djinns*
B. *Maximum City*
C. *Ministry of Utmost Happiness*
D. *White Tiger*

21. The movie *Gone Girl* is based on a novel by:

A. Rhys Adrian B. Angela Carter
C. Gillian Flynn D. Caryl Churchill

22. Amitav Ghosh's *Jungle Nama* is:

A. A novel
B. A collection of Short Stories
C. A book in verse
D. A play

23. The first attempt at writing a monolingual Dictionary in English was made by:

A. Dr. Samuel Johnson
B. Alexander Pope
C. Ben Jonson
D. T.S. Eliot

24. A word or sentence that remains the same if read backward is known as:

A. Acronym B. Palindrome
C. Portmanteau D. Homonym

25. A novel not written by Amitav Ghosh is:

A. *River of Smoke*
B. *The Circle of Reason*
C. *Sea of Poppies*
D. *Red Earth and Pouring Rain*

26. Mark the odd one among the following:

A. A Conceit B. An Allusion
C. A Paradox D. An Ode

11. A	**12.** C	**13.** A	**14.** C	**15.** B	**16.** A	**17.** B	**18.** B
19. D	**20.** B	**21.** C	**22.** C	**23.** A	**24.** B	**25.** D	**26.** D

27. The film *Maqbool* is an adaptation of Shakespeare's play:

A. *Macbeth* B. *Hamlet*
C. *The Tempest* D. *King Lear*

28. OTT stands for:

A. Online Television Transmission
B. Other-Transmission Terminal
C. Open Time Transmission
D. Over-The-Top

29. Two same sounding words with different meanings are called:

A. Homograph B. Homonym
C. Synonym D. Antonym

30. The following is not true about the novel *Robinson Crusoe*:

A. It was written by Daniel Defoe
B. It is based on the life of Alexander Selkirk
C. Crusoe's companion is called 'Monday'
D. It is credited as marking the beginning of realistic fiction

31. A Biblioklept is one who:

A. steals books B. loves books
C. worships books D. fears books

32. A work that depicts an imaginary place where life is extremely bad because of deprivation or oppression or terror is called:

A. Satire B. Utopia
C. Allegory D. Dystopia

33. The word that has the same meaning as 'precarious' is:

A. Secure B. Elevated
C. Uncertain D. Confident

34. ________ is a Dalit autobiography.

A. *The Outcaste*
B. *Untouchable*
C. *The Fall of a Sparrow*
D. *A Shot at History*

35. A phrase, poem or a quotation set at the beginning of a section, chapter or book is called:

A. Monograph B. Epigraph
C. Epitaph D. Epigram

36. The opening of a story that establishes the context and may reveal some background is called:

A. Interlude B. Foreword
C. Prologue D. Preface

37. The phrase 'It's Greek to me' comes from Shakespeare's play:

A. *Hamlet* B. *Julius Caesar*
C. *Twelfth Night* D. *Cymbeline*

38. Neologism is:

A. A word with roots in a native language
B. A word whose meaning changes over a period of time
C. An obsession with new words and phrases
D. A newly coined word or a word used in a new sense

39. Salim Sinai is the central character in the novel:

A. *Heart of Darkness*
B. *Midnight's Children*
C. *Kim*
D. *The Secret Sharer*

40. *Wings of Fire* is a famous autobiography written by:

A. Vandana Shiva
B. Maulana Abul Kalam Azad
C. APJ Abdul Kalam
D. Saleem Ali

27. A	**28.** D	**29.** B	**30.** C	**31.** A	**32.** D	**33.** C
34. A	**35.** B	**36.** C	**37.** B	**38.** D	**39.** B	**40.** C

EXPLANATORY ANSWERS

1. **(D): Devdutt Pattanaik:** He is an Indian author who writes extensively on Indian mythology and has penned over 50 books. Notable works include 'Jaya: An Illustrated Retelling of the Mahabharata' (2010) and 'Sita: An Illustrated Retelling of the Ramayana' (2013). His writing often interprets ancient myths for a contemporary readership.

2. **(A): Spondee:** It is a metrical foot with two consecutive stressed syllables (e.g., "heartbeat"). Villanelle, Sonnet, and Canzone are poetic forms, making Spondee the odd one out. Spondee focuses on stress patterns rather than structural form.

3. **(A): A character speaks to the audience unheard by other characters:** This device allows a character to reveal thoughts or motives directly to the audience. It creates dramatic irony because the other characters on stage remain unaware of the aside.

4. **(A): Robert Ludlum:** The original Bourne novels, beginning with 'The Bourne Identity' (1980), were written by Ludlum. The movie adaptations starring Matt Damon derive from these spy thriller novels, which have sold millions of copies globally.

5. **(D): Metaphor:** "From what I've tasted of desire" (from Robert Frost's poem "Fire and Ice") compares desire to something that can be tasted. This figurative expression vividly links an abstract emotion with a physical sense, enhancing the poem's impact.

6. **(C):** The publication order is 'Harry Potter and the Philosopher's Stone' (1997), 'Harry Potter and the Prisoner of Azkaban' (1999), 'Harry Potter and the Goblet of Fire' (2000), and 'Harry Potter and the Half-Blood Prince' (2005). Each of these was a massive bestseller, often setting pre-order records.

7. **(C): Simone de Beauvoir:** 'The Second Sex' (1949) is a landmark feminist text examining the construction of womanhood. It influenced feminist theory worldwide and introduced the famous line "One is not born, but rather becomes, a woman."

8. **(D): John Keats:** "Ode on a Grecian Urn," published in 1819, is one of Keats's most famous Odes. It contrasts the eternal beauty of art with the fleeting nature of human life, encapsulated in the line "Beauty is truth, truth beauty."

9. **(C): Mary Shelley:** 'Frankenstein; or, The Modern Prometheus' (1818) is a seminal work of Gothic and early science fiction literature. It explores themes of scientific ambition, creation, and moral responsibility, written when Shelley was just 18.

10. **(B): Prospero:** In Shakespeare's 'The Tempest,' first performed in 1611, Miranda is Prospero's daughter. Isolated on an island, she displays innocence and compassion, which powerfully contrasts her father's obsession with power and retribution.

11. **(A): O. Henry:** He wrote the short story "The Last Leaf," first published in 1907. Known for his surprise endings, O. Henry depicts a poignant tale of hope and friendship set in Greenwich Village. His works have been translated into numerous languages and remain widely read.

12. **(C): An Elegy:** A poem of mourning or lament, often written for the dead. Famous examples include "Lycidas" by

John Milton (1637) and "In Memoriam A.H.H." by Alfred Tennyson (1850). Elegies generally explore themes of grief, loss, and consolation.

13. **(A): A Sonnet:** A poem of fourteen lines, typically written in iambic pentameter. This form became prominent in Renaissance literature, especially in the works of Shakespeare, who wrote 154 sonnets. Sonnets often follow specific rhyme schemes like the Shakespearean or Petrarchan pattern.

14. **(C): "Among School Children":** This poem was written by W.B. Yeats in 1926, not by T.S. Eliot. Eliot wrote works such as "Gerontion" (1919), "Journey of the Magi" (1927), and "Four Quartets" (completed in 1942). Eliot received the Nobel Prize in Literature in 1948.

15. **(B): Annie Ernaux:** She was awarded the Nobel Prize in Literature in 2022 for what the committee described as "the courage and clinical acuity" in her writing. She is known for autobiographical works like "La Place" (1983) and "Happening" (2000). Her literary style merges personal experience with broader social commentary.

16. **(A): Twilight in Delhi:** Published in 1940, it is a notable novel by Ahmad Ali, portraying the cultural and social fabric of Delhi during the early 20th century. It highlights the decline of Muslim aristocracy under British colonial rule. This work is considered an important piece of Indo-Islamic literary heritage.

17. **(B): Kannada:** Girish Karnad wrote extensively in both English and Kannada, contributing significantly to modern Indian drama. His famous Kannada plays include "Tughlaq" (1964) and "Hayavadana" (1971). He received the Jnanpith Award in 1998 for his contributions to literature.

18. **(B): Julius Caesar:** Mark Antony is a central figure in this Shakespearean tragedy, famous for his funeral oration beginning with "Friends, Romans, countrymen." First performed in 1599, the play dramatizes real historical events from Roman history and explores themes of power and betrayal.

19. **(D): Ambiguous:** It means something that can be interpreted in more than one way. In literary and rhetorical contexts, ambiguity can add depth and complexity to a text. Its opposite would be clarity or definiteness.

20. **(B): Maximum City:** Written by Suketu Mehta, this nonfiction work explores life in Mumbai, not Delhi. "City of Djinns," "The Ministry of Utmost Happiness," and "The White Tiger" each depict aspects of Delhi in their narratives. "Maximum City" was a Pulitzer Prize finalist in 2005.

21. **(C): Gillian Flynn:** Her novel "Gone Girl" (2012) was adapted into a film directed by David Fincher in 2014, earning over $369 million worldwide. It follows the mysterious disappearance of a wife and the ensuing media frenzy, exploring themes of deception. The book topped The New York Times bestseller list for eight weeks.

22. **(C): A book in verse:** Published in 2021, "Jungle Nama" by Amitav Ghosh is a verse adaptation of a Bengali folklore from the Sundarban region. It uses rhyming couplets and illustrations to retell the legend of Bon Bibi. Its form blends poetry with narrative storytelling.

23. **(A): Dr. Samuel Johnson:** "A Dictionary of the English Language," published in 1755, is regarded as the first major authoritative monolingual English dictionary. It included around 42,773 entries and set standards for lexicography until the completion of the Oxford English Dictionary in 1928.

24. (B): Palindrome: It reads the same forwards and backwards (e.g., "madam," "racecar"). Such words or phrases mirror letter arrangements symmetrically. Palindromes are found in various languages, showcasing linguistic playfulness.

25. (D): Red Earth and Pouring Rain: Written by Vikram Chandra, published in 1995, it won the Commonwealth Writers' Prize for Best First Book. The other options—"River of Smoke," "The Circle of Reason," and "Sea of Poppies"—were authored by Amitav Ghosh.

26. (D): An Ode: Conceit, Allusion, and Paradox are figures of speech or rhetorical devices, whereas an Ode is a lyric poem in praise of someone or something. Famous odes include "Ode on a Grecian Urn" by John Keats (1819).

27. (A): Macbeth: "Maqbool" (2003), directed by Vishal Bhardwaj, is a cinematic adaptation of Shakespeare's "Macbeth." It transplants the play's themes of ambition and guilt into the Mumbai underworld, earning critical acclaim for its performances and direction.

28. (D): Over-The-Top: Refers to content platforms delivering media over the Internet, bypassing traditional cable or satellite TV. Examples include Netflix, Amazon Prime Video, and Disney+, each serving millions of subscribers globally.

29. (B): Homonym: Two same-sounding words with different meanings (and possibly different spellings) are called homonyms. Examples include "right" (correct) and "rite" (ceremony). They often cause confusion but enrich language play.

30. (C): Crusoe's companion is called 'Monday': This is untrue; in Daniel Defoe's "Robinson Crusoe" (1719), the companion Crusoe rescues is named Friday. The novel, influenced by Alexander Selkirk's real-life story, is credited with inaugurating the tradition of realistic fiction in English.

31. (A): Biblioklept: It refers to a person who steals books. This term comes from the Greek words 'biblio' (books) and 'kleptes' (thief). Instances of bibliokleptomania have been recorded historically, highlighting how some individuals compulsively hoard stolen books.

32. (D): Dystopia: It depicts a nightmarish society or environment characterized by oppression, deprivation, or extreme distress. Works like George Orwell's "1984" (1949) and Aldous Huxley's "Brave New World" (1932) exemplify dystopian themes, warning about the dangers of totalitarian rule or unchecked technology.

33. (C): Uncertain: "Precarious" suggests insecurity or instability, such as a precarious foothold on a mountain ledge. Synonyms include "tentative," "unstable," or "risky," highlighting the underlying threat or risk in a given situation.

34. (A): The Outcaste: Written by Sharankumar Limbale and originally published in Marathi as "Akkarmashi" (1984). It is a Dalit autobiography that recounts Limbale's personal experiences of caste-based discrimination in India, contributing significantly to Dalit literature.

35. (B): Epigraph: A phrase, quotation, or short poem placed at the beginning of a book, chapter, or section. Authors like T.S. Eliot and F. Scott Fitzgerald often used epigraphs to set the tone or theme for their works, inviting readers to interpret the text in light of the chosen lines.

36. (C): **Prologue:** It serves as the opening of a story or play, establishing context and possibly revealing background details. In dramatic works, it can be delivered by a Chorus or a narrator figure, preparing audiences for the subsequent narrative.

37. (B): **Julius Caesar:** The phrase "It's Greek to me" appears in Act 1, Scene 2, spoken by Casca referring to Cicero's speech. Shakespeare's usage popularized this expression to mean something that is unintelligible or not understood.

38. (D): **A newly coined word or a word used in a new sense:** Neologisms arise as languages evolve, responding to cultural or technological changes. Examples include words like "blog" or "Brexit," which entered common use relatively recently.

39. (B): **Midnight's Children:** Published in 1981 by Salman Rushdie, it follows Salim Sinai who is born at midnight at the moment of India's independence (1947). The novel blends magic realism with historical events, and it won the Booker Prize in 1981.

40. (C): **APJ Abdul Kalam:** "Wings of Fire" (1999) recounts his journey from humble beginnings to becoming a leading scientist in India's space and missile programs. Co-authored with Arun Tiwari, it has inspired millions, reflecting Kalam's vision and philosophy for national development.

Previous Papers (Solved)

JAMIA MILLIA ISLAMIA

B.A. (HONS.) ENGLISH

Entrance Exam, 2022*

PART—A

Directions: *Choose the correct options in the Objective Type questions given below:*

1. Neftali Ricardo Reyes Basoalto is the real name of which famous poet?
A. C.P. Cavafy
B. Pablo Neruda
C. George Seferis
D. Gabriela Mistral

2. "The Proposal" is the name of a famous one-act play by:
A. Bertolt Brecht
B. George Bernard Shaw
C. Anton Chekov
D. August Strindberg

3. In which language did Harishankar Parsai write originally?
A. Gujarati
B. Marathi
C. English
D. Hindi

4. Which poet is known as the pioneer of the ghazal form in English?
A. Imtiaz Dharker
B. Agha Shahid Ali
C. Ahmed Ali
D. Tabish Khair

5. Who wrote the famous play, *Chandalika*?
A. Mahesh Dattani
B. Rabindranath Tagore
C. Girish Karnad
D. Vijay Tendulkar

6. *Death of a Salesman,* the iconic American play, was written by _______ .
A. Tennessee Williams
B. Eugene O'Neill
C. Arthur Miller
D. John Osborne

7. The first black woman to win the Nobel Prize in literature was _______ .
A. Maya Angelou
B. Toni Morrison
C. Pearl S. Buck
D. Jamaica Kincaid

8. Which of the following books was short-listed for the JCB Prize for Literature last year?
A. Daribha Lyndem's *Name Place Animal Thing*
B. H.M. Naqvi's *Home Boy*
C. Mamang Dai's *The Black Hill*
D. Kynpham Sing Nongkynrih's *Funeral Nights*

* Exam held on 22-06-2022.

9. From which country was the author, Seima Lagerlof?
A. Finland
B. Sweden
C. Norway
D. Denmark

10. "The Road Not Taken" is a famous poem by ________ .
A. Allen Ginsberg
B. Walt Whitman
C. Lawrence Ferlinghetti
D. Robert Frost

11. *Dubliners* is a book written by _______ .
A. Sean O'Casey
B. Oscar Wilde
C. James Joyce
D. Joyce Carol Oates

12. Besides being a poet, A.K. Ramanujan was a:
A. Translator
B. Professor
C. Folklorist
D. All of the above

13. "Kubla Khan" is a famous poem by:
A. Lord Byron
B. Samuel Taylor Coleridge
C. Cardinal Newman
D. Leigh Hunt

14. "The Bet" is a famous short story by ______.
A. Guy de Maupassant
B. H.M. Munro 'Saki'
C. Isaac Bashevis Singer
D. Anton Chekhov

15. "I have a dream" is a speech by:
A. Nelson Mandela
B. Barack Obama
C. Gopal Krishna Gokhale
D. Martin Luther King Jr.

16. Who wrote the novel, *The Plague*?
A. Orhan Pamuk
B. Albert Camus
C. Jean Paul Sartre
D. Charles Dickens

17. Which of the following won the Nobel prize for Literuatre but lost the election for the post of President of the country?
A. Mario Vargas Llosa
B. Gabriel Gracia Marquez
C. Valcav Havel
D. Leopold Senghor

18. "Fire and Ice" is the name of a famous poem by:
A. William Carlos Williams
B. Allen Ginsberg
C. Robert Frost
D. Camilo Jose Cela

19. "For Anne Gregory" is a famous poem by:
A. Stephen Spender
B. Phillip Larkin
C. Seamus Heaney
D. William Butler Yeats

20. *Joseph Anton : A Memoir* is written by _______ .
A. Sudeep Sen
B. Judith Wright
C. Salman Rushdie
D. Robert Kroetsch

21. In which language did Rahul Sankrityayan write originally?
A. Konkani
B. Kannada
C. Hindi
D. Bengali

22. Who received the Nobel Prize for Literature 2021?
A. Peter Handke
B. Ngugi wa Thiong'o
C. Ivo Andric
D. Abdulrazak Gurnah

23. Which book won the JCB Prize for Literature 2021?
A. M. Mukundan's *Delhi : A Soliloquy*
B. Benyamin's *Jasmine Days*
C. O.V. Vijayan's *The Legends of Khasak*
D. Jayanth Kaikini's *No Presents Please*

24. Which of the following North East authors is both a recipient of the Padma Shri as well as Akademi Award?
A. Temsula Ao
B. Robin Ngangom
C. Nabanita Kanungo
D. Desmond Kharmawphlang

25. 'Malgudi' is a fictional town in the works of ______.
A. Ashokamitran
B. U.R. Ananthamurthy
C. R.K. Narayan
D. Vaikom Muhammad Basheer

26. "The Ghat of the Only World" is a famous tribute written by Amitav Ghosh for ______.
A. A.K. Ramanujan
B. Agha Shahid Ali
C. Arun Kolatkar
D. Dilip Chitre

27. Which of the following is a recipient of the Nobel Prize for Literature?
A. Marcel Proust
B. James Joyce
C. Vladimir Nabokov
D. Olga Tokarczuk

28. Who among the following is a recipient of the Commonwealth Poetry Prize?
A. Jerry Pinto
B. Sujata Bhatt
C. Ranjit Hoskote
D. Vijay Nambisan

29. Which of the following is a recipient of the Sahitya Akademi Award?
A. *Chronicle of a Corpse Bearer* by Cyrus Mistry
B. *Doongaji House* by Cyrus Mistry
C. *The Radiance of Ashes* by Cyrus Mistry
D. *The Prospect of Miracles* by Cyrus Mistry

30. *The Golden Gate* is a novel written by ______.
A. Vikram Chandra
B. Vikram Seth
C. Vikas Swarup
D. Hoshang Merchant

31. "Let Me Not to the Marriage of True Minds" is a/an ______.
A. Ode
B. Sonnet
C. Villanelle
D. Ghazal

32. *"Hawk roosting"* is a famous poem by ______.
A. Ted Hughes
B. A.K. Ramanujan
C. Sylvia Plath
D. Gopalakrishna Adiga

33. "Love is not love which alters when it alteration finds" is a line from a famous poem by ______.
A. John Donne
B. William Wordsworth
C. William Shakespeare
D. John Keats

34. Who wrote the famous novel, *Heart of Darkness?*
A. Chinua Achebe
B. H. Rider Haggard
C. John Fowles
D. Joseph Conrad

35. Which of the following is a well-known Indian English woman poet?
A. Rajathi Salma
B. Kamala Das
C. Malika Amar Shaikh
D. Jerry Pinto

36. Which of the following has won the Pulitzer Prize for fiction?
A. Salman Rushdie
B. Aravind Adiga
C. Amitav Ghosh
D. Jhumpa Lahiri

37. Who wrote the famous novel, *Kanthapura*?
A. Manohar Malgaonkar
B. Mulk Raj Anand
C. Raja Rao
D. R.K. Narayan

38. "To be or not to be" is a famous quote from the play, ________.
A. *Othello*
B. *Macbeth*
C. *King Lear*
D. *Hamlet*

39. William Shakespeare was born in ________ .
A. 1562
B. 1563
C. 1564
D. 1565

40. *Sacred Games,* the novel, was written by ________ .
A. Tishani Doshi
B. Raja Rao
C. Thirty Umrigar
D. Vikram Chandra

ANSWERS

1	2	3	4	5	6	7	8	9	10
B	C	D	B	B	C	B	A	B	D
11	**12**	**13**	**14**	**15**	**16**	**17**	**18**	**19**	**20**
C	D	B	D	D	B	A	C	D	C
21	**22**	**23**	**24**	**25**	**26**	**27**	**28**	**29**	**30**
C	D	A	A	C	B	D	B	A	B
31	**32**	**33**	**34**	**35**	**36**	**37**	**38**	**39**	**40**
B	A	C	D	B	D	C	D	C	D

Previous Paper (Solved)

JAMIA MILLIA ISLAMIA (JMI)

B.A. (HONS.) ENGLISH ENTRANCE EXAM 2021*

PART—A

Directions: *Choose the correct options in the Objective Type questions given below:*

(1 mark each)

1. Which novel won the Booker Prize 2021?
A. So Many Different Modes
B. At Night All Blood is Black
C. In Memory of Memory
D. The Employees

2. Who has written the book My Seditious Heart?
A. Amitav Ghosh
B. Arundhati Roy
C. Kiran Desai
D. Arvind Adiga

3. Which writer created the famous fictional character of Count Dracula?
A. Agatha Christie B. Bram Stoker
C. R.L. Stevenson D. Wilkie Collins

4. Which U.S. President has authored the book The Audacity of Hope?
A. George Bush B. Joe Biden
C. Barack Obama D. Donald Trump

5. *What You Can Do to Avoid AIDS* is a brilliant book by a basketball player. Name the player.
A. Kobe Bryan B. Magic Johnson
C. Bill Bradley D. Sam Smith

6. Tweedledee and Tweedledum are fictional characters from which Children's book?
A. Alice in Wonderland
B. The Wing in the Willow's
C. The Secret Garden
D. Winnie the Pooh

7. Rip Wan Winkle is written by:
A. Henry James
B. Washington Irving
C. Ralph Ellison
D. Nathaniel Hawthorne

8. 3 Idiots movie is an adaptation of:
A. The 3 Mistakes of My Life
B. Five Point Someone
C. One Night at the Call Centre
D. Two States

9. Name the autobiography of Kamala Das:
A. My Endless Days
B. My Story So Far
C. My Story
D. My Story Retold

10. Name the American poet who read a poem at John F Kennedy's inauguration ceremony:
A. Walt Whitman B. Robert Frost
C. Lucille Clifton D. Langston Hughes

11. Who is the first French writer to win the Booker prize?
A. David Diop B. Andre Breton
C. Alain Badiou D. Francois Bon

12. Name the poet who read the poem 'The Hill We Climb' in Joe Biden's inauguration ceremony.
A. Maya Angelou
B. Greta Thunberg
C. Amanda Gorman
D. Amanda Lawrence

*Exam held on 12-08-2021.

13. Nobel Prize for Literature 2020 was bagged by:
A. Katherine Woodcock
B. Louise Gluck
C. Olga Tokarezuk
D. Peter Handke

14. Name the poet who won the Sahitya Akademi Award 2020 for the poetry collection *When God is a Traveller*:
A. Veerappa Moily
B. Gian Singh
C. Arundhati Subramaniam
D. Anamika

15. Who has written the novel An Era of Darkness?
A. V.S. Naipaul
B. Shashi Tharoor
C. Arundhati Roy
D. William Darlymple

16. Willy Wonka is a fictional character from the novel:
A. Charlie and the Chocolate Factory
B. Rip Wan Winkle
C. TinTin
D. Little Women

17. Revolution 2020 is the latest novel by:
A. Shashi Tharoor B. Chetan Bhagat
C. Boman Desai D. Devdutt Patnaik

18. The Heights of Machchu Pichchu is a poem by:
A. Gabriel Mistral
B. Pablo Neruda
C. Gabriel Garcia Marquez
D. Mario Vargas Llosa

19. *Of Woman Born* is a feminist book by:
A. Adrienne Rich B. Virginia Woolf
C. Mary Shelley D. Germaine Greer

20. Who has authored the memoir The World Within World?
A. W.H. Auden B. Stephen Spender
C. Philip Larkin D. Walt Whitman

21. 'On First Looking into Chapman's Homer' is a sonnet by:
A. P.B. Shelley
B. Byron
C. John Keats
D. William Wordsworth

22. Vishal Bharadwaj's movie Haider is an adaptation of the Shakespearean play:
A. Othello
B. Macbeth
C. Hamlet
D. The Merchant of Venice

23. The idiom 'Pot calling the kettle black' was first used in the novel:
A. Don Quixote B. Tom Jones
C. Pamela D. Little Women

24. The idiom 'Break the ice' was used first in the Shakespearean play:
A. The Merchant of Venice
B. The Taming of the Shrew
C. The Tempest
D. Othello

25. 1984 is a novel by:
A. George Eliot B. George Orwell
C. Aldous Huxley D. Wilkie Collins

26. Catch 22 is a novel by:
A. Joseph Heller
B. John Steinbeck
C. Somerset Maugham
D. William Faulkner

27. Mark Twain's real name was:
A. Jack Griffith Chaney
B. Mark Samuel Porter
C. Samuel Clemens Langhorne
D. Samuel Tiffin Lawrence

28. Anaphora means:
A. repetition of words
B. repetition of sounds
C. repetition of consonants
D. repetition of rhyme

29. Synecdoche means:
A. Whole representing part
B. Part representing whole
C. Contradictory terms put together
D. Exaggeration

30. Neologism means:
A. New logic
B. Use of a term that has been newly created
C. Usage of old words
D. New science

31. What is the seventh and final installment in J.K. Rowling's Harry Potter series?
A. Harry Potter and the Sorcerer's Stone
B. Harry Potter and the Deathly Hallow's
C. Harry Potter and the Half-Blood Prince
D. Harry Potter and the Order of the Phoenix

32. Who is the author of The Time Machine?
A. R.L. Stevenson B. H.G. Wells
C. Daniel Defoe D. Henry Fielding

33. Octave is an:
A. Eight line stanza
B. Nine line stanza
C. Three line stanza
D. Two line stanza

34. Burlesque is a:
A. narrative poem B. satiric poem
C. pastoral poem D. comedic poem

35. Miss Havisham is a popular fictional character of:
A. Charless Dickens B. Harper lee
C. Jane Austen D. George Eliot

36. Déjà vu is a French word which means:
A. Already heard B. Already seen
C. Already done D. Already eaten

37. The word sizzle is an example of:
A. onomatopoeia B. ellipsis
C. repetition • D. refrain

38. What is Xenophobia?
A. fear of strangers B. fear of dark
C. fear of needles D. fear of open spaces

39. Euthanasia means:
A. mercy killing B. ideal place
C. death sentence D. good thought

40. The famous speech 'I have a Dream' was delivered by:
A. John F Kennedy
B. Martin Luther King Jr.
C. Jawahar Lal Nehru
D. Maulana Azad

ANSWERS

1	2	3	4	5	6	7	8	9	10
B	B	B	C	B	A	B	B	C	B
11	**12**	**13**	**14**	**15**	**16**	**17**	**18**	**19**	**20**
A	C	B	C	B	A	B	B	A	B
21	**22**	**23**	**24**	**25**	**26**	**27**	**28**	**29**	**30**
C	C	A	B	B	A	C	A	B	B
31	**32**	**33**	**34**	**35**	**36**	**37**	**38**	**39**	**40**
B	B	A	D	A	B	A	A	A	B

Previous Paper (Solved)

JAMIA MILLIA ISLAMIA (JMI)

B.A. (HONS.) ENGLISH ENTRANCE EXAM 2020

PART—A

Directions: *Choose the correct options in the Objective Type questions given below:*

(1 mark each)

1. What does the rhetorical term "carpe diem" mean?

A. It means "seize the day", i.e., time is short so make the most of it

B. It means an intentional drop from the serious to the trivial

C. It means an expression that is stereotyped or hackneyed

D. It means a comparison between two dissimilar things

2. What does the rhetorical term "comic relief" mean?

A. It means the use of short, humorous episodes in a serious or tragic work

B. It means an intentional drop from the elevated to the trivial or ridiculous

C. It means a form of low comedy that evokes laughter through ridiculous situations

D. It means the humorous use of a word so that it suggests two or more meanings

3. What does the rhetorical term "oxymoron" mean?

A. It means a form of understatement

B. It means a comparison between two dissimilar things

C. It means a roundabout or indirect way of writing

D. It means the combination of two contrary terms

4. Which of the following lines is an example of "malapropism"?

A. She's as headstrong as an allegory on the banks of the Nile

B. Is life worth living? That depends on the liver

C. The pen is mightier than the sword

D. O my love's like a red, red rose

5. What does the rhetorical term "alliteration" mean?

A. A formal and elborate prose style

B. The use of a mild or vague term, in stead of a blunt term

C. A bold overstatement or exaggeration used for serious or comic effect

D. A repetition of sounds in a sequence of nearby words

6. What does the rhetorical term "onomatopoeia" mean?

A. The use of words or expressions that have become obsolete

B. A contrast or opposite in meaning between two words

C. An expression employed in everyday sppech of writing

D. A word that imitates the sound is represents

7. Which of the following lines is an example of "metaphor"?

A. I burn and freeze

B. Is he smart? Why, the man is an Einstein

C. It is the star to every wand ring bark

D. Flowers are lovely, love is flowerlike

8. Who wrote *The Canterbury Tales*?

A. William Langland

B. Geoffrey Chaucer

C. John Gower
D. Sir Thomas Malory

9. Who wrote *The Fairie Queene*?
A. Edmund Spenser B. John Donne
C. John Dryden D. Sir Philip Sidney

10. Who wrote *Doctor Faustus*?
A. Robert Greene
B. Robert Nash
C. William Shakespeare
D. Christopher Marlowe

11. Who wrote *The Merchant of Venice*?
A. William Shakespeare
B. Ben Jonson
C. William Congreve
D. John Dryden

12. Who ruled England when Shakespeare became known for his dramas?
A. King Henry VIII B. King Richard II
C. Queen Elizabeth I D. Queen Mary Tudor

13. When was the King James Version (KJV) of the Bible published?
A. 1603 B. 1615
C. 1611 D. 1620

14. Which blind poet wrote a sonnet about his own blindness?
A. George Herbert B. John Milton
C. John Donne D. Henry Vaughan

15. Who, among the following, was not a Romantic poet?
A. William Wordsworth
B. Percy Bysshe Shelley
C. Alfred Tennyson
D. Lord Byron

16. Which woman writer wrote *Sense and Sensibility*?
A. Jane Austen B. Mary Shelley
C. Maria Edgeworth D. Emily Bronte

17. What was the real name of George Eliot?
A. Louisa May Alcott
B. Mary Ann Evans
C. Amantine L.A. Dupin
D. Charlotte Bronte

18. Who wrote the poem, *In Memoriam*, on the death of his friend?
A. Alfred Tennyson
B. Robert Browning
C. Dante Gabriel Rossetti
D. Henry Wadsworth Longfellow

19. Who wrote the novel, *Oliver Twist*, on the Victorian workhouses?
A. Samuel Richardson
B. William Makepeace Thackeray
C. George Meredith
D. Charles Dickens

20. Who wrote *A Passage to India?*
A. Rudyard Kipling B. George Orwell
C. E.M. Forster D. Rider Haggard

21. Who wrote *Lady Chatterley's Lover*?
A. James Joyce B. Virginia Woolf
C. E.M. Forster D. D.H. Lawrence

22. Who wrote *The Return of the Native*?
A. Bret Harte B. Sir Walter Scott
C. Thomas Hardy D. William Morris

23. Who wrote *The Heart of Darkness*?
A. Joseph Conrad B. Henry James
C. Samuel Butler D. George Moore

24. When did Rabindranath Tagore win the Nobel Prize for Literature?
A. 1910 B. 1920
C. 1913 D. 1915

25. For which book did Arundhati Roy win the Booker Prize?
A. *The Ministry of Utmost Happiness*
B. *The End of Imagination*
C. *Listening to Grasshoppers*
D. *The God of Small Things*

26. Who won the Nobel Prize for Literature in 2019?
A. Peter Handke B. Olga Tokarczuk
C. Kuzuo Ishiguro D. Bob Dylan

27. Which novel was authored by the African writer, Ngugi wa Thiong'o?
A. *Cry, the Beloved Country*
B. *Weep Not, Child*

C. *Things Fall Apart*
D. *The Interpreters*

28. Who was the first African writer to win the Nobel Prize for Literature in 1986?
A. Wole Soyinka
B. Chinua Achebe
C. Ngugi wa Thiong'o
D. Ben Okri

29. Who wrote the autobiography, Wings of Fire?
A. Dadabhai Naoroji B. A.P.J. Abdul Kalam
C. J.R.D. Tata D. C.V. Raman

30. Who wrote the autobiography, My Experiments with Truth?
A. Jawaharlal Nehru B. Vallabhai Patel
C. M.K. Gandhi D. B.R. Ambedkar

31. Which character dies at the end of Dickens' novel, A Tale of Two Cities?
A. Charles Darney B. Sydney Carton
C. Doctor Manette D. Lucie Manette

32. Which essayist has written: "Reading maketh a full man; conference a ready man; and writing an exact man."?
A. Francis Bacon B. Roger Ascham
C. Thomas Hobbes D. Jeremy Taylor

33. Which playwright had said: "I have nothing to declare except my genius."?
A. Eugene O'Neill
B. William Shakespeare
C. George Bernard Shaw
D. Oscar Wilde

34. Which poet has written: "I have measured out my life with coffee spoons."?
A. Ted Hughes B. Sylvia Plath
C. T.S. Eliot D. W.B. Yeats

35. Which philosopher has written: "I think; therefore I am."?
A. Socrates B. Plato
C. Descartes D. Voltaire

36. In which novel does a race of horses rule over their human slaves?
A. George Orwell's *Animal Farm*
B. Jonathan Swift's *Gulliver's Travels*
C. Mary Shelley's *Frankenstein*
D. Ann Radcliffe's *The Mysteries of Udolpho*

37. In which novel does the white hero have a loyal black slave named Friday?
A. Henry Fielding's *Tom Jones*
B. Charles Dickens' *Nicholas Nickleby*
C. Daniel Dafoe's *Robinson Crusoe*
D. Tobias Smollett's *Roderick Random*

38. Which scientist wrote *On the Origin of Species?*
A. Thomas Henry Huxley
B. Charles Darwin
C. Isaac Asimov
D. Carl Sagan

39. Which Feminist writer wrote *The Second Sex*?
A. Simone de Beauvoir
B. Audre Lorde
C. Germaine Greer
D. Gloria Steinem

40. Which psychologist wrote *The Interpretation of Dreams?*
A. Carl Jung B. Sigmund Freud
C. Josef Breuer D. Jean Piaget

ANSWERS

1	2	3	4	5	6	7	8	9	10
A	A	D	A	D	D	A	B	A	D
11	**12**	**13**	**14**	**15**	**16**	**17**	**18**	**19**	**20**
A	C	C	B	C	A	B	A	D	C
21	**22**	**23**	**24**	**25**	**26**	**27**	**28**	**29**	**30**
D	C	A	C	D	A	B	A	B	C
31	**32**	**33**	**34**	**35**	**36**	**37**	**38**	**39**	**40**
B	A	D	C	C	B	C	B	A	B

Previous Paper (Solved)

JAMIA MILLIA ISLAMIA (JMI)

B.A. (HONS.) ENGLISH ENTRANCE EXAM 2019

PART—A

Directions: *Choose the correct options in the Objective Type questions given below:*

(1 mark each)

1. A limerick is a:
A. A six-line poem rhyming aaabbb
B. A five-line poem rhyming aabba
C. A seven-line poem rhyming aabbcca
D. An eight-line poem rhyming ababcdcd

2. A haiku is a:
A. A short poem of 10 syllables
B. A short poem of 15 syllables
C. A short poem of 17 syllables
D. A short poem of 19 syllables

3. A fable is a:
A. A short story with animal characters
B. A short story with fantastical beast characters
C. A short story with gods and demi-gods
D. A short story with fairies and magicians

4. The Nobel Prize in Literature for the year 2017 was awarded to:
A. Margaret Atwood
B. Doris Lessing
C. Haruki Murakami
D. Kazuo Ishiguro

5. Rabindranath Tagore was awarded the Nobel Prize in Literature for the year:
A. 1905 B. 1910
C. 1913 D. 1920

6. *A Suitable Boy* is written by:
A. Amitav Ghosh
B. Vikram Seth
C. Salman Rushdie
D. Arvind Adiga

7. *Malgudi Days* is written by:
A. Upamanyu Chatterjee
B. Raja Rao
C. R.K. Narayan
D. Mulk Raj Anand

8. *The Untouchable* is written by:
A. Raja Rao
B. Mulk Raj Anand
C. Amrita Pritam
D. Munshi Premchand

9. *Midnight's Children* is written by:
A. Vikram Seth
B. Salman Rushdie
C. Amitav Ghosh
D. Arundhati Roy

10. *Train to Pakistan* is written by:
A. Khushwant Singh
B. Arundhati Roy
C. Anita Desai
D. Amrita Pritam

11. *Ice-Candy Man* is written by:
A. Bapsi Sidhwa
B. Alamgir Hashmi
C. Saadat Hasan Manto
D. Agha Shahid Ali

12. *The Kite Runner* is written by:
A. Paulo Coelho
B. Khaled Hosseini
C. Yann Martel
D. George Orwell

13. *Decolonizing the Mind* is written by:
A. Wole Soyinka
B. Chinua Achebe

C. Ngugi wa Thiong'o
D. Amos Tutuola

14. *The Life of Pi* is written by:
A. Joseph Conrad
B. Paulo Coelho
C. Yann Martel
D. Harper Lee

15. *The Mahabharata* is written by:
A. Vatsyayan B. Bharata Muni
C. Ved Vyas D. Kalidas

16. *Iliad* and *Odyssey* are written by:
A. Cicero
B. Homer
C. Socrates
D. Aristotle

17. *Rubaiyyat* is written by:
A. Saadi Shirazi B. Omar Khayyam
C. Al-Biruni D. Rumi

18. *Cry, the Beloved Country* is written by:
A. Alan Paton
B. Nadine Gordimer
B. Joseph Conrad
D. J.M. Coetzee

19. "Lihaaf" is written by:
A. Attia Hosain
B. Ismat Chugtai
C. Rashid Jahan
D. Eunice De Souza

20. "Draupadi" is written by:
A. Githa Hariharan
B. Mahasweta Devi
C. Nayantara Sehgal
D. Anita Desai

21. *A House for Mr. Biswas* is written by:
A. Ruth Prawer Jhabvala
B. Bapsi Sidhwa
C. Amitav Ghosh
D. V.S. Naipaul

22. *Lady Chatterley's Lover* is written by:
A. Thomas Hardy
B. D.H. Lawrence
C. James Joyce
D. Agatha Christie

23. Mary Ann Evans was a novelist better known by her pen name:
A. Acton Bell
B. A.M. Barnard
C. George Eliot
D. Harper Lee

24. The first woman novelist of England was:
A. Mary Shelley
B. Aphra Behn
C. Elizabeth Gaskell
D. Jane Austen

25. A ballad is:
A. A short poem or song that is humorous
B. A short poem or song that has nymphs and satyrs
C. A short poem or song that has a dreamlike quality
D. A short poem or song that narrates a romantic story

26. An epic is:
A. A long poem with heroic characters
B. A long poem with animal characters
C. A long poem with humorous characters
D. A long poem with nymphs and satyrs

27. The film, *My Fair Lady,* is based on the G.B. Shaw play:
A. *Saint Joan*
B. *Pygmalion*
C. *Candida*
D. *Major Barbara*

28. Which one of these creatures in J.K. Rowling's novels is not based on classical mythology?
A. Fluffy
B. Mrs. Norris
C. the Phoenix
D. the Hippogriff

29. In which Hardy novel does a girl fail to get married because she goes to the wrong church?
A. *Far From the Madding Crowd*
B. *The Return of the Native*
C. *The Mayor of Casterbridge*
D. *Tess of the D'Urbervilles*

30. In which Coleridge poem is a ship condemned to wandering endlessly on the seas after a sailor kills a large bird?
A. Kubla Khan
B. Christabel
C. The Rime of the Ancient Mariner
D. Frost at Midnight

31. In which Kafka story does a man wake up to find himself transformed into a giant insect?
A. The Judgment
B. The Metamorphosis
C. In the Penal Colony
D. A Common Confusion

32. In which Dickens novel does a child get punished because he asks for more food?
A. *Nicholas Nickelby*
B. *David Copperfield*
C. *Great Expectations*
D. *Oliver Twist*

33. In which Shakespearean play does a moneylender demand a pound of flesh from his debtor?
A. *The Two Gentlemen of Verona*
B. *The Merchant of Venice*
C. *Measure for Measure*
D. *Cymbeline*

34. *Anna Karenina* is written by:
A. Anton Chekhov B. Alexander Pushkin
C. Maxim Gorky D. Leo Tolstoy

35. *Crime and Punishment* is written by:
A. Fyodor Dostoyevsky
B. Ivan Turgenev
C. Alexander Pushkin
D. Nikolai Gogol

36. *The Scarlet Letter* is written by:
A. Langston Hughes
B. Ernest Hemingway
C. Nathaniel Hawthorne
D. Emily Dickinson

37. *The Adventures of Tom Sawyer* is written by:
A. Mark Twain
B. Ernest Hemingway
C. William Faulkner
D. Herman Melville

38. Which Dickens novel begins with the words, "It was the best of times, it was the worst of times ...."
A. *Great Expectations*
B. *A Tale of Two Cities*
C. *The Pickwick Papers*
D. *Barnaby Rudge*

39. Which modern novel ends with the words, "Frankly, my dear, I don't give a damn."
A. *To Kill a Mockingbird*
B. *Murder on the Orient Express*
C. *The Other Side of Midnight*
D. *Gone with the Wind*

40. The famous speech "I Have A Dream" was delivered by:
A. Winston Churchill
B. Abraham Lincoln
C. Emmeline Pankhurst
D. Martin Luther King Jr.

ANSWERS

1	2	3	4	5	6	7	8	9	10
B	C	A	D	C	B	C	B	B	A
11	**12**	**13**	**14**	**15**	**16**	**17**	**18**	**19**	**20**
A	B	C	C	C	B	B	A	B	B
21	**22**	**23**	**24**	**25**	**26**	**27**	**28**	**29**	**30**
D	B	C	B	D	A	B	B	A	C
31	**32**	**33**	**34**	**35**	**36**	**37**	**38**	**39**	**40**
B	D	B	D	A	C	A	B	D	D

English Literature & Media Knowledge

- English Literature at a Glance
- Glossary of Literary Terms
- Multiple Choice Questions
- Literary and Media Knowledge
- Muliple Type Questions

English Literature at A Glance

THE OLD ENGLISH PERIOD (I) (ANGLO-SAXON PERIOD) (450-1050)

Beowulf is probably the oldest epic of the Teutonic world. It is believed to be belonging to the first half of the sixth century.

Some important works of the Anglo-Saxon period (Pre-Christian Era).

Some important works of the Anglo-Saxon period are: *The Ruined Burg, The Lover's Message. The Maiden's Complaint, The Wanderer* and *the Seafarer.*

'The Wanderer is also known as *'Widsith'*. The work is based on the wandering life of the gleeman.

Belonging to this period, we also have *"Deor's Lament"*, which, according to Long is, "much more poetic than *'Widsith,'* and is the one perfect lyric of the Anglo-Saxon period.

In the *Seafarer*, we have glimpses of hard sea life along with the call of the sea, which we, in our times, find more pronouncedly, but perhaps less picturesquely, in Masefield's *"Sea-Fever"*.

Some Christian writers of the Anglo-Saxon period.

Whereas the pagan literature of the Anglo-Saxon period was chiefly in the form of oral legends which they had brought with them from the foreign lands which they previously inhabited, the Christian writing mainly came into existence as a result of the teachings of the monks who had come under the influence of two schools—the Augustinian School (from Rome) and Northumbrian School (from Ireland).

While the former, did not produce much lasting works, the latter produced a number of good and great writers, *e.g.,* **The Venerable Bede (673-735), Caedmon (seventh century)** and **Cynewulf (eighth century)**.

Besides the poets mentioned above, we have **Alfred (848-90)** who is chiefly known as a translator.

ANGLO-NORMAN PERIOD (1066-1350)

Some important works of the Anglo-Norman period.

One important work of this period is *Geoffrey's "Historic Regum Britanniae"* (1137) commonly known as *"History"*. Geoffrey is believed to have died in 1154.

Geoffrey's work which became immensely popular in his own life, is a mixture of pagan and Christian legends and is based more on lies than on real historical events.

However, the said work has its literary value for its poetry and romance pertaining to king Arthur and his Knights, and hence, it became a source of inspiration and scintillating subject matter for such illustrious authors as Malory, Shakespeare and Tennyson.

Geoffrey's work was in Latin verse. Thereafter appeared *"Layman's Brut"* (c. 1200) which has its main interest in giving Arthur's legends in (Anglo-Saxon) English itself.

Then there appeared what are known as *"Metrical Romances"* which were based on the "matter" of France, Rome and Britain.

While in the *Matter of France,* **Charlemagne's** exploits dominated and in the *Matter of Rome*

Alexander's adventures and the war of Troy were the main subjects, in the *Matter of Britain*, exploits of Arthur and his knights of the Round Table were chief subject matter. There were a number of cycles pertaining to the knights of Arthur, among them being **Sir Gawain (1350)** *Quest of the Holy Grail, Death of Arthur, Merlin, etc.*

Besides the above, other works of the period included ballads, lyrics and such poems as the *Owl and the Nightingale, Ormulum, Cursor Mundi (1320), The Pearl, Patience, Cleanness, etc.* Also **Roger Bacon's** *"Opus Majus"* appeared in 1267.

THE AGE OF CHAUCER (1340-1400)

The Hundred years war between England and France had already started in 1338 when **Chaucer** was born in **1340**.

In the earlier years of the war, England was all-powerful and under Edward III it won victories over France at Sluys in 1340 and Crecy in 1346, culminating in the capture of Calais in 1347.

Another thumping victory was won by the Black Prince, Edward III's son in 1356 by defeating the French at Poitiers.

As a result of the English victories, the English foreign trade began to flourish, particularly in the export of wool to Flanders, which filled the coffers of the English king and the people also became richer, as we notice conspicuously in **Chaucer's** *Canterbury Tales* when we consider the lot of so many characters, particularly those belonging to landed aristocracy.

This picture is also graphically depicted in **Trevelyan's** *British History of Six Centuries.*

It was unfortunate for England that in the moment of its glory it was overtaken by plague, the Black Death which took a heavy toll of life all over Europe in 1348-49.

As a result of the Black Death, most of the labourers who escaped death, left the country, and this caused an intense scarcity of the availability of essential commodities at cheap rates. To meet this menace, the Parliament tried to force the labourers to accept the same wages as they were getting before the Black Death, and it all finally precipitated into the well-known Peasants' Revolt during the reign of Richard II.

In spite of the passage of certain statutes purported to safeguard the English clergy against the undue domination of the Pope, the low simmering of wrath among the clergymen for several reasons, there emerged in the "Lollards Movement" under the leadership of the redoubtable Wyclif.

Another prominent feature, this one in the literary world, was the slow advent of the spirit of New Learning from Italy and drastic changes in the structure of the English language which had already been continuing as the inevitable outcome of the Norman conquest at Hastings in 1066.

These were the general conditions in which the most significant writers of the age—**Chaucer, Langland, Dunbar,** etc. lived and flourished, thus heralding a new age slowly, but boldly and surely.

MAJOR AUTHORS AND THEIR WORKS OF CHAUCER'S AGE

Sir Thomas More (1478-1535)

Utopia (English Version)

William Tyndale (1485-1536)

New Testament

Geoffrey Chaucer (1340-1400)

The Boke of the Duchesse
The Romaunt of the Rose
The House of Fame
Troylus Cryseyde
The Canterbury Tales
Legends of Good Women
The Parliament of Fouls

Wyclif (1320-1384)

The Bible

John Heywood (1564-1627)

Four P's

Thomas Sackville and Thomas Norton : (1536-1608) (1532-1584)

Gorboduc

THE SEVENTEENTH CENTURY

THE RENAISSANCE (1578-1625)

The Renaissance of English Literature coincides with the Age of Queen Elizabeth I. Hence, in the history of English literature, this period is also called as the *Elizabethan Age*. The inspiration for the great works of this period came from the prolific translations into English of works of ancient Rome and Greece. Thus, Plutarch's *Lives* was translated by **Sir Thomas North (1579)** from the French version. Montaigne's Essays was translated by **John Florio (1603)**. In verse, Ovid's *Metamorphoses* was translated by **Arthur Golding (1565, 1567)**. Among other works of foreign origin translated into English were Ariosto's *Orlando Furioso* by **Harrington (1591)**, and Homer's *Iliad* by **'George Chapman (1598)**.

The rising English stage and the English novel borrowed from Boccaccio, Cinthio, Bandello and Straparola — the Italians. Attracted though England was to Italian art, it resisted the evil influences of debauchery, crime and passions that the Italian spirit represented. Yet, the time was ripe in England for the full development of every art and literary form. Renaissance means *a flowering again of art and culture*. It inculcated a sense of wonder in things. England also wanted to rival Spain, France and Portugal in her navigational triumphs. Thus in 1578, Sir Francis Drake circumnavigated the world, and in 1588, the English navy destroyed the Armada. The same spirit of adventure moved literature. In *Apologie for Poetrie*, Sidney described the poet — of all sciences'the monarch'. Poets were encouraged to innovate new styles and rhythms.

Poetry

Three great men of letters led the Renaissance in England — Spenser, Sidney and Lyly.

Edmund Spenser (1552-1599) wrote the *Shepheardes Calendar* (1579)—an allegory. The union of line and metre is varied and rich. In *Hymnes In honour of Love and Beautie*, he sets forth his philosophy, the conflict in his mind between paganism and Christianity. He also wrote a satire named, *Mother Hubberd's Tale* to denounce the neglect of arts and letters. His pastoral, *Colin Clout's Come Home Again* describes his stay in London in 1589. His *Amoretti* (1595) are sonnets on love and his *Epithalamion* is an ode, But his masterpiece is the *Faerie Queene* (1589, 1595), an allegory in which characters represent virtues and vices. In it his lyrical quality and colour-effects are at their best. The *Faerie Queene* is Queen Elizabeth. The nine-line stanza he used is now called the *Spenserian stanza*.

Sir Philip Sidney (1554-1586) was a scholar, knight and courtier. In 1580 he wrote *Arcadia* which has a blend of pastoral and heroic elements It is a romance of chivalry and love. The language is characterized by *pathetic fallacy* — endowing inanimate objects with feelings and sensations. William Shakespeare borrowed from this style. His other poem, *Astrophel and Stella* (1591) describes his lost love for the daughter of an Earl. His *Apologie for Poetrie* (1595) written in an unaffected prose, is a plea for poetry.

John Lyly (1554-1606) invented an artistic, flowery style called *euphuism* through his famous romance, *Euphues, the Anatomy of Wit* (1579). This style was adopted by the refined people of the Court. The style is characterized by the use of alliteration and antithesis, fantastic metaphors and similes based on mythology, and natural history of flora and fauna.

The works of these three trail-blazed many poets and sonneteers like Samuel Daniel, Michael Drayton, Thomas Watson, Henry Constable and Thomas Lodge. Notable works from 1590 to 1603 were **Samuel Daniel's (1562-1619)** *The Civil Wars* (1595) describing the *War of the Roses*, **Michael Drayton's (1563-1631)** *Idea, the Shepherd's Garland*, *The Baron's Wars, England's Heroicall Epistles* (1603) and *Poly-Olbion*, a long description of England in 15,000 alexandrines or lines of twelve syllables. England came to be known as *"a nest of singing birds"* because of the great number of lyrics and poems written in this period. **Thomas Campion (1567-1620)** published an anthology called *Two Books of Ayres* (1612). Many of the best poems are found in plays by Ben Jonson, Thomas Dekker, Beaumont and Fletcher, and Webster. But those of William Shakespeare are probably the most beautiful. In his *Sonnets*, he describes his love for a married woman who betrays him. Other poems of this period are Marlowe's Hero and Leander (1598), Shakespeare's *Venus and Adonis* (1593) and *The Rape of Lucrece* (1594).

After Elizabeth's reign, in James I rule, poetry became religious and didactic. The Protestant spirit dominated the literary works. The poems of George Wither, William Browne, the Fletcher brothers and William Drummond show the influence of Spenser still.

Ben Jonson (1573-1637) was the greatest humanist of the time. He was mainly a playwright but wrote poems also. His poetry is found in collections like Epigrams and The Forest (1616) and The Underwoods (1640). He was a satirist and neo-classicist being influenced by the Latin classics.

John Donne's (1573-1631) poetry is revolutionary. He disobeys the laws of rhythm and uses a device called the metaphysical conceit in which strangely opposite ideas are juxtaposed.

Prose

Much of the prose of the period is poetical, influenced by euphuism. Robert Greene, Thomas Lodge, Thomas Nashe, Thomas Deloney, and Thomas Dekker are the major writers. **Robert Greene's (1558-1592)** works include *Mamilia* and *Menaphon* and **Thomas Lodge's (1558-1625)** include *Rosalynde: Euphues Golden Legacie* (1590). **Thomas Nashe (1567-1601)** wrote pamphlets like The *Anatomie of Absurdities* and *The Terrors of the Night*. **Thomas Dekker's (1572-1632)** *The Gils Horne booke* is famous for its picturesque prose. Most of the poets and prose writers of this period were also dramatists. Shakespeare used prose for homely and humorous scenes and verse for tragic ones.

Many writers of the English Renaissance were inspired by the literary criticism of the Continent to write some themselves. Stephen Gosson's *The Schoole of Abuse* (1579) and *Sidney's Apologie for Poetrie* are good examples. Sidney eulogizes the poet as a law-giver. The period also saw works of religious prose. **Richard Hooker's (1554-1600)** pamphlet on the Marlin Marprelate controversy is a famous one. Hooker's *Of the Laws of Ecclesiastical Polity* (1594) is a masterpiece of English prose. The most seminal work of the period is the authorized version of the Bible published in 1611. The work was commissioned by James 1. A beautiful prose minus archaism is used by the revisers. The diction was to influence the English language very deeply. It is the language of daily speech, yet fresh and lofty.

Side by side with religious literature, secular and philosophical literature, mostly written by **Francis Bacon (1561-1626)**, came out. He had taken all knowledge as his province and elaborated his doctrines in his *Novum Organum* (1620). His ideas influenced the formation of *The Royal Society for Improving Natural Knowledge* in 1645. His most popular work is his *Essays* written on diverse topics in a terse, epigrammatic style. The English writers quote copiously from Bacon today. His sentences are household terms. Take for example, "*He that hath wife and children hath given hostages to fortune*". "*Some books are to be tasted, others to be swallowed and some few to be chewed and digested*".

Another great prose-writer of the period was **Robert Burton (1577-1640)** whose *The Anatomy of Melancholy* (1621) is full of pedantry. He borrowed from numerous sources and is full of melancholy and jests; his style abounds in synonyms and epithets.

Drama

Drama thrived in the Renaissance. Foreign influence, especially of Italy, predominated. Plays were written so that the public would enjoy them and applaud the stage. There was a great variety of plays written — pure tragedy, tragi-comedy, historical drama, romantic comedy, comedy of errors, farce, pastoral, etc. The stage was a simple structure, circular in form with a courtyard open to the sky. A platform projected into the courtyard. Boys played the female roles. The public consisted of groundlings and courtiers on galleries. The unities of time, place and action were disregarded. Farce and tragedy were found in succession.

Several mythological allegories were acted before the court. **John Lyly's** euphuistic romances like *Campaspe* (1584), *Sapho and Phao, Endymion* (1592), *Midas* were praises of the queen. **George Peele (1558-1598)** wrote *The Araygnement of Paris* (1584) and *The Old Wives' Tale*. There were violent plays like **Thomas Kyd's (1558-1594)** The *Spanish Tragedie* (1585) and **Christopher Marlowe's (1564-1593)** *Tamburlaine, the Great* (1587) and *Doctor Faustus* (1592). *Doctor Faustus* is an allegory on the Renaissance love of power. It shows how Doctor Faustus, the scientist, sells his soul to the devil for twenty-four years of full power to satisfy every desire. In the end his agony increases as the devil approaches to claim his soul. Marlowe also wrote *The Jew of Malta*, which shows the unbridled love for wealth, and the historical play Edward II. Marlowe crafted the blank verse (mighty line as Shakespeare called it and used). This was suited to the fiery speeches of his characters.

The towering genius of the age was certainly **William Shakespeare (1564-1616)**. He was versatile and wrote about 36 plays and 144 sonnets. "Shakespeare was not of an age but for all times" and "Poets are born not made", wrote Ben Jonson about him. He created a gallery of nearly 800 characters who typify personalities found through human history. Julius Caesar's pride and ambition, Macbeth's unbridled ambition, King Lear's dotedness, and Othello's susceptibility to suspicion against his wife — are tragic flaws that govern men even today.

Shakespeare was not educated except for a few years at a grammar school. He had 'little Latin and less Greek' and read books in translation from Latin and Greek. He adapted the stories into a World entirely his own, instinct with life and vibrancy. Shakespeare began his career by acting for the stage. Then he wrote plays and staged them, mainly to seek court patronage. His great success made him the envy of his contemporaries like Robert Greene. In his tragedies he depicts the fall of great men owing to a tragic flaw in their character. Although they had the will to change their destiny, a fate controlled them. He used the beliefs of his time like the supernatural powers and phenomena to capture the interest of his audience. Some of his historical plays are *Richard II* (1596) and *King John* (1595). Among the romantic comedies *As You Like It* (1600), *The Merchant of Venice* (1596) and *Twelfth Night* (1601) are popular. *A Midsummer Night's Dream* (1595) is a fairy play. *Romeo and Juliet* (1594) is a tragicomedy. He used prose and blank verse.

His *Henry IV* (I & 2) (1597, 1598) contain much more blank verse than his other plays. In depth of psychological insight, and power of style *Hamlet* (1601), one of Shakespeare's great tragedies, stands supreme. *The Tempest* (161I) is one of his last plays which shows the dramatist's mellowed maturity.

Even after 400 years, Shakespeare's plays are very popular, being translated into almost every important language. *"Age cannot wither her nor custom stale her infinite variety"*; Shakespeare described Cleopatra in these words. The same may be said about his plays also.

Ben Jonson was Shakespeare's antithesis. He borrowed the style of the classics and was very erudite. He carefully studied society and wrote about it. He took the different 'humours' or dominating characteristics of men and satirized them in *Every Man in his Humour* (1598) and *Every Man out of his Humour* (1599), *Volpone, or the Fox* (1605) and *The Alchemist* (1605). He also wrote the historical tragedies, *Sejanus His Fall* (1603)' and *Catiline His Conspiracy* (1611). The plays are very true to history. John Marston, Thomas Dekker, Thomas Heywood and Middleton were other playwrights of the age. John Webster (1580-1625) is famous for horror plays like *The White Devil* (1609-1612) and *The Duchess of Malfi* (1613-1614).

MAJOR AUTHORS AND THEIR WORKS

Edmund Spenser (1552-1599)
The Faerie Queene
The Shepheardes Calendar
Amoretti
Epithalamion
Prothalamion
Mother Hubberd's Tale
The Ruins of Time
The Tears of the Muses
Astrophel

Phillip Sidney (1554-1586)
Arcadia
Astrophel and Stella
An Apologie for Poetrie

Ben Jonson (1573-1637)
Every Man in His Humour
Every Man Out of His Humour
Volpone Or the Fox
Cynthia's Revels
The Alchemist
Bartholomew Fayre
Epicaene or the Silent Women
Sejanus His Fall
Catline His Conspiracy
The Poetaster
The Devil as an Ass
The Masque of Beauty

Samuel Daniel (1562-1619)
Delia
Civil Wars between the Two Houses of Lancaster and York

Michael Drayton (1563-1631)
The Battle of Agincourt
England's heroic Epistles
The Barons' Wars
Polyolbion

William Shakespeare (1564-1616)
The Two Gentlement of Verona
The Merry Wives of Windsor
Measure for Measure
The Comedy of Errors
Love's Labour's Lost
The Taming of the Shrew
All's Well that Ends Well
A Midsummer Night's Dream
The Merchant of Venice
Much Ado About Nothing
As You Like it
Twelfth Night
Romeo and Juliet
Macbeth
Hamlet
King Lear
Othello
Antony and Cleopatra
Julius Caesar
Timon of Athens
Coriolanus
Titus Andronicus
Troilus and Cressida
King John
King Richard the Second
King Henry the Fourth-Part First
King Henry the Fourth-Second Part
King Henry the Fifth
King Henry the Sixth-First Part
King Henry the Sixth-Second Part
King Henry the Sixth-Third Part
King Richard the Third
King Henry the Eighth
Cymbeline
Pericles
The Winter's Tale
The Tempest
Venus and Adonis and Rape of Lucrece (Narrative Poems)
Sonnets (154 in number).

Christopher Marlowe (1564-1593)
Tamburlaine the Great
Edward II
Doctor Faustus
The Jew of Malta
The Tragedy of Dido, Queen of Carthage.

George Peele (1558-1597)
The Araygnement of Paris
The Famous Chronicle of King Edward I

Robert Greene (1560-1592)
Frier Bacon and Frier Bungey
Orlando Furioso
Pandosto

Thomas Nashe (1567-1601)
The Unfortunate Traveller Or The Life of Jack Wilton

Thomas Lodge (1558-1625)
The Wounds of Civil War
Rosalynde

Thomas Kyd (1557-1595)
The Spanish Tragedy

John Lyly (1554-1606)
Euphues, The Anatomy of Wit
Euphues and His England
Endymion

Francis Bacon (1561-1626)
Essays
The Advancement of Learning
The New Atlantis
Novum Organum

John Webster (1580-1625)
The White Devil
The Duchess of Malfi
The Devil's Law Case.

Thomas Heywood (1575-1650)
A Woman Killed with Kindness
The English Traveller
The Captives

Robert Burton (1577-1640)
The Anatomy of Melancholy

Sir Thomas Browne (1605-1682)
Religio Medici
Vulgar Errors
Hydrotaphia or Urne Burriale
Christian Morals

Thomas Hobbes (1588-1679)
Leviathan

Jeremy Taylor (1613-1667)
The Liberty of Prophesying
Holy Living
Holy Dying

END OF THE RENAISSANCE (1625-1660)

Prose

Puritanism set the trend for the literature during the reign of Charles 1. The Bible was the guiding spirit which may be best seen in Milton's works. The zealous Calvinists enforced Presbyterianism. The passionate curiosity for life which characterized the Renaissance gave place to a search for salvation. **Sir Thomas Browne (1605-1682)** was a scientist, but in his *Pseudodoxia Epidemica or Vulgar Errors* (1646), we see his belief in miracles. His *Religio Medici* (1642) speaks of the vanity of earthly life. **George Herbert's (1596-1633)** *The Country Parson* and **Jeremy Taylor's (1613-1667)** *Holy Living* (1650) and *Holy Dying* (1651) are sermons championing religious freedom. **John Milton (1608-1674)**, who is famous as a poet, wrote numerous pamphlets in favour of divorce which are models of beautiful prose. His *Areopagitica* (1644) is a speech for the liberty of unlicensed writing.

Another great prose-writer was **Thomas Hobbes (1588-1679)** whose *Leviathan* (1651) is a famous work. He was an empiricist and realist and believed that sensations and ideas are caused by physical reasons. Numerous works of ethics, sociology and history were written. *The History of the Rebellion and Civil Wars in England* was written by **Edward Hyde (1609-1674). Izaac Walton (1593-1683)** wrote the biographies of John Donne and George Herbert.

The Compleat Angler (1653) is his famous work on the post-Civil War scene and contains descnptions of the English countryside.

Poetry

Two types of poets existed then — the Cavaliers, who were the Royalists, and the religious or Metaphysical poets. Thomas Carew, Sir John Suckling, John Cleveland, Robert Herrick were Cavalier poets who displayed epicurean tastes. Imagination and sensuous imagery predominate their poems. Among the religious poets, Herbert, Crashaw, Vaughan and Marvell stand out. They were mystics. **George Herbert's (1593-1633)** style is simple and expresses Christian piety in his anthology The Temple (1633). His poems *The Pulley and Love* are very popular. **Richard Crashaw (1613-1649)** used fantastic conceits; e.g. he describes the maudlin St Mary Magdalene's eyes as "walking baths, compedious oceans", **Henry Vaughan (1622-1695)** was a mystic and his poem The Retreat is a nostalgic longing for the blissful heavenly state of childhood.

John Milton's greatest achievement was his *Paradise Lost* (1667). In theme it deals with the fall of man. In form, it follows the strict unity of the classical epic. His other poems are *L'Allegro* (1632), *II Penseroso* (1632), *Comus* (1634), *Lycidas* (1637), *Samson Agonistes* (1671), etc.

RESTORATION LITERATURE (1620-1734)

Prose

In 1660, Charles II returned to the throne and the Puritan republic ended. The year is also marked as the beginning of the modem literature. **John Bunyan's (1628-1688)** works, *Grace Abounding* (1666) and *The Pilgrim's Progress* (1678) are the last surviving works of Puritan faith. The Pilgrim's Progress is an allegory describing the trials and tribulations on the way to salvation as faced by a Christian. Bunyan's prose is a blend of common speech and the grandeur of the revised Bible.

The scientific spirit took over the reign. The Royal Society of London for the Improvement of Natural Knowledge, to which Bacon and William Harvey (who discovered the circulation of blood) had contributed, now had many learned men. **Sir Isaac Newton** published Principia in 1687. He discovered the laws of gravity, of the diffraction of white light and the theory of fluxions.

John Locke (1632-1704) propounded a new philosophy of commonsense and intelligent reasoning in his *An Essay Concerning Human Understanding* (1690). It lays stress on development of character. It was to influence the English thought. Voltaire was one of his French disciples.

Poetry

Restoration literature was derived from pre-Commonwealth national literature and was a reaction against Puritan oppression. It rejected severe moral codes of conduct and was chiefly satiric in nature. **Samuel Butler's (1612-1680)** poem, *Hudibras* published in three parts (1663, 1664 & 1678), is a typical work of this period. It is inspired by *Don Quixote*. He satirizes Sir Hudibras as a grotesque Presbyterian with a squire called Ralpho. It lays bare all the human follies in octosyllabic couplets. Many court poets like **Andrew Marvell (1621-1678)** and **John Oldham (1653-1683)** were veterans of the Republican era and satirize the follies of the new age.

The great poet of the period was **John Dryden (1631-1700)**. He excelled in almost every kind of composition. He wrote a series of heroic stanzas in honour of Cromwell on his death. He was a disciple of the metaphysical poets displaying their far-fetched images and conceits. In *Astraea Redux* (1660), he celebrated the return of Charles II and in *Annus Mirabilis* (1667) he commemorated the Great Fire of London and the war with Holland. He was a staunch Tory and his famous satires are *Absalom and Achitophel* (1681), *The Medal and Mac-Flecknoe*. In this last work he satirizes Shadwell, the Whig poet. *The Hind and the Panther* (1687) is an allegory on Catholicism and Anglicanism. Dryden also translated the classics, chiefly Persuis and Juvenal. He turned Virgil's *Aeneid* into brilliant couplets. His *Alexander's Feast* is an ode in honour of St. Cecilia.

Drama

The dramatic works of the Restoration were licentious and full of cynicism. They regarded the moral code of the Puritans as a matter of ridicule. Scenery now played an important part on the stage and actresses, not boys, played the female roles. The theatre was regarded as a place of vice and evil. Shakespeare's plays were rewritten and his tragedies like *Romeo and Juliet* given happy endings. French influence dominated and extraordinary superhuman feats were described. Heroes were presented as ideals and were made to give pompous speeches.

Dryden wrote many plays like *Aureng-zebe* or *The Great Mogul* (1675) and The Conquest of Granada (1669, 1670) which abound in rhetoric.

The tragedians were **Thomas Otway (1651-1685)**, Nathaniel Lee (1653-1692) and **Nicholas Rowe (1674-1718)**. The comedy of this period reflects the gay intrigues of the society. Caricature and farce were used and obscenity also touched it. The main aim was to amuse. **Sir George Etheredge (1635-1691)** was an innovator and **William Wycherley (1640-1715)** was a moralist playwright. **William Congreve (1670-1729)** wrote a series of masterpieces including *The Way of the World* (1700). **John Vanbrugh** (1664-1726) and **George Farquhar (1678-1707)** were other comedy writers of the period.

Criticism

Dryden was the first English critic. *The Essay of Dramatick Poesie* (1668) is his longest single prose work and a major piece of English literary criticism. It is in the form of a discussion between four characters, one of whom is Dryden himself. It deals with topics related to theatre and evaluates the works of the Elizabethan dramatists, especially of Shakespeare.

The Diarists of the Restoration Period

One of the sources of information and genres of prose writing during the Restoration were diaries. The important names are those of John Evelyn, Samuel Pepys and Roger North. **John Evelyn (1620-1706)** was a rich man who had cultured tastes. He was a member of the Royal Society and had wide interests in diverse fields like gardening, forestry, navigation and architecture. His *Diary* which was written almost throughout his lifetime throws a floodlight on the major social and national events of the time like the Galley Slaves and the Great Fire. It is written in a plain, graphic style. **Samuel Pepys (1633-1703)** had a chequered career. Coming from the middle classes, he joined the civil services and rose to be the secretary of the Admiralty. He also became the President of the Royal Society and a member of Parliament. His famous *Diary*, covering a period of ten years, is in the form of confessions. It was written in laconic sentences like the messages of a telegram and was in a sort of code which was deciphered only in 1825. The diary shows him to be a man of versatile interests like music, science and literature. But the most controversial aspect is the detailed confessions of his life. Nobody seemed to guess he was a libertine, a morally debauched character who could stoop to low means. When we read the diary, it seems he is writing of another person. **Roger North** belonged to an elite family. He was a Tory gentleman and was engaged in the politics of the times. His famous work is *North's Lives of the Norths* containing biographies of three relatives and an autobiography. His pen pictures and anecdotes are in colloquial style.

MAJOR AUTHORS AND THEIR WORKS

Robert Herrick (1591-1574)
Noble Numbers
Hesperides

Thomas Carew (1598-1639)
Poems
'He that loves a rosy cheek'

Sir John Suckling (1660-1642)
'Ballad upon a Wedding'
'Why so pale and wan, Fond Lover'?

Andrew Marvell (1621-1678)
'To His Coy Mistress'
'The Rehearsal Transprosed'

'Ode upon Cromwell's Return from Ireland'
New Letters (a Prose Work)

George Herbert (1593-1633)
The Temple
Affliction
Easter Wings
The Collar
Man

Richard Crashaw (1613-1649)
Carmen Deo Nostro
The Infant Morturs
Steps to the Temple

John Milton (1608-1674)
Paradise Lost (in twelve Books)
Paradise Regained
Comus
Lycidas
Samson Agonistes
L'Allegro
Ill Penseroso
Areopagitica (Prose Work)
Ode on the Morning of Christ's Nativity
Sonnets (including) :
'On His Blindness'
'On the Late Massacre in Piedmont'
'When the Assault was Intended to the City'
'On His Having Arrived at the Age of Twenty-three'
A large number of Tracts and Pamphlets in support of the Parliament

John Donne (1573-1631)
Songs and Sonnets
Aires and Angels
A Nocturnall upon Lucies Day
A Valediction : Forbidding Mourning
The Extasie
Devotions (Sermon in Prose)
Ignatius His Enclave (a Prose Work)
Of the Progress of the Soul
Death's Duell

Abraham Cowley (1618-1667)
Pyramus and Thisbe
The Mistress
The Davideis
Pindarique Odes
Constantia and Philetus
Discourse by Way of Vision
Concerning the Government of Cromwell (a Prose Work)

Henry Vaughan (1622-1695)
Poems
Regeneration
The Retreat
Olor Iscanus
Thalia Redivia
Silex Scintillans

John Dryden (1631-1700)
(i) Heroic Stanzas on the Death of Oliver Cromwell
Astraea Redux (on the Restoration of Charles II)
Absalom and Achitophel
Religio Laici
The Hind and the Panther
The Fables
Annus Mirabilis
The Medal
Mac Flecknoe
Alexander's Feast
Prefaces to His Plays (in Prose)
An Essay of Dramatic Poesy
(ii) Dryden's Plays
Tyrannic Love
Conquest of Granada
All for love
The Rival Ladies
The Indian Emperor
Aureng-Zeb
Don Sebastian
Cleomenes
Love Triumphant

John Vanbrugh (1664-1726)
The Relapse
The Provoked Wife
The Confederacy

George Farquhar (1678-1707)
The Recruiting Officer
The Beaux Stratagem

Thomas Otway (1652-1685)
Orphan
Venice Preserved
Don Carlos
Alcibiades

Nathaniel Lee (1653-1692)
Nero
The Rival Queens
Sophonisba

John Bunyan (1628-1688)
The Pilgrim's Progress
Grace Abounding
The Life and Death of Mr. Badman
The Holy War

John Locke (1632-1704)
Essay on the Human Understanding
Treatise on Government
Thoughts on Education

John Evelyn (1620-1706)
Diary

Samuel Pepys (1633-1703)
Diary

MULTIPLE CHOICE QUESTIONS

1. Who wrote the *Faerie Queene?*
A. John Lyly B. Edmund Spenser
C. Ben Jonson D. Shakespeare

2. What is the nine-line stanza used in the *Faerie Queene* called?
A. Alexandrine B. Shakespearean
C. Spenserian D. Petrarchan

3. *The Anatomy of Melancholy* is written by:
A. Robert Burton B. John Dryden
C. Thomas Dekker D. Milton

4. *Doctor Faustus* is a story of:
A. a scientist
B. revenge
C. the Renaissance love of power
D. a greedy Jew

5. Marlowe invented:
A. sprung rhythm B. sonnet
C. allegory D. blank verse

6. *Romeo and Juliet* is a:
A. tragedy B. comedy
C. tragi-comedy D. history

7. *Every Man in His Humour* is written by:
A. Ben Jonson B. Dryden
C. John Donne D. Marston

8. Dryden wrote:
A. *Sejanus*
B. *The Compleat Angler*
C. *Aureng-zebe*
D. *Principia*

9. The song *Drink to me only with thine eyes* is written by:
A. Lyly B. Ben Jonson
C. Shakespeare D. Spenser

10. The Puritan Parliament closed the theatres in:
A. 1638 B. 1632
B. 1606 D. 1642

11. *The Shoemaker's Holiday* is a play written by:
A. Shakespeare
B. Marlowe
C. Thomas Dekker
D. Marston

12. Ben Jonson's *The Poetaster* is a satire on:
A. Marston and Dekker
B. Marlowe
C. Kyd
D. Greene

13. The main theme of Webster's plays is his:
A. humour
B. satire
C. preoccupation with death
D. social life

14. Marlowe, Kyd, Lyly and Greene were known as:
A. Humorists
B. University Wits
C. The Rivals of Shakespeare
D. The Decadents

15. The person who collaborated with Beaumont for many plays was:
A. Fletcher B. Shakespeare
C. Marston D. Greene

16. Herrick, Carew, Suckling and Lovelace were collectively called:
A. Metaphysical Poets
B. Religious Poets
C. Puritans
D. Cavalier Poets

17. The *Horatian Ode* by Andrew Marvel is addressed to:
A. Cromwell B. Charles II
C. Queen Elizabeth D. Shakespeare

18. *Comus* by Milton is a/an:
A. masque B. ode
C. epic D. lyric

19. *Lycidas* is an elegy by Milton on:
A. Arthur Hallam B. Edward King
C. Cromwell D. Ben Jonson

20. *The Compleat Angler* is written by:
A. Milton B. Robert Burton
C. Izaak Walton D. Thomas Fuller

21. *Leviathan* is written by:
A. Milton B. Marvel
C. Thomas Hobbes D. Farquhar

22. *The Pilgrim's Progress* by John Bunyan is a/an:
A. book of philosophy
B. treatise on education
C. masque
D. allegory

23. Samuel Butler's satire on Puritanism is:
A. *Hudibras* B. *Way of the World*
C. *Utopia* D. *Paradise Lost*

24. John Evelyn's *Diary* is famous for:
A. describing major social events of his times
B. describing personal experiences
C. scholarly research
D. noting facts and figures

25. Samuel Pepys' *Diary* is mainly:
A. social B. confessional
C. descriptive D. argumentative

ANSWERS

1	2	3	4	5	6	7	8	9	10
B	C	A	C	D	C	A	C	B	D
11	**12**	**13**	**14**	**15**	**16**	**17**	**18**	**19**	**20**
C	A	C	B	A	D	A	A	B	C
21	**22**	**23**	**24**	**25**					
C	D	A	A	B					

THE EIGHTEENTH CENTURY

THE AUGUSTAN AGE (1700-1740)

In general, the eighteenth century was the age of understanding and enlightenment. The emphasis was on the advancement of the human mind. Sensibility was the guiding principle. This age borrowed the humour and poetic technique of the previous century.

This age is generally called *The Augustan Age* or *The Age of Queen Anne* because the queen patronized the men of letters. The period is also known as the Classical Age. It Was an age of tolerance and harmony and was guided by reason. Dryden still wrote and was a contemporary of French authors Corneille, Racine and Moliere. Many English works were translated by the French. Poctry was still for aristocrats and the courts, but prose spread among the common public. People demanded instructions and information and practical hints for living. This led writers to use a simple style to be comprehensible to all.

Poetry

Matthew Prior (1664-1721) began by writing a parody of The Hind and the Panther in which he expounded his opinions on politics. **Sir Samuel Garth (1661-1791)** and **Joseph Addison (1672-1719)** used the heroic couplet of Dryden. Addison described Marlborough's victory at Blenheim in his poem *The Campaign* (1704). But the poetical luminary of the period was **Alexander Pope (1688-1744)**. He polished Dryden's couplet and used it as a weapon of satire, like in the famous *An Essay on Man* (1732-1734). His *An Essay on Criticism* (1711) and *The Rape of the Lock* (1712, 1714) are other great works. The latter is in mock-heroic style and describes the anger of a lady whose lock of hair had been cut off. Pope also translated the Iliad. He wrote *The Dunciad* (1728) to castigate bad poets. His *Imitations of Horace* (1733-1737) is highly admired even today.

Jonathan Swift, usually known as a prose writer, also showed a gift or versification like in his poem *On the Death of Dr. Swift.* **John Gay (1685-1732)** was popular for his fables like *The Hare with Many Friends* and his songs in *The Beggar's Opera.* **Edward Young's (1683-1765)** *The Commaint, or Night Thoughts on Life, Death, and Immortality* (1742), is a poet's delight in meditation underlining the vanity of all earthly glory.

Prose

This period saw an increasing demand for the circulation of facts and ideas among the public. **Daniel Defoe (1659-1731)** was a trail-blazer as a Journalist and his popular works are *The True-Born Englishman* (1701) and *The Shortest way with the Dissenters* (1702). Defoe wrote the first English nove! Robinson Crusoe (1719), which is a children's classic or collection of adventure stories. He cultivated the art of reporting and presented his stories as historical narratives which are precise and practical.

Steele, Addison, Swift, Arbuthnot were the other great prose-writers of the time. They introduced a style adorned by figures of speech. The periodicals of Steele and Addison contain essays which deal with practica1 moral questions and reflect the morals of the time.

Richard Steele (1672-1729) led a dissipated life and was full of remorse for it. He extols the Bible as a guide in life in his work *The Christian Hero*. He launched the journal *The Tatler* in 1709. **Joseph Addison** propagated rational and moderate ideas He collaborated with Steele on *The Tatler*. Steele then founded *The Spectator* in 1711 and Addison again collaborated. Here they were merely the spectators of the society and its foibles. It epitomizes the whole nation. The character of Sir Roger de Coverley is a masterpiece, a comic personality with eccentricities. Other characters, Sir Andrew Freeport. Will Honeycomb, Captain Sentry capture the imagination of the readers.

Jonathan Swift (1667-1745) enjoyed ridicule rather than correction. He lays bare all the vices of man as something that are beyond correction. He ridiculed the modern authors in his The *Battle of the Books* (1704) and attacked the Papists and Presbyterians in *The Tale of a Tub* (1704). His most popular work is a children's classic, *Gulliver's Travels* (1726), which is also a satire on politics, religions, science and nature of man.

John Arbuthnot (1667-1735) was another humanist and man of wit and is known for his *The History of John Bull* (1712), an amusing allegory on the politics of the time.

During this period a number of deists like Locke, Collins and Tindal propounded a philosophy advocating reasoning rather than superstitious beliefs as advocated by orthodox Christians. Earl of Shaftesbury (1671-1713), Lord Bolingbroke (1678-1751) and Mandeville were other rationalists of the time who wrote many prose works.

THE AGE OF TRANSITION (1740-1800)

Like all other periods of transition, this age was also disturbed and confused. Two movements can be clearly observed in the writings of the time: (*i*) the allegiance to the old order of classicism, and (*ii*) the search after the new order of Romanticism. The period was marked by new learning, new philosophy, growth of historical research and new realism.

This period is also known as the *Age of Johnson* because **Samuel Johnson (1709-1784)**, the greatest English man of letters, flourished during this period. Samuel Johnson was a versatile man of letters translator, journalist, commentator, critic, novelist, biographer and poet. He created two satirical poems, *London* (1738) and *The Vanity of Human Wishes* (1749). He had a supple style and describes his personal reflections in his essays *The Rambler* (1750-1752) and *The Idler* (1758-1760). His *Dictionary of English Language* (1747-1755) shows remarkable precision in definition and a feeling for the correct use of words. Besides the novel *Rasselas, Prince of Abyssinia* (1759) his best works are biographical and literary studies and his edition of *Shakespeare* (1765). His *Lives of the Poets* (1777-1781) is a biographical work. His admirer James Boswell's famous biography of Johnson has made him immortal. He is described here in candid details. His prejudices, excellences and demerits are all laid bare.

Poetry

Poetry showed the influence of Dryden and Pope. It was mainly didactic and satirical and the couplet still was the major form.

Oliver Goldsmith's (1728-1774) *Deserted Village* (1770) is a masterpiece of the period. **James Thomson's (1700-1748)** *The Seasons* (1730) is a praise of the beauties of Nature in all her diversity. Other noteworthy poems of the period are **William Collins' (1721-1759)** *Ode to Evening*, a delightful lyric, and **Thomas Gray's (1716-1771)** *Elegy Written in a Country Churchyard* (1751).

A general belief in human liberty was seen as the French Revolution proceeded. **William Cowper** (1731-1800) who wrote *The Ballad of John Gilpin,* **George Crabbe (1754-1832)**, the Scotsman **Robert Burns (1759-1796)** and the mystic **William Blake (1757-1827)** echoed the sentiments of the period. Burns was a farmer and wrote in original racy dialect thus causing a break from convention. Blake was a visionary and his poems are collected in *Songs of Innocence* (1789) and *Songs of Experience* (1794). In *The Tyger,* he uses the Lamb as a symbol of innocence and of Jesus, and the Tiger as the symbol of evil in the world, of the evil seen in the French Revolution where thousands were sent to the guillotine.

Novel

The period saw the development of the novel. A series of masterpieces came out. In the novel, the author could describe events in detail. Defoe's novels so far were based on strange subjects. Now they concentrated on commonplace events of family life and society. Adventure of earlier novels gave place to character portrayal. The novels were very long and filled with minute details. **Samuel Richardson (1689-1761)** wrote *Pamela, or Virtue Rewarded* (1740) and *Clarissa Harlowe* (1747-1748). **Henry Fielding (1707-1754)** is famous for *Joseph Andrews* (1742) and *Tom Jones* (1749), **Tobias Smollet (1721-1771)** wrote *The Adventures of Roderick Random* (1748) and *The Expedition of Humphry Clinker* (1771), **Laurence Sterne (1713-1768)** wrote *Tristram Shandy* (1760), and **Oliver Goldsmith** *The Vicar of Wakefield* (1766).

Letter

There were famous letter writers also, like **Lord Chesterfield (1694-1773). Horace Walpole (1719-1797), Thomas Gray and Richardson**. Frequently, a series of letters was bound into book-form. Collections of this kind were the letters of **Lady Mary Wortley Montagu (1689-1762)**, written to Pope from Constantinople, and of Thomas Gray, from the Lake District. Chesterfield's letters to his son contain comments on political and social matters. Richardson's *Pamela* is entirely in letter-form.

Drama

The century was the age of the great novels. Drama lost originality and talent. People saw Shakespeare's plays enacted, but what attracted them was the genius of the actors. However, there were a few good plays written. For instance, Johnson's *Irene* (1749), Fielding's *The Miser*, Goldsmith's anti-sentimental comedy *She Stoops to Conquer* (1773), and Sheridan's *The School for Scandal* (1777) and *The Rivals* (1775).

Historical Work

Towards the last part of the century the history of England was rocked by many revolutionary changes the impact of which were felt in English literature. Till the mid-18th century Victorian England reigned supreme. She was mistress of the seas and her imperial rule covered many colonies. In 1776, America declared her independence and the British Parliament was divided on the issue. Many Britishers favoured the American claims. In 1789, the French Revolution broke out and here too the Britishers were divided into two camps. Inspired by the writings of Rousseau, many believed the Revolution was being fought for the right causes. The Parliament resounded with the speeches of the famous. Some even accused Warren Hastings for his extortion policies in India and some others were against slave-trade.

Treatises on philosophy by **David Hume (1711-1776)** and histories by **William Robertson (1721-1793)** and political economy (*Wealth of Nations*) by **Adam Smith (1723-1790)** came out.

Edmund Burke (1729-1797) read law and began writing to propound his views on human feelings and emotions. His language is as oratorical in Parliament at the trial of Warren Hastings as in his famous writing *A Philosophical Inquiry into the Origin of our Ideas of the Sublime and the Beautiful* (1756).

Other orators who expressed themselves in writing were Tom Paine, Godwin and Jeremy Bentham. **William Godwin (1756-1836)** advocated the elimination of government in *Enquiry Concerning Political Justice* (1793). He proscribed law, marriage, gratitude, everything that limited liberty. His monumental work is *The Decline and Fall of the Roman Empire* (1776-1788) in which he describes the growth of Christianity and his belief in reason rather than the divine. At the same time **William Paley (1743-1805)** wrote *A View of the Evidences of Christianity* (1794) to prove the existence of miracles by logic.

MAJOR AUTHORS AND THEIR WORKS

Alexander Pope (1688-1744)

Pastorals

An Essay on Criticism

Windsor Forest

The Rape of the Lock
Dunciad
Translation of Iliad and Odyssey
To Lord Bathrust
On the Use of the Riches
An Essay on Man
Epistle to Dr. Arbuthnot
Of the Knowledge and Characters of Men
Of the Characters of Women
The Messiah
Satires and Epistles of Horace Imitated

Matthew Prior (1664-1721)
Solomon on the Vanity of the World
Alma : or the Progress of the Mind
The Town and Country Mouse

John Gay (1685-1732)
Fables
The Shepherd's Week
The Rural Sports
Trivia
The Beggar's Opera
The Streets of London

Edward Young (1683-1765)
Night Thoughts

Dr. Samuel Johnson (1709-1784)
The Vanity of Human Wishes
London
The Lives of the Poets
Preface to Shakespeare
Dictionary of the English Language
A journey to the Western Islands of Scotland
The Rambler
Rasselas
Prince of Abyssinia
The Life of Savage
The Adventurer
The Idler

Daniel Defoe (1661-1731)
Robinson Crusoe
Mall Flanders
Colonel Jack
The Memoirs of a Cavalier
Captain Singleton
Journal of the Plague Year
Roxana

Jonathan Swift (1667-1745)
The Battle of the Books
A Tale of a Tub
Gulliver's Travels
Journal to Stella
The Drapier's Letters
Cadenus and Vanessa

Joseph Addison (1672-1719)
The Spectator
The Campaign
Public Credit
The Vision of Mirza
Cato
Rosamond
The Drummer

Richard Steele (1672-1729)
The Tatler
The Guardian
The Funeral
The Lying Lover
The Tender Husband
The Conscious Lover

Thomas Gray (1716-1771)
Elegy Written in a Country Churchyard
On a Distant Prospect of Eton College
On the Death of a Favourite Cat
The Bard
The Progress of Poesy
The Fatal Sisters
The Descent of Odin

MULTIPLE CHOICE QUESTIONS

1. *The Hind and the Panther* is a parody about:
   A. religion
   B. society
   C. politics
   D. human beings in general
2. Which poem is in mock-heroic style?
   A. *The Rape of the Lock*
   B. *The Christian Hero*
   C. *On the Death of Dr. Swift*
   D. *The Hare with Many Friends*
3. Who was the first journalist of the age?
   A. Dryden B. Daniel Defoe
   C. Swift D. Arbuthnot
4. Who wrote the first English dictionary?
   A. Goldsmith B. Boswell
   C. Webster D. Samuel Johnson
5. Lord Chesterfield is famous as a:
   A. Novelist B. Letter-writer
   C. Playwright D. Poet
6. The novel written in epistolary or letter form is;
   A. *Joseph Andrews* B. *Pamela*
   C. *Vicar of Wakefield* D. *Tom Jones*
7. Johnson's biographer was:
   A. Boswell B. Irene
   C. Swift D. Edmund Burke
8. A play which describes heroes as virtues personified and is full of pompous speeches is:
   A. Heroic play
   B. Sentimental Comedy
   C. Anti-Sentimental Comedy
   D. Tragi-Comedy
9. Edmund Burke was:
   A. poet and scholar B. playwright
   C. orator and writer D. lexicographer
10. *The Decline and Pall of the Roman Empire* is written by:
    A. Paley B. Smith
    C. Johnson D. Godwin
11. The main reason why papers came out in Queen Anne's time was:
    A. People were hungry for information about current events
    B. People wanted to contact businessmen
    C. People wanted to improve their writing style
    D. People liked sensational fiction stories
12. The characters Sir Andrew Freeport, Captain Sentry and Sir Roger are featured in:
    A. *The Tatler*
    B. *The London Gazette*
    C. *The Spectator*
    D. *The Review*
13. The countries that influenced British literature and art in the 18th century were:
    A. Germany and Holland
    B. Sweden and Norway
    C. Austria and France
    D. France and Italy
14. The religious revival of the 18th century started by John and Charles Weslay was known as:
    A. Methodism B. Deism
    C. Presbyterianism D. Evangelism
15. *The Hind and the Panther Transvers'd to the Story of the Country and City Mouse* is a poem by:
    A. Dryden B. Matthew Prior
    C. Pope D. John Gay
16. John Gay is famous for a musical drama named:
    A. *The Beggar's Opera*
    B. *Polly*
    C. *The Secretary*
    D. *Fables*
17. *The Ballad of John Gilpin* is written by:
    A. Thomas Gray
    B. William Cowper
    C. William Blake
    D. Robert Burns

18. The son of a British Prime Minister is famous for his letters and *The Castle of Otranto*, a gruesome play. His (the son's) name was:
A. Robert Walpole
B. Horace Walpole
C. William Pitt
D. Churchill

19. *Wealth of Nations* is written by:
A. Joshua Reynolds B. Adam Smith
C. Godwin D. David Hume

20. Sheridan was a:
A. poet B. dramatist
C. novelist D. musician

21. *The Rivals* is a play by:
A. Sheridan B. Goldsmith
C. Johnson D. David Garrick

22. *Origin of our Ideas of the Sublime and the Beautiful* is an essay by:
A. Edmund Burke B. Godwin
C. Thomas Paine D. Hume

23. The greatest Scottish poet of the 18th century is:
A. Robert Burns B. Walter Scott
C. William Cowper D. John Gay

24. The lines, *"O My luve's like a red, red rose,/ That's newly sprung in June;...."* are attributed to:
A. William Blake B. Fergusson
C. Robert Burns D. Macpherson

25. Who was known as the "Man of Feeling" after his sentimental novel *The Man of Feeling*?
A. Francis Burney B. Ann Rediliffe
C. Matthew Lewis D. Henry Mackenzie

ANSWERS

1	2	3	4	5	6	7	8	9	10
C	A	B	D	B	B	A	B	C	D
11	**12**	**13**	**14**	**15**	**16**	**17**	**18**	**19**	**20**
A	C	D	A	B	A	B	B	B	B
21	**22**	**23**	**24**	**25**					
A	A	A	C	D					

THE NINETEENTH CENTURY

THE ROMANTIC AGE (1798-1830)

The eighteenth century literature of England was inspired by reason, but the nineteenth century was the age of imagination. The Preface to the *Lyrical Ballads* by William Wordsworth and Samuel Taylor Coleridge in 1798, heralds the period of English Romanticism. The authors of this work were disgusted with the excesses of the French Revolution, they condemned the Rationalist Movement. England turned away from the literature of France and transferred her sympathies to Germany. The philosophical doctrine of Romanticism was inspired by Germany. Romanticism was essentially poetic. Although poles apart in their political beliefs, Wordsworth and Shelley both considered the poet as the guide, prophet and seer of mankind.

Poetry

For the great Romantics — Wordsworth, Shelley, Keats, Byron — the study of the wondrous world of feelings, senses, instincts, of Man' relation to Nature, were of prime importance. Romanticism is shot with *metaphysics*. As M. Lanson puts it, *tout traverse de frissons metaphysique* Alexander Pope had used poetry to depict the thoughts of the philosophers in his *Essay on Man.* The Romantics, dedicated to Romantic imagination — *the esemplastic imagination* as Coleridge called it — were convinced that what was revealed to their poetic intuitions, was right, the Truth. Mysterious forces divine in origin moved the earth, not cold rationalist cause and effect. Pope's couplet was dull and too precise governed by convention. The Romantics sought a lyrical form using unusual images and association of words. They found models for these in the Renaissance and the old popular poetry.

William Wordsworth (1770-1850) is aptly called the "High Priest of Nature". He saw Nature as the *'Stern Daughter of the voice of God',* man's conscience whose balmy presence never disappointed. He was born in 1770 in the picturesque Lake District of England. Here he spent happy years of his childhood in communion with God and Nature. After study at Cambridge, he went to France in 1791 and was enthused by the cause of the Revolution. But when the Reign of Terror came and thousands died at the guillotine, his fine sensibilities, his search for human equality and peace received a rude shock. He engaged himself in the philosophy of William Godwin for sometime. Finding no solution to the problem of human pain, he finally turned to the study of Nature. In the poems of the Lyrical Ballads he describes the mundane happenings of country life, the activities of humble people. He used their common dialect with its flawed grammar as his style. He decries the coming of the industrial era which mechanized English life. With no ornament, his poetry draws its power from the intensity of his feelings and imagination, In The Prelude (1805), a long poem, Wordsworth set out to look back and retrospect on his life. He follows the growth, the turnings of his poetic genius since childhood, ruminates on his errors and recalls the corrective lessons of Nature. In his great moral poem, The Excursion (1814), he uses a philosophy to refute the pessimism that the Revolution had brought.

Samuel Taylor Coleridge (1772-1834) was Wordsworth's "Spirits Brother". He was guided by the same philosophy of the imagination. While Wordsworth's imagination gave him a special vision of the common things of rustic life, Coleridge stirred up the supernatural. To apprediate his poetry peopled with strange, translunary beings like the Ancient Mariner, one needs *'that willing suspension of disbelief that constitutes poetic faith',* In *The Rime of the Ancient Mariner,* Coleridge describes tne strange adventures of a sailor in a ship. Having killed an albatross, the mariner suffers from hallucinations. The poem, with strange rhythm and cadences, creates a wondrous world. Coleridge was a master of lyrical style. His other famous poems are *Christabel* (1816), and *Kubla Khan* (1816). *Kubia Khan* was written as a result of an opium dream and described the wonderful, strange palace of the Chinese king, Kubla Khan. Coleridge certainly fulfils the meaning of *'Renaissance'* as *'a renascence of wonder'.*

Robert Southey (1774-1843) wrote poetry based on outlandish settings and myths like *Thalaba, the Destroyer* (1801), *The Curse of Kehama* (1810), and *Roderick, the Last of the Goths* (1814). His descriptions are rich and graphic and he uses a great variety of verse forms. He wrote a number of poems in ballad form.

Walter Scott (1771-1832) also had an interest in ballad poetry. He translated the *Lenore* from German (1796). His *The Minstrelsy of the Scottish Border* (1802) shows a great romantic interest in the Middle Ages and the days of chivalry.

The second generation of great Romantic poets include Shelley, Keats and Byron.

Percy Bysshe Shelley (1792-1822) gave up his title and wealth to write poetry. His aim was to awaken mankind to the millenium, the coming future, which would remove human anguish and sorrow. His famous ode, *Ode to the West Wind* is an impassioned exhortation — *Make me thy lyre eu'n as the forest is ...... If Winter comes, can Spring be far behind?* He came under the influence of William Godwin, the philosopher. He proclaimed himself an atheist at the age of 21. His works include *Queen Mab* (1813), *Prometheus Unbound* (1818-1819), which shows human revolt against false gods, *To a*

Skylark, Adonais (1821), which is an elegy to Keats, and The Cenci (1819). Shelley's style is a mixture of abstractions and visual images.

John Keats (1795-1821) was the most sensuous of the great Romantic poets. As we read his poems, richly laden with imagery and associations, all the senses are stirred up the visual, olfactory, auditory and tactile. It is said he tasted pepper in wine to describe certain lines. His famous odes are *To a Nightingale, To Autumn* and *On a Grecian Urn.*

Lord George Gordon Byron (1788-1824) was a wealthy nobleman who shunned the popular beliefs of his times. He was notorious as a dilletante. At the age of 19, he wrote Hours of Idleness (1807). With the publication of *Childe Harold's Pilgrimage* (1812) he became famous. Childe Harold was Byron himself, the figure of the disillusioned man, the hero fed up of pleasures and debauches. He lives an outlawed life and is rebellious in spirit. He took on more incarnations in his poems, *The Giaour* (1813), *The Corsair* (1814), *The Siege of Corinth* (1815). In these he displayed his own passions and eccentricities. In 1816, divorced from his wife, he retired to Switzerland and then to Italy. He wrote a number of plays — *Manfred* (1817), *Cain* (1821) and *The Deformed Transformed* (1824). The crowning work was his lyrical, satirical *Don Juan* (1819-1823). He went to Greece to fight for its independence, but died of illness. His satire is political, against England and also against English hypocrisy and cant. His licentious descriptions caused scandals. Don Juan, his magnum opus, is written in ottava rima or eight-line stanzas and is full of wit and mockery.

Thomas Moore (1779-1852), Thomas Campbell (1777-1844), Samuel Rogers (1763-1855), Jamess Hogg (1770-1835), Walter Savage Landor (1775.1864) and **Leigh Hunt (1784-1859)** were other poets of the time.

Novel

Novels of terror and mystery prospered from 1800 to 1830. **Matthew Gregory Lewis** (1775-1818) wrote *Tales of Terror* (1800) and *Tales of Wonder* (1801). **Charles Lamb's (1775-1834)** *Tales from Shakespeare* (1807) is very popular even today. *Mrs Shelley,* the poet's wife, wrote the classic *Frankenstein* in which a scientist creates a monster that turns on its creator and destroys his most beloved ones. It is a novel of prophetic fear. **Miss Mary Mitford** wrote on country life and **Maria Edgeworth (1767-1849)** brought out educational novels like Belinda (1801) and *Tales of Fashionable Life* — novels for children.

Jane Austen (1775-1817) produced half a dozen novels which are drawing-room comedies of life. They study the passion and distress of young ladies and the life of country-folk. The novels — *Pride and Prejudice* (1813), *Sense and Sensibility* (1811), *Emma* (1816), *Persuasion* (1818), *Mansfield Park* (1814), *Northanger Abbey* (1818) — are realistic and witty, full of bracing dialogue.

Walter Scott was Scotland's greatest novelist recreating the past of his country's myths and ballads with rich humour. *Waverly* (1814), *Guy Mannering* (1815), *The Heart of Midlothian* (1818) contain history and direct observation. In *Ivanhoe* (1820), he describes the history of England in the days of the legendary Richard, the Lion Heart. *Kenilworth* (1821), *Quentin Dunward* (1823) were his other famous historical novels. He imbued the Romantic era with a love for the Middle Ages.

Prose/Criticism

The Romantic Age saw a number of reviewers and critics like **Jeremy Bentham (1748-1832)**, who expounded utilitarian doctrines, **Sydney Smith (1771-1845)**, and **William Cobbett (1762-1835)**. Coleridge, the poet, interpreted the doctrines of Kant and Schelling which show the distinction between pure reason and practical reason.

Lamb, Hazlitt, De Quincey and Leigh Hunt were Romantic critics of literature. **Charles Lamb's** essays on Shakespeare's tragedies state that we cannot do justice to them by staging them since the passions which are to be felt in their intensity are torn to tatters by the gimmickry of the actors. **William Hazlitt's (1778-1830)** criticism of some of Shakespeare's characters like Falstaff — *he laughs three inches below the flesh* — is a masterpiece.

Coleridge's famous work of criticism, *Biographia Literaria* (1817), marvellously analyses Wordsworth's poetry. The Romantics believed that Shakespeare's art was organic like a work of Nature and *"esemplastic'* — able to blend different elements by imagination. **Thomas De Quincey's (1785-1859)** style is penetrating and incisive when criticizing the poets in *The Confessions of an English Opium Eater* (1821).

MAJOR AUTHORS AND THEIR WORKS

William Wordsworth (1770-1850)

The Lyrical Ballads
The Prelude
The Excursion
Tintern Abbey
Ode on Intimations of Immortality
Michael
The Solitary Reaper
Loadamia
Ode to Duty
To Milton
The Leech-Gatherer
Upon Westminster Abbey
The Rainbow
We Are Seven
The World Is Too Much with Us
To the Cuckoo
The Daffodils
Lucy Gray
Simon Lee
Early Spring
Strange Fits of Passion Have I Known

Walter Scott (1771-1832)

The Bride of Lammermoor
Ivanhoe
Quentin Durward
The Heart of midlothian
Old Mortality
The Antiquity
Guy Mannering
Waverly
Rob Roy
Kenilworth
Red Gauntlet
The Black Dwarf
The Monastery
The Abbot
The Pirate
The Fortunes of Night
The Betrothed
The Talisman
Woodstock
Lives of the Novelists
Life of Napoleon
Tales of Grandfather
The Lay of the Last Minstrel
The Minstrelsy of the Scottish Border
Marmion
The Lady of the Lake
Rockeby

Robert Southey (1774-1843)

Joan of Arc
Wat Tyler
After Blenheim
The Holly Tree
The Scholar
A Vision of Judgement
Madoc
Life of Nelson
Thalaba the Destroyer
Roderick
The Curse of Kehama

S.T. Coleridge (1772-1834)

Biographia Literaria
Table Talk
Aids to Reflection
Christabel
Kubla Khan
The Rime of the Ancient Mariner
France : An Ode
Destiny of Nations

Frost at Midnight
Dejection : An Ode
Youth and Age
Religious Musings

Lord Byron (1788-1824)

Childe Harold's Pilgrimage
Don Juan
The Bride of Abydos
Manfred
The Giaour
Hours of Idleness
The Vision of Judgement
The Prisoner of Chillon
Lara
Marino Faliero
English Bards and Scotch Reviewers
The Siege of Corinth
The Corsair
Cain

P.B. Shelley (1792-1822)

On the Necessity of Atheism
The Revolt of Islam
Prometheus Unbound
The Mask of Anarchy
Hellas
The Cenci
The Witch of Atlas
The Indian Serenade
Ozymandias of Egypt
Epipsychidion
Alaster
Queen Mab
Adonais
Ode to the West Wind
The Cloud
Ode to a Skylark
O World! O Life! O Time!
Defence of Poetry (a Prose Work)
To Night
The Sensitive Plant
A Lament

John Keats (1795-1821)

Endymion
Lamia
Hyperion
The Eve of St. Agnes
Isabella
The Eve of St. Mark
La Belle Dame Sans Merci
Ode to a Nightingale
Ode to Autumn
Ode On a Grecian Urn
Ode to Psyche
On Melancholy
On First Looking into Chapman's Homer
Bright Star

Jane Austen (1775-1871)

Sense and Sensibility
Pride and Prejudice
Mansfield Park
Emma
Persuasion
Northanger Abbey

Charles Lamb (1775-1834)

Essays of Elia
The Last Essays of Elia
John Woodvil
Tales from Shakespeare
Specimens of English Dramatic Poets
The English Comic Writers
The Old Familiar Faces

William Hazlitt (1778-1830)

Characters of Shakespeare's Plays
The English Poets
The English Comic Writers
The Dramatic Literature of the Age of Elizabeth
The Round Table : A Collection of Essays
Table Talk on Men and Manners
The Spirit of the Age

Thomas De Quincey (1785-1859)

Confessions of an English Opium Eater
Joan of Arc
English Mail Coach
Dream Fugue
Murder Considered as One of the Fine Arts
Suspiria de Profundis

Samuel Rogers (1763-1855)
Pleasures of Memory
Italy

James Hogg (1770-1835)
Kilmeny
The Queen's Wake

Thomas Campbell
Pleasures of Hope
Theodoric
Gertrude of Wyoming
Lachiel
Lord Ullin's Daughter
The Last Man
Ye Mariners of England
Hohenlinden
The Battle of Baltic

Thomas Moore (1779-1852)
Lalla Rookh
Irish Melodies

Leigh Hunt (1784-1859)
Story of Rimini
Autobiography

Walter Savage Landor (1775-1864)
Gebir
Hellenics
Imaginary Conversations
The Citations of William Shakespeare
Pericles and Aspasia

THE VICTORIAN ERA (1830-1880)

During this era, the conflict between religion and science, mysticism and rationalism, became intense. There were those who, influenced by Darwin's theory of evolution as expounded in his *On the Origin of Species,* lost their faith in the biblical explanation of man's descent from Adam and Eve. They wanted to shun dogma and accept the scientific spirit. Others lamented the loss of faith and the rising consumer values. Mat thew Arnold in his poem *Dover Beach* writes:

> *"The Sea of Faith was once too at the full.....*
> *But now I only hear its long withdrawing melancholy roar......"*

Prose

Carlyle and Ruskin echoed the prophecies of the Romantic era in their prose works. **Thomas Carlyle (1795-1881)**, the Scotsman, abandoned orthodoxy and came under the influence of the German writers Schiller, Novalis, Richter and Goethe. His work *Sartor Resartus* (1833-1834) is a sort of allegory based on a German professor who has written a treatise on clothes. He penetrates through the clothes to the essence of the man's being. Carlyle was also a historian. His historical works are *The French Revolution* (1837) and *The History of Frederich II of Prussia, called frederik the Great* (1858-1865). These are satirical and prophetic, expounding how man and society are organized. He was against materialism and praised the Magi and prophets of the past. He advocates strength and power.

John Ruskin (1819-1900) was indignant about the ugliness of existence brought in by industrialism and the machine. *Unto This Last* (1860), which influenced Gandhiji's economic theories, describes his disgust for soulless labour. He was a student of arts. *Modern Painters* (1843, 1860) is about landscape painters like Turner. He also wrote *The Seven Lamps of Architecture* (1849) and *The Stones of Venice* (1851-1853), praising Gothic art.

Matthew Arnold (1822-1888), the poet, wanted his countrymen to inculcate classical qualities to become harmonious in morals and in ereative works. The English must break away from their insular moorings by imbibing the teachings of Greece and the French. He is *the detector-general of the intellectual failings of his own nation.* Poetry, according to him, is important in character formation, and culture is *"the minister of the sweetness and light essential to the perfect character"*. His works include *On translating Homer, The Study of Celtic Literature and Essays in Criticism* (1865, 1889). He wrote St. Paul and Protestantism advocating that dogma should be removed from Christianity and it should adjust itself to the findings of science.

A number of philosophers, historians and scholars wrote in this period. Charles Darwin's theory of evolution dramatically affected human thought. **John Stuart Mill (1806-1873)** expounded the processes of logic and political economy. **Herbert Spencer (1820-1903)** and **Thomas Henry Huxley (1825-1895)** were scientists. **Thomas Babington Macaulay (1800-1859)** was a poet, essayist and historian who advocated English education in India. The Oxford Movement gave rise to religious writers like **John Keble (1792-1866)** and **John Henry Newman (1801-1890)**. Newman's famous work is *Apologia pro Vita Sua* (1864) in which he explains why he had converted to the Roman Church.

Novel

The transition from Walter Scott's novels to Charles Dicken's first novel in 1836 is a great one. When Queen Victoria ascended the throne, **Frederick Marryat (1792-1848)** produced sea-stories; **Edward BulwerLytton (1803-1873)** wrote about Byronic heroes, attractive criminals and historical novels like *The Last Days of Pompeii* (1834); **Benjamin Disraeli** (1804-1881), the Prime Minister of England, wrote *Coningsby: or The New Generation* (1844) and *Sybil: or The Two Nations* (1845) to show that the aristocrats of the society had a duty towards the unfortunate ones. In Disraeli's novels, one finds the politics of Queen Victoria's reign.

Perhaps the greatest Victorian novelist is **Charles Dickens (1812-1870)**, whose identification with the underdog in society was unmatched by any writer. One reason for this is his own troubled childhood led in penury under the shadow of a father who was in debtor's prison. The part of his life comes through vividly in his novel *David Copperfield* (1849-1850) which is also an indictment of the cruel, unimaginative schools of his times. He was a master craftsman in character delineation. A host of characters and their dialogues have become household in the English-speaking world. Thus the incorrigible optimist Micawber, Geakle, Pickwick, Fagin and others are types of characters that may be seen all around us anywhere. Dickens had a forgiving sense of humour. He never let bitterness creep into his recreations of painful events of the past. Among his famous novels are: *Pickwick Papers* (1836; in the picaresque style), *Barnaby Rudge* (1841) and *A Tale of Two Cities* (1859; based on the French Revolution), *Oliver Twist* (1837) and *Hard Times* (1854); novels exposing social conditions. He has a picturesque style and concrete imagination.

William Makepeace Thackeray (1811-1863) made a penetrating analysis of upper middle class and aristocratic society. He was a master of irony. In *The Book of Snobs* (1849), he ridicules the tendency to fawn on nobility and to imitate their manners. *Vanity Fair* (1847-1848), *History of Pendennis* (1848-1850), *The Newcomes* (1853-1855), *The History of Henry Esmond* (1852) and *The Virginians* (1857-1859) are pictures of contemporary life in which he depicts human eccentricities and follies. He was adept at reproducing jargon and idiolects.

The Romantic spirit was still alive in the works of the Bronte sisters. **Charlotte Bronte (1816-1855)** wrote *Jane Eyre* (1847), the story of a governess in a terrifying house. Her sister **Emily Bronte (1818-1848)** wrote *The Wuthering Heights* (1847), set in a wild landscape. Powerful passions and characters have made this one of the greatest novels of all times.

George Eliot (1819-1880), a pen-name for Mary Ann Evans, wrote Adam Bede (1859), the story of a girl who was forced to murder her own baby. *The Mill on the Floss* (1860) and *Romola* (1863) are other novels by her. In *Middlemarch, a Study of Provincial Life* (1871-1872), the novelist builds up, from the lives of a great number of deeply studied characters, the complex picture of the life of a small town.

Poetry

The poetry of this period still shows the influence of the Romantic Era. **Alfred, Lord Tennyson (1809-1892)** was an eclectic, selecting the best of his forerunners. He was first interested in style and metre, but later on ideas started interesting him. A great many poems by him are flawlessly beautiful. If *The Lotus Eaters* is softly languorous, *Ulysses* has a striking severity. Tennyson also experienced the intellectual crisis of his times and shared its anxieties. For instance, *The Princess* (1847) is occupied with the question of feminism. *In Memoriam* (1850) is one of his most beautiful poems. It is an elegy on the premature death of his friend Arthur Hallam. It concerns itself with the belief in immortality, the conflict between the hopes of Christianity and the rationalism of science. It is composed of octosyllabic quatrains. He shows a type of Byronic revolt in Locksley Hall (1886) and Maud (1855). In *Idylls of the King* (1859, 1869, 1889) he took Arthurian legends as his theme.

Robert Browning (1812-1889) was famous for using the technique of dramatic monologue in his poems. Through the protagonists of his poems he gives vent to his feelings, passions and aspirations. Thus in *Paracelsus* (1835), he describes the highly ambitious hero who wanted to transform man's life. We find here Browning's views on truth and philosophy. His other poems include *Sordello* (1840), *Pippa Passes* (1841), *My Last Duchess, Porphyria's Lover* and his masterpiece, *The Ring and the Book* (1868-1869). In his works we find an excess of thought and a rare vocabulary. He uses blank verse dexterously. His brusque speech, broken syntax and uneven rhythm are in contrast to Tennyson's. As Pound and Eliot have said, Browning brought verse nearer to modem colloquial speech. Browning's characters are remote in time and culture. Some of these are Rabbi Ben Ezra, Fra Lippo Lippi and Andrea del Sarto. In *The Ring and the Book* he takes as his subject an Italian crime and explores the minds of all his characters. He strikes a note of hope in his poems. The lines *"God's in his heaven/ And all's well with the world"* lay bare his beliefs. But in general, Browning is considered a difficult poet.

Matthew Arnold (1822-1888) was a reflective poet with a melancholic bent. A deep brooding pensiveness informs his poetry. Dover Beach shows his concern with the loss of faith in a world of science. His epic poem *Sohrab and Rustum, Tristram and Iseult, The Scholar Gypsy* are other famous works.

Dante Gabriel Rossetti, William Morris and Algernon Charles Swinburne together are known as the Pre-Raphaelite poets. They affected Raphael, the Renaissance painter, in their desire to paint sonorous wordpictures which may not have much content to conveyor any philosophy to reveal. It was in accordance with the aestheticism of Ruskin. In fact Rossetti and Morris were painters as well as poets. They worshipped beauty like John Keats did. Robert Buchanan attacked these poets as belonging to *the fleshly school of poetry*.

Dante Gabriel Rossetti (1828-1882) translated the Italian poet Dante's *Vita Nuova*. His *The Blessed Damozel* is an exquisite poem and his best sonnets are contained in *The House of Life* in which he extols his young and beautiful wife. They are full of rich sounds and images and mystic symbols. Rossetti was inspired by the ballads of the Middle Ages. Like the primitive Italian painters, he uses rich colours and depicts warm sensuous feelings.

William Morris (1834-1896) was enchanted by Gothic art of the Middle Ages. His poems drew inspiration from those of Froissart, Chaucer and Malory. He borrowed stories from Scandinavia and Iceland. His poems are like frescoes and are very lyrical in quality. The famous ones are *The Earthly Paradise* (1868-1870) and *The Life and Death of Jason* (1867). These works show rhythm and use of archaism. He strove to bring civilization back to art from the utilitarian industrialization.

Algernon Charles Swinburne (1837-1909) was a prodigy. He was a musician, and a sonority of rhymes filled his poetry. He took romantic themes like revolt against society, hatred of monarchy and struggle against traditional morality. His *Atalanta in Calydon* (1865) is his masterpiece and is known for its choral passages.

To these poets of the Victorian Age must be added the name of **Edward Fitzgerald (1809-1883)** whose **The Rubaiyat of Omar Khayyam (1859)** is a classic.

MAJOR AUTHORS AND THEIR WORKS

Alfred Lord Tennyson (1809-1892)

The Princess
In Memoriam
Maud
Enoch Arden
Idylls of the King
Queen Mary
Harold
Backet
Akbar's Tomb
Crossing the Bar
Locksley Hall
Locksley Hall Sixty Years After
Dora
Poems by Two Brothers
The Falcon
The Cup
Poems Chiefly Lyrical
Ulysses
Poems Chiefly Lyrical
Ulysses
The Lotos-Eaters
The Death of Oenone and Other Poems

Robert Browning (1812-1889)

Pauline
Paracelsus
Strafford
Sordello
Bells and Pomegranates
Christmas Eve and Easter Day
Men and Women
Dramatis Personae
The King and the Book
Asolando
Pippa Passes
Fra Lippo Lippi
Andrea del Sarto
King Victor and King Charles
Dramatic Lyrics
Dramatic Romances and Lyrics

Matthew Arnold (1822-1888)

Sohrab and Rustum
Tristram and Iseult
Balder Dead
Empedocles on Etna
Stanzas from the Grande Chartreuse
The Strayed Reveller and Other Poems
Dover Beach
Thyrsis
Scholar Gypsy
On Translating Homer
New Poems
On the Study of Celtic Literature
Essays in Criticism
Culture and Anarchy
Literature and Dogma
Mixed Essays
Friendship's Garland
God and the Bible

D.G. Rossetti (1828-1882)

The Blessed Damozel
World's Worth
Ave
The White Ship
Sister Helen
Eden Bower
The House of Life
Ballads and Sonnets

Christina Georgina Rossetti (1830-1894)

The Goblin Market
The Prince's Market
A Pageant and Other Poems

William Morris (1834-1896)

The Defence of Guenevere

The Life and Death of Jason
The Earthly Paradise
A Dream of John Bull
News from Nowhere
A Tale of the House of the Wolfings
The Roots of the Mountains
The Story of the Glittering Plain
The Sundering Flood
Hope and Fears for Art
Signs of Change

A.C. Swinburne (1837-1909)

Atalanta in Calydon
Erechtheus
Tristram of Lyonesse
Chasteland
Bathwell
Mary Stuart
William Blake : A Critique
A Study of Shakespeare
A Study of Ben Jonson
Songs Before Sunrise

Edward Fitzgerald (1809-1883)

Euphranor : A Dialogue on Youth
Translation of Rubaiat

Thomas Carlyle (1795-1881)

Sartor Resartus
The French Revolution
Heroes and Hero-Worship
Past and Present
The Letters and Speeches of Oliver Cromwell
Latter-day Pamphlets
Life of John Sterling
History of Frederick the Great
Chartism

John Ruskin (1819-1900)

The Modern Painters
Salsette and Elephanta
The Seven Lamps of Architectur
The Stones of Venice
The Two Paths
Unto This Last
Munera Pulveris
Time and Tide by Wear and Tyne
Fors Clavigera
Sesame and Lilies
The Crown of Wild Olive

T.B. Macaulay (1800-1859)

History of England from the Accession of James II
Lays of Ancient Rome

Charles Dickens (1812-1870)

Pickwick Papers
Nicholas Nickleby
Martin Chuzzlewit
Dombey and Son
David Copperfield
Bleak House
A Tale of Two Cities
Great Expectations
Our Mutual Friend
Edwin Drood
Oliver Twist
Little Dorrit
Baraby Rudge
The Uncommercial Traveller
A Christmas Carol
Hard Times
Old Curiosity Shop

William Makepeace Thackeray (1811-1863)

Vanity Fair
Barry Lyndon
Pendennis
Henry Esmond
The New Comes
The Virginians
Adventures of Philip
The Book of Snobs
The History of Pendennis
Lovel the Widower
The Round about Papers
The English Humorists of the Eighteenth Century

The Four Georges
Rebecca and Rowena
The Rose and The Ring
Ivanhoe—the Legend of the Rhine

George Meredith (1828-1909)

The Ordeal of Richard Feveral
Evan Harrington
Emilia in England
Rhoda Fleming
Vittoria
The Adventures of Harry Richmond
Diana of the Crossways
One of Our Conquerous
The Amazing Marriage
The Egoist
Beauchamp's Career
The Tragic Comedians

Charlotte Bronte (1816-1855)

Jane Eyre
Shirley
The Professor
Villette

Emily Bronte (1818-1848)

Wuthering Heights

George Eliot (1810-1880)
(Mary Ann Evans)

Adam Bede
The Mill on the Floss
Silas Marner
Scenes of Clerical Life
Life of Jesus
Romola
Fleix Holt the Radical
Daniel Deronda
Middlemarch

Benjamin Disraeli (1804-1881)

Vivian Gray
Sybil : Or the Two Nations
The Voyage of Captain Popavilla
Henrietta Temple
Coningsby : or the New Generation
Tancred : or the New Crusade
The Wondrous Tale of Alroy and the Rise of Iskander
Contarini Fleming : A Psychological Autobiography

R.L. Stevenson (1850-1894)

Travels with a Donkey in the Cevennes
An Inland Voyage
Virginibus Pueresque
New Arabian Nights
Treasure Island
The Strange Case of Dr. Jackyll and Mr. Hyde
Kidnapped
The Black Arrow
The Master of Ballantrae
Catriona
Underwords
A Child's Garden of Verses

Thomas Hardy (1840-1828)

Under the Greenwood Tree
Desperate Remedies
A Pair of Blue Eyes
Two on a Tower
Far From the Madding Crowd
The Return of the Native
The Mayor of Casterbridge
Tess of the D'Urbervilles
Jude the Obscure
The Hand of Ethelberta
The Trumpet Major
The Woodlanders
The Well-beloved
A Laodicean
A Group of Noble Dames
Life's LIttle Ironies
Wessex Poems
The Dynasts
A Changed Man
Winter Words
The Waiting Supper and Other Tales

MULTIPLE CHOICE QUESTIONS

1. *"Bliss was it in that dawn to be alive, But to be young was very heaven!"* These lines have been attributed to:
   A. Wordsworth B. Shelley
   C. Keats D. Byron
2. *The Essays of Elia* is written by
   A. De Quincey B. Charles Lambs
   C. Hazlitt D. Cobbett
3. The publication of Wordsworth's Lyrical Ballads coincides with the
   A. French Revolution
   B. War for American Independence
   C. Industrial Revolution
   D. Invention of the steam engine
4. The poem Coleridge wrote as a result of an opium-induced dream was:
   A. *The Solitary Reaper*
   B. *Christabel*
   C. *Rime of the Ancient Mariner*
   D. *Kubla Khan*
5. Byron's poem, *The Vision of Judgment,* is an attack on the works of:
   A. Coleridge B. Keats
   C. Shelley D. Southey
6. *Childe Harold* is a poem by:
   A. Coleridge C. Southey
   B. Byron D. Shelley
7. *Prometheus Unbound* is written by:
   A. Browning B. Tennyson
   C. Shelley D. Spenser
8. *Adonais* is an elegy on:
   A. Keats B. Arthur Hallam
   C. Byron D. Shakespeare
9. John Keats is famous for his:
   A. odes B. plays
   C. blank verse D. masques
10. *Tales from Shakespeare* was written by:
    A. Coleridge
    B. Lamb and his sister Mary
    C. Wordsworth
    D. Byron
11. *Confessions of an English Opium Eater* is written by:
    A. De Quincey B. Coleridge
    C. Byron D. Leigh Hunt
12. William Godwin was a:
    A. Psychologist B. Statesman
    C. Scotsman D. Philosopher
13. *Don Juan* by Byron is written in:
    A. blank verse B. rhyming couplets
    C. ottava rima D. quatrains
14. The educational novel written by Maria Edgeworth is:
    A. *Waverly*
    B. *Belinda*
    C. *Ivanhoe*
    D. *Northanger Abbey*
15. Coleridge's *Biographia Literaria* critically analyzes the works of:
    A. Byron B. Wordsworth
    C. Keats D. Shelley
16. *The Stones of Venice* is a book about:
    A. History of Venice
    B. Landscapes
    C. Romantic Literature
    D. Gothic Art
17. Hopkins and Patmore were:
    A. religious poets B. nature poets
    C. war poets D. critics
18. Swinburne, Rossetti and Morris together were known as the:
    A. Decadent poets
    B. Pre-Raphaelite poets
    C. War poets
    D. Absurd poets
19. Christina Rossetti's work containing poems for children is:
    A. *The Earthly Paradise*
    B. *Scholar Gypsy*
    C. *Goblin Market*
    D. *The House of Life*

20. Swinburne's masterpiece known for its choral passages is:
A. *Atalanta in Calydon*
B. *Cain*
C. *Sohrab and Rustam*
D. *Queen Mab*

ANSWERS

1	2	3	4	5	6	7	8	9	10
A	B	C	D	D	B	C	A	A	B
11	**12**	**13**	**14**	**15**	**16**	**17**	**18**	**19**	**20**
A	D	C	B	B	D	A	B	C	A

THE MODERN AGE (1880 ONWARDS)

As the 20th century dawned, new values replaced the old ones and shaped the literature of Great Britain. England fast lost its imperial image as her colonies revolted and fought for independence. Industrialization progressed by leaps and bounds and the two World Wars brought economic depression. All this affected the content of literature. Writers sought new vehicles of expression. The findings of **Sigmund Freud** in the realms of psychology took novelists to the subconscious mind. A great number of writers who became famous men of letters in English came from Ireland **(G.B. Shaw, W.B. Yeats, James Joyce and Samuel Beckett)** and from America **(T.S. Eliot and Ezra Pound)**. Socialism became a practising creed and feminism raised her head. Dogmatic Christianity was more or less ignored. Although great strides were made in scientific inventions, science could not provide suitable answers to the deep questioning of the human mind resulting in ethical philosophy. The age saw the end of feudalism. Victorian reticence and prudery gave way to decadence in literature. English writers came under the influence of the French Parnassians and Symbolists. Scandinavia and Russia represented by **Ibsen** and **Tolstoy** also influenced the British men of letters. Many a poet wished to fight free from the fixed rules of versification and wrote in free verse. Many imitated the American poet **Walt Whitman**. English literature became more expansive in its concerns. The life and culture of foreign lands were depicted. Although **Kipling** was an imperialist, his works go beyond England. Being born in India, his works give a graphic view of the country. The great Celtic Revival under Yeats brought a new strain to English literature. Finally, the theatre, lying dormant for a century, now woke up with renewed vigour.

Criticism

The Age began with scholarly works in literary history. **Leslie Stephen (1832-1904)** wrote biographical and critical essays. He produced *The English Utilitarians and the Dictionary of National Biography*. He was an agnostic and rationalist. **A.C. Bradley (1851-1935), H.J.C. Grierson (1866-1960)** and **Edward Dowden (1843-1913)** were other famous critics. Bradley is famous for his critical work on Shakespeare's tragedies.

Walter Horatio Pater (1839-1894) propounded the literary doctrine *Art for Art's Sake* which was a quest for the most refined pleasure. The exquisite in art came from a reflection of the past. He eulogized the accomplishments of the Renaissance. His prose style was rich, musical and classical. His works include *Studies in the History of the Renaissance* (1873) and *Marius the Epicurean* (1885).

John Addington Symonds (1840-1893) was another admirer of the Renaissance. **Oscar Wilde (1856-1900)**, more known as a novelist and dramatist, gave a wider dimension to the theory of Art for Art's Sake by spicing it with wit and paradox. **George Saintsbury (1845-1933)** and **Sir Walter Raleigh (1861-1922)** were other famous critics.

Poetry

Most of the poetry written in this period are the works of those more renowned as novelists: Robert Louis Stevenson, Rudyard Kipling and Thomas Hardy. William Butler Yeats, who pioneered the Celtic Revival, Thomas Steams Eliot, whose *Wasteland* is a watershed leading to modern poetry, Gerard Manley Hopkins, the Catholic poet, are the famous poets of this period.

Rudyard Kipling (1865-1936) wrote on imperialist themes in *Barrack Room Ballads* (1892), *The Seven Seas* (1896) and *Five Nations* (1903). These poems were aimed by their rugged music to rouse people to protest. He combined folk-music with music-hall chorus. It had the sound of drum beats and bugle-calls and even the refinements of chamber music. The poetry of imperialism, heroism of national policy, contained slang and even biblical allusions. In fact, his popularity was that of Walt Whitman, the national poet of America. Many of his subjects were from India, like the poem *Gunga Din*.

W.E. Henley (1849-1903) also wrote poetry which praised Britain's colonial power. *The Song of the Sword, For England's Sake* and *London Voluntaries* are some of his better-known poems.

There were also a group of poets called the Decadents. They were aesthetes and their doctrine was 'Art for Art's Sake'. **Oscar Wilde** was the leading poet of the group. *The Ballad of Reading Gaol* (1898) is his famous work inspired by his crime and imprisonment.

A group of poets had a pessimistic view of life. **John Davidson (1857-1909), Ernest Dawson (1867-1900)** and **A.E. Housman (1859-1936)** are some of these poets. But the leading pessimist of the age was **Thomas Hardy (1840-1928)**, better known as a novelist. He published *Wessex Poems* (1898) after the novel *Jude the Obscure* failed to receive public acclaim. His poetry was musical and highly individual. He had a disillusioned view of life. From 1903 to 1908, he produced the vast poetical work *The Dynasts*, written under the background of Napoleon's struggle against Europe combining real history with symbolic flashes. His poem, *To an Unborn Pauper Child,* reveals his utter dejection with life: *'Breathe : hid heart',* it begins.

Francis Thompson (1859-1907) and **Gerard Manley Hopkins (1844-1889)** were religious poets of the beginning of the twentieth century. Thompson's poem, *The Hound of Heaven* is a masterpiece. It describes God as a Heavenly Hound chasing man to capture his soul and man fleeing Him in the pleasures of life. The Jesuit, Hopkins invented a new type of verse called *'sprung rhythm'.* It was filled with strange word coinages and is difficult for the ordinary reader to understand. His poetry reflects the conflirt within him between his attraction to Roman Catholicism and his joy tor the beautiful creation. He wrote a number of religious poems of which *The Wreck of the "Deutschland"* is one of the best. It describes the death of five Franciscan nuns on board the ship, *Deutschland.*

Irish, English and Continental influences met in **W.B. Yeats (1865-1939)**. He Was born in Ireland but came to live in London. He was influenced by the strange mystical visions of William Blake, by pre-Raphaelite refinement and even the mysticism and occultism of the Orient, especially of India. His poetry is an attempt to revive Celtic mysticism and Irish mythology. Apparently it Was Yeats who introduced Rabindra Nath Tagore to the West. He also came under the influence of Verlaine, a French symbolist poet. His best poetry is in *The Wild Swans at Coole* (1919), *The Tower* (1928) and *The Winding Stair* (1933). Some of his well-known poems are: *Easter* (1916), *The Second Coming, Byzantium, A Prayer for my Daughter, Leda and Swan, Sailing to Byzantium, Meru, Lapis Lazudili, Among School Children,* etc. His progress as a poet can be assessed by comparing the beautiful but simple *Lake Isle of Innisfree* with the beautiful and profound *Byzantium.*

The towering poet of the 20th century is **Thomas Steams Eliot (1888-1965)**. Eliot came on to the scene when the West was passing through tremendous upheavals — belief in religion, especially of the Church was fading, democracy was the new experiment in politics, and many modernist trends were noticeable in literature. Eliot proclaimed himself" a royalist in politics, an Anglo-Catholic in religion and a classicist in literature". Tradition, according to him, was not the dead past but the past living in the present. In his essay *Tradition and the Individual Talent*, he states that "the talent of an artist shows itself not where he differs from the ancients but where, in his work, they assert their immortality". Eliot's poetry shows metaphysical, symbolist and imagist strains, but his individual talent shines forth unmistakeably. An eclectic philosophy, borrowed from his own Christianity and Buddhism and the Upanishads informs his poetry. His poetry, especially *The Wasteland* (1922) is a poem that describes the zeitgeist (spirit of the times) and the *angoisse metaphysique* (metaphysical anguish) of life in post-World War Europe. It begins with the sentence *"April is a cruel month"* and this sets the strain lor the whole poem. A brooding sense of futility and human inanity pervades modern life. Eliot achieves this effect by a combination of literary allusions to the past which stirs associations, and by what is called as the *objective correlative*. This last technique means that images are described which call up an emotion or a feeling. His other poems are *The Lave Song of J. Alfred Prufrock* and *Four Quartets* (1944). These lines from the *Four Quartets* may sum up the disillusionment of the times: *"Footfalls echo in the memory/Down the passage one could not take / To the door one could not open"*. Eliot was a poet of spiritual regeneration.

As the century proceeds, a host of poets make their mark **Stephen Spender (1909-1995), W.H. Auden (1907-1973), C. Day Lewis (1904-1972), Louis MacNeice (1907-1963)** — all of them wrote with a Social awareness, exposing the horror of the bourgeois culture and capitalist exploitation and the terror of totalitarianism.

We cannot end this section of the early modern twentieth century without a reference to **Rupert Brooke (1887-1915), Wilfred Owen (1893-1918)** and **Siegfried Sassoon (1886-1967)** popularly known as the "War poets". They had served the Armed Forces in the First World War, and after 1918, disillusioned by the horrors they had witnessed took their pens to write against the war. The poem *The Soldier* is one of the finest lyrics in the English language. It describes the poet's sense of impending death in battle and his love for his country: *"If I should die/Think only this of me/That there is a part of England/Buried in some foreign land"*. Another poem is Sassoon's *Everyone Sang,* which describes the exultation felt by the soldiers returning home after the General Armistice was signed. They are described as *freed birds.*

Novel

Just like poetry, the novel of this century reflects the great passions and strivings of the age. The discoveries of **Sigmund Freud (1856-1939)** revealed the relationship of man's behaviour to his subconscious mind. The subconscious contains impressions of past experiences which influence a person's attitudes and behaviour. These discoveries led not only to new methods of psychiatric treatment but also to new dramatic techniques in the art of the novel. The stream-of-consciousness method used by James Joyce and Virginia Woolf spring from these discoveries. The modem novel is more and more concerned with an analysis of human behaviour. The focus shifts from a description of the external atmosphere to the thoughts of the characters.

Thomas Hardy's works are tinged with a gloomy pessimism reminiscent of Schopenhauer, and an analogy may be found in his works to Flaubert and Zola from France. Hardy's country Dorsetshire and the surroundings become the 'Wessex' of his novels. His work is full of realistic descriptions of the countryside. The places, full of pre-historic and Roman remains, heaths, have a character, and influence the people living there. The pre-historic past presses on the life of today. He is adept at delineating rustic characters. Man is a puppet of fate and an uncontrollable destiny drives him along life. A bitter helplessness pervades his novels *Far* *from the Madding Crowd* (1874), *The Return of the Native* (1878), *The Mayor of Casterbridge* (1886), and *Jude the Obscure* (1895). His success reached a climax with *Tess of the d'Urbervilles* (1891). His *Tess of the D'UrberviUes* and *Jude the Obscure,* because of their frank handling of sex and religion, aroused the hostility of the reading public. These two books, however, present Hardy's most moving indictments of the human situation.

The works of George Robert Gissing (1857-1903) produce a sense of absolute dejection. He worked as an ill-paid hack in the poor districts of London and described these places vividly in his books. Although impressed by Charles Dickens, his writings show none of Dickens' humour. One bitter, wretched world, a miserable London, exists in his works. Thus *Demos, a Story of English Socialism* (1886) describes the futility of socialist agitation, *The Nether World* (1889), the wretchedness of the London slums, *New Grub Street* (1891), the hopeless lot of a penniless writer, and *The Odd Women* (1893), the plight of unmarried women. His style is as bare and unaffected as his ideas.

Robert Louis Stevenson (1850-1894) stands in contrast to Hardy and Gissing in his recreation of the life of action and adventure. Although he suffered from an incurable malady, he did not lose faith in himself. He brought out *An Inland Voyage* (1878), *Travels with a Donkey in the Cevennes* (1879), *The Silverado Squatters, Treasure Island* (1833), *Kidnapped* and *The Master of Ballantrae* (1889) among others. The last three are very popular among children the world over. He also wrote children's adventure classics like *The Treasure Island* (1883), *Dr Jekyll and Mr. Hyde* (1886) and *Kidnapped* (1886). In *Dr. Jekyll and Mr Hyde* he touches upon the dual nature of man his good and evil aspects. His style is vivid and full of interesting details.

Another great novelist was the Pole, **Joseph Conrad (1857-1924)**, who perfected his knowledge of English and wrote in a vivid style with a strong foreign accent. His experience of sailing life and work in the English merchant service gave him the ideas to write masterpieces like *The Nigger of the Narcissus* (1897), and *Lord Jim: A Tale* (1900). Like the Slavs he was preoccupied with the problem of human misery. *Lord Jim* and *The Heart of Darkness* (1902) show his anger at what the white man had done to exploit Africa and other nations. A trait of his narrative technique is the gradual picture of his character formed from fragmentary descriptions of witnesses. He has a rich, sensuous prose style full of striking imagery.

Rudyard Kipling wrote stories about Indian life: *Plain Tales from the Hills* (1888) and *Soldiers Three* (1888). *Plain Tales from the Hills* depicts an Englishman's encounter with the strange East. Kipling was born in Bombay and spent his early life in India. He knew the land and its customs, its people and languages. His best book is *Kim* (1901), the story of a half-Irish boy, who speaks the language of the rustics of India and accompanies a Buddhist Lama on his search for "Nirvana" or Salvation. Kipling is adept at describing the sights and smells of India and its colourful people with their racy dialects. He also wrote two animal epics entitled, *The Jungle Book* (1894) and a series of short stories for children like *Captains Courageous* (1897), just *So Stories* (1902) and *Puck of Pook's Hill* (1906). Kipling was influenced by Carlyle's doctrine of energy. As a spokesman of the Imperialist theme he believed that it was ideal for a person to sacrifice himself for his tribe. He believed that especially the white man was ordained to rule and lead nations. His works praise Britain's hegemony over her colonies.

Shortly after Kipling, came H. G. Wells and John Galsworthy who were Socialists and criticized the English society. **H.G. Wells** (1866-1946) began by writing stories with a semi-scientific flavour like *The Time Machine* (1895), *The Island of Dr Moreau* (1896), *The Invisible Man* (1897) and *The War of the Worlds* (1898). The stories are ingenuously plotted and thrill and disturb the readers. Later on Wells' interest shifted to social problems. He became a member of the Fabian Society. He wrote *Mankind in the Making* (1903) describing how society would look like when reformed by socialism. He also satirized the society in *Love and Mr Lewisham*

(1900), *Kipps* (1905). *Tono-Bungay* (1909) and *Marriage* (1912). He does not glorify Britain's past and he scorns the existing institutions of his country. He wrote a number of remarkable books after the outbreak of World War I in 1914. These show his restless self-examining spirit. Some of these are *Mr Britling Sees it through* (1916) and *The Undying Fire* (1919).

In the works of **John Galsworthy (1867-1933)** we find an artistic conscience. Like Wells, he also attacked the concept of property and commercialism in his novels. He too exposed and criticized national prejudices, especially those existing among his own class, the landed gentry. He was widely read in Continental Literature and was especially influenced by France and Russia. Turgenev with his noble realism was his ideal. He is a detached and impartial observer of his country's decadent values. He advocates a fearless search for truth. *In The Island Pharisees* (1904) he exposes the stagnation of thought among English privileged classes. A similar theme is touched in other novels like *The Country House* (1907), *The Patrician* (1911) and *The Dark Flower* (1913) where country squires, aristocracy and artists are critically studied. *The Forsyte Saga* (1922) is his masterpiece. It is a natural history of the rich upper-middle class family. He describes their attitude to events like the Great War, the growth of socialism, unemployment and the coal strike.

Enoch Arnold Bennett (1867-1931) wrote a number of different types of novels presenting a detailed picture of an industrial district in the provinces. He is a realist like the French nationalists. His masterpiece is *The Old Wives' Tale* (1908).

G.K. Chesterton (1874-1936) was a champion of tradition and he refuted and opposed the attacks of his contemporaries against English society in *Orthodoxy* (1908), *The Napoleon of Notting Hill* (1904). He believed in tradition sanctified by ages of experience and even in the religious bond between men. His style is effective with the use of imagery and comparison and he spices it with plenty of humour.

James Joyce (1882-1941) pioneered a new type of novel with the *stream-of-consciousness* technique. Characters in *Ulysses* (1922) unreel themselves by a sort of interior monologue. Speech is mimicked and styles are parodied. *Ulysses* is modelled on the *Odyssey* of Homer and set in the slums of Dublin. The thousand pages of this novel cover just one day in the life of Leopold Bloom and Stephen Dedalus. Joyce coined words from several languages and was a master craftsman with wit and conceits. His other famous work is the autobiographical *A Portrait of the Artist as a Young Man* (1916) which describes his adolescence and sensuous tendencies.

Virginia Woolf (1882-1941) continued the stream-of-consciousness technique. Her works *To the Lighthouse* (1927) and *Mrs Dallaway* (1925) reveal the hidden inner life of her characters.

E.M. Forster (1879-1970) was the novelist of cultural relations. In **A Passage to India** (1924) he studies the conflict between the west and the east and takes a favourable stand for the latter. *Where Angels Fear to Tread* (1905) studies how the cultural divide between an Italian girl and her English husband leads to the ruination of their marriage and life.

D.H. Lawrence (1885-1930) was a prolific writer. His outspoken views on sexual relations raised much hue and cry. He considered sex the religion of the blood. His novels were dubbed pornographic. He believed in the free expression of human personality, in being guided by unrestrained primitive instincts. In *Sons and Lovers* (1913) he studies the relationship of son and mother and the social disparity of a father, a coalminer and a mother, a teacher. The novel is autobiographical. Other works by him are *The Rainbow* (1915), *Women in Love* (1921), and *The Plumed Serpent* (1926). *The Rainbow,* suppressed as obscene, treats the conflict between man and woman. *Lady Chatterley's Lover* (1928) was canned for being obscene.

George Orwell (1903-1950) wrote novels which were an indictment of totalitarian government: *Animal Farm* (1945) and *Nineteen Eighty-Four* (1949). **Aldous Huxley's** *Brave New World* (1932) is a prophetic book about the future of civilization in the context of scientific advancement.

Drama

After Shakespeare, **George Bernard Shaw (1856-1950)** is the great playwright whose works enlivened the British stage. Shaw, like Ibsen, believed in drama as a vehicle for ideas. He had a rich Irish sense of humour and his plays are satires on various social and philosophical themes. His general technique was to discuss the problem of his play first in its preface. Often this preface is longer than the play itself. *Widowers' Houses* (1892) was his first play. In this he discusses the problem of Housing. In *Mrs Warren's Profession* (1894) he lays bare the profession of a prostitute. In *Arms and the Man* (1894) the theme is the chocolate-cream soldier. Shaw was an iconoclast breaking well-established idols or myths. Thus this play disillusions us of the romantic image of a soldier. He is not one who is willing to die for his country, but one who loves his life. When the enemy is weak, he attacks, but withdraws and takes to his heels if the enemy is strong. George Bernard Shaw had a keen interest in the English language and formulated a standard pronunciation for it. He studies the theme of how language can influence one's rise in the social ladder. Professor Higgins succeeds in teaching a flower-girl to rid herself of a cockney accent and to speak well enough to pass for royalty! In *Man and Superman* we see Shaw as a master conversationalist. Ideas are discussed without much action taking place in the play. *The Apple Cart* (1929) shows the weaknesses of democracy. Although an Irish man, Shaw did not write on Irish themes as such.

Oscar Wilde reminds one of the Restoration playwrights Sheridan and Congreve in his comedy of manners. His style is full of paradox and verbal wit. Some of his famous plays are *Lady Windermere's Fan* (1892), *A Woman of No Importance* (1893) and *The Importance of Being Ernest* (1895).

John Galsworthy's plays *Sfrife* (1909), *Justice* (1910) and *Loyalties* (1922) were based on the theme of class exploitation.

W.B. Yeats contributed to the Irish drama. His Celtic theme comes through in *The Countess Cathleen* (1892) and *The Land of Heart's Desire* (1894). **Sean O'Casey** (1884-1964) and **J. M. Synge** (1871-1909) were other noted Irish playwrights. The latter's plays, *The Playboy of the Western World* (1907) and *Riders to the Sea* (1904) are famous.

T.S. Eliot's contribution to the modern theatre were religious and moral plays. He uses the Greek "chorus" style in *Murder in the Cathedral* (1935) to heighten the dramatic effect of the murder of Thomas Becket by the Archbishop of Canterbury's men. *The Family Reunion* (1939) is a play about sin and expiation. Eliot pruned verse to sound like prose. This is done dexterously in *The Cocktail Party* (1949) and *The Confidential Clerk* (1953) where characters speak verse which sounds like prose.

A group of playwrights came to be known as the "Angry Young Men". **John Osborne (1929-1994)** was the most prominent of them. His play *Look Back in Anger* (1956) catches the mood of the frustrated youth in post-War England. In his plays, he exposes the wretchedness of the working class.

Harold Pinter (1930-2008) mixes comedy and horror in his plays like *The Birthday Party* (1958).

Another group of dramatists drew their inspiration from France. *The Absurd Theatre*, as it was called, began in France with Albert Camus, Jean Genet anJ Ionesco as its pioneers. In England, **Samuel Beckett (1906-1989)** was the Irish dramatist of this school. His plays *Endgame* (1955), *Krapp's Last Tape* (1958) and *Waiting For Godot* (1906) show the meaninglessness of human action and the unrelieved gloom of existence.

MAJOR AUTHORS AND THEIR WORKS

George Bernard Shaw (1856-1950)

Widowers' Houses

Candida

You Never Can Tell

Man and Superman

Back to Methuselah

Saint Joan

Heartbreak House

The Philanderer

Mrs. Warren's Profession
Caesar and Cleopatra
John Bull's Other Island
Major Barbara
The Doctor's Dilemma
Getting Married
The Apple Cart
Pygmalion
The Dark Lady of the Sonnets
Plays Pleasant and Unpleasant
The Millionaire
The Intelligent Woman's Guide to Socialism
Everybody's Political What is What
Cashel Byron's Profession
Love Among the Artists
Androcles and the Lion
The Devil's Disciple
The Man of Destiny

W.B. Yeats (1865-1939)

The Land of Heart's Desire
The Countess Cathleen
The Shadowy Waters
The Hour-glass
The Resurrection
The King's Threshold
On Baile's Strand
The Cat and the Moon
Ideas of Good and Evil
Discoveries
The Wind among the Reeds
The Wanderings of Oisin
The Tower
The Winding Stair and Other Poems
Lake Isle of Innisfree
Byzantium

John Galsworthy (1867-1933)

The Silver Box
Strife
The Skin Game
The Man of Property
Justice
Loyalties
Escape
The Inn of Tranquility
The Forsyte Saga
The Country House
Fraternity
The Patrician
The Dark Flower
Saint's Progress
Maid in Waiting
Flower Wilderness

Rudyard Kipling (1865-1936)

Kim
The Jungle Book
Barrack-room Ballads
Departmental Ditties
The Seven Seas
The Five Nations
Tales from the Hills
Soldiers Three
Life's Handicap
The Phantom Rickshaw
Many Inventions
The Day's Work
Just-so Stories for Little Children
Rewards and Fairies
Debits and Credits

H.G. Wells (1866-1946)

The Time Machine
Love and Mr. Levisham
Kipps
The History of Mr. Polly
Mr. Britling Sees It Through
Christina Albertas Father
The Wonderful Visit
The Island of Dr. Moreau
The Invisible Man
The War of the Worlds
The First Men in the Moon

The Food of the Gods
Marriage
Experiment in Autobiography
The Contemporary Novel

Joseph Conrad (1857-1924)

The Nigger of the 'Narcissus'
Typhoon
Lord Jim
Victory
Almayer's Folly
An Outcast of the Islands
Youth
Heart of Darkness
The Secret Agent
The Shadow of Line
Suspense-A Napoleonic Novel

Arnold Bennett (1867-1931)

The Old Wives' Tale
Clayhanger
Riceyman Steps
Buried Alive
Hilda Lessways
These Twain
Sacred and Profane Love
The Pretty Lady
The Love Match
The Author's Craft

Walter de la Mare (1873-1956)

Peacock Pie
Memoirs of a Midget
Songs of Childhood
Bells and Grass
The Traveller
Early the Morning
Love

T.S. Eliot (1888-1965)

The Waste Land
Prufrock and Other Observations
Gerontion
The Hollow Men
Ash Wednesday
Four Quartets
Sweeney Agonistes
Murder in the Cathedral
The Rock
The Family Reunion
The Cocktail Party
The Confidential Clerk
The Sacred Wood
After Strange Gods
The Elder Statesman
The Idea of a Christian Society
What is a Classic?
For Lancelot Andrews
The Use of Poetry and the Use of Criticism
Elizabethan Essays
Points of View

Virginia Woolf (1882-1941)

The Voyage Out
Jacob's Room
Mrs. Dalloway
To The Light House
The Waves
Flush
Orlando : A Biography
The Common Reader
Roger Fry
The Death of the Moth
Mr. Bennett and Mrs. Brown
A Room of One's Own
Between the Acts (Unfinished)

E.M. Forster (1879-1970)

Abinger Harvest
Two Cheers for Democracy
A Passage to India
Howard's End
The Hill of Devi
The Celestial Omnibus
Collected Short Stories
Where Angels Fear to Tread

The Longest Journey
The Story of the Siren
A Room with a View
The Eternal Moment

James Joyce (1882-1941)

Ulysses
Portrait of the Artist as a Young Man
Finnegans Wake
Dubliners

D.H. Lawrence (1885-1930)

Sons and Lovers
Woman in Love
Lady Chatterly's Lover
The Rainbow
The White Peacock
Kangaroo
The Plumed Serpent

Aldous Huxley (1894-1963)

Point Counter Point
The Burning Wheel
Those Barren Leaves
Brave New World
After Many a Summer
Eyeless in Gaza
Antic Hay
Time Must Have a Stop
Crome Yellow
The Defeat of Youth
The Perennial Philosophy
The Devils of Loudun

George Orwell (1903-1950)

The Animal Farm
The Road to Wigan Pier
Nineteen Eighty-Four
Burmese Days
Keep the Aspidistra Flying

Oscar Wilde (1854-1900)

The Sphinx
The Ballad of Reeding Gaol
The Canterville Ghost
De Profundis
The Duchess of Padua
The Importance of Being Earnest
An Ideal Husband
Lady Windermere's Fan
Salome
The Picture of Dorian Gray
The Happy Prince and the Other Tales

Harold Pinter (1930-2008)

The Birthday Party
The Dumb Waiter
The Care Taker
A Night Out
The Home Coming
Old Times
Silence

MULTIPLE CHOICE QUESTIONS

1. The Celtic Revival was begun by:
A. George Bernard Shaw
B. W.B. Yeats
C. J,M. Synge
D. James Joyce

2. *The Wasteland* is written by:
A. T.S. Eliot B. John Galsworthy
C. Thomas Hardy D. Virginia Woolf

3. Hardy is famous for his poem:
A. *The Hound of Heaven*
B. *The Dynasts*
C. *Four Quartets*
D. *Wild Swans of Coole*

4. The Irish dramatist, who wrote absurd plays, was
A. W.B. Yeats

B. Samuel Beckett
C. Sean O'Casey
D. J.M. Synge

5. *Everyone Sang* is a poem about:
A. socialism B. music
C. war D. death

6. *The Old Wives'* Tale is written by:
A. Robert Gissing B. Galsworthy
C. H.G. Wells D. Arnold Bennet

7. Robert Louis Stevenson wrote stories about:
A. adventure B. human nature
C. war D. nature and man

8. *The Invisible Man* is written by:
A. D.H. Lawrence B. H.G. Wells
C. Kipling D. Dickens

9. *Nigger of the Narcissus* is written by:
A. Hardy B. Eliot
C. Lawrence D. Conrad

10. Sex was considered the religion of the blood by:
A. D.H. Lawrence B. Ibsen
C. G.B. Shaw D. Oscar Wilde

11. The British novelist and poet who described India best was:
A. Virginia Woolf
B. Graham Greene
C. Rudyard Kipling
D. Aldous Huxley

12. Rupert Brooke, Wilfred Owen and Siegfried Sassoon are together known as:
A. Flower Poets B. War Poets
C. Poets of Revolt D. Patriotic Poets

13. Walt Whitman was the national poet of:
A. England B. Poland
C. America D. France

14. *The Wreck of the Deutschland* is a:
A. war poem B. historical poem
C. romantic poem D. religious poem

15. *Sprung rhythm* was invented by:
A. Gerard Manley Hopkins
B. T.s. Eliot
C. Auden
D. Yeats

16. *The Family Reunion* — a play, is written by:
A. W.B. Yeats
B. T.S. Eliot
C. Cecil Day Lewis
D. Louis MacNiece

17. Gissing's *The Odd Women* is a work on:
A. plight of unmarried women
B. poverty of slum-dwellers
C. war and love
D. the life force

18. *Ulysses* is written by:
A. Virginia Woolf B. George Orwell
C. Arnold Bennett D. James Joyce

19. *The Patrician* is written by:
A. Kipling B. H.G. Wells
C. Henry James D. Galsworthy

20. *Look Back in Anger* is written by:
A. A. J. Cronin
B. Aldous Huxley
C. D. H. Lawrence
D. John Osborne

ANSWERS

1	2	3	4	5	6	7	8	9	10
B	A	B	B	B	D	A	B	D	A
11	**12**	**13**	**14**	**15**	**16**	**17**	**18**	**19**	**20**
C	B	C	D	A	B	A	D	D	D

Indian Writing in English

ANAND, MULKRAJ (1905-2004)

He was greatly influenced by Premchand on the one hand and Tagore on the other.

Works

Some of his famous novels are :

1. The Village (1939)
2. Across the Black waters (1940)
3. The Sword and the sickle (1942)
4. Untouchable (1933) (his first novel)
5. Seven summers (1951)
6. Private Life of an Indian Prince (1953)
7. The Big Heart (1945)
8. Coolie (1936) (It was recast in seventies)
9. Two Leaves and a Bud (1937)
10. The Old Woman and the Cow (1960)
11. The Road (1961)
12. Death of a Hero (1963)
13. Confession of a Lover (1976)
14. Morning Face (1968)

AUROBINDO, GHOSE (1872-1950)

- He was known as the "firebrand" of India.
- He was a poet, a saint, a philosopher, statesman, yogi and a prophet.
- He is one of the pre-Independence Titanic trio of Indian poets—Tagore, Aurobindo and Sarojini Naidu.
- He is chiefly known for his
  - *(i)* Savitri (1953) a poetic epic on a grand scale.
  - *(ii)* The Life Divine (1939-40)
  - *(iii)* Essays on Gita
- He is a great exponent and proponent of ancient Indian thought.
- According to R. K. Singh, "Aurobindo is sympathetic to the modernist trends in writing and study of poetry and, in fact, himself adopts some of the methods followed by the modern poets."
- To quote Mr. Singh again, "In Aurobindo's literary order, poetry is a means of spiritual expression that helps to open the consciousness..."

CHATTERJEE, BANKIM CHANDRA (1838-94)

- He is generally called 'The Father of Bengali fiction.'
- Today he is most known for his patriotic bent of mind.
- In all he wrote 14 novels.
  - *(i)* Some of them are historical.
  - *(ii)* Others are social.
  - *(iii)* Still others are philosophical with stress on renunciation and non-attachment.
- Some of his novels are :
  - *(i)* *The Poison Tree (1884):* It is a story of Hindu life in Bengal of the period
  - *(ii)* Kapalkundala (1885)
  - *(iii)* Durgeshnandini (1890)
  - *(iv)* Krishnakanta's Will (1895)
  - *(v)* The Two Rings (1897)
  - *(vi)* Rajmohan's Wife (1904) (published posthumously)
  - *(vii)* Anand Math (1884)

CHAUDHURI, NIRAD, C. (1897-1999)

- He came into limelight with the publication of his "The Autobiography of an Unknown Indian." (1951).
- His other important works are:
  - *(i)* A Passage to India (1959)
  - *(ii)* Continent of Circe (1966) (He received the Duff Cooper Memorial Prize).
  - *(iii)* The Intellectual in India (1967)
  - *(iv)* To Live or Not to Live (1970)
- He is known for his most correct and chaste prose for which he has earned much acclaim from the scholars and critics, including Khushwant Singh.

DESAI, ANITA (Born-1937)

- She is a renowned novelist and short story writer.
- Some of her famous novels are :
  - *(i)* Cry, the Peacock (1963)
  - *(ii)* Voices in the City (1965)
  - *(iii)* Bye-Bye, Blackbird (1971)
  - *(iv)* Fire on the Mountain (1977)
  - *(v)* Clear Light of Day (1980)
- Her collection of short stories is captioned "Games at Twilight" (1978)

GANDHI, M.K. (1869-1948)

1. His famous work in English is "My Experiments with Truth."
2. The work is an important autobiographical writing which is held in high esteem for its truthfulness, frankness, simplicity and directness of expression in non-ornamental effective English.

MARKANDAYA, KAMALA (1924-2004)

1. She is one of the modern novelists and is known for her:
   - *(i)* Nectar in a Sieve (her first novel) (It is a novel on miserable rural life).
   - *(ii)* Some Inner Fury (1955) (It is a novel of violence and destruction)
   - *(iii)* A Silence of Desire (1960) (It is a novel urging the readers to speak out frankly to unburden their hearts).
   - *(iv)* Possession (1963) (The problem of possession is discussed in this novel).
   - *(v)* A Handful of Rice (1966) (It depicts the life of the poor classes in Madras).
   - *(vi)* The Coffer Danus (1969)
   - *(vii)* The Nowhere Man (1972)
   - *(viii)* Two Virgins (1973)
   - *(ix)* The Golden Honeycomb (1977)
   - *(x)* Pleasure City (1982).

KHUSHWANT SINGH (Born-1915)

- He is known for his novels :
  - *(i)* Train to Pakistan (his masterpiece)
  - *(ii)* I Shall Not Hear the Nightingale (1959). (It describes the social life of a Sikh family during the pre-Independence period).
- "The Mark of Vishnu" is another of his well-known works.
- Some of his known stories
  - *(a)* Karma
  - *(b)* When Sikh Meets Sikh
  - *(c)* The Rape, etc.
- He is also known for his:
  - *(i)* A History of the Sikhs
  - *(ii)* Translation of Japji Sahib, etc.
- His regular columns appear weekly in some dailies, *e.g.* :
  - *(i)* 'With Malice Towards One And All'—The Hindustan Times.
  - *(ii)* 'This Above All'—The Tribune.
- Mulk Raj Anand is stated to have said that Khushwant Singh's "Train to Pakistan" is likely to last, while about his other creative literary work, one may have some doubts.
- Among his latest work is "Truth, Love and Little Malice."

MULLER, MAX (1823-1900)

- He was a famous Indologist, German orientalist and linguist, who unearthed a lot of ancient Indian history and Sanskrit scriptures, the Rig Veda, in particular, of which he published six colossal volumes, for which he had got an assignment from the East India Company in 1847.
- Actually he was a student of Sanskrit, who started comparative study of languages and "Avesta" (in 1845) which is the renowned sacred book of the Zoroastrians.
- He gave seven lectures on Indian and ancient Indian philosophy at Cambridge University, which have now been published by Rupa & Co. under the caption: "India : What Can it Teach Us?"

- He distnguishes the highest wisdom of Greece and India by using the terms "to know ourselves" and "to know our self", respectively.
- Muller makes very appreciative comments on the Rig Veda and the Vedic Religion.

NAIDU, SAROJINI (1879-1946)

- She is a well-known Indian English poet who started writing poetry at a very early age and she was inspired by Edmund Gosse to choose Indian themes and scenery rather than imitating the English classics.
- She is now known as 'The Nightingale of India.'
- She took a keen interest in India's struggle for freedom.

Some of her works are :

1. The Golden Threshold (1905)
2. The Bird of Time (1912)
3. The Broken Wing (1917)
4. The Sceptred Flute (1946)
5. The Feather of the Dawn (1961) (It appeared posthumously)

Some of her famous poems are :

1. The Queen's Rival
2. Palanquin Bearers
3. To My Fairy Fancies
4. The Pardah Nashin
5. Awake
6. Village Song
7. The Soul's Prayer
8. Fishermen of Coromondel
9. It You Call Me
10. Caprice
11. Summer Woods
12. Songs of Radha
13. The Bird Sanctuary, etc.

NANDY, PRITISH (Born-1947)

- He was the editor of the 'Illustrated Weekly of India' and has now Telecast a T.V. serial over the Doordarshan: "Hungama Unlimited."
- *(i)* He is a prolific poet, though he is still not considered one of the best.
  (ii) Most of his poetry has been dismissed by critics as mere experimental gimmickry. Such was Saleem Peeradina.
  (iii) Even Nissim Ezekiel dubbed him to be a poetaster.
- Some of his works are :
  (i) Gods and Olives (1967)
  (ii) On Either Side of Arrogance (1968)
  (iii) From the Outer Bank of the Brahmputra (1969)
  (iv) Riding the Midnight River (1975)
  (v) In secret Anarchy (1979), etc.
- He has written a number of anthologies and translated a number of poets including Agyeya, Amrita Pritam, Kaifi Azmi etc.
- He has also written some short stories and a verse play.

NARAYAN, R.K. (906-2001)

- Of the three great novelists, Narayan, Anand and Rao, it is Narayan who has won the maximum accolade both in India and abroad.
- One of his great achievements is his creation of the famous town of Malgudi like Hardy's Wessex.
- Narayan is the true master of humour, irony, realism, romance and artistry.
- Most of his novels and stories depict the life of people of South India.
- It is sometimes held that Narayan lacks true pathos, genuine depth of feeling, realistic description of poverty and misery, the elements which go in for making a novelist a great one.
- However, he has earned much popularity as a novelist, and within the range of his own art, he cannot be taken except with due regard and attention.

Some of his famous novels are :

1. Swami and Friends (1935)
2. Bachelor of Arts
3. The English Teacher

4. The Financial Expert
5. Mr. Sampath (1949)
6. The Guide (1958)
7. The Man-eater of Malgudi
8. The Dark Room (1939)
9. Waiting for the Mahatma
10. The Vendor of Sweets
11. The Painter of Signs (1976)

(He won the Sahitya Akademi Award for 'Guide' in 1961)

R.K. NARAYAN (as a short story writer)

- Some of his stories have appeared in the following collections:
  - *(i)* Malgudi Days
  - *(ii)* Dodu and Other Stories
  - *(iii)* Cyclone and Other Stories
  - *(iv)* Gods, Demons and Others

Narayan has written a few hundred stories, most of them quite interesting and highly readable:

Some of his famous short stories are :

1. The Golden
2. A Career
3. The Snake Song
4. Man Hunt
5. A Willing Slave
6. An Astrologer's Day
7. The Doctor's word
8. God of Troubles, etc.

NEHRU, JAWAHARLAL (1889-1964)

- He needs no introduction as a freedom fighter, statesman and first Prime Minister of India.
- Some of his literary works are :
  - *(i)* An Autobiography (1936)
  - *(ii)* Glimpses of World History (1939)
  - *(iii)* Discovery of India (1946)
- Children enjoy reading his "Letters from Father to His Daughter."
- He is known for his simple, chaste, poetic English which is a model of natural style.

PRITAM, AMRITA (1919-2005)

- She is the most famous Punjabi Author.
- She won the Jnanpith Award for her "Kagaj Te Kenvas" in 1981.
- Her best known autobiographical work which appeared in the seventies is "Rasidi Ticket."
- *(i)* Her "Shadows of words : An Auto-biography" (a transcreation of the Hindi original by Jyoti Sabharwal) has been published by Macmillan in 2002.

  (ii) The book presents "an inner journey down the memory lane" presented by the author, who considers old age the best part of her life, like the last sips of tea, which are "usually the sweetest."

RADHAKRISHAN, SARVAPALLI (1888-1975)

- He is known as an outstanding educationist and a philosopher who presented the Hindu/Indian viewpoint to the world.
- His works include
  - *(i)* An Idealist View of Life (Lectures)
  - *(ii)* Indian Philosophy (1923,1927)
  - *(iii)* The Hindu View of Life (1932)
  - *(iv)* An Idealist View of Life (1932)
  - *(v)* Eastern Religious and Western Thought (1939)
- He wrote in a very simple, intelligible prose-style.

RAO, RAJA (1908-2006)

- His famous works are:
  - *(i)* The Serpent and the Rope (1960)
  - *(ii)* Kanthapura (1938)
  - *(iii)* The Cat and Shakespeare (1965-66)
- *(i)* He was awarded the Sahitya Akademi Award for his 'The Serpent and the Rope' in 1964.

  (ii) He was also decorated with Padma Bhushan in 1969.

Raja Rao as a short story writer

- He is also a well-known short story writer.
- His first collection of short stories was "Jauni" which was published in France in 1930.

- The collection: "The Cow of the Barricades" was published in 1947

 Some of his famous short stories are :
 1. Akkayya
 2. The Little Gram-shop
 3. Kanaka Pal
 4. Narsiga

ROY, ARUNDHATI (Born-1961)

She made her debut with her novel: "The God of Small Things" which won her the Booker Prize in 1997, besides a handful amount running into crores as royalty for less than four hundred pages which comprise the said novel.

DE, SHOBHA (Born-1948)

- She is a renowned contemporary Indian English novelist and T.V. serial script writer.
- Some of her novels are prescribed in universities in England and Australias.
- Her T.V. serial "Swabhiman" which ran into numerous episodes was telecast over the Doordarshan.
- *(i)* She has become even more popular with her serial "Kittie Party" telecast over the Zee T.V.

 (ii) According to the Tribune, it "is a clever insight into the mind of today's urban Indian women poised at the crossroads of modernity and tradition."

TAGORE, RABINDRANATH (1861-1941)

Tagore was a versatile genius. He was a :

(i) poet
(ii) novelist
(iii) short story writer
(iv) dramatist
(v) musician
(vi) actor (in dramas)
(vii) painter
(viii) statesman and a host of other things.

Some of his famous novels are :
1. The House and the World (1919)
2. The Wreck (1921)
3. Gora (1923)

VIVEKANANDA, SWAMI (1863-1902)

He is a well-known Indian seer, prophet, recluse preacher, lecturer and poet, who:

(i) made the ancient Indian philosophy known to the whole world at the Parliament of Religious in Chicago, USA.

(ii) Brought about a wave of resurgence among the Indian masses through his stirring spiritually inspired speeches which were also full of:
 (a) patriotic fervour
 (b) love for universal brotherhood.
 (c) spirit of social uplight, etc.

SOME LITERARY MASTERPIECES

CANTERBURY TALES

by Chaucer

'Canterbury Tales' is a collection of stories in verse by Chaucer. These tales are told by twenty-nine pilgrims who are going on a visit to the shrine of St. Thomas-a-Becket at Canterbury.

Each tale is a complete unit in itself without being intended to be linked with other tales. But, in the narration which is fictional in essence, we have head-links which are actually connecting passages. The headlinks are descriptions of the pilgrims as well as the events that take place in the course of the journey besides valuable digressions.

In those days, the people were very fond of pilgrimages for the sake of religious devotion and fun and they generally travelled in groups to face the dangers of the journey. The tales are written and descriptions of pilgrims given as if Chaucer himself had met such characters and had some experiences like those given.

The pilgrims meet at the Tabard Inn in Southwark on the eve of their departure and there they plan the journey. Chaucer himself is one of the pilgrims and the host of the Inn, Harry Bailly, not only gives a hearty welcome to the pilgrims but also accompanies them to the shrine.

Since the journey is quite tedious, each pilgrim is required to tell two tales on the journey towards the shrine and two during the return journey. But, Chaucer could complete only twenty four tales during his life time and in this sense, the Canterbury Tales is only a fragment.

An important aspect of the tales which brings Chaucer near to a dramatist and a novelist is that the tales differ in character as widely as do those by whom they are told.

The Knight tells, a chivalrous tale, the Clerk a devotional tale while the Miller's and the Reeve's tales are coarse and farcical in complete harmony with their own characters.

UTOPIA

by Thomas More

The period when Renaissance was in full bloom, Utopia was written by Sir Thomas More who lived from 1478-1535. He was imbued with the spirit of humanism.

The Greek word "Utopia" means "nowhere". Hence, it is in this light that Sir More tried to present an imaginary ideal republic of his dreams, which was of course, impossible to be achieved on this earth.

Utopia was originally written in Latin and was published in 1516. Later, it was translated into Italian and French. It was much later, after death of More, that its English translation appeared.

The Important characters in the book are :

1. The writer himself.
2. Peter Giles—writers's friend
3. Raphael Hythloday—a Portuguese traveller.

The book comprises two parts. In part one the protagonist (Hythloday) describes his voyaging with the explorer, Amerigo Vespucci.

In part two Hythloday describes the country of Utopia.

Comments :

Utopia glorifies

1. A democratic society.
2. A socialistic society with public control over wealth.
3. Religious tolerance
4. Economic equality
5. Peace and prosperity (upto a limit)
6. Love of this world.
7. Love of nature and natural way of living.
8. Love of beauty.
9. Love of the common man.
10. Love of human dignity.

Utopia condemns

1. Aristocracy
2. Elitism
3. Asceticism and stoicism
4. Other worldliness
5. Fanaticism and bigotry.
6. False Chivalry
7. A Luxurious way of life
8. Scholasticism
9. Narrow-mindedness
10. War, Jingoism and Chauvinism.

GORBODUC

by Thomas Norton & Thomas Sackville

The other name of Gorboduc is Ferrex and Porrex. It is known for being the first regular English tragedy. It was written by Thomas Norton and Thomas Sackville and was first staged in 1562, that is, two years before the birth of Shakespeare. The work became a model for the Renaissance dramatists. It is, in essence, a Senecan tragedy of revenge.

The important characters in this tragedy are :

1. Gorboduc, The king of England
2. Ferrex—Gorboduc's elder son
3. Porrex—Gorboduc's younger son
4. Videna—The Queen
5. The murderers of the king and the queen
6. The nobles
7. The common people, etc.

The story in a nutshell: After the king divides his kingdom between his two sons, the latter begin to quarrel as a result of which Porrex kills Ferrex. The latter is so much loved by the queen that she kills Porrex. The people rise in revolt and kill the king and the queen. The nobles thereafter kill the murderers of the royal couple. This leads to a bloody civil war. There is chaos and anarchy as the question of success remains unsolved.

Senecan Features

1. Division into five acts.
2. Revenge as the chief motive.
3. A chain of murders—one murder leading to the other.
4. A ghost as one of the characters.
5. Lack of humour and any comic relief.
6. All-pervading seriousness and blood and thunder.
7. Avoidance of bloodshed on the stage, as it is reported by the characters through dialogues and monologues.
8. A plethora of rhetorical speeches by the characters.
9. Appearance of the chorus at the end of each act.

The use of blank verse in a drama was for the first time made in Gorboduc.

ASTROPHEL AND STELLA

by Philip Sidney

Astrophel and Stella is a sonnet series written by Sir Philip Sidney, Sidney is known more as a critic for his 'Apologie for Poetry' than as a poet, though his poetic claim is not altogether rejectable. His chief position as a poet rests on Astrophel and Stella.

Significance

1. The work is significant in the sense that it is perhaps the first work in English literature written in the white heat of passion, arising out of a personal and intimate experience.
2. In spite of artificiality of certain sonnets and general Petrarchan extravagance in the series, the work, having arisen out of real experience and genuine feelings, does not altogether look unreal.
3. It sounds real in several respects as in the apostrophe to the moon, in minute, vivid details and descriptions, etc.
4. Though the excessive use of conceits, hyperboles and embellishments mars the series in certain respects, yet its overall significance for the English literature cannot be underestimated.
5. Sidney was, no doubt, influenced by Petrarch. Yet he tries to assert himself every now and then by following a rhyme scheme other than the Petrarchan.
6. His most frequently used rhyme scheme is abba, abba, cdcd, ee. In other words, his sonnets end with a couplet in the Shakespearean style.

DOCTOR FAUSTUS

by Christopher Marlowe

The play opens with the chorus which announces the theme of the play i.e., the story of a scholarly doctor who has his end because of excessive lust for knowledge in the fields of magic and necromancy.

At the start Faustus looks at several fields of study such as Logic, Medicine, Law, Divinity, etc. But he finally settles at Magic. Then appear the Good Angel and the Evil Angel. The former warns Faustus against studying Magic book. He asks him to study the holy books. But the latter encourages him to study the Magic book.

The End of Faustus: His end is as tragic as it can be. He has not indulged or little indulged in sensual pleasures. What makes his sin more serious in theological circles in his association with Satan and the Satanic forces-demons, ghosts, devils etc. So, he gets no forgiveness and relief of any kind despite all his wailings and is taken away to hell by the Devils.

THE WINTER'S TALE

by Robert Green

Robert Greene's prose novel 'Pandosto' or 'The Triumph of Time' was published in 1588 and reprinted in 1607. This became the source for Shakespeare's *The Winter's Tale* which seems to have been composed in 1610 or 1611.

The title signifies an old wives' tale told to the curious children before they go to bed. Hence, such a tale can contain fairy-tale, exaggerative or legendary elements which may be far from reality because of some romantic, imaginary, unreal, absurd persons, incidents and situations.

Characters

Polixenes—the King of Bohemia, Leontes—the King of Sicilia, Hermione—Leontes's wife, Mamillus—Son of Leontes, Camillo—a Gicilian Lord, Cleomenes & Dion—courtiers, Paulina—Antigonus's wife, Emilia—the queen's lady, Florizel—the son of the king of Bohemia, Florizel—known as Doricles, Paulina.

BARTHOLOMEW FAIR

by Johnson

It is one of the most famous of Jonson's comedies which pleases all but hurts none. It is an authentic picture of the London of Queen Elizabeth's times. It was first staged in 1624, in manuscript form. It was published later in 1631.

There is a broad spectrum of humanity in the work at all levels, chiefly low level. Thus we have in the play gallants, gulls, cutpurses and bawds, lovers, squires, servants and justices of peace, etc.

Important Characters

1. **Bartholomew Cokes:** He is a foolish young squire.
2. **Waspe:** He is servant to Cokes who accompanies him to the fair.
3. **Grace Wellborn:** She is the fiancee of Waspe.
4. **Edgeworth:** He is a cutpurse.
5. **Nightingale:** a ballad singer and companion and accomplice of Edgeworth.
6. **Adam Overdo:** a justice of peace.
7. **Zeal-of-the Land Busy:** He is a Puritan who becomes an object of mockery.
8. **Dame Purecraft:** She is a rich widow.
9. **Winwife:** He is a London gallant who is Busy's rival in wooing Purecraft.
10. **Quarlous :** He is a gamester but he is guised as a madman. He is Busy's friend, with whom he finds himself in a quarrel. He at last wins the hand of Purecraft.

Plot: There is virtually no plot in the play but only a presentation of a plethora of incidents and episodes which are mostly left undeveloped. Jonson's chief aim is to hold a mirror to the London life of his times.

The main incidents are

1. Cokes being relieved of purse, sword, cloak and marriage licence at the hands of Edgeworth.
2. Overdo being taken for a pickpocket and put in the stocks.
3. Waspe and Busy being put in the stocks for fighting and creating nuisance.
4. Overdo's escape from the stocks.
5. Quarlous's disclosing to Overdo the real face of Edgeworth.
6. Overdo's invitation to all to dinner.
7. Quarlous's winning of the hand of Purecraft.

Thus, the play proves Jonson to be a gentle satirist who has an ocean of sympathy with his characters of all kinds.

PARADISE LOST

by John Milton

Needless to say that the said Epic is the greatest heroic poem in English literature and one of the greatest of its kind in world literature.

A true epic on classical lines though with several diversional elements, as it is, it has twelve books.

A bookwise "Argument of Paradise Lost" is given by W.J. Long, which may be summarised as under :

Book I

It contains *inter alia*,

(*i*) a statement of the subject, the Fall of Man, and

(*ii*) a noble invocation for light and divine guidance.

Thereafter, in it, we have—

(*i*) description of Satan and the rebel agents. Satan's physical size, his gigantic shield, etc. are on supernatural lines, as can be visualised for a devil of his kind, as in a true epic in particular.
Satan's great power of oratory is also there before us.

(*ii*) the ouster of the rebel angels from heaven by the Almighty.

(*iii*) the diabolical plot of the rebel angels to wreak their vengeance on God by beguiling Adam and Eve, God's children and first parents of mankind, from their state of innocence by bringing about their fall by eating the forbidden fruit in the Eden.

(*iv*) a description of the sulphurous hell-fire and the eternal agonies undergone by the damned spirits there.

(*v*) the raising of Satan's palace, Pandemonium.

Book II

It contains, *inter alia*,

(*i*) a description of the council of devils in the Pandemonium.

(*ii*) Satan's desire to take up the task of beguiling Adam and Eve upon himself.

(*iii*) his journey to the gates of hell, guarded by Sin and Death.

Book III

It contains *inter alia*—

(*i*) God's behest to Raphael to warn Adam and Eve of the imminent danger of disobedience to them.

(*ii*) Son of God's offer to take upon himself the sin of the impending disobedience of man.

(*iii*) Satan's meeting with Uriel, the Angel of the sun, for the purpose of learning the way to earth, the abode of God's new creation.

(*iv*) Satan's journey to the earth in the guise of an angel of light.

Book IV

It contains, *inter alia*—

(*i*) The scenes of Paradise and of Adam and Eve being in the state of innocence.

(*ii*) Eden being guarded by an angel.

(*iii*) The arrest of Satan when he is trying to tempt Eve in a dream.

(*iv*) the setting free of Satan in an unconvincing way.

Book V

It contains, *inter alia*—

(*i*) the description by Eve of her dream to Adam.

(*ii*) Adam and Eve's routine life.

(*iii*) Raphael's visit to Eden.

(*iv*) Raphael's description of the revolt of the fallen angels.

Book VI

It contains, *inter alia*—

a continuation of Raphael's description of the revolt of the fallen angels.

Book VII

It contains a description of the story of creation by Raphael.

Book VIII

It contains Adam's description to Raphael of himself and his meeting with Eve.

Book IX

It contains an account of Satan's temptation of Eve.

Book X

It contains, *inter alia*—

(*i*) God's judgement on Adam and Eve.

(*ii*) Sin and Death's construction of a highway through chaos to the earth.

(*iii*) Satan's return to Pandemonium.

(*iv*) Adam and Eve's repentance.

(*v*) the turning of fallen angels into serpents.

Book XI

(i) Acceptance of Adam's repentance by God.

(ii) Michael's departure to bring into effect Adam and Eve's banishment from Eden.

(iii) Michael's prophecy regarding the destiny of man.

Book XII

It contains *inter alia*—

(i) Continuation of Michael's prophecy.

(ii) Learning by Adam and Eve of future redemption of mankind.

(iii) Adam and Eve's departure out of Eden.

Given below are some extracts from Book I:

The lines given below state the theme: The Fall of Man and present an Invocation to the Muse and the Holy spirit (*i.e.* the spirit of God):

THE WAY OF THE WORLD

by Congreve

As the play opens, we find two men Mirabell and Fainall talking to each other in a Chocolate House.

We learn that Fainall is married to Lady Wishfort's daughter, Arabella who is referred to as Mrs Fainall in the play. We also learn, that Mirabell loves Lady Wishfort's niece, Millament. Lady Wishfort is not only Millament's aunt but also her guardian.

It is learnt that Mirabell often went to Wishfort's house ostensibly to court her but actually to meet Millament. This pretence of Mirabell is at last exposed by Mrs. Marwood.

An enigmatic situation is now created for Millament. Since Lady Wishfort has learnt about Mirabell's sham, she forbids any meeting between him and Millament, Further, in order to inherit the lady's wealth, she has to marry according to her wish. This means that if she marries Mirabell against her wishes, she is likely to be deprived of the fortune of the lady who is fifty-five.

Mirabell has his own plot. He arranges marriage between his servant, Waitwell and Lady Wishfort's maid servant, Foible. The purpose of this marriage is that Waitwell is presented by Mirabell as his (imaginary) uncle, named Sir Rowland.

As Foible has been taken into confidence, she would impress upon Lady Wishfort that Sir Rowland, a wealthy man, has in his heart a deep love and wants to marry her. Through this plan Mirabell wanted to cause embarrassment to Lady Wishfort by revealing the identify of Sir Rowland later and thus compelling her to allow Millament to marry him.

A hindrance is created in the execution of the plot when Mrs. Marwood, Fainall's mistress comes to know about the plan, and she makes her lover aware of it. Besides, not only Millament but also Mrs. Fainall know about this plot.

Mrs. Fainall had once been Mirabell's mistress and in her heart of hearts, she still loves him. Hence, she also does not want that Mirabell should marry Millament, as her heart is burning with the fire of jealousy.

Mr. Fainall is a mean fellow, and he finds it an easy opportunity to blackmail Lady Wishfort. For this, he threatens to divorce Mrs. Fainall. It is further another proof of his avaricious nature that in a deed which is in his possession, he has already arranged the settlement of major part of Mrs. Fainall's estate in his own favour.

It is at the most critical moment when Sir Rowland and Lady Wishfort are busy in constructive prospects and Mirabell and Millament have agreed to marry each other, that Fainall makes his appearance.

Thus Mirabell's apple-cart is disturbed. However Foible reveals the secret of Fainall's love affair with Mrs. Marwood. However, Fainall, rising on the crest of the situation sets forth certain conditions to remain silent. The conditions concern the fortunes of Mrs. Fainall and Millament and the marriage of Lady Wishfort.

Just then Waitwell presents a deed which is executed by Mrs. Fainall before her marriage with Fainall. In it, she has conferred her then estate on Mirabell. Thus the deed with Fainall becomes infructuous.

The net result of this *deus ex machina* is that Mirabell and Millament now have no obstacle in tying the nuptial knot to each other.

SENSE AND SENSIBILITY AND PRIDE AND PREJUDICE

by Jane Austen

In essence, the novel *Sense and Sensibility* is a satire on sentimentalism. Elinor represents sense, while sensibility is represented by her sister Marianne. The story, like all stories of Jane Austen, is very simple, but interesting.

Mrs. Henry Dashwood with her three daughters Elinor, Marianne and Margaret, is left in a very straitened situation on the death of her husband. They have to retire to Devonshire where they begin to live in a very humble cottage.

Edward Ferrars is the brother of Mr. John Dashwood. John is the step son of Mr. Henry Dashwood. He had been entrusted by the latter to take care of his wife and daughter after his death. But he does not discharge his responsibilities in this respect.

Edward and Elinor fall in love with each other. Marianne falls in love with a poor, unscrupulous young man, John Willoughby.

Willoughby suddenly leaves for London. Marianne and Elinor go after him. But Willoughby says that he is going to be married to a rich heiress. Elinor also learns that even her lover, Edward, has been untrue to her, as he is already engaged to Lucy Steel who is the niece of Edward.

Edward's mother is not happy with his engagement to Lucy, and settles her property on his younger brother, Robert, who is a fool of the first water. Then Robert and Lucy are married, while Edward stands rejected. Then Edward marries Elinor. Marianna who has been wooed by Colonel Brandon, marries him.

Immature style of Jane Austen is evident in this novel, but her future greatness and maturity is also visible here in seed form. The novel was completed in 1797, though it was published in 1813.

The story of Pride and Prejudice which is regarded as her best work and was published in 1813 is well-known to all scholars and need not be given here. It is in this novel that all the plot and stylistic perfection of Jane Austen comes into play. It is here that the dialogues are most lively, characters life like and her humour at its best.

Whereas in Sense and Sensibility, her characters such as Mrs. Jennings, her stupid daughter, her uncouth son-in-law and Mr. Palmer are some of the humorous characters they are no match for Mr. Collins, Mrs. Bennet, Catherina de Borough and others of Pride and Prejudice.

DAVID COPPERFIELD (1849-50)

by Charles Dickens (1812-70)

David Copperfield is perhaps the most popular novel of Dickens. It is an autobiographical novel in which Dickens's power of characterization, depicting humorous and pathetic situations and characters is perhaps the best brought out. The novel is told in the first person.

THE MAYOR OF CASTERBRIDGE

by Thomas Hardy

It was published serially in 1886. It is the story of a man who brings doom upon himself.

THE MILL ON THE FLOSS (1860)

by George Eliot (1819-80)

The Mill on the Floss is the most popular novel of Gorge Eliot. It is also perhaps her most autobiographical novel. The story represents the typical Victorian problem of morality and a moral order which spares nobody.

The Mill mentioned in the title of the novel is the imaginary mill 'Dorlcote Mill' owned by Mr. Tulliver. The mill is situated on the river Floss.

The two main characters in the novel are:

(i) Tom Tulliver, and

(ii) Maggie Tulliver.

THE WASTELAND

by T.S. Eliot

When the Wasteland was published in book form in 1922, it was soon realized to be the beginning of the emergence of the Modernist Poetry.

Earlier the Georgians and the Imagists had appeared and disappeared but their effect, particularly that of the latter, had been retained in the inner recesses of the minds of the writers, poets included, even though superficially the movement of Imagism had all but spent itself.

It was because Ezra Pound who had occupied a pivotal position in the movement which had such protagonists as Hilda Doolittle and Aldington, also was instrumental in giving the final shape, as were now have, to Eliot's poem.

The Wasteland depicts the collapsing civilization of Europe and, connotatively, the fall of values in the modern world. The poem is highly realistic in this sense, but it promises vaguely some possibility of redemption through some everlasting philosophies such as that of the Buddha and the Upanishadas.

It cannot be disputed that the overwhelming picture of pessimism, death and desolation in the poem is to a great extent the result of the annihilation and mayhem which was witnessed in the First World War that ended in 1917. Then there emerged a particularly distressing mood in the twenties and this mood of depression of the entire period all over the world is very deftly brought about in the poem.

The poem's merit does not lie just in depicting a particular mood, but in its employment of complex symbolism and references to mythology, history, culture, religion and literature from varied sources in modern and medieval world and even the remote ancient times.

SAINT JOAN

by G.B. Shaw

It is one of the most famous plays of G.B. Shaw. It is this play which won him the Nobel Prize. The play was first produced in 1923.

Historical Background to Saint Joan: Saint Joan is a historical play which is based on the life and career of a real character, Joan of Arc. She was a common country girl, who was born in 1412. As a girl, she heard divine voices and had divine visions. But she was sent to the stake on the charges of heresy in 1431.

Social, political and religious conditions of the period are closely related to the story of Joan of Arc.

It was in 1415 that the English forces under the leadership of their young king, Henry V defeated Charles VI, the French King at Agincourt—a decisive battle which aroused waves of nationalism in England.

As a result of this humiliating defeat, the French king had to accept certain most unpleasant terms such as :

1. He had to sign a treaty with the English King in 1420.
2. According to it, he had to :
   (i) disown his own son, the Dauphin, declaring him as illegitimate.
   (ii) marry his infant daughter to the English king.
   (iii) allow the English to keep with them large area of France which they had conquered.

It is to be noted that at that time, France was not one united country. It consisted of a number of estates which were under the control of different feudal lords or barons.

TO THE LIGHT HOUSE

by Virginia Woolf

Virginia Woolf's most famous novel, Mrs. Dalloway was published in 1925. Two years later, another masterpiece of hers was published in 1927.

It is the only novel of Mrs. Woolf which has a Three Part Structure :

(i) Part I: The Window
(ii) Part II: Time Passes
(iii) Part III: The Lighthouse.

The main characters in the novel are:

1. **Mrs. Ramsay:** She is a middle-aged charming woman, a mother of eight children. She is the central figure in the novel.
2. **Mr. Ramsay:** He a scholar and philosopher of great repute and has won several academic honours.
3. **Charles Tansley:** He is an intelligent young student of Mr. Ramsay.
4. **Minta Doyle:** He is a young man who loves Paul Rayley.

5. **Paul Rayley:** She loves Doyle.
6. **Augustus Carmichael:** He is an old man and poet.
7. **Lily Briscoe:** She is a painter.
8. **William Bankes:** He is an old friend of Mr. Ramsay's.
9. **James Ramsay:** He is six year old child of Ramsays.
10. **Cam :** Janes's sister.

The scene is laid in the island of Skye in the Hebrides.

The story is autobiographical in nature in the sense that:

(i) Mr. and Mrs. Ramsay resemble Mrs. Woolf's parents.

(ii) Lily Briscoe greatly resembles Mrs. Woolf herself.

The novel whether more artistic than Mrs. Dalloway or not, has earned as much if not more popularity than Mrs. Woolf's other masterpiece.

The novel is written on the stream-of-consciousness technique:

(i) In the *Window,* not only the personality of Mrs. Ramsay is revealed, but also we have the personality of Mr. Ramsay before us which is laid bare through the eyes of Lily Briscoe, Charles Tansley, William Bankes, etc.

(ii) In *Time Passes*, we learn more about Mrs. Ramsay and others through the memory of the Charwoman, Mrs. Mc Nab.

(iii) In *Lighthouse* we have another focus on Mrs. Ramsay through the memory of Lily Briscoe.

The novel is poetic, as usually all of Mrs. Woolf's novels are

ADVENTURES OF HUCKLEBERRY FINN

by Mark Twain

The novel opens with a warning to the reader:

"Persons attempting to find a moral in it will be banished; persons attempting to find a plot in it will be shot."

Although Mark Twain wrote this novel as a companion to Tom Sawyer, yet it is much more than that. However, a link with the earlier novel is established in the first chapter.

Huck is adopted by the widow Douglas to "civilize" him. The money which is found at the end of Tom Sawyer is put by Judge Thatcher on interest and it fetches a dollar to each boy 'all the year round.'

Huck is not much interested in Douglas' prescriptions of a strict disciplined moral life. Twain attains a technical tour de force by shifting narrative to the first person. This enables Twain to establish *point of view*. Huck is the model of *radical innocence* and *instinctive knowledge*.

SONS AND LOVERS

by D. H. Lawrence

The family of Morels lived in the mining village of Betswood. Mrs. Morel who has had a puritan nourishment, still upholds the values of refinement and nobility. She gets enamoured of Morel's rich ruddy face and merry laughter as well as wavy black hair. Mr. Morel is also captivated by her. The two get married.

The two have an antithetical nature and temperament. Whereas Mrs. Morel is a puritan lady, Mr. Morel is fond of a sensuous, luxurious life. He tries to domineer over his wife. But she rebels against this and the result is that even the children dislike Mr. Morel.

The estrangement between the couple becomes intense when one day, out of jealousy, Mr. Morel clips off the curls of the young William, whom his mother loves so such.

Mrs. Morel does not give up her efforts to reform her husband. But he rather goes more and more astray in his fondness for drinking, etc.

The couple had two more children. Morel tries to entertain the children, but often, the more Mrs. Morel instigates them against him, the more he teases them.

Mrs. Morel is frightened of her estranged relationship with her husband and focuses all her attention on her sons. She wants to possess her first child William whose love affair with Lily she condemns. But the boy dies of pneumonia.

Then Paul Morel, the third child, and the hero of the novel, falls ill. He is suffering from bronchitis. She nurses him tenderly and virtually treats him as her lover. This is how the famous Oedipus complex gets manifested in the novel.

Paul has relationship with three women, that is, his mother, Miriam and Clara. Among these, Miriam is his beloved.

The relationship between Paul and Miriam develops as Paul goes to the Willey Farm with his mother. He offers to teach her French and algebra and thus a friendship develops between the two. But, as Lawrence himself points out, their friendship is "chaste" and purely spiritual.

This relationship between Paul and Miriam cannot become an everlasting one since Mrs. Morel is afraid that Miriam is going to suck Paul's soul and she herself can ill-afford to lose her son. Paul too realises that as long as his mother is alive, his relationship with any woman cannot be permanent.

Paul is interested not only in a spiritual relationship with Miriam. He wants to have with her a physical contact also, but this she denies to him.

Since Paul cannot get physical satisfaction from Miriam, he enters into physical union with a married woman, Clara, who lives separately from her husband. But, the problem is that the woman is unable to satisfy Paul spiritually. The result is that Paul is thrashed by Clara's husband to his complete discomfiture.

Since Paul feels that his failure with both the women, Miriam and Clara, has been because of his mother's possessive nature towards his soul, he begins to hate her. But, when she falls ill with cancer, he tries to arrange the best medical treatment for her.

Being no longer able to witness the agonising misery of his mother, he ends the story of her life by administering morphia to her.

Now, it was impossible for Paul to establish relationship with any woman. He had to be lonely, and there was no escape for him from this state of affairs.

HAMLET

by Shakespeare

Introduction: The king of Denmark has recently died. On his death, his son, Hamlet, the Prince of Denmark, who is a student at the University of Wittenberg, is summoned to the Danish Court.

Hamlet feels miserable that his father's throne has been seized by his uncle, Claudius and his mother has married him.

Ophelia: Another shock comes to Hamlet when his beloved, Ophelia, rejects his suit on the advice of his father, Polonius.

The Ghost: Hamlet learns from his friend, Horatio, and two officers that they have sighted his father's ghost. As Hamlet himself encounters the ghost, the latter tells him the reality that his father had been poisoned by his uncle. The ghost also burdens Hamlet with the responsibility of avenging his death.

The spies: Claudius appoints two spies, Rosencrantz and Guildenstern to keep a watch on Hamlet. The latter arranges the staging of a play "The Murder of Gonzago" to which the king is also invited. The king's abnormal behaviour while watching the play (in which the murder of a king in a manner similar to that in which Hamlet's father is killed is staged) convinces Hamlet of Claudius's guilt.

Having been convinced of Claudius's and his mother's collusion in the murder of his father, Hamlet scolds his mother in a closed room. But as he hears an echo from behind the curtain, he thrusts his rapier at the person hidden. This is how Polonius who was eavesdropping gets killed.

Cause of Hamlet's Madness: Claudius tries his best to know the real cause of Hamlet's "madness," "ecstasy" or distraction, but having failed in his effort, he decides to send him out to England.

In the Ship: In the ship with the two spies, Rosencrantz and Guildenstern, Hamlet opens the sealed letter which contains the orders for his execution on his reaching England. He cleverly replaces these orders for the execution of the spies who lose their life in the venture.

Ophelia's Madness and Death: On learning about the death of her father, Ophelia goes mad, while her brother Laertes burns with the desire for revenge which is sharpened by Claudius.

The Duel: As Ophelia's dead body is being lowered in the grave, Hamlet grapples with Laertes. The two have a bloody duel in which both of them are badly wounded.

Claudius's end: When the two fighters are dying the villainy of Claudius is divulged by Laertes and Gertrude, the Queen. Hamlet kills Claudius with his poisoned rapier and soon Fortinbras arrives to be the next ruler of Denmark.

A Dialogue between the ghost and Hamlet

There are several extremely interesting scenes in Hamlet. Hamlet's dialogue with the ghost of his father is one of them. Here are the following lines which need no explanation.

MACBETH

by Shakespeare

Macbeth was the Lord of Glamis. He was related to Duncan, the king of Scotland. As the play begins, he returns with another general, Banquo, after crushing the rebellion of the Lord of Cawdor.

The Three Witches: When the two generals were returning, they met three witches, one of whom addressed Macbeth as the Lord of Cawdor. Macbeth felt greatly excited as he heard the witches' prophecies that he would soon be king and Banquo's descendants would also be kings. Thereafter, they disappeared.

Macbeth's Promotion: Soon thereafter, Macbeth was informed by two nobles that he had been made Lord of Cawdor by the king. This further thrilled Macbeth as he realized that the prophecy of the witches had come out true. He was so curious and enthusiastic that he wanted that the second prophecy of the witches that he would become the king should also turn true as early as possible.

Duncan's visit to Macbeth's Castle: The king Duncan wanted to visit Macbeth's castle to honour him. Meanwhile, Macbeth informed his wife through a letter regarding the witches' prophecies.

Lady Macbeth's Ambition: Lady Macbeth was even more ambitious than Macbeth and wanted to see him king. As Macbeth reached home, at the earliest, she incited her husband to murder Duncan to make the prophecy come out true. Macbeth was hesitant in accepting this advice.

Duncan was warmly welcomed by the Macbeth couple. He loved the peaceful atmosphere of the castle and went to sleep peacefully and without an iota of suspicion in his mind.

Lady Macbeth continued inciting her husband and even called him a coward when he expressed hesitation and his feeling of non-propriety in killing a guest who was also one of their kins.

The couple drugged the guards and they went into a sound sleep. Then Lady Macbeth herself went to kill Duncan, but now the king's face seemed to her as that of her father. So, she could not execute her plan.

The Bloody Dagger: Thereafter, Macbeth went into the king's room, but as he saw the vision of a bloody dagger, he changed his mind. Yet again, he took courage and struck a dagger into Duncan's heart and killed him.

The Voice: As Macbeth told his wife about the deed, he heard a voice: "Macbeth shall sleep no more." As Macbeth was now terribly overtaken by fear and madness, Lady Macbeth, showing greater courage, put the blood-covered dagger by the side of the guards and stained their clothes with blood to put the blame on them.

The Porter: Soon, the gate knocked. As the porter opened the gate, two of Duncan's nobles entered and went into the king's room where they found him dead.

Duncan's sons: As the news of the king's murder was conveyed to Macbeth, he killed the two guards. Meanwhile, as the news reached Scotland, the king's sons began to run for safety. The elder one, Malcom fled to England. Macbeth was then proclaimed king of Scotland.

Banquo: Macbeth was satisfied that the witches' second prophecy had also turned out to be true, but he feared Banquo. It was because the witches had also prophesied that Banquo's descendants would be kings. Hence, to perpetuate his kingdom Macbeth made up his mind to kill not only Banquo but also his son, Fleance.

The Banquet: Macbeth hit upon a plan. He invited all the nobles to a banquet. As Banquo and his son were on their way to Macbeth's castle, two assassins hired by Macbeth waylaid Banquo and his son. In the attempt, Banquo was killed but his son escaped.

Banquo's Ghost: Macbeth saw Banquo's ghost seated in a chair at the banquet. He even heard the ghost's whispers. Those present there were surprised to note Macbeth's strange behaviour.

For a brief period, the ghost disappeared, but soon it appeared again. Macbeth began to tremble and cry wildly. His such behaviour made him a suspect in the eyes of the guests.

The Witches Again: Macbeth went to consult the witches again. As he saw them, they called three ghosts. Macbeth was told the following three prophecies in turn :

(i) Macbeth should beware of Macduff.

(ii) No man born of woman could harm Macbeth.

(iii) Macbeth could never be defeated until Birnam Wood came to Dunsinane hill.

Lady Macbeth's mental state: Lady Macbeth was in an extremely depressed mood. As such she committed suicide. Macduff had run away to England. It was reported to Macbeth that the Birnam wood was marching towards Dunsinane hill. Macbeth felt puzzled. Soon, it was known that the green branches of the wood were being carried by Malcom's soldiers who were marching towards Macbeth.

Macbeth and Macduff: A fight started between Macbeth and Macduff face to face besides their soldiers fighting with their opposites. As Macduff told Macbeth that he was taken from his mother's womb, Macbeth felt so much discouraged that he got killed without a fight. The witches' prophecies had come full circle on Macbeth, as all his ambition was finally dashed to the ground with true poetic justice meeting out to him, which is perhaps not present in any other of Shakespeare's plays.

Macbeth is a great poet and *inter alia,* Macbeth is a wonderful piece of lyrical and dramatic poetry.

ARMS AND THE MAN

by G. B. Shaw

The young, romantic Raina is standing in her balcony to enjoy the beauty of the night in that month of November in 1885. She has all the romantic ideas of heroism of her lover Major Sergius Saranoff who is out taking part in the war between the Bulgarians and the Serbs.

Suddenly, there comes an intruder. He is a Swiss officer, Captain Bluntschli. He threatens Raina with his pistol and orders her to keep quiet.

Soon, a Russian army officer enters Raina's room to search for the fugitive. Raina hides Bluntschli behind the curtain. She tells the officer that nobody has entered her room.

As the officer goes away, Raina offers some chocolate cream to the fugitive. He tells her that he always carries chocolates to the war in place of cartridges. Then he goes to sleep.

It is the 6th of March, 1886. As Major Petkoff, Raina's father returns from the war, he is welcomed by Raina and her mother, Catherine. Major Sergius also comes. He has resigned from the army as he has not been given promotion.

The two family servants, Nicola, the man-servant and Louka, the maid-servent are already engaged. But when Sergius and Louka are alone, Sergius embraces Louka. She tells him that Raina loves a Swiss officer and would marry him.

Bluntschli comes to return the coat lent to him by Raina and Catherine. Major Petkoff instructs Bluntschli to prepare papers for sending three regiments. The papers are then delivered to the messengers.

Raina has already learnt from Bluntschli about non-heroic part of Sergius in the army. Sergius thinks that she is no longer loyal to him.

At last Raina is married to Bluntschli to which both Petkoff and his wife agree. Louka gets married to Serguis.

In this way, the myth of both the heroism of a soldier and the romance of love is exploded by Shaw in his own inimitable, interesting and simple way.

THE PORTRAIT OF A LADY

by Henry James

It is perhaps Henry James' most important novel which was written in 1881. James believed in images rather than in a story. Yet, if the novel is to be studied as a story, it can be said to be the psychological study of Isabel Archer a young American girl who leaves America with her aunt Mrs. Touchett and goes to Europe in a sort of what may be called her spiritual odyssey.

Note :

1. While portraying Isabel, Henry James had the model of his cousin Mary Temple called "Minny" in his mind. The young girl died in 1870 when she was only 24.
2. The European tour is arranged as once dreamed by Minny, though she got no opportunity to fulfil her dream.
3. Minny had died of T.B.; here we find Ralph dying of the same disease.
4. Gardencourt is a 16th Century English mansion– the kind of architecture Henry cherished.
5. Henry was particularly fond of painting and architecture.
6. Isabel's European odyssey comprises a visit to several countries, *e.g.* England, Italy, France, Greece, Turkey and Egypt.
7. It is to be noted that Henry James had a high regard for the European culture with its vast history, but he had no fondness for his native, American culture which had no history except that worth the name.
8. Isabel is shown as having fondness for Browning and George Eliot, as Minny also had. Besides she is also interested in the German philosophy.

THE GUIDE

by R.K. Narayan

Written in 1958, The Guide which won R.K. Narayan the Sahitya Akademi Award is one of his best novels and a masterpiece giving ample proof of his *tour de force* in the matter of artistic technique.

There are two distinct aspects of the story of The Guide. One half of it is supposed to be told by Raju, the hero, to one of his followers (as he turns from a tourist guide to a saint). The entire life story of Raju is however put in a flashback and told as such by the author. This technical achievement is a rare triumph in the modern artistic style.

Again, to understand more clearly, the story of Raju as saint forms the objective aspect and that of Raju as a tourist guide the autobiographical aspect. This artistic pattern is woven in the entire novel and this is what makes it artistically unique.

Simply speaking, it is the story of Raju's life and death. Raju has to indulge in several vocations and avocations, such as:

(i) as a food vendor at the railway station.
(ii) as a tourist guide.
(iii) as a sentimental adulterer.
(iv) as a manager to a dancing girl, Rosy.
(v) as a prisoner.
(vi) as a reluctantly holy martyred saint.

The setting is, as usual with Narayan, Malgudi town. It is at the newly set up railway station that Raj becomes a vendor. As a tourist guide also, he is quite successful.

One day Rosy, the dancer, and Marco, her husband, an archaeologist, engaged Raju as their guide. There were often quarrels between the husband and the wife.

Raju fell in love with Rosy and spent most of his time with her. He wanted to make her a famous dancer. Rosy's husband at last left her and she now lived with Raju. She was his 'snake-girl'.

Raju who was too ambitious, crossed the limit of propriety. He got addicted to habits such as gambling, drinking, etc. But when he forged the signature of Rosy on an important document, he was caught by Rosy's husband. He had to spend two years in jail. Then Rosy parted ways with him.

After completing his jail term, Raju went to a village, Mangal. There the people mistook him for a saint. Raju, depending on the art of simulation and dissimulation, found it a golden opportunity to be something, and if still dilly-dallying, he willy-nilly took it upon himself to be a holy man.

It was Raju's misfortune that his test was too near and too hard and it was beyond his imagination and comprehension. As usual, the villages were a superstitious lot, and as the famine hit the village, they expected of Raju to do some miracle to appease the rain God.

Raju had no grounding in such machinations of the so-called holy men and he had to go on a fast into death to cause the rain god to show his mercy. Once started, it was now impossible to give up the fast, as the whole area had been converted into a hubbub of pilgrims, tourists, visitors and mediamen who were reporting every now and then on Raju's determination and condition.

The days passed by and yet there was no sign of a cloud. It was the twelfth day of his fast. Raju was too weak to walk or even talk. Somehow he managed to reach the bank of the river, the venue of his prayer for rain. He collapsed uttering the words, "Velan, it's raining in the hills. I can feel it coming up under my feet, up my legs."

GORA

by R.N. Tagore

Written in 1923, it is perhaps the most famous novel of Tagore. It is a patriotic novel which expresses the voice of Resurgent India which is arousing to shake up the shackles of slavery. The novel expresses true secularism and a fusion of the oriental and the occidental. Even Gourmohan, the hero, the son of an English lady is brought up in a Hindu household and stands for that universal blend of ideologies and cultures which is so characteristic of Tagore.

❑❑❑

Glossary of Literary Terms

Abridged edition

Condensed or shortened version of a work.

Absence

1. It is a modern term which is used to explain a work of art on the basis of aspects which are absent rather than those which are manifestly present in the work.

Acronym

1. A word formed from the initial letters of other words, *e.g.*

   NOIDA for New Okhla Industrial Development Authority.

2. The word may be considered synonymous to 'acrostic'.

Acrostic

1. It is a form of literary exercise in which the first letters of each line in a poem form a word as we read downwards.
2. Here are two Acrostics by H.S. Bhatia :

   (i) "Wait, O little child, wait!
   In the wind lies thy message,
   Not in the hubbub of the worldly;
   Else you may repent, says the sage."
   (The word formed is "WINE"

Act

Major division in a dramatic work.

Adage

Maxim or proverb.

Addendum

Addition or appendix to a book.

Aesthetic Realism

1. *(i)* According to Hudson, "Esther Waters" by George Moore was a landmark in this movement toward aesthetic realism.

   (ii) This movement was the vehicle of the new realists of which Moore and Gossing were representatives.

   (iii) According to Hudson, "they mistook mere ugliness for frankness and "seeing life steadily and seeing it whole."

Alexandrine

1. It is a line of six iambic feet instead of five.
2. It is not known for certain how this line originated.
3. It appears that it was evolved by Spenser by adding the Alexandrine to the eight-line stave (a b a b b c b c) of Chaucer that he used in the Monkeys Tale.

Alienation Effect

It was a term devised by the famous German playwright, Bartolt Brecht, who wanted to bring home the need, for realization of a kind of 'alienation' of the audience and the actors from the stage during the performance of a play, as the play being a play and not a part of real life.

Allegory

1. When the abstract or spiritual ideas are presented through living images, the result is the allegory.

Examples of Allegorical Works

1. The Pilgrim Progress
2. The Scarlet Letter
3. The Faery Queene
4. Morality Plays, such as "Everyman".
5. Seven Deadly Sins in Dr. Faustus, etc.

Alliteration

1. It signifies the repetition of initial consonant sounds, *e.g.*

   The furrow followed free.

Almanac

Book or table comprising a calendar of days, weeks and months indicating special occasions or events.

Anagnorisis

It means Discovery or Reversal in a Tragedy.

Anagram

Letters or word or phrase which, when re-arranged, form a new word.

Anapaest

It comprises two unaccented syllables followed by an accented one:

(i) Redeploy

(ii) Introduce

(iii) Camouflage

Androcentrism

The term implies the predominance of man in all social and intellectual activities.

Anecdote

Brief account or story about an individual.

'Angry Young Men'

It was a movement which came into existence in the second half of the twentieth century, mainly as a result of Osborn's play: "Look Back In Anger."

Annotation

Textual comment on a book.

Anthology

Collection of poetry or prose from diverse sources.

Anticipated Future

See 'Prosopopaeia'

Antithesis

1. It signifies the setting of one thing against another, often of opposite sense *e.g.*

   'A *friend never* betrays, an *enemy always* does.
2. 'Antithesis' can be expressed in literature also by presenting two aspects (of life) side by side, *e.g.* the real and the marvellous.

Aphorism

Short statement of a truth or dogma couched in memorable terms.

Apostrophe

It implies an exclamatory address to a person. (usually a dead one), some inanimate object or an abstract idea, *e.g.*

"Milton! thou shouldst be living with us at this hour..."

Archaism

It is a word or phrase which is no longer in use, *e.g.* loon, quoth, yclept, eftsoon(s), etc.

Archetypal Approach to Criticism

1. This Approach is also called Mythological, Ritualistic or Totemic Approach.
2. It endeavours to study literature on the basis of myth.

Areopagitica

This is the name of Milton's famous prose pamphlet, pleading for freedom, freedom of the press, in particular.

Argot

Slang or coarse vernacular language.

Aside

1. It is a kind of device similar to "soliloquy" (being probably comparatively brief) when a character speaks to himself.
2. The best example of an "aside" may be Shylock's words : "How like a fawning publican he looks" in Act, I sc. 3 of The Merchant of Venice.

Assonance

Unlike the alliteration (which signifies the repetition of consonant sounds), it signifies the repetition of vowel sounds, *e.g.*

1. I *hear* him *bear* the mark of a *seer* on his head.

Autobiography

An account of a person's life by himself or herself.

Avant-garde

Without going into historical aspects of the word, one can say that it implies those (persons) who support or create the newest ideas, fashions (generally literary or artistic), techniques, styles, etc. in an art, piece of literature, etc.

Ballad

1. Broadly-speaking, there are two kinds of ballads:
   (i) Traditional Ballads such as those pertaining to Robin Hood, Chevy Chase, etc.
   (ii) Modern Ballads, such as The Rime of Ancient Mariner, etc.

Bathos

1. It is a term to denote anticlimax.
2. It is generally used when there is sudden descent or fall from the sublime to the trite or ridiculous, *e.g.*

   Delay not thine departure hence,

   For thou mightst have a hot pudding, Awaiting thee.

Belles lettres

Essays on literary studies and the aesthetics of literature.

Bibliography

List of works on a particular subject or author.

Biography

An account of a person's life.

Blank verse

Poetry with unrhymed line endings (usually written in iambic pentameters).

Blurb

These are the words of praise or description of a book in a nutshell, inserted usually by the publisher on the cover page or jacket of the book, to attract the reader's eye.

Bound verse

Verse based on metrical pattern.

Burlesque

It is a way of writing which generates irony, humour and satire, *e.g.* Cervantes' Don Quixote, Samuel Butler's Hudibras, etc.

Bowdlerize

To 'cleanse' a work by omitting or cutting out indecent passages, phrases or words.

Cacophony

When the excessive use of high sounding words is made such that the meaning is lost or diminished in value in the sound, the result is cacophony instead of euphony.

Cadence

Rhythm and phrasing of language.

Caesura

1. In classical prosody, 'Caesura' means "break between words within a metrical foot." (Concise Oxford).
2. In English prosody, it means "pause about middle of line." (ibid.).
3. A Caesura "which does not immediately follow the ictus" is known as 'Feminine Caesura" (Chambers 20th century).

   (**Note :** In modern connotation, Caesura implies natural pause in a line of verse and not an unnatural or forced one)

Canon

Collection of works established as genuine.

Canto

Division of an epic or narrative poem.

Caption

Short description accompany-ing an illustration.

Caricature

The chief characteristics of characters are sometimes so exaggerated by the author that the characters look like some humorous or even funny creatures. The result is the creation of caricatures. This is what Dickens (more than any other author) has done.

Catalogue

List of books or works.

Catastrophe

1. It signifies the complete (often sudden) devastation of the fortunes of a character (often the hero and/or the heroine) in a play or piece of fiction.

Catharsis

This is the term used for the ousting of the emotions of pity and fear in the tragedy.

Chronicle Plays

1. These are the plays based on (English) History.
2. Such plays became very popular among the people in the sixteenth century.
3. These plays contain almost every important character, real or legendary, in the period of the times concerned.

Cipher

Writing that employs sub-stitution or transposition of letters.

Classic

(i) A classic (in reality, any book) is "the expression of man" as an individual.

(ii) It is also the expression of his mindset and the stance taken by him.

Cliche

Any word, phrase or expression that has lost its real effect for having been too frequently used by authors or laymen is called a cliche which may otherwise be quite lovable, *e.g.*

(i) The news is too good to be true.

(ii) The sorrow was too deep for tears.

(iii) Thanking you in anticipation, etc.

Climax

1. It is the main point of interest in a play or novel which is reached usually in the third act (or sometimes 4th of a 5 act of a play) or towards the end.
2. The resolution often takes place after the Climax or the forces for it start working or increase their intensity after it.

Colloquial

1. In speech, we sometimes make use of certain words and phrases which are not acceptable in standard speech
2. Such colloquial expressions should be avoided in all formal speech or writing.

Colonialism

1. The term differs from 'colonization' as the term may imply political or economic control of policies in a political unit without real annexation of land.

Colonisation

Literarily, the most significant modernist theories in the matter of

(i) colonisation

(ii) post colonisation

(iii) decolonisation, and

(iv) neo-colonisation have been provided and practised by—

(a) Ngugiwa Thiong'o

(b) Soyinka

(c) Achebe Chinua, etc.

Comedy

Humorous dramatic piece; *high comedy* has welldrawn characterization and witty dialogue; *low comedy*, or *slapstick* has absurd situations and boisterous action; *farce* is exaggerated comedy; *tragi-comedy* is a blend of the tragic and comic; *satire* uses sarcasm and wit to ridicule people's follies and vices (originally in verse).

Comic Relief

1. It is the name given to the brief light or comic dramatic action within the performance of a regular serious play to bring about a relief to the spectators to regain their real selves, for a short while to relax their strained nerves and prepare for further action, often more serious and culminating into breath-taking, gasping climax before denouement.

Conceit

1. A conceit is a far-fetched or highly complex and even obscure or unintelligible comparison between two, often dissimilar, persons or objects.
2. It was commonly used by the Elizabethans particularly the Metaphysical poets, especially Donne.

Concordance

Alphabetical index of words in a work, or works by a single author.

Confidant/Confidante

1. In a play when a character takes upon himself/herself the task of some secret or information characteristic about a character to another, the character indulging in such an activity is known as a "confidant" (mas.) or "confidante" (fem.)
2. Such information or secret is generally in the matter of love.
3. A good example of a 'confidante' is Nerissa in the Merchant of Venice.

Connotation

1. It signifies the suggested or implied meaning of word as against the transparent or literary meaning.
2. Connotative devices are brought into play by the artists, poets in particular to enhance pleasure and acceptability conveyed by words and other expressions.
3. Poets like Keats and T.S. Eliot frequently resort to the device of suggestiveness which is akin to connotation.

Consummation

1. When a work achieves complete satisfaction on all counts-literary as well as artistic, it is consummation that results.
2. An artist who has the knack, calibre or skill to make this achievement, is a consummate artist.

Copyright

Protective law to prevent pirating or plagiarism of an author's work.

Couplet

Two successive rhyming lines in poetry.

Court Comedy

1. It is opposed to the Domestic Comedy in the sense that instead of domestic scenes it contains other elements which attract a different kind of audience, *e.g.*
   (i) endless play of words
   (ii) elaborate dialogues
   (iii) repartees, jests, retorts, etc.

Cycle

Group of works united by an overall theme.

Dactyl

1. Dactyl means one accented syllable followed by two unaccented ones, e.g.
   (i) Lazily
   (ii) Separate
   (iii) Unspoken.

Decayed (or Constant) Metaphor

See Metaphor

Deism

1. A "deist" is a theist who believes in the existence of God but rejects the idea of a revealed religion.

Denouement

1. It is the final resolution of the problem in a piece of dramatic performance.

2. The best document comes about when it arises naturally out of the action of the play and not through the 'Deus ex machina'.

Detonation

When a word refers to its literal meaning independent of the meaning which the author may intend to convey, it is the device of "Detonation" which is at play.

Diabolus Ex Machina

1. The term literally means "devil out of the machine".
2. When all of a sudden a person or an event spoils the whole good game, causing unmitigated misery, it is the work of "Diabolus Ex Machina".
3. Thus, the term signifies sudden, unexpected turn of events for a plightful situation.

Dialect

Manner of speaking pertaining to a particular class or geographical region.

Dialectic

1. It was used originally to refer to the nature of a logical argument.
2. Later, it began to be linked to Kant, Hegel and Marx in varying forms.
3. The three generally accepted aspects of 'dialectic' are:
   - *(i) Thesis:* It is akin to the (original) idea.
   - *(ii) Antithesis:* It implies the inherent opposition in the thesis, which may operate after some time.
   - *(iii) Synthesis:* It implies the resolution of the conflict to evolve a higher (or final) truth.

Dialogue

1. Dialogue is something very important in any poetic or prose play or a piece of prose fictions.
2. *(i)* The nature of the dialogue, including its language depends upon the kind of the play—a tragedy, comedy, romance, etc. or the kind of the scene prevailing there at the time and place of the dialogue.
   (ii) Much also depends upon the taste of the spectators or audience which again is related to the spirit of the age :

A Dialogical Novel

1. It is a kind of novel in which a number of voices, interactive in the scheme, operate in work, resulting in a kind of dialogue (or series of dialogues) as against the Monologic Presentation.

Diary

Sequential private record of personal and other events kept by an individual.

Diction

1. It refers to the selection, arrangement and order of words.
2. The term which has become more popular in literary world is "Poetic Diction" to which a lot of space has been devoted by Wordsworth in his "Preface to Lyrical Ballads."

Dictionary

Book containing the words of a language, and their definitions, alphabetically; two-language dictionaries contain the corresponding words of both languages and their meanings, also alphabetically; any book that gives words and phrases about a particular subject, arranged alphabetically.

Didactic

A work is didactic in nature when it undertakes to teach a moral, *e.g.* much of Wordsworth's poetry.

Digest

Publication where works are abridged.

Digression

1. When a writer, instead of carrying on the main plot or incident, starts indulging in a side story, dialogue or descriptive narration, it is digression that results.

2. Digression gives extraneous pleasure which is not inherent in or indispensable to the main story.
3. Digression can sometimes enhance the value of a work but more often it mars its spirit.

Documentary

Form of fiction or drama based on documentary evidence provided by newspapers, recent historical reports or other contemporary or recent factual evidence.

Doggerel

Rough, ill-constructed verse.

Domestic Comedy

1. One of the earliest examples of the Domestic Comedies is "Gammer Gurton's Needle" (Cir. 1562)
2. It presents realistic life of the peasant class of its times.
3. It is full of fun and coarse humour.

Double entendre

Ambiguity in a word or expression, one of whose meanings is usually bawdy or frivolous.

Drama

Work to be performed on a stage by actors.

Dramatic Irony

It is a device occurring in a drama when a character on the stage is unaware of a fact which the audience know and understand.

Dramatic Monologue

1. It is a kind of drama or piece of dramatic poetry in which only one character speaks out throughout the performance and script.

Dramatis Personae

Characters in a play.

Duologue

Conversation between two characters in a play, story or poem.

Edition

Total number of copies of a book printed from unchanged set of type.

Electicism

The term implies the gleaning of facts or ideas from different sources instead of depending on just one source (or a few sources).

Elegy

Serious meditative poem; often lamenting death.

Empathy

In a play or novel, when the reader or spectator begins to feel like the hero/heroine or some particular character as if he/she were that character, it is "empathy" which is at play.

Empiricism

Empiricism implies the importance of experiment and experience in the matter of gaining knowledge,

Encyclopedia

Comprehensive work encompassing and describing many aspects of knowledge; specialist work covering comprehensively a subject or discipline.

Epic

Long narrative poem incorporating myth, legend, folklore and history, about the deeds of heroes, warriors, important people; a grandiose treatment of an individual's or nation's story.

Epic Style

1. It is a style which is dignified and exalted (as grand style is), as:
   (i) Paradise Lost by Milton
   (ii) Aeneid by Virgil
   (iii) Iliad by Homer
   (iv) Hyperion by Keats, etc.
2. Sometimes, it is, also referred to as 'heroic' style.'

Epigram

1. It signifies some brief, witty word, saying or piece of writing.

2. Pope's work, for instance, is a model of "Epigrammatic" style.
3. Bacon's essays are a bundle of Epigrams.

Epilogue

It is the last item in a work of art (as in a drama) which often declares or comments upon the conclusion of the work.

Epistle

Direct address to another person, a 'letter' in the form of verse.

Epitaph

Valediction to dead person or persons; inscription on a tomb or grave.

Epithet

1. It comprises a word or group of words to describe the chief characteristics of a person, *e.g.*
   (i) Alexander the Great
   (ii) The Holy Bible.

Eponymous

Person whose name becomes the title of the work.

Erastianism

1. It implies the doctrine that the state should have supremacy over the church in ecclesiastical matters.
2. Erastianism was one of the doctrines which was vehemently opposed by the followers of the Oxford Movement
3. The doctrine is probably wrongly ascribed to Erastus.

Essay

Short composition, usually in prose, discussing a topic or variety of topics.

Euphemism

1. When an unpleasant expression has to be made in a comparatively pleasant or less harsh way, the mellowed or toned down words which are used express euphemism, *e.g.*
   (i) Instead of saying about a person "He acted foolishly, we can say, "He should have acted more wisely."
   (ii) Instead of saying about a person that he has died, we sometimes say, "God Almighty has called him" or "He has left for his heavenly abode."

Euphony

1. It signifies the pleasant combination of words which create desirable rhythms and tonal effects without interfering with the intended meaning.
2. An excessive use of such devices can lead to tautology or bombasticism and sound superficial or facile.
3. The generally accepted antonym of euphony is "Cacophony".

Euphuism

1. An ornate, floral style of writing popularized by Lyly.

Exposition

It signifies a way of writing where explanations are not withheld or suppressed but manifestly made clear to the reader for immediate response based on clarity.

Fable

A short narrative in prose or verse, often with animals, that points a moral.

Fiction

General term for an imaginative work, usually in prose.

Figure of Speech (or of Rhetoric)

It signifies the unusual use of words to heighten their effect.

First person

Style of novel, etc., in which narrator is a character.

Flashback

1. When a writer while presenting a situation suddenly refers to a past situation or event, it is the device of "flashback" that he exploits.
2. Browning, T.S, Eliot and Stream of consciousness novelists, in particular, take advantage of this device.

Folk tale

Story handed down by word of mouth from generation to generation.

Foot

In poetry, rhythmic unit of two or three syllables.

Foreshadowing

1. It is a device in which the author himself prepares the spectators (or readers) for the catastrophe or some important event which may be on the cards.
2. Such a device checks the readers, etc. from suffering from the malady of disbelief.
3. Shakespeare is probably one of the greatest masters of this device, and it is sometimes believed that one of the main reasons of Shakespeare's grand success was his convincing mastery over the technique of foreshadowing.

Foreword

Short introduction to a work.

Free verse (vers libre)

Poetry free from mechanical restrictions such as metre and rhyme, cadenced according to meaningful stress.

Fustian

It means the use of pompous, ornate, Euphuist or bombastic language.

Gazetteer

Geographical dictionary or index.

Ghost writer

Person who undertakes literary work for another who takes the credit.

Glossary

Alphabetical list of unfamiliar or uncommon words, usually appended to work in which they appear.

Haiku

According to Oxford Dictionary, "A Haiku is a Japanese poem of seventeen syllables, in three lines of five, seven and fine traditionally evoking images of the natural world."

Haplology

"Omission in utterance of a sound resembling a neighbouring sounds (as 'idolatry' for 'idololatry') (ibid.)

Haplography

"The inadvertent writing once of what should have been written twice." (Chambers 20th Century Dictionary)

Heroic Couplet

1. A couplet written in iambic pentametre is known as a 'heroic couplet'.

Heroic verse

1. A poem written in heroic couplets is known as 'heroic verse,' *e.g.* Pope's poems such as:
   (i) Essay Man
   (ii) Essay in Criticism
   (iii) The Rape of the Lock, etc.

Homily

1. It is a term pertaining to a work which instead of laying stress on artistic or aesthetic standards, undertakes to urge the readers on to a high moral life.
2. It is just like a sermon in a church.
3. Such are the most of the poems of Longfellow.

Homograph

1. It implies a word which has the same spelling and pronunciation as another, but is different in meaning and origin from the other, *e.g.* :
   (i) bear (*n*) an animal
   (ii) bear (*v*) (to) tolerate
   (iii) bear (*v*) (to) carry

Homonym

1. (i) It is "a word having the same sound and perhaps the same spelling as another, but a different meaning and origin" (Chambers.....)

   (ii) Hence, *Homonymous* means: " having the same name : having different *significations* and origin but the same sound." (ibid.)

Hurd, Bishop

1. He aroused great interest in the Gothic and imaginative literature with his "Letters on Chivalry and Romance" (1762)

Hyperbole

1. It is a figure of speech which expresses an exaggerated statement to heighten the effect of a rhetorical statement, *e.g.*
   (i) O child, may you never die!
   (ii) Child is Father of the Man

Idiom

Form of expression of phrase peculiar to its language and possessing a meaning other than its literal one.

Idolatry

1. It means the worship of an image which is believed to be the abode of a superhuman being.

Idyll

Short pastoral poem conveying mood of happy innocence.

Imagism

School of poetry (early 1900s) concerned with precise language, direct treatment, and freedom of form.

Imperialism

1. It means the state policy for a country (as of England and certain other European countries, in particular during certain periods of history) to expands its area by annexing foreign lands and sub-during the natives.

Impersonality

1. It means that the author himself should not be palpably visible in a piece of literature, in other words, the work should be done on highly objective lines.

Indianism

When an expression is commonly used in India but is not used by the English, it is called an "Indianism," *e.g.*

(i) 'demise' instead of 'death'

(ii) 'bearer' instead of 'waiter'

(iii) 'left for his heavenly abode' instead of 'died,' etc.

Interior Monologue

1. It is a device, as used by James Joyce in Ulysses, to express the thoughts, feelings and emotions of a character on usually more than one levels of consciousness.
2. It is a sort of inner debate which may or may not be conflict in essence.

Interludes

1. Just as Miracles passed into Moralities, the latter gradually passed into Interludes, as the people wanted entertainment along with instruction.

Introduction

Essay stating author's intention to reader.

Inversion

It is the figure of speech (much used by Milton but ridiculed by many modern critics) in which words are presented in their unnatural order, *e.g.*

O God's glory I sing,
And to His Mercy I pray.

Irony

1. It is a device used to convey a meaning which is the opposite of the apparent meaning, *e.g.* What a brave son of India Jai Chand was!

Jingle

Verse or verses with strong rhyme and rhythm.

Journal

Paper, periodical or magazine.

Judicial Criticism

1. It is the kind of criticism which is a sort of judgement on a writer or his work of art.
2. Such kind of best example is Pope's "Essay on Criticism".

Legend

Story about a particular person containing myth and historical fact; explanation of symbols on a map or chart.

Lexicon

Dictionary, especially for Classical and Middle Eastern languages.

Limerick

1. It is a kind of humorous verse written in five jingling lines.
2. The form seems to have derived "from a refrain formerly used, referring to 'Limerick' in Ireland." (Chambers 20th Century Dictionary)

Linguistics

The scientific study of language.

Litotes

1. It is akin to "understatement" which is sometimes used by writers to emphasise the desired meaning, *e.g.* India is not lagging in Information Technology.
2. However, more often it is an "understatement used ironically, especially using a negative to express the category as :

   'I shan't be sorry when it's over' meaning 'I shall be very glad', or 'It was no easy matter' for 'It was very difficult.'"

   (Advanced Learner's Dictionary)

Lyric

Usually short, song-like poem in which the poet expresses personal feelings.

Manuscript

Book or work written by hand.

Maxim

Short statement or even sentence containing a general truth about human conduct and human nature.

Melodrama

1. It was a crude form of drama which appealed to the groundings who were not much interested in the artistic minuteness such as the plot, characterization, etc.
2. They wanted only entertainment through striking scenes and absorbing movement of incidents and situations.

Metaphor

1. It is a kind of simile when a comparison is suggested rather than explicitly stated, such that 'as' or 'like' is not used in such a case, *e.g.*

   (i) Lala Lajpat Rai was the Lion of Punjab.

   (ii) I see a lily on thy face.

Meter

Patterns of stressed and unstressed syllables in verse.

Metonymy

1. It implies the use of the name of some person or thing for another person or thing, *e.g.*

   (i) Have you studied 'Milton'?
   (Milton here means Milton's works).

   (ii) In the 'light' of these remarks:
   ('light' here means in view of....)

   (iii) Sceptre and Crown (i.e. monarchy)
   Must tumble down.

Metre

It may not be possible or even necessary to describe it here in full detail, but we can have a cursory look at the following :

1. *Monometre :* It means a line (or verse) with a single iamb (foot)
2. *Dimetre:* It means a line with two iambs.
3. *Trimetre:* It means a line with three iambs.
4. *Tetrametre:* It means a line with four iambs.
5. *Penta metre:* It means a line with five iambs.
6. *Hexta metre:* It means a line with six iambs.
7. *Hepta metre:* It means a line with seven iambs.

Miracle and Mystery Plays

1. These plays were sponsored by the church and were originally held within the premises of the church, but later, as the number of audience swelled, the boundaries of the church seemed too limited and the plays began of be held outside the church.
2. *(i)* The Miracle plays represented the lives of saints, and later for any biblical theme.

   (ii) The Mystery plays represented scenes from the life of Jesus Christ.

Mock Heroic

When an apparent epic is presented in a light vein, it is known as a "mock heroic" poem piece of fiction, etc., *e.g.*

(i) The Rape of the Lock

Modernism

1. Towards the close of the 20th century, a movement against such modes as realism and naturalism started in all forms of literature and art such as poetry, drama, novel, music, painting, architecture, sculpture, etc. which continued unabated during the first world war period and partly upto the middle of the century.

Modulation

1. Of necessity poetry is musical.
2. As in music, to avoid poetry from falling into "monotony," there is the system of "modulation" which here means, changing the key or tone, to introduce the element of variety to give or enhance pleasure.

Monologue

Single person addressing an audience alone, in drama, verse or prose. *Interior monologue*: unspoken but thought speech in verse or prose.

Moralities or Morality Play

1. They were basically allegories on the same lines as Miracles, or Mysteries but without direct represent of scriptural or Christ-concerned events or personages.
2. In Moralities abstract virtues and vices like Wisdom, Goodness, Justice, Evil, Vice, Greed, Lethargy, Lust, etc. were personified and presented on stage as persons.

Myth

Non-factual story that embodies explanation of how something comes to exist, usually involving supernatural or superhuman creatures.

Narrative

Story or tale in prose or verse.

Narratology

1. It means the study of different forms and structures of a narrative work in the matter of its various syntactical, literary and grammatical frameworks.

Neoclassicism

Movement of late 17th and 18th century reviving classical values in English literature, emphasizing discipline, reason and clarity.

Neologism

Newly-coined word.

New Wave (la Nouvelle Vague)

Movement in literature and cinema originating in France in late 1950s that attempted to eschew fixed values, revealing a character by the way he experienced objects and events, which were often meticulously described.

Nom de plume

Term used to indicate a fictitious name used by a writer to represent his work.

Novel

Extended piece of prose fiction.

Novelette

Long short story of some 15,000 words.

Novella

Prose fiction longer than a short story, shorter than a novel (about 30,000 words), concentrating upon a single event.

Obscurity

1. When a writer's language is not (or not easily) intelligible to the reader, the work concerned is termed as obscure.

Ode

Lyric poem describing an event or feelings about a person, object or event. *Pindaric Ode* (Greece) written for choral recitation in units of three stanzas; *Horatian Ode* (Rome) consisted of succession of stanzas following pattern of first one.

Omniscient Author

It is a device used by some outstanding modern novelists to move freely from the objective narrative to the internal or subjective psyche of a character or characters and then comment freely and apparently unattached on the significance, possibility or outcome of any or some events.

Onomatopoeia

When the very sound (pronunciation) of a word conveys the sense of the object producing such sound, the use of onomatopoeia becomes clear *e.g.,*

(i) The *lashing* of waves on the sea-shore
(ii) The *rustle* of leaves
(iii) The *hissing* of the snake
(iv) The *jungle* of coins
(v) The *clanging* of arms.

Oxymoron

1. It is a figure of speech in which two apparently contradictory words or terms are used to convey, a paradoxical sense, e.g.

   (i) 'busy-idle days' (Lamb in Dream children)
   (ii) Life in Death (Coleridge in 'Rime.....').

Pantomime

1. Pantomimes became popular in England particularly in the first quarter of the 18th century.
2. A Pantomime is a dramatic representation pertaining to some myth, legend or traditional tale (or it may have some fairy element in it).

Parable

A story which conveys a moral lesson is known as a parable, as for instance, the biblical parables.

Paradox

It is a figure of speech in which a truth is brought home through the use of self-contradictory statement, *e.g.*

(i) Cowards die many a time before their death.
(ii) Discretion is the better part of valour.
(iii) After death, we awake into an eternal life.

Parallelism

1. It is a rhetorical device where balancing sentences, phrases or words are used to enhance effect, e.g.

   What is important is not what you say, but what is important is what you mean.
2. Excessive use of this device leads to monotony and superficiality.

Parody

Comic imitation of serious words, style, sense, subject of a writer to make them appear ridiculous.

Pastoral

Literature depicting idealized rural life.

Pathetic Fallacy

When nature is shown as sympathising with human lot, the device used is called "pathetic fallacy," *e.g.*

(i) Byron's description of the battle of Waterloo in Childe Harold's Pilgrimage.
(ii) The behaviour of slow-moving nature in Tennyson's "Lotos-eaters".

Pedantry

1. The term refers to the excessive display of knowledge such as:
   (i) Foreign words and phrases
   (ii) Allusions
   (iii) Archaic words
   (iv) high sounding and sesquipedalian words
   (v) cataloguing, etc.

   when these are not strictly needed within the context of the work.

Periodic Sentence

A sentence in which the Principal clause occurs at the end when it is preceded by one or more subordinate clauses, such that the sense is clear only when the whole sentence is read, is known as a 'periodic sentence'.

Periodical

Magazine or journal published regularly.

Periphrasis

1. It means a round about way of saying a thing, *e.g.* An idle singer of an empty day, etc.
2. The term is close to circumlocution and euphemism in sense and effect.

Personification

1. It is a device where inanimate objects are shown as those having life and behaving likewise, *e.g.*

   "But yonder comes the powerful *king* of day."

   —*Thomson*

Pessimists

Although in English literature, we have a number of pessimist poets or a good number of poets expressing at times pessimistic ideas or writing sometimes in a pessimistic mood, yet two of the poets are known in particular, as "Pessimists." They are:

(i) Thomas Hardy

(ii) A.E. Housman

Philology

Study of literature, language and linguistics.

Picaresque

Chronicle of adventures of a rogue; originated in 16-century Spain.

Plagiarism

Wrongful appropriation and publication of another's work as one's own.

Platitude

It means a truth or generalization which is too well-known mainly because of its overuse, *e.g.*

Truth is evergreen.

Pleonasm

(a) It means the use of words more than those which are absolutely necessary, *e.g.*

1. He sat *down* on the ground.
2. He looked up *high* towards the sky.
3. He has got *sole* monopoly over such kind of business.

(b) In essence, it is akin to Tautology or circumlocution.

Plot

Plan or organization of events and characters in a play, work of fiction or poem as to induce curiosity and suspense in the audience or reader.

Poem

Literary work which may be in rhyme, blank verse or a combination of the two.

Poetic Diction

1. Diction stands chiefly for choice of words.
2. In poetry, poetic diction is unavoidable as mere metre is not enough to make a poem a literary piece of work.
3. In other words, mere versification or combination of words in rhyme or any other verse form does not make poetry.

4. The poets resort to several devices in this regard, some of which are :
   (i) Use of similes, metaphors, symbols, inversions, and other figures of speech as such as hyperbole, irony, antithesis, personification, etc.
   (ii) Omission of some parts of speech or grammatical rules.
   (iii) Use of archaic or uncommon words.
   (iv) Change in order of words, etc.
   (v) Use of picturesque phrases and expressions
   (vi) Use of other ornamental devices such as epithets
   (vii) Use of highly musical lies, fanciful flights etc.

Poetic Justice

1. It means the reward or punishment handed down to the characters at the end of a work of art according to their deeds.

Poetry

Any kind of metrical composition in a literary work.

Pornography

Work in which there is a deliberate emphasis on the sexual behaviour of characters, in order to arouse sexual excitement.

Potboiler

Work written essentially to gain the author a livelihood.

Precis

Concise statement; short summary of a work.

Preface

Introduction to a work.

Prologue

It is often the original statement by the writer (as in a drama) which highlights the chief aim of the work which is going to be unfolded or staged.

Propaganda

Work devoted to the dissemination of an idea or belief, usually biased.

Prose

Writings not in verse.

(Modern) Prose Style

1. The English prose style started by Bacon, flourished in the hands of Addison and Steele and numerous essayists and prose stylists that followed.
2. As a fine example of the latest modern prose style, Naipaul who won the Nobel Prize for Literature in 2001 deserves to be mentionéd.

Prosody

Study of the handling of language in poetry.

Prosopopaeia

1. This figure of speech is used when:
   (i) The past (called the Historic Present) is written in the present tense:
   Sohrab and Rustam clash with their full might.
   (ii) The (anticipated) future is written in the present tense:
   Here, we go to our new house tomorrow with all our belongings carried in a lorry and then tucked in elegant mahogany almirahs.

Pseudonym

Name other than the true one used by an author to represent his work.

Psychological Process

It is the process applied to the study of a piece of literature to penetrate another's mind and to study the activities, utterances, etc. of various characters, as, for instance, to arrive at the exact nature of Hamlet's madness whether there was "method" in it or not.

Pun

1. When a word gives several meanings (often for fun) as in a play, it is the "pun" that is used.
2. Shakespeare is a great master of this device.

3. **Example :**
   (*i*) This is the *book.*
   (*ii*) It means
      (*a*) any book
      (*b*) a holy book, often the Bible.

Realism

Literature that attempts to depict life objectively and faithfully.

Refrain

Phrase, line or lines repeated at intervals or at the end of a stanza in poetry.

Review

Notice or critical article on musical, artistic or literary work.

Revue

Theatrical entertainment made up of sketches, dances, songs, recitals and improvised pieces, usually humorous, satirical or topical.

Rhetoric

Art of using language, in speaking or writing, to persuade. The persuasive style (rather than the content) of a work.

Rhythm

1. It signifies the measured regular beat or movement of sounded words in language.
2. Rhythm is a must in poetry as well as prose, as it introduces or enhances the element of pleasure, interest and curiosity.

Rhyme

Echoing sound or audible similarity in two or more words, especially at endings. Device used to construct much poetry.

Riddle

Puzzle, question or enigma; conundrum.

Roman a clef

Novel based upon actual people under disguised names.

Romance

Tale of chivalry, originally written in verse (Medieval times); term applied now to any wonderful or mysterious tale far removed from reality.

Romance Languages

1. Languages which have emerged straightaway from Latin and/or Greek, are called Romance Languages.

Romanticism

Movement originating in late 18th century as revolt against neoclassicism, emphasizing imaginative style.

Saga

Lengthy prose work, sometimes in several parts, describing the history and events surrounding medieval kings, warrriors and, recently, fictitious families.

Satire

Any work in which wickedness, folly, vice and corruption in individuals and society is exposed by ridicule and scorn.

Science fiction

Literature based on scientific fact or fantasy, on earth or on other worlds in space, often set in periods in the distant future.

Semantics

Branch of linguistics dealing with meaning, and the change of meaning, in words.

Semiology

General study or science of signs with which humans communicate with each other (including words and their use in every context).

Sermon

Verbal instruction of some length, usually religious.

Short story

Work of fiction usually revolving around single event.

Sic

Included in brackets after a printed word or quoted passage to indicate that it is quoted accurately, however actually incorrect.

Simile

1. When we draw comparison between two persons by using (usually 'like', as-so or as) it is the 'simile' that we make use of, *e.g.*
   (i) As red as a rose
   (ii) As happy as a lark
   (iii) She looked like a violet, half-hidden behind the rock.
2. *An Exaggerated Simile:* It is a simile in which the sense is clearly exaggerated, *e.g.*
   (i) He ran as fast as lightning
   (ii) He has in himself the force as much as there is in ten horses.

Slang

Colourful and vernacular language of the street, marketplace, barrackroorn, workplace, sportsplace and playground.

Soliloquy

Kind of monologue in which a stage character expresses his thoughts and feelings.

Song

Poem or verse set to music.

Sonnet

14-line poem of set rhyme-scheme; Elizabethan (Shakes-pearean) *ababcdcdefefgg*, Italian *abbaabba cdcdcd* (or *cdecde*).

Stanza

Group of lines of verse in definite pattern, usually repeated in a poem.

Strophe and Anti Strophe

1. Strophe is "the song sung by the chorus (in a Greek play) as it moved towards one side, answered by an exact counterpart." (Chambers 20th Century Dictionary)
2. Anti-Strophe is the term for the Strophe, "as it returned : part of any ode thus answered..." (*ibid.*)

Style

Characteristic manner of expression in prose or verse; the way in which a thing is written by an author.

Stock Material

Material necessary for a writer to write.

Stock Characters

Characters that are commonly found in most of pieces of dramas or fiction.

Stock Situations

Situations which are frequently presented byauthors in their works.

Synthesis, Poetry of

The term "Poetry of Synthesis" is referred to by I.A. Richards, and it has been thus explained by Cleanth Brooks—

"... a poetry which does not leave out what is apparently hostile to its dominant tone, and which, because it is able to fuse the irrelevant and disordant, has come to terms with itself and invulnerable to irony."

Structure

"The structure meant is a structure of meaning, evaluations and interpretations : and the principle of unity which informs it seems to one of balancing and harmonizing connotations, attitudes and meanings."

Tragedy of Blood (And Thunder)

1. It was basically a melodramatic presentation of horrible, gory scenes.
2. The first famous tragedy of this kind is Kyd's "Spanish Tragedy".

Sublimity

1. It is a term which is used to describe inexplicable beauty which is beyond any rules to describe or measure.

Symbolism

French poetic movement of late 19th century that developed as revolt against realism, concentrating on evoking emotions by use of indirect suggestion (symbol and metaphor); flourished in Russia at turn of century as literary movement, and later in British novel.

Synecdoche

1. This figure of speech is used when the understanding of one thing by means of another is employed.
2. This can be done in several ways, some of which are mentioned below :
   (i) When a part stands for a whole or genus, e.g.
   We have fifty *hands* in our factory.
   (hands = workers)
   (ii) When a whole or genus stands for a part, e.g. He belongs to a different *world* from yors (world = category, social set-up, economic status, etc.)
   (iii) When an individual represents a class, *e.g.*
   He is the *Nestor* of our village.
   (Nestor = the oldest man)

Syntax

It means :

(i) The way a sentence is constructed
(ii) Arrangement of words in writing (or in speech) according to the rules of grammar
(iii) Rules pertaining to this system or arrangement.

Synonym

A word similar in meaning to another.

Synopsis

Outline of the main points of a work; a summary.

Tale

Spoken or written narrative.

Tautology

Overuse of synonyms or repetition of ideas in sentence.

Theme

Central idea of a work, rather than its subject.

Thesis

Long essay or treatise on a subject, usually expository; work presented to examiners for academic qualification.

Third person

Style of novel, etc., in which narrator is outside action.

Tract

Short printed treatise on religious or political subject.

Tragedy

It is "a drama in which the principal characters are involved in desperate circumstances or led by overwhelming passions. It is invariably serious and dignified. The movement is always stately, but grows more and more rapid as it approaches the climax ; and the end is always calamitous, resulting in death or dire misfortune of the principals."

Tragic Flaw

1. In Shakespeare's tragedies, in particular, we often find a particular flaw in the character of the hero which ultimately leads to the fall of his destiny, along with the fall of his state or estate.

Transferred Epithet

When an epithet is transferred from a person to a thing, it is known as a 'transferred epithet', *e.g.*

(i) It is a *foolish* idea
(ii) Let *happy* days come.

Translation

Rendering of a work into another language.

Treatise

Formal work examining a subject and the principles underlying it.

Trochaic Line Metre

1. A line in verse is known as a *"trochaic" line* when the first, third and other odd syllables

in it are accented (as in the 'Iambic metre') irrespective of the length of the line.

2. A poem comprising such lines is known as having been written in the "Trochaic" metre.

Understatement

1. It is practically the opposite of hyperbole and is sometimes used by the writers to emphasise indirectly the desired meaning.

Vade mecum

Manual or handbook carried for frequent reference.

Verisimilitude

It is the likeness of truth presented in a work of art that makes it similar to the characteristics or situation in real life and that enables the readers to accept it ungrudgingly as truth (and may be, sometimes, more than real happening in life).

Vernacular

Domestic or native language.

Versification

Study of how traditional verse is constructed.

Wit

(*i*) Dryden defines (in "Annus Mirabilis") wit as "delightful imagining of persons, actions, passions or things."

Yarn

Story or tale, sometimes improbable and far-fetched.

❑❑❑

Multiple Choice Questions

1. Who wrote *Don Juan*?
   A. Shakespeare B. Tennyson
   C. Byron D. T.S. Eliot
2. Who wrote *The Life of Johnson*?
   A. Boswell B. Macaulay
   C. Churchill D. Sir Walter Raleigh
3. *Priest's Nun's Tale* was written by
   A. Spenser B. Charles Lamb
   C. Tennyson D. Chaucer
4. Who is said to have first used the term "Metaphysics"?
   A. Matthew Arnold B. Sidney
   C. Donne D. Dr. Johnson
5. The writer of *Volpone* is
   A. Johnson B. Milton
   C. Jonson D. Shelley
6. Which is the correct chronological sequence?
   A. Spenser—Chaucer—Milton—Donne
   B. Spenser—Wordsworth—Tennyson—T.S. Eliot
   C. Milton—Shakespeare—Philip Larkin—Keats
   D. Auden—Eliot—Shelley—Keats
7. *Pilgrim's Progress* was written by
   A. Milton B. Shelley
   C. Swinburne D. John Bunyan
8. The writer of the line : *"Stone walls do not a prison make"* is
   A. Lovelace B. Milton
   C. W.B. Yeats D. T.S. Eliot
9. *"Monkey's Paw"* is a
   A. Poem B. Drama
   C. Short story D. Novel
10. Lyrical Ballads appeared in
    A. 1690 B. 1798
    C. 1802 D. 1800
11. The writer of *'A Pair of Blue Eyes'* is
    A. Thackeray B. Dickens
    C. George Eliot D. Thomas Hardy
12. *Hard Times* was written by
    A. Thackeray B. Dickens
    C. Trollope D. Marquese
13. Which of the following poets was most impressed by the German philosophy?
    A. Chaucer B. Wordsworth
    C. Coleridge D. Southey
14. The two cities referred to in *"A Tale of Two Cities"* are
    A. London and Paris
    B. London and Rome
    C. Rome and Paris
    D. Moscow and Rome
15. *The Peasant's Bread* is a story by
    A. Maupassant B. Tagore
    C. R.K. Narayan D. Tolstoy
16. *The Financial Express* was written by
    A. Raja Rao B. R.K. Narayan
    C. Tagore D. Mulk Raj Anand
17. *"Negative Capability"* is a term associated with
    A. Tagore B. Shelley
    C. Keats D. Coleridge
18. The most impressive treatment of "imagination" has been given by
    A. Coleridge B. Shelley
    C. Eliot D. Yeats
19. *Lady Chatterley's Lover* was banned because it was considered
    A. obscene B. revolutionary
    C. obscurantist D. None of these
20. *For Whom The Bell Tolls* was written by
    A. Marquese B. Hemingway
    C. Hawthorne D. None of these
21. The writer of : *"A Pair of Mustachios"* is
    A. Anand B. Tagore
    C. Raja Rao D. Anita Desai
22. The writer of *Scarlet Letter* is
    A. Henry James B. James Joyce
    C. Hawthorne D. None of these

23. Rousseau is associated with
A. French Revolution
B. American War of Independence
C. Russian (Bolshevik) Revolution
D. None of these

24. Who wrote *'Train to Pakistan'*?
A. Narayan
B. Manohar Malgaon
C. Khushwant Singh
D. Anand

25. Who is the writer of *Azadi*?
A. R.K. Narayan B. Khushwant Singh
C. Tagore D. Chaman Nahal

26. *"The God of Small Things"* is written by
A. R.K. Narayan B. Hemingway
C. Graham Greene D. Arundhati Roy

27. Who wrote the poem *"Listeners"*?
A. Tennyson
B. Thomas Hood
C. Goldsmith
D. Walter de la Mare

28. In writing *"Canterbury Tales"* Chaucer was influenced by
A. Decameron
B. The Divine Comedy
C. The Holy Bible
D. None of these

29. *'Animal Farm'* was written by
A. James Joyce B. Virginia Woolf
C. George Orwell D. Hemingway

30. Shobha De is a
A. poet B. dramatist
C. novelist D. an actress

31. Dunciad was written by
A. Dryden B. Pope
C. Tennyson D. Shelley

32. Bernard Shaw got the Nobel Prize for
A. Pygmalion
B. Man and Superman
C. Saint Joan
D. None of these

33. The Victorian Period is marked by
A. Great political upheavals
B. Great social security
C. Great wars
D. Economic deprivation

34. Swift is known mainly as
A. an essayist B. a poet
C. a satirist D. a short story writer

35. Who is the writer of the novel *"The Village"*?
A. Khushwant Singh B. Anita Desai
C. Mulk Raj Anand D. R.K. Narayan

36. The most famous writer of the heroic couplet is
A. Dryden B. Chaucer
C. Spenser D. Pope

37. *Macflecknoe* is a poem written by
A. Dryden B. Pope
C. Tennyson D. Yeats

38. Who wrote *'Everyman in His Humour'*?
A. Shakespeare B. Jonson
C. Milton D. Keats

39. *'Indian Jugglers'* is an essay by
A. De Quincey B. Gardiner
C. Hazlitt D. Lamb

40. Who wrote *'The Gropes of Wrath'*?
A. Pearl Buck B. Hemingway
C. Virginia Woolf D. John Steinbeck

41. Who rendered into English the ancient Greek tragedy *"Atlanta in Calydon"*?
A. Swinburne B. Shelley
C. Tennyson D. Arthur Hugh Clough

42. *The Deserted Village* was written by
A. Cowper B. Goldsmith
C. Keats D. Johnson

43. *'Savitri'* is an epic written by
A. Tagore
B. Prem Chand
C. Aurobindo
D. Bankim Chandra Chatterjee

44. The anthem *"Vande Mataram"* occurs in
A. Godan B. Anand Math
C. Gora D. Train to Pakistan

45. *'All Fool's Day'* is an essay written by
A. Charles Lamb B. Hazlitt
C. A.G. Gardiner D. R.C. Stevenson

46. The drama *Tamburlaine* is written by
A. Shakespeare B. Marlowe
C. Lyly D. Green

47. The book *"Appreciations"* was written by
A. Morris B. Arnold
C. Walter Pater D. Christina Rossetti

48. *"The Admirable Crichton"* was written by
A. Steinbeck B. T.S. Eliot
C. Trollope D. James Barrie

49. *"The Death of a Salesman"* was written by
A. James Barrie B. Eugene O'Neill
C. Arthur Miller D. None of these

50. The Restoration period is said to have started from
A. 1660 B. 1676
C. 1625 D. 1645

51. Who wrote *"The Lady's Not for Burning"*?
A. Barrie B. Christopher Fry
C. Robert Bridges D. T.S. Eliot

52. Who wrote the poem *"Brahma"*?
A. T.S Eliot B. Emerson
C. Whitman D. Frost

53. The writer of *Walden* is
A. Tennyson B. Whitman
C. Thoreau D. Frost

54. In *'Sons and Lovers'* Lawrence has depicted the life of
A. factory workers B. miners
C. farmers D. animals

55. Who wrote *Kim*?
A. Kipling B. Tagore
C. Lawrence D. Narayan

56. *'The Hairy Ape'* is a famous play by
A. Barrie B. Eugene O'Neill
C. Christopher Fry D. T.S. Eliot

57. Who is the writer of *Frankenstein*?
A. George Eliot B. Jane Austen
C. Mary Shelley D. Emile Bronte

58. Who wrote the *'Cries of Children'*?
A. Robert Browning B. Elizabeth Barrett
C. Thomas Hood D. Cowper

59. Which poet is known as poet's poet?
A. Shakespeare B. Milton
C. Spenser D. Shelley

60. Who wrote the maximum number of sonnets?
A. Shakespeare B. Milton
C. Sidney D. Wordsworth

61. *Adonais* is the eulogy written on the death of
A. Coleridge B. Byron
C. Keats D. Wordsworth

62. Who wrote *Mother*?
A. Tolstoy B. Maxim Gorky
C. Chekhov D. Hardy

63. Who is associated with *Malgudi*?
A. Narayan
B. Anand
C. Manohar Malgonkar
D. Anita Desai

64. The author of *Beowulf* is
A. Bede B. Cynewulf
C. Chaucer D. Unknown

65. The Anglo-Saxon period is often said to be from 450 to ......
A. 900 B. 1000
C. 1050 D. 1100

66. *"To a Mountain Daisy"* is a poem by
A. Wordsworth B. Shelley
C. Keats D. Burns

67. Who wrote: *"The Devil's Disciple"*?
A. Galsworthy B. Barrie
C. Shaw D. Fry

68. Who wrote *"The Decline and Fall of the Roman Empire"*?
A. Walter Raleigh B. Trollope
C. Smollett D. Edward Gibbon

69. Richard Hooker was a prose writer of the
A. Victorian period B. Romantic period
C. Elizabethan period D. Chaucerian age

70. Alexander Dumas was
A. an English writer B. an American writer
C. a French writer D. a German writer

71. Which one was not one of the Lake poets?
A. Shelley B. Wordsworth
C. Southey D. Coleridge

72. *The Theory of Catharsis* is associated with
A. Plato B. Dryden
C. Aristotle D. Sidney

73. Who wrote *'In Defence of Poetry'*?
A. T.S. Eliot B. Yeats
C. Keats D. Shelley

74. *'The Playboy of the Western World'* is a play by
A. Barrie B. Synge
C. Fry D. Eliot

75. *'Silent Woman'* is a play by
A. Marlowe B. Shakespeare
C. Ben Jonson D. Lyly

76. The Scene of *Beowulf* is laid in
A. England B. France
C. Spain D. None of these

77. *"Kidnapped"* was written by
A. Dickens B. Thackeray
C. Hardy D. R.L. Stevenson

78. *'The Prisoner of Zenda'* was written by
A. Sterne B. Trollope
C. Anthony Hope D. George Eliot

79. What was the full name of Cervantes?
A. Jim Cervantes
B. John Cervantes
C. Miguel de Cervantes
D. Sir Roger Cervantes

80. Besides being a poet, Chaucer was
A. a trader B. a manufacturer
C. a teacher D. a diplomat

81. The name of William Golding's first novel is
A. The Inheritors B. Lord of the Flies
C. Pincher Martin D. The Pyramid

82. The author of *Erewhon* is
A. Hardy B. Marquese
C. Samuel Butler D. Cervantes

83. Which of the following is a *Comedy of Manners*?
A. The Way of the World
B. The Duchess of Malfi
C. The Lady's Not for Burning
D. The Hairy Ape

84. Which one among the following is not a pessimist?
A. Gissing B. Browning
C. Hardy D. Thomson

85. Charles Reade's drama *"Drink"* was adapted from a work of
A. Goethe B. Zola
C. Mallarwe D. Tennyson

86. Which one among the following was not a utilitarian?
A. Rousseau B. James Mill
C. Ricardo D. Bentham

87. *'The Praise of Folly'* was written by
A. Walter Raleigh B. Thomas Moore
C. Charles Lamb D. Ruskin

88. Who wrote: *"In Praise of Idleness"*?
A. Bertrand Russell B. Thomas More
C. Charles Lamb D. Hazlitt

89. The real name of Saki is
A. H.H. Munro B. Samuel Butler
C. George Orwell D. The Duke

90. Who started: *"The Tatler"*?
A. Addison B. Swift
C. Steele D. Stevenson

91. The poem *'The Song of the Shirt'* was written by
A. Mrs. Browning B. Pope
C. Shelley D. Thomas Hood

92. *Sir Roger* was originally the creation of
A. Addison B. Dryden
C. Steele D. Milton

93. Who wrote: *"Areopagitica"*?
A. Charles Lamb B. Hazlitt
C. De Quincey D. Milton

94. *'The Selfish Giant'* is a story written by
A. Tagore B. Oscar Wilde
C. Maupassant D. Tolstoy

95. Who wrote : *"Four Quartets"*?
A. T.S. Eliot B. W.B. Yeats
C. W.H. Auden D. Philip Larkins

96. Who wrote : *"Look Back in Anger"*?
A. Steinbeck B. Christopher Fry
C. John Osborne D. Barrie

97. Who wrote : *"The Devils of Loundun"*?
A. Bertrand Russell B. Aldous Huxley
C. J.B. Priestley D. Hazlitt

98. Who wrote : *"Principles of Human Knowledge"*?
A. Milton B. John Bunyan
C. Nash D. George Berkeley

99. Who wrote : *"Liber Amoris"*?
A. Lamb B. Hazlitt
C. Byron D. Wordsworth

100. *"A Railway Clerk"* is a poem by
A. Keki N. Daruwallah
B. Nissim Ezekiel
C. Shiv K. Kumar
D. Jayanta Mahapatra

101. Who won The Booker of Bookers?
A. Arundhati Roy B. Khushwant Singh
C. Mulk Raj Anand D. Salman Rushdie

102. Who wrote: *"The Battle of Books"*?
A. Bacon B. Hazlitt
C. Swift D. None of these

103. Who wrote: *"Nectar in a Sieve"*?
A. Mulk Raj Anand
B. Manohar Malgonkar
C. Kamala Markandaya
D. Pearl S. Buck

104. *'The Good Earth'* was written by
A. Raja Rao
B. R.K. Narayan
C. Pearl S. Buck
D. Kamala Markandaya

105. The writer of *'The Dove Found No Rest'* is
A. Pearl S Buck B. Hemingway
C. Raja Rao D. Dennis Stoll

106. Who wrote: *"So Many Hungers"*?
A. Bhabani Bhattacharya
B. Kamala Markandaya
C. Manohar Malgonkar
D. Chaman Nahal

107. Who is the writer of *"The Middleman and Other Stories "*?
A. Mulk Raj Anand
B. Bharati Mukherjee
C. Tagore
D. Prem Chand

108. Cicero was a Roman
A. philologist B. physician
C. orator D. None of these

109. Who is the writer of *"Gita Rahasya"*?
A. Tulsi Das B. Vivekananda
C. Shivananda D. B.G. Tilak

110. *'The Rubaiyat of Omar Khayyam'* was translated into English by
A. Robert Browning B. Tennyson
C. Fitz Gerald D. Hopkins

111. Mayakovsky was the famous poet of
A. France B. Italy
C. Austria D. Russia

112. Marquese originally wrote his *"One Hundred Years of Solitude"* in
A. French B. German
C. Spanish D. Italian

113. Identify Emile Bronte's novel in the following
A. Persuasion
B. Wuthering Heights
C. Jane Eyre
D. Middlemarch

114. Which one is believed to be the first English tragedy?
A. Gorboduc
B. The Spanish Tragedy
C. Dr. Faustus
D. The Jew of Malta

115. Which of the following works is not by Milton?
A. Paradise Lost B. Il Penseroso
C. Lycidas D. Maud

116. *'Music At Night'* is a book of essays by
A. A.G. Gardiner B. Bertrand Russell
C. Aldous Huxley D. Chesterton

117. The character of Sherlock Holmes was created by
A. Arthur Conan Doyle
B. Hazlitt
C. I.A. Richards
D. Agatha Christie

118. Who wrote the Preface to the *Gitanjali*?
A. W.B. Yeats B. T.S. Eliot
C. Auden D. Philip Larkin

119. What can be said to be the tragic flaw in *Hamlet*?
A. Revenge B. Indecisiveness
C. Hastiness D. Suspicion

120. Who wrote *'The Spanish Tragedy'*?
A. Shakespeare B. Thomas Kyd
C. Marlowe D. Lyly

121. Name the author of *"1984"*
A. George Orwell B. Graham Greene
C. Naipaul D. James Joyce

122. Who is the creator of *Wessex*?
A. Dickens B. Smollett
C. Meredith D. Hardy

123. Whose novel *"The Foundation Pit?"* was discovered only a few years ago?
A. Andrey Platanov B. Cherneshevysky
C. Jane Austen D. George Eliot

124. The novel *"We"* was written by
A. Andrey Platanov B. Tolstoy
C. Maxim Gorky D. Zamayatin

125. Name the writer of *"What Is To Be Done"*
A. Zamayatin B. Gorky
C. Cherneshevysky D. Chekhov

126. Name the writer of the novel *"Les Miserables"*
A. Virginia Woolf B. Mrs. Radcliffe
C. Victor Hugo D. James Joyce

127. Which of the following novels is not by Salman Rushdie?
A. Midnight's Children
B. Grimus
C. The Moor's Last Sigh
D. The Lighthouse

128. A sonnet comprises
A. 16 lines B. 14 lines
C. 12 lines D. 20 lines

129. Who is renowned for his outstanding work *"Holy Sonnets"*?
A. Donne B. Herrick
C. Milton D. Pope

130. Which of the following is not written by Hugo Charteris?
A. Pictures in the wall
B. A Piece of String
C. The Old Boys
D. The Boarding House

131. Which of the following works is by H.G. Wells?
A. All in a Garden Fair
B. The Invisible Man
C. A Child of the Jago
D. Point Counter Point

132. Who wrote : *"The Ideal of a Christian Church"*?
A. John Keble
B. Newman
C. Nash
D. William George Ward

133. Which of the following odes is not by Keats?
A. Ode on Intimations of Immortality
B. Ode to a Nightingale
C. Ode on a Grecian Urn
D. Ode to Autumn

134. Which of the following works is not that of David Hume?
A. Treatise of Human Nature
B. The Rise and Fall of the Roman Empire
C. Political Discourses
D. History of Great Britain

135. Who is the writer of *'The School for Scandal'*?
A. Ben Jonson B. R.B. Sheridan
C. Congreve D. Webster

136. Who is the writer of the poem *"The Canonization"*?
A. Milton B. Dryden
C. Donne D. Chaucer

137. Name the writer of the poem *"Wind Hour"*?
A. Hopkins B. Eliot
C. Dryden D. Yeats

138. Who is the writer of the poem *"Adam's Course"*?
A. Eliot B. Tagore
C. Yeats D. Shelley

139. Who wrote the poem: *"Lay Your Sleeping Head"*?
A. Auden B. Yeats
C. Stephen Spender D. Ted Hughes

140. The play *"The Birthday Party"* is written by
A. G.B. Shaw B. Galsworthy
C. Harold Pinter D. Osborne

141. Who is believed to be the writer of *"On the Sublime"*?
A. Aristotle B. Longinus
C. Plato D. M. Arnold

142. Name the author of *"An Essay on Dramatic Poesie"*
A. Dryden B. Sidney
C. Shelley D. Arnold

143. Who is the writer of *"Culture and Society"*?
A. Cleanth Brooks
B. Eliot
C. Bertrand Russell
D. Raymond Williams

144. The writer of the *'Mirror and the Lamp'* is
A. Hume B. Lionel Trilling
C. M.H. Abrams D. Sean Lucy

145. The writer of *"Provide Provide"* is
A. Whitman B. Frost
C. Yeats D. Auden

146. Who wrote *"Desire Under the Elms"*?
A. Arthur Miller B. Osborne
C. Eugene O'Neill D. Shaw

147. Who is the writer of *"A Severed Head"*?
A. Iris Murdoch B. Paul Scott
C. Goldwing D. Huxley

148. *'Das Kapital'* is written by
A. Engel B. Freud
C. Marx D. Lawrence

149. *"Waiting for Godot"* is written by
A. Samuel Beckett B. Ibsen
C. Brecht D. Chekhov

150. Who is the writer of *"A House for Mr. Biswas"*?
A. Salman Rushdie B. V.S. Naipaul
C. Vikram Seth D. R.K. Narayan

151. Name which is not the work of Marlowe
A. Richard I B. Tambarlaine
C. The Jew of Malta D. Dr. Faustus

152. Name the writer of the poem *"The Weary Blues"*
A. Longfellow B. Whitman
C. Frost D. Langston Hughes

153. Which of the following poems is not written by Robert Lowell?
A. In the Cage B. Dolphin
C. Good Morning D. The Old Flame

154. Which of the following poems is written by Wallace Stevens?
A. Red Sun Blues B. Sunday Morning
C. From Survivor D. "Going"

155. Which of the following poems is not written by Philip Larkin?
A. Art Grass B. Sad Steps
C. Traveller D. Church going

156. *Oedipus Rex* was written by
A. Sophocles B. Homer
C. Seneca D. Aeschylus

157. Flaubert's famous work is
A. Odysseus B. Madame Bovary
C. The Trial D. The Outsider

158. Northrop Fry is basically a
A. Dramatist B. Novelist
C. Poet D. Critic

159. The writer of *"The Beauty in a State"* is
A. Raja Rao
B. Tagore
C. Shelley
D. Ananda Coomaraswami

160. The most important work of K.R. Srinivas Iyengar is
A. Indian Way of Writing
B. Indians Under the Foreign Rule
C. Indian Writing in English
D. Indian Literary Scene

161. The writer of *"The Swan and the Eagle"* is
A. M.K. Naik
B. C.D. Narasimhaiah
C. Bruce King
D. V.K. Gokak

162. Who wrote the poem: *"The Lake Isle of Innisfree"*?
A. Yeats B. Eliot
C. Spender D. Auden

163. Who wrote : *"The Lives of the Poets"*?
A. Boswell B. Hazlitt
C. Macaulay D. Dr. Johnson

164. Who wrote: *"The Interpretation of Dreams"*?
A. Marx B. Jung
C. Freud D. Darwin

165. Who wrote : *"Principles of Literary Criticism"* (in 1924)?
A. T.R. Leavis B. Kenneth Brooke
C. I.A. Richards D. A.G. Gardiner

166. Whose book "Language" (1933) is considered *"The Bible of American Linguistics"*?
A. Robert A. Hall B. Bloomfield
C. Bernard Bloch D. Edward Sapir

167. Which of the following poems is not by Frost?
A. Design B. Birches
C. Reluctance D. Michael

168. The famous soliloquy *"To be or not to be"* occurs in
A. Macbeth B. King Lear
C. Hamlet D. Othello

169. Which is the *'Odd man out'* in the following?
A. Paradise Lost B. The Ramayana
C. Essay on Man D. Iliad

170. Which Italian poet is most famous for his sonnets?
A. Petrarch B. Dante
C. Ovid D. None of these

171. What figure of speech has been used in the following line?
"Milton! thou shouldnt be living with us at this hour." ***—Wordsworth***
A. Hyperbole B. Simile
C. Metaphor D. Apostrophe

172. Which figure of speech has been used in the term : *"immemorial elms"*?
A. Allegory B. Rhyme
C. Alliteration D. Oxymoron

173. Which play of Shaw is also sometimes called *"The Chocolate Soldier"*?
A. Arms and the Man B. Candida
C. Pygmalion D. Saint Joan

174. Which one among the following cannot be deemed to be a writer of the *"Problem Play"*?
A. G.B. Shaw
B. Galsworthy
C. Harley Granville-Barker
D. Eliot

175. Who is the writer of *"Metamorphoses"*?
A. Ovid B. Dante
C. Petrarch D. Virgil

176. The book *"Euphues"* was written by
A. Greene B. Jonson
C. Dryden D. John Lyly

177. Who can be said to be the greatest writer of the *Comedy of Humours*?
A. Dryden B. Ben Jonson
C. Congreve D. Etherege

178. Which one among the following is not a play by Ben Johnson?
A. Volpone
B. Alchemist
C. Every man out of His Honour
D. The Way of the World

179. Who is the writer of the book *"Prince"*?
A. Ovid B. Boccaccio
C. Machiavelli D. Montaigne

180. Who is the writer of the essay *"Simulation and Dissimulation"*?
A. Montaigne B. Lamb
C. De Quincey D. Bacon

181. Name the figure of speech for which Lyly is chiefly remembered
A. Malapropism B. Euphuism
C. Melodramaticism D. None of these

182. *Utopia* was written by
A. Walter Raleigh
B. Sir Thomas Moore
C. Daniel Defoe
D. None of these

183. The other name for *Euphues* is
A. The Anatomy of Melancholy
B. The Anatomy of Joy
C. The Anatomy of Wit
D. None of these

184. *Ferrex and Porrex* is the other name for
A. The Spanish Tragedy
B. Dr. Faustus
C. Goboduc
D. None of these

185. Which one among the following belongs to the group known as University Wits?
A. Shakespeare B. Congreve
C. Dryden D. Marlowe

186. *Astrophel and Stella* is a
A. play B. novel
C. sonnet sequence D. short story

187. What is the Greek meaning of *'Utopia'*?
A. An ideal place
B. A healthy place
C. A lovely place
D. Not a place (=*ou*=not; *topos*=a place)

188. The word "Volksgeist" means
A. The spirit of the age
B. (As per) tradition, custom and consensus
C. The essence of something
D. None of these

189. Which one of the following was a contemporary of Chaucer?
A. Spenser B. Herrick
C. Robert Graves D. John Gower

190. The famous work of Boccaccio is
A. Decameron
B. Divine Comedy
C. Essays
D. A collection of sonnets

191. What is meant by *"Grub Street"*?
A. The literary scene of hacks' crowds during Pope's period.
B. Unhygienic streets of London
C. Streets full of worms
D. Plague-infested streets

192. Who wrote: *"Idylls of the King"*?
A. Tennyson B. Browning
C. Spenser D. Keats

193. What could be another name for Renaissance?
A. The New Learning B. The Reformation
C. The Prostantism D. Humanism

194. Who wrote: *'Hudibras'*?
A. Butler B. Addison
C. Steele D. Goldsmith

195. *"London"* by Dr. Johnson is
A. An epic B. A verse satire
C. A prose satire D. A critical work

196. Who wrote *Moll Flanders*?
A. Richardson B. Fielding
C. Smollett D. Defoe

197. *The Gothic novel* was primarily a novel of
A. Pity
B. Terror
C. Love
D. Description of nature

198. *'Unto This Last'* is a work by
A. Carlyle B. Pater
C. Oscar Wilde D. John Ruskin

199. Who is the writer of *"The Blessed Damozel"*?
A. Christina Rossetti B. Emile Bronte
C. D.G. Rossetti D. W.B. Yeats

200. Who among the following was not a critic?
A. M. Arnold B. Ruskin
C. Dryden D. Tennyson

201. Which one among the following was not a contemporary or predecessor of Shakespeare?
A. Marlowe B. Kyd
C. Fry D. Greene

202. Who among the following was not a prose writer?
A. Ascham B. Coleridge
C. Hooker D. Raleigh

203. Who among the following was not a character writer?
A. Wordsworth
B. Joseph Hall
C. John Earle
D. Sir Thomas Overbury

204. Who among the following was not an essayist of the seventeenth century?
A. Halifax
B. Sir Thomas Browne
C. Hazlitt
D. Sir William Temple

205. About whom has it been said :
"He knew small Latin and less Greek"
A. Ben Jonson B. Shakespeare
C. Milton D. Aristotle

206. Who said about Shakespeare:
"He was not of age but of ages"?
A. Jonson B. Johnson
C. Dryden D. Arnold

207. Who wrote: *'Modern Painters'*?
A. Rossetti B. Reynolds
C. Hazlitt D. Ruskin

208. Which one of the following is not the work of Lamb?
A. Of Style B. All Fools' Day
C. Dream Children D. Grace Before Meat

209. Who is stated to have said :
"veni, vidi, vici"?
A. Julius Caesar B. Alexander
C. Napoleon D. Homer

210. Who wrote : *"The Advancement of Learning"*?
A. Pope B. Tennyson
C. Bacon D. Eliot

211. Who wrote: *"We are hollow men."*?
A. Eliot B. Yeats
C. Tagore D. Ezekiel

212. By which character is the following line in Shakespeare's Julius Caesar spoken?
"I'm well-armed in honesty"?
A. Caesar B. Cassius
C. Brutus D. Cicero

213. *'The Way of All Flesh'* was written by
A. Swift B. Congreve
C. Butler D. Addison

214. Who is the writer of *"The Good Companions"*?
A. A.G. Gardiner B. Chatterton
C. Hazlitt D. J.B. Priestley

215. Who is the writer of the poem *'Vagabond'*?
A. MacNeice B. Masefield
C. Sir Henry Newbolt D. Rupert Brooke

216. *"Gallathea"* in written by
A. Spenser B. Herbert
C. Lyly D. Shelley

217. Who wrote: *"The Harp of India"*?
A. Govind Chunder Dutt
B. Michael Madhusudan Dutt

C. Henry L.V. Derozio
D. V.K. Gokak

218. *"King Porus—A Legend of Old"* is written by
A. Henry Derozio
B. Toru Dutt
C. Sarojini Naidu
D. Michael Madhusudan

219. Who is the writer of the poem *"The Dance of the Eunuchs"*?
A. Nissim Ezekiel B. Kamala Das
C. Daruwallah D. A.K. Ramanujan

220. Which Indian poet wrote the poem *"The Trojan War"*?
A. Vikram Seth B. Keki N. Daruwalla
C. Sri Aurbindo D. Tagore

221. Who wrote: *"Jonathan Wild"*?
A. Richardson B. Smollett
C. Defoe D. Fielding

222. *"Of Revenge"* is one of the essays of
A. Lamb B. Hazlitt
C. Gardiner D. Bacon

223. Who wrote: *"The Confessions of An English Opium-Eater"*?
A. Coleridge B. Shelley
C. De Quincey D. James Joyce

224. Who wrote the poem *"Rhapsody on a Windy Day"*?
A. Yeats B. Spenser
C. Eliot D. Housman

ANSWERS

1	2	3	4	5	6	7	8	9	10
C	A	D	D	C	B	D	A	C	B
11	**12**	**13**	**14**	**15**	**16**	**17**	**18**	**19**	**20**
D	B	C	A	D	B	C	A	A	B
21	**22**	**23**	**24**	**25**	**26**	**27**	**28**	**29**	**30**
A	C	A	C	D	D	D	A	C	C
31	**32**	**33**	**34**	**35**	**36**	**37**	**38**	**39**	**40**
B	C	A	C	C	D	A	B	C	D
41	**42**	**43**	**44**	**45**	**46**	**47**	**48**	**49**	**50**
A	B	C	B	A	B	C	D	C	A
51	**52**	**53**	**54**	**55**	**56**	**57**	**58**	**59**	**60**
B	B	C	B	A	B	C	B	C	D
61	**62**	**63**	**64**	**65**	**66**	**67**	**68**	**69**	**70**
C	B	A	D	C	D	C	D	C	C
71	**72**	**73**	**74**	**75**	**76**	**77**	**78**	**79**	**80**
A	C	D	B	C	D	D	C	C	D
81	**82**	**83**	**84**	**85**	**86**	**87**	**88**	**89**	**90**
B	C	A	B	B	A	B	A	A	C
91	**92**	**93**	**94**	**95**	**96**	**97**	**98**	**99**	**100**
D	C	D	B	A	C	B	D	B	B
101	**102**	**103**	**104**	**105**	**106**	**107**	**108**	**109**	**110**
D	C	C	C	D	A	B	C	D	C

111	112	113	114	115	116	117	118	119	120
D	C	B	A	D	C	A	A	B	B
121	122	123	124	125	126	127	128	129	130
A	D	A	D	C	C	D	B	A	B
131	132	133	134	135	136	137	138	139	140
B	D	A	B	B	C	A	C	A	C
141	142	143	144	145	146	147	148	149	150
B	A	D	C	B	C	A	C	A	B
151	152	153	154	155	156	157	158	159	160
A	D	C	B	C	A	B	D	D	C
161	162	163	164	165	166	167	168	169	170
B	A	D	C	C	B	D	C	C	A
171	172	173	174	175	176	177	178	179	180
D	C	A	D	A	D	B	D	C	D
181	182	183	184	185	186	187	188	189	190
B	B	C	C	D	C	D	B	D	A
191	192	193	194	195	196	197	198	199	200
A	A	A	A	B	D	B	D	C	D
201	202	203	204	205	206	207	208	209	210
C	B	A	C	B	A	D	A	A	C
211	212	213	214	215	216	217	218	219	220
A	C	C	D	B	C	C	D	B	C
221	222	223	224						
D	D	C	C						

❑❑❑

Literary and Media Knowledge

NOBEL PRIZE FOR LITERATURE 2000–2017

Year	Laureate	Country	Language	Genre(s)
2000	Gao Xingjian	China, France	Chinese	novel, drama, literary criticism
2001	V. S. Naipaul	United Kingdom Trinidad & Tobago	English	novel, essay
2002	Imre Kertesz	Hungary	Hungarian	novel
2003	J. M. Coetzee	South Africa	English	novel, essay, translation
2004	Elfriede Jelinek	Austria	German	novel, drama
2005	Harold Pinter	United Kingdom	English	drama
2006	Orhan Pamuk	Turkey	Turkish	novel, screenplay, essay
2007	Doris Lessing	United Kingdom	English	novel, drama, poetry, short story, memoirs
2008	J. M. G. Le Clezio	France Mauritius	French translation	novel, short story, essay
2009	Herta Muller	Germany Romania	German	novel, poetry
2010	Mario Vargas Llosa	Peru Spain	Spanish drama	novel, short story, essay
2011	Tomas Transtromer	Sweden	Swedish	poetry, translation
2012	Mo Yan	China	Chinese	novel, short story
2013	Alice Munro	Canada	English	short story
2014	Patrick Modiano	France	French	novel
2015	Svetlana Alexievich	Belarus (Born in Ukrainian SSR)	Russian	history, essay
2016	Bob Dylan	United States	English	poetry, songwriting
2017	Kazuo Ishiguro	United Kingdom (born in Japan)	English	novel

MAN BOOKER PRIZE (2000–2017)

Year	Winner	Book	Genre	Country
2000	Margaret Atwood	The Blind Assassin	Novel	Canada
2001	Peter Carey	True History of the Kelly Gang	Historical novel	Australia
2002	Yann Martel	Life of Pi	Fantasy novel	Canada
2003	DBC Pierre	Vernon God Little	Novel	Australia, Mexico
2004	Alan Hollinghurst	The Line of Beauty	Historical novel	United Kingdom
2005	John Banville	The Sea	Novel	Ireland
2006	Kiran Desai	The Inheritance of Loss	Novel	India
2007	Anne Enright	The Gathering	Novel	Ireland
2008	Aravind Adiga	The White Tiger	Novel	India
2009	Hilary Mantel	Wolf Hall	Historical novel	United Kingdom
2010	Howard Jacobson	The Finkler Question	Novel	United Kingdom
2011	Julian Barnes	The Sense of an Ending	Novel	United Kingdom
2012	Hilary Mantel	Bring Up the Bodies	Historical novel	United Kingdom
2013	Eleanor Catton	The Luminaries	Historical novel	New Zealand
2014	Richard Flanagan	The Narrow Road to the Deep North	Historical novel	Australia
2015	Marlon James	A Brief History of Seven Killings	Historical/ experimental novel	United Kingdom
2016	Paul Beatty	The Sellout	Satirical novel	United States of America
2017	George Saunders	Lincoln in the Bardo	Historical/ experimental novel	United States of America

SAHITYA AKADEMI AWARDS–2017

Name	Language	Name	Language
Jayanta Madhab Bora	Assamese	Rajen Toijamba	Manipuri
Afsar Ahmed	Bengali	Shrikant Deshmukh	Marathi
Rita Boro	Bodo	Bina Hangkhim	Nepali
Shiv Mehta	Dogri	Gayatri Saraf	Odia
Mamang Dai	English	Nachhattar	Punjabi
Urmi Ghanshyam Desai	Gujarati	Neeraj Daiya	Rajasthani
Ramesh Kuntal Megh	Hindi	Niranjam Mishra	Sanskrit
T.P. Ashoka	Kannada	Bhujanga Tudu	Santali
Autar Krishen Rahbar	Kashmiri	Jagdish Lachhani	Sindhi
Gajanan Jog	Konkani	(Late) Inqulab	Tamil
Udaya Narayana Singh 'Nachiketa'	Maithili	Devipriya	Telugu
K.P. Ramanunni	Malayalam	Baig Ehsas	Urdu

JNANPITH AWARD WINNERS (2000-2017)

Award Winners	Year	Award Winners	Year
Dr. Indira Goswami (Assamese)	2000	Amar Kant & Shrilal Shukla (Hindi)	2009
Rajendra Keshav Lal Shah (Gujarati)	2001	Chandrasekhar Kambar (Kannada)	2010
D. Jayakanthan	2002	Pratibha Ray (Odiya)	2011
Vinda Karandikar (Marathi)	2003	Ravuri Bharadhwaja (Telugu)	2012
Rehman Rahi (Kashmiri)	2004	Kedarnath Singh (Hindi)	2013
Kunwar Narain (Hindi)	2005	Bhalchandra Nemade (Marathi)	2014
Ravindra Kelekar (Konkani) and Satyavrat Shastri (Sanskrit)	2006	Raghuveer Chaudhari (Gujarati)	2015
O.N.V. Kurup (Malayalam)	2007	Shankha Ghosh (Bengali)	2016
Akhlaq Khan Shahryar (Urdu)	2008	Krishna Sobti (Hindi)	2017

FAMOUS BOOKS AND AUTHORS

Book	Author
A Secular Agenda	Arun Shourie
A Suitable Boy	Vikram Seth
Accession of Extinction	D.R. Mankekar
Adam Beda	George Eliot
Adhe Adhure	Mohan Rakesh
Adonis	P.B. Shelley
Adventures of Huckleberry Finn	Mark Twain
Adventures of Sherlock Holmes	Arthur Conan Doyle
Adventures of Tom Sawyer	Mark Twain
Advise and Consent	Allen Drury
Affluent Society	J.K. Galbraith
After the Dark Night	S.M. Ali
Age of Reason	Jean Paul Sartre
Agni Pariksha	Acharya Tulsi
Agni Veena	Kazi Nazrul Islam
The Agony and the Ecstasy	Irving Stone
Ain-i-Akbari	Abul Fazal
Ajat Shatru	Jai Shankar Prasad
Akbarnama	Abul Fazal
Alchemist, The	Ben Jonson
Alice in Wonderland	Lewis Carroll
All is Well that Ends Well	William Shakespeare
All things Bright and Beautiful	James Herroit
Amar Kosh	Amar Singh

Book	Author
Ambassador's Journal	J.K. Galbraith
Ambassador's Report	Chester Bowles
An American Tragedy	Theodore Drieser
An Autobiography	Jawaharlal Nehru
An Eye to China	David Selboume
An Idealist View of Life	Dr. S. Radhakrishnan
An Unknown Indian	Nirad C. Choudhury
Anandmath	Bankim Chandra Chatterjee
Ancient Mariner	Samuel Taylor Coleridge
And Quiet Flows the Don	Mikhail Sholokhov
Androcles and the Lion	George Bernard Shaw
Animal Farm, The	George Orwell
Anna Karenina	Count Leo Tolstoy
Another Life	Derek Walcott
Answer of History	Mohammed Raza Pahlavi
Antony and Cleopatra	William Shakespeare
Ape and Essence	A. Huxley
Apple Cart	George Bernard Shaw
Arabian Nights	Sir Richard Burton
Area of Darkness	V.S. Naipaul
Arms and the Man	George Bernard Shaw
Around the World in Eighty days	Jules Verne
Arrangement, The	Elia Kazan
Arrival and Departure	Arthur Koestler
Arrowsmith	Sinclair Lewis
Arthashastra	Kautilya
As You Like It	William Shakespeare
Ascent of the Everest	Sir John Hunt
Ashtadhyayi	Panini
Asian Drama	Gunnar Myrdal
Asia and Western Dominance	K.M. Panikkar
Atoms of Hope	Mohan Sundara Rajan
August 1914	Alexander Solzhenitsyn
August Coup, The	Mikhail S. Gorbachev
Autumn Leaves	O. Pulla Reddi
Avanti Sundari	Dandi
Babur Nama	Zaheeruddin Mohammed Babur
Babbit	Sinclair Lewis
Back of Methuselah	George Bernard Shaw
Backward Place, A	Ruth P. Jhabwala

Book	Author
Bandicoot Run	Manohar Malgonkar
Bang-i-Dara	Mohammed Iqbal
Bangla Desh The Unfinished Revolution	Lawrence Liftschultz
Banyan Tree, The	Hugh Tinker
Beast and Man	Murry Midgely
Beginning of the Beginning	Acharya Rajneesh
Betrayal of Pearl Harbour	James Rusbridge and Eric Nave
Bend in the Ganges, A	Manohar Malgonkar
Ben Hur	Lewis Wallace
Bermuda Triangle	Charles Berlitz
Berry Patches	Yevgeny Yevtushenko
Best and the Brightest, The	David Halberstan
Between the Lines	Kuldip Nayar
Beyond Modernisation, Beyond Self	Sisir Kumar Ghose
Bharat Bharati	Maithili Sharan Gupta
Bharatiya Parampara Ke Mool Swar	Govind Chandra Pande
Big Breach, The	Richard Tomlinson
Big Fisherman, The	Lloyd C. Douglas
Biopgraphia Literaria	Samuel Taylor Coleridge
Bisarjan	Rabindra Nath Tagore
Birth and Death of Sun	George Gamow
Bitter Sweet	Noel Coward
Black Arrow, The	Robert Louis Stevenson
Blind Ambitions	John Dean
Blind Beauty	Boris Pasternak
Blind Men of Hindustan ! Indo-Pak Nuclear War	General K.S. Sundarji
Bliss was it in that Dawn	Minoo Masani
Bloodline	Sidney Sheldon
Blue Bird	Maurice Macterlink
Bone People, The	Kerl Hulme
Born Free	Joy Adamson
Bread, Beauty and Revolution	Khwaja Ahmed Abbas
Breakthrough	Gen. Moshe Dayan
Bride for the Sahib and other Stories, A	Khushwant Singh
Bride's Book of Beauty, The	Mulk Raj Anand
Broken Wings	Sarojini Naidu
Brothers Karamazhov	Fyodor Dostoevsky
Bubble, The	Mulk Raj Anand

Book	Author
Bhudha Charitam	Ashvaghosha
Bunch of Old Letters, A	Jawaharlal Nehru
Butterfield-8	John O' Hara
By Love Possessed	James Cozzens
Caesar and Cleopatra	George Bernard Shaw
Cancer Ward	Alexander Solzhenitsyn
Candida	George Bernard Shaw
Candide	Voltaire
Canterbury Tales	Geoffery Chaucer
Cardinal, The	Henry M. Robinson
Centennial	James Michener
Chandalika	Rabindra Nath Tagore
Chemmeen	Thakazhi Sivasankar Pillai
Cherry Orchard	Anton Chekov
Chesaplake	James A. Michener
Chidambara	Sumitra Nandan Pant
Chikaveera Rajendra	Masti Venkatesh Iyengar
Children of Gebelawi	Naguib Mahfouz
Childe Herolds Pilgrimage	Lord Byron
China Passage, A	J.K. Galbraith
China's Watergate	Leo Goodstadt
Chinese Betrayal	B.N. Mullick
Chitra	Rabindra Nath Tagore
Chittirappaval	P.V. Akilandam
Chomas Drum	K. Shivaram Karnath
Chronicle of a Death Foretold	Gabrel Garcia Marquez
Class, The	Eric Segal
Climate of Treason	Andrew Boyle
Comedy of Errors	William Shakespeare
Common Sense	Thomas Paine
Comus	John Milton
Communist Manifesto	Karl Marx
Confessions	J.J. Rousseau
Confessions of a Lover	Mulk Raj Anand
Confessions of an Opium Eater, The	Thomas Dequicey
Confidential Clerk	T.S. Eliot
Conquest of Self	M.K. Gandhi
Conservationist, The	Ms. Nadine Gordimer
Continent of Circle	Nirad C. Choudhury

Book	Author
Coolie	Mulk Raj Anand
Coup, The	John Updike
Count of Monte Cristo	Alexander Dumas
Court Dancer	Rabindra Nath Tagore
Covertly Papers	Joseph Addison
Cresent Moon	Rabindra Nath Tagore
Crescent over Kashmir	Anil Maheshwari
Crime and Punishment	Fyodor Dostoevsky
Crisis into Chaos	E..M.S. Namboodiripad
Crisis in India, The	Ronald Segal
Critique of Pure Reason, A	Immanuel Kant
Crown and the Loincloth, The	Chaman Nahal
Crown of Wild Olive, The	John Ruskin
Cry My Beloved Country	Alan Patan
Culture in the Vanity Bag	Nirad C. Choudhury.
Curtain Raisers	K. Natwar Singh
Dangerous Summer, The	Ernest Hemingway
Darkness at Noon	Arthur Keostler
Dark Room, The	R.K. Narayan
Dashkumar Charitam	Dandi
Das Kapital	Karl Marx
Daughter of the East	Benazir Bhutto
David Copperfield	Charles Dickens
Day in Shadow, The	Nayantara Sehgal
Days of His Grace	Eyvind Johnson
Dean's December	Saul Below
Death of a City	Amrita Pritam
Death of a Patriot	R.E. Harrington
Death of a President	William Manchester
Death, The Supreme Friend	Kakasaheb Kalelkar
Debacle	Emile Zola
Decameron	Giovanni Boccaccio
Decline and Fall of the Roman Empire	Edward Gibbon
Decline and Fall of Indira Gandhi	D.R. Mankekar and Kamala Mankekar
Decline of the West	O Spengier
Deewan-i-Ghalib	Mirza Ghalib
Delhi	Khushwant Singh
Democracy Means Bread and Freedom	Piloo Mody
Democracy Redeemed	V.K. Narsimhan

Book	Author
Descent of Man	Charles Darwin
Deserted Village	Oliver Goldsmith
Devdas	Sharat Chandra Chatterjee
Die Blendung	Elias Canetti
Dilemma of our Time	Harold Joseph Laski
Diplomacy in Peace and War	J.N. Kaul
Discovery of India	Jawaharlal Nehru
Distant Drums	Manohar Malgonkar
Distant Neighbours	Kuldip Nayar
Divine Comedy	A. Dante
Divine Life	Swami Sivananda
Doctor's Dilemma	George Bernard Shaw
Dolls's House, A	Ibsen
Don Juan	Lord Byron
Don Quixote	Saavedra Miguel de Cervantes
Double Helix, The	J.D. Watson
Dragon's Teeth	U.B. Sinclair
Dream in Hawaii, A	Bhabani Bhattacharya
Dream of Fair to Middling Women	Samuel Beckett
Dreams Roses and Fire	Eyvind Johnson
Dr. Jekyll and Mr. Hyde	Robert Louis Stevenson
Durgesh Nandini	Bankim Chandra Chatterjee
Dynamics of Social Change	Chandra Shekhar
Earth	Emile Zola
Earth Mother, The	Pupul Jayakar
Economic Planning of India	Ashok Mehta
Economics of the Third World	S.K. Ray
Eduction of Public Man	Hubert Humphery
Eight Lives	Raj Mohan Gandhi
Elegy Written in a Country Church Yard	Thomas Grey
Emile	J.J. Rousseau
Emma	Jane Austen
End of Era	C.S. Pandit
Ends and Means	Aldous Huxley
Envoy to Nehru	Escott Reid
Essays for Poor to the Rich	John Kenneth Galbraith
Essays of Elia	Charles Lamb
Essays on Gita	Sri Aurobindo Ghosh
Eternal Himalayas	Major H.P.S. Ahluwalia

Book	Author
Eternal India	Indira Gandhi
Executioner's Song	Norman Mailer
Expanding Universe	Arthur Stanley Eddington
Eye of the Storm, The	Patric White
Face to Face	Lasse & Mrs. Lisa Berg
Faces of Everest	Maj. H.P.S. Ahluwalia
Facts are Facts	Khan Abdul Wali Khan
Fall of a Sparrow, The	Salim Ali
Family Reunion	T.S. Eliot
Far From the Madding Crowd	Thomas Hardy
Far Pavilions, The	M.M. Kaye
Faraway Music, The	Svetlana Allilueva
Farewell the Trumpets	James Morris
Farewell to Arms, A	Ernest Hemingway
Farm House	George Orwell
Father and Sons	Ivan Turgenev
Faust	J.W. Von Goethe
Fidelio	L. Beethoven
Fifth Horseman, The	Larry Collins and Dominique Lapierre
Final Days, The	Bob Woodward and Carl Bernstein
Finding a Voice-Asian Women in Britain	Amrit Wilson
Fire Next Time, The	James Balbwin
First Circle	Alexander Solzhenitsyn
Flames form the Ashes	P.D. Tandon
Flounder, The	Gunter Grass
Food Nutrition and Poverty in India	V.K.R.V. Rao
For Whom the Bell Tolls	Ernest Hemingway
Forbidden Sea, The	Tar Ali Baig
Forsyte Saga	John Galsworthy
Forty Nine Days	Amrita Pritam
Freedom At Midnight	Larry Collins and Dominique Lapierre
French Revolution	Thomas Carlyle
Friends and Foes	Sheikh Mujibur Rehman
Friends not Masters	Ayyub Khan
From Here to Eternity	James Jones
From India to America	L. S. Chandrashekhar
From Raj to Rajiv	Mark Tully & Zaheer Masani
Ganadevata	Tara Shanker Bandopadhyay
Gandhi and Stalin	Louis Fisher

Book	Author
Gardener	Rabindra Nath Tagore
Gathering Storm	Winston Churchill
Geeta Govinda	Jaya Dev
Ghasiram Kotwal	Vijay Tendulkar
Gita Rahasya	Bal Gangadhar Tilak
Glimpses of World History	Jawaharlal Nehru
Godan	Munshi Prem Chand
Godfather, The	Mario Puzzo
God of Small Things, The	Arundhati Roy
Gold Bat, The	P.G. Wodehouse
Golden Gate	Vikram Seth
Golden Threshold, The	Sarojini Naidu
Gone with the Wind	Margaret Mitchel
Good Earth	Pearl S. Buck
Gora	Rabindra Nath Tagore
Grammar of Politics	Harold Joseph Laski
Grapes of Wrath	John Steinbeck
Great Challenge, The	Louis Fishcer
Great Depression of 1990, The	Ravi Batra
Great Expectations	Charles Dickens
Great Gatsby	F. Scott Fitzgerald
Great Illusion	Norman Angel
Great Tragedy	Z.A. Bhutto
Guide, The	R.K. Narayan
Gulag Archipelago	Alexander Solzhenitsyn
Gul-i-Naghma	Raghupati Sahai (Firaq) Gorakhpuri
Gulistan and Bostan	Sheikh Saadi
Gulliver's Travels	Jonathan Swift
Gurusagaram	O.P. Vijayan
Hamlet	William Shakespeare
Handful of Dust, A	Evelyn Waugh
Harry Potter*	J.K. Rowling
Harsha Charita	Ban Bhatt
Heat and Dust	Ruth P. Jhabwala
Heir Apparent	Dr. Karan Singh
Henderson, the Rain King	Saul Below
Henry Esmond	William Thackeray
Hero of our Times	Richard Hough
Heroes and Hero Worship	Thomas Carlyle

Book	Author
Higher than Hope	Fatima Meer
Himalayan Blunder	Brigadier J.P. Dalvi
Hindu Civilization	J.M. Barrier
Hinduism	Nirad C. Choudhury
Hindu View of Life	Dr. S. Radhakrishnan
Hounds of Baskervilles, The	Arthur Conan Doyle
House Divided	Pearl S. Buck
House for Mr. Biswas, A	V.S. Naipaul
Huckieberry Finn	Mark Twain
Human Factor	Graham Greene
Humboldt's Gift, The	Saul Bellow
Humour	Ben Johnson
Hunchback of Notre Dame	Victor Hugo
Hungary Stones	Rabindra Nath Tagore
I Am Not an Island	K.A. Abbas
I Follow the Mahatma	K.M. Munshi
Idiot, The	Fyodor Dostoevsky
Idols	Sunil Gavaskar
Idylls of the King	Alfred Teennyson
If I am Assassinated	Z.A. Bhutto
Illiad	Homer
Importance of Being Earnest	Oscar Wilde
In Afghanistan's Shadow	Salig S. Harrison
In Evil Hour	Gabriel Garcia Marquez
In a Free State	V.S. Naipaul
In Memorium	Alfred Lord Tennyson
In Search of Gandhi	Richard Attenbrough
In Search of Identity	Anwar-al-Sadat
India A Wounded Civilization	V.S. Naipaul
India Changes	Taya Zinkin
India Discovered	John Keay
India Divided	Rajendra Prasad
India from Curzon to Nehru and After	Durga Das
India Remembered	Percival and Margaret Spear
India of Our Dreams	M.V. Kamath
India, The Critical Years	Kuldip Nayar
India Today	Rajni Palme Dutt
India We Left	Humphry Trevelyan
India Wins Freedom	Maulana Abul Kalam Azad

Book	Author
Indian Home Rule	M.K. Gandhi
Indian Muslims	Mohammed Mujeeb
Indian Muslims The Need For a Positive Outlook	Wahiduddin Khan
Indian Philosophy	Dr. S. Radhakrishnan
Indian War of Independence	V.D. Savarkar
India's China War	Neville Maxwell
India's Priceless Heritage	N.A. Palkhivala
India	Magasthenes
Indira's India	S. Nihal Singh
Indira Gandhi's Emergence and Style	Nayantara Sehgal
Inheritance of Loss, The	Kiran Desai
Inner Circle, The	Jonathan Frost
Inside Asia (also, Inside Europe and Inside Africa)	John Gunter
Inside Third Reich	Albert Spencer
Intimacy	Jean Paul Sartre
Invisible Man	H.G. Wells
Iron in the Soul	Jean Paul Sartre
Isabella	John Keats
Islamic Bomb	Stev Weissman and Herbert Krounsney
Island in the Steams	Ernest Hemingway
Is Paris Burning	Larry Collins And Dominique Lapierre
Ivanhoe	Sir Walter Scott
Jane Eyre	Charlotte Bronte
Jazz	Toni Morison
Jean Christopher	Roman Rolland
Jinnah-India-Partition Independence	Jaswant Singh
Jobs for Millions	V.V. Giri
Judgement, The	Kuldip Nayar
Judge's Miscellany, A	M. Hidayatullah
Jullius Caesar	William Shakespeare
Jungel Book	Rudyard Kipling
Justice of Peace Ke Aansu	Janardan Prasad Singh
Kadambari	Bana Bhatt
Kagaz te Kanwas	Amrita Pritam
Kali Aandhi	Kamleshwar
Kamayani	Jai Shanker Prasad
Kamasutra	S.J. Vatsyayan
Kanthapura	Raja Rao

Book	Author
Kapal Kundala	Bankim Chandra Chatterjee
Kashmir-Behind the Vale	M.J. Akbar
Kaya Kalp	Munshi Prem Chand
Kayar	Thakazhi Sivasankara Pillai
Ken Attendant Godot	Samuel Backett
Kenilworth	Sir Walter Scott
Khak-i-Dil	Jan Nissar Akhtar
Kidnapped	Robert Louis Stevenson
Killer Angels	Michael Shaara
Kim	Rudyard Kipling
King of Dark Chamber	Rabindra Nath Tagore
King Lear	William Shakespeare
Kipps	H. G. Wells
Kissinger Years, The	T.N. Kaul
Kitni Navon Main Kitni Bar	S.H. Vatsyayan
Kore Kagaz	Amrita Pritam
Kublai Khan	Samuel Taylor Coleridge
Kulliyat-i-Iqbal	M. Iqbal
Kumar Sambhava	Kalidas
L'Allegro	John Milton
La Divine Comedia	A. Dante
Lady Chatterley's Lover	D.H. Lawrence
Lady of the Lake	Sir Walter Scott
Lajja	Ms. Taslima Nasreen
Last Days of Pompeii	Edward George Lytton
Last Maharaja, The	Jean Louis Nou and Jacques Pouchepadass
Last Thing	C.P. Snow
Laws Versus Justice	V.R. Krishna Iyer
Lead Kindly Light	Vincent Shean
Le Contract Social (The Social Contract)	J.J. Rousseau
Leaders	Richard Nixon
Leaves of Grass	Walt Whiteman
Letters from the Field	Margaret Mead
Les Miserables	Victor Hugo
Leviathan	Thomas Hobbes
Life Divine	Aurbindo Ghosh
Life of Dr. Johnson	James Boswell
Light that Failed	Rudyard Kipling
Lines of Fate	Marek Kharitonov

Book	Author
Lipika	Rabindra Nath Tagore
Living Room	Graham Greene
Lolita	V. Nabokov
Long Walk to Freedom	Nelson Mandela
Look Back in Anger	John Osborne
Lord of the Files	William Golding
Lost Child	Mulk Raj Anand
Lost Honour	John Dena
Lotus Eaters	A Tennyson
Love Story	Eric Segal
Lycidas	John Milton
Macbeth	William Shakespeare
Magic Mountain	Maharishi Ved Vyas
Main Street	Sinclair Lewis
Major Barbara	George Bernard Shaw
Making of a Midsummer Night's Dream, The	David Selbourne
Malgudi Days	R.K. Narayan
Malti Madhav	Bhavabhuti
Malavikagnimitra	Kalidas
Man and Superman	George Bernard Shaw
Man Eaters of Kumaon	Jim Corbett
Man of Destiny	George Bernard Shaw
Mankind and Mother Earth	Arnold Toynbee
Man, The Unknown	Lewis Carroll
Man for All Seasons, A	Robert Bolt
Man for Moscow	G. Wynne
Many Worlds	K.P.S. Menon
Marriage and Morals	Bertrand Russel
Masters, The	C.P. Snow
Mati Matal	Gopinath Mohanty
Maurice	E.M. Forster
Mayor of Casterbridge	Thomas Hardy
Meghdoot	Kalidas
Mein Kampf	Adolf Hitler
Memories of Hope	Charles de Gaulle
Memories of Malgudi	R.K. Narayan
Men who Kept the Secrets	Thomas Powers
Men who Killed Gandhi, The	Manohar Malgonkar
Merchant of Venice	William Shakespeare

Book	Author
Middle Ground, The	Margaret Drabble
Middle March	George Eliot
Midnight's Children*	Salman Rushdie
Midsummer Night's Dream, A	William Shakespeare
Mill on the Floss	George Eliot
Miser, The	Moliere
Mistaken Identify	Nayantara Sehgal
Moby Dick	Hermann Melville
Modern Painters	John Ruskin
Moon and Six Pence	W. Somerset Maugham
Moonlight Sonata	L Beethoven
Mookhajiva Kanasugalu	K. Shivram Karnath
Mother	Maxim Gorky
Mother India	Katherine Mayo
Mountbatten and Independent India	Larry Collins & Dominique Lapierre
Mountbatten and The Partition of India	Larry Collins & Dominique Lapierre
Mrinalini	Bankim Chandra Chatterjee
Mrs. Gandhi's Second Reign	Arun Shourie
Much Ado About Nothing	William Shakespeare
Mudra Rakshasa	Vishakhadatta
Murder in the Cathedral	V.S. Eliot
Muslim Dilemma in India	M. K. A. Baig
My Days	R.K. Narayana
My Early Life	M.K. Gandhi
My Experiments with Truth	M.K. Gandhi
My India	S. Nihal Singh
My Life and Times	V.V. Giri
My Music, My Love	Ravi Shankar
My Own Boswell	M. Hidayatullah
My Presidential Years	R.Venkata Raman
My Struggles	E.K. Nayanar
My Truth	Indira Gandhi
Mysterious Universe	James Jens
Naked Came the Stranger	Penelope Ashe
Naked Face, The	Sidney Sheldon
Naked Triangle, The	Balwant Gargi
Naku Thanthi	D.R. Bendre
Nana	Emile Zola
Nature of Mass Poverty, The	J.K. Galbraith

Book	Author
Natya Shastra	Bharat Muni
Neela Chand	Shiv Prasad Singh
Nehru Family and Sikhs	Harbans Singh
Netaji Dead or Alive	Samar Guha
New Dimensions of India's Foreign Policy	Atal Behari Vajpayee
Nine Days' Wonder	John Mansfield
Nineteen Eighty-four	George Orwell
1999-Victory Without War	Richard Nixon
Nisheeth	Uma Shanker Joshi
Niti-Sataka	Bharatrihari
Nixon in White House	Seymour M. Hersh
Non-Violence in Peace and War	M.K. Gandhi
Nuclear India	G.G. Mirchandani and P.K.S. Namboodari
O'Jerusalem	Larry Collins and Dominique Lapierre
Occasion for Loving	Nadine Gordimer
Oddakkuzal	G. Shankara Kurup
Odyssey	Homer
Of Human Bondage	W. Somerset Maugham
Old Man and the Sea	Ernest Hemingway
Oliver Twist	Charles Dickens
Omeros	Derek Walcott
One Day on the Life of Ivan Denisovich	Alexander Solzhenitsyn
One Hundred Years of Solitude	Gabriel Marquez
One World	Wendell Wilkie
One World to Share	Sridath Ramphal
Origin of Species	Charles Darwin
Oru Desattinte Katha	S.K. Pottekkatt
Oscar and Lucinda	Peter Carey
Othello	William Shakespeare
Other Side of Midnight, The	Sidney Sheldon
Our Films, Their Films	Satyajit Ray
Paddy Clarke Ha Ha Ha	Roddy Doyle
Pakistan Papers	Mani Shankar Aiyer
Painted Veil	W. Somerset Maugham
Painter of Signs	R.K. Narayan
Pair of Blue Eyes, A	Thomas Hardy
Pakistan Crisis	David Loshak
Pakistan Cut to Size	D.R. Mankekar
Pakistan, The Gathering Storm	Benazir Bhutto

Book	Author
Panchatantra	Vishnu Sharma
Paradise Lost	John Milton
Paradise Regained	John Milton
Passge to England, A	Nirad C. Choudhury
Passage to India, A	E.M. Forster
Past and Present	Thomas Carlyle
Pather Panchali	Bibhuti Bhushan Bandhopadhayaya
Patriot, The	Pearl S. Buck
Personal Adventure, A	Theodore H. White
Peter Pan	J. M. Berrie
Pickwick Papers	Charles Dickens
Pilgrim's Progress	John Bunyan
Pinjar	Amrita Pritam
Plans for Departure	Nayantara Sehgal
Portrait of India	Ved Mehta
Post Office	Rabindra Nath Tagore
Power and Glory	Graham Greene
Power That Be	David Halberstan
Pratham Pratishruti	Ashapurna Devi
Prelude	William Wordsworth
Prem Pachisi	Munshi Prem Chand
Premonitions	P.N. Haksar
Price of Power	Kissinger
Pride and Prejudice	Jane Austen
Prince	Nicolo Machiaveli
Principla	Issac Newton
Prison and Chocolate Cake	Nayantara Sehgal
Prison Diary	Jaya Prakash Narayan
Prisoner of Zenda	Anthony Hope
Prisoner's Scrapbook, A	L.K. Advani
Prithviraj Raso	Chanda Bardai
Professor, The	Charlotte Bronte
Promises to Keep	Chester Bowels
Pygmalion	George Bernard Shaw
Pyramids of Sacrifice	Peter L. Berger
Radharani	Bankim Chandra Chatterjee
Rage of Angels	Sidney Sheldon
Raghuvansha	Kalidas
Ragtime	E.L. Doctorow

Book	Author
Rainbow, The	Pearl S. Buck
Rains Came	Louis Bromefield
Rajtarangini	Kalhana
Ram Charita Manas	Tulsidas
Ramayana	Maharishi Valmiki
Rangbhoomi	Munshi Prem Chand
Rang-i-Shairi	Raghupati Sahai (Firaq Gorakhpuri)
Rape of Bangladesh	Anthony Mascarenhas
Rape of the Lock	Alexander Pope
Ratnavali	Harsh Vardhan
Razor's Edge	W. Somerset Maugham
Rebel, The	Albert Camus
Rebirth	Leonid Brezhnev
Red and Black, The	Stendhal
Red Badge of Courage	Stephan Crane
Red Star over China	Edgar Snow
Reflections of the French Revolution	Edmund Burke
Reminiscences of the Nehru Age	M.O. Mathai
Reprieve	Jean Paul Sartre
Republic	Plato
Resurrection	Count Leo Tolstoy
Return of the Native, The	Thomas Hardy
Returning to the Source	Acharya Shree Rajneesh
Revenue Stamps, The	Amrita Pritam
Rich Like Us	Nayantara Sehgal
Riding the Storm	Harold MacMillan
Rights of Man	Thomas Paine
Rise and Fall of the Great Powers	Paul Kennedy
Ritu Samhara	Kalidas
Rivals, The	R.B. Shridan
Road to Folly	Leslie Ford
Robe, The	Lloyd C. Douglas
Robinson Crusoe	Daniel Defoe
Romeo and Julliet	William Shakespeare
Rubaiyat	Omar Khayyam
Rubaiyat-i-Omar Khayyam	Edward Fitzgerald
Sadar-i-Riyasat	Karan Singh
Saket	Maithili Sharan Gupta
Sakha Ram Binder	Vijay Tendulkar

Book	Author
Samler's Planet	Saul Bellow
Sands of Time	Sidney Sheldon
Satanic Verses	Salman Rushdie
Sanctuary	William Faulkner
Satyartha Prakash	Swami Dayanand
Savitri	Sri Aurobindo Ghosh
Scarlet Letter	Nathaniel Hawthorne
Scarlet Pimpernal	Baroness Orczy
Sceptred Flute	Sarojini Naidu
Scholar Extraordinary	Nirad C. Choudhury
School for Scandal, The	R.B. Sheridan
Scope of Happiness, The	Vijayalakshmi Pandit
Search for Home, A	Sasthi Brata
Sense and Sensibility	Jane Austen
Sense of Time, A	H.S. Vatsyayan
Sesame and Lilies	John Ruskin
Seven Lamps of Architecture	John Ruskin
Seven Summers	Mulk Raj Anand
Shadow from Ladakh	Bhabani Bhattacharya
Shahnama	Firdausi
Shakuntala	Kalidas
Shalimar	Manohar Malgonkar
Shall We Tell the President	Jeffrey Archer
Shape of Things to Come	H.G Wells
Shame	Salman Rushdie
She Stoops to Conquer	Oliver Goldsmith
Ship of Fools	Katherine Anne Porter
Shivaji, The Great Patriot	Lala Lajpat Rai
Shoes of the Fisherman, The	Morris West
Silas Marner	George Eliot
Six Characters in Search of an Author	Lugi Pirandello
Slave, The	Issac Bashevis Singer
Small Land	Leonid Brezhnev
Sohrab and Rustam	Matthew Arnold
Song of India, The	Sarojini Naidu
Sonnets, The	William Shakespeare
Sons and Lovers	D.H. Lawrence
Sound and the Fury, The	William Faulkner
Soz-i-Watan	Munshi Prem Chand

Book	Author
Spaniard in the Works, A	John Lennon
Spirit of the Age	William Hazlitt
Spy Catcher	Peter Wright
St. John	George Bernard Shaw
Story of My Life	Moshe Dayan
Story of Real Man	Nikolayev Polevol
Strangers and Brothers Omnibus	C.P. Snow
Sunny Days	Sunil Gavaskar
Study of History, A	Arnold Toynbee
Swami and Friends	R.K. Narayan
Swapnavasvadatta	Bhasa
Sword and the Sickle	Mulk Raj Anand
Tale of a Tub, A	Jonathan Swift
Tale of Two Cities, A	Charles Dickens
Tales from Shakespeare	Charles Lamb
Talisman	Sir Walter Scott
Tamas	Bhisham Sahni
Tarzan of the Apes	Edger Rice Burroughs
Tears of D'Urbervilles	Thoms Huardy
Tempest, The	William Shakespeare
Thank You, Jeeves	P.G. Wodehouse
The Garden of Life	Naveen Patnaik
The White Tiger*	Arvind Adiga
Thieves in the Night	Arthur Koestler
Thirteenth Sun	Amrita Pritam
Three Musketeers	Alexander Dumas
Thorn Birds	Colleen McCollough
Thousand Days, A	Arthur M. Shlesinger
Through the Indian Looking Glass	David Selbourne
Through the Looking Glass	Lewis Carroll
Times Machine	H.G. Wells
Time to be Happy	Nayantara Sehgal
To Live or not to Live	Nirad C. Choudhury
Tom Jones	Henry Fielding
Train to Pakistan	Khushwant Singh
Traveller, The	Olive Goldsmith
Treasure Island	Robert Louis Stevenson
Trial, The	Franz Kafka
Trinity	Leon Uris
Triumph	John Kenneth Galbraith

Book	Author
Tropic of Cancer	Henry Miller
Tryst with Destiny	L. S. Gopalan
Twelfth Night	William Shakespeare
Twenty Years After	Alexander Dumas
Two Leaves and a Bud	Mulk Raj Anand
Two Women	Alberto Moravia
Ulysses	James Joyce
Uncle Tom's Cabin	H.B. Stowe
Unhappy India	Lala Lajpat Rai
Universe Around Us	James Jeans
Unto this Last	John Ruskin
Untold Story	General B.M. Kaul
Upturned Soil, The	Mikhail Sholokhov
Urvashi	Ramdhari Singh Dinkar
Utopia	Thomas More
Uttar Ramcharita	Bhava Bhuti
Valley of Dolls	Jacqueline Susann
Vanity Fair	William Thackeray
Vendor of Sweets, The	R.K. Narayan
Vicar of Wakefield	Oliver Goldsmith
Victim, The	Saul Bellow
View From Delhi, A	Chester Bowles
View From the UN	U. Thant
Village by the Sea, A	Anita Desai
Village , The	Mulk Raj Anand
Vinay Patrika	Tulsidas
Virangana	Maithili Sharan Gupta
Virginians, The	William Thackeray
Vish Vriksha	Bankim Chandra Chatterjee
Voice of Conscience	V.V. Giri
Voice of Freedom , A	Nayantara Sehgal
Voice of the Voiceless	Ruth Harring
Waiting for Godot	Thomas Becket
Wake up India	Annie Besant
Walls of Glass, The	K.A. Abbas
War and Peace	Count Leo Tolstoy
War of the Worlds, The	H.G. Wells
Waste Land	T.S. Eliot
Way to all Flesh	Samuel Butler

Book	Author
Way of the World, The	William Congreve
Wealth of Nations	Adam Smith
Week With Gandhi, A	Louis Fisher
We Indians	Khushwant Singh
We, the People	N.A. Palkivala
Where the Grass is Greener	David M. Smith
White House Years	Henry Kissinger
Wings of Fire	A.P.J. Abdul Kalam*
Willhelm Meister	J.W. Von Goethe
Without Fear or Favour	Neelam Sanjiva Reddy
Witness to an Era	Frank Moraes
Woman's Life, A	Guy de Maupassant
Wonder That Was India, The	A.L. Basham
Worthy it is	Odysseus Elytis
Wreck , The	Rabindra Nath Tagore
Wuthering Heights	Emile Bronte
Yajnaseni	Pratibha Roy
Yama	Mahadevi Verma
Yashodhara	Maithili Sharan Gupta
Yayati	V.S. Khandekar
Year of the Upheaval	Henry Kissinger
Year of the Vulture, The	Amita Malik
Yesterday and Today	K.P.S. Menon
Zhivago, Dr.	Boris Pasternak
Zulfi, My Friend	Piloo Mody

FAMOUS AUTHORS IN DIFFERENT LANGUAGES

English	William Shakespeare, John Milton, Chaucer, Spenser, Lord Byron, P.B. Shelley, John Keats, Francis Bacon, T.S. Eliot, Cecil Dlay Lewis, Alduous Huxley, W.B. Yeats Bunyan, Dryden, Dr. Johnson, Alexander Pope, Robert Browning, Charles Lamb, Charles Dickens, Thomas Hardy, W.M. Thackeray, George Eliot, Alfred Tennyson, Robert Bridges, George Bernard Shaw, D.H. Lawrence, Oliver Goldsmith, Sheridan, Walter Scott, William Wordsworth, S.T. Coleridge, Henry Fielding, Somerset Maugham, J.K. Rowling.
French	Imile Zola, Gustave Flaubert, Moliere, Proudhon, Jean Paul Sartre, Le Sage, Victor Hugo, Alexander Dumas, Balzac.
German	Goethe, Hoffman, Lessing, Schelling, Schaupenhuer, Heinrich Heine, Guenter Grass
Russian	Tolstoy, Mikhail Solokhov, Turgenev, Dostoevsky, Maxim Gorky, Techov, Alexander Salzhenitsyn, Boris Pasternak

Greek	Homer, Aesop, Aristophanes, Euripedes, Herodotus, Hesoid, Theocritus, Xenophon, Aeschylus, Sophocles
Latin	Dante, Boccacio, Terence, Virgil, Ovid, Horace, Seneca
Norwegian	John Bojer, Ibsen
Persian	Ghalib, Umar Khyyam, Abul Fazal, Amir Khusro, Faiz, Firdausi, Mohd. Iqbal Saddi
Spanish	Juan Valera, Lope De Vega, Cervantes

FAMOUS CHARACTERS AND THEIR CREATORS

Character	Creator	Character	Creator
Adam	Milton	Juliet	William Shakespeare
Alice	Lewis Carroll	Jessica	William Shakespeare
Ancient Mariner	Coleridge	Jean Valjin	Victor Hugo
Ariel	William Shakespeare	Jacques	William Shakespeare
Antonio	William Shakespeare	Jeeves	P.G. Wodehouse
Anna Karenina	Leo Tolstoy	King Arthur	Tennyson
Bassomio	William Shakespeare	Kim	Rudyard Kipling
Bertie Wooster	P.G. Wodehouse	Long John Silver	R.L. Stevenson
Brutus	William Shakespeare	Macbeth	William Shakespeare
Beatrix	Thackery	Micawber	Charles Dickens
Beatrice	William Shakespeare	Miranda	William Shakespeare
Christian	John Bunyan	Mephistopheles	J.W. Von Goethe
Cordelia	William Shakespeare	Mellors	D.H. Lawrence
Cleopatra	William Shakespeare	Malaprop	Sheridian
Clare	Thomas Hardy	Oliver Twist	Charles Dickens
Claudius	William Shakespeare	Peggotty	Charles Dickens
David Copperfield	Charles Dickens	Priyangbada	Kalidas
Dushyanta	Kalidas	Portia	William Shakespeare
Don Quixote	Cervantes	Pip	Charles Dickens
Eliza Doolittle	George Bernard Shaw	Perry Mason	Erle Stanley Gardner
Estella	Charles Dickens	Pickwick	Charles Dickens
Faust	J.W. Von Goethe	Rip Van Winkle	Washington Irving
Gora	Rabindranath Tagore	Sam Weller	Charles Dickens
Hamlet	William Shakespeare	Surpanakha	Valmiki
Harry Potter	J.K. Rowling	Shylock	William Shakespeare
Hyde	R.L. Stevenson	Sherlock Halmes	Arthur Conan Doyle
Hercule Poirot	Agatha Christie	Shakuntala	Kalidas
Hawkins	R.L. Stevenson	Sancho Panza	Cervantes Saavedra
Hector	Homer	Tess	Thomas Hardy
Ivanhoe	Sir Walter Scott	Watson	Arthur Conan Doyle
Iago	William Shakespeare	Zhivago	Boris Pasternak
James Bond	Ian Fleming		

GREAT POETS

Language	Poet
Hindi	Surdas, Tulsidas, Keshav
Sanskrit	Valmiki, Vedvyas, Kalidas
Bengali	Rabindra Nath Tagore
Urdu	Mirza Ghalib
Persian	Sheikh Saadi
Latin	Virgil
Greek	Homer
English	Shakespeare
German	Goethe
Italian	Dante
French	Sully Proudhone
Punjabi	Waris Shah

GREAT INDIAN AUTHORS AND POETS

Language	Authors and Poets
Assamese	Birendra Kumar Bhattacharya; Hem Chandra Barua; Hem Chandra Goswami; Madhavkandali.
Bengali	Ashapoorna Devi; Bankim Chandra Chatterjee; Bibhuti Bhushan Bandopadhyaya; Bishnu Dey; Pramendra Mitra; Rabindra Nath Tagore; R.C. Dutt; Michael Madhusudan Datt; Kazi Nazrul Islam; Tarashankar Bandopadhyaya.
English	Kamala Das; Manohar Malgonkar; R.K. Narayan; Raja Rao; Mulk Raj Anand; Bhabani Bhatacharya; Sasthi Brata; Arun Joshi; Chaman Nahal; K.A. Abbas; Anita Desai; R. Prawer Jhabwala; Kamla Markandaya; Khushwant Singh; Manoj Dass.
Gujarati	K.M. Munshi; Mirabai; Narmada Sagar; Narsingh Mehta; Govardhan Ram; Uma Shankar Joshi.
Hindi	Tulsidas; Surdas; Kesav Das; Bihari; Kabir; Sumitra Nandan Pant; Jai Shankar Prasad; Maithili Sharan Gupta; Munshi Prem Chand; Upendra Nath Ashk; Suryakant Tripathi 'Nirala', Acharya Chatursen; Mohan Rakesh; Harivansh Rai Bachchan; Mahadevi Verma; Bhagwati Charan Verma; Ramdhari Singh Dinkar.
Kannada	K.V. Puttappa; B.M. Pampan; Panna; Ramchandra Bendre; K.S. Karanth; Purandar Das.
Malayalam	C.V. Raman Pillai; S.K. Pottekkatt; G. Sankara Kurup; Thakazhi Sivasankara Pillai; O. Chandu Menon; Vallathol; Kumaran Asan.
Marathi	Hari Narayan Apte. Tikaram Mahay; Tukaram; V.S. Khandekar.
Oriya	Gopalbandhu Das; Gopi Nath Mohanty; Radha Nath Roy.
Punjabi	Sheikh Farid; Bhai Veer Singh; Dhani Ram Chatrik; Amrita Pritam; Nanak Singh; Balwant Gargi; Waris Shah; Bulle Shah.
Sanskrit	Maharishi Valmiki; Maharishi Ved Vyas, Shreeharsh; Ashvaghosh; Shudrak; Bharvi; Jaidev; Bhartrihari; Kalidas; Banabhatta; Bhavabhuti; Dandi.
Tamil	P.V. Akilandam, Subramaniam Bharati; Ramalingam.
Telugu	Lakshmi Narasimhan; Triputi; V. Satyanarayana.
Urdu	Assadulla Khan 'Ghalib'; Mohammed Iqbal; Mir Taqui Mir; Prem Chand; 'Firaq' Gorakhpuri; Rajinder Singh Bedi; Krishan Chander; Qurrat-ul-Ain Hyder; Sardar Jafri; Qazi Abdul Sattar.

WELL KNOWN QUOTATIONS

1. A thing of beauty is a joy for ever; Its loveliness increases; It will never pass into nothingness. — *Keats: Endymion*
2. A little knowledge is a dangerous thing — *Pope*
3. Beauty is truth, truth beauty that is all. Ye know on earth, all all ye need to know — *Keats: Ode on a Grecian urn*
4. All the world is a stage and all the man and women merely players — *Shakespeare: As you like it*
5. Some books are to be tested, others to be swallowed and some few to be chewed and digested — *Bacon*
6. Better to reign in hell than serve in heaven — *Milton: Paradise lost*
7. The child is father of the man — *Wordsworth: My heart leaps up*
8. A single step for man — a giant leap for mankind — *Neil Armstrong*
9. Dilli Chalo— *Netaji Subhash Chandra Bose*
10. To be or not to be — that is the question. — *Shakespeare: Hamlet*
11. Only free men negotiate. I shall never negotiate while I am still a prisoner — *Nelson Mandela*
12. Truth and non-violence are my God — *Mahatama Gandhi*
13. Let a hundred flowers bloom and let a thousand schools of thought contend — *Mao Tse-tung*
14. Jai Jawan, Jai Kisan— *Lal Bahadur Shastri*
15. Eureka! Eureka! — *Archimedes*
16. Some are born great, some achieve greatness and some have greatness thrust upon them — *Shakespeare*
17. Where wealth accumulates, men decay — *Goldsmith*
18. Power tends to corrupt and absolute power corrupts absolutely — *Lord Acton*
19. Man is by nature a political animal — *Aristotle*
20. I have nothing to offer but blood, toil, tears and sweat — *Winston Churchill*
21. I came, I saw, I conquered — *Julius Ceaser*
22. For fools rush in where angels fear to tread — *Pope*
23. Generations to come, it may, will scarce believe that such a one as this ever in flesh and blood walked upon this earth — *Einstein*
24. Government of the people, by the people, for the people — *Lincon*
25. East is east and west is west and never the twain shall meet — *Kipling*
26. Swaraj is my birth right — *Bal Gangadhar Tilak*
27. Cowards die many times before their death: The valiant never taste of death but once — *Shakespeare: Julius Ceaser*
28. Where ignorance is bliss, It is folly to be wise — *Grey*
29. I know nothing except the fact of my ignorance — *Socrates*
30. We are such stuff as dreams are made of and our little life is rounded with a sleep — *Shakespeare: The Tempest*
31. What's in a name? That which we call a rose By any other name would smell as sweet — *Shakespeare: Merchant of Venice*
32. Patriotism is the best refuge of a scoundrel — *Samuel Johnson*
33. Reading maketh a full man; conference a ready man; and writing an exact man — *Francis Bacon*
34. It is excellent to love a giant's strength but it is tyrannous to use it like a giant — *Shakespeare: Measure to Measure*

35. Water, water everywhere
Not any drop to drink
— *S.T. Coleridge: The Ancient Mainer*

36. It is strange but true, for truth is always strange
— *Byron: Don Juan*

37. Virtue is its own reward
— *Cicero: De Fintibus*

38. Frailty, thy name is woman
— *Shakespeare: Hamlet*

39. We don't fear to negotiate, but we do not negotiate out of fear — *J.F. Kennedy*

40. Give us good mothers and I shall give you good nation — *Napoleon*

41. The woods are lovely, dark and deep
But I have promises to keep
And miles to go before I sleep
— *Robert Frost*

42. We have made a tryst with destiny
— *Pt. Nehru*

43. Eli, Eli, Lamma Sabcathani (My God, my God, why last thou forsaken me)
— *Jesus Christ at the Cross*

44. If winter comes can spring be for behind
— *Shelley*

45. Man does not live by bread alone
— *Bible*

46. Nothing is good or bad, thinking makes it so
— *Shakespeare: Hamlet*

47. Garibi hatao — *Indira Gandhi*

48. Aram haram hai — *Jawaharlal Nehru*

49. Quit India — *Mahatma Gandhi*

50. Jai Jawan, Jai Kisan, Jai Vigyan
— *Atal Behari Vajpayee*

❑❑❑

Multiple Type Questions

BOOKS & AUTHORS

1. Who are the authors of following works?
   A. *Hidden Love*
   B. *My Book of Human Rights*
   C. *Devil May Care*
   D. *A Prisoner of Birth*
2. Who was the first English writer to win Nobel Prize for Literature?
3. Whose autobiography is titled *Freedom in Exile*?
4. Who wrote *The Dream of the Red Chamber,* China's greatest novel?
5. Name the author of following Books—
   A. *Reconciliation, Islam, Democracy and the West;*
   B. My Country: My Life (Autobiography);
   C. *Good-bye Shahzadi: A Political Biography of Benazir Bhutto.*
6. Which Indian freedom-fighter and staunch nationalist's work is *India Wins Freedom*?
7. Who has written the Tales Of The Future?
8. Which American historian wrote the 10-volume *History of the United States*?
9. *Songs of Innocence* is the work of which English poet, philosopher and artist?
10. Who is the author of *'The Enchantress of Florence'*?
11. Name the sister of forceful novelist Charlotte Bronte who wrote *Wuthering Heights.*
12. Which Libyan leader and military dictator wrote *The Green Book*?
13. Which former British Prime Minister's autobiography is titled *Full circle*?
14. Which is the longest biography in publishing history?
15. Who is the author of best sold series of Harry Potter?
16. What is the pen name of K.K. Nair, who wrote a 10 volume *History of Literature*?
17. Who is the author of *'The Kalam Effect – My Years with the President'*?
18. Which is the longest single-volume novel of the 20th century?
19. Which Pakistani Prime Minister's autobiography is titled *Daughter of the East?*
20. Name the Russian-American novelist, poet, and an authority on butterflies, whose *Lolita* is world famous.
21. Which Indian diplomat and author's work is *The Flying Troika*?
22. Name the Indian author and journalist, settled in New York, who became blind at the age of 3, and is a writer for *New Yorker.*
23. Who is credited to have authored the first modern Indian novel in English, *Rajmohan's Wife*?
24. Which British Prime Minister (1951-55), won Nobel Prize for literature?
25. Name the Indian writer and social critic, whose work includes *Autobiography of an Unknown Indian.*
26. Which English satirist's work is *Gulliver's Travels?*
27. Which India-born British writer's controversial book *The Satanic Verses* made Iran's spiritual

leader Ayatollah Khomeini sentence him to death?

28. Which French novelist and dramatist's works include *Jean-Christophe* (a ten-volume novel), biographies of Mahatma Gandhi and Vivekananda?

29. Which Indian president authored the *Hindu View of Life?*

30. Which Hindi writer's real name was Dhanpat Rai?

31. Which Greek Philosopher and educator's work, *Dialogues,* includes the *Republic,* the longest and one of the most celebrated works?

32. What do you call the art of compiling dictionaries?

33. What was the pseudonym of Lewis Carroll?

34. Give the title of the book Jim Corbett wrote on animals.

35. Who is called the Father of English poetry?

36. What is the term for 'the fear of books'?

37. Which former Indian Prime Minister's autobiography is titled *The Insider*?

38. What is the title of famous Musician Pt. Ravi Shankar's autobiography?

39. A. Which book is considered China's greatest novel?
B. Who wrote it?

40. A. Who wrote *Mahatma Gandhi and his Apostles*?
B. What was the title of the book on Mahatma Gandhi by Romain Rolland?

41. Name the German poet who wrote a poem appreciating Kalidasa's *Shakuntala*.

42. Who created the character 'Tarzon'?

43. In Arthur Conan Doyle's novels, who narrates the Sherlock Holmes stories?

44. Which English novelist and playwright wrote detective thrillers including *The Four Just Men* and *The Ringer*?

45. This 19th century Irish author and dramatist authored *An Ideal Husband*. Who was he?

46. Who wrote the following books:
A. Confessions
B. Confessions of a Lover
C. Confessions of an English Opium Eater

47. Who wrote the following two books :
A. *A Passage to England*
B. *A Passage to India*

48. Which famous character, created by Jonathan Swift, found himself lying on the island of Laputa?

49. Name the British jounalist and author of best-sellers like *Day of the jackal, The Odessa File* and *The Dogs of War.*

50. Which German philosopher wrote *Critique of Pure Reason*?

51. Name the Hungarian author of *Darkness at Noon.*

52. Name the ghost who narrates the stories to king Vikramaditya.

53. Who wrote the famous sea-story *The Cruel Sea*?

54. Which country is the setting for the famous story of *Alibaba and the Forty Thieves*?

55. Name the authors of the following books:
A. *Making Peace with Partition*
B. *The Grapes of Wrath*

56. Who wrote the book *Pather Panchali*?

57. Which staunch socialist leader of India wrote *Prison Diary*?

58. Who wrote *Small is Beautiful: A study of Economics as if people Mattered*?

59. Who is considered the Father of comedy?

60. Who wrote the book *Somnium*, regarded by some people as the first science fiction to be written?

61. Who wrote the book *The Great Indian Novel*?

62. Who wrote the famous sea-story *The Rover*?

63. Dr. Samuel Johnson's biography was written by..........................

64. Name the Sanskrit writer who wrote the famous *Kamasutra.*

65. Which English author is known for his works like *The Time Machine, Kipps* and *The Outline of History*?

66. Which English writer developed the stream-of-consciousness technique and is known for works like *To the Lighthouse, Mrs. Dalloway* and *Orlando*?

67. Which Indian authored *Bread, Beauty and Revolution*?

68. A business tycoon of world fame, authored *Business @ the Speed of Thought*. Name him.

69. Who wrote the following books:
A. *Conquest of Self*
B. *Devdas*

70. Give the names of the authors of following books:
A. *The Book of Negroes*
B. *The God of Small Things*
C. *Hungary Stones*
D. *The Water Babies*

71. Name the British historian who authored the adage "power tends to corrupt and absolute power corrupts absolutely".

72. Which Indian Sanskrit scholar and poet wrote *Kadambari* and *Harsha Charita*?

73. Which Italian author and humanist, also called the Father of the Novel, wrote *Life of Dante*?

74. Who said it— "All the world is a stage And all the man and women merely players"?

75. Name the French educationist, who as a (blind) teacher of the blind, devised the touch system of reading and writing for blind.
(**Clue:** She died in the year 2000.)

76. Name the authentic book on statecraft by Chanakya (Kautilya) (4th century B.C.).

77. Which English poet wrote *The Canterbury Tales*?

78. Who wrote the following books:
A. Secrets of the World's Inspirational Women (Westland);
B. Gandhi : A Political and Spiritual Life
C. *Brushes with History : Autobiography of Dr. K.K. Birla*

79. Which football player's autobiography, released in 2007, is titled 'Moments'?

80. Along which famous road is Rudyard Kipling's novel *Kim* set?

81. In *Alice in Wonderland,* a fictional work of Lewis Caroll, to which animal does Alice first speak in French?

82. In which book of the Old Testament were the Ten Commandments first listed?

83. Name the musical maestro whose work is '*The Secret of My Life*'.

84. Name the author of the following works.
A. My Truth
B. India Divided

85. Name the Indian aristocrat whose work is 'India– *From Midnight to the Mellenium*'.

86. Who is the author of *'The Post American World'*?

87. Name the Indian-born American who authored the prize winner book 'The Namesake'?

88. Who is the author of the prize winner book 'The White Tiger'?

ANSWERS

1. A. Angshumita Deka.
B. Jaya-shree Gupta.
C. Sebastian Faulks.
D. Jeffrey Archer.

2. Rudyard Kipling, in 1907.

3. Dalai Lama.

4. Cao Chan (he wrote 80 of the 120 chapters). Following his death in 1763, Kao Eh finished it.

5. A. Mrs. Benazir Bhutto;
B. Lal Krishna Advani;
C. Shyam Bhatia.

6. Abul Kalam Azad (1888-1958).
7. Jayant Narlikar.
8. George Bancroft (1800-1891).
9. William Blake (1757-1827).
10. Salman Rushdie.
11. Emily Bronte (1818-48).
12. Col. Muammar al Gaddafi (1924-2011). (He took power in a coup in 1969 and became President in 1977).
13. Sir Anthony Eden.
14. The ongoing biography of Sir Winston Churchill, coauthored by his son Randolph and the historian Martin Gilbert (both UK).
15. J.K. Rowling.
16. Krishna Chaitanya.
17. P.M. Nair.
18. *A Suitable Boy* (p. 1349) by Vikram Seth.
19. Benazir Bhutto.
20. Vladimir Nabokov (1899-1977).
21. Kumara Padmanabha Shivashankar Menon (1898-1982).
22. Ved Mehta (b. 1934).
23. Bankim Chandra Chattopadhyaya (1834-94). He is often called the 'Father of the Indian novel'.
24. Sir Winston Churchill (1874-1965).
25. Nirad C. Chaudhary (1897-1999).
26. Jonathan Swift (1667-1745).
27. Salman Rushdie (b. 1946).
28. Romain Rolland (1866-1944).
29. Dr. Sarvepalli Radhakrishnan (1888-1975).
30. Munshi Premchand (1880-1936).
31. Plato (427-347 B.C.). He was a pupil of legendary Socrates and teacher of Aristotle.
32. Lexicography.
33. Charles Lutwidge Dodgson.
34. *Man-eaters of Kumaon.*
35. Geoffery Chaucer.
36. Bibliophobia.
37. P.V. Narasimha Rao.
38. *My Music and My Life.*
39. A. *The Dream of the Red Chamber.*
    B. Cao Chan wrote 80 of the 120 chapters of the book. Following his death in 1763, Kao Eh finished it.
40. A. Ved Mehta.
    B. *Mahatma Gandhi.*
41. J.W. Von Goethe.
42. Edgar Rice Burroughs.
43. Dr. Watson.
44. Edgar Wallace (1875-1932).
45. Oscar Wilde (1854-1900).
46. A. J.J. Rousseau.
    B. Mulk Raj Anand.
    C. Thomas De Quincey.
47. A. Nirad C. Choudhuri.
    B. E.M. Forster.
48. Gulliver.
49. Fredrick Forsyth (b.1939).
50. Immanuel Kant (1724-1804).
51. Arthur Koestler (1905-83).
52. Betaal.
53. Nicholas Monsarrat.
54. Persia.
55. A. Radha Kumar.
    B. John Steinbeck.
56. Bibhuti Bhushan.
57. Jayaprakash Narayan.
58. Ernst Schumacher.
59. Aristophanes.
60. Johannes Kepler.
61. Shashi Tharoor.
62. Joseph Conrad.
63. James Boswell.
64. Vatsyayana (5th century A.D.).
65. Herbert George Wells (1866-1946).

66. Virginia Woolf (1882-1941).

67. Khwaja Ahmad Abbas.

68. Bill Gates.

69. A. Mahatma Gandhi.
B. Sarat Chandra.

70. A. Lawrence Hill.
B. Arundhati Roy.
C. Rabindranath Tagore.
D. Charles Kingsley.

71. John Acton (1834-1902).

72. Banabhatta (7th Century).

73. Giovanni Boccaccio.

74. Shakespeare.

75. Louis Braille (1809-52).

76. *Artha Shastra.*

77. Geoffrey Chaucer.

78. A. Zerbanoo Gifford.
B. Kathryn Tidrick.
C. Sonia Gandhi.

79. Christiano Ronaldo.

80. Grand Trunk Road.

81. The Mouse.

82. Exodus.

83. Zubin Mehta.

84. A. Smt. Indira Gandhi.
B. Dr. Rajendra Prasad.

85. Shashi Tharur.

86. Farid Zakaria.

87. Jhumpa Lahiri.

88. Arvind Adiga.

THE CINEMA

1. The film in which Laurel and Hardy (characters) both appeared for the first time was________.

2. Who called Caniflas the "World's greatest comedian"?

3. Which popular heroine of the silent film turned her popularity into power by co-founding United Artists along with Charlie Chaplin, Fair Banks and Griffith?

4. Name the title of first sound Mickey Mouse film?

5. Which famous cartoon character is generally regarded as the fore runner of Mickey Mouse?

6. A. Which Shakespeare play was filmed entirely in the Round House in London (1969)?
B. Name who played the leading role in the film.

7. Which term is used to describe films which are sombre in mood and portrays under-world corruption and crime?

8. Who is the first and youngest child to win an Oscar?

9. Name the lead pair (hero and heroine) in the first Hindi film (Talkie).

10. Name the only play written by Charlie Chaplin?

11. Which soccer wizard did feature in the *Escape to Victory,* with Michael Caine, Sylvester Stallone and Mav von Sydow?

12. Which film-star became the President of the United States?

13. Which film-star was the first to become the Chief Minister of Andhra Pradesh?

14. Which British actor-director's *Gandhi* won 8 Oscars?

15. The first Oscar for the Best Actress was won by ________.

16. Which film was based on Graham Green's *The Power and The Glory*?

17. Name the first film-star to appear on a postage stamp?

18. Who was the first woman film-star of India to enter into the *Rajya, Sabha*?

19. Can you name one of the great classical actors and the finest speaker of Shakespearean verse in the history of theatre, who acted even at 90?

20. Which was the first talkie film?

21. On which book the film *A Place in the Sun* is based?

22. Which Indian won a National Award for a film acting at the age of 80?

23. Name the first cinemascope film?

24. Name the first black man to win an Oscar for the Best Actor.

25. Name the play of G.B. Shaw that inspired *My Fair Lady*.

26. Under what title, Granam Greene's classic *The power and the Glory* was filmed in 1947?

27. Give the title of the first major 3D film feature.

28. Which was the first film that appeared in Cinemascope?

29. She won a special Juvenile award from the Academy on 25 February, 1935, at the age of 6 years 310 days. In 1935 itself, she became the youngest person to reach No.1 at the box office. She also became the youngest, self-made millionairess in 1938. Who was she?

30. In which 1979 film, Holmes pursued a real-life criminal?

31. Name the film in which Steven Spielberg made a guest appearance.

32. Name the first Technicolour all-talking film.

33. In how many films did Sean Connery played the character James Bond, upto and including *Never Say Never Again*?

34. For which film Marlon Brando turned down the Oscar?

35. Name the first film to win an Oscar.

36. What was the cinema's first western feature?

37. Name the comic genius who received an Honorary Oscar in 1974, when he was 83 years 182 days old—making him the oldest winner of an Honoray Oscar.

38. What was the title of the first sound Mickey Mouse film?

39. Who was the first Count Dracula on screen?

40. Give the name of the imaginary country in Charlie Chaplin's masterpiece *Great Dictator*, in which Fuerher Hynkel ruled.

41. Who gave the music for Richard Attenborough's internationally acclaimed film *Gandhi*?

42. Name the first Indian film to be nominated for an Oscar.

43. Name the institution that awards Oscars every year.

44. Name the first full length animated cartoon film in the world.

45. Name the cartoonist who created Fantoche, the first well-known cartoon figure. The inventor produced more than a hundred cartoons between 1908 and 1918.

46. When did Walt Disney make the first sound Mickey Mouse film?

47. Name the famous conductor who collaborated with Disney on the production of *Fantasia*.

48. Name the final personally produced feature cartoon.

49. What was the nickname of the 'real' Dracula?

50. Name the India's longest serving film star, who made his debut in 1936 and is noted for his films like *Achhut Kanya* and *Kismet*.

51. Name the child artist, who at 6, co-starred with Charlie Chaplin in *The Kid* and was the youngest millionaire.

52. *The China Syndrome* deals with a scientific disaster. What was that?

53. Name the first star to appear nude on the screen.

54. The only survivor at the end of *Alien* was....................

55. With which of the following film adaptations of Shakespearean plays, Laurence Olivier has not been associated?

A. *Romeo and Juliet* B. *Othello*
C. *As You Like it* D. *Macbeth*

56. Who created the cartoon character Bugs Bunny?

57. Name the film which won 11 Oscar awards in different category in 2004.

58. For the first time on the Indian screen, in which 1913 Phalke film did women apear before the camera?

59. Which science-fiction epic of James Cameroon set a new global box office record in January 2010 sinking 'Titanic' to become the biggest earning film of all time?

60. The actor who flew an F-series plain (an-F15) in *Top Gun*?

61. Which film won a score of 8 Oscar awards out of 10 nominations in 9 categories in 81st Annual Academy Awards, 2009?

62. Name the Indian music maestro who won two oscar awards in two different categories in 81 Annual Academy Awards, 2009.

63. Ben Hur was banned in China in 1930 for containing propaganda of ....

64. Who wanted to be an artist but had to work as a house painter?

65. The film in which the first screen kiss was performed?

66. Who won Best Actor Oscar Posthumously?

ANSWERS

1. Hal Roch's 45 *minutes from Hollywood.*

2. Charlie Chaplin.

3. Mary Pickford (Glady Marie Smith) (1893-1979) (Toranto).

4. *Streamboat Willie*, produced during 1928-29.

5. 'Felix, the cat'. It's animator was Pat Sullivan.

6. A. *Hamlet.*
B. Nicol Williamson played the leading role.

7. The *Film noire.*

8. Shirley Temple, at 6. (Honorary Oscar).

9. Master Bittal and Zubaida.

10. *Twelve Just Men*

11. Pele.

12. Ronald Reagon (b. 1911). (Tenure : 1981-88).

13. N.T. Rama Rao.

14. Sir Richard Attenborough (b. 1923).

15. Janet Gaynor for *Seventh Heaven*, *Sunrise and Street Angel* (1927-28).

16. The Fugitive (1947).

17. Grace Kelly (1929-1982). Following her marriage to Prince Rainier III of Monaco, a special stamp was issued in her honour at their first wedding anniversary.

18. Nargis Dutt (1929-81).

19. Sir John Gielgud (1904-2000).

20. *Jazz Singer* (1927).

21. *An American Tragedy.*

22. Premji.

23. *The Robe.*

24. Sidney Poitier (Film: *Guess Who's Coming to Dinner*).

25. *Pygmalion.*

26. *The Fugitive.*

27. *The Power of Love*, screened first in 1922. It starred Bedford and Noah Beery.

28. *The Robe.*

29. Shirley Temple (USA).

30. *Murder by Decree*. The criminal was Jack the Ripper and Holmes was played by Christopher Plummer.

31. *The Blues Brothers.*

32. *On With the Show* (1929).

33. Seven times.

34. *The Godfather.*

35. *Wings* (1927-28).

36. *The Great Train Robbery.*

37. Groucho Marx (USA). He died on 19 August, 1977.

38. *Steamboat Willie* (1928-29).

39. Bela Lugozi.

40. Tomania.

41. Pandit Ravishankar.

42. *Mother India.*

43. Academy of Motion Picture Arts and Sciences.

44. *Snow White and the Seven Dwarfs.*

45. Emile Cohn.

46. 1928-29.

47. Leopold Stokowski.

48. *The Jungle Book*, premiered in 1967.

49. Tepes (the Impaler).

50. Ashok Kumar (1911-2002).

51. Jackie Coogan.

52. The breakdown of a nuclear power station.

53. Annette Kellerman in *Daughter of the Gods* (1916).

54. Sigourney Weaver, as Ripley.

55. D.

56. Chuck Jones, with the help of other animators in his department the Warner's.

57. The Lord of the Rings : The Return of the King.

58. Mohini Bhasmasur.

59. 3D blockbuster *'Avatar'*.

60. Tom Cruise.

61. Danny Boyle's *Slumdog Millionaire.*

62. A.R. Rahman.

63. Superstitious beliefs namely Christianity.

64. Hitler.

65. The Kiss.

66. Peter Finch.

WHO SAID IT? (QUOTATIONS)

1. Which French monarch said, "A leader is a dealer in hope"?

2. Which ancient thinker said, "*Non omnia possumus omnes*— We are not all capabable to everything"?

3. Who wrote, "Accidents will occur in the best-regulated families"?

4. Whose words are these: "If a thing is worth doing it is worth doing badly"?

5. Who wrote, "You can tell the ideals of a nation by its advertisements"?

6. Whose famous words are these: "That one small step for man, but a gaint leap for mankind"?

7. Whose words are these: "I came, I saw, I conquered"?

8. Who wrote: "In heaven an angel is nobody in particular"?

9. Who wrote: "Four legs good, two legs bad"?

10. Whose words are these: "The golden rule is that there is no golden rule"?

11. Name the famous Nobel Laureate who remarked, "If everyone were to act, where would the audience be"?

12. Which American President felt that "the ballot is stronger than the bullet"?

13. Which Chinese leader said, "Let a hundred flowers bloom"?

14. Whose famous words are these: 'Do you believe in astrology?' 'I don't even believe in astronomy'?

15. Which famous scientist, after being forced to recant his doctrine that the Earth moves round the Sun, remarked, "*E pur si muove*— Yet it does move"?

16. Whose remarks are these: "The battle of Waterloo was won on the playing fields of Eton"?

17. Which English writer word's are these: "What use are catridges in battle? I always carry chocolate instead"?

18. Whose words are these: "Beauty in distress is much the most affecting beauty"?

19. "The flowers anew, returning season bring! But beauty faded has no second spring": whose words are these?

20. "The nearer the church the farther from God." Whose words are these?

21. Who made the following speech on the eve of Indian independence: "Long years ago we made a tryst with destiny, and now the time comes when we shall redeem our pledge"?

22. Whose words are these: "She knows there's success like failure. And that failure's no success at all"?

23. Who called English a "Nation of Shopkeepers"?

24. Who wrote, "The faith that stands on authority is not faith"?

25. Whose words are these: "Fame is like a river, that beareth up things light and swollen, and drowns things weighty and solid"?

26. Who said, "I awoke one morning and found myself famous"?

27. In which of his work William Shakespeare (1564-1616) wrote:

"It is a wise father that knows his own child"?

28. Name the famous Spanish writer who wrote: "Fear has many eyes and can see things underground"?

29. To whom is attributed the following sentence: "There is no terror in a bang, only in the anticipation of it"?

30. Who wrote, "The proper study of mankind is man"?

31. Who made the statement, "One man's meat is another man's poison"?

32. Name the person who made the following statement: "Man is born free, but everywhere he is in chains"?

33. Name the woman novelist whose one of the poem's lines are:

"Riches I hold in high esteem,
And Love I laugh to scorn;
And lust of fame was but a dream
That vanished with the morn".

34. Which famous poet wrote:

"Heard melodies are sweet
But those unheard are sweeter"?

35. "All the world is a stage
And all men and women merely players"
—Whose lines are these?

36. "Whom the God loves dies young".— these word are of a poet who died at the age of 39. Who was he?

37. Whose words were the: "Morality which is based on ideas or an ideal is an unmitigated evil"?

38. "Everything's got a moral, if only you can find it": who said it?

39. Name the person who wrote, "Some are born great, some achieve greatness and some have greatness thrust upon them".

40. Which scientist said, "Genius is one per cent inspiration and ninety-nine per cent perspiration"?

41. "No authority can be founded on authority, even if the authority were divine"?

42. Whose title of an essay was "Murder Considered as One of the Fine Arts"?

43. Name the person who said, "The English may not like music—but they absolutely love the noise it makes"?

44. Whose words are these: "Music says nothing to the reason: it is a kind of closely structured nonsense"?

45. Who claimed, "We are not amused"?

46. Who said, "A nickname is the heaviest stone that the devil can throw at a man"?

47. Whose words are these: "My country is the world, and my religion is to do good"?

48. Whose words are these: “The way to win an atomic war is to make certain it never starts”?

49. Which writer wrote, “Whatever was required to be done, the circumlocution office was beforehand with all the public departments in the art of perceiving— HOW NOT TO DO IT”?

50. To whom these words are attributed: “Old age is woman’s hell”?

51. “All good things which exist are the fruits of originality”: whose words are these?

52. “I am dying with the help of too many physicians”: who said this?

53. From which religious text following words are borrowed: “Wine is a mocker, strong drink is raging”?

54. Who said this about Charlie Chaplin: “I can’t once remember him still. He was always standing up as he sat down and going out as he came in”?

55. Which British Prime Minister said, “You (Hitler) do your worst, and we will do our best”?

56. Who said, “Houses are built to live in and not to look on”?

57. According to which religious book, “Haste is of the devil”?

58. Whose words are these: “Ability and necessity dwell near each other”?

59. According to whom, “History is more or less bunk”?

60. Which English author remarked, “There is a history in all men’s lives”?

61. Who said, “We are always getting ready to live, but never living”?

62. Who wrote, “Humility is the key to quick success”?

63. Name the American President who said, “The administration of justice is the firmest pillar of government”?

64. Who wrote, “Justice without generosity, may easily become Shylock’s Justice”?

65. Which Indian leader said, “A true lawyer is one who places truth and service in the first place and the emolument of the profession in the next place only”?

66. Who wrote, “Morality in Europe today is animal-morality”?

67. Which Indian Prime Minister’s words are these: “Eternal vigilance is the price of liberty”?

68. Name the author who commented, “Casting my mind’s eye over the whole of fiction, the only absolutely original creation I can think of is Don Quixote”?

69. Which famous English writer’s words are these: “It is easier to replace a dead man than a good picture”?

70. Whose words are these, that has been quoted in Aristotles’s *Nicomachean Ethics*: “Even God cannot change the past”?

71. Whose words are these:"Tell me what you eat: I will tell you what you are"?

72. What is the source of following sentence: "Even your best friends won't tell you"?

73. From which religious text, following sentence has been quoted : "A faithful friend is the medicine of life"?

74. Name the writer whose words follow:"I have lost friends, some by death.........others through sheer inability to cross the street."

75. Who wrote, "The only reason people want to be masters of the future is to change the past"?

76. Who wrote, "If there were two birds sitting on a fence, he would bet you which one would fly first"?

77. Which famous author wrote, "Men are as chancy as children in their choice of playthings"?

78. Who asked, "What is a weed?" and then answered himself by saying, "A plant whose virtues have not yet been discovered"?

79. Who said, "Let a hundred flowers bloom and let a thousand school of thought contend."

80. Which famous personality's words are: "Civilization has made the peasantry its pack animal"?

81. Who said, " Do not judge, and you will never be mistaken"?

82. Name the Indian who said, "Every village has to become a self-sufficient republic"?

83. Which American President said, "Freedom to learn is the first necessity of guaranteeing that man himself shall be self-reliant enough to be free"?

84. Which English poet said, "Half of the harm that is done in this world is due to people who want to feel important"?

85. Which British Prime Minister said, "I am eager to learn, but I am not prepared to be taught"?

86. Name the Russian writer, whose words follow: "I can't understand how anyone can write without rewriting everything over and over again. I scarcely ever re-read my writing, but if by chance I come across a page, it always strikes me. All this must be re-written; this is how I should have written."

87. Which Nobel winning physicist said, "I do not believe in the God of theology who rewards good and punishes evil"?

88. Whose words are there, "Reading maketh a full man; conference a ready man: and writing an exact man."

89. Whose words are these, "Eli, Eli, Lamma Sabcathani (My God, my God, why last there forsaken me)."

90. Which 20th century scientist's words are these:" It is more difficult to disintegrate a prejudice than an atom"?

91. "Machinery has its place, it has come to stay. But it must not be allowed to displace necessary human labour."—who said it?

92. Which American President said, "Ask not what your country can do for you, but what you can do for your country"?

93. Name the great personality who said,"I have nothing to offer, but blood, toil, tears and sweat"?

94. Who said,"Men are cruel, but man is kind"?

95. Which American President's words are these:"No matter how much cats fight, there always seem to be plenty of kittens"?

ANSWERS

1. Nepolean.
2. Virgil (70-19 B.C.).
3. Charles Dickens (1812-70) (*David Copperfield*).
4. G.K. Chesterton (1874-1936).
5. Norman Douglas (1868-1952).
6. Neil Armstrong (b. 1930), while setting foot on the moon, (Apollo XI mission) on 21 July 1969.
7. Julius Caesar (102-44 B.C.)
8. George Bernard Shaw (1856-1950).
9. George Orwell (1903-50), in *Animal Farm*.
10. Bernard Shaw, *Maxims of Revolutionists*.
11. Rabindranath Tagore.
12. Abraham Lincoln.
13. Mao Tse-Tung.
14. Peter de Vries (1910-93).
15. Galileo Galilei (1564-1642).
16. Duke of Wellington (1769-1852).
17. George Bernard Shaw.
18. Edmund Burke (1729-97).
19. Ambrose Philips (c. 1674-1749).
20. Lancelot Andrewes (1565-1626).

21. Jawaharlal Nehru (1889-1964).
22. Bob Dylon (b. 1941, song: love minus zero/ no limit)
23. Nepolean Bonaparte.
24. Ralph Waldo Emerson (1803-82).
25. Francis Bacon (1561-1626).
26. Lord Byron (1788-1824), on instantaneous success of *Childe Harold*.
27. *The Merchant of Venice*.
28. Miguel Cervantes (1547-1616), in *Don Quixote*.
29. Alfred Hitchcock (1899-1980).
30. Alexander Pope.
31. Hippocrates.
32. Jean Jacques Rousseau.
33. Emily Bronte.
34. John Keats.
35. Shakespeare (in *As You Like It*).
36. Lord Byron.
37. D.H. Lawrence (1885-1930).
38. Lewis Carroll (1832-98).
39. William Shakespeare.
40. Thomas Edison.
41. A.J. Ayer (1910-89).
42. Thomas de Quincey (1785-1859).
43. Sir Thomas Beecham.
44. Anthony Burgess (1917-93).
45. Queen Victoria.
46. William Hazlitt (1778-1830).
47. Thomas Paine (1737-1809).
48. General Omar Bradley (1893-1980).
49. Charles Dickens (1812-70).
50. Ninon de Lenclos (1620-1705).
51. John Stuart Mill (1806-73).
52. Alexander the Great (356-323 B.C.).
53. The *Bible*.
54. Louis Brooks (1908-85).
55. Winston Churchill (1874-1965).
56. Francis Bacon (1561-1626).
57. The *Koran*.
58. Pythagorus.
59. Henry Ford (1863-1947).
60. William Shakespeare (1564-1616).
61. Ralph Waldo Emerson (1803-82).
62. Mahatma Gandhi.
63. George Washington.
64. Mahatma Gandhi.
65. Mahatma Gandhi.
66. Friedrich Nietzsche (1844-1900).
67. Jawaharlal Nehru.
68. W. Somerset Maugham (1874-1965).
69. George Bernard Shaw (1856-1950).
70. Agathon (447?-401 B.C.).
71. Jean Anthelme Brillat-Savarin (1775-1826).
72. Advertisement for Listerine mouthwash, 1920s.
73. The *Bible*.
74. Virginia Woolf (1882-1941)
75. Milan Kundera (1929) in *The Book of Laughter and Forgetting*.
76. Mark Twain (1835-1910), in *The Celebrated Jumping Frog*.
77. Rudyard Kipling (1865-1936) in *Kim*.
78. Ralph Waldo Emerson (1803-82) in *Fortune of the Republic*.
79. Mao-Tse-tung
80. Leon Trotsky.
81. Rousseau.
82. Mahatma Gandhi.
83. Franklin D. Roosevelt.
84. T.S. Eliot (1888-1965).
85. Winston Churchill (1874-1965), British Prime Minister (1940-45 and 1951-55).
86. Leo Tolstoy (1828-1910).
87. Albert Einstein (1879-1955).
88. Francis Bacon
89. Jesus Christ at the cross.

90. Albert Einstein.

91. Mahatma Gandhi.

92. John Fitzgerald Kennedy (1917-63), 35th U.S. President (1961-63).

93. Winston Churchill.

94. Rabindranath Tagore (1861-1941).

95. Abraham Lincoln (1809-65), sixteenth President of the USA (1861).

PROVERBS

1. What is that makes 'most noise'?
2. Fill up the blanks:
   A. Better pay up the butcher than the ———————.
   B. A tale twice told is cabbage ——— sold.
3. The bare foot is better than ———.
4. Who according to Clarke "best loved furthest off"?
5. What would you require to kill a butterfly?
6. A cat has how many lives?
7. As the saying goes, "If you go to Rome, what are you advised to do?"
8. "Look before you leap"—What does that mean?
9. Complete the following : "Man proposes ———".
10. What is a great promoter of admiration?
11. Who said the following : "Do not quarrel with your bread and butter"?
12. What is required to be healthy, wealthy and wise?
13. Fill up the blanks :
    A. Envy and wrath shorten ———.
    B. Envy is ———.
    C. Envy is more implacable than ———.
14. Complete the following Hindi proverb:
    Do not try to save the world
    ————————————.
15. Do your best
    And leave the rest——to whom?
16. He who knows others is learned;
    He who knows himself is———.
17. Who is the one who is soon parted with from his money?
18. Who die young?
19. Whom would you attribute the following words:" It is an ill air where we get nothing"?
20. What is its own reward?
21. You should not wash your dirty linens in ———.
22. Without what "Learning is labour lost"?
23. What is meant by, "Least said soonest mended"?
24. If someone is lucky at cards, when will he be unlucky?
25. No one is rich enough to do without a ————.
26. No pillow is as soft as a ———— .
27. What should never be dated?
28. What is after the darkest hour?
29. Who should not throw stones at someone's house?
30. What one should strike when it is hot?
31. Put the appropriate name of animal in the following blank:
    "Trust in God, but tie your ————."
32. What is that maketh a ready man?
33. What one should not put in one basket?
34. When one is in the greatest in danger?
35. What is the meaning of the following: "Old birds are not caught with chaff"?
36. What was not built in a day?

37. For what, no one should be punished twice?
38. Once in........................., always in debt. (Fill up the blank.).
39. Something old is like........................
40. Once bitten,...............shy. (Fill up the blank.)
41. Who can not be choosers?
42. Blessed is the man who finds wisdom as well as........................
43. According to a chinese proverb, what never come in pairs, and what never come alone?
44. What is not much better than begging?
45. What takes no other hue?
46. According to a Latin saying, beware of whom bearing gifts?
47. Blue eyes say," Love me or I die." But what do the black eyes say?
48. If one is lucky at cards, when will he be unlucky?
49. If a good archer is not known by his arrows, then he is known for what?
50. A man apt to promise, is apt to........................
51. "A man of.........................begs his bread on Sundays." (Fill up the blank.)
52. When do you say," Billy has found a pin"?
53. Whose word is as good as his bond?
54. Beauty without what avails nought?
55. What do you mean by, "Looking from under Brent Hill"?
56. What is the soul of wit?
57. What does, 'Booked for Bucknall' mean?
58. What is Brough Hill weather?
59. In which sea, every man is a pilot?
60. The chain is no stronger than its ....
61. What that melts the wax will harden the clay?
62. Coffee should be black as............, strong as............, and sweet as........... (Fill up the blanks.)
63. Along with love, which common ailment can not be hidden?
64. What is a tyrant that's always attended with fear?
65. What is bad farming?
66. What is the darkest hour?
67. What is Davie Debet?
68. What type of dealing is praised more than practised?
69. What cures more than doctors?
70. What is the mother of good luck (success)?
71. Who is Doctor Dodipoll?
72. Who will make a doctor his heir?
73. A new broom is good for how many days?
74. What proves the rule?
75. One eye-witness is better than how many ear-witnesses?
76. What are pillars of suçcess?
77. The coin that is most current among us is........................
78. "A good hay year a bad fog year." What does the word "fog" here mean?
79. What between keeps friendship green?
80. What is Hobson's choice?
81. What are green afar off?
82. About whom is said, "As hollow as a key"?
83. Without what, knowledge is like light without warmth?
84. The better workman, the worse........................
85. Whose advice should you write down, though you like it not at present?
86. What is a pleasure in young man, but a fault in an old?
87. Who:
    A. makes proverbs, and
    B. (Who) repeat them?
88. What is the best policy?
89. Whom do the hounds and horses devour?
90. When men will let you abuse them?
91. Why I believe it?
92. Who is the devil's cushion (or playfellow)?

93. What is a voluntary misfortune as well as the mother of devotion?

94. What is the mother of invention?

95. If Jack's in love, he's no judge of whose beauty?

96. Jack of all trades and master of..........................

97. What should you be before you are generous?

98. "To keep the band in the nick".—What does this mean?

99. "He who handles a nettle tenderly is soonest stung". What is the meaning of the proverb?

100. Who said: "The who has a thousand friends has not a friend to spare. And he who has one enemy shall meet him everywhere"?

ANSWERS

1. Empty vessel.
2. A. Doctor.
   B. Twice.
3. None.
4. The Men.
5. A musket.
6. Nine.
7. Do as Romans do.
8. It means, 'think before acting'.
9. God disposes.
10. Distance.
11. Swift.
12. Go early to bed and be early to rise.
13. A. Life.
    B. Blind.
    C. Hatred.
14. Save yourself for the world.
15. To God.
16. Wise.
17. A fool.
18. Those whom the God love.
19. Herbert (1640).
20. Virtue.
21. Public.
22. Thought.
23. It means that the best method to stop a quarrel is to stop discussing the current topic.
24. In love.
25. Neighbour.
26. Clear conscience.
27. Women and music.
28. The dawn.
29. People who live in glass houses.
30. Iron.
31. Camel.
32. Conference.
33. All the eggs.
34. When one thinks himself to be the safest.
35. It means that 'Experienced men are difficult to deceive'.
36. Rome.
37. One crime.
38. Debt.
39. Gold. (Old is gold).
40. Twice.
41. Beggars.
42. Wealth.
43. Blessings (not in pairs), misfortune (never alone).
44. Borrowing.
45. Black.
46. Greeks.
47. "Love me or I kill thee."
48. In love.
49. His aim.
50. Forget.
51. Many trades.

52. Said, when a man makes a great stir about a matter and it ends in nothing that is significant.

53. A honest man's word.

54. Bounty.

55. It is said of a sullen, frowning person in an ill humour. Brent Hill indicates the eyebrows.

56. Brevity.

57. Going to be married.

58. It's stormy weather, which often occurs at fair time.

59. Calm sea.

60. Weakest link.

61. (The same) Heat.

62. Hell, death, love.

63. Cough.

64. Cruelty.

65. Cursing the weather.

66. Before the dawn.

67. Debt personified or a bailiff.

68. Plain dealing.

69. Diet.

70. Diligence.

71. Doctor Dodipoll is a proverbial name for a simpleton.

72. Only a fool.

73. Three days.

74. Exception.

75. Ten.

76. Failures.

77. Flattery.

78. The aftermath.

79. A hedge.

80. No choice at all.

81. Hills.

82. Said of a deceitful man.

83. Zeal.

84. Husband.

85. The advice of him who loves you.

86. To woo.

87. A. Wise men.
B. Fools.

88. Honesty.

89. Their masters.

90. If only you will make them laugh.

91. Because it is absurd; because it is impossible.

92. An idle person.

93. Ignorance.

94. Necessity.

95. Jill's beauty.

96. None.

97. Be just.

98. To make things meet.

99. The proverb means that 'one dealing with mentally crooked people should avoid the use of humane methods'.

100. Emerson.

MISCELLENEOUS

1. Who is regarded as the King of the Gods in Roman mythology?
2. Name the winged horse of the Gods.
3. According to the Greek mythology, who was the first ruler of the world?
4. According to the Greek mythology, who were the nine Muses?
5. According to the Roman mythology, who was the Great Earth Mother?
6. Who was the Sun God in the Roman mythology?
7. Who was the Goddess of love in the Greek mythology?
8. Who was the Greek God of the Sea?

9. According to the Greek mythology, who was the ruler of the winds?
10. Who is the Greek Goddess of Wisdom?
11. Name the legendary Greek craftsman who along with his son Icarus tried to escape from captivity on wings.
12. The owl is associated with which Greek God?
13. Which was the mountain home of Jupiter?
14. What was the name of the ferryman in the Greek mythology, who rowed the dead over the river Styx to Hadés?
15. Who was the Greek Messenger of the Gods?
16. The character corresponding to Hercules of Greek mythology in the Roman mythology is called_________.
17. According to the *Bible*, who is the 'Prince of Peace'?
18. Prince of Darkness is another name for...................
19. What do you call the Jewish holiday in February or March to commemorate the deliverance of the Jews from the massacre planned by Haman?
20. What is Reynard or Renard?
21. Name the legendary Greek king of Corinth who was condemned in the underworld eternally to roll a boulder to the top of a hill, from where it always rolled down.
22. Who was the Greek God of the sea?
23. Mars is associated with which mythology?
24. Which famous character in Greek mythology died from an arrow in the heel?
25. What was the mountain home of Zeus?
26. In the *Bible,* who lived till the age of 969, and is said to have been the oldest person who ever lived?
27. In Greek mythology, which Trojan princess was cursed with a gift of prophecy than no one would believe?
28. In Greek mythology, which goddess sprang from chaos and became the mother of all things?
29. In which book of Old Testament were the Ten commandments first listed?
30. Which narcotic is named after the Greek god of sleep and dreams?
31. In Greek mythology, which seven daughters of Atlas, when pursued by Orion, were turned into stars?
32. Who is supposed to be the most prolific painter of the world?
33. *Mona Lisa is* the creation of which celebrated artist?
34. Which work of Michelangelo is a representation of Mary with the dead Christ across her knees?
35. What was the greatest work of Michelangelo in painting?
36. Which painter's work is 'The Fall of Man'?
37. Which is the world's heaviest statue?
38. Which is the world's tallest statue?
39. Name the well known Indian artist, who made a film titled 'Gajagamini'.
40. Which Italian artist's work is *The Last Judgement*?
41. What was the nationality of Picasso?
42. Where would you find the largest art gallery?
43. The famous "Unfinished Symphony" was written by.........
44. Michael Jackson's autobiography "Moonwalk" is dedicated to.......
45. Where would you find *The Statue of the Little Mermaid*?
46. Who painted the famous painting 'Creation of Adam'?
47. What do you call a vessel used in sea for trips as well as racing?
48. Which word or phrase is nearest in meaning to 'Atavistic'?
49. What is Spelology?
50. What is Vexillology?
51. What is a 'Biological Clock'?

52. What do you call a lyric poem, lofty in feeling and style and usually in the form of an address?

53. Who is indifferent to pleasure or pain, having austere impassivity and limited wants?

54. What is a 'Fable'?

55. Which type of writing holds upto ridicule the vices and follies of its age?

56. What is 'Byte', in computer terminology?

57. What do you call the organized collection of information stored on a magnetic disk or other direct-access storage device?

58. What is 'Operating System' in computer terminology?

59. What term is used when a king, queen or somebody renounces the office by choice?

60. What term is used for universities and schools by their past and present pupil?

61. What do you call an annual calendar of months and days, usually with astronomical data and other information?

62. Which term is used for the organic life on the Earth comprising living material and dead objects?

63. Which substance nullifies the effect of poison?

64. Which chemical destroys germs?

65. Which type of medicine relieves pain?

66. Which branch of army manages guns mounted on carriages?

67. In which old system of trade one commodity is exchanges for another?

68. What is Chauvinism?

69. What do you call the Chamber of pilot and co-pilot in an aeroplane?

70. What do you call an inscription on a tomb or monument?

71. The animals are collectively called——————.

72. What is a Freeport?

73. What is described as the Fourth Estate?

74. What are carcinogens?

75. What is a Personal Computer?

76. What do you call the physical parts of a computer system?

77. The part of a computer that stores information is called————.

78. Which term is used to describe biosterous way of expressing patriotism?

79. If technical or area-specific words are used in talk, it is called————.

80. What is Lampooning?

81. What is Melodrama?

82. Which term is used for a person traitor to his motherland?

83. What term is used for an act of stealing the writing or creative work of others?

84. What does 'vaccine' mean?

85. What is Acrophobia?

86. Who is a Vagabond?

87. Who is a 'Vacuous'?

88. What is Cibophobia?

89. Which Russian term brought in use by Gorbachev, implies the restructuring of the system to increase productivity?

90. The annual financial statement of the government is also known as————.

91. Optics is the study of————.

92. Acoustics is the study of————.

93. What is an Oasis?

94. What is an Affidavit?

95. What is Xenophobia?

96. What is the term for the fear of sexual abuse?

97. What was the ancient Science of Buildings called?

98. Whom do misogynists hate?

99. What do you call the funel-shaped clouds with violent whirlwinds?

100. What are Tusks?

101. A group of foxes is called————.

102. What does the term Caligynephobia mean?

103. What is the legal term for the complainant, the one that brings the matter to the notice of court?

104. Under what arrangement complaints and grievances are heard by a neutral person or agency to give impartial judgement?

105. By what popular name, a declaration of intention, programmes and policies to be followed by a political party before elections, is known?

106. What is Franchise?

107. By what popular name, a small bomb or explosive, usually thrown by hand, is known?

108. By which process a criminal or accused is handed over by one country to the other to face legal action?

109. Which imaginary line round the Earth divides it into two equal parts, the northern and southern hemisphere?

110. What is a decree?

111. What do you call a consignment of goods forbidden to be imported or traded, without government's approval?

112. It is a motion by a member in a legislature to draw attention of the executive to a matter of urgent public importance. Name it?

113. What was *Magna Carta*?

114. What is a hurricane?

115. What do you call a region of low rainfall and low productivity?

116. Give the term for the number of individuals per unit area?

117. What is Demography?

118. Who is an ecologist?

119. Which term is applied to those who are anti-Jewish in their outlook?

120. At the end of invitation letters, you find the letters "R.S.V.P.". What do they mean?

121. Washington D.C. is the capital of America. But what does D.C. stand for?

122. What does the A.T.M. stand for in banking?

123. What does VIRUS stand for?

124. What is the full name of SMS?

125. What does the AIDS stand for?

ANSWERS

1. Jupiter.

2. Pegasus.

3. P'an-ku.

4. The nine Muses were the daughters of Zeus and Memory. Presiding over one of the arts, their names were : Clio, Euterpe, Thalia, Melpomene, Terpischore, Erato, Polyhymnia, Urania and Calliope.

5. Juno.

6. Apollo.

7. Aphrodite.

8. Poseidon.

9. Aedus.

10. Athena.

11. Daedalus. Icarus is said to have flew too near the Sun and the wax holding his wings together melted. He fell into the sea and was drowned. However, his father (Daedalus) managed to reach to safety.

12. Athena, the Greek Goddess of Wisdom.

13. Mount Parnassus.

14. Charon.

15. Hermes.

16. Heracles.

17. The future Messiah, held by most christians to be Christ.

18. Satan.

19. *Purim.*

20. A name for fox, used in fables, etc.

21. Sisyphus.

22. Poseidon.

23. Roman.

24. Achilles.

25. Mount Olympus.

26. Methuselah.

27. Cassandra.

28. Gaia.

29. Exodus.

30. Morphine.

31. Pleiades.

32. Pablo Ruiz Picasso (1881-1973) (Spain). His full name : Pablo Diego Jose Francisco de Paula Juan Nepomuceno de los Remedios Crispin Cipriano de la Santisima Trinidad Ruiz y Picasso.

33. Leonardo da Vinci. **34.** *Pieta*.

35. Decoration of the ceiling of the Sistine Chapel in Vatican.

36. Michelangelo.

37. The Statue of Liberty (USA). It weighs 24,635 tonnes.

38. The Statue of Buddha (in bronze), Tokyo (Japan). It's 394ft. (120m) high and 115ft (35m) wide.

39. Maqbool Fida Hussain (1915-2011).

40. Michelangelo. **41.** Spanish.

42. In the Winter palace at the state hermitage museum, St. Petersburg, Russia. It's 322 galleries contain nearly three million works of art and objects of archaeological interest.

43. Schubert. **44.** Fred Astaire.

45. Copenhagen. **46.** Michaelangelo.

47. Yacht.

48. Primitive characteristic.

49. Spelology is the study of caves.

50. Vexillology is the study of flags.

51. The rhythmic occurence of processes within organisms at periodic intervals.

52. Ode. **53.** A Stoic person.

54. A brief story constructed to bring out a lesson or moral.

55. A Satire. (Example: Bernand Shaw's *Arms and the Man,* a satire on war).

56. Byte is a group of bits (binary digits, which may be either the digit 0 to 1) that act as a single unit of information, such as a letter or numeral.

57. Database.

58. Operating system is a type of software that controls the operation of a computer system.

59. Abdication. **60.** *Alma Mater*.

61. Almanac. **62.** Biosphere.

63. Antidote. **64.** Antiseptic.

65. Analgesic. **66.** Artillery.

67. Barter System.

68. Chauvinism is a term applied to any excessive devotion to cause, particularly a patriotic or military one.

69. Cockpit. **70.** Epitaph.

71. Fauna.

72. It is a port which is exempted from custom duties and regulation.

73. Press.

74. Cancer-inducing substances.

75. Personal computer is a desktop or handheld computer designed for general purpose use.

76. Hardware. **77.** Memory.

78. Jingoism. **79.** Jargon.

80. It is a phenomenon of writing satire against a person.

81. It is a drama that appeals to emotions.

82. Quisling. **83.** Plagiarism.

84. The word 'vaccine' has been derived from Latin word 'vacca' meaning cow. It's a suspension of dead attenuated, or otherwise modified micro organisms for inoculation to produce immunity to a disease by stimulating the production of antibodies.

85. Fear of height.

86. A person with no fixed home.

87. One who is bereft of ideas or intelligence.

88. Fear of food. **89.** *Perestroika*.

90. The Budget. **91.** Light.

92. Sound.

93. A part of the desert where water and vegetation are found.

94. It's written or printed statement of facts sworn to or affirmed before a notary public or any other person qualified to administer an oath.

95. Fear of strangers. **96.** Contreltophobia.

97. *Vastushastra.* **98.** Women.

99. Tornado. It whirls with great velocity and does great damage over a small area.

100. Tusks are a pair of very long pointed teeth (incisors)— that project from the mouth of certain animals, e.g., Elephant, Walrus and Wild boar.

101. A skulk.

102. Fear of beautiful women.

103. Plaintiff.

104. Ombudsman. In India, *Lokpal* and *Lokayuktas* are equivalent to Ombudsman.

105. Manifesto.

106. It's the right to vote.

107. Hand Grenade.

108. Extradition.

109. Equator.

110. It is the decision of a court or arbitrator.

111. Contraband.

112. Adjournment Motion.

113. The *Magna Carta* was a Charter of Rights granted to the English people in A.D. 1215 by King John II.

114. A hurricane is a storm with violent wind, thunder and lightning.

115. Desert. **116.** Density.

117. The mathematical study of populations.

118. The one who studies ecology.

119. Anti-semitism.

120. "Respondez S'il vous plaft" or Please answer.

121. District of Columbia.

122. Automatic Teller Machine.

123. Vital Information Resources Under Siege.

124. Short Message Service.

125. Acquired Immuno-Deficiency Syndrome.

❑❑❑

English

1 Spelling Errors

The most common errors in English are of spellings of words. Even the most learned men are sometimes confused about the correct spellings of some words. One must keep and use a dictionary religiously. Never ignore and let pass a new word casually.

A number of question to test your knowledge of spellings are compiled here. Try to solve as many as you can.

Multiple Choice Questions

Directions: *Find the correctly spelt word out of the four options in each question.*

1. A. Accompalish B. Ackmplesh C. Acomplush D. Accomplish
2. A. Acommodation B. Acomodation C. Accomodation D. Accommodation
3. A. Astonished B. Astronished C. Astoneshed D. Asstonished
4. A. Benefeted B. Benefitted C. Benifited D. Benefited
5. A. Belligerent B. Beligirent C. Belligarant D. Belligerrent
6. A. Chancelery B. Chancellery C. Chancellary D. Chancelary
7. A. Discriminate B. Discremineta C. Discremenate D. Discriminat
8. A. Damage B. Dammage C. Damaige D. Dammege
9. A. Efficiant B. Effécient C. Efficient D. Eficient
10. A. Extravagant B. Extreragent C. Extreregant D. Extravegent
11. A. Efflorascence B. Eflorescene C. Effllorescence D. Efflorescence
12. A. Equinimity B. Equanimmity C. Equannimity D. Equanimity
13. A. Farmament B. Farmement C. Fermament D. Fremament
14. A. Grieff B. Grief C. Grieef D. Grrief
15. A. Guarantee B. Garuntee C. Guaruntee D. Gaurantee
16. A. Hypocritical B. Hypocretical C. Hypocriticel D. Hypocirticel
17. A. Humurous B. Humorous C. Humoreus D. Humorrous
18. A. Itenerary B. Itinarery C. Itinarary D. Itinerary
19. A. Indipenseble B. Indispansible C. Indispensable D. Indipensable

20. A. Imprecticability B. Impracticebility C. Impracticibility D. Impracticability

21. A. Incradulous B. Incredulous C. Incridulous D. Incredalous

22. A. Juddicious B. Judiceous C. Judicious D. Judiceus

23. A. Kleptomonia B. Kleptemonia C. Kleptomania D. Klaptomania

24. A. Lackdaisical B. Lackadaisical C. Lckadaisicle D. Lackadisical

25. A. Licentious B. Licontious C. Licenttious D. Licientious

26. A. Meddicine B. Medicine C. Medicene D. Medicinne

27. A. Meritricious B. Merefrecious C. Meretricious D. Merritricious

28. A. Missunderstood B. Miesunderstood C. Misunderstood D. Misunderstod

29. A. Occurad B. Occurred C. Ocurred D. Occured

30. A. Osttentatious B. Ostentetious C. Ostentatious D. Ostenttatious

31. A. Obnosious B. Obnoxeous C. Obnoxious D. Obnoseous

32. A. Omenous B. Ominous C. Ommineous D. Omineous

33. A. Pecification B. Pacification C. Pecifacation D. Pecefication

34. A. Prograssive B. Progressive C. Progresive D. Prograsive

35. A. Pasiveness B. Passiveness C. Passeveniss D. Passivines

36. A. Polyendry B. Poliendry C. Pollyendry D. Polyandry

37. A. Puerille B. Puerrile C. Puerile D. Purrile

38. A. Pesanger B. Passenger C. Pessenger D. Pasanger

39. A. Querrelsome B. Quarrelsame C. Quarrelsome D. Querralsome

40. A. Rigourous B. Rigerous C. Rigorous D. Regerous

41. A. Survellance B. Surveilance C. Surveillance D. Survaillance

42. A. Schedule B. Schdule C. Schedale D. Schedeule

43. A. Sepalchrle B. Sepalchral C. Sepulchrle D. Sepulchral

44. A. Sympathetic B. Smypathetic C. Sympothetic. D. Sympethetic

45. A. Sincerely B. Sencerely C. Sincerelly D. Sincerrely

46. A. Satellite B. Sattellite C. Satelite D. Sattelite

47. A. Teracherous B. Treacherous C. Treacheraus D. Treachereans

48. A. Uncivilized B. Uncevilized C. Uncivillized D. Uncevelized

49. A. Vainglorious B. Vaniglorious C. Vaniglerious D. Vaingloreus

50. A. Vulnarable B. Valnerable C. Velnerable D. Vulnerable

ANSWERS

1	2	3	4	5	6	7	8	9	10
D	D	A	B	A	C	A	A	C	A
11	12	13	14	15	16	17	18	19	20
D	D	C	B	A	A	B	D	C	D
21	22	23	24	25	26	27	28	29	30
B	C	C	B	A	B	C	C	B	C
31	32	33	34	35	36	37	38	39	40
C	B	B	B	B	D	C	B	C	C
41	42	43	44	45	46	47	48	49	50
C	A	D	A	A	A	B	A	A	D

2 Spotting Errors

The most common errors in English are of spellings, grammar and usage of words. By regular practice, the errors can be easily spotted and minimised.

Common Errors with Nouns and Noun-Phrases

Incorrect	Correct
1. I have bought new *furnitures.*	I have bought new *furniture.*
2. The wages of sin *are* death.	The wages of sin *is* death.
3. She told these *news* to her mother.	She told her mother this *news.*
4. He took *troubles* to do his work.	He took *trouble* (or pains) over his work.
5. The *cattles* were grazing.	The *cattle* were grazing.
6. He showered *many abuses* on me.	He showered *much abuse* on me.
7. I spent the holidays with my *family members.*	I spent the holidays with my *family.*
8. There is no *place* in this compartment.	There is no *room* in this compartment.
9. Write this new *poetry* in your *copy.*	Write this new *poem* in your *note-book.*
10. He took *insult* at this.	He took *offence* at this.
11. Put your *sign* here.	Put your *signatures* here.
12. She is my *cousin sister.*	She is my *cousin.*
13. *Sunil's* my *neighbour's* house was burgled.	*Sunil* my *neighbour's* house was burgled.
14. I lost a *ten-rupees* note.	I lost *a ten-rupee* note.
15. Road closed for *repair.*	Road closed for *repairs.*
16. His house is out of *repairs.*	His house is out of *repair.*
17. What is the *reason* of an earthquake?	What is the *cause* of an earthquake?
18. This building is made of *stones.*	This building is made of *stone.*
19. I disapprove of *these kinds* of games.	I disapprove of *this kind* of games.
20. Veena's and Sheela's father is ill.	Veena and Sheela's father is ill.
21. His *son-in-laws* are doctors.	His *sons-in-law* are doctors.
22. *Alms* is given to the *poor.*	*Alms* are given to the poor.
23. He always keeps his words.	He always keeps his *word.*
24. I carried the *luggages.*	I carried the *luggage.*
25. *Two-third* of the work is left.	*Two-thirds* of the work is left.

Common Errors with Pronouns

Incorrect	Correct
1. Both did not go.	Neither went.
2. We all did not go.	None of us went.
3. Each of these boys play.	Each of these boys plays.
4. Whoever does best he will get a prize.	Whoever does best will get a prize.
5. One should not waste his time.	A man should not waste his time.
6. I and she are sisters.	She and I are sisters.
7. He is wiser than me.	He is wiser than I.
8. Between you and I, Anil is not to be trusted.	Between you and me, Anil is not to be trusted.
9. Nobody was there but I.	Nobody was there but me.
10. Who is there ? It is me.	Who is there ? It is I.
11. Only he and me can use this card.	Only he and I can use this card.
12. Let you and I go now.	Let you and me go now.
13. Everyone got one's pay.	Everyone got his pay.
14. Everyone is frightened when they see a tiger.	Everyone is frightened when he sees a tiger.
15. These two friends are fond of one another.	These two friends are fond of each other.
16. I did not like him coming at that hour.	I did not like his coming at that hour.
17. Who do you think I met?	Whom do you think I met?
18. You should avail this opportunity.	You should avail yourself this opportunity.
19. When you have read these books, please return the same to me.	When you have read the books, please return them to me.
20. They that are humble need fear no fall.	Those that are humble need fear no fall.

Common Errors with Adjectives

Incorrect	Correct
1. These all oranges are good.	All these oranges are good.
2. He held the book in the both hands.	He held the book in both hands.
3. Both men have not come.	Neither man has come.
4. That man should do some or other work.	That man should do some work or other.
5. He is elder than I.	He is older than I.
6. Shakespeare is greater than any other poets.	Shakespeare is greater than any other poet.
7. He is a coward man.	He is a cowardly man.
8. Many villagers cannot write his own name.	Many villagers cannot write their own name.
9. Each of us loves our home.	Each of us loves his home.
10. Much efforts bring their reward.	Much effort brings its reward.
11. He found hundred rupees.	He found a hundred rupees.
12. He had leave of four days.	He had four days leave.

Incorrect	Correct
13. This is a worth seeing sight.	This is a sight worth seeing.
14. He will spend his future life here.	He will spend the rest of his life here.
15. There is a best teacher in that class.	There is a very good teacher in that class.
16. Of the two plans this is the best.	Of the two plans this is the better.
17. He is becoming strong every day.	He is becoming stronger every day.
18. He is worst than I.	He is worse than I.
19. Jaipur is hot than Delhi.	Jaipur is hotter than Delhi.
20. In our library the number of books is less.	In our library the number of books is small.

Common Errors with Verbs

Incorrect	Correct
1. He asked had we taken our luggage.	He asked if we had taken our luggage.
2. She asked what are you doing.	She asked what we were doing.
3. Rama asked to Anil why he is angry.	Rama asked Anil why he was angry.
4. He does not care for his money.	He does not take care of his money.
5. He does not care for his work.	He takes no care over his work.
6. No one cared for him after his mother died.	No one took care of him after his mother died.
7. He got angry before I said a word.	He got angry before I had said a word.
8. I met a man who was my tutor 20 years ago.	I met a man who had been my tutor twenty years ago.
9. I had been for walking yesterday.	I went for a walk yesterday.
10. If I shall do this I shall be wrong.	If I do this I shall be wrong.
11. I have left trekking.	I have given up trekking.
12. I came to know as to how he did this.	I learnt how he did this.
13. I came to know why he was sad.	I found out why he was sad.
14. He knows to swim.	He knows how to swim.
15. The criminal's head was cut.	The criminal's head was cut off.
16. I said to him to go.	I told him to go.
17. I told the teacher to excuse me.	I asked the teacher to excuse me.
18. He is troubling me.	He is giving me trouble.
19. I have got a hurt on my leg.	I have hurt my leg.
20. She gave a speech.	She made a speech.

Common Errors in Subject-Verb Agreement

Incorrect	Correct
1. The owners of this factory *is* very rich.	The owners of this factory *are* very rich.
2. The pleasures of nature that one can experience at Shimla *is* beyond description.	The pleasures of nature that one can experience at Shimla *are* beyond description.

Incorrect	Correct
3. There *is* no street lights in our colony.	There *are* no street lights in our colony.
4. He and I *am* entrusted with the job.	He and I *are* entrusted with the job.
5. Rice and curry *are* his favourite dish.	Rice and curry *is* his favourite dish.
6. The honour and glory of our country *are* at stake.	The honour and glory of our country *is* at stake.
7. Time and tide *waits* for none.	Time and tide *wait* for none.
8. All the passengers with the driver *was* killed.	All the passengers, with the driver, *were* killed.
9. The teacher, with her students, *were* going out.	The teacher, with her students, *was* going out.
10. I as well as they *am* tired.	I as well as they *are* tired.
11. Not only the soldiers but their captain also *were* captured.	Not only the soldiers but their captain also *was* captured.
12. Neither you nor I *were* selected.	Neither you nor I *was* selected.
13. Either of these two applicants *are* fit for the job but neither want to accept it.	Either of these two applicants *is* fit for the job but neither wants to accept it.
14. One of these students are sure to stand first.	One of these students *is* sure to stand first.
15. Everyone of these workers want a raise.	Everyone of these workers wants a raise.
16. None of these letters has been answered so far.	None of these letters *have* been answered so far.
17. None of the girls were present at the party.	None of the girls *was* present at the party.
18. Many a battle were fought on Indian soil.	Many a battle *was* fought on Indian soil.
19. A lot of work remain to be done.	A lot of work *remains* to be done.
20. The majority of these girls likes music.	The majority of these girls *like* music.

Common Errors in the Use of Modals/Auxiliary Verbs

Incorrect	Correct
1. When I shall see him I shall tell him this.	When I *see* him, I shall tell him this.
2. If I should do wrong, he would punish me.	If I *did* wrong, he would punish me.
3. Until he will have confessed his fault, he will be kept in prison.	Until he *has* confessed his fault, he will be kept in prison.
4. She will obey me.	She *shall* obey me.
5. You would work hard.	You *should* work hard.
6. You shall find him in the garden.	You *will* find him in the garden.
7. He must have died of exposure, but we cannot be certain.	He *might* have died of exposure, but we cannot be certain.
8. You might not show disrespect to your elders.	You *must* not show disrespect to your elders.
9. You may take exercise in order to maintain good health.	You *must* take exercise in order to maintain good health.
10. He must be a crook for all we know.	He *may* be a crook for all we know.

Common Errors in the Use of Adverbs

	Incorrect	*Correct*
1.	He is very much angry.	He is *very* angry.
2.	She was very good enough to help me.	She was *good enough* to help me.
3.	She runs much fast.	She runs *very* fast.
4.	She runs very faster than Seema.	She runs *much* faster than Seema.
5.	It is bitter cold today.	It is *bitterly* cold today.
6.	He is a much learned man.	He is a very learned man.
7.	She is thinking very hardly.	She is thinking very hard.
8.	To tell in brief the film was boring.	*In short* the film was boring.
9.	He told the story in details.	He told the story *in detail.*
10.	I did it anyhow.	I *managed to do* it somehow.
11.	Aeroplanes reach Europe soon.	Aeroplanes reach Europe quickly.
12.	Before long there were dinosaurs on the earth.	*Long ago,* there were dinosaurs on the earth.
13.	This book is too interesting.	This book is *very* interesting.
14.	He lives miserly.	He lives in *a miserly* way.
15.	Just I had gone when she came.	I had just gone when she came.
16.	He sings good.	He sings *well.*
17.	He sings good than I.	He sings *better* than I.
18.	Really speaking it is cold.	*As a matter of fact* it is cold.
19.	He is enough tall to reach the ceiling.	He is *tall enough* to reach the ceiling.
20.	He went directly to his college.	He went *direct* to his college.

Common Errors in the Use of Conjunctions

	Incorrect	*Correct*
1.	As he is fat so he runs slowly.	As he is fat *he* runs slowly.
2.	If he is fat then he will run slowly.	If he is fat, he will run slowly.
3.	Though he is fat still he runs fast.	Though he is fat, *he runs* fast.
4.	*As* I pulled the trigger at the sametime he shook my arm.	As I pulled the trigger, he shook my arm.
5.	No sooner I had spoken than he left.	No sooner *had* I spoken than he left.
6.	Not only he will go, but also he will stay there.	Not only *will he* go, but he *will also* stay there.
7.	Neither he comes nor he writes.	Neither *does he* come nor *does he* write.
8.	Scarcely he entered the room than the telephone rang.	Scarcely *had* he entered the room *when the* telephone rang.
9.	Hardly she had left the house than it began to rain.	Hardly *had she* left the house *when* it began to rain.
10.	He is the fastest runner and he comes last.	He is the fastest runner *but* he comes last.
11.	She is as innocent as if she looks.	She is as innocent as she looks.
12.	Until he does not try he must be punished.	He must be punished unless he tries.
13.	I want to know as to why you are late.	I want to know why you are late.

Incorrect	Correct
14. I am fond of Chinese food as for example sweet and sour prawns.	I am fond of Chinese food, for example, sweet and sour prawns.
15. He was angry therefore I ran away.	He was angry so I ran away.
16. I was trying to work, at that time he was disturbing me.	While I was trying to work, he was disturbing me.
17. Supposing if he is late, what will happen?	Supposing he is late (or if he is late) what will happen?
18. He asked me that why I was late.	He asked me why I was late.
19. Let us catch a taxi lest we should not get late.	Let us catch a taxi lest we should get late.
20. She dresses herself like the teacher does.	She dresses herself as the teacher does.
21. Wait while I come.	Wait *until* (or *till)* I come.
22. Until, there is corruption in India, there can be little progress.	*As long* as there is corruption in India there can be little progress.
23. I have never told a lie nor cheated anybody.	I have never told a lie *nor have I* cheated anybody.
24. Both Mohan as well as Arun are responsible for this action.	Both Mohan *and* Arun are responsible for this action.
25. Hindus and Muslims both are to blame for the riots.	*Both Hindus* and Muslims are to blame for the riots.

Common Errors in the Use of Prepositions

Incorrect	Correct
1. I will not listen him.	I will not listen *to* him.
2. Copy this word by word.	Copy this word *for* word.
3. He enquired from her where she lived.	He enquired *of* her where she lived.
4. Sign here with ink.	Sign here *in* ink.
5. Has she come in train or by foot?	Has she come *by* train or *on* foot?
6. She said this at his face.	She said this *to* his face.
7. Open the book on page one.	Open the book *at* page one.
8. I was invited for lunch.	I was *invited to* lunch.
9. I am ill since three months.	I have been *ill for* three months.
10. This paper is inferior than that.	This paper is inferior *to* that.
11. This resembles to that.	This *resembles* that.
12. My brother is superior than you in strength.	My brother is superior *to* you in strength.
13. He wrote me.	He wrote *to* me.
14. I shall explain them this.	I shall explain this *to* them.
15. Send this letter on my address.	Send this letter *to* my address.
16. He suggested me this.	He suggested this *to* me.
17. He goes *on his* work.	He goes *to his* work.
18. He *reached to* Nagpur.	He *reached* Nagpur.
19. He told *to me* to go.	He told *me* to go.
20. The term begins *from* July 1st.	The term begins *on* July 1st.

Miscellaneous Errors

Incorrect	*Correct*
1. Many *homes* are lying vacant.	Many *houses* are lying vacant.
2. It is cool in the *shadow* of the tree.	It is cool in the *shade* of the tree.
3. She *keeps* good health.	She *enjoys* good health.
4. My leg is *paining*.	*I am feeling pain* in my leg.
5. *See* this word in the dictionary.	*Look up* this word in the dictionary.
6. The train will arrive *just now.*	The train will arrive *shortly.*
7. They are *pulling* on well.	They are *getting* on well.
8. The river has *over flown* its bank.	The river has *over flown* its banks.
9. He was appointed *on* the post.	He was appointed *to* the post.
10. Last but not *the least,* we have to discuss the problem of over population.	Last but not *least,* we have to discuss the problem of over population.
11. *Cities* after *cities* fell.	*City* after *city* fell.
12. What is the use Munir going there?	What is the use of Munir going there?
13. He *did many mischief.*	He *made much mischief.*
14. It is exact five *in* my watch.	It is exact five *by* my watch.
15. I will dine with them on *next Sunday.*	I will dine with them *Sunday next.*
16. Misfortunes when faced bravely and *manly* become less troublesome.	Misfortunes when faced bravely and *manfully* become less troublesome.
17. I am *laid down* with fever.	I am *laid up* with fever.
18. He is habituated to smoking.	He is *addicted* to smoking.
19. *According to my opinion* he is right.	*In my opinion* (or according *to me)* he is right.
20. Could you please *open* this knot?	Could you please *untie* this knot?

Multiple Choice Questions

Directions: *In this section, each sentence has three parts, indicated by (A), (B) and (C). Read each sentence to find out whether there is an error. If you find an error in any one of the parts (A, B, C), indicate your response by marking the letter related to that part. If a sentence has no error, indicate this by marking '(D)' which stands for "No error". Errors may belong to grammar, usage or idiom. Ignore errors of punctuation, if any.*

1. (A) Beware of/(B) a fair-weather friend/(C) who is neither a friend in need nor a friend indeed/ (D) No error.

2. (A) Copernicus proved/(B) that Earth/(C) moves round the Sun./(D) No error.

3. (A) Seldom we have been treated/(B) in such a rude manner/(C) by the police personnel./(D) No error.

4. (A) Some men are born great,/(B) some achieve greatness/(C) and some had greatness thrust on them./(D) No error.

5. (A) The property/(B) was divided/(C) among the two brothers./(D) No error.

6. (A) I am quite certain/(B) that the lady is not only greedy/(C) but miserly./(D) No error.

7. (A) The aircraft overloaded/(B) there was something wrong of the battery/(C) and the engine was making a queer noise/(D) No error.

8. (A) A thorough inquiry of the misappropriation of funds/(B) is now imperative/(C) to bring the guilty to book/(D) No error.

9. (A) The brilliant success in the examination/ (B) as well as his record in sports/(C) deserves high praise/(D) No error.

10. (A) While travelling by a train/(B) on a cold winter night/(C) an argument rose between two passengers in our compartment/(D) No error.

11. (A) I cannot find/(B) where has he gone/(C) though I have tried may best/(D) No error.

12. (A) If I was/(B) the Prime Minister of India/(C) I would work wonders/(D) No error.

13. (A) Amit's severe bout of flu/(B) debilitated him so much/(C) that he was too tired to do for work for a week./(D) No error.

14. (A) This is the crux of the entire problem;/(B) everything centres on/(C) it being resolved./ (D) No error.

15. (A) One of the major aims of the Air Force/(B) was the complete demolition of all means of transportation/(C) by the bombing of rail lines and terminals./(D) No error.

16. (A) His strong voice cut over/(B) the hum of conversation/(C) like a knife through butter./ (D) No error.

17. (A) Even though they weren't expecting us/ (B) they managed to knock up/(C) a marvellous meal./(D) No error.

18. (A) The celebrated singer was/(B) surrounded by the usual crowd/(C) of lackeys and hanger-ons./(D) No error.

19. (A) If it weren't/(B) for you,/(C) I wouldn't be alive today./(D) No error.

20. (A) He looked like a lion/(B) baulked from/ (C) its prey./(D) No error.

21. (A) Widespread flooding/(B) is effecting/(C) large areas of the villages./(D) No error.

22. (A) She regards/(B) negotiating prices with customers/(C) as her special preserve./(D) No error.

23. (A) Often in political campaigns, a point is reached at which/(B) the candidates take out their gloves./(C) and start slugging with bare fists./(D) No error.

24. (A) If we really set to/(B) we can get the whole house/(C) cleaned in an afternoon./(D) No error.

25. (A) Pieces of rock plummeted/(B) down the mountainside/(C) in the ground below./(D) No error.

26. (A) Since the two parties each won/(B) the same number of seats,/(C) the minority party holds the balance of power./(D) No error.

27. (A) It's arrogant for you/(B) to assume you'll/ (C)win every time./(D) No error.

28. (A) We've paid for our travel and accommod-ation,/(B) so we need only to take/(C) some pocket-money with us./(D) No error.

29. (A) There's no evidence to show/(B) that information technology secrets are more/(C) vulnerable in India than Britain or the US./(D) No error.

30. (A) It is shameful that hunting/(B) is still considered sport/(C) by some unscrupulous people in the civilized world./(D) No error.

31. (A) The Prime Minister's good looks won him/ (B)the election but he has still to prove/(C) that he's not a just pretty face./(D) No error.

32. (A) The two books are the same/(B) except for the fact that this/(C) has an answer in the back./ (D) No error.

33. (A) He estimated his income tax bill/(B) by extrapolation over figures/(C) submitted in previous years./(D) No error.

34. (A) The modern office block/(B) sticks out like a sore thumb/(C) among the old buildings in the area./(D) No error.

35. (A) I will try to put over/(B) some feelers to gauge/(C) people's reactions to our proposal./ (D) No error.

36. (A) A major contribution of Mathura sculptors/ (B)of that period were the creation and popularization/(C) of the Buddha's image in human form./(D) No error.

37. (A) Amit has been deceiving Mona/(B) for many years but she/(C) has not still tumbled to it./(D) No error.

38. (A) Mahavira was an advocate of nonviolence and vegetarianism,/(B) who revived and reorganized the Jain doctrine/(C) and established rules for their monastic order. (D) No error.

39. (A) Microwaves are the principle carriers/(B) of television, telephone and data transmissions/ (C)between stations on earth and between the earth and satellites./(D) No error.

40. (A) An unit is an abstract idea,/(B) defined either by reference to/(C) a randomly chosen material standard or to a natural phenomenon./ (D) No error.

41. (A) With the crisis deepening,/(B) the critics sense an opportunity/(C) about putting in place a more radical strategy./(D) No error.

42. (A) The salesman gave us/(B) a big spiel about why/(C) we should buy his product./(D) No error.

43. (A) I will need several weeks/(B) to invent the lie of the land before/(C) I can make any decision about the future of the business./(D) No error.

44. (A) You should be cautious/(B) and make a few discrete enquiries about/(C) the firm before you sign anything./(D) No error.

45. (A) Your husband doesn't/(B) believe that you are older/(C) than I./(D) No error.

46. (A) We are meeting today afternoon/(B) to discuss the matter/(C) and reach a compromise./ (D) No error.

47. (A) Either Ram or/(B) you is responsible/(C) for this action./(D) No error.

48. (A) The student flatly denied/(B) that he had copied/(C) in the examination hall./(D) No error.

49. (A) By the time you arrive tomorrow/(B) I have finished/(C) my work./(D) No error.

50. (A) The speaker stressed repeatedly on/(B) the importance of improving/(C) the condition of the slums./(D) No error.

51. (A) The captain with the members of his team/ (B) are returning/(C) after a fortnight./(D) No error.

52. (A) After returning from/(B) an all-India tour/ (C) I had to describe about it/(D) No error.

53. (A) The teacher asked his students/(B) if they had gone through/(C) either of the three chapters included in the prescribed text./(D) No error.

54. (A) Although they are living in the country/ (B) since they were married/(C) they are now moving to the town./(D) No error.

55. (A) Do you know/(B) how old were you/(C) when you came here?/(D) No error.

ANSWERS

1	2	3	4	5	6	7	8	9	10
D	B	A	C	C	C	B	A	D	C
11	**12**	**13**	**14**	**15**	**16**	**17**	**18**	**19**	**20**
B	A	C	C	B	A	A	C	C	C
21	**22**	**23**	**24**	**25**	**26**	**27**	**28**	**29**	**30**
C	A	A	A	C	A	A	B	D	B
31	**32**	**33**	**34**	**35**	**36**	**37**	**38**	**39**	**40**
C	C	C	D	A	B	C	C	A	A
41	**42**	**43**	**44**	**45**	**46**	**47**	**48**	**49**	**50**
C	D	D	D	C	A	B	D	B	A
51	**52**	**53**	**54**	**55**					
B	C	C	B	D					

❑❑❑

3 Articles

Definite and Indefinite Articles

(*i*) 'A' and 'an' are Indefinite Articles.

(*ii*) 'The' is Definite Article.

(*iii*) 'A' and 'an' modify a noun in a general way.

(*iv*) 'The' particularises it. *e.g.*,

Mohan has **a pen.**

The pen which you gave me was expensive.

Vowel and Consonant Sounds

(*i*) 'A' is used before words starting with the sound of a consonant.

(*ii*) 'An' is used before a vowel sound (vowels a, e, i, o, u) *e.g.*,

a book, a cat, a useful thing, a European girl, a university,

but an FDR, an MA, an honest boy, an hour, an owl, an egg, an umbrella, etc.

Use of Articles 'A' and 'An'

A cat mews. (*i.e.*, every cat)

The cat of my neighbour mews day and night. (*i.e.*, a particular cat)

He gave me **an** egg. (Here 'an' means 'one')

Use of Article 'The'

1. 'The' is used before names of rivers, mountains, seas, oceans:

   The Himalayas, the Ganga, the Yamuna, the Bay of Bengal, the Indian Ocean, the Nile, the English Channel, *etc.*

2. Names of newspapers and magazines:

   The Times of India, the Tribune, The Sun, *etc.*

3. Names of the famous and holy books:
   The Guru Granth Sahib, The Gita, The Ramayana, *etc.*

4. Names of creations of nature:
   the sun, the earth, the moon, the sky, *etc.*

5. While using Adjectives as Nouns:
   The poor should be helped by **the rich.**

6. Sometimes with the Comparative Degree:
   The more you think, **the more** you worry.

7. With the Superlative Degree:
   She is **the most intelligent** girl in our school.

8. Before the imaginary lines and directions:

   The Latitude, The Equator, the east, the west, etc.

9. Before the names of musical instruments:
   the violin, the piano, the flute, etc.

10. While using a Proper Noun as a Common Noun:

    Mohan is **the Sachin** of our team.

Omission of Article 'The'

1. Before some Nouns used to convey general sense, articles are not used but are used to particularise them:
   Man is mortal.

2. Before Proper Nouns:
   Rakesh is an intelligent boy.

3. With Abstract Noun:
   Childhood is the prime time of one's life.
   The childhood of Sohan was full of sorrow.

4. With Material Nouns:
   Milk is an essential food.
   The milk of the cow is sweet.

5. Usually no article is used before names of diseases:
   Cancer is a fatal disease.
   However, when we talk about a disease figuratively, we use an article before its name, *e.g.*
   Corruption is a cancer.
6. Names of games and language:
   I like football.
   I can speak Punjabi, Hindi and English.
7. Gold is a precious metal.

   NOTE: As you must have noted above, the definite article 'the' has been used where a noun is particularised.

Double Use of Article 'The'

Read the following sentences carefully to understand this :

1. The poet and novelist has been honoured.
   (The same person is the poet as well as novelist)
2. The poet and the novelist have been honoured.
   (The poet and the novelist are two different persons).
3. I have a black and white dog.
   (that is, one dog)
4. I have a black and a white dog.
   (that is, two dogs)

Multiple Choice Questions

Directions : *Fill in the blanks with suitable articles. Mark 'D' if no article required.*

1. Do you know .... boy in white?
A. a B. an
C. the D. No article

2. She is .... girl I am looking for.
A. a B. an
C. the D. No article

3. Have you read .... Mahabharat?
A. a B. an
C. the D. No article

4. ....rich are not always happy.
A. A B. An
C. The D. No article

5. Oranges are sold by .... dozen.
A. a B. an
C. the D. No article

6. Milk is sold by .... litre.
A. a B. an
C. the D. No article

7. .... Amazon is the longest river in the world.
A. A B. An
C. The D. No article

8. .... higher you climb, the colder it gets.
A. A B. An
C. The D. No article

9. She is .... untidy girl.
A. a B. an
C. the D. No article

10. I am .... M.A. is English.
A. a B. an
C. the D. No article

11. I have already spent .... few rupees I had.
A. a B. an
C. the D. No article

12. .... English are very hard-working.
A. A B. An
C. The D. No article

13. April is the fourth month of .... year.
A. a B. an
C. the D. No article

14. Rice is sold by .... kilogram
A. a B. an
C. the D. No article

15. She is .... best of the three girls.
A. a B. an
C. the D. No article

16. .... man in the car is a friend of mine.
A. A B. An
C. The D. No article

17. Brevity is .... soul of wit.
A. a B. an
C. the D. No article

18. .... thing of beauty is a joy for ever.
A. A B. An
C. The D. No article

19. .... little learning is a dangerous thing.
A. A B. An
C. The D. No article

20. .... best sauce for food is hunger.
A. A B. An
C. The D. No article

21. Birds of .... feather flock together.
A. a B. an
C. the D. No article

22. He makes .... living by begging.
A. a B. an
C. the D. No article

23. It is .... pity that he died so young.
A. a B. an
C. the D. No article

24. What .... nuisance it is?
A. a B. an
C. the D. No article

25. Delhi is .... London of India.
A. a B. an
C. the D. No article

26. Where is .... will, there is a way.
A. a B. an
C. the D. No article

27. Her father is .... physician and surgeon.
A. a B. an
C. the D. No article

28. This will benefit .... poor.
A. a B. an
C. the D. No article

29. ....bird in hand is better than two in a bush.
A. A B. An
C. The D. No article

30. As he is hard-working, he will win .... prize.
A. a B. an
C. the D. No article

31. .... water of this well is dirty.
A. A B. An
C. The D. No article

32. Only .... wearer knows where the shoe pinches.
A. a B. an
C. the D. No article

33. .... action will be taken against you.
A. A B. An
C. The D. No article

34. .... sun rises in the east.
A. A B. An
C. The D. No article

35. She was promoted to .... highest post.
A. a B. an
C. the D. No article

36. Did you see .... Taj Mahal?
A. a B. an
C. the D. No article

37. He is .... one-eyed man.
A. a B. an
C. the D. No article

38. This is .... useful book.
A. a B. an
C. the D. No article

39. Cloth is sold by .... metre.
A. a B. an
C. the D. No article

40. The sun sets in .... west.
A. a B. an
C. the D. No article

41. Amar bought......umbrella yesterday.
A. a B. an
C. the D. No article

42. Surinder is ...... honest boy.
A. a B. an
C. the D. No article

43. She wrote ...... book in French.
A. a B. an
C. the D. No article

44. ...... lion roars.
A. A B. An
C. The D. No article

45. ..... apple a day keeps the doctor away.

A. A B. An
C. The D. No article

46. John bought ...... car yesterday.

A. a B. an
C. the D. No article

47. His father is ..... engineer in the U.S.A.

A. a B. an
C. the D. No article

48. It is hard for ..... owl to fly during the day times.

A. a B. an
C. the D. No article

49. She had ..... rimmed hat.

A. a B. an
C. the D. No article

50. My uncle is ..... heart specialist.

A. a B. an
C. the D. No article

51. He looks as foolish as .... ass.

A. a B. an
C. the D. No article

52. Did you go to .... prison to visit him?

A. a B. an
C. the D. No article

53. I found .... one-rupee note in the market.

A. a B. an
C. the D. No article

54. It is a pleasure to meet such .... efficient man.

A. a B. an
C. the D. No article

55. The Sanyasi lived in a cave in .... Himalayas.

A. a B. an
C. the D. No article

56. There is .... union in our factory.

A. a B. an
C. the D. No article

57. He hit his wife on the head with .... umbrella.

A. a B. an
C. the D. No article

58. I caught him by .... collar.

A. a B. an
C. the D. No article

59. Child is .... father of man.

A. a B. an
C. the D. No article

60. He gazed at .... moon for two hours.

A. a B. an
C. the D. No article

ANSWERS

1	2	3	4	5	6	7	8	9	10
C	C	C	C	C	C	C	C	B	B
11	**12**	**13**	**14**	**15**	**16**	**17**	**18**	**19**	**20**
C	C	C	C	C	C	C	A	A	C
21	**22**	**23**	**24**	**25**	**26**	**27**	**28**	**29**	**30**
A	A	A	A	C	A	A	C	A	A
31	**32**	**33**	**34**	**35**	**36**	**37**	**38**	**39**	**40**
C	C	B	C	C	C	A	A	C	C
41	**42**	**43**	**44**	**45**	**46**	**47**	**48**	**49**	**50**
B	B	A	A	B	A	B	B	A	A
51	**52**	**53**	**54**	**55**	**56**	**57**	**58**	**59**	**60**
B	C	A	B	C	A	B	C	C	C

❑❑❑

4 Prepositions

A Preposition is a word that comes before a Pronoun or a Noun and expresses the relationship between Noun or Pronoun and some part of the remaining sentence.

(*a*) He is busy **with** his work.
(*b*) The boy jumped **into** the river.
(*c*) The birds are chirping **in** the trees.

In these sentences the words **with**, **into** and **in** show the relationship between the verbs **busy, jumped** and **chirping** with the nouns **work, river** and **trees** respectively.

Position of the Preposition

A. A Preposition usually precedes its object.
(*i*) He laughs **at** the poor.
(*ii*) He is angry **with** you.
(*iii*) She agrees **with** me.

B. In the case of Relative Pronouns it comes after the subject.
(*i*) This is the boy whom I was looking **for**.
(*ii*) That is the pen whose mention I was making **of**.

C. In the following cases, the Preposition comes after its object.
(*i*) Where is the boy you were complaining **against**?
(*ii*) What things are there you are looking **for**?
(*iii*) Who is there, you are waiting **for**?

Omission of the Prepositon

In many cases when the sentences contain Nouns of Time or Place, the Prepositions **from**, **in** and **for** are often omitted.

(*i*) He walked many kilometres.
(*ii*) He came to see me last year.
(*iii*) As I could not find my puppy anywhere, I looked here and there.

Prepositions are small words that show the relationship between one word and another. Prepositions in the following sentences show the position of the paper in relation to the desk, the book, hand and the door.

The paper is **on** the desk.
The paper is **under** the book.
The paper is **in** his hand.
The paper is **by** the door.

Common Prepositions

about	at	by
in	onto	toward
above	before	concerning
inside	out	under
across	behind	despite
into	over	until
after	below	down
like	since	up
against	beneath	during
near	through	upon
along	beside	except
of	throughout	with
amid	between	for
off	till	within
among	beyond	from
on	to	without

Multiple Choice Questions

Directions: *Select the most appropriate preposition from the given alternatives to fill in the blanks and make the sentence meaningfully complete.*

1. Don't try to be an advocate ..... these criminals.
A. for B. with
C. across D. in

2. The audience admired him ..... his sweet voice.
A. to B. on
C. for D. at

3. I want to check your bag ..... fake currency notes.
A. to B. for
C. upon D. on

4. The dew drops clung .... the blades of grass.
A. for B. on
C. to D. in

5. The thief was chased ..... by the police.
A. on B. after
C. into D. at

6. Please carry this bag ..... my room.
A. on B. for
C. to D. in

7. A lorry bumped ..... a car.
A. on B. over
C. into D. to

8. They were begging ..... food.
A. for B. on
C. to D. after

9. She always boasts ..... her wealth.
A. of B. for
C. on D. after

10. She banged ..... the door violently.
A. for B. to
C. on D. down

11. I applied ..... the post of a clerk.
A. for B. on
C. in D. to

12. I applied ..... the Principal for the post of a teacher.
A. to B. on
C. with D. for

13. I begged ..... him not to divulge the secret.
A. for B. of
C. with D. to

14. You had better borrow a pen ..... Rakesh.
A. over B. into
C. from D. by

15. I baked a cake ..... the guests.
A. to B. for
C. on D. of

16. She is confident ..... (her) success.
A. with B. on
C. of D. for

17. The doctor will cure you ..... malaria.
A. of B. with
C. for D. from

18. This law is common ..... all.
A. to B. upon
C. over D. at

19. She was condemned ..... her bad hand writing.
A. on B. for
C. into D. of

20. In summer there will be a great demand ..... desert cooler.
A. on B. with
C. for D. of

21. We shall wait ..... you.
A. on B. for
C. towards D. after

22. Tom displayed his injury ..... all his friends.
A. for B. upon
C. to D. at

23. She distributed the sweets ..... the two brothers.
A. among B. between
C. for D. in

24. Please distribute these apples ..... all.
A. among B. to
C. for D. at

25. It rarely happened that he defended ..... an innocent person.
A. against B. for
C. upon D. at

26. The parents were disappointed ..... the performance of their son.
A. on B. with
C. at D. of

27. Common salt dissolves ..... water.
A. for B. in
C. with D. by

28. This medicare is free ..... sugar.
A. on B. to
C. from D. of

29. The manager granted leave ..... the clerk.
A. to B. on
C. into D. for

30. The air was heavy ..... aroma of perfumes.
A. on B. with
C. into D. from

31. She had a quick glance ..... the magazine.
A. at B. from
C. into D. to

32. The climate of Kashmir is favourable ..... me.
A. with B. in
C. to D. for

33. They hate you ..... your poverty.
A. for B. on
C. in D. of

34. He is eligible ..... this post.
A. for B. to
C. with D. at

35. The smoke was emerging ..... down the foot of the hill.
A. on B. to
C. from D. at

36. The criminal managed to escape ..... the prison.
A. upon B. from
C. with D. of

37. You should educate your friends ..... the benefits of living in villages.
A. on B. towards
C. upon D. in

38. She made a lot of efforts ..... win the match.
A. for B. to
C. upon D. at

39. The new inspector will enquire ..... the murder case.
A. on B. for
C. into D. at

40. The retired soldiers were exempted ..... all taxes.
A. from B. to
C. on D. of

41. She was adept ..... journalism.
A. at B. on
C. with D. in

42. She is afraid ..... snakes.
A. on B. to
C. of D. with

43. I agree ..... your proposal.
A. for B. on
C. to D. with

44. The children were amazed ..... so big a python.
A. at B. on
C. in D. with

45. She was anxious ..... the final match.
A. about B. on
C. with D. for

46. He apologized ..... his being late.
A. towards B. for
C. on D. as

47. The children were amused ..... his jokes.
A. for B. to
C. at D. on

48. She is angry ..... you.
A. to B. with
C. on D. for

49. She is angry ..... your teasing remark.
A. at B. in
C. for D. with

50. A big patch of land was allocated ..... the refugees.
A. to B. for
C. in D. upon

ANSWERS

1	2	3	4	5	6	7	8	9	10
A	C	B	C	B	C	C	A	A	C
11	**12**	**13**	**14**	**15**	**16**	**17**	**18**	**19**	**20**
A	A	B	C	B	C	A	A	B	C
21	**22**	**23**	**24**	**25**	**26**	**27**	**28**	**29**	**30**
B	C	B	A	A	C	B	C	A	B
31	**32**	**33**	**34**	**35**	**36**	**37**	**38**	**39**	**40**
A	C	A	A	C	B	A	B	C	A
41	**42**	**43**	**44**	**45**	**46**	**47**	**48**	**49**	**50**
A	C	C	A	A	B	C	B	A	A

❑❑❑

5 Synonyms & Antonyms

There are thousands of words in English language. No one can remember their meanings easily but with regular practice one can memorise most of them. A number of words with their Synonyms and Antonyms are compiled here. Try to learn as many as you can and answer the questions thereafter.

Words	*Synonyms*	*Antonyms*
Abandon	Cease, Forsake	Continue
Abhor	Hate, Loathe, Detest	Like, Love
Abiding	Enduring, Durable	Fleeting
Able	Proficient, Competent	Incompetent, Unfit
Ability	Skill, Power	Disability, Inability
Abortive	Fruitless, Futile	Fruitful, Successful
Abolish	Destroy, Undo	Restore, Revive
Abridge	Shorten, Curtail	Lengthen, Expand
Absolve	Forgive, Pardon, Excuse	Condemn
Accelerate	Hasten	Retard
Accord	Agreement, Harmony	Discord, Disagreement
Accumulate	Collect, Store, Amass	Distribute, Scatter
Adamant	Hard, Inflexible	Flexible
Adversity	Misfortune, Distress	Prosperity
Adept	Expert, Skilful	Inexpert, Unskillful
Aggravate	Heighten, Intensify	Quell, Suppress
Agile	Nimble	Clumsy, Undeft
Alert	Vigilant	Heedless
Allay	Calm, Soothe, Assuage	Arouse
Ameliorate	Improve, Advance, Amend	Worsen, Deteriorate
Ambiguous	Vague, Unclear	Clear
Amiable	Lovable, Agreeable	Disagreeable
Annihilate	Destroy	Create
Arduous	Hard, Strenuous	Easy

Words	Synonyms	Antonyms
Attacks	Assault	Defend
Audacity	Boldness	Cowardice
Auspicious	Favourable, Propitious, Lucky	Ominous, Inauspicious, Unlucky
Austere	Harsh, Severe, Rigorous	Easy-going
Authentic	True, Genuine	Spurious, False
Avarice	Greed	Generosity
Averse	Unwilling, Loath, Disinclined	Willing, Inclined
Aversion	Hostility, Hatred	Affinity, Liking
Base	Low, Mean, Ignoble	Noble, Exalted
Boisterous	Noisy, Stormy	Calm, Quiet
Brave	Courageous, Daring, Bold, Plucky	Cowardly, Dastardly, Timid
Brief	Short, Concise, Laconic	Lengthy, Diffuse
Bright	Vivid, Radiant	Dull, Dark
Brutal	Savage, Cruel	Humane, Kindly
Callous	Hard, Cruel, Indifferent	Soft, Tender, Concerned
Cautious	Careful, Wary	Rash, Reckless, Foolhardy
Censure (*n*)	Blame, Condemnation	Praise
Censure (*vb*)	Blame, Condemn	Praise, Commend
Circumscribed	Restricted, Confined, Limited	Unconfined, Unrestricted
Civil	Polite, Courteous, Gracious, Urbane	Rude, Uncivil, Impolite, Ungracious
Coerce	Compel, Force	Volunteer
Compassionate	Pitiful, Sympathetic, Merciful	Unsympathetic, Merciless, Cruel
Compress	Condense, Abbreviate	Expand, Lengthen
Conspicuous	Noticeable, Manifest	Inconspicuous
Constant	Steady, Steadfast, Uniform	Inconstant, Variable
Cordial	Friendly, Warm, Hearty	Cold, Unfriendly
Covert	Hidden, Secret	Overt, Open
Cruel	Savage, Ruthless, Vicious	Kind, Gentle, Benevolent
Cursory	Rapid, Superficial	Thorough, Exhaustive, Intensive
Credible	Believable, Probable, Plausible	Incredible, Unbelievable, Fantastic
Crafty	Cunning, Sly	Artless, Simple, Ingenuous
Costly	Expensive, Dear	Cheap, Inexpensive
Confidence	Trust, Reliance	Distrust, Doubt
Death	Decease, Demise	Existence, Life
Dearth	Scarcity, Lack, Want, Paucity, Shortage	Plenty, Abundance
Decay	Dissolution, Decline, Decomposition, Disintegration	Regeneration

Words	Synonyms	Antonyms
Deference	Respect, Reverence	Disrespect, Irreverence
Deficient	Lacking, Inadequate	Complete, Sufficient
Desolate	Lonely, Deserted	Crowded, Occupied
Destitute	Wanting, Needy •	Rich, Affluent
Diligence	Industry, Perseverance	Idleness
Disgrace	Dishonour, Discredit	Honour, Credit
Dwindle	Decrease, Shrink	Grow, Increase
Earthly	Terrestrial, Mundane	Celestial, Heavenly, Unearthly
Eligible	Qualified, Suitable	Ineligible, Unsuitable
Emancipate	Liberate, Free	Enslave
Excited	Impassioned, Stimulated	Composed, Cool, Impassive
Extraordinary	Uncommon, Remarkable, Marvellous	Commonplace, Ordinary
Extravagant	Lavish, Prodigal, Wastrel, Spendthrift	Thrifty, Economical, Frugal
Fabricate	Construct, Make	Destroy
Fabulous	Fictitious, Mythical	Actual, Real
False	Untrue, Mendacious	True, Genuine
Famous	Well-known, Renowned	Obscure, Unknown
Fantastic	Fanciful, Imaginative, Visionary	Practical, Down to earth
Fearful	Nervous, Anxious, Afraid, Scared	Fearless, Dauntless
Felicity	Happiness	Sorrow
Gaiety	Joyousness, Hilarity	Mourning, Dullness
Garrulous	Talkative, Loquacious	Taciturn, Silent, Reserved
Generous	Liberal, Magnanimous	Stingy, Miserly
Gigantic	Huge, Colossal	Minute, Small
Graphic	Vivid, Pictorial, Meaningful	Vague
Guest	Visitor	Host
Guile	Fraud, Trickery	Artlessness, Ingenuousness
Gratitude	Gratefulness	Ingratitude, Ungratefulness
Gratuitous	Voluntary, Spontaneous, Unwarranted	Involuntary, Forced
Hamper	Hinder, Obstruct	Facilitate, Ease
Haughty	Arrogant, Proud	Humble, Modest
Hazardous	Dangerous, Perilous	Safe, Secure Protected
Headstrong	Obstinate, Stubborn	Weak-willed, Flexible

Words	*Synonyms*	*Antonyms*
Hope	Belief, Conviction, Expectation	Despair, Hopelessness
Improvident	Prodigal, Carelessness	Provident, Economical
Incessant	Unceasing, Continuous	Discontinuous
Indolent	Slothful, Lethargic	Active, Energetic
Joy	Delight, Pleasure	Sadness, Gloom
Jolly	Jovial, Merry	Gloomy, Sad
Judicious	Discreet, Prudent	Indiscreet, Injudicious
Knowledge	Enlightenment, Learning	Ignorance, Stupidity
Laborious	Industrious, Assiduous	Slothful, Lazy
Laxity	Slackness, Looseness	Firmness
Lenient	Mild, Forbearing	Strict, Stern
Lethal	Deadly, Fatal, Mortal	Life-giving, Vital, Vivifying
Liberal	Generous, Tolerant	Intolerant, Illiberal
Liberty	Freedom, Independence	Slavery, Bondage
Lively	Animated, Active	Dull, Listless
Loyal	Faithful, Devoted	Treacherous, Disloyal, Unfaithful
Lucky	Fortunate	Unlucky, Unfortunate
Lucrative	Profitable	Unprofitable
Magnanimous	Generous, Largehearted	Ungenerous, Stingy
Malady	Illness, Ailment	Health
Manifest	Noticeable, Obvious	Obscure, Puzzling
Meagre	Small	Plentiful, Large
Mean	Low, Abject	Noble, Exalted
Mendacious	False, Untruthful	Truthful
Misery	Sorrow, Distress	Happiness, Joy
Morbid	Sick, Diseased	Healthy
Mournful	Sorrowful, Sad	Joyful, Happy
Negligent	Careless, Heedless	Careful
Notorious	Infamous, Disreputable	Reputable
Obedient	Submissive, Compliant, Docile	Disobedient, Recalcitrant, Wayward
Obsolete	Antiquated, Out-of-Date	Current, Modern
Opportune	Timely, Seasonable	Inopportune
Opulence	Wealth, Riches	Penury, Poverty
Onerous	Heavy, Burdensome	Light, Easy
Palatable	Tasty, Delicious	Unpalatable
Pathetic	Touching	Joyous, Cheery
Persuade	Urge, Induce	Dissuade
Praise (*vb*)	Applaud, Eulogise	Condemn

Words	*Synonyms*	*Antonyms*
Praise (*n*)	Applause, Eulogy	Condemnation
Precarious	Risky, Uncertain	Safe, Certain
Pretence	Pretext, Excuse	Candour, Frankness
Propagate	Breed, Circulate	Terminate, Restrict
Quaint	Odd, Singular	Usual, Ordinary
Quell	Suppress, Subdue	Agitate, Arouse
Rare	Uncommon, Scarce	Common, Ordinary
Refined	Polished, Elegant	Crude, Coarse
Remote	Distant	Near, Close
Renown	Fame, Reputation	Infamy, Notoriety
Rigid	Stiff, Unyielding	Flexible, Yielding
Remorseful	Regretful, Repentant	Unrepentant
Rebellion	Revolt, Mutiny, Insurgency	Loyalty
Scared	Holy, Consecrated	Profane, Unholy
Sane	Sensible, Sound	Insane
Scold	Chide, Rebuke	Praise
Serious	Grave, Earnest	Frivolous
Shy	Bashful	Bold, Impudent
Simple	Plain, Artless	Complex, Cunning, Shrewd
Solitary	Single, Lonely, Secluded	Numerous, Multitude
Shallow	Superficial	Deep
Solace	Comfort, Relief	Discomfort, Grief
Spurious	Sham, False	Genuine, Authentic
Stagnant	Still, Motionless	Moving
Surplus	Excess	Deficit, Shortage
Tame	Gentle, Mild, Domesticated	Savage, Wild
Teacher	Instructor, Educator	Student, Pupil
Tedious	Wearisome, Monotonous	Agreeable, Lively
Temporal	Worldly, Secular	Spiritual
Temperate	Moderate	Immoderate, Intemperate
Tortuous	Winding, Circuitous	Straight, Direct
Tough	Hard, Strong	Tender, Soft, Flexible
Transient	Temporary, Fleeting	Lasting, Durable, Permanent
Trusworthy	Reliable	Unreliable, Untrustworthy
Tranquil	Calm	Agitated
Ugly	Unsightly, Repulsive	Beautiful, Attractive
Useful	Advantageous, Serviceable	Useless
Vehemence	Passion, Force	Apathy, Indifference

Words	Synonyms	Antonyms
Vindictive	Revengeful	Forgiving
Wholesome	Healthy	Unwholesome, Morbid, Unhealthy, Diseased
Wicked	Evil, Impious	Pious, Good
Wise	Sagacious, Erudite	Foolish, Stupid
Wrath	Anger, Fury, Rage	Love, Peace, Calm
Wreck	Ruin, Destroy	Create, Construct
Yield	Surrender, Submit	Resist, Revolt
Yielding	Submissive, Supple	Inflexible, Intractable
Yoke	Oppression, Bondage	Freedom
Zeal	Passion, Fervour	Apathy, Indifference
Zest	Relish, Enthusiasm	Distaste, Disrelish

Multiple Choice Questions

Directions (Qs. 1 to 50): *In the following questions choose the word which best expresses the MEANING of the given word.*

1. TEPID
   A. Hot B. Warm
   C. Cold D. Boiling

2. MAYHEM
   A. Jubilation B. Havoc
   C. Excitement D. Defeat

3. TIMID
   A. Fast B. Slow
   C. Medium D. Shy

4. CANTANKEROUS
   A. Quarrelsome B. Rash
   C. Disrespectful D. Noisy

5. PRECARIOUS
   A. Cautious B. Critical
   C. Perilous D. Brittle

6. TACITURNITY
   A. Dumbness B. Changeableness
   C. Hesitation D. Reserve

7. INEBRIATE
   A. Dreamy B. Stupefied
   C. Unsteady D. Drunken

8. HARBINGER
   A. Massenger B. Steward
   C. Forerunner D. Pilot

9. INTIMIDATE
   A. To hint B. Frighten
   C. Bluff D. Harass

10. IRONIC
    A. Inflexible
    B. Bitter
    C. Good-natured
    D. Disguisedly sarcastic

11. STRINGENT
    A. Tense B. Stringy
    C. Strict D. Causing to shrink

12. ECSTATIC
    A. Animated B. Bewildered
    C. Enraptured D. Willful

13. COMMENSURATE
    A. Measurable B. Proportionate
    C. Beginning D. Appropriate

14. DESTITUTION
    A. Humility B. Moderation
    C. Poverty D. Beggary

15. ASCEND
A. Leap B. Grow
C. Deviate D. Mount

16. UNCOUTH
A. Ungraceful B. Rough
C. Slovenly D. Dirty

17. LYNCH
A. Hang B. Madden
C. Killed D. Shoot

18. LAUD
A. Lord B. Eulogy
C. Praise D. Extolled

19. CORRESPONDENCE
A. Agreements B. Contracts
C. Documents D. Letters

20. VENUE
A. Place B. Agenda
C. Time D. Duration

21. STERILE
A. Barren B. Arid
C. Childless D. Dry

22. SYNOPSIS
A. Index B. Mixture
C. Summary D. Puzzle

23. GERMANE
A. Responsible B. Logical
C. Possible D. Relevant

24. PONDER
A. Think B. Evaluate
C. Anticipate D. Increase

25. CANNY
A. Obstinate B. Handsome
C. Clever D. Stout

26. ABUNDANT
A. Ripe B. Cheap
C. Plenty D. Absent

27. CONSEQUENCES
A. Results B. Conclusions
C. Difficulties D. Applications

28. SHIVER
A. Shake B. Rock
C. Tremble D. Move

29. DILIGENT
A. Progressive B. Brilliant
C. Inventive D. Hard-working

30. DISTANT
A. Far B. Removed
C. Reserved D. Separate

31. FORAY
A. Excursion B. Contest
C. Ranger D. Intuition

32. FRUGALITY
A. Foolishness B. Extremity
C. Enthusiasm D. Economy

33. GARNISH
A. Paint B. Garner
C. Adorn D. Abuse

34. VIGOUR
A. Strength B. Boldness
C. Warmth D. Enthusiasm

35. CANDID
A. Apparent B. Explicit
C. Frank D. Bright

36. BRIEF
A. Limited B. Small
C. Little D. Short

37. GARRULITY
A. Credulity B. Senility
C. Loquaciousness D. Speciousness

38. FURORE
A. Excitement B. Worry
C. Flux D. Anteroom

39. NEUTRAL
A. Unbiased B. Non-aligned
C. Undecided D. Indifferent

40. LAMENT
A. Complain B. Comment
C. Condone D. Console

41. ADVERSITY
A. Failure B. Helplessness
C. Misfortune D. Crisis

42. TURN UP
A. Land up B. Show up
C. Crop up D. Come up

43. DEIFY
A. Flatter B. Challenge
C. Worship D. Face

44. ERROR
A. Misadventure B. Misgiving
C. Ambiguity D. Blunder

45. SHALLOW
A. Artificial B. Superficial
C. Foolish D. Worthless

46. MASSACRE
A. Murder B. Stab
C. Assassinate D. Slaughter

47. COMBAT
A. Conflict B. Quarrel
C. Feud D. Fight

48. VORACIOUS
A. Wild B. Hungry
C. Angry D. Quick

49. IMPROMPTU
A. Offhand B. Unimportant
C. Unreal D. Effective

50. RABBLE
A. Mob B. Noise
C. Roar D. Rubbish

Directions (Qs. 51 to 100): *In the following questions choose the word which is the exact OPPOSITE of the given words.*

51. STRINGENT
A. General B. Vehement
C. Lenient D. Magnanimous

52. FLIMSY
A. Frail B. Filthy
C. Firm D. Flippant

53. BUSY
A. Occupied B. Engrossed
C. Relaxed D. Engaged

54. ADAPTABLE
A. Adoptable B. Flexible
C. Yielding D. Rigid

55. LOVE
A. Villainy B. Hatred
C. Compulsion D. Force

56. BALANCE
A. Disbalance B. Misbalance
C. Debalance D. Imbalance

57. RELINQUISH
A. Abdicate B. Renounce
C. Possess D. Deny

58. MOUNTAIN
A. Plain B. Plateau
C. Precipice D. Valley

59. FICKLE
A. Courageous B. Sincere
C. Steadfast D. Humble

60. PERENNIAL
A. Frequent B. Regular
C. Lasting D. Rare

61. RARELY
A. Hardly B. Definitely
C. Frequently D. Periodically

62. STARTLED
A. Amused B. Relaxed
C. Endless D. Astonished

63. ADHERENT
A. Detractor B. Enemy
C. Alien D. Rival

64. QUIESCENT
A. Indifferent B. Troublesome
C. Weak D. Unconcerned

65. CONDENSE
A. Expand B. Distribute
C. Interpret D. Lengthen

66. BENIGN
A. Malevolent B. Soft
C. Friendly D. Unwise

67. OBSCURE
A. Implicit B. Obnoxious
C. Explicit D. Pedantic

68. HYPOCRITICAL
A. Gentle B. Sincere
C. Amiable D. Dependable

69. EVASIVE
A. Free B. Honest
C. Liberal D. Frank

70. INDUSTRIOUS
A. Indifferent B. Indolent
C. Casual D. Passive

71. EXTRICATE
A. Manifest B. Palpable
C. Release D. Entangle

72. LUCID
A. Glory B. Noisy
C. Obscure D. Distinct

73. INSIPID
A. Tasty B. Stupid
C. Discreet D. Feast

74. OBEYING
A. Ordering B. Following
C. Refusing D. Contradicting

75. VICTORIOUS
A. Defeated B. Annexed
C. Destroyed D. Vanquished

76. COMMISSIONED
A. Started B. Closed
C. Finished D. Terminated

77. VANITY
A. Pride B. Humility
C. Conceit D. Ostentious

78. ZENITH
A. Acme B. Top
C. Nadir D. Pinnacle

79. TANGIBLE
A. Ethereal B. Concrete
C. Actual D. Solid

80. REPRESS
A. Inhibit B. Liberate
C. Curb D. Quell

81. EPILOGUE
A. Dialogue B. Prelude
C. Post script D. Epigram

82. FRAUDULENT
A. Candid B. Direct
C. Forthright D. Genuine

83. LOQUACIOUS
A. Reticent B. Talkative
C. Garrulous D. Verbose

84. NIGGARDLY
A. Frugal B. Thrifty
C. Stingy D. Generous

85. PERTINENT
A. Irrational B. Irregular
C. Insistent D. Irrelevant

86. FAINT-HEARTED
A. Warm-hearted B. Full-blooded
C. Hot-blooded D. Stout-hearted

87. VIOLENT
A. Humble B. Harmless
C. Gentle D. Tame

88. STATIONARY
A. Active B. Mobile
C. Rapid D. Busy

89. HONORARY
A. Dishonourable B. Reputed
C. Paid D. Official

90. COMMON
A. Rare B. Small
C. Petty D. Poor

91. REPEL
A. Attend B. Concentrate
C. Continue D. Attract

92. ARTIFICIAL
A. Red B. Natural
C. Truthful D. Solid

93. CAPACIOUS
A. Limited B. Caring
C. Foolish D. Changeable

94. PROVOCATION
A. Vocation B. Pacification
C. Peace D. Destruction

95. METICULOUS
A. Mutual B. Shaggy
C. Meretricious D. Slovenly

96. ABLE
A. Disable B. Inable
C. Unable D. Enable

97. COMFORT
A. Uncomfort B. Miscomfort
C. Discomfort D. None of these

98. GAIN
A. Loose B. Fall
C. Lost D. Lose

99. SYNTHETIC
A. Affable B. Natural
C. Plastic D. Cosmetic

100. ACQUITTED
A. Freed B. Burdened
C. Convicted D. Entrusted

ANSWERS

1	2	3	4	5	6	7	8	9	10
B	B	D	A	B	D	D	C	B	D
11	**12**	**13**	**14**	**15**	**16**	**17**	**18**	**19**	**20**
C	C	B	C	D	A	C	C	D	A
21	**22**	**23**	**24**	**25**	**26**	**27**	**28**	**29**	**30**
A	C	D	A	C	C	A	C	D	A
31	**32**	**33**	**34**	**35**	**36**	**37**	**38**	**39**	**40**
A	D	C	A	C	D	C	A	A	A
41	**42**	**43**	**44**	**45**	**46**	**47**	**48**	**49**	**50**
C	B	C	D	B	D	D	B	A	A
51	**52**	**53**	**54**	**55**	**56**	**57**	**58**	**59**	**60**
C	C	C	D	B	D	C	D	C	D
61	**62**	**63**	**64**	**65**	**66**	**67**	**68**	**69**	**70**
D	B	B	A	C	A	C	B	B	B
71	**72**	**73**	**74**	**75**	**76**	**77**	**78**	**79**	**80**
D	C	A	A	A	D	B	C	A	B
81	**82**	**83**	**84**	**85**	**86**	**87**	**88**	**89**	**90**
B	D	B	D	D	D	C	B	C	A
91	**92**	**93**	**94**	**95**	**96**	**97**	**98**	**99**	**100**
D	B	A	B	D	C	C	D	B	C

❑❑❑

6 One Word Substitutions

There are many words in English language which can be perfectly used for a number of words. These words help in expressing ideas in a short and correct manner for the right occasion. Such words not only enhance the vocabulary but also enable you to economise in the use of words to a great extent. Try to learn as many as you can.

Denoting Numbers

- A collection of poems — *anthology*
- A number of merchant ships protected by warships (in war-time) — *convoy*
- A number of stars grouped together — *constellation*
- A number of hired applauders, *i.e.* persons paid to clap — *claque*
- A number of people at church — *congregation*
- A number of people gathered together for some common purpose — *gathering, assembly, society*
- A group of people who get together to work for some cause of common interest — *coterie*
- A number of workmen, prisoners, thieves — *gang*
- A number of sheep — *flock*
- A number of geese — *gaggle*
- A number of leopards — *leap*
- A number of lions, monkeys — *pride, troop*
- A number of herrings, mackerel — *shoal*
- A number of fish taken in a net — *catch, haul*
- A number of whales, porpoises — *school, gam*
- A number of oxen or horses (two or more) harnessed together — *team*
- A number of ships, cars, buses — *fleet*

Denoting Places

- A place where bees are kept — *apiary*
- A place where birds are kept — *aviary*
- A place where fishes are kept — *aquarium*
- A dwelling-place of an animal underground — *burrow*
- A squirrel's home — *drey*
- A nest of a bird of prey — *eyrie, aerie*

- A place where spirituous liquors are produced *distillery*
- A place where clothes are washed and ironed *laundry*
- A place where Government records are kept *archives*
- A place where treasures of art, curiosities, etc. are preserved or exhibited *museum*
- A place where fruit trees are grown *orchard*

Pertaining to the Literary Sphere

- A work whose writer is unknown *anonymous*
- A record of one's life written by oneself *autobiography*
- The history of the life of a person *biography*
- The heading or short description of a newspaper article, chapter of a book etc. *caption*
- A humorous play, having a happy ending *comedy*
- A list of books in a library *catalogue, bibliography*
- A book in which the events of each day are recorded *diary*
- A books containing the words of a language with their definitions, in alphabetical order *dictionary*
- A book of names and addresses *directory*
- A short speech by a player at the end of a play *epilogue*
- A brief summary of a book *epitome*
- A book containing information on all branches of knowledge *encyclopedia*
- To remove the offensive portions of a book *expurgate*
- A speech delivered without earlier preparation *extempore*
- A noisy or vehement speech intended to excite passions *harangue*
- A written account, usually in book form of the interesting and memorable experiences of one's life *memoirs*
- A note to help the memory *memorandum*
- A declaration of plans and promises put forward by a candidate for election, political party or a sovereign *manifesto*
- A short speech by a player at the beginning of a play *prologue*
- Literarv theft, or passing off an author's original work as one's own *plagiarism*
- Speaking aloud to oneself *soliloquy*
- A play with a sad or tragic end *tragedy*

Pertaining to Religion

- One who believes that man can have no knowledge of God but only of natural phenomena *agnostic*
- One who renounces his religious vows or forsakes his religious principles *apostate*
- One who does not believe in existence of God *atheist*
- One intolerantly devoted to a particular creed *bigot*
- To utter profane language against God or anything holy *blaspheme*
- A breaker of church images *iconoclast*
- Worship of images or idols *idiolatory*

- One who believes in God — *theist*
- One who believes in only one God — *monotheist*
- One who believes in many Gods — *polytheist*

Pertaining to Government

- To give up a throne or other office of dignity — *abdicate*
- Absence of government — *anarchy*
- Government by Sovereign of uncontrolled authority — *autocracy, despotism*
- Government by departments of states — *bureaucracy*
- Government of the people, for the people and by the people — *democracy*
- Government by the nobility — *aristocracy*
- The right of self-government — *autonomy*
- Government by a few — *oligarchy*
- Government by the wealthy — *plutocracy*
- Government by divine guidance — *theocracy*
- To decide a political question by the direct vote of the whole electorate — *referendum*
- Sweeping governmental change — *revolution*
- The science of government — *politics*

Pertaining to Professions

- One who attends to the diseases of the eye — *oculist*
- One who tests eyesight and sells spectacles — *optician*
- One who attends to the teeth — *dentist*
- One skilled in the care of hands and feet — *chiropodist*
- A physician who assists women at child-birth — *obstetrician*
- One who drives a motorcar — *chauffeur*
- One who makes or sells candles — *chandler*
- One who preserves the skins of animals and mounts them so as to resemble the living animals — *taxidermist*
- One who compiles a dictionary — *lexicographer*
- One who writes books — *author*
- One skilled in the treatment of diseases of animals — *veterinarian*
- A tradesman who manages funerals — *undertaker*
- One who draws up contracts and lends money on interest — *scrivener*
- One who lends money and keeps goods as security — *pawnbroker*
- A teacher who travels from place to place to give instruction. — *peripatetic*
- One who travels from place to place selling miscellaneous articles — *hawker, pedlar*
- One who collects postage stamps — *philatelist*
- One who lends money at exorbitant interest — *usurer*
- One who takes care of a building — *janitor*
- One who sells sweets and pastries — *confectioner*
- One who works in a coalmine — *collier*
- One who flies an aeroplane — *pilot, aviator*

- One who studies rocks and soils — *geologist*
- One who shoes horses — *farrier*
- A professional rider in horses races — *jockey*
- One who deals in silks, cotton, woollen, and linen goods — *mercer*
- One who deals in wines — *vintner*
- One who deals in fish — *fishmonger*
- One who deals in iron and hardware — *ironmonger*
- One who sells fruits, vegetables, etc. from a barrow — *costermonger*
- One who sets type in a printing office — *compositor*

Pertaining to Medicine

- A substance which destroys or weakens germs — *antiseptic*
- Any medicine which produces insensibility — *anaesthetic*
- A medicine to counteract poison — *antidote*
- Want or poorness of blood — *anaemia*
- A medicine which alleviates pain — *anodyne*
- To cut off a person's body a part which is infected — *amputate*
- One who is recovering from illness — *convalescent*
- To be able to tell the nature of disease by its symptoms — *diagnose*
- A disease affecting many persons at the same place and time — *epidemic*
- A disease confined to a particular district or place — *endemic*
- To disinfect by smoke — *fumigate*
- Free or exempt from infection — *immune*
- A person who is sick — *invalid*
- A cure for all diseases — *panacea*
- A disease widely epidemic — *pandemic*
- Confinement to one place to avoid spread of infection — *quarantine*

Pertaining to Characteristics and Actions

- One who devotes his life to the welfare and interests of other people — *altruist*
- One who can use both hands with equal ease — *ambidexterous*
- One who fishes with a rod — *angler*
- One who kills secretly or by surprise — *assassin*
- A person who collects things belonging to ancient times — *antiquary*
- One who is always finding faults — *censorious*
- One living at the same time as another — *contemporary*
- One who sneers at the aims and beliefs of his fellowmen — *cynic*
- One who delights in speaking about oneself — *egotist*
- One who exalts his own opinion — *egoist*
- One who dies for a noble cause — *martyr*
- One who retires from society to live a solitary life — *recluse, hermit*
- One who maliciously sets fire to buildings — *incendiary*

- One who is banished from his home or his country — *exile*
- One who takes refuge in a foreign country — *refugee, alien*
- One who runs away from justice or the law — *fugitive*
- One who walks in his sleep — *somnambulist*
- One who looks on the bright side of things — *optimist*
- One who looks on the dark side of things — *pessimist*
- A hater of mankind — *misanthropist*
- One who knows everything — *omniscient*
- One who is all powerful — *omnipotent*
- One who is present everywhere — *omnipresent*
- One who devotes his service or wealth for the love of mankind — *philanthropist*
- One new to anything — *novice, tyro, neophyte*
- One who engages in any pursuit for the love of it, and not for gain — *amateur*
- One who journeys to a holy place — *pilgrim*
- A leader of the people who can sway his followers by his oratory — *demagogue*
- One who has special skill in judging art, music, tastes, etc. — *connoisseur*
- One whose reasoning is clever yet false — *sophist*
- One who makes a display of his learning — *pedant*
- One who is indifferent to pain or pleasure — *stoic*
- One who loves his country and serves it devotedly — *patriot*
- One devoted to the pleasures of eating and drinking — *epicure*
- One who poses to be what he is not — *hypocrite, impostor*
- One who foretells events — *prophet*
- One who pretends to know a great deal about everything — *mountebank, charlatan, quack*
- One versed in many languages — *linguist*
- One who cannot pay one's debts — *insolvent*
- One who takes over after another in office or employment — *successor*
- One who has been before another in office or employment — *predecessor*
- One who is opposed to intellectual progress — *obscurant*
- One who abstains from alcoholic drinks — *teetotaller*
- One who hides away on a ship to obtain a free passage — *stowaway*
- One who spends very little — *miser*
- One who spends too much — *spendthrift*

Pertaining to War

- An unprovoked attack by an enemy — *aggression*
- Shells, bombs, military stores — *ammunition*
- A place where naval or military weapons are made or stored — *ordnance*
- An agreement between belligerents to stop fighting — *armistice*
- A general pardon of offenders — *amnesty*
- To reduce to nothing — *annihilate*
- Nations carrying on warfare — *belligerents*

- To surround a place with the intention of capturing — *besiege*
- To camp in the open air without tents or covering — *bivouac*
- To seize for military use — *commandeer*
- A person who is forced by law to become a soldier — *conscript*
- An order prohibiting ships to leave the ports — *embargo*
- A number of firearms being discharged continuously — *fusillade*
- To make an examination or preliminary survey of enemy territory for military objectives — *reconnoitre*

Pertaining to Marriage and Children

- One who marries a second wife or husband while the legal spouse is alive — *bigamist*
- One vowed to a single or unmarried life — *celibate*
- One engaged to be married — *fiancé, fiancee*
- A child whose parents are dead — *orphan*
- A hater of marriage — *misogamist*
- One who has more than two wives at a time — *polygamist*

Pertaining to Death

- Dead and decaying flesh (esp. of animals) — *carrion*
- A monument set up for persons who are buried elsewhere — *cenotaph*
- To preserve a dead body from putrefaction — *embalm*
- Words inscribed on a tomb — *epitaph*
- An examination of dead body — *postmortem, autopsy*
- An account in the newspaper of the funeral of one deceased — *obituary*
- The property left to someone by a will — *legacy*
- Occurring after death — *posthumous*
- The act of killing a human being — *homicide*
- Murder of a new born child — *infanticide*
- Murder of a brother — *fratricide*
- Murder of a sister — *sororicide*
- Murder of a mother — *matricide*
- Murder of a father — *patricide*
- Murder of a parent — *parricide*
- Murder of a king — *regicide*

Pertaining to Sciences and Arts

- The study of all heavenly bodies and the earth in relation to them — *astronomy*
- The science of land management — *agronomics*
- The study of mankind — *anthropology*
- The study of physical life or living matter — *biology*
- The study of plants — *botany*
- The art of beautiful handwriting — *calligraphy*

- The science which deals with the varieties of human race *ethnology*
- The study of the origin and history of words *etymology*
- The study of coins *numismatics*
- The study of human face *physiognomy*
- The art of making fireworks *pyrotechnics*
- The study of birds *ornithology*
- The study of languages *philology*
- At home equally on land or in water *amphibious*
- The inside of a nut *kernel*
- The central or innermost part of fruit *core*
- The animals of a certain region *fauna*
- The plants and vegetation of a certain region *flora*
- Absence of rain for a long time *drought*
- To supply land with water by artificial means *irrigate*
- One who studies plant and animal life *naturalist*
- A cud-chewing animal, *e.g.* the cow *ruminant*
- A gnawing animal, *e.g.* the rat *rodent*
- A four-footed animal *quadruped*
- Animals which carry their young in a pouch, *e.g.* kangaroo *marsupials*
- Soil composed largely of decayed vegetable matter *humus*
- A preparation for killing insects *insecticide*
- A plant or animal growing on another *parasite*
- Living for many years *perennial*

Miscellaneous

- Loud enough to be heard *audible*
- Not distinct enough to be heard *inaudible*
- Fit for food *edible*
- Unfit for human consumption *inedible*
- Fit to be chosen or selected *eligible*
- Not having the qualities for being chosen *ineligible*
- Writing that is easy to read *legible*
- Writing that is difficult to decipher *illegible*
- Able to read *literate*
- Unable to read *illiterate*
- Born of married parents *legitimate*
- Born of unmarried parents *illegitimate*
- To send back a person to his own country *repatriate*
- To banish from one's country *expatriate*
- To move from one country to another *migrate*
- One who leaves his country to settle in another *emigrant*
- One who comes into a foreign country to settle there *immigrant*

❑ Incapable of being redeemed from evil, *i.e.* beyond correction	*incorrigible*
❑ That which cannot be rubbed out or blotted out	*ineffaceable, indelible*
❑ That which cannot be conquered	*invincible*
❑ Incapable of making errors	*infallible*
❑ That which cannot be avoided or prevented	*inevitable*
❑ Incapable of being burnt	*incombustible*
❑ That which easily catches fire	*inflammable, flammable*
❑ That which cannot be seen	*invisible*
❑ Living for ever	*immortal*
❑ Increase the gravity of an offence	*aggravate*
❑ Ordinary or commonplace remark	*platitude*
❑ That which cannot be satisfied	*insatiable*
❑ That which cannot be repaired	*irreparable*
❑ That which cannot be imitated	*inimitable*
❑ Persons (or efforts) that cannot be wearied	*indefatigable*
❑ One who eats too much	*glutton*
❑ To destroy completely	*annihilate*
❑ A statement open to more than one interpretation	*ambiguous*
❑ A round about way of speaking	*circumlocution*
❑ Cautious observation of events, etc.	*circumspection*
❑ That which cannot be hurt	*invulnerable*

Multiple Choice Questions

Directions: *Below are given some statements each of which is capable of being expressed by one word only. Each statement is followed by four such words of which only one is correct. Out of the given alternatives A, B, C and D choose the correct word which very closely fits each definition.*

1. A set of papers giving information about a person or event:
A. editorial B. agenda
C. dossier D. clippings

2. List and explanations of technical, difficult, etc. terms:
A. preface B. glossary
C. bibliography D. appendix

3. One who pays too much care to his clothes and personal appearance:
A. conscious B. dandy
C. cynosure D. leer

4. A child born after death of father:
A. effeminate B. immature
C. fatherless D. posthumous

5. A person who is hard to please:
A. insensible B. hypocrite
C. egoist D. fastidious

6. Complete failure in something attempted:
A. fiasco B. vain
C. falsies D. flop

7. A word which can be interpreted in any way:
A. confusing B. misnomer
C. ambiguous D. precise

8. A group of persons united by common interests:
A. society B. class
C. clique D. coterie

9. A person who is inexperienced and easily deceived:
A. fool B. immature
C. blackhorn D. greenhorn

10. Instruction by question and answer:
A. interrogatory B. catechism
C. bulletin D. alibi

11. Record of events by someone with first hand knowledge:
A. novice B. report
C. memoir D. itinerary

12. A mode of talk familiar to a particular group or profession:
A. jargon B. colloquial
C. slang D. abuses

13. Person who is crazy:
A. lackadaisical B. tarter
C. scrupulous D. loony

14. A person who readily believes others:
A. hasty B. immature
C. credulous D. credible

15. One who eats human flesh:
A. beast B. cannibal
C. maneater D. carnivorous

16. Intentional destruction of racial groups:
A. genocide B. homicide
C. fratricide D. communal riot

17. One with weakness of mind caused by old age:
A. dastard B. dotard
C. fop D. philanderer

18. Study of insects:
A. zoology B. philology
C. entomology D. etymology

19. A critical judge of any art particularly fine arts:
A. connoisseur B. veteran
C. philistine D. dilettante

20. One who introduces items of an entertainment:
A. consort B. compere
C. director D. introducer

21. A combination of business firms:
A. enterprise B. franchise
C. cartel D. autonomous

22. Freeing of suppressed emotions:
A. catastrophe B. catharsis
C. epilogue D. chagrin

23. One who believes in the power of fate:
A. optimist B. pessimist
C. fearful D. fatalist

24. The murder of brother:
A. genocide B. homicide
C. salvage D. fratricide

25. Additional to proper payment:
A. premium B. overtime
C. ex-gratia D. fringe

26. A person or thing used to tempt somebody into a position of danger:
A. decoy B. provocateur
C. jinx D. scapegoat

27. Custom of having more than one husband at the same time:
A. polygamy B. polyandry
C. bigamy D. sexagenary

28. A person of refined taste in food and drink:
A. emeritus B. epicure
C. glutton D. gourmand

29. A tombstone inscription:
A. epithet B. encomium
C. epistle D. epitaph

30. An office which has no work but high salary:
A. fortuitous B. gratuitous
C. sinecure D. ceremonial

31. One who is indifferent to pains and pleasure of life:
A. stoic B. metaphysical
C. pessimist D. sceptic

32. List of names of persons showing duties to be performed by each in turn:
A. notice B. bulletin
C. roster D. agenda

33. Long angry speech of criticism or accusation:
A. track record B. tirade
C. taut D. outburst

34. One who is in favour of never drinking alcoholic drinks:
A. idealist B. uxorious
C. teetotaller D. unalcoholic

35. Trying to win favour by flattery and charm:
A. smarmy B. shrewish
C. toady D. loquacious

36. A decision on which one cannot go back:
A. incorrigible B. irrevocable
C. rigid D. invulnerable

37. The science that studies the varieties of human race:
A. phrenology B. physiology
C. sociology D. ethnology

38. A person who hates women:
A. philogynist B. philatelist
C. misogamist D. misogynist

39. A group of people in a particular grade in an organisation:
A. colleague B. staff
C. echelon D. commission

40. Honourably discharged from service:
A. emeritus B. latitudinarian
C. infallible D. meritorious

41. One who does not believe in the existence of God:
A. atheist B. altruist
C. agnostic D. flippant

42. The large money paid for an early retirement:
A. goldmine B. golden handshake
C. gratuity D. lion's share

43. A hater of learning and knowledge:
A. misologist B. misogynist
C. philologist D. philanthropist

44. One who lives and acts for the welfare of others:
A. misanthrope B. credulous
C. altruist D. gregarious

45. Mental weariness for want of occupation:
A. desperate B. depression
C. fatigue D. ennui

46. That which makes it difficult to recognise the presence in real of somebody or something:
A. cover B. mask
C. make-up D. camouflage

47. To bear a hand in one's new business:
A. partnership B. interfere
C. assist D. join

48. One who renounces the world and practices self-discipline in order to attain salvation:
A. devotee B. ascetic
C. theist D. parsimonious

49. A place where gambling is practiced:
A. hotel B. motel
C. casino D. stadium

50. A sad song is a:
A. dirge B. elegy
C. ditty D. knell

ANSWERS

1	2	3	4	5	6	7	8	9	10
C	B	B	D	D	A	C	C	D	B
11	12	13	14	15	16	17	18	19	20
C	A	D	C	B	A	B	C	A	B
21	22	23	24	25	26	27	28	29	30
C	B	D	D	D	A	B	B	D	C
31	32	33	34	35	36	37	38	39	40
A	C	B	C	A	B	D	D	C	A
41	42	43	44	45	46	47	48	49	50
A	B	A	C	D	D	C	B	C	A

❑❑❑

7 Idioms and Phrases

- An idiom is a group of words established by usage as having a meaning different from the individual words.
- A phrase is a small group of words standing together as an idiomatic expression.

Learn and practise as may as you can.

Idioms and Idiomatic Phrases

✦ **ABC** (basic principles)
She does not know the ABC of photography.

✦ **At one's beck and call** (ready to obey)
He had a dozen men at his beck and call.

✦ **At sixes and sevens** (in disorder)
The drawing room articles were lying at sixes and sevens on the floor.

✦ **A wet blanket** (a discouraging person)
Don't allow Rakesh to accompany you to the hunting trip because he is a wet blanket.

✦ **A big gun** (an important person)
Mr Smith is a big gun in our city.

✦ **At a stone's throw** (at a short distance from)
My school is at a stone's throw from my house.

✦ **A man of word** (a person who keeps his promise)
Mr Sharma is a man of word.

✦ **A man of a few words** (a remarkable person)
Gandhiji was a man of a few words.

✦ **At arm's length** (to keep away)
We should always keep bad boys at arm's length

✦ **A bolt from the blue** (a sudden and unexpected event)
The news of my friend's death came to me like a bolt from the blue.

✦ **A man of letters** (a scholar)
Radha Krishnan was a man of letters.

✦ **A hard nut to crack.** (a puzzling problem)
To get a win over American basket ball team is a hard nut to crack for India.

✦ **A yeoman's service** (service which is beneficial to the human beings)
He did yeoman's service through his life.

✦ **A snake in the grass** (a hidden foe)
Beware of him because he seems to be a snake in the grass.

✦ **Acid test** (hard test)
The election will be an acid test for the ruling party.

✦ **A wolf in sheep's clothing** (a hypocrite)
You should not keep company with him because he is a wolf in sheep's clothing.

✦ **At the eleventh hour** (at the last moment)
The war was about to start but fortunately at the eleventh hour a messenger came to the PM with a message of peace.

✦ **A great card** (an important person)
Mr Sood is a great card in the ministry of finance.

✦ **A fool of the first water** (one completely foolish)
Being a fool of the first water he could not solve even the simplest sum.

✦ **A bone of contention** (to be the cause of quarrel)
Kashmir is the bone of contention between India and Pakistan.

✦ **A green hand** (not very much experienced)
We shall pay a little to a green hand.

✦ **All in all** (completely)
Rajesh is all in all in this office.

✦ **A bed of roses** (a comfort)
Life is not a bed of roses.

✦ **An apple of discord** (to be the cause of)
Kashmir is an apple of discord between India and Pakistan.

✦ **A white elephant** (of no use)
This sort of glib talker always proves a white elephant in the end.

✦ **A red letter day** (An important day)
15th August is a red letter day for the Indians.

✦ **By hook or by crook** (by any means fair or foul)

✦ **Black sheep** (a traitor)
Later on Mr XYZ proved a black sheep.

✦ **By dint of** (by means of)
By dint of hard work, she earned a lot of money.

✦ **Break ones back** (to work hard to get something)
He broke his back to earn his livelihood.

✦ **Break the back of** (accomplish the hardest part of a certain job)
There is nothing to be worried about as we've already broken the back of the problem.

✦ **Beat about the bush** (to go on talking on some worthless topic)
Stop this beating about the bush, come to the main task.

✦ **Beyond one's means** (beyond one's budget)
He is living beyond his means, therefore, he is sure to get ruined.

✦ **Cut loose** (Keep away)
India should cut loose from bad politics.

✦ **Chips of the same block** (having the same taste)
They are the chips of the same block.

✦ **Cut-throat competition** (a stiff competition)
There is a cut-throat competition among the publishers in the market.

✦ **Come what may** (no matter what happens)
I'll do it come what may.

✦ **Drop someone a line** (send a letter, etc.)
Please drop me a line of your well-being.

✦ **Dull the edge of** (reduce the intensity of)
Take this pill and it will dull the edge of pain.

✦ **From hand to mouth** (without any saving)
The poor factory worker is living from hand to mouth.

✦ **Fair and square** (clean)
One must be fair and square in one's dealing.

✦ **Hard of hearing** (somewhat deaf)
She is a bit hard of hearing.

✦ **In the good books of** (be good in one's mind)
Jack is in the good books of his teachers.

✦ **In black and white** (in written)
Don't give him anything in black and white.

✦ **In cold blood** (mercilessly)
The old woman was murdered in cold blood.

✦ **In a crack** (all of a sudden or rapidly)
The thief left the place in a crack.

✦ **In full swing** (in full force)
The studies of the students are going on in full swing.

✦ **In the twinkling of an eye** (quickly)
The monkey ate up grams in the twinkling of an eye.

✦ **Keep the ball rolling** (to maintain the progress of some activity)
After the death of his father he had to take the charge of his office to keep the ball rolling.

✦ **Neck and neck** (even)
There is a neck and neck fight between the two boxers.

✦ **Once in a blue moon** (seldom)
She visits her brother once in a blue moon.

✦ **Slow and steady** (slowly but continually)
Slow and steady wins the race.

✦ **To cut a sorry figure** (present oneself in a bad way)
She cut a sorry figure on the stage.

✦ **To give a red carpet reception** (to give a warm welcome)
The PM was given a red carpet reception in America.

✦ **To dance one's tune** (to follow someone submissively)
He always dances to his brother's tune.

✦ **To turn a deaf ear to** (to disregard)
She turned a deaf ear to her parents' advice.

✦ **To call a spade a spade** (to speak the truth)
Gandhiji always called a spade a spade.

✦ **To bring to book** (to scold)
The naughty boy was brought to book by the teacher.

✦ **To cut short** (to reduce)
Smoking will cut short your life.
He wants to get money by hook or by crook.

✦ **To grease the palm of** (to bribe)
Rohit greased the palm of the clerk and got the file moved.

✦ **Through thick and thin.** (under all circumstances)
We'll stand by you through thick and thin.

✦ **To die by inches** (to die a painful death)
The old man died by inches.

✦ **To eat one's words** (to retract one's statement)
You'll have to eat your words because you have spoken without thinking.

✦ **To burn the midnight oil** (to work hard)
You'll have to burn the midnight oil if you want to get good marks.

✦ **To poke one's nose into** (to meddle with)
It is bad to poke your nose into others' affair.

✦ **To fall flat** (to have no effect)
His father's advice fell flat on him.

✦ **To make a clean breast of** (to confess)
He made a clean breast of his involvement in the bomb blast.

✦ **To get the better of** (overcome)
Anger got the better of him.

✦ **To break somebody's back** (to give too much work to him to do)
She broke his back by giving him so much hard work to do.

✦ **Throw cold water on** (to discourage)
She tried to throw cold water on his plan but he was well-determined.

✦ **The long and short of** (in brief)
The long and short of his lecture is that we should live like brothers.

✦ **To burn one's fingers** (to get oneself in trouble)
You have burnt your fingers by speaking against him.

✦ **To turn over a new leaf** (to change the course of life)
He has turned over a new leaf in his life.

✦ **To have one's own axe to grind** (to have vested interest)
He has his own axe to grind in this matter.

✦ **To take to one's heels** (to run away)
The thief took to his heels as soon as he saw the policeman.

✦ **To move heaven and earth** (to make too much effort)
The young man moved heaven and earth to find a job.

✦ **To be caught red handed** (to be caught at the time of committing a crime)
The clerk was caught red handed when he was accepting bribe from Mr ABC.

✦ **To receive with open arms** (to give a warm welcome)
The new president of the club was received with open arms by the members.

✦ **To be born with a silver spoon in one's mouth** (to be born in a rich family)
Mr. J. L. Nehru was born with a silver spoon in his mouth.

✦ **To come to light** (to be known)
A new disease has recently come to light.

✦ **To be the apple of one's eye** (be very dear)
He is the apple of his parent's eye.

✦ **To make fun of** (laugh at)
The children made fun of the waiter in the hotel.

✦ **To let the cat out of the bag** (to divulge secret)
It was Sohan who let the cat out of the bag by telling the real matter.

✦ **To open a new chapter** (to start some habit, etc.
By drinking, you've opened a new chapter in your life.

✦ **To make the flesh creep** (to terrify)
The story made my flesh creep.

✦ **To lose ground** (to retreat)
After fighting for some time the Pakistani army began to lose ground.

- **To bring to book** (to punish)
The student was brought to book by the teacher.
- **To show a clean pair of heels** (to run away)
The thief showed a clean pair of heels as soon as he saw the policeman approaching.
- **To gain ground** (to be established)
He gained ground in India in a few years.
- **To get wind of** (to get information)
I got wind of his secret plans.
- **Under a cloud** (be in trouble or in a state of disgrace or suspicion)
His company seemed to be under a cloud as it had no funds to pay the wages to the workers.

Verbal Phrases

- **Act upon** (to follow)
I acted upon my father's advice.
- **Act upto** (to perform within limits)
He acted upto his conscience.
- **Act beyond** (to perform crossing limits)
We should not act beyond our capacity.
- **Act for** (to perform in place of someone else)
The vice principal acted for the principal.
- **Back up** (to make a queue)
The vehicles began to back up.
- **Back down** (withdraw claim in the presence of opposition)
The leader backed down from his previous statement.
- **Back off** (draw back some plan or action)
They backed off from building a flyover.
- **Back out** (withdraw from a promise, etc.)
The government backed out of its promise.
- **Break down** (stop working) My car broke down on the highway.
- **Break into** (enter in certain premises by breaking the door, etc.)
Last night a thief broke into my neighbour's.
- **Break off** (stop all of a sudden)
She broke off and began to think over about her/his hand.
- **Break out** (spread)
Cholera has broken out in the town.
- **Break out of** (escape from)
A prisoner broke out of the prison last night.
- **Break up** (disperse)
The cloud of fog began to break up as the sun rose.
- **Break something up** (Cause something to break into small pieces)
She broke up the chocolate to distribute it among the girls.
- **Break with** (Cut off connection after quarrelling with someone)
He has broken with his brother.
- **Call on** (pay a visit to somebody)
I'll call on Mohan's today.
- **Call out** (to start)
The workers have called out a strike.
- **Call off** (to stop the strike etc.)
The workers have called off the strike.
- **Call at** (to visit someone's house)
I called at his house yesterday.
- **Call in** (send for)
Please call in the doctor.
- **Carry on** (continue)
Please carry on your work.
- **Carry something out** (perform a task)
Our company is carrying out a big deal with a foreign company.
- **Carry something over** (postpone)
The fancy dress competition had to be carried over till Monday)
- **Carry someone off** (kill somebody)
Cancer carried her off on the day of her 20th birthday.
- **Come of age** (get established)
As our company has come of age, so, there is no problem in selling our goods.
- **Come of** (belong to)
She comes of a royal family.
- **Come over** (surmount)
We at last came over all our problems.

✦ **Come off** (to take place)
The marriage of my brother comes off in the next month.

✦ **Come round** (agree)
At last he came round to my views.

✦ **Come under** (fall in the category of)
All these animals come under the same species.

✦ **Come down with** (suffer from)
She came down with whopping cough.

✦ **Come from** (be the nature of)
She came from London.

✦ **Come about** (happen)
The explosion came about when the worker struck the match to light a cigarette.

✦ **Cut off** (die)
The princess was cut off in the prime of her life.

✦ **Cut down** (reduce)
The prices of consumer goods should be cut down.

✦ **Cut someone out** (exclude someone)
His father cut him out of his will.

✦ **Fall in**
She fell in love with the prince.

✦ **Fall down** (fail)
The deal fell down for lack of transparency.

✦ **Fall out** (quarrel)
She fell out with his elder brother.

✦ **Fall through** (fail)
The project fell through for lack of funds.

✦ **Get away** (escape)
She got away with her life.

✦ **Get by** (to accomplish something with great difficulty)
She is not rich. She has just enough to get by.

✦ **Get on** (perform)
How are you getting on with your studies?

✦ **Get out** (become known)
The news got out that the PM was paying a visit to Russia.

✦ **Get over** (overcome)
At last I got over all obstacles.

✦ **Get up** (rise)
When do you get up in the morning?

✦ **Give up** (stop)
He gave up smoking.

✦ **Give out** (emit)
Garlic gives out a pungent smell.

✦ **Give in** (collapse)
The bridge gave in under the heavy load.

✦ **Give away** (distribute)
The Principal gave away the prizes.

✦ **Give out** (announce)
It was given out that the President of India would visit the place soon.

✦ **Go off** (explode)
The gun went off suddenly.

✦ **Go on** (continue)
She went on about how she flew the aeroplane.

✦ **Go through** (examine)
I'll go through this book later on.

✦ **Go up** (be built)
The construction of the house is going up.

✦ **Grind on** (continue for a long time in a tedious way)
The discussion over political issues ground on.

✦ **Grind something out** (produce something a tedious way)
She will grind some more short stories.

✦ **Look out** (be careful)
Look out! there is a snake.

✦ **Look down upon** (hate)
We should not look down upon the poor.

✦ **Look at** (watch)
Look at the blackboard.

✦ **Look after** (take care of)
We ought to look after our old parents.

✦ **Look into** (investigate)
The new police inspector will look into the matter.

✦ **Look up** (rise)
The prices of consumer goods are looking up.

✦ **Look back** (think of the past)
It made her feel disolate when she looked back on things of the past.

✦ **Make up** (to fulfil)
I'll make up my deficiency in Mathematics.

✦ **Make out** (understand)
I could not make out what she said.

✦ **Make up one' mind** (to resolve)
I have made up my mind to settle in the USA.

✦ **Make off** (leave hurriedly)
She made off without informing anybody.

✦ **Make something over** (transfer)
She should make her property over to her sons.

✦ **Make over** (hand over)
He made over the charge of the file to Mr Robert.

✦ **Pull back** (retreat)
The government has pulled back from its previous policy.

✦ **Pull something down** (demolish)
The authorities concerned pulled down a few building which were illegally built on government land.

✦ **Pull out** (pluck)
The child pulled out a few petals of the flower.

✦ **Pull through** (recover)
The patient will pull through.

✦ **Push on** (continue a journey)
It was getting darker but we pushed on.

✦ **Push at** (exert force)
He pushed at the bell, but it did not ring.

✦ **Push for** (demand persistently)
The workers have been pushing for the installation of new machines for five years.

✦ **Put out** (extinguish)
She put out the light.

✦ **Put on** (wear)
He put on an overcoat.

✦ **Put off** (postpone)
The plan had to be put off.

✦ **Put by** (spare something for future)
We must put by some money for future.

✦ **Put up with** (stay)
Your aunt is out of town for a couple of days, you may put up with us till she comes.

✦ **Put something down** (record something)
She put a new idea down on the paper.

✦ **Take after** (resemble)
He takes after his father.

✦ **Take off** (remove)
He took off his shoes.

✦ **Take something out** (obtain)
You may take out some money from Rohit if you want to purchase this car.

✦ **Take to** (fall into the habit of)
He took to gambling.

✦ **Turn something down** (reject something)
The judge turned down his appeal.

✦ **Turn on** (attack)
The thief turned on him with a knife.

Multiple Choice Questions

Directions: *Some idioms/phrases are given below with their probable meanings. Select the options with their correct meanings.*

1. **Carry out**
   A. To take from one place to another
   B. To continue
   C. To obey
   D. To make efforts

2. **In the same boat**
   A. A worn out choice
   B. Indifferent
   C. In identical circumstances
   D. Carry off

3. **In one's good book**
   A. A costly book
   B. A priceless treasure

C. In one's favour
D. An enchanting beauty

4. Keep a straight face
A. To do make up
B. To change clothes
C. Assume responsibility
D. To remain serious

5. To be above board
A. To have a good height
B. To be honest in any business deal
C. To have no debts
D. To try to be beautiful

6. On the face of it
A. To agree B. From an action
C. More than enough D. Apparently

7. Let the bygones be bygones
A. In one's favour B. To pretend
C. To forget the past D. Other choice

8. To split hairs
A. Major distinctions
B. Hair with two ends
C. To make minute distinction
D. Without distinction

9. Bread and butter
A. Both bread and butter
B. Something essential
C. Livelihood
D. Relevant things

10. To bell the cat
A. To catch a cat and tie a bell round its neck
B. To make an effort
C. To be quick
D. To face a risk

11. Hard and fast
A. Strict B. Solid
C. Fast moving D. Some hard surface

12. Part and parcel
A. The part of a parcel
B. An essential part
C. A missing parcel
D. Some part of a machine sent by parcel

13. Null and void
A. Something invalid
B. Something that can be avoided
C. Something that can be nullified
D. Something evil

14. To make clean breast of
A. To gain prominence
B. To praise oneself
C. To confess without reserve
D. To destroy before it blooms

15. Trump card
A. A powerful means of achieving an object
B. Resourcefulness
C. The best gamble to attain success
D. None of these

16. Tall talk
A. A discussion continued for a long time
B. A high sounding talk
C. A meaningful talk
D. A useless talk

17. Small talk
A. Gossip
B. A discussion carried on for a long time
C. A brief discussion
D. None of these

18. Throw out of gear
A. To replace B. Hinder, disturb
C. To decide D. Take up tune

19. To and fro
A. Back and forth B. Puzzled
C. Amazed D. Reprove

20. To bell the cat
A. To do an easy job
B. To be indifferent to
C. To undertake a difficult job
D. To clarify

21. To be under cloud
A. Puzzle
B. Enjoy the favour
C. Talk thoughtlessly
D. To be under suspicion

22. A labour of love
A. A tragic end
B. A funny thing
C. Not fruitful
D. Work done without payment

23. Follow suit
A. Follow an example B. Wear a new dress
C. Irrelevant D. A gay person

24. Foul play
A. Bad intentions
B. A play not well acted
C. A play not liked by the audience
D. None of these

25. To pick holes
A. To find some reason to quarrel
B. To destroy something
C. To criticise someone
D. To cut some part of an item

26. To smell a rat
A. To see signs of plague epidemic
B. To get bad smell of a dead rat
C. To suspect foul dealings
D. To be in a bad mood

27. To put a spoke in one's wheel
A. To encourage
B. Act without restraint
C. Risk something
D. To obstruct one's progress

28. To pull one's leg
A. To give up B. Take care of
C. To befool D. To know

29. To play with fire
A. Grasp the truth
B. To handle something dangerous
C. To ridicule
D. To flee away

30. To reckon with
A. Take up time
B. Make an inventory
C. To deal with
D. Submit to punishment

31. To run short
A. Talk until one is tired at
B. Apply to oneself
C. To get rid of
D. To have or be too little

32. A man of letters
A. A postman B. A learned man
C. A hypocrite D. An ignorant man

33. A maiden speech
A. A speech made in the parliament
B. A speech made before unmarried girls
C. A speech made by a political leader
D. A speech made for the first time

34. Order of the day
A. An order passed on a particular day
B. A current law
C. Something common or general
D. None of these

35. To end in smoke
A. To make completely understand
B. To ruin oneself
C. To excite great applause
D. None of these

36. To give vent to
A. To allow to flow forth
B. To prove a failure
C. To amass wealth
D. To evade

37. To eat humble pie
A. To apologise or confess
B. To order
C. To flatter
D. To get rid of

38. A black sheep
A. An unlucky person
B. A negro
C. An ugly person
D. None of these

39. To catch a tartar
A. To trap wanted criminal with great difficulty
B. To catch a dangerous person
C. To meet with disaster
D. To deal with a person who is more than one's watch

40. Sit on fence
A. To remain neutral
B. To show contempt
C. To enjoy the surroundings
D. To become fond of

41. Pay off old scores
A. To repay the debt
B. To have revenge
C. To invite
D. Secretly

42. Turn turtle
A. To cheat
B. To be lopsided
C. To frustrate
D. To dance to the tune

43. Wash one's hands of
A. To refuse
B. To assist
C. To abuse
D. To refuse to be

44. Under duress
A. Under compulsion
B. Willing
C. To elicit information
D. To demand

45. To turn the tables
A. To ruin someone
B. To turn the situation to one's own side
C. To reverse the situation
D. To move from one point to another

46. On the cards
A. Possibly
B. Probably
C. Openly
D. Likely

47. To leave someone in the lurch
A. To come to compromise with someone
B. Constant source of annoyance to someone
C. To put someone at ease
D. To desert someone in his difficulties

48. To play second fiddle
A. To be happy, cheerful and healthy
B. To reduce importance of one's senior
C. To support the role and view of another person
D. To do back seat driving

49. To yearn for
A. To weep for
B. To remember
C. To admire
D. To long for intensely

50. Call off
A. To finish
B. To withdraw
C. To postpone
D. To cry

ANSWERS

1	2	3	4	5	6	7	8	9	10
C	C	C	D	B	D	C	C	C	D
11	**12**	**13**	**14**	**15**	**16**	**17**	**18**	**19**	**20**
A	B	A	C	C	B	A	B	A	C
21	**22**	**23**	**24**	**25**	**26**	**27**	**28**	**29**	**30**
D	D	A	A	C	C	D	C	B	C
31	**32**	**33**	**34**	**35**	**36**	**37**	**38**	**39**	**40**
D	B	D	C	D	A	A	D	B	A
41	**42**	**43**	**44**	**45**	**46**	**47**	**48**	**49**	**50**
B	B	D	A	C	D	D	C	D	B

❑❑❑

8 Narration

Direct and Indirect Narration/Speech

The exact words spoken by the speaker are known as Direct Speech.

The words spoken by somebody and expressed by someone else with some modification are known as Indirect Speech.

(*a*) Ram says to me, "You do not help me."

(*b*) Ram tells me that I do not help him.

The sentence (*a*) shows the words spoken by Ram. So, it is a sentence of Direct Speech.

The sentence (*b*) shows the words spoken by Ram and expressed by someone else with certain modification. So, it is a sentence of Indirect Speech.

The following points should be noted while changing Direct Speech into Indirect speech:

1. The verb outside the inverted commas is called the Reporting Verb.
2. The verb or sentence inside the inverted commas is called the Reported Speech.
3. If the Reporting verb is in the Present or Future Tense, there is no change in the tense in the Reported Speech.
4. If the Reporting Verb is in the Past Tense, the Tense in the Reported Speech is changed.
5. The Reporting verb may be in any Tense, in it the Pronouns are changed as under:
   (*i*) First Person according to Subject
   (*ii*) Second Person according to Object
   (*iii*) Third Person, No change.
6. If the Reporting verb is in the Past Tense the Adverb will change as under in the Indirect Speech.

Direct	***Indirect***
now	then
here	there
after	before
today	that day
yesterday	the previous day
these	those
tomorrow	the next day
last week	the previous week
this	that

7. Adjectives/Determiners are changed as under:

Direct	***Indirect***
this	that
these	those

Rules for Change of Tense

Reporting Verb	Reporting Speech	Change of Tense
Present Tense	Any Tense	No change
Future Tense	Any Tense	No change
Past Tense	Present/Future Tense	Change into corresponding Past Tense
Past Tense	Past Indefinite Tense	Change into Past Perfect Tense
Past Tense	Past Continuous Tense	Change into Past Perfect Continuous Tense
Past Tense	Past Perfect/Perfect Continuous Tense	No change
Past Tense	Universal Truth	No change
Past Tense	Proverb	No change

Transformation of Speech Based on Special Rules

1. Rule Related to Interrogative Sentence

- If the answer of an interrogative sentence is possible in yes-no manner.

Illustration.

Dhoni said to Sachin, "Will you help me?"

Dhoni asked Sachin whether he would help him.

(**Note :** The answer of R.S. is possible in yes-no manner)

Rule of Transformation from Direct to Indirect speech

Step I : Change R.V. into ask.

Step II : In place of comma use 'if/whether'.

Step III : Change interrogative sentence into assertive sentence.

- If the answer of an interrogative sentence is not possible in yes-no manner.

Illustration:

Sachin said to Dhoni, "What do you want?"

Sachin asked Dhoni what he wanted.

(**Note :** Only in Step II, you have to avoid comma and inverted comma and rest will be same as mentioned above).

2. Rule related to Imperative Sentence

- Imperative sentence is a sentence which shows Order/Advice/Request

Illustration:

My teacher said to me, "Go there".

My teacher ordered me to go there.

Rule of Transformation from Direct to Indirect Speech

Step I : Change R.V. as per meaning/sense of R.S. into order/request/advise.

Step II : In place of comma, use 'to'.

Step III : Rest portion will be same.

3. Rule related to Optative Sentence

- Optative sentence is a sentence which expresses the feeling of bless/curse/pray/wish.

Illustration:

Mother said to me, "May you live long!"

Mother blessed me that I might live long.

Rule of Transformation from Direct to Indirect Speech

Step I : Change R.V. as per meaning/sense of R.S. into bless/curse/pray/wish.

Step II : In place of comma, use 'that'.

Step III : Change optative sentence into assertive sentence.

4. Rule related to Exclamatory Sentence

- Exclamatory sentence is a sentence which takes note of exclamatory (!) mark in that sentence showing inner feeling.

Illustration:

She said, "Alas! I am ruined".

She exclaimed with sorrow that she was ruined.

Rule of Transformation from Direct to Indirect Speech

Step I : Change R.V. as per meaning/sense of R.S. into exclaim/exclaims/exclaimed/will or shall exclaim + joy/sorrow/anger/surprise/applause/contempt.

Step II : Change comma into that.

Step III : Change note of exclamation (!) into full stop (.)

Step IV : Change exclamatory sentence into assertive sentence.

Universal, Historical truth, etc.

If the Reported Speech expresses a Universal or Historical or Habitual truth, its Tense will not change.

1. The teacher said to the students, "The sun rises in the east."

   The teacher told the students that the sun rises in the east.

2. My father said to me, "The First Battle of Panipat was fought in 1526."

   My father told me that the First Battle of Panipat was fought in 1526.

Multiple Choice Questions

Directions (Qs. 1 to 13): *Select the correct Indirect Speech for the following sentences:*

1. I said to him, "I shall help you."
- A. I told him that I can help him.
- B. I told him that I would help him.
- C. I told him that I will help him.
- D. I told him that I shall be helping him.

2. My Teacher said to me, "The earth revolves round the sun."
- A. My teacher told me that the earth revolves round the sun.
- B. My teacher told me that the earth revolve round the sun.
- C. My teacher told me that the earth had been revolving round the sun.
- D. My teacher told me that the earth has been revolving round the sun.

3. I said to my friend, "My father daily goes for a walk."
- A. I told my friend that my father daily goes for a walk.
- B. I told my friend that my father daily went for a walk.
- C. I told my friend that my father has to go for a walk.
- D. I told my friend that my father had gone for a walk.

4. He said to me, "May God bless you!"
- A. He requested that God can bless me.
- B. He prayed that God can bless me.
- C. He prayed that God might bless me.
- D. He prayed that God will bless me.

5. The patient said, "Thank you, doctor."
- A. The patient thanked the doctor.
- B. The patient requested the doctor with thanks.
- C. The patient told the doctor thanks.
- D. The patient suggested the doctor thanks.

6. Satish said, "No, I shall not talk to him."
- A. Satish told that he should not talk to him.
- B. Satish suggested that he would not have talked to him.
- C. Satish exclaimed with sorrow that he would not talk with him.
- D. Satish refused to talk to him.

7. The child said, "What a lovely place!"
- A. The child exclaimed with sorrow that it was a lovely place.
- B. The child thought that the place was lovely.
- C. The child exclaimed with joy that the place was very lovely.
- D. The child suggested that the place was lovely.

8. He said, "What a fool I have been!"
- A. He told himself with sorrow that he was a fool.
- B. He confessed with regret that he had been a great fool.
- C. He said himself a fool.
- D. He suggested that he could be a fool.

9. He said, "Alas! I am ruined."
- A. He told me that he had been ruined.
- B. He exclaimed with joy that he had been ruined.
- C. He exclaimed with sorrow that he was ruined.
- D. He told me that he should not be ruined.

10. The accused said, "I am not guilty."
- A. The accused exclaimed with sorrow that I am not guilty.
- B. The accused exclaimed with joy that he was not guilty.
- C. The accused stated that he was not guilty.
- D. The accused told me that he has not been guilty.

11. My teacher said, "The earth is round".
- A. My teacher said that the earth was round.
- B. My teacher says that the earth is round.
- C. My teacher said that the earth is round.
- D. My teacher ordered that the earth is round.

12. He said, "What a place it is!"

A. He said that it was a very fine place.
B. He said that is a very fine place.
C. He said that the place is fine.
D. He exclaimed with joy/surprise that it was a very fine place.

13. Ria said, "Shall I thread the needle?"

A. Ria asked if she should thread the needle.
B. Ria asked if she shall thread the needle.
C. Ria ordered if she should thread the needle.
D. Ria says that if she would thread the needle.

Directions (Qs. 14 to 33): *Pick out the correct alternative that completes the incomplete sentence which is changed into Indirect Narration.*

14. She said to me, "I shall see you as soon as I get time."
She told me:

A. that she will see me as soon as she will get time.
B. that she would see me as soon as she would get time.
C. she would see me whenever she got time.
D. that she would see me whenever she gets time.

15. My secretary said to me, "Your plane will leave if you do not go at once."
My secretary told me that:

A. her plane would leave if she did not go at that time.
B. her plane would leave if I do not go at once.
C. my plane would leave if I did not go at that very time.
D. my plane will leave if I did not go at that time.

16. My mother said to me, "Don't quarrel among yourselves".
My mother:

A. forbade me to quarrel among ourselves.
B. asked me not to quarrel among ourselves.
C. asked me that not to quarrel among ourselves.
D. asked me to quarrel not among ourselves.

17. Her father said to her mother, "Excuse the daughter."
Her father:

A. requested her mother to excuse the daughter.
B. asked her mother to excuse the daughter.
C. asked her mother to have excused the daughter.
D. asked her mother to have been excused.

18. He said to his friend, "Wait here till father comes."
He requested his friend:

A. to wait here till father had come.
B. that to wait there till his friend came.
C. to wait there till father came.
D. to wait here until his friend came.

19. She said to her maid, "Run and catch the thief."
She ordered her maid:

A. ran and catch the thief.
B. that to run and to catch the thief.
C. ran and caught the thief.
D. to run and catch the thief.

20. Anita said to Sunita, "What are you doing?"
Anita asked Sunita:

A. what she will be doing.
B. that what she is doing.
C. that what she was doing.
D. what she was doing.

21. She said to me, "Are you meeting me today?"
She enquired of me:

A. whether I am meeting her that day.
B. whether I was meeting her today.
C. whether I was meeting her that day.
D. I was meeting her that day.

22. Nitish said to me, "When did you buy this pen?"
Nitish asked me:

A. when I was to buy that pen.
B. when I would buy that pen.
C. when I had bought that pen.
D. when I was buying that pen.

23. She said to me, "Are you going to market?"
She enquired of me:
A. I am going to market.
B. I was going to market.
C. if I was going to market.
D. if I had been going to the market.

24. Damini said, "Why did not you change your clothes?"
Damini asked me:
A. why I had not changed my clothes.
B. why I did not change my clothes.
C. why I would not change my clothes.
D. why I have not been changing my clothes.

25. Umesh said to me, "Have you read that novel?"
Umesh asked me:
A. if he was reading that novel.
B. if he had read that novel.
C. if I had read that novel.
D. if I was reading that novel.

26. She said to me, "I shall forgive you."
She told me:
A. that she will forgive me.
B. that she was going to forgive me.
C. that she will not forgive me.
D. that she would forgive me.

27. I said to her, "It was very hot last night."
I told her:
A. that it had been very hot the previous night.
B. that it was very hot the previous night.
C. that it has been very hot the last night.
D. that it had been very hot this night.

28. She said to me, "I thank you for the help you have given."
She:
A. told me that she thanked me for the help I had given.
B. thanked me for the help I have given.
C. thanked to me for the help I have given.
D. thanked me for the help I had given.

29. Mohini said to me, "Trust in God."
Mohini advised me:
A. that I should trust in God.
B. should trust in God.
C. trusted in God.
D. to trust in God.

30. I said to him, "Let us go to school."
I told him:
A. we would go to school.
B. we shall go to school.
C. that we would go to school.
D. that we should go to school.

31. Rajni said, "May God bless you?"
Rajni:
A. exclaimed with wish that God might bless me.
B. expressed a wish that God might bless me.
C. asked God to bless me.
D. shouted with joy to bless me.

32. My mother said me, "Do not have so many friends."
My mother forbade me:
A. to have so many friends.
B. not to have so many friends.
C. to have been so many friends.
D. to possess so many friends.

33. Ram said, "Pay attention to me."
Ram asked:
A. pay attention to him.
B. paid attention to him.
C. having paid attention to him.
D. to pay attention to him.

Directions (Qs. 34 to 50): *In questions below, the sentences have been given in Direct/Indirect Speech. Out of the four alternatives suggested select the one which best expresses the given sentence in Indirect/Direct Speech.*

34. She said that her brother was getting married
A. She said, "Her brother is getting married."
B. She told, "My brother is getting married"
C. She said, "My brother is getting married".
D. She said, "My brother was married".

35. "Please don't go away", she said.
A. She said to please her and not go away.
B. She told me to go away.
C. She begged me not to go away.
D. She begged that I not go away.

36. "If you don't keep quiet I shall shoot you", he said to her in a calm voice.
A. He warned her to shoot if she didn't keep quiet calmly.
B. He said calmly that I shall shoot you if you don't be quiet.
C. He warned her calmly that he would shoot her if she didn't keep quiet.
D. Calmly he warned her that be quiet or else he will have to shoot her.

37. I told him that he was not working hard.
A. I said to him, "You are not working hard."
B. I told him, "You are not working hard."
C. I said, "You are not working hard."
D. I said to him, "He is not working hard."

38. She said that she would finish the work the next day.
A. She said, "I will finish the work the next day."
B. She said, "I will finish the work tomorrow."
C. She said, "You will finish the work tomorrow."
D. She said, "I finished the work."

39. She said to him, "Why don't you go today?"
A. She asked him why he did not go that day.
B. She said to him that why he don't go today.
C. She asked him not to go today.
D. She asked him why he did not go today.

40. "Are you alone, my son?" asked a soft voice close behind me.
A. A soft voice asked that what I was doing there alone.
B. A soft voice said to me are you alone son.
C. A soft voice from my back asked if I was alone.
D. A soft voice behind me asked if I was alone.

41. My cousin said, "My room-mate had snored throughout the night."
A. My cousin said that her room-mate snored throughout the night.
B. My cousin told me that her room-mate snored throughout the night.
C. My cousin complained to me that her room-mate is snoring throughout the night.
D. My cousin felt that her room-mate may be snoring throughout the night.

42. He asked Rama if he needed his help then.
A. He said to Rama, "Do you need my help?"
B. He told Rama, "Tell me if you need help."
C. He asked Rama, "Do I need your help?"
D. He said to Rama, "Do you need my help now?"

43. Nita ordered her servant to bring her a cup of tea.
A. Nita told her servant, "Bring a cup of tea."
B. Nita said, "Bring me a cup of tea."
C. Nita said to her servant, "Bring me a cup of tea."
D. Nita said to her servant, "Bring her that cup of tea."

44. He exclaimed with joy that India had won the Sahara Cup.
A. He said, "India has won the Sahara Cup."
B. He said, "India won the Sahara Cup."
C. He said, "How! India will win the Sahara Cup."
D. He said, "Hurrah! India has won the Sahara Cup."

45. The boy said, "Who dare call you a thief?"
A. The boy enquired who dared call him a thief.
B. The boy asked who called him a thief.
C. The boy told that who dared call him a thief.
D. The boy wondered who dared call a thief.

46. The little girl said to her mother, "Did the sun rise in the East?
A. The little girl said to her mother that the sun rose in the East.
B. The little girl asked her mother if the sun rose in the East.
C. The little girl said to her mother if the sun rises in the East.
D. The little girl asked her mother if the sun is in the East.

47. Dhruv said that he was sick and tired of working for that Company.
A. Dhruv said, "I am sick and tired of working for this Company."
B. Dhruv said, "He was tired of that Company."
C. Dhruv said to me, "I am sick and tired of working for this Company."
D. Dhruv said, "I will be tired of working for that Company."

48. He said to his father, "Please increase my pocket-money."
A. He told his father, please increase the pocket-money.
B. He pleaded his father to please increase my pocket-money.
C. He requested his father to increase his pocket-money.
D. He asked his father increase his pocket-money.

49. She said to her friend, "I know where is everyone."
A. She told that she knew where was everyone.
B. She told her friend that she knew where was everyone.
C. She told her friend she knew where is everyone
D. She told her friend that she knows where was everyone.

50. His father ordered him to go to his room and study.
A. His father said, "Go to your room and study."
B. His father said to him, "Go and study in your room."
C. His father shouted, "Go right now to your study room."
D. His father said firmly, "Go and study in your room."

ANSWERS

1	2	3	4	5	6	7	8	9	10
B	A	A	C	A	D	C	B	C	C
11	**12**	**13**	**14**	**15**	**16**	**17**	**18**	**19**	**20**
C	D	A	B	C	A	B	C	D	D
21	**22**	**23**	**24**	**25**	**26**	**27**	**28**	**29**	**30**
C	C	C	A	C	D	A	A	A	D
31	**32**	**33**	**34**	**35**	**36**	**37**	**38**	**39**	**40**
B	A	D	C	C	C	A	B	A	D
41	**42**	**43**	**44**	**45**	**46**	**47**	**48**	**49**	**50**
A	D	C	B	A	B	A	C	B	A

❑❑❑

9 Voice

A sentence in active voice focuses on the person or thing doing the action. A sentence in passive voice focuses on the person or thing affected by the action. *e.g.*,

The idol was built. (Active voice)
Someone built the idol. (Passive voice)

Transformation of Voice

- Voice and Tense are closely associated with each other.
- Tense plays an important role while transforming the voice.

On the basis of following points, voice can be transformed from active to passive voice.

The Present Indefinite Tense

Active voice: Subject + V_1 + Object

Passive voice: Subject + is, am, are + V_3 + by + Object

1. **Active voice:** He sings sweet songs.
   Passive voice: Sweet songs are sung by him.
2. **Active voice:** She does not cause any hindrance in my work.
   Passive voice: No hindrance in my work is caused by her.
3. **Active voice:** Do they love their country?
   Passive voice: Is their country loved by them?

The Present Continuous Tense

Active voice: Subject + is/am/are + V_1 + ing + Object.

Passive voice: Subject + is/am/are + being + V_3 + by + Object.

1. **Active voice:** She is cooking food.
   Passive voice: Food is being cooked by her.
2. **Active voice:** Rita is not knitting a sweater.
   Passive voice: A sweater is not being knitted by Rita.
3. **Active voice:** Is Meena baking a cake?
   Passive voice: Is a cake being baked by Meena?

The Present Perfect Tense

Active voice: Subject + has/have + V_3 + Object.

Passive voice: Subject + has/have + been + V_3 + by + Object.

1. **Active voice:** I have written an essay.
   Passive voice: An essay has been written by me.
2. **Active voice:** They have not whitewashed the fence.
   Passive voice: The fence has not been whitewashed by them.
3. **Active voice:** Have you cut the cake?
   Passive voice: Has the cake been cut by you?

The Past Indefinite Tense

Active voice: Subject + V_2 + Object

Passive voice: Subject + was/were + V_3 + by + Object

1. **Active voice:** He composed a new song.
   Passive voice: A new song was composed by him.
2. **Active voice:** He did not operate the computer.
   Passive voice: The computer was not operated by him.
3. **Active voice:** Did she catch a fish?
   Passive voice: Was a fish caught by her?

The Past Continuous Tense

Active voice: Subject + was/were + V_1 + ing + Object
Passive voice: Subject + was/were + being + V_3 + by + Object

1. **Active voice:** The farmers were ploughing the fields.
   Passive voice: The fields were being ploughed by the farmers.
2. **Active voice:** He was not administering the new drug to the patient.
   Passive voice: The new drug was not being administered to the patient by him.
3. **Active voice:** Was she sewing a dress?
   Passive voice: Was a dress being sewn by her?

The Past Perfect Tense

Active voice: Subject + had + V_3 + Object.
Passive voice: Subject + had + been + V_3 + by + Object

1. **Active voice:** He had issued me an import licence.
   Passive voice: I had been issued an import licence.
2. **Active voice:** We had not visited the Taj.
   Passive voice: The Taj had not been visited by us.
3. **Active voice:** Who had taught you English?
   Passive voice: By whom had you been taught English?

The Future Indefinite Tense

Active voice: Subject + will/shall + V_1 + Object.
Passive voice: Subject + will/shall + be + V_3 + by + Object.

1. **Active voice:** He will remove the dust from the shelf.
   Passive voice: The dust from the shelf will be removed by him.
2. **Active voice:** He will not open the main gate.
   Passive voice: The main gate will not be opened by him.
3. **Active voice:** Will you help us?
   Passive voice: Shall we be helped by you?

The Future Perfect Tense

Active voice: Subject + will/shall + have + V_3 + Object.
Passive voice: Subject + will/shall + have + been + V_3 + by + Object.

1. **Active voice:** They will have sold their house by then.
   Passive voice: Their house will have been sold by them by then.
2. **Active voice:** He will not have informed the police about it.
   Passive voice: The police will not have been informed about it by him.
3. **Active voice:** Will they have accepted the deal?
   Passive voice: Will the deal have been accepted by them?

Imperative Sentences

1. **Active voice:** Open the window.
   Passive voice: You are ordered to open the window.

   Or

   Let the window be opened.
2. **Active voice:** Please/kindly open the window.
   Passive voice: You are requested to open the window.
3. **Active voice:** Never make a noise.
   Passive voice: A noise should never be made.

Infinitives

1. **Active voice:** It is time to open the shop.
   Passive voice: It is time for the shop to be opened.
2. **Active voice:** He begged the officer to forgive him.
   Passive voice: He begged the officer to be forgiven.
3. **Active voice:** He has to break the door.
   Passive voice: The door has to be broken by him.

Prepositional Verb

1. **Active voice:** She laughed at the beggar.
   Passive voice: The beggar was laughed at by her.
2. **Active voice:** He listened to the news.
   Passive voice: The news was listened to by him.
3. **Active voice:** They called in the doctor.
   Passive voice: The doctor was called in by them.

Double Object

1. **Active voice:** He gave me a pen.
   Passive voice: A pen was given to me by him.
   Or
   I was given a pen by him.
2. **Active voice:** She told us a story.
   Passive voice: A story was told (to) us by her.
   Or
   We were told a story by her.

Use of Preposition other than 'by'

1. **Active voice:** The jug contains juice.
   Passive voice: Juice is contained in the jug.
2. **Active voice:** The audience thronged the hall.
   Passive voice: The hall was thronged with the audience.
3. **Active voice:** I know her.
   Passive voice: She is known to me.

Quasi Passive Verbs

1. **Active voice:** Quinine tastes bitter.
   Passive voice: Quinine is bitter when tasted.
   Or
   Quinine is bitter when it is tasted.
2. **Active voice:** Sugar is sweet (to taste).
   Passive voice: Sugar is sweet when tasted.
   Or
   Sugar is sweet when it is tasted.

Implied Sentences

1. **Active voice:** The driver drove the bus.
   Passive voice: The bus was driven.
2. **Active voice:** Someone read the news.
   Passive voice: The news was read.
3. **Active voice:** They say work is worship.
   Passive voice: It is said that work is worship.

Multiple Choice Questions

Directions (Qs. 1 to 20): *In the following questions, a sentence has been given in Active/Passive Voice. Out of the four alternatives suggested, select the one that Best Expresses the same sentence in Passive/Active Voice.*

1. Circumstances will oblige me to go.
A. I will oblige the circumstances and go.
B. I shall be obliged to go by the circumstances.
C. Under the circumstances, I should go.
D. I shall be obliged by the circumstances to go.

2. We waste much time on trifles.
A. Much time was wasted on trifles.
B. Much time will be wasted on trifles.
C. Much time is wasted by us on trifles.
D. Much time is wasted on trifles.

3. Mohan gave the beggar an old shirt.
A. An old shirt was given to Mohan by the beggar.
B. An old shirt was given to the beggar by Mohan
C. The begger was gave an old shirt by Mohan.
D. An old shirt was gave to the beggar by Mohan.

4. They have made him a king.
A. A king has been made by him.
B. He was made a king by them.
C. They have been made kings by him.
D. He has been made a king by them.

5. Who taught you English?
A. By whom English was taught to you?
B. By whom you were taught English?
C. By whom was English taught to you?
D. By whom are you taught English?

6. Was he knocking at the door?
A. Was the door being knocked at by him?
B. Was the door being knocked by him?
C. Was the door knocked by him?
D. Was the door knocking at him?

7. What was Rani doing?
A. What was done by Rani?
B. What was Rani being done?
C. What was being done by Rani?
D. What was being doing Rani?

8. Why were you wasting your time?
A. Why was your time being wasted?
B. Why was your time being wasted by you?
C. Why was your time wasted by you?
D. Why was your time wasted?

9. She has laid out a small garden.
A. A small garden has been laid by her.
B. A small garden has laid her.
C. A small garden being laid by her.
D. A small garden has been laid out by her.

10. She had already solved all the sums.
A. All the sums had already been solved by her.
B. All the sums have already been solved by her.
C. All the sums have been solved by her.
D. All the sums are solved by her.

11. He will have posted the letter.
A. The letter has been posted by him.
B. The letter will be posted by him.
C. The letter will have been posted by him.
D. The letter is posted by him.

12. They will have sold all the books by 4 P.M.
A. All the books will be sold by 4 P.M.
B. All the books will have been sold by 4 P.M.
C. All the books were being sold by 4 P.M.
D. All the books must be sold by 4 P.M.

13. Do you speak English?
A. Is English spoken by you?
B. Does English spoken by you?
C. Is English being spoken by you?
D. Does English being spoken by you?

14. Had they seen me before?
A. Had myself been seen by them before?
B. Had me being seen by them before?
C. Had I been seen by them before?
D. Had I being seen by them before?

15. May I take this pen?
A. May this pen will be taken by me?
B. May this pen shall be taken by me?
C. May this pen should be taken by me?
D. May this pen be taken by me?

16. Can we send it by air?
A. Can this be sent by air?
B. Can it be sent by air?
C. Can it go by air?
D. Can it be send by air?

17. Who wrote this book?
A. By whom was this book written?
B. By whom is this book written?
C. By whom was this book being written?
D. By whom is this book being written?

18. What did you buy?
A. What is bought by you?
B. What is being bought by you?
C. What was bought by you?
D. What was being bought by you?

19. Whom do you want?
A. Who is wanted by you?
B. Who is being wanted by you?
C. You are wanted by whom?
D. You are being wanted by whom?

20. When will you raise this question?
A. When this question will be raised by you?
B. When will this question be raised by you?
C. When this question is being raised by you?
D. When is this question being raised by you?

Directions (Qs. 21 to 35): *In each of the following questions, a sentence is given in Active Voice. Below it are given four alternatives suggesting the Passive Voice form of the above sentence. Choose the correct alternative.*

21. Who did this?
A. This was done by whom?
B. By whom was this done?
C. Who has done this?
D. By whom this was done?

22. One should keep ones promises.
A. Promises should be kept.
B. Ones promises should be kept by one.
C. Promises must be kept.
D. Ones promises one should keep.

23. Give the order.
A. Order given.
B. Order be given.
C. Let the order be given.
D. Order may be given by you.

24. You will have to do it.
A. It will be done by you.
B. It will have to be done by you.
C. It has to be done by you.
D. It would have to be done by you.

25. Keep to the left.
A. You are ordered to keep to the left.
B. You ought to keep to the left.
C. You are advised to keep to the left.
D. You must keep to the left.

26. They will arrange a party.
A. A party will have to be arranged by them.
B. A party they will have to arrange.
C. A party will be arranged by them.
D. A party by them will be arranged.

27. Someone has picked my pocket.
A. My pocket is picked.
B. My pocket has picked.
C. My pocket has been picked.
D. My pocket was picked.

28. He kept me waiting.
A. I kept waiting for him.
B. I kept waiting by him.
C. I was waiting for him.
D. I was kept waiting by him.

29. Why do you tell a lie?
A. Why is a lie told by you?
B. Why is told a lie by you?
C. Why is told by you a lie?
D. Why has a lie been told by you?

30. I have written a letter.
A. A letter is written by me.
B. A letter has been written by me.
C. A letter was written by me.
D. A letter had been written by me.

31. They will have helped you.
A. You will have helped by them.
B. You will have been helped by them.
C. You will be helped by them.
D. You will be helped by them.

32. Open the door.
A. Door may be opened.
B. Let the door be open.
C. Let the door be opened.
D. Door be opened.

33. I am reading a book.
A. A book is read by me.
B. A book is being read by me.
C. A book has been read by me.
D. A book in been read by me.

34. Why did your brother write such a letter?
A. Why your brother wrote such a letter?
B. Why was by brother written such a letter?
C. Why was such a letter written by your brother?
D. Why was written such a letter by your brother?

35. Did you run a great risk?
A. Was a great risk run by you?
B. Was run a great risk by you?
C. Was by you run a great risk?
D. Had you run a great risk?

Directions (Qs. 36 to 45): *In each of the following questions, a sentence is given in Passive Voice. Below it are given four alternatives suggesting the Active Voice form of the above sentence. Choose the correct alternative.*

36. He was made king.
A. He became king.
B. They made him king.
C. They had made him king.
D. He has been made king.

37. Good news is expected by us.
A. We are expecting good news.
B. We have been expecting good news.
C. We had expected good news.
D. We expect good news.

38. The child must be looked after.
A. The child you must look after.
B. You must look after the child.
C. You must look the child after.
D. You may look after the child.

39. What is wanted by you?
A. What you want?
B. What did you want?
C. What do you want?
D. What you do want?

40. Your father is known to me.
A. I am known to your father.
B. I know your father.
C. I have known your father.
D. I knew your father.

41. She may be told the story by you.
A. The story may be told by you to her.
B. You may tell the story to her.
C. You may tell her the story.
D. You may tell to her the story.

42. Duty ought to be done.
A. Let duty be done.
B. One ought to do one's duty.
C. One should do his duty.
D. Do you duty.

43. Is English spoken by you?
A. Did you speak English?
B. Do you speak English?
C. Have you spoken English?
D. Do you know how to speak English?

44. Gold coins are contained in this box.
A. This box contains gold coins.
B. This box has contained gold coins.
C. This box is containing gold coins.
D. This box has gold coins.

45. Character is revealed by manners.
A. Manners revealed character.
B. Manners reveal character.
C. Manners have revealed character.
D. Manners do reveal character.

ANSWERS

1	2	3	4	5	6	7	8	9	10
D	C	B	D	C	A	C	B	D	A
11	**12**	**13**	**14**	**15**	**16**	**17**	**18**	**19**	**20**
C	B	A	C	D	B	A	C	A	B
21	**22**	**23**	**24**	**25**	**26**	**27**	**28**	**29**	**30**
B	A	C	B	C	C	C	D	A	B
31	**32**	**33**	**34**	**35**	**36**	**37**	**38**	**39**	**40**
B	C	B	C	A	B	D	B	C	B
41	**42**	**43**	**44**	**45**					
C	B	B	A	B					

❑❑❑

10 Sentence Completion

Filling the blanks is such an exercise that starts with the primary schools and continues at the highest level of competitive examinations. One must practise it regularly to score well.

Multiple Choice Questions

Directions: *Pick out the most effective word(s) from the given words to fill in the blanks and make the sentence meaningfully complete.*

1. One requires great .... to teach and handle little children who are restless.
A. patience B. attitude
C. determination D. knowledge

2. The researchers will .... some of the causes of increasing poverty in the state.
A. fund B. investigate
C. promote D. circulate

3. I usually perform .... when nobody is watching me.
A. alone B. good
C. better D. hard

4. It was .... to everyone that the minister had been drinking.
A. observed B. known
C. discovered D. realised

5. I would rather stay indoors .... the rain stops.
A. so B. waiting
C. until D. usually

6. The process should be completed as far as possible within a week, ... which the matter should be brought to notice of the officer concerned.
A. following B. failing
C. realizing D. referring

7. The officers are ..... to regular transfers.
A. free B. open
C. subject D. available

8. All letters received from Government should ..... be acknowledged.
A. suddenly
B. obviously
C. immediately
D. occasionally

9. Mumbai office ..... a meeting of senior officials to discuss the high incidence of frauds.
A. attended B. convened
C. reported D. registered

10. The note should be ..... to all the concerned departments for their consideration.
A. regulated B. requested
C. carried D. forwarded

11. Your present statement does not .... what you said last week.
A. accord to B. accord in
C. accord with D. accord for

12. I had a vague .... that the lady originally belonged to Scotland.
A. notion B. expression
C. imagination D. theory

13. The prisoner showed no .... for his crimes.
A. hatred B. obstinacy
C. remorse D. anger

14. It is inconceivable that in many schools children are subjected to physical .... in the name of discipline.
A. violation B. exercise
C. violence D. security

15. We have not yet fully realised the .... consequences of the war.
A. happy B. pleasing
C. grim D. exciting

16. Happiness consists in being .... what we have.
A. contented to B. contented with
C. contented for D. contented in

17. His rude behaviour is a .... his organization.
A. disgrace for
B. disgrace on
C. disgrace upon
D. disgrace to

18. No child is .... understanding. One has to wait and provide proper guidance.
A. dull to B. dull in
C. dull of D. dull for

19. I am fully .... the problems facing the industry.
A. alive with B. alive to
C. alive for D. alive on

20. The Romans were .... science.
A. bad in B. bad to
C. bad for D. bad at

21. Although I was .... of his plans, I encouraged him, because there was no one else who was willing to help.
A. sceptical B. remorseful
C. fearful D. excited

22. You have no business to .... pain on a weak and poor person.
A. inflict B. put
C. direct D. force

23. Her uncle died in a car accident. He was quite rich. She suddenly .... all her uncle's money.
A. succeeded B. caught
C. gave D. inherited

24. There was a major accident. The plane crashed. The pilot .... did not see the tower.
A. likely B. probably
C. scarcely D. hurriedly

25. The car we were travelling in .... a mile from home.
A. broke off B. broke down
C. broke into D. broke up

26. What are you .... in the kitchen cupboard?
A. looking in B. looking on
C. looking to D. looking for

27. I did not see the point of .... waiting for them, so I went home.
A. hanging around B. hang on
C. hang together D. hanging up

28. He lost confidence and .... of the deal at the last minute.
A. backed out B. backed on
C. backed down D. backed onto

29. To the dismay of all the students, the class monitor was ..... berated by the principal at a school assembly.
A. critically B. ignominiously
C. prudently D. fortuitously

30. All attempts to revive the fishing industry were ..... failure.
A. foredoomed to B. heading at
C. predicted for D. estimated to

31. There are ..... parked outside than yesterday.
A. fewer cars
B. few cars
C. less cars
D. a small number of cars

32. The minister had to ..... some awkward questions from reporters.
A. fend B. fend at
C. fend out D. fend off

33. The ..... of evidence was on the side of the plaintiff since all but one of the witnesses testified that his story was correct.
A. propensity B. force
C. preponderance D. brunt

34. Attention to detail is ..... of a fine craftsman.
A. hallmark B. stamp
C. seal of authority D. authenticity

35. Behaving in a .... and serious way, even in a .... situation, makes people respect you.
A. calm, difficult
B. steady, angry
C. flamboyant, tricky
D. cool astounding

36. Along with a sharp rise in ...., a recession would eventually result in more men, women, and children living in ....
A. crime, apathy
B. fatalities, poor
C. deaths, slums
D. unemployment, poverty

37. The government has .... to provide financial aid to the ones .... by severe floods in the city.
A. desired, troubled B. promised, havoc
C. failed, affected D. wanted, struck

38. An airplane with .... passengers on board made an unscheduled .... as the airport to which it was heading was covered with thick fog.
A. imitable, slip B. faulty, stop
C. variety, halt D. numerous, landing

39. Deemed universities .... huge fees, but have not been successful in providing .... education to our students.
A. collect, maintaining
B. pay, better
C. ask, good
D. charge, quality

40. If the banks desire to .... profit, they should get rid of .... measures.
A. lose, concentrate
B. increase, populist
C. earn, unhealthy
D. maximise, traditional

41. Leadership defines what the future should look like and ...... people with that vision.
A. aligns B. develops
C. trains D. encourages

42. We upset ourselves by responding in an ...... manner to someone else's actions.
A. unabashed B. irrational
C. arduous D. arguable

43. All the people involved in that issue feel a great ...... to his suggestion.
A. contradiction B. adherence
C. indifference D. repugnance

44. These elections will be remembered as much for its anti-incumbency mood as for its ...... mandate.
A. invincible B. rational
C. unprecedented D. deliberate

45. How do you expect us to stay in such a ...... building even if it can be hired on a nominal rent?
A. scruffy B. disperate
C. fragmented D. robust

46. ...... efforts from all concerned are required to raise the social and economic conditions of our countrymen.
A. Perpetual B. Dynamic
C. Massive D. Exploring

47. Many companies see technology as a ...... for a whole host of business problems.
A. consideration B. preference
C. linking D. panacea

48. Known as devout and serious person, she also has ...... sense of humour.
A. better B. plentiful
C. quick D. good

49. The matter would have become serious if ...... action had not been taken.
A. hasty B. fast
C. timely D. unusual

50. The ...... with which he is able to yield the paint brush is really remarkable.
A. ease B. practice
C. majesty D. sweep

51. You must ensure the correctness of the information before ....
A. drawing B. enabling
C. learning D. jumping

52. The rocket .... the target and did not cause any casualty.
A. sensed B. reached
C. missed D. exploded

53. It is desirable to take .... in any business if you want to make profit.
A. advice B. risk
C. loan D. recourse

54. They wasted all the money on purchase of some .... items.
A. excellent B. important
C. significant D. trivial

55. When he found the wallet his face glowed but soon it faded as the wallet was ....
A. empty B. vacant
C. recovered D. stolen

56. He has served the country by .... many significant positions.
A. appointing
B. creating
C. developing
D. holding

57. The frequent errors are a result of the student's ....
A. talent B. smartness
C. carelessness D. perception

58. The robbers eventually .... in breaking into the house.
A. succeeded B. decided
C. caught D. trained

59. I finally .... her to stay another day.
A. advised B. persuaded
C. suggested D. called

60. Most of the people who .... the book exhibition were teachers.
A. witnessed B. presented
C. conducted D. attended

ANSWERS

1	2	3	4	5	6	7	8	9	10
A	B	C	A	C	B	C	C	B	D
11	**12**	**13**	**14**	**15**	**16**	**17**	**18**	**19**	**20**
C	A	C	C	C	B	D	B	B	D
21	**22**	**23**	**24**	**25**	**26**	**27**	**28**	**29**	**30**
B	C	C	B	C	C	D	A	B	A
31	**32**	**33**	**34**	**35**	**36**	**37**	**38**	**39**	**40**
A	D	D	A	A	D	C	D	C	B
41	**42**	**43**	**44**	**45**	**46**	**47**	**48**	**49**	**50**
A	A	D	C	A	A	D	D	C	A
51	**52**	**53**	**54**	**55**	**56**	**57**	**58**	**59**	**60**
A	C	B	D	A	D	C	A	B	D

11 Sentence Improvement

One may use the same words in many ways but the best way is only one that makes the perfect usage of the words and conveys the proper meaning of the expression. Try it yourself in the following questions.

Multiple Choice Questions

Directions: *In these questions, a part of the sentence is bold. Below are given alternatives to the bold part at A, B and C which may improve the sentence. Choose the correct alternative. In case no improvement is needed, your answer is 'D'.*

1. Discreet salience **is extremely important** to create that 'irresistible-yet-unattainable' image for brands that want to take India seriously

A. was extremely important
B. is mainly important
C. was important extremely
D. No Improvement

2. This, over a designer outfit that he wanted for a friend's party and **that his sensitive** parents refused him.

A. which his sensitive
B. which his insensitive
C. that his insensitive
D. No Improvement

3. Goa was full of non-Goa property hunters **rushing about buying up the place** like tomorrow was an expired lease.

A. rushing in buying up the place
B. rushed about buying up the place
C. rushing about to buy up the place
D. No Improvement

4. Property hunting is a **tired and hungry** making business.

A. is a tiresome and hungry
B. is a tiring and hungry
C. is a tiring and waste
D. No Improvement

5. Cultural differences aside, **till luxury need speaks** in a manner that befits.

A. luxury still needs to speak
B. luxury still need to speak
C. luxury till need to speak
D. No Improvement

6. Indian food—the culinary avatar of the subcontinent's social history presented on a platter—**is without doubt the best food** in the world.

A. is undoubtedly the greatest food
B. is without doubt greatest food
C. is best food without doubt
D. No Improvement

7. It must retain the language of poetry. **It needed to create** stories, and not statements.
A. It needed creating
B. It needs creating
C. It needs to create
D. No Improvement

8. This year, Asia-Pacific has become the first region **to reach aggregate profiting** in biotech.
A. to reach aggregated profitability
B. to reach aggregate profitability
C. to reach aggregate of profit
D. No Improvement

9. India is deviating to embrace the West. If Western luxury brands deviate a little, **albeit selectively**, they will find rich Indian arms open far and wide.
A. though selectively
B. however selectively
C. albeit selectedly
D. No Improvement

10. China and India continued to attract attention and deals, motivated by the desire to increase access to these **largest and growing** drug markets and by the need to lower the costs of drug development.
A. larger and growing
B. large and growing
C. larger and grown
D. No Improvement

11. Luxury brands are **still above of the** clover curve here, with their elite (small) audiences.
A. still ahead of the
B. still in the
C. still far of the
D. No Improvement

12. Agencies **hence needed to be** sure of returns before investing, say admen.
A. hence needs to be
B. so needs to be
C. hence need to be
D. No Improvement

13. India is still a nascent market and that's the spirit everyone's **looking at it**.
A. looking for it B. looking in it
C. looking with it D. No Improvement

14. Questioning the state's move to allow women to serve liquor but not dance in bars **of the ground that** dancing aroused physical lust.
A. on the grounds that
B. of the grounds that
C. over the grounds that
D. No Improvement

15. For England the positives from their crushing series lose come in the shape of James Anderson and Kevin Pietersen, **both of which** have made significant strides up the rankings.
A. both of which B. both of whom
C. both of who D. No Improvement

16. International campaigns can work well for luxury here, **but context cannot be** ignored.
A. so context cannot be
B. but context cannot
C. but context couldn't
D. No Improvement

17. For one, the Indian luxury context, **while evolved rapidly**, still has its own meaning, and its own implications.
A. while evolved rapid
B. which evolving rapidly
C. while evolving rapidly
D. No Improvement

18. But too much of availability can compromise a luxury brand or **made it lose** its lustre.
A. make her lose B. make him lose
C. make it lose D. No Improvement

19. Still, it's under-the-upper **layers themselves who** are aspiring for slivers of luxury.
A. layers themselves which
B. layer itself who
C. layers themself which
D. No Improvement

20. It is like saying Hindi movies, with skimpily dressed dancers, would **effect public** order.
A. effect your B. affect public
C. affected public D. No Improvement

21. The court held that a few women being involved in prostitution was no **justice to deny other** bar girls the right to livelihood.

A. justification to declare other
B. justification to deny other
C. justice to let other
D. No Improvement

22. All-rounder cricketer has also made some progress **over the** player rankings.

A. above the B. at the
C. up the D. No Improvement

23. Former minister on Sunday **joined hands** with a suspended Lok Sabha member to float a new political outfit.

A. folded hands
B. walked hand in hand
C. shaked hands
D. No Improvement

24. Pakistan's former ministers will meet in London on Monday **to ask** a strategy to return home from exile.

A. to chalk out
B. to negotiate
C. to create
D. No Improvement

25. It's a family potboiler, medical thriller and political drama **all in one**—except that it's all too real and all too grim.

A. all 3 in one
B. all coupled into one
C. all rolled into one
D. No Improvement

26. India's efforts to get international support for its civil nuclear energy programme got **a go ahead on** Sunday as Germany indicated it would not come in the way of the India-US nuclear deal.

A. a life in B. a boost on
C. a boost at D. No Improvement

27. Is it time for old bungalows to **bite the dust**?

A. go down B. get down
C. come down D. No Improvement

28. The bungalows was an outward manifestation of a certain **way in life**, and with that era gone.

A. way for life B. way of life
C. way at life D. No Improvement

29. The builder Mittals will reportedly **raise their money**-raking high-rise behind it.

A. highten their money
B. rise their money
C. raise there money
D. No Improvement

30. The impatient present has usually demolished **more of the** past before we wake up to the irretrievable loss.

A. much of B. much of their
C. much of the D. No Improvement

31. Preservation is a romantic notion; demolition **quiet** more practical reasons.

A. has many, B. had many,
C. have many, D. No Improvement

32. You must get back to your **charming self** and impress the audience with your social skills.

A. own self B. main self
C. own uniqueness D. No Improvement

33. Stay focused on your goals and don't **get disturbed by** non-materialistic possessions.

A. get involved by
B. get betrayed by
C. get distracted by
D. No Improvement

34. You may appear more optimistic than your detractors **may want it to be.**

A. want you to be
B. wish yourself to be
C. seek you be
D. No Improvement

35. There are a number of mineral springs in the Czech territory, which **has been used** for medicinal purposes since the early 15th century.

A. have been used B. had been used
C. has being used D. No Improvement

36. The picturesque mountains **offer**s excellent bungee jumping spots.
A. shows B. provides
C. offer D. No Improvement

37. Begin your **meal with** traditional faves like potato soup, beef soup with liver dumplings or dill soup made from sour milk.
A. meals with B. meal in
C. meals of D. No Improvement

38. You can also **go to the** National Museum building and the famous Prague State Opera.
A. went to B. visit the
C. saw D. No Improvement

39. If they close the Gulf for a **length of time** to shipping, then certainly we could look at $150, probably higher.
A. larger amount of time
B. larger duration of time
C. larger amount of hours
D. No Improvement

40. **More of them** are owned by the state and even the privately-owned ones are open to the public.
A. Most of which B. Most of them
C. Most of all D. No Improvement

41. Constructed in the ninth century by the Prince Booivoj, the castle has transformed **oneself** from a wooden fortress surrounded by earthen bulwarks to the imposing form it has today.
A. himself B. herself
C. itself D. No Improvement

42. Apart from frequent art exhibitions, **their are also** permanent collections devoted to archaeology, anthropology, mineralogy, natural history and numismatics.
A. there is also B. there are also
C. their are also D. No Improvement

43. You can visit the Czech Museum of Fine Arts, **at a** permanent exhibition on Czech Kubism.
A. with a
B. for a
C. in a
D. No Improvement

44. Tensions **above** Iran come at a time of strong demand for energy.
A. under B. inside
C. over D. No Improvement

45. Because its shores line the narrow Straits of Hormuz, Iran **could quickly hit** both military and commercial shipping.
A. will quickly hit
B. shall quickly hit
C. will be quick hitting
D. No Improvement

46. For most people who exercise **at the** morning, there is no getting around the question: Eat and run? Or run and eat later?
A. in the
B. in
C. at the time of
D. No Improvement

47. Are ad agencies even attempting to peer into the keyhole of this indulgence sanctum to garner consumer insights **ahead of** the curve?
A. above
B. over
C. within
D. No Improvement

48. Too many people rush into the world of credit and don't stop to think about how **their actions could affect their** credit score and ability to qualify for credit in the future.
A. their actions may affect their
B. their actions might affect their
C. their actions will affect their
D. No Improvement

49. According to the report, **number of deal with** vaccines were energized by concerns around avian flu, SARS, and biodefence products, while looming patent expirations led to more deals in generics.
A. number of deals in
B. number of deal in
C. number of deals with
D. No Improvement

50. This is how the Bombay High Court responded to the state government's purported **moral stand which** dance bars were causing grave harm to society.
A. moral stand in
B. moral stand at
C. moral stand that D. No Improvement

51. If you have a high credit limit, use **at least a** third of it.
A. atleast a
B. at last a
C. utmost a
D. No Improvement

52. Fitness experts will say that **first eating provides** fuel for a proper workout.
A. eating in the beginning provides
B. first eat provides
C. eating first provides
D. No Improvement

53. One study that examined the claim directly in 1995 found that a group of people did **burned much calories from fat on days** when they exercised on an empty stomach than on days when they had a small breakfast first.
A. burn more calories from fat on days
B. burn more calorie from fat on days
C. burnt more calories from fat on days
D. No Improvement

54. Carefree children spent their afternoons **to run about barefoot**, their clothes dusty, and telltale twigs of the neighbour's mango tree in their hair.
A. running barefoot in the sun
B. run about barefoot in the sun
C. running about barefoot in the sun
D. No Improvement

55. A year ago, a 13-year-old girl attempted suicide because her mother **refuses to pay his** mobile bills.
A. refuses to pay her
B. refused to pay her
C. refused to pay his
D. No Improvement

ANSWERS

1	2	3	4	5	6	7	8	9	10
D	C	D	B	A	D	C	C	D	B
11	**12**	**13**	**14**	**15**	**16**	**17**	**18**	**19**	**20**
C	C	D	A	C	D	C	C	C	C
21	**22**	**23**	**24**	**25**	**26**	**27**	**28**	**29**	**30**
B	C	C	A	C	B	D	B	D	C
31	**32**	**33**	**34**	**35**	**36**	**37**	**38**	**39**	**40**
A	D	C	A	D	C	A	B	D	B
41	**42**	**43**	**44**	**45**	**46**	**47**	**48**	**49**	**50**
C	B	A	C	D	A	D	C	A	C
51	**52**	**53**	**54**	**55**					
C	C	A	C	B					

❑❑❑

12 Reordering Words & Sentences

Different words form a sentence and convey their meaning only when arranged in a proper order. A Paragraph is formed from sentences, it will convey its true meaning and purpose only when the sentences are arranged in a proper manner. Try and practise it in this exercise.

Multiple Choice Questions

Directions (Qs. 1 to 20): *In the following questions, some parts of the sentence have been jumbled up. You are required to rearrange these parts which are labelled P, Q, R and S to produce the correct sentence. Choose the option with proper sequence.*

1. We are doing
P : to the people
Q : to give relief
R : all we can
S : but more funds are needed
The correct sequence should be
A. P Q R S B. R Q P S
C. Q P R S D. S P Q R

2. The man
P : when he was
Q : in the office last evening
R : could not finish
S : all his work
The correct sequence should be
A. P Q R S B. Q R S P
C. R Q P S D. R S P Q

3. The people decided
P : they were going
Q : how much
R : to spend
S : on the construction of the school building
The correct sequence should be
A. Q P R S B. P Q R S
C. P R Q S D. S Q P R

4. The man said that
P : those workers
Q : would be given a raise
R : who did not go on
S : strike last month
The correct sequence should be
A. P Q R S B. P R S Q
C. Q P R S D. R S P Q

5. I think
P : the members
Q : are basically in agreement
R : of the group
S : on the following points
The correct sequence should be
A. R Q P S B. S Q R P
C. P R Q S D. P Q S R

6. While it was true that
P : I had
Q : to invest in industry
R : some lands and houses
S : I did not have ready cash

The correct sequence should be

A. P Q R S B. P R S Q
C. S Q P R D. Q P R S

7. P : But for your help
Q : to finish this work
R : it would not have been possible
S : in time

The correct sequence should be

A. P R Q S B. S P Q R
C. R P Q S D. P Q R S

8. The boy
P : in the competition
Q : who was wearing spectacles
R : won many prizes
S : held in our college

The correct sequence should be

A. P Q R S B. R P S Q
C. Q R P S D. Q P S R

9. About 200 years ago,
P : in the south of India
Q : an old king
R : ruled over a kingdom
S : called Rajavarman

The correct sequence should be

A. Q S R P B. P Q R S
C. Q P S R D. Q S P R

10. P : his land
Q : a wooden plough
R : the Indian peasant still uses
S : to cultivate

The correct sequence should be

A. R Q P S B. Q P S R
C. S R Q P D. R Q S P

11. He was a man,
P : even if he had to starve
Q : who would not beg
R : borrow or steal
S : from anyone

The correct sequence should be

A. P Q R S B. P R Q S
C. Q R S P D. Q P R S

12. P : in the progress of
Q : universities play a crucial role
R : our civilization
S : in the present age

The correct sequence should be

A. S Q P R B. Q R S P
C. Q R P S D. S Q R P

13. P : far out into the sea
Q : for the next two weeks there were further explosions
R : which hurled
S : ashes and debris

The correct sequence should be

A. Q R P S B. R S P Q
C. Q R S P D. S R P Q

14. William Shakespeare,
P : in his lifetime
Q : the great English dramatist
R : wrote thirty-five plays
S : and several poems

The correct sequence should be

A. P Q R S B. R S P Q
C. Q S R P D. Q R S P

15. Whenever I am,
P : with an old friend of mine
Q : in New Delhi
R : to have dinner
S : I always try

The correct sequence should be

A. S Q P R B. Q S R P
C. R P S Q D. P R Q S

16. P : I don't know
Q : must have thought
R : what people sitting next to me
S : but I came away

The correct sequence should be

A. R S Q P B. R Q S P
C. P Q R S D. P R Q S

17. P : in estimating the size of the earth
Q : but they were hampered by the lack of instruments of precision
R : ancient astronomers
S : used methods which were theoretically valid

The correct sequence should be

A. R P Q S B. P R Q S
C. R S Q P D. R P S Q

18. P : It is a pity that
Q : by offering a handsome dowry
R : a number of parents think that
S : they will be able to ensure the happiness of their daughters

The correct sequence should be

A. S Q R P B. P R S Q
C. P S R Q D. P R Q S

19. The common man
P : in nurturing
Q : a more active role
R : communal harmony
S : should play

The correct sequence should be

A. P R S Q B. S Q P R
C. S Q R P D. P R Q S

20. The doctor
P : able to find out
Q : what has caused
R : the food poisoning
S : has not been

The correct sequence should be

A. S P R Q B. P R Q S
C. P R S Q D. S P Q R

Directions (Qs. 21 to 40): *A number of sentences are given below which when properly sequenced form a coherent paragraph. Each sentence is labelled as abcdef...... Choose the most logical order of sentences from among the given choices to construct a coherent paragraph:*

21. (a) Parts of northern region were pounded by heavy rains today,
(b) Vehicular traffic came to a near halt.
(c) As mid and high altitude areas of Himachal Pradesh were in grip of severe cold wave with snow lashing the tribal areas and mid ranges receiving showers.
(d) As the sky remained heavily overcast with dark clouds reducing the visibility considerably.
(e) A large number of tourists were forced to buy heavy woollens and stay indoors due to inclement weather.

A. ecabd B. adecb
C. edabc D. acbde

22. (a) The idea is that students should be able to find employment for themselves after the course.
(b) The Central Board of Secondary Education is planning a revamp of its vocational courses.
(c) For this it is necessary to tie up with the industry as well as mobilise schools for their support.
(d) While others will be made less academic and more in tune with the needs of the industry.
(e) A number of courses have been identified as 'deadwood' and will be done away with.

A. bedac B. abcde
C. acebd D. baced

23. (a) Clearly, age is not a deterrent in one's choice of learning.
(b) Perhaps, it was because of her childhood desire.
(c) When Rachna came to Delhi eight years back, she had not anticipated a career in the field of art.
(d) She has been successful in the various exhibitions that she has been part of in terms of business.
(e) She had got into expressing her thoughts with the help of a brush and colours only because her daughter refused to get initiated into it.
(f) She feels that her use of colour appeals to people.

A. aedcbf B. cdefba
C. cebadf D. acdebf

24. (a) The rehabilitation record has been dismal.
(b) It has been two years years since the earthquake rudely rattled the people of Gujarat.
(c) And since then, life has been a constant struggle.
(d) The quake set Gujarat's clock back by 10 years.
(e) Things changed forever.

A. bedca B. bcade
C. dbace D. edcba

25. (a) In fact, success in exams depended on rote learning from old notes.
(b) when he was studying civil engineering in a college in Gujarat.
(c) He was detained for lack of attendance.
(d) Lectures were soporific, classes rarely worth attending and 80 per cent attendance compulsory.
(e) The college became a trap he hated.
(f) His is a plight many engineers across India would identify with.
(g) He found the going tough.
A. abcdgef B. bgdacef
C. fabcdge D. abcdefg

26. (a) In a country that has close to 600 recognised engineering colleges, there are only seven IITs.
(b) Barring a few exeptions, the academic atmosphere in these is moribund.
(c) The very best students usually get there.
(d) many waste themselves in frustration.
(e) Most of those who get into engineering are good students.
(f) but about 1.25 lakh others and up in the remaining colleges.
A. aecfbd B. abecdf
C. abcdef D. acfbed

27. (a) Whatever the job market, common wisdom says that IIT graduates will find jobs where others have failed.
(b) The IIT brand name is a ticket to success.
(c) When recruiters go headhunting, the IITs are still top of their list.
(d) Its possessor is understood to have an excellent academic record and the will to succeed.
(e) In the job market, that counts.
A. bdeac B. abcde
C. abdce D. dbace

28. (a) It will pave the way ....
(b) signalling a new beginning in strategic ties......
(c) for a tangible Indian economic presence in Iran and Central Asia.
(d) Iran has offered India valuable road linkages to central Asia ......
(e) aimed at promoting peace and economic cooperation in the region.
A. dbeac B. debca
C. acebd D. abced

29. (a) A good college is essential for a successful career and admissions are based on marks.
(b) The marks-based system followed by all the boards in the country recognises only a small percentage of students as successful.
(c) The marks one scores in the crucial board exams dictate the path his life takes.
(d) Anyone scoring below a certain percentage is automatically branded a 'failure'.
(d) So if you cannot make it into the best college, your career is over even before it has started.
A. abcde B. bcdea
C. bdcae D. abdec

30. (a) The project has already started on an experimental basis in the west district.
(b) A website is soon going to be launched where application forms can be downloaded and submitted.
(c) Standing in a queue at a government office to submit application form will be a thing of the past.
(d) A unique code will be alloted while submitting the form which will help in finding the status of the application.
A. abcd B. dabc
C. cbda D. badc

31. (a) To curb bio-terrorism is a difficult task.
(b) To check these attacks and lessen their impact, we need an impartial team of sincere, strong and dedicated men.
(c) The media can play a strong role in stopping this unnecessary spread of panic.
(d) Since bio-terrorism is not visible or easily detectable, it can be used often.
(e) Men who honour the lives of their fellow countrymen before their own.

A. abcde B. dabce
C. adbec D. acbed

32. (a) He was dying.
(b) No one was ready to touch him as even shifting him from one place to another would lead to profuse bleeding.
(c) He was a five-day old infant, premature and bleeding profusely.
(d) Even if injected one small needle, blood would ooze out and continue to flow for an hour at a stretch.
(e) This small being had haematoma, a thick blood clot in his brain.
A. edbca B. cabde
C. eacdb D. cedba

33. (a) The day I don't treat a patient, I feel ....
(b) I have enough to eat, I crave for blessings now.
(c) But if a financially weak patient gives me only ₹ 50, I don't mind.
(d) Each month I do three to four operations free of cost.
(e) I have lost something in life.
(f) My consultation fee is ₹ 300.
A. fcdeab B. dfcbae
C. fcabde D. bdfcea

34. (a) When he was rushed to the nearby Primary Health Centre after his fall, the doctor referred him to a hospital.
(b) This worsened his injury.
(c) Had a little precaution been exercised after the accident, Tarun would have continued with his gymnastic classes.
(d) He was paralysed from waist downwards when he fell from the vaulting horse while doing gymnastics.
(e) However, the doctor forgot to tell Tarun's parents to take him on a stretcher as he had suffered spinal injuries.
(f) Tarun is wheelchair bound for two years.
A. fdeabc B. abcdef
C. fdcaeb D. fdbcae

35. (a) As the temperature rises, staying hydrated can become a greater challenge for people exercising both indoors and out.
(b) Several things can influence this process, including age, gender, physical conditioning. humidity and a lack of sufficient fluids.
(c) In hot weather, individuals can lose as much as two quarts of sweat per hour.
(d) As we age, we have a lower perceived level of thirst in response to fluid loss and early stages of dehydration.
(e) If not replenished, this can lead to dehydration, heat exhaustion and even heatstroke.
A. abcde B. dbcae
C. cbdea D. acebd

36. (a) The leopard was discovered in the servant quarters of a farmhouse.
(b) The injuries appeared to have been caused by the paws of the leopard, and were not teeth wounds.
(c) It took the wild life officials, Delhi Police and Delhi zoo vets eight hours to capture the leopard that had wandered into a factory in south Delhi.
(d) The leopard then jumped into the factory where the workers managed to lock it in a small generator room before calling in the police.
(e) Before its capture, the leopard attacked two women and a man in the farmhouse.
A. aebdc B. bdaec
C. eadbc D. adbec

37. (a) Police suspect a carpenter working at John's house as he has not reported for work since the day the boy went missing.
(b) John did not return home in the afternoon.
(c) John's mother had herself put the boy on the vehicle in the morning.
(d) John smiled at him and was last seen walking up to him.
(e) His parents called the school and were told John had not been to school at all and had been marked absent.
(f) He was about to enter the school when someone called out his name.

A. cfdbea B. debfca
C. bfdaec D. abcdef

38. (a) However, the mayhem over the last few months is deeply shocking.
(b) Yet I do not agree with the prophets of doom who see nothing but disaster ahead.
(c) When I came back to my motherland India after a stay in Switzerland, I felt I was trading a hotbed of intense religious and political violence for peace and quiet.
(d) I think our nation is searching for an identity.
(e) And a new vision of the future will emerge from this.
A. abcde B. cabde
C. cebad D. bedca

39. (a) An integrated and combined approach was required to reveal the mystery of the brain —its structure, composition and function.
(b) Since the early 80's, scientists were clear that the brain would be the final frontier to conquer.
(c) The initiative was flagged off and came to be known as the Human Brain Project.
(d) But that wasn't easy because understanding the brain involved completely integrating information from the level of the gene to the level of behaviour.
(e) To fulfill this requirement a group of American scientists from various disciplines decided to work together.
A. acbed B. bdaec
C. abdec D. badec

40. (a) A product is something that is made in a factory, a brand is something that is bought by a consumer.
(b) The trick therefore, lies in the brand positioning.
(c) For a consumer, the satisfaction of becoming associated with a name that is the 'best' and the 'leader' is far more important and at times makes him ignore the price factor.
(d) Brands come and go.
(e) Still there are those who manage to stay and develop an affinity with consumers.
A. aebcd B. debac
C. decab D. aecdb

ANSWERS

1	2	3	4	5	6	7	8	9	10
B	D	A	B	C	C	A	C	A	D
11	**12**	**13**	**14**	**15**	**16**	**17**	**18**	**19**	**20**
C	A	C	D	B	D	C	B	B	D
21	**22**	**23**	**24**	**25**	**26**	**27**	**28**	**29**	**30**
D	A	C	A	B	D	A	A	C	C
31	**32**	**33**	**34**	**35**	**36**	**37**	**38**	**39**	**40**
C	D	B	C	D	A	A	B	B	B

❑❑❑

13 Comprehension Passages

PASSAGES

Directions: *Read the following passages and answer the questions given below each.*

PASSAGE-1

In the Roman times, defected enemies were generally put to death as criminals for having offended the emperor of Rome. In the middle ages, however, the practice of ransoming of returning prisoners in exchange for money became common. Though some saw this custom as a step towards a most humane society, the primary reasons behind it were economic rather than humanitarian.

In those times, rulers had only a limited ability to raise taxes. They could neither force their subject to fight nor pay them to do so. The promise of material compensation in the form of goods and ransom was therefore the only way of inducing combatants to participate in a war. In the middle ages, the predominant incentive for the individual soldiers was the expectation of spoils. Although collecting ransom clearly brought financial gain, keeping a prisoner and arranging for his exchange had its cost. Consequently, procedures were devised to reduce transaction costs.

One such device was a rule asserting that the prisoner had to assess his own value. This compelled the prisoner to establish a value *without too much distortion;* indicating too low a value would increase, the captive's chances of being killed, while indicating too high a value would either ruin him financially or create a prohibitively expensive ransom that would also result in death.

1. It can be inferred from the passage that a medieval soldier

A. was less likely to kill captured members of opposing armies than was a soldier of the Roman Empire

B. was similar to a 20th century terrorist in that he operated on a basically independent level and was motivated solely by economic incentives

C. had few economic options and chose to fight because it was the only way to earn an adequate living

D. was motivated to spare prisoners' lives by humanitarian rather than economic ideals

2. Which of the following best describes the change in policy from executing prisoners in Roman times to ransoming prisoners in the middle ages?

A. The emperors of Rome demanded more respect than did medieval rulers and thus Roman subjects went to greater lengths to defend their nation

B. It was a reflection of the lesser degree of direct control medieval ruler had over subjects

C. It became a show of strength and honour warrior of the middles ages to be able to capture and return their enemies

D. Medieval soldiers were not as humanitarian as their ransoming practices might have indicated

3. The primary purpose of the passage is to
   A. discuss the economic basis of the medieval practice of exchanging prisoners for ransom
   B. examine the history of the treatment of prisoner of war
   C. emphasize the importance of a warrior's code of honour during the middle ages
   D. explore a way of reducing the cost of ransom
4. The author uses the phrase *"without too much distortion"* in order to
   A. indicate that prisoners would fairly assess their worth
   B. emphasize the important role medieval prisoners played in determining whether they should be ransomed
   C. explain how prisoners often paid more than an appropriate ransom in order to increase their chances for survival
   D. suggest that captors and captives often had understanding relationships

PASSAGE-2

The world dismisses curiosity by calling it idle or mere idle curiosity—even though curious persons are seldom idle. Parents do their best to extinguish curiosity in their children because it makes life difficult to be faced everyday with a string of unanswerable questions about what makes fire hot or why grass grows. Children whose curiosity survives parental discipline are invited to join our university. With the university, they go on asking their questions and trying to find the answers. In the eyes of a scholar, that is what a university is for. Some of the questions which the scholars ask, seem to the world to be scarcely worth asking, let alone answering. They asked questions too minute specialised for you and me to understand without years of explanation. If the world inquires of one of them why he wants to know the answer to a particular question he may say especially if he is a scientist, that the answer will in some obscure way make possible a new machine or weapon or gadget. He talks that way because he knows that the world understands and respects utility.

But to you who are now part of the university, he will say that he wants to know the answer simply because he does not know it, the way the mountain climber wants to climb a mountain, simply because it is there. Similarly a historian asked by an outsider why he studies history may come out with the argument that he has learnt to repeat on such occasions, something about knowledge of the past making it possible to understand the present and mould the future. But if you really want to know why a historian studies the past, the answer is much simpler, something happened and he would like to know what. All this does not mean that the answers which scholars find to their questions have no consequences. They may have enormous consequences but these seldom form the reason for asking the questions or pursuing the answers. It is true that scholars can be put to work answering questions for the sake of the consequences as thousands are working, now, for example, in search of a cure for cancer. But this is not the primary function of the scholars. For the consequences are usually subordinate to the satisfaction of curiosity.

1. According to the passage, the children make life difficult for their parents
   A. by their ceaseless curiosity
   B. by unceasing bombardment of questions
   C. by asking irrelevant questions
   D. by posing profound questions
2. The common people consider some of the questions that the scholars ask unimportant
   A. as they are too lazy and idle
   B. as they are too modest
   C. as it's beyond their comprehension
   D. as it is considered a waste of time
3. A historian really studies the past
   A. to comprehend the present and to reconstruct the future
   B. to explain the present and plan the future
   C. to understand the present and make fortune
   D. to understand the present and mould the future

4. Children whose curiosity survives parental discipline means
   A. children retaining their curiosity in spite of being discouraged by their parents
   B. children pursuing their mental curiosity
   C. children's curiosity subdued due to parents' intervention
   D. children being disciplined by their parents

5. According to the passage, parents do their best to discourage curiosity in their children
   A. because thev have no time
   B. because they have no patience to answer them
   C. because they feel that their children ask stupid questions continuously
   D. because they are unable to answer all their questions

PASSAGE-3

The factor of geographical distribution is equally, possibly even more, significant that English is spoken as first or native language in at least four continents of the world, Russian in two, Chinese and the Indian languages in one. English is without question the closest approach to a world language today. It goes without saying that no two persons ever have an identical command of their common language. Certainly, they have not precisely the same vocabulary. There are at least minor differences in pronunciation, indeed the same individual will not pronounce his vowels and consonants in absolutely identical fashion everytime he utters them. Everyone possesses, in addition, certain individual traits of grammatical form and syntactical order, constituting that peculiar and personal quality of language which we term as style. All of this is implicit in the well-known phrase, 'Style is the man.' No men are identical, no two styles are the same. If this be true of but two persons, the potential of differences resident in a language spoken by more than 200 million truly staggers imagination.

1. The author argues that English is the closest approach to a world language because
   A. there are more native speakers of English than of any other language
   B. English has less number of mutually unintelligible dialects
   C. the geographical distribution of English covers a much greater area
   D. other languages are much too complex to be world languages

2. The fact that the same individual will not pronounce his vowels and consonants identically everytime shows that
   A. literary style varies from person to person
   B. mutual intelligibility is a myth
   C. vocabulary varies from individual to individual
   D. no two persons speak the same language exactly the same way

3. It is evident from the passage that style is
   A. a strange type of language
   B. a language where one does not have to be particular about correctness and grammar
   C. language used in a particular way by an individual
   D. a question of grammatical and syntactic correctness

4. According to some authorities
   A. more people speak Chinese dialect than English
   B. more people speak English as an auxiliary language than as a first language
   C. more people speak English in the UK than in England
   D. about one-fourth of the world's population speaks English

5. The overall implication of the passage is that
   A. to suppose that 230 million people speak English as a native language would certainly be an underestimate
   B. the 55 million inhabitants of the British Isles speak like the 30 million inhabitants of the dominions and colonies
   C. a little less than half the native English speakers in the world live in the US

D. about one-tenth of the total English-speaking world population lives in British dominions and colonies

PASSAGE-4

What is the future which awaits our children? The underlying assumption of the question, that Indian children have a common future, is itself dubious. It can legitimately be asked whether a student who is well-fed, attending a boarding school in the salubrious climate of the hills and learning to use computers has any future in common with a malnourished child who goes to a school with no blackboards, if indeed he does go to school. The latter may have no worthwhile future at all. And it might be worthwhile to analyse the significance of this marginalisation of more than 75 per cent of the children of this country.

The failure to provide an infrastructure for primary education in the villages of India more than 40 years after independence is in sharp contrast with the sophisticated institutions, for technical institutes of higher education are funded by the government, which essentially means that the money to support them comes from taxes. And, since indirect taxation forms a substantial part of the taxes collected by the government, the financial burden is borne by all the people. L.K. Jha put it graphically when he observed that 25 paise of every rupee spent on educating an IIT student comes from the pockets of men and women whose children may never enter a proper classroom.

1. The author is trying to highlight which of the following?

A. Faulty system of direct taxes

B. The greatness of L.K. Jha

C. Need of sophisticated education for rural poor

D. Need to have common future for Indian children

2. Which of the following pairs have been termed as 'sharp contrast' by the author?

(*i*) Infrastructure for technical education

(*ii*) Lack of infrastructure for rural primary schools

(*iii*) 25 paise of every rupee earned by Government is spent on education

(*iv*) The financial burden of higher technical education is borne by all people

(*v*) 75% of children have limited opportunities

A. (*ii*) and (*iv*) B. (*ii*) and (*iii*)

C. (*iii*) and (*iv*) D. (*i*) and (*ii*)

3. Which of the following statements is not true?

(*i*) The author welcomes Govt.'s initiative on primary education

(*ii*) 75% of the children have a bright future

(*iii*) 25% cost of educating a technocrat comes from poor people

A. Only (*i*) B. Only (*ii*)

C. Only (*iii*) D. Only (*i*) and (*ii*)

4. According to the author, who among the following does not have a hopeful and prosperous future?

(*i*) All students from technical institutes

(*ii*) All students financially supported by the Government

A. Only (*i*) B. Only (*ii*)

C. Both (*i*) and (*ii*) D. Neither (*i*) nor (*ii*)

5. What seems to be the likely answer of the author to the question posed by him in the first sentence of the passage?

(*i*) There is no common future for the Indian children

(*ii*) The future is worthwhile for majority of Indian children

(*iii*) The majority may never enter a proper classroom

A. Only (*i*) B. Only (*ii*)

C. Only (*iii*) D. Both (*i*) and (*ii*)

6. What seems to be the purpose of the author in writing this passage?

A. Setting goals for children of upper middle class

B. Questioning the legitimacy of public schools

C. Highlighting lack of infrastructural facilities for primary education

D. Focusing on inequality in educational opportunities

PASSAGE-5

Cyber crime is the branded stigma defacing the culture and magnanimity of computer technology. It is upkeeping the flag with indomitable triumph against developing computer technology worldwide.

Modern age is striding with marching steps of technology revolution beating the past decade of ancestral belief with ultimate care. Computer invention has unfolded the mystery of quick access with the objective of minimum manpower and cutting the time consumption parameters.

As each coin has dual face of its portrait, likewise computer technology is sick of creeping virus. Synthetic man-made dilemma of site hackers activation is causing setback to the expanding anchor of revolutionary device with great loss of time, economy and data profile as suffered by consumers. A recent report from Internet security firm Websense estimates that 85.6 per cent of all the unwanted e-mails contained links to spam sites. The company's data suggests that the number of malicious sites grew 233 per cent in the last six months and saw 671 per cent growth in the number of malicious sites during the last year. In June alone, the total number of e-mails detected as containing viruses increased by 600 per cent compared to May.

Chat rooms, blogs and message-boards where the users post comments have been identified as the top targets of hackers and spammers due to the high traffic these attract. According to Websense, 95 per cent of user-generated comments to blogs, chat rooms and message-boards during the first half of the year were malicious.

It is advisable not to click on spurious links and stay away from keying in passwords at unknown sites as they are most likely to be spammed. Hackers can steal your passwords and log in to your account and access critical information like account numbers and contact details among other things.

1. The above passage is:
A. an advisory for the computer users.
B. an advisory for the Internet users.
C. a warning against possible threat to the Internet users.
D. related to chat rooms, blogs and message boards.

2. People who use chat rooms and blogs,
A. are safe and have no threats from spam.
B. are more prone to malicious e-mails.
C. create virus and hack the accounts of others.
D. are unsafe.

3. According to the writer, it is not safe to:
A. log on to spurious links.
B. access one's own account frequently.
C. have essential information stored in a computer.
D. include data-stealing code.

4. Hackers and spammers, according to the writer, are:
A. a new threat to the Internet users and the economy.
B. only pranksters and not serious threat to the system.
C. rained, professional technocrats who are an asset.
D. not expert professionals.

5. Which word in the passage is synonym of *weblog*?
A. blog B. password
C. site D. e-mail

6. Which agency has assessed the data record with spam sites?
A. Microsoft
B. Internet security from Google
C. Websense
D. Spammers

7. Which month dominates the e-mails detection data record?
A. May B. June
C. Last six months D. Last year

PASSAGE-6

Progress in life depends a good deal on crossing one threshold after another. Some time ago, a man watched his little nephew try to write his name. It was hard work, very hard work. The little boy had arrived at an effort threshold. Today he writes his name with comparative ease. No new threshold confronts him. This is the way with all of us. As soon as we cross one threshold, as soon as we conquer one difficulty, a new difficulty appears, or should appear. Some people make the mistake of steering clear of thresholds. Anything that requires genuine thinking and use of energy, they avoid. They prefer to stay in a rut where thresholds are not met. Probably, they have been at their job a number of years. Things are easy for them. They make no effort to seek out new obstacles to overcome. Real progress stops under such circumstances.

Some middle-aged and elderly people greatly enrich their lives by continuing to cross thresholds. One man went into an entirely new business when he was past middle life and made success of it, De Morgan didn't start to write novels until he was past sixty. Psychologists have discovered that man can continue to learn throughout his life. And it is undoubtedly better to try and fail than not to try at all. There one can be placed in the category of the Swiss mountaineer of whom it was said, *"He died climbing"*. When a new difficulty arises to obstruct your path, do not complain. Accept the challenge. Determine to cross this threshold as you have crossed numerous other thresholds in your past. In the words of a poet, do not rest but strive *to pass from dream to grander dream.*

1. What obstructs real progress in life?
A. Remaining at one and the same post
B. Avoiding the thinking and energy
C. Shunning every work
D. Stopping education

2. What does progress in life depend upon?
A. Good habits
B. Hardwork
C. Overcoming one difficulty after another
D. Spirit of service and cooperation

3. What does *'He died climbing'* signify?
A. He died when he was climbing the hill
B. He died before getting at the top
C. He strove hard till the last moment of life
D. He climbed the hill and then died

4. What does *'to pass from dream to grander dream'* mean?
A. Always having greater and greater aspiration in life
B. Seeing one good dream and then greater aspiration in life
C. Making plan after plan
D. Seeing one dream after the other

5. What did the man entering a new business past middle life do of his business?
A. He miserably failed in it
B. He achieved partial success
C. He dropped the business after some time
D. He achieved good success in it

6. How can you accomplish the most difficult tasks?
A. By mobilizing all possible resources
B. By avoiding all obstacles
C. By sticking to hardwork
D. By doing it bit by bit and persisting in the effort

7. What does De Morgan's life teach?
A. That it is futile to learn many things
B. That one is never old in case he has vigour
C. That it is never too late to learn
D. That creative writing can be made even late in life

8. How do middle-aged and elderly people add brilliance to their lives?
A. By overcoming difficulty one after another
B. By getting sycophants to surround them
C. By making fine speeches
D. By acquiring resourcefulness

9. What should we do when a new difficulty obstructs our path?
A. Run away from it
B. Be bold and face it
C. Manoeuvre to get it removed
D. Enlist other people's help to get it over

10. When did De Morgan start to write novels?
A. When he was sixty years old
B. When he was below sixty
C. When he studied psychology
D. None of these

PASSAGE-7

It is *heartening* to know that if one had not had any heart attack earlier and he stops smoking, his chances of having a heart attack *drop* to that of a non-smoker in about six months' time. Stopping of smoking is also the single most effective means of secondary prevention (recurrence of a heart attack) in heart patients.

Smoking leads to pain and stiffness in the legs while walking. No amount of drugs can help. The only remedy is to give up smoking. If women smoke during pregnancy, there is an increased risk of death of the baby in the womb or soon after birth. Even where the baby survives, there is likelihood of delayed physical and intellectual development of the baby till it reaches 11 years of age.

Still worse the fact about smoking is that passive smoking is equally dangerous. Passive smokers are those who do not smoke but being in the company of smokers have to inhale smoke exhaled by the smokers They are equally prone to heart diseases, lung cancer and bronchitis, for no fault of theirs. It is seen that the incidence of these diseases is greater among women whose husbands are *heavy* smokers As such, every non-smoker has a fundamental right to safeguard himself against the danger of passive smoking. "Your smoking is injurious to my health and I have a right to stop you from smoking" could be the slogan against passive smoking. It is a great threat to the health of the individual, the family and the society. In fact one has to choose between health and smoking including passive smoking. *One cannot have both.*

Another matter of *grave concern* about smoking is the long time interval between the start of smoking habit and the manifestation of deadly diseases like cancer, chronic bronchitis and heart attack. People are generally not aware of the link between smoking and the misery they have to undergo years later and younger people often fall victim to this menacing habit under the wrong impression that they are *immune* to its disastrous effects, not realising that they are *heading* towards catastrophe. The prolonged incubation period of many tobacco-related diseases has prevented recognition of the size of the threat and the *grim* picture of chronic and life-threatening diseases.

1. What is "passive smoking"?

A. Giving up the habit of smoking abruptly
B. Exhaling smoke by a non-smoker
C. Unintended intake of smoke exhaled by smokers
D. Smoking cigarettes which are harmless in nature

2. The effects of passive smoking are more and more prominently observed among

A. the children
B. the smokers
C. the wives of smokers
D. the non-smokers

3. Which of the following is a heartening thing, according to the author?

A. People who have had a heart attack stop smoking
B. It takes only six months for any person to quit smoking
C. The smoker carries the risk of heart attack for six months
D. None of these

4. Which of the following statements is/are false in the context of the passage?

(*i*) Passive smokers are not free from risk of heart diseases
(*ii*) Intake of certain medicines helps recover pain and stiffness in legs caused by smoking
(*iii*) Younger people are immune to the disastrous effects if their regular smoking is under control

A. (*i*) and (*ii*) only B. (*ii*) and (*iii*) only
C. (*ii*) only D. (*iii*) only

5. Which of the following is not mentioned in the passage as a likely result of smoking by women during pregnancy?

A. Death of baby before birth
B. Death of baby after birth
C. Survival of baby with some abnormality
D. Abnormal delay in the childbirth

6. Which of the following is considered by the author as a matter of "grave concern"?

A. Inordinate delay in appearance of symptoms of hazards of smoking

B. Long time required for giving up the habit of smoking

C. Manifestation of deadly diseases like cancer, bronchitis, etc.

D. Lack of awareness of people regarding the hazards of smoking

7. The youth feel that they are immune to the hazardous effects of smoking because

A. these effects of smoking are not visible within a short time span

B. they do not realise that they are heading towards disaster

C. they feel a great thrill in acquiring the habit of smoking

D. the link between smoking and its disastrous effects cannot be established

8. Which factor prevents people from realising the extent of threat of smoking hazards?

A. Their lack of awareness of civic responsibilities

B. Their firm belief that they are not immune to these hazards

C. The less disastrous effects of tobacco-related diseases

D. None of these

9. The last sentence of the third para *"One cannot have both"* means

A. active smoking and passive smoking

B. smoking and risk of heart diseases

C. threat to the individual and also to the family

D. None of these

Directions (Qs. 10 to 12): *Choose the word which is most nearly the* ***SAME*** *in meaning as the word given in bold capitals as used in the passage.*

10. HEADING

A. crowning B. marching

C. adorning D. title

11. HEAVY

A. excessive B. bulky

C. large D. thick

12. DROP

A. roll B. escape

C. remove D. reduce

Directions (Qs. 13 to 15): *Choose the word which is most nearly the* ***OPPOSITE*** *in meaning of the word given in bold capitals as used in the passage.*

13. GRIM

A. dim B. dark

C. presentable D. pleasant

14. IMMUNE

A. free B. vulnerable

C. powerful D. weak

15. HEARTENING

A. cheerful B. miserable

C. frightening D. dangerous

PASSAGE-8

The happy man is the man who lives objectively, who has free affections and wide interests, who secures his happiness through these interests and affections and through the fact that they, in turn, make him an object of interest and affection to many others. To be the recipient of affection is a potent cause of happiness, but the man who demands affection is not the man upon whom it is *bestowed.* The man who receives affection is, speaking broadly, the man who gives it. But it is useless to attempt to give it as a calculation, in the way in which one might lend money at interest, for a calculated affection is not genuine and is not felt to be so by the recipient.

What then can a man do who is unhappy because he is encased in self? So long as he continues to think about the causes of his unhappiness, he continues to be self-centred and therefore does not get outside the vicious circle, if he is to get outside it, it must be genuine interests, not by simulated interests adopted merely as a medicine. Although this difficulty is real, there is nevertheless much that he can do if he has rightly diagnosed his trouble. If, for example, his trouble is due to a sense of sin, conscious or unconscious, he can first persuade his conscious mind that he has no reason to feel sinful and then proceed, to plant his rational conviction in his unconscious mind, concerning himself meanwhile with some more or less neutral activity. If he succeeds in *dispelling* the sense of sin, it is possible that genuine objective interests will arise spontaneously. If his trouble is self-pity, he can deal with it in the same manner after first persuading himself that there is nothing extraordinarily unfortunate in his circumstances.

If fear is his trouble, let him practise exercises designed to give courage. Courage has been recognised from time immemorial as an important virtue, and a great part of training of boys and young men has been devoted to producing a type of character capable of fearlessness in battle. But moral courage and intellectual courage have been much less studied, they also, however, have their technique. Admit to yourself everyday at least one painful truth, you will find this quite useful. Teach yourself to feel that life still be worth living even if you were not, as of course you are, immeasurably superior to all your friends in virtue and in intelligence. Exercises of this sort prolonged through several years will at last enable you to admit facts *without flinching* and will, in so doing, free you from the empire of fear over a very large field.

1. Who according to the passage is the happy man?
A. who is encased in self
B. who has free affection and wide interests
C. who is free from worldly passions
D. who has externally centre passions

2. According to the passage, calculated affection
A. appears to be false and fabricated
B. makes other pen-on to love you
C. turns into permanent affection over a period of time
D. leads to self-pity

3. Which of the following virtues, according to the passage, has been recognised for long as an important virtue?
A. Patriotism B. Sacrifice
C. Courage D. Self-consciousness

4. Which of the following, according to the passage, has not been studied much?
A. Feeling of guilt and self-pity
B. The state of mind of an unhappy man
C. How to get absorbed in other interests
D. Moral and intellectual courage

5. If a man is suffering from a sense of sin
A. he should invite opinion of others
B. he should admit his sin at once
C. he should consciously realize that he has no reason to feel sinful
D. he should develop a fearless character

6. What happens to a man who demands affection?
A. His feelings are reciprocated by others
B. He tends to take a calculated risk
C. He becomes a victim of a viscious circle
D. None of these

7. What should a man do who is suffering from the feeling of self-pity?
A. He should control his passions and emotions
B. He should persuade himself that everything is alright in his circumstances
C. He should seek affection from others
D. He should develop a feeling of fearlessness

8. How to get out of the viscious circle mentioned in the passage?
A. By practicing skills of concentration
B. By inculcating the habits of self-absorption
C. Being true to others and one's internal circumstances
D. None of these

9. Which of the following statements is not *true* in the context of the passage?
A. Happy man has wide interests
B. Courage has been recognized as an important virtue
C. Unhappy man is encased in self

D. Issue of intellectual courage has been extensively studied

10. Which of the following words is ***SIMILAR*** in meaning of the word **'bestowed'** as used in the passage?

A. Conferred B. Accommodated
C. Trusted D. Withdrawn

11. Which of the following statements is *true* in the context of the passage?

A. All passions stem from unhappiness
B. The happy man lives in subjectively
C. Any virtue has a dark side also
D. One feels happy if one receives affection

12. Which of the following words is ***SIMILAR*** in meaning to the word **'flinching'** as used in the passage?

A. Wincing B. Convincing
C. Explaining D. Debating

13. What happens when you think about cause of your unhappiness?

A. You try to introspect and look critically at yourself
B. You realize that the life can be lived in different ways
C. You try to practice exercise designed to give courage
D. You remain a self-centred person

14. What according to the passage is the real cause of happiness?

A. Material rewards and incentives received
B. Critical analysis of the happy state of mind
C. Affection received from others
D. Calculated risks taken

15. Which of the following words is ***OPPOSITE*** in meaning of the word **'dispelling'** as used in the passage?

A. Giving B. Accumulating
C. Projecting D. Scattering

PASSAGE-9

Education, particularly higher education, is the obvious but crucially important instrument for nation building. As Confucious has said:

"If you are thinking of one year, plant rice. If you are thinking of a decade, plant trees. If you are thinking of a century, educate the people."

When we set about the task of higher education, we should be absolutely clear in our perception of the goals of education in the specific context of our nation's development. No *doubt,* one of the important aims of education would be to create the required range and nature of trained manpower assessed to be needed by different sectors of national growth. The entire educational apparatus must be geared progressively to fulfill the requirements of different phases of our growth in every sector—primary, secondary and *tertiary.* The aim must be to ensure that our country does not experience either *paucity,* or a *surfeit* of trained manpower in any specific segment of our economy. The requirements of our country, as a free, democratic, secular, socialist, nation, *aspiring* for rapid development, *entail* a specific recipe for our educational institutions. Today's educational institutions must therefore be developed accordingly and must regulate themselves to give the country the precise nature and quantum of trained manpower as projected by the requirements of our planned economy.

1. The author has quoted thoughts of Confucious to stress

A. importance of planting trees for human beings
B. the worthless efforts in planting rice
C. the benefits of investing in education
D. the need for assessing manpower requirement

2. Which statement cannot be made on the basis of the passage?

A. Higher education should keep in view the requirements of national economy
B. Higher education has not been employed for nation building
C. All levels of education have a role to play in nation's growth
D. In our country we need to have a specially planned educational system

3. The writer believes that
   A. there are no problems related to higher education
   B. investment in education is of long-range
   C. higher education should be used to assess manpower needs
   D. aims of higher education in India are absolutely clear
4. The author's expectations from higher education, are essentially
   A. unrealistic B. confusing
   C. critical D. vague
5. The writer indicates that
   A. higher education did not play any role in national growth
   B. primary education did not play any role in national growth
   C. our nation experiences paucity of trained manpower in many sectors
   D. today's higher education has no precise goals to achieve
6. Author has used the word 'apparatus' to indicate the
   A. scientific nature of education
   B. complicated organization demanded by education
   C. readily visible benefits of education
   D. entire equipment of education to perform particular function
7. Which of the following has not been conveyed by the passage?
   A. Education at any level can contribute in nation building
   B. Manpower needs in many areas can be fulfilled through higher education
   C. Rapid development of our nation is possible through higher education
   D. Present higher education does not ensure surfeit of trained manpower
8. This passage is likely to be addressed to
   A. politicians only
   B. scientists only
   C. students only
   D. cannot be said
9. Choose a suitable title to the passage:
   A. Manpower Planning in India
   B. Importance of Higher Education
   C. Demands of Higher Education
   D. Role of Higher Education in India

Directions (Qs.10 to 12): *Choose the word which is most nearly the **SAME** in meaning as the word given in bold capitals as used in the passage.*

10. **DOUBT**
    A. suspicion B. certain
    C. definite D. sure
11. **TERTIARY**
    A. last B. important
    C. third D. terminal
12. **ASPIRING**
    A. inquiring B. awaiting
    C. involving D. striving

Directions (Qs.13 to 15): *Choose the word which is most **OPPOSITE** in meaning as the word given in bold capitals as used in the passage.*

13. **PAUCITY**
    A. moderate B. enormity
    C. mediocrity D. littleness
14. **SURFEIT**
    A. abundance B. redundancy
    C. repletion D. lack
15. **ENTAIL**
    A. entitled B. ensure
    C. dismiss D. retain

PASSAGE-10

Books are a great treasurehouse of knowledge. They are the living examples of man's *march* on the path to higher and higher civilisation. The great men who died long ago, live in their books. We feel their very personality and existence when we read their books. We feel as if they were conversing with us.

Books not only store civilization but also carry it forward. All coming generations get the light of knowledge from the books written by their ancestors and try to improve upon that knowledge. Civilization cannot make much *headway* in a country where there are not many *great* books. We get through books the latest knowledge in the fields of arts, science, commerce, etc. This knowledge is helpful to us and *enables* us to achieve success in the field of our choice.

Books are never failing friends. They never *desert* us, not even when all fair-weather friends have deserted us. They dispel the dark clouds of gloom from our minds and increase our happiness if we are already happy. Through the ages, the scriptures and other great books have provided immeasurable *solace* to the wounded and strife-torn humanity.

There may be books prescribed for some course or profession, but then there are books for general study. The books of literature—poetry, drama, novel, short stories, etc., are generally highly thrilling and inspiring if they are written by a good author. There may be tragic, comical or humorous books. The question is that of an individual's choice.

To be a lover of books, though not to be bookworm, is a sign of good luck. A voracious reader gets much *more pleasure* from reading books than a miser gets in hoarding money. The knowledge embedded in books is valueless; so is pleasure obtained from reading them. A good book absorbs the whole spirit of man; the reader's pleasure is indescribable.

1. Which of the following, according to the passage, is not true about books?
   A. They are source of inspiration
   B. They are source of knowledge
   C. They are source of happiness
   D. They are means of livelihood

2. How do the books help in progress of civilization?
   A. Based on the earlier books new knowledge is obtained
   B. The books provide solution to many problems
   C. The books inspire the scientists
   D. Not mentioned in the passage

3. How do the books make people more happy?
   A. They help the reader to overcome the shadows of uncertainty
   B. They help bring in joy by amusing the reader through their content
   C. They help the reader to understand the darker side of life
   D. Not mentioned in the passage

4. Which of the following is the author's view about the knowledge and pleasure derived from books?
   (*i*) We get more of knowledge and less of pleasure
   (*ii*) We get more of pleasure and less of knowledge
   (*iii*) We get knowledge and pleasure in equal measure
   A. only (*i*) B. only (*ii*)
   C. either (*i*) or (*ii*) D. only (*iii*)

5. The high quality of books produced by a country indicates:
   A. it has a high rate of literacy
   B. it has a progressive civilization
   C. it is not an industrialised nation
   D. it has learned ancestors

6. Why are the books, according to the passage, called never-failing friends?
   A. Books do not betray individuals
   B. Books are inanimate
   C. Books always give companionship to the reader
   D. Books are available in the market anytime unlike others

7. How do the books help in bringing peace in the minds of people?
   A. Books provide information about the past civilization
   B. Books help people learn to take correct steps with the help of the recorded information
   C. Books act as a window to the minds of the great men
   D. Not mentioned in the passage

8. Which of the following has been described as a sign of good luck?
   A. Being a miser
   B. Having lot of money
   C. Advancing the culture
   D. A passion for books

Directions (Qs. 9 to 12): *Choose the word which is most nearly the* ***SAME*** *in meaning as the word given in bold capitals as used in the passage.*

9. **SOLACE**
   A. peace B. tranquillity
   C. calmness D. console

10. **ENABLES**
   A. helps B. succeeds
   C. promotes D. stops

11. **HEADWAY**
   A. higher B. forge
   C. movement D. improve

12. **MARCH**
   A. move B. progress
   C. pass D. register

Directions (Qs. 13 to 15): *Choose the word which is most* ***OPPOSITE*** *in meaning of the word given in bold capitals as used in the passage.*

13. **GREAT**
   A. small B. thin
   C. short D. ordinary

14. **PLEASURE**
   A. displeasure B. pain
   C. happiness D. hardship

15. **DESERT**
   A. waterhole B. bitter
   C. accompany D. propel

ANSWERS

PASSAGE-1

1	2	3	4
A	B	A	A

PASSAGE-2

1	2	3	4	5
A	C	D	A	D

PASSAGE-3

1	2	3	4	5
A	D	C	D	A

PASSAGE-4

1	2	3	4	5	6
D	A	D	A	A	D

PASSAGE-5

1	2	3	4	5	6	7
A	D	A	A	A	C	B

PASSAGE-6

1	2	3	4	5
A	C	C	A	D
6	**7**	**8**	**9**	**10**
D	B	A	B	D

PASSAGE-7

1	2	3	4	5
C	C	D	B	D
6	**7**	**8**	**9**	**10**
A	A	D	D	B
11	**12**	**13**	**14**	**15**
A	D	D	B	C

PASSAGE-8

1	2	3	4	5
B	A	C	D	C
6	**7**	**8**	**9**	**10**
D	B	D	D	A
11	**12**	**13**	**14**	**15**
D	D	D	C	B

PASSAGE-9

1	2	3	4	5
D	D	C	D	D
6	**7**	**8**	**9**	**10**
D	A	D	B	A
11	**12**	**13**	**14**	**15**
C	D	B	D	C

PASSAGE-10

1	2	3	4	5
D	A	D	D	B
6	**7**	**8**	**9**	**10**
A	D	D	D	A
11	**12**	**13**	**14**	**15**
D	B	D	B	C

❑❑❑

14 Cloze Test

A cloze test is a procedure in which a person is asked to supply words that have been removed from a passage as a test of his ability to comprehend text. Practise it regularly to score well.

PASSAGES

Directions: *In each of the following passages some numbered blank spaces are given. For each numbered blank space four answer choices are given. Pick out the one which is the most appropriate for that blank space, keeping the trend of the passage in mind.*

Passage-1

Mankind's most ....(1).... treasure of thoughts is carefully preserved in the golden casket of books. The ....(2).... of books is as vast as the universe, for there is no corner of it which they have left ....(3).... . There is no ....(4).... of books on any topic, be it as simple as the composition of sodium nitrate or as ....(5).... as the mechanism of a spacecraft rocketing towards Mars. The ....(6).... of books is not only most easily available but is enlightened, dependable and lifelong. In times of distress they make us stoically ....(7).... of the object that causes uneasiness and we learn to ....(8).... with the sting of adversity.

Questions

1. A. costly B. important C. valuable D. vast

2. A. area B. scope C. storage D. kingdom

3. A. unexplored B. unseen C. untouched D. unapproached

4. A. lack B. dearth C. shortage D. insufficiency

5. A. extricate B. intricate C. intrinsic D. internecine

6. A. company B. assistance C. friendship D. companionship

7. A. defiant B. defendant C. defensible D. delusive

8. A. adapt B. adopt C. exist D. co-exist

Passage-2

Though the government has tried to ....(1).... Naxalism with all its might, much more needs to be done to totally root out the ....(2).... of Naxalism. The roots of Naxalism ....(3).... economic backwardness and social exploitation of the peasants and the weaker classes. Thus, the best way to ....(4).... Naxalism is to bring the naxals ....(5).... the mainstream. ....(6).... policies and schemes should be implemented effectively ....(7).... the Naxals economically stable. They should be ....(8).... to participate in democratic processes. The government has to ....(9).... the social upliftment of the Naxals. Use of force in ....(10).... Naxalism will yield little success.

Questions

1. A. crush B. handle C. tackle D. suppress
2. A. menace B. whole C. gamut D. stems
3. A. lies in B. are in C. abound in D. exist in
4. A. crash B. crush C. break D. defy
5. A. in B. on C. into D. within
6. A. Current B. Latest C. Occurring D. Existing
7. A. so that B. so as to make C. such that D. to make
8. A. insisted B. brought C. encouraged D. forced
9. A. assure B. insure C. guarantee D. ensure
10. A. countering B. defying C. banishing D. desecrating

Passage-3

We are living in very exciting ....(1).... . The ....(2).... change is dizzying and the impact this progress is having on our present and — more importantly — on our future is difficult to ....(3).... in its ...(4).... . This is the age of ....(5).... micro-processors, sophisticated software, new hardware technology and high bandwidth, high-speed networks. The PC gave us a new way to work, play and ....(6).... . In fact, it brought ....(7).... our desktops computing power, which until a few years ....(8).... had only been available to corporates. With the ....(9).... of the internet, the PC ....(10).... us the most convenient and flexible way to head on to the Net.

Questions

1. A. periods B. days C. phase D. times
2. A. phase B. pace C. sphere D. drastic
3. A. guess B. forecast C. comprehend D. approximate
4. A. whole B. entirety C. fruition D. fullness
5. A. strong B. changing C. powerful D. sonorous
6. A. convey B. communicate C. entertain D. enjoy
7. A. onto B. to C. on D. at
8. A. back B. earlier C. behind D. before
9. A. addendum B. adherence C. afoot D. advent
10. A. allowed B. privileged C. brought D. offered

Passage-4

What is required today in our country is ....(1).... of a new political culture based on full respect for human liberty, on pluralism and on a better social deal for all. The major ....(2).... facing us today is to carry out democratic transformation in all the ....(3)...., social, cultural, economic and political. The events of the 20th century ....(4).... one thing absolutely clear that human ....(5)...., everywhere, specially in countries whose political structures were ....(6).... to reflect the revolutionary aspirations of the people ....(7).... not only under stress and strain but are ....(8).... vast upheavals because of the ....(9).... of democracy. At the same time it has also to be understood that democracy cannot be ....(10).... into a static mould.

Questions

1. A. growing B. developing C. creating D. creation
2. A. development B. crisis C. challenge D. drawback
3. A. corners B. context C. realm D. spheres
4. A. have made B. has made C. had made D. made

5. A. travails B. traverse
C. traps D. transverse

6. A. supposed B. meant
C. caused D. forced

7. A. were B. was
C. are D. have been

8. A. developing B. evolving
C. experiencing D. faced with

9. A. denial B. rebuff
C. rebuttal D. absence

10. A. shaped B. flex
C. frozen D. caused

Passage-5

For centuries, women not only in India but all over the world ....(1).... treated as ....(2).... secondary position to men. ....(3).... human history men ....(4).... far greater power then women to name, classify, and order the worlds in which they both live. ....(5).... studies in various parts of the world point out to a wide ....(6).... in male and female roles ....(7).... cultures and demonstrate the possibility of change in these sex-determined roles. The 20th century in particular ....(8).... the cause of gender justice by internationalizing struggles for equality ....(9).... women and other oppressed people. Women's struggles against their ....(10).... were intertwined in ....(11).... degrees with ideologies and movements based on the values of freedom, self-determination, equality, democracy and justice.

Questions

1. A. has been B. have been
C. had been D. were

2. A. occupying B. taking
C. possessing D. serving

3. A. All through B. Throughout
C. Since D. From

4. A. have B. had
C. have had D. enjoy

5. A. Sociological B. Anthropological
C. General D. Practical

6. A. concord B. repulsion
C. disagreement D. variation

7. A. among B. across
C. between D. of

8. A. developed B. evolved
C. promoted D. entertained

9. A. for B. to
C. among D. by

10. A. subsidiary B. subsequent
C. subservience D. subordination

11. A. various B. varying
C changing D. differing

Passage-6

Visualisation is a strong ....(1).... to memory. Those persons who ......(2)..... a powerful memory cannot do so without taking the help of visualisation. Such persons have developed the skills to ....(3).... visualisation even in such ....(4).... tasks as remembering names and numbers. These persons have the names and numbers ....(5).... in their brain even after hearing those names and figures only once. On the other hand those who take the help of revising to memorise ....(6).... to forget it once they have ....(7).... the practice of revising ....(8).... the ones who have applied visualisation to memorise. Psychologists ....(9).... in visualisation a powerful tool for personality development. The more you visualise, the more you are ....(10).... your attitude and behaviour to the blue prints of your vision and ....(11).... more you are inching towards success.

Questions

1. A. way B. path
C. aid D. symptom

2. A. command B. master
C. rule D. enjoy

3. A. use B. apply
C. put D. place

4. A. trivial B. difficult
C. mundane D. unscrupulous

5. A. impress B. imprinted
C. impinge D. store

6. A. bent B. incline
C. prone d. tend

7. A. dropped B. left
C. gave up D. given up

8. A. unlike B. opposite
C. contrary D. not like

9. A. found B. have found
C. sees D. finds

10. A. shaping B. moulding
C. making D. attuning

11. A. actually B. factually
C. subsequently D. consequently

Passage-7

The development of an area depends on the resources ....(1).... in the area, the needs and ....(2).... of the people living there and the technological skill ....(3).... by them. Humans play an important and decisive role in the ....(4).... of development of an area. We choose the ....(5).... of resources which could be developed to our ....(6).... . The natural ....(7).... available in an area ....(8).... value as a resource only when people find a use for them. There are ....(9).... where large potential resources are available, but they ....(10).... developed for economic reasons. Lack of capital for investments, roads and railway lines, and other ....(11).... facilities may stand in the way of resource development.

Questions

1. A. present B. prevalent
C. available D. exist

2. A. inspirations B. aspirations
C. ambitions D. curiosity

3. A. handled B. practised
C. availed D. possessed

4. A. system B. design
C. pattern D. style

5. A. class B. group
C. variety D. types

6. A. good B. advantage
C. approach D. favour

7. A. secrets B. phenomenon
C. products D. endowments

8. A. get B. acquire
C. possess D. takes

9. A. instances B. events
C. circumstances D. happenings

10. A. have not yet been
B. haven't been
C. are not yet
D. yet have not been

11. A. common B. general
C. infrastructural D. structural

Passage-8

The Naxal problem in India is basically socio-economic in ....(1).... . The main reasons ....(2).... the Naxal movement in India are the ....(3).... of peasants and their weak social and economic position. ....(4).... of the peasants are landless labourers whose lands have been ....(5).... occupied by the landlords. Moreover, the landlords give ....(6).... wages to the peasants. Their ....(7).... suffering at the hands of the landlords thus encourage many peasants to take law ....(8).... their own hands. Due to their poor economic condition the peasants easily ....(9).... the trap of the naxal leaders who have their ....(10).... interests. Illiteracy, unemployment, police excesses, corruption and ....(11).... administration further ....(12).... this complex problem.

Questions

1. A. form B. shape
C. behaviour D. nature

2. A. for B. of
C. in D. behind

3. A. complaisance B. exploitation
C. domination D. exculpation

4. A. Many B. Much
C. Most D. All

5. A. imperiously B. imperatively
C. forcefully D. forcibly

6. A. improper B. small
C. inadequate D. insufficient

7. A. long B. brutal
C. pathetic D. great

8. A. in B. into
C. on D. by

9. A. fall into B. fall in
C. fell in D. fell into

10. A. selfish B. vested
C. vicious D. vindictive

11. A. failed B. improper
C. inefficient D. bureaucratic

12. A. heighten B. deepen
C. add D. worsen

Passage-9

No doubt various ....(1).... and Acts are there to eliminate the ....(2).... practice of child labour. But the ....(3).... is that, these are not being implemented in both letter and spirit, for which the ....(4).... of the problem remains as it was. Therefore a judicious, pragmatic, integrated and time-bound ....(5).... supplemented by ....(6).... follow-up action is essential to ....(7).... the problem that ....(8).... deep root in our Society. It is true that child labour can't be ....(9)... with a magic wand. If we ....(10).... time-bound goals and follow, of course, with the ....(11).... assistance of ILO and UNICEF, it is possible to eliminate the problem of child labour. With strong political will power and people's backing nothing is ....(12).... . Rather ....(13).... the bud we should let it blossom and spread its fragrance all around. ....(14).... lies the progress and prosperity of the society.

Questions

1. A. means B. methods
C. source D. provisions

2. A. unjust B. inhuman
C. mal D. illegal

3. A. anxiety B. abrasion
C. tragedy D. conclusion

4. A. magnitude B. depth
C. gravity D. soaring

5. A. approach B. analysis
C. survey D. scheme

6. A. continuous B. thorough
C. throughout D. regular

7. A. outroot B. uproot
C. downroot D. grassroot

8. A. have B. has
C. had D. has taken

9. A. wipe out B. wipe off
C. wipe up D. wiped

10. A. keep B. put
C. put up D. set

11. A. ongoing B. continuing
C. unending D. frequent

12. A. insurmountable B. intangible
C. inscrutable D. incorrigible

13. A. killing B. hurting
C. destroying D. nipping

14. A. Here B. There
C. Therein D. Herein

Passage-10

Every action we perform ....(1).... a result. And, naturally, we lay claim ....(2).... the results or fruits ....(3).... from that action in the ....(4).... that it is we who perform the action. This is .....(5).... ignorance because ....(6).... is it the Lord who ....(7).... the result of any action, it is by His will ....(8).... that even the action is accomplished. The will of the Lord ....(9).... whether we cooperate with His will or strive ....(10).... . If God wills that an action takes place, he arranges for the ....(11).... for it to happen. It is ....(12).... experience that sometimes despite our best efforts we ....(13).... achieve the results we desire, and at other times the seemingly most ....(14).... situations mysteriously get ....(15).... . ....(16).... way man chooses to act, both the act and the outcome of the cost are dependent ....(17).... on the will of the Lord.

Questions

1. A. produce B. produces
C. causes D. undergoes

2. A. on B. at
C. to D. for

3. A. occurring B. obtaining
C. deriving D. falling

4. A. belief B. hope
C. fantasy D. folly

5. A. sheen B. keen
C. sheer D. sheathe

6. A. alone B. only that
C. not only D. for only

7. A. declares B. decides C. ordains D. ornate

8. A. completely B. entirely C. only D. alone

9. A. prevails always
B. prevails everywhere
C. is prevalent
D. always prevails

10. A. alone B. always C. constantly D. independently

11. A. wherewithal B. whereabouts C. whatsoever D. wherefore

12. A. usual B. general C. universal D. common

13. A. does not B. may not C. do not D. might not

14. A. intractable B. intangible C. internecine D. intricate

15. A. subsided B. resolved C. solved D. converted

16. A. Whatever B. All the C. All those D. Whichever

17. A. mainly B. actually C. entirely D. generally

ANSWERS

PASSAGE-1

1	2	3	4	5	6	7	8
C	D	A	B	B	D	A	D

PASSAGE-2

1	2	3	4	5	6	7	8	9	10
C	A	A	B	C	D	B	C	D	A

PASSAGE-3

1	2	3	4	5	6	7	8	9	10
D	B	C	B	C	B	A	D	D	D

PASSAGE-4

1	2	3	4	5	6	7	8	9	10
D	C	D	A	A	B	C	C	A	C

PASSAGE-5

1	2	3	4	5	6	7	8	9	10	11
B	A	B	C	B	D	B	C	D	D	B

PASSAGE-6

1	2	3	4	5	6	7	8	9	10	11
C	A	B	C	B	D	A	A	B	D	D

PASSAGE-7

1	2	3	4	5	6	7	8	9	10	11
C	B	D	C	D	B	D	B	A	A	C

PASSAGE-8

1	2	3	4	5	6	7	8	9	10	11	12
D	A	B	C	D	C	A	B	A	B	C	D

PASSAGE-9

1	2	3	4	5	6	7	8	9	10	11	12	13	14
D	B	C	A	A	D	B	D	B	D	B	A	D	C

PASSAGE-10

1	2	3	4	5	6	7	8	9	10	11	12	13	14	15	16	17
B	C	B	A	C	C	C	D	D	D	A	D	C	A	B	D	C

Comprehension Skills

- Comprehension
  - I. Cloze Test
  - II. Passages
  - III. Poetry
- Writing Critical Review
- Styles and Forms of Narration
- Essay Writing

Comprehension

Comprehension is a very important part of English paper. The questions on comprehension lay particular stress on understanding a given passage. You are required to read a passage or poem and answer a few questions based on it. Various comprehension questions are set solely with the objectives named below:

1. To test your ability to detect the central idea or the focal point in the given passage.
2. To test your ability to understand and interpret the given passage or poem.
3. To judge your capability to pick out the various arguments put forward by the writer for or against something.
4. To test your accuracy and richness of vocabulary.
5. To test your academic ability to understand the implied and the clearly and fully expressed ideas of the writer of the passage or poem.
6. To test, occasionally, your power of appreciating critically the views contained in the given passage or poem.

While answering comprehension questions, you must comply with the following important points:

1. First, read the whole passage or poem attentively, carefully and quickly.
2. Read it for the second time, slowly but steadily.
3. Work out the probable meaning of new words, from the context in which they have been used.
4. Underline and look for transitional words and phrases as an aid to comprehension.
5. The process of elimination should be used while selecting the correct answer.
6. Your answers should be brief and to the point, where-ever required.

I. CLOZE TEST

A cloze test is a procedure in which a person is asked to supply words that have been removed from a passage as a test of his ability to comprehend text. Practise it regularly to score well.

Directions: *In each of the following passages some numbered blank spaces are given. For each numbered blank space answer choices are given. Pick out the one which is the most appropriate for that blank space. Keep the trend of the passage in mind.*

PASSAGE-1

A drug which has been ....(1).... promoted here for fever and pain ....(2).... has invited medical ....(3).... over its ....(4).... side-effects following adverse reactions and its ....(5).... withdrawal in certain European countries. The scientific advisory committee has issued a ....(6).... advice on the ....(7).... of the drug ....(8).... some serious ....(9).... in the liver. While most doctors in India ....(10).... there is not need to ....(11).... yet, they also admit that they ....(12).... ....(13).... about it as most studies on the drug are industry ....(14).... .

QUESTIONS

1. A. aggressively B. astonishingly C. surprisingly D. immensely

2. A. treatment B. relief C. cure D. removal

3. A. concern B. criticism C. discussion D. debate

4. A. probable B. probably C. possible D. possibly
5. A. unconditional B. immediate C. consequent D. subsequent
6. A. precautionary B. preliminary C. formal D. informal
7. A. sell B. purchase C. recommendation D. marketing
8. A. reminding B. following C. thinking D. caring
9. A. complications B. problem C. complexity D. consequences
10. A. suggest B. insist C. lay D. say
11. A. worry B. react C. panic D. exorbitant
12. A. think B. know C. knew D. known
13. A. a bit B. a little C. a few D. little
14. A. based B. sponsored C. surveyed D. experimented

PASSAGE-2

I believe the biggest challenge ....(1).... the world is that of ....(2).... poverty across a large ....(3).... of the ....(4).... population and the continued ....(5).... between the rich and poor nations. The globalisation ....(6).... of the Nineties was ....(7).... to change all that and it has not made a significant impact as yet. Indeed, poverty today is the single biggest ....(8).... of place and democracy. It is high time that even the most ....(9).... rich citizen or indeed all of us ....(10).... people, realise that the only way to ....(11).... prosperity is to defeat poverty.

QUESTIONS

1. A. confronting B. facing C. spoiling D. destroying
2. A. acute B. continued C. general D. common
3. A. proportion B. share C. portion D. fraction
4. A. universal B. en bloc C. entire D. global
5. A. disputation B. disparity C. discrimination D. tensile
6. A. struggle B. efforts C. wave D. air
7. A. considered B. perpetually C. supposed D. perhaps
8. A. curse B. enemy C. hurdle D. obstruction
9. A. complacent B. compliant C. fatuous D. inconsiderate
10. A. well-to-do B. cultured C. privileged D. developed
11. A. defend B. debilitate C. protect D. save

PASSAGE-3

What the daily newspapers nowadays ....(1).... carry are the reports of ...(2).... murders, killings, genocides and ....(3).... cleansing all over the world. India is not an exception ...(4).... . For a moment one is sure ....(5).... the principle of religious tolerance, peace and ....(6)...., which were the ....(7).... of Indian society, that are now slowly but steadily ....(8).... hatred, anger, distrust and religious intolerance. Making things worse are the divisive practices being ....(9).... by some ....(10).... minds that have led to the rise of religious fundamentalism. And this is a ....(11)...., which is ....(12)..... in the form of hundreds of innocent lives being lost in all corners of the country.

QUESTIONS

1. A. usually B. generally C. regularly D. casually
2. A. huge B. massive C. brutal D. mass
3. A. ethnic B. ethical C. evasive D. eventual

4. A. to it B. in it
C. for it D. on it

5. A. of thinking B. to think about
C. to think of D. thinking about

6. A. conscientious B. compassion
C. rapacity D. sagacity

7. A. heart B. core
C. cornerstones D. milestones

8. A. are replaced with
B. replaced by
C. being replaced by
D. being replaced with

9. A. precluded B. precipitated
C. predisposed D. fabricated

10. A. perverted B. scrupulous
C. nefarious D. ruthless

11. A. calumny B. bane
C. crass D. denouncement

12. A. visible B. coming
C. taking its toll D. resulting its toll.

PASSAGE-4

The outstanding ....(1).... of the development of science and technology can neither be realised nor enriched in an atmosphere with disturbed ....(2).... balance, ...(3).... to pollution hazards. The ....(4).... of pollution and conservation of the natural ecosystems in all the development efforts are ....(5).... not merely for the growth of our ....(6).... but for our very existence on this earth. It demands the ....(7)... that it deserves. Although ....(8).... is expressed in various circles for ....(9).... the environmental balance and ....(10).... of forests, but at the same time there is a large scale ....(11).... of forests, as ....(12).... evidenced in several river valley projects ....(13).... at the national level.

QUESTIONS

1. A. capacity B. potential
C. possibility D. advancement

2. A. economical B. natural
C. ecological D. polluting

3. A. susceptible B. adversely
C. salubrious D. pernicious

4. A. removal B. eradication
C. discarding D. evolution

5. A. imperil B. imminent
C. impulsive D. imperative

6. A. status B. sociability
C. economy D. environment

7. A. importance B. attention
C. value D. care

8. A. interest B. enthusiasm
C. deep concern D. anxiety

9. A. maintaining B. evolving
C. developing D. rising

10. A. growing B. maintaining
C. maintenance D. regeneration

11. A. degeneration B. degradation
C. deprivation D. dereliction

12. A. blatantly B. vitally
C. vividly D. indiscreetly

13. A. executed B. planned
C. organised D. undertaken

PASSAGE-5

India is a country where women ....(1).... worshipped and ....(2).... at the same time. If mantras have been chanted to ....(3)... the Goddesses, ...(4).... have also been hurled at a domestic wife questioning her devotion and ....(5).... . Their position has remained more or less the same ....(6).... . Though women have taken ....(7).... since the country achieved independence, they still are a ....(8).... of political, socio-economic and legal neglect. The current year has seen a number of government ....(9).... to empower women. Though these are ....(10)...., much will depend on the ....(11).... implementation of these schemes or else they ....(12).... achieve the targets, they have set for themselves.

QUESTIONS

1. A. are B. were
C. has been D. have been

2. A. cursed B. blamed
C. crucified D. insulted

3. A. placate B. please
C. plead D. respect

4. A. curses B. expletives
C. obscenity D. objurgation

5. A. virginity B. purity
C. chastity D. fecundity

6. A. till date
B. over time
C. till now
D. until now.

7. A. remarkable progress
B. advancement
C. rapid strides
D. important steps

8. A. object B. subject
C. matter D. victim

9. A. machinery B. initiatives
C. project D. plannings

10. A. laudable B. languor
C. lascivious D. lassitude

11. A. efficient B. thorough
C. appropriate D. effective

12. A. would not B. should not
C. will not D. cannot

PASSAGE-6

We are ....(1).... about our success and failure in every field. No doubt, we start our actions with ....(2).... but still in a corner of our mind ....(3).... about success and failure and ....(4).... makes us tense. And this tension sometimes ....(5).... that it effects our efficiency and performance. So, we ....(6).... remember that the mind is efficient ....(7).... it is cool, not hot or tense. The tease or excited mind ....(8).... produce rational concepts or ....(9).... thought processes. A calm person has his senses fully ....(10).... with the environment ....(11).... he places himself. A restless person ....(12).... notice anything, consequently he gets into trouble with himself and others and ....(13).... everything.

QUESTIONS

1. A. always worried B. anxious always
C. curious always D. in doubt-always

2. A. over-confidence B. full confidence
C. full enthusiasm D. full effort

3. A. a doubt remains still
B. remains a doubt
C. still remians a doubt
D. a doubt still remains

4. A. intentionally B. unnecessarily
C. necessarily D. unconsciously

5. A. become so intense
B. grow so much
C. become so intensive
D. become so serious

6. A. must B. have to
C. will have to D. shall have to

7. A. when B. when only
C. only then when D. only when

8. A. can never B. could not
C. connot D. possibly

9. A. obnoxious B. obligatory
C. objective D. orderly

10. A. engrossed B. paralleled
C. identified D. sunk

11. A. on which B. in which
C. at which D. where

12. A. do not B. does not
C. did not D. cannot

PASSAGE-7

Great books do not spring from something ....(1).... in the great men who wrote them. They are the ....(2).... of their very core, the ....(3).... of the life itself of the authors. And literature cannot be said to ....(4).... its true purpose. Until it ....(5).... translated into the actual life of him who reads. Literature is the ....(6).... of true ideas and high emotions and life is ....(7).... of ideas and emotions. In a world ....(8).... of literature, the intellectual and emotional activity of all ....(9)... exceptionally gifted men would quickly sink and ....(10).... to a narrow circle. The broad, the noble, the generous would tend to disappear ....(11).... accessible storage. And life would be ....(12).... degraded, because the ....(13).... idea and the pretty emotion would never feel the upward pull of the ideas and emotions of genius.

QUESTIONS

1. A. accidental B. remarkable C. strange D. superficial

2. A. affluence B. effluence C. excellence D. magnificence

3. A. outcome B. offspring C. flow D. expression

4. A. have served B. done C. achieve D. accomplished

5. A. is B. has been C. gets D. has

6. A. store B. stock C. vast reservoir D. huge collection

7. A. expression B. expansion C. storage D. constituted

8. A. devout B. devolve C. deterrent D. deprived

9. A. but few B. except C. but a few D. people

10. A. die B. spoil C. dissolve D. retract

11. A. for want of B. desiring C. searching D. for

12. A. altogether B. correspondingly C. contrarily D. actually

13. A. beautiful B. ornamental C. stupid D. fallacious

PASSAGE-8

Patriotism is one of the qualities that touches the heart of the ....(1).... countrymen. When a soldier fights and dies in saving his country from the enemy, his sacrifice in this way is termed as ....(2).... and attains the ....(3).... worthy of worship. Thus in a war the soldier gets ....(4).... without surrendering, by which he ....(5).... saved his life, ...(6).... the hearts of his fellow being. This situation is true not only in ....(7).... an enemy but anyone who struggles to acheive a ....(8).... aim without surrendering and ....(9).... his life. He ....(10).... succeeded but he leaves a ....(11).... for others to follow who will definitely win and attain the victory ....(12).... the adversaries..

QUESTIONS

1. A. humble B. rustic C. fellow D. sophisticated

2. A. intelligent B. virtuous C. supreme D. courageous

3. A. death B. martyrdom C. end D. goal

4. A. vanquished B. vanguard C. reward D. award

5. A. would have had B. would be able to C. would have D. could have

6. A. attracting B. winning C. taking D. getting

7. A. struggling B. killing C. winning D. fighting

8. A. esteemed B. high C. patriotic D. laudable

9. A. offers B. sacrifices C. lays D. present

10. A. could have B. could not have C. may have D. may not have

11. A. trail B. trial C. goal D. situation

12. A. upon B. over C. on D. against

PASSAGE-9

Our beautiful sunbright ....(1).... is being systematically damaged by industrial pollution ....(2).... into rivers like the Ganga and Jamuna, ...(3).... wastes from atomic plants ....(4).... into-the world's oceans, and poisonous gases ....(5).... with the ozonosphere. ....(6)...., tropical rain forests and green pastures are ....(7).... under the pressure of a ....(8).... population. Rivers like the Narmada are being dammed to change nature's ....(9).... surface ....(10).... between flora and fauna, and sloping mountain terrain is being ....(11).... into mini oceans to supply electricity to the ....(12).... industrial stomach of our age.

QUESTIONS

1. A. ecology
   B. ecosystem
   C. environment
   D. physical phenomena
2. A. directed B. channelled C. scattered D. accumulated
3. A. atomic B. scientific C. nuclear D. bumptious
4. A. diverted B. routed C. outstretched D. overflown
5. A. channelled B. routed C. scattered D. mixed
6. A. Besides B. Instead C. Addition to D. Above all
7. A. diminishing B. reducing C. minimising D. disappearing
8. A. proliferating B. profiting C. projecting D. pronounceable
9. A. smooth B. well balanced C. rough D. unequal
10. A. equilibrium B. equality C. equation D. equity
11. A. contracted B. convulsed C. conjured D. converted
12. A. hungry B. greedy C. vacant D. ever starving

PASSAGE-10

Only ....(1)...., people find a long journey by motor-car ....(2).... . Mostly a long journey by train is much more comfortable and ....(3).... . The tracks, the coaches and the smooth though swift motion ....(4).... the pleasantness of the train journey. ....(5).... at the beautiful countryside from a window seat in a fast moving train has a ....(6).... of its own. A night journey ....(7).... its pleasures too. One can experience a sense of adventure ....(8).... a restful sleep. Modern railway travel being ....(9)... comfortable than in the past, ...(10).... the childhood excitement of ....(11).... the train and its engine as ....(12).... of visual and imaginative delight.

QUESTIONS

1. A. exceptionally B. ordinarily C. unusually D. abnormally
2. A. disagreeable B. unenjoyable C. strange D. agreeable
3. A. enjoyable B. suitable C. appropriate D. enjoying
4. A. hike B. jolt C. contribute D. all add to
5. A. Observing B. Enjoying C. To look D. Looking
6. A. comfort B. complacence C. delight D. satisfaction
7. A. had B. has C. have D. has have
8. A. alongwith B. together with C. addition to D. adding to
9. A. highly B. extensively C. exceptionally D. so much more
10. A. revives B. vibrates C. regenerates D. enliven
11. A. fancying B. enjoying C. feeling D. dreaming
12. A. subjects B. objects C. centre D. focus

PASSAGE-11

Women were earlier considered as the kitchen keepers and house keepers – that was ....(1).... as their ....(2)... field of activity. ....(3)... women began to get educated and came out ....(4)... the social and potitical field and today they are there in all fields and are ....(5)... equal emloyment as the menfolk. Not only this they are ....(6)... themselves in those fields. Two important reasons behind the changed ....(7)... are : firstly, Womens are ....(8)... themselves duly qualified and want to use-their talents to seek an employment; and secondly, with the price-index ....(9).... everyday it is found necessary for the middle class families that the wife having ....(10).... academic qualifications working and ....(11).... the family income. This while giving them a social status, also helps the family to have a better standard of living, which everyone ....(12).... for and rightly too.

QUESTIONS

1. A. recognised B. realized C. regarded D. looked
2. A. exclusive B. only C. working D. one
3. A. Day by day B. Slowly C. Later D. Gradually
4. A. on B. in C. at D. to
5. A. finding B. seeking C. enjoying D. sharing
6. A. distinguishing B. proving C. mastering D. struggling
7. A. scenario B. circumstances C. society D. culture
8. A. thinking B. finding C. educating D. proving
9. A. excelating B. intensifying C. changing D. escalating
10. A. registered B. recognised C. requisite D. minimum
11. A. substituting B. segment C. influencing D. suplement
12. A. do crave B. does crave C. starve D. do starve

PASSAGE-12

Importance of music especially in today's hum drum life cannot be ....(1)..... Today man is surrounded by ....(2).... worries and listening to music ....(3).... his nerves. Music acts as a ....(4).... and soothes the nerves. It is a fine art and groups of all ages ....(5).... to its sweet sound. A person gifted with aesthetic ....(6).... finds music as a food for his soul. Some of the great musicians of the world ....(7).... in high esteem ....(8).... of the kind of they produce western, oriental, classical, pop or light. These musicians ....(9).... concerts which attract people from all walks of life. If people are ....(10).... to balming music, they will definitely find life a rich and healthy ....(11)..... In this way, the importance of music is really ....(12).... .

QUESTIONS

1. A. overstated B. understated C. irrelevant D. relevant
2. A. varied B. innumerable C. different D. variegated
3. A. calm B. cure C. soothe D. please
4. A. stimulant B. catalyst C. machinery D. device
5. A. are attracted B. get attracted C. are pleased D. feel pleasure
6. A. beauty B. blessing C. capabilities D. knowledge
7. A. were held B. are held C. are taken D. are received
8. A. no matter B. considering C. respectively D. irrespective
9. A. popularize B. organize C. form D. propagate
10. A. forced B. brought C. introduced D. exposed
11. A. stage B. experience C. achievement D. thing
12. A. considerable B. unavoidable C. imimense D. recognisable

PASSAGE-13

There are groups of people in ....(1).... developing countries who are in poverty line and who became the victims and ....(2).... in a self-fulfilling vicious of poverty. ....(3).... of the parents in the society ....(4).... afford to send their children to school. ....(5)...., the children often go to the labour force ....(6).... in order to ....(7).... the family income and to help the economic ....(8).... of the family. The Indian Government and educational ....(9).... are taking adequate steps for their standard of living and ....(10).... opportunities for schooling with full day food and other required ...(11)... .

QUESTIONS

1. A. each B. all C. whole D. every
2. A. engulfed B. surrounded C. trapped D. fall
3. A. line B. circle C. frame D. structure
4. A. can't B. couldn't C. cannot D. can never
5. A. Though B. Despite C. Instead D. Even so
6. A. at an early age B. in his growing stage C. in his childhood D. at his childhood
7. A. add B. supplement C. hike D. improve
8. A. servility B. survivality C. conditon D. situation
9. A. activist B. executives C. planners D. propagonist
10. A. approving B. alloting C. distributing D. providing
11. A. privileges B. facilities C. necessities D. factors

PASSAGE-14

What is urgently, ...(1).... in our country is a proper survey and a planned assessment of what sort of jobs ....(2).... demand both in the public as well as in the private sector and there ....(3).... a controlled enrolment in institutes and institutions which should be training young men in such needed jobs. It is a ....(4).... task, no doubt, but when the government and the private agencies ....(5).... make large scale survey for so many other problems of the country why cannot this grave problem of unemployment be ....(6).... at a priority basis and money and manpower be invested and ....(7).... to make an assessment of the requirements and then the process of their fulmilment ....(8).... . What is actually needed is not only scheming and planning but actually to have a ....(9)... to find the root of the ....(10).... . Only then can the ....(11).... be found out.

QUESTIONS

1. A. demanded B. needed C. prevalent D. lacking
2. A. are of B. are at C. are most in D. currently
3. A. needs to be B. is C. are D. shall be
4. A. labourious B. Herculean C. time taking D. stupendous
5. A. can B. could C. are out to D. readily
6. A. noticed B. surveyed C. treated D. observed
7. A. used B. employed C. organised D. treated
8. A. be worked out B. be taken up C. be decided D. be developed
9. A. spirit B. will C. motive D. strength
10. A. malady B. grievances C. curse D. paradox
11. A. treatment B. cure C. remedy D. solution

PASSAGE-15

A sudden flood of ....(1).... dangerous toys like swords and bow and arrow make their ....(2).... in the market during the Dussehra festival. ....(3)...., eyes can and do get injured ....(4).... by these toys and ....(5)...., the victims aare innocent children. ....(6).... by the Ram Lila and similar television serials, children ....(7).... swords at each other or fire arrows from bows which ....(8).... to permanent blindness if ....(9).... to hit the eye. This happens ....(10).... if the injury is servere and not managed properly. Any injury in and around the eye ....(11).... taken seriously land managed on an emergency basis.

QUESTIONS

1. A. potentially B. instantly C. constantly D. inevitably
2. A. arrival B. appearance C. place D. position
3. A. unknowingly B. undoubtedly C. undauntedly D. unfortunately
4. A. advertently B. inadvertently C. unfortunately D. unknowingly
5. A. almost B. almost always C. all the time D. very often
6. A. Motivated B. Inspired C. Encouraged D. Taught
7. A. attack B. take out C. brandish D. home
8. A. can lead B. could lead C. would lead D. lead
9. A. it targets B. it comes C. they happen D. they are
10. A. usually B. generally C. commonly D. more often
11. A. are to be B. is to be C. shall be D. may be

PASSAGE-16

The scientist of today is a man of ....(1).... ambition. He is not contented with ....(2).... he has achieved, but wants to be a creator of new and surprising things so that the common people may ....(3).... at the marvels of his ....(4)...., feel thrilled and go away ....(5).... by his superior wisdom and his ....(6).... inventiveness. The new and challenging scientific forces now ....(7).... by him in the universe will continue to work ....(8).... in ever increasing numbers, to lead mankind to ....(9).... material progress, and to ....(10).... in its hand unlimited power for conquering ....(11).... territories of knowledge and experience.

QUESTIONS

1. A. increasing B. elevating C. soaring D. diversing
2. A. what B. whatever C. those D. that
3. A. broad B. work C. gape D. deride
4. A. invention B. genius C. life D. achievement
5. A. impressed B. dejected C. attracted D. motivated
6. A. enviable B. reliable C. unavoidable D. considerable
7. A. brought B. given C. let loose D. realised
8. A. fruitfully B. miracles C. magic D. wonders
9. A. unscathed B. unrelenting C. unmitigated D. unprecedented
10. A. keep B. allot C. load D. place
11. A. greater B. varied C. unknown D. more and more

PASSAGE-17

Education of the future has to ....(1).... human values and see that the human factor is not neglected. The task of education is to help the individual to know himself. ....(2).... as the individual is ignorant of his ....(3)...., his potentialites and his mission of life, he ....(4).... contribute in a creative manner ....(5).... his own growth and development of the society. It is often said that, as education is the ....(6).... of the thinking elite of the nation, ...(7).... the nation's future depends on its system of education. This is true to some ....(8).... .But ....(9)...., the general outlook of society has also a strong ....(10).... on education itself so that education can only be reformed when a ....(11).... change has already begun in society.

QUESTIONS

1. A. consider B. protect C. care D. preserve

2. A. Till then B. So long C. Uptill then D. Till that time

3. A. own B. credibilities C. nature D. real self

4. A. can't B. could not C. could never D. cannot

5. A. in B. throughout C. to D. towards

6. A. developing process B. development C. building up D. guidance

7. A. much of B. many of C. mostly D. mainly

8. A. limit B. horizon C. context D. extent

9. A. conversely B. alternately C. actually D. outwardly

10. A. hearing B. relation C. opposition D. affinity

11. A. consequent B. corresponding C. subsequent D. similar

PASSAGE-18

Every action we perform ....(1).... a result. And, naturally, we lay claim ....(2).... the results or fruits ....(3).... from that action in the ....(4).... that it is we who perform the action. This is .....(5).... ignorance because ....(6).... is it the Lord who ....(7).... the result of any action, it is by His will ....(8).... that even the action is accomplished. The will of the Lord ....(9).... whether we cooperate with His will or strive ....(10).... If God wills that an action takes place, he arranges for the ....(11).... for it to happen. It is ....(12).... experience that sometimes despite our best efforts we ....(13).... achieve the results we desire, and at other times the seemingly most ....(14).... situations mysteriously get ....(15).... . ....(16).... way man chooses to act, both the act and the outcome of the cost are dependent ....(17).... on the will of the Lord.

QUESTIONS

1. A. produce B. produces C. causes D. undergoes

2. A. on B. at C. to D. for

3. A. occuring B. obtaining C. deriving D falling

4. A. belief B. hope C. fantasy D. folly

5. A. sheen B. keen C. sheer D. sheathe

6. A. alone B. only that C. not only D. for only

7. A. declares B. decides C. ordains D. ornate

8. A. completely B. entirely C. only D. alone

9. A. prevails always B. prevails everywhere C. is prevalent D. always prevails

10. A. alone B. always C. constantly D. independently

11. A. wherewithal B. whereabouts C. whatsoever D. wherefore

12. A. usual B. general C. universal D. common

13. A. does not B. may not C. do not D. might not

14. A. intractable B. intangible C. internecine D. intricate

15. A. subsided B. resolved C. solved D. converted

16. A. Whatever B. All the C. All those D. Whichever

17. A. mainly B. actually C. entirely D. generally

10. A. subsidiary B. subsequent C. subservience D. subordination

11. A. various B. varying C changing D. differeing

PASSAGE-19

For centuries, women not only in India but all over the world ....(1).... treated as ....(2).... secondary position to men. ....(3).... human history men ....(4).... far greater power then women to name, classify, and order the worlds in which they both live. ....(5).... studies in various parts of the world point out to a wide ....(6).... in male and female roles ....(7).... cultures and demonstrate the possibility of change in these sex-determined roles. The 20th century in particular ....(8).... the cause of gender justice by internationalizing struggles for equality ....(9).... women and other oppressed people. Women's struggles against their ....(10).... were interwined in ....(11).... degrees with ideologies and movements based on the values of freedom, self-determination, equality, democracy and justice.

QUESTIONS

1. A. has been B. have been C. had been D. were

2. A. occupying B. taking C. possessing D. serving

3. A. All through B. Throughout C. Since D. From

4. A. have B. had C. have had D. enjoy

5. A. Sociological B. Anthropological C. General D. Practical

6. A. concord B. repulsion C. disagreement D. variation

7. A. among B. across C. between D. of

8. A. developed B. envolved C. promoted D. entertained

9. A. for B. to C. among D. by

PASSAGE-20

What is required today in our country is ....(1).... of a new political culture based on full respect for human liberty, on pluralism and on a better social deal for all. The major ....(2).... facing us today is to carry out democratic transformation in all the ....(3)...., social, cultural, economic and political. The events of the 20th century ....(4).... one thing absolutely clear that human ....(5)...., everywhere, specially in countries whose political structures were ....(6).... to reflect the revolutionary aspirations of the people ....(7).... not only under stress and strain but are ....(8).... vast upheavals because of the ....(9).... of democracy. At the same time it has also to be understood that democracy cannot be ....(10).... into a static mould.

QUESTIONS

1. A. growing B. developing C. creating D. creation

2. A. development B. crisis C. challenge D. drawback

3. A. corners B. context C. realm D. spheres

4. A. have made B. has made C. had made D. made

5. A. travails B. traverse C. trapse D. transverse

6. A. supposed B. meant C. caused D. forced

7. A. were B. was C. are D. have been

8. A. developing B. evolving C. experiencing D. faced with

9. A. denial B. rebuff C. rebuttal D. absence

10. A. shaped B. flex C. frozen D. caused

PASSAGE-21

We are living in very exciting ....(1).... . The ....(2).... change is dizzying and the impact this progress is having on our present and – more importantly – on our future is difficult to ....(3).... in its ...(4).... . This is the age of ....(5).... micro processors, sophisticated software, new hardware technology and high bandwith, high-speed networks. The PC gave us a new way to work, play and ....(6).... . In fact, it brought ....(7).... our desktops computing power, which until a few years ....(8).... had only been available to corporates. With the ....(9).... of the internet, the PC ....(10).... us the most convenient and flexible way to head on to the Net.

QUESTIONS

1. A. periods B. days
   C. phase D. times
2. A. phase B. pace
   C. sphere D. drastic
3. A. guess B. forecast
   C. comprehend D. approximate
4. A. whole B. entirety
   C. fruition D. fullness
5. A. strong B. changing
   C. powerful D. sonorous
6. A. convey B. communicate
   C. entertain D. enjoy
7. A. onto B. to
   C. on D. at
8. A. back B. earlier
   C. behind D. before
9. A. addendum B. adherence
   C. afoot D. advent
10. A. allowed B. privileged
    C. brought D. offered

PASSAGE-22

Visualisation is a strong ....(1).... to memory. Those persons who ...... (2) ..... a powerful memory cannot do so without taking the help of visualisaton. Such persons have developed the skills to ....(3).... visualisation even in such ....(4).... tasks as remembering names and numbers. These persons have the names and numbers ....(5).... in their brain even after hearing those names and figues only once. On the other hand those who take the help of revising to memorise ....(6).... to forget it once they have ....(7).... the practice of revising ....(8).... the ones who have applied visualisation to memorise. Psychologists ....(9).... in visualisation a powerful tool for personality development. The more you visualise, the more you are ....(10).... your attitude and behaviour to the blue prints of your vision and ....(11).... more you are inching towards success.

QUESTIONS

1. A. way B. path
   C. aid D. symptom
2. A. command B. master
   C. rule D. enjoy
3. A. use B. apply
   C. put D. place
4. A. trivial B. difficult
   C. mundane D. unscrupulous
5. A. impress B. imprinted
   C. impinge D. store
6. A. bent B. incline
   C. prone d. tend
7. A. dropped B. left
   C. gave up D. given up
8. A. unlike B. opposite
   C. contrary D. not like
9. A. found B. have found
   C. sees D. finds
10. A. shaping B. moulding
    C. making D. attuning
11. A. actually B. factually
    C. subsequently D. consequently

PASSAGE-23

....(1).... people today remember the war that was fought after China invaded India in 1962. Not because the war was never really ....(2).... . Nor because it was ....(3).... almost before it began. The reason is ....(4).... that most of us were yet to be born. The main reason for the Chinese attack seems to ....(5).... to establish the ....(6).... order, expose our ....(7)...., put us in our place. The official reason, ...(8)...., was the territorial dispute, ...(9).... more than 100,000 square kilometres. ....(10).... speaking, India borders Tibet, not China. The McMohan Line ....(11).... the border with Tibet in what is now Arunachal Pradesh was the result of a 1914 treaty ....(12).... British India and Tibet. This was not ....(13).... to the Chinese the result was a .....(14)..... nose. The Chinese attack was ....(15).... fast and furious. ....(16).... brave soldiers ....(17).... down their lives, but India was simply unable to halt the ....(17).... . Panic quickly ....(18)....

QUESTIONS

1. A. A few B. Few C. Fewer D. A little
2. A. joined B. combined C. acted D. approved
3. A. finished B. ceased C. over D. stopped
4. A. simple B. simply C. common D. commonly
5. A. had been B. have C. had D. have been
6. A. pecking B. unavoiding C. powerful D. selfish
7. A. projections B. pretensions C. presumption D. pretending
8. A. more over B. probably C. perhaps D. however
9. A. effecting B. causing C. affecting D. influencing
10. A. Formally B. Informally C. Broadly D. Technically
11. A. relating B. dividing C. defining D. laying
12. A. among B. between C. of D. by
13. A. favourable B. favoured C. acceptable D, accepting
14. A. angry B. bloody C. honed D. blitz
15. A. quick B. prick C. sudden D. unassuming
16. A. Some B. Few C. Many D. A lot of
17. A. onrush B. onset C. omnipotence D. omen
18. A. come in B. gone in C. set in D. set out

PASSAGE-24

Man has always been ....(1).... with flying because it ....(2).... a sense of freedom, of romance and thrill-something too ....(3).... to resist. It is the task of the ....(4).... of the skies to safeguard Indian air-space from unwelcome ....(5)..... . The Indian Air Force ....(6).... a chequered and glorious history. From its ....(7).... days of single-engine aeroplanes like Tempests and Spitfires to the state of the art multi-engine, supersonic MIG and Sukhoi fighters, the Indian Air Force ....(8).... a long way. In addition to the already existing ....(9).... of aircraft and weapon systems, plans are ....(10).... to enhance its air defence power and ....(11).... capability through upgradation and ....(12).... .

QUESTIONS

1. A. fascinated B. moved C. inspired D. fancied
2. A. generates B. cultivates C. reaps D. evokes
3. A. envisaging B. impressing C. enchanting D. laudable
4. A. sentiness B. sedulous C. venturous D. fervid
5. A. emigrants B. intruders C. foreigners D. tourists
6. A. had B. have C. have had D. has had

7. A. early B. undeveloped
C. growing D. embryonic

8. A. had come B. has come
C. have come D. came

9. A. invention B. inventory
C. mechanism D. technique

10. A. progressive B. afresh
C. afoot D. affluent

11. A. combat B. increase
C. intensify D. ensure

12. A. acquistion
B. acknowledgement
C. acquiescence
D. accumulation

PASSAGE-25

Libraries were never ....(1).... the place to ....(2).... They never will be. But those who've visited libraries for the ....(3).... pleasure of it will testify to the feeling of ....(4).... on entering the labyrinth ....(5).... high with books. Suddenly, a ....(6).... spent reading seems the ideal. It's a similar experience to ....(7).... in a bookshop. The difference : in the second situation, despair ....(8).... you as your eyes zoom ....(9).... on the price; in the first there is the ....(10).... that all these books are yours for the asking. Today, ...(11).... liberary use is almost ....(12).... necessity-based. The reading room is ....(13).... full with students poring ....(14).... their books..

QUESTIONS

1. A. realised B. seen
C. recognised D. considered

2. A. hung out B. hang out
C. hang out in D. hung out in

3. A. mere B. sheer
C. trivial D. trifle

4. A. exhilaration B. exhaustion
C. expedition D. extrapolation

5. A. going B. moving
C. pik D. towering

6. A. long time B. whole life
C. life time D. life long

7. A. browsing B. move about
C. move D. stroll

8. A. swamps B. swab
C. swoon D. swoop

9. A. at B. on
C. in D. upon

10. A. idea B. surity
C. certainty D. knowledge

11. A. although B. however
C. in fact D. moreover

12. A. wholly B. partially
C. outwardly D. purely

13. A. tight B. completely
C. over crowded D. cramped

14. A. into B. onto
C. over D. upon

PASSAGE-26

The ....(1).... of a country does not depend on the abundance of its revenue but more ....(2).... by its citizens; its men of education, enlightenment and character. It is for the ....(3).... of higher learning to ....(4).... an academic environment of equity, justice and fair play where those ....(5).... in the ....(6).... task of nation building can ....(7).... their responsibilities in a spirit of sincerity, dedication and commitment. Higher education in India ....(8).... great strides after independence. The ideal of education is to ....(9).... for self-preservation but which also prepares us to recognise and ....(10).... the rights of others and to shoulder our ....(11).... as responsible citizens.

QUESTIONS

1. A. prospects B. fortune
C. protrusion D. gaiety

2. A. illustrated B. emancipated
C. defined D. apprehended

3. A. institute B. centre
C. college D. university

4. A. encourage B. embark
C. promote D. polish

5. A. employed B. recruited
C. held D. engaged

6. A. paramount B. ardous
C. lucrative D. laudable

7. A. dispense B. disburse
C. carry D. discharge

8. A. have taken B. had taken
C. has taken D. is taking

9. A. evoke B. prepare
C. encourage D. cultivate

10. A. concede B. preserve
C. coddle D. clung

11. A. obligations B. obduracy
C. obsequiousness D. portfolio

PASSAGE-27

Observation is one of the key ....(1).... of modern corporate behaviour. Indeed it has long been the ....(2).... for humans and animals generally. It is essential for every corporate citizen to be able to taste the ....(3).... of what is happening around him all the time, not merely to survive but to ....(4).... . ....(5).... the corporate corridors to check which way the wind is blowing ! Know when it is appropriate to get your ....(6).... in and when it is ....(7).... to maintain a low profile. To ....(8).... a career with the ease and ....(9).... of a winner, you need to be able to ....(10).... a disaster before it happens ! You need to take an advantage before someone else ....(11).... . You need to be at the right place before someone else ....(12).... there. Observation or paying attention to what's happening around us is essential ....(13).... . We need to take the time to ....(14).... the habit of paying attention so that we can make our work ....(15).... and so that we can stand at ease! Career ....(16).... will be the happy outcome!

QUESTIONS

1. A. approach B. method
C. tactics D. means

2. A. rule B. norm
C. convention D. technique

3. A. presence B. essence
C. events D. problem

4. A. thrive B. throb
C. fare D. blow

5. A. Sniff B. Snuffle
C. Spin-off D. Splutter

6. A. shore B. oar
C. objective D. ogle

7. A. correct B. right
C. prudent D. prudish

8. A. carry B. initiate
C. continue D. conduct

9. A. caprice B. comfort
C. over-confidence D. aplomb

10. A. forecast B. apprehend
C. guess D. foretell

11. A. do B. does
C. takes D. gets

12. A. come B. comes
C. get D. gets

13. A. everytime B. alltime
C. everywhere D. forever

14. A. reap B. sow
C. cultivate D. grow

15. A. easy B. easier
C. easiest D. simple

16. A. advancement B. progression
C. achievement D. cultivation

PASSAGE-28

The ....(1).... Euphoria over the ....(2).... fall in the cost of domestic air travel has ....(3).... to a more realistic appraisal of what is on offer. The aggressive ....(4).... schemes offered since the beginning of July have certainly been good news for certain categories of passengers who probably value .....(5).... above anything else. For them, the heavily discounted fare ....(6).... enables them to afford air travel for the first time. In fact, the ....(7).... of the fare cut ....(8).... such that in specific instances air travel compares

....(9).... to the fares charged by the Railways for upper class travel. Obviously, it ....(10).... for a change in mindset to switch to air travel in ....(11).... to, say, rail transport in India. Economy and affordability will certainly be key ....(12).... but they must be made available ....(13).... a fairly long period. To put it differently, cheaper air travel or at least a ....(14).... fare structure ....(15).... institutionalised in the country.

QUESTIONS

1. A. embryonic B. early
C. ending D. initial

2. A. casual B. sudden
C. surprising D. dramatic

3. A. raised B. caused
C. given way D. gave way

4. A. lucrative B. lofty
C. laudable D. promotional

5. A. expenses B. affordability
C. comfort D. time

6. A. scheme B. structure
C. system D. circular

7. A. portion B. ratio
C. magnitude D. proportion

8. A. are B. is
C. has been D. have been

9. A. very slightly B. very favourably
C. specifically D. generally

10. A. causes B. calls
C. invites D. lures

11. A. choice B. favour
C. preference D. alternative

12. A. determinants B. detrimenetals
C. performers D. issues

13. A. over B. for
C. to D. through

14. A. different B. distinctive
C. reducing D. differential

15. A. must be B. has to be
C. ought to be D. have to be

PASSAGE-29

"I need a break" is a common ..... (1) ..... among the ....(2).... middle and elite classes – under ....(3).... pressure to perform, to live up to their own artificial standards, to earn, and earn some more and ....(4).... some more. But in this vortex, time is at a ....(5)...., and the much needed break ....(6).... materialises because harried professionals are unable to stay away from work long enough ....(7).... from the city and breathe in some fresh air—metaphorically and literally. And weekends? They are ....(8).... lazing at home, ...(9).... on chores, or may be watching some mind numbing television programme. Because it would be hard to think of a place you ....(10).... escape to that was far enough from the city to be ....(11).... and yet close enough to ....(12).... as a weekend break.

QUESTIONS

1. A. restrain B. refrain
C. remark D. saying

2. A. hurried B. harried
C. worried D. busy

3. A. continuous B. consequent
C. constant D. stable

4. A. even B. add
C. farther D. then

5. A. premium B. minimum
C. limitation D. restriction

6. A. never often B. often never
C. although never D. sometimes do not

7. A. to stay away B. to escape
C. to go away D. to get moved

8. A. there B. for
C. those D. some

9. A. getting B. catching
C. catching up D. catching down

10. A. can B. ever
C. would D. could

11. A. refreshed B. refreshing
C. resting D. rejoining

12. A. consider B. anticipate
C. contemplate D. meditate

PASSAGE-30

Every monsoon I'm reminded of an incident that ....(1).... many years ago when I was a young man ....(2).... my first job in Mumbai. I was staying with my sister in those days. On one wet and windy night I ....(3).... with friends, and as it happens when you are in pleasant company, the ....(4).... . It was past ten when I finally bid goodby to my companions and moved towards my sister's house. It had rained the whole day, and it ....(5).... to drizzle again. The rain had ....(6).... people indoors earlier than usual and the dimly-lit street I was walking along was ....(7).... . I had heard that the road was ....(8).... . They said one could hear a woman calling for help on some nights. As I proceeded, I suddenly saw a figure walking ....(9).... me. A bandicoot chose to ....(10).... across my path, just then she seemed to have ....(11).... into thin air. Then I heard a faint ....(12).... for help. This frightened me and as such I turned and fled. The next morning I came to know from my sister that the bandicoot was no other but her friend who had mistakenly thought she was being ....(13).... . Out of fear she was looking behind and walking when she ....(14).... into a ditch. Now every monsoon, I'm reminded of my ....(15).... on that wet night.

QUESTIONS

1. A. happened B. occured
C. took place D. had taken place
2. A. in B. on
C. working at D. working with
3. A. had been out B. went for outing
C. had gone D. was out
4. A. time passes B. time runs
C. time flies D. time files
5. A. has B. was
C. began D. had begun
6. A. pushed B. sent
C. send D. driven
7. A. calm B. peace
C. lonely D. deserted
8. A. mysterious B. ghostly
C. haunted D. devilish
9. A. before B. in front of
C. a head D. near
10. A. scuttle B. scurry
C. scuff D. scrouge
11. A. faded B. vanished
C. vaporised D. melted
12. A. sound B. voice
C. cry D. whisper
13. A. followed B. chased
C. pursued D. caught
14. A. fall B. stumbied
C. threw D. jumped
15. A. foolishness B. ignorance
C. confusion D. cowardice

PASSAGE-31

Most of India's educational institutions, ...(1).... by hiring people who are ....(2).... qualified to be teachers. They are ....(3).... an unhappy group, which is ill-paid and which commands ....(4).... respect. Sadly, it is these men and women who have the enormous duty of ...(5).... tomorrow's society, a responsibility that remains ...(6)... . Children are ....(7).... in this terrifying circle : they are ....(8).... into submission, their innocence is destroyed and their lives become ....(9).... joyless. What follows is still ....(10).... . A violent childhood ....(11).... a violent adulthood. A child who faces the ....(12).... of an adult grows up ....(13).... that violence is the answer to all problems. They become ....(14).... individuals and often their intellectual development ....(15).... in the absence of congenial peace.

QUESTIONS

1. A. get away B. manage
C. run D. go away
2. A. not really B. really not
C. virtually not D. not actually

3. A. commonly B. mainly
C. specifically D. usually
4. A. scant B. scanty
C. scarce D. rare
5. A. forming B. moulding
C. framing D. making
6. A. unsatisfied B. unprecedented
C. unfulfilled D. unrequited
7. A. taught B. caught
C. captured D. chained
8. A. battered B. split
C. squeezed D. shaped
9. A. universally B. utterly
C. wholly D. complete
10. A. unfavourable B. bad
C. not good D. worse
11. A. may lead to
B. may grow to
C. may reach to
D. would develop to
12. A. consequences B. wrath
C. grief D. wretch
13. A. thinking B. supposing
C. infering D. believing
14. A. complex B. complicated
C. rough D. sanguine
15. A. slows down B. moves slowly
C. hampers D. brakes

PASSAGE-32

Men ....(1).... the maker of their own destinies and they ....(2).... make the destiny of the society and the nation. Life is a great gift of God to men and man ....(3).... making constant efforts to live a ....(4).... life right from the stone age to the modern one. But it is man who ....(5).... to think out how to live well. The ....(6).... before mankind today is between self-preservation and self-destruction. Science has given men all the powers that they need but the new millennium ....(7).... new challenges. We are ....(8).... what nature has given us—forests are being cut down, slums are being ....(9)...., rivers are being polluted. Medical science has made great ....(10)....; but the population is growing in a geometrical ....(11).... . Our natural resources like coal and oil are being ....(12).... . Atomic energy is our only hope. The ....(13).... welcome of the new millennium lies in our determination and hope for self-preservation ....(14).... self-destruction.

QUESTIONS

1. A. are B. have been
C. being D. had been
2. A. unitedly B. ultimately
C. conjointly D. co-exist to
3. A. have been
B. are
C. has been
D. have had been
4. A. congenial
B. cordial
C. congregational
D. congruent
5. A. have B. is
C. are D. has
6. A. optional B. choice
C. possibilities D. probabilities
7. A. presents B. places
C. offers D. puts forth
8. A. destroying B. ignoring
C. neglecting D. wasting
9. A. developed B. constructed
C. created D. manufactured
10. A. advancement B. advances
C. achievement D. inventions
11. A. dimension B. angle
C. index D. proportion
12. A. deported B. deplored
C. depleted D. disposed
13. A. actual B. real
C. warm D. innate
14. A. upon B. over
C. on D. above

II. PASSAGES

Directions: *Read each of the following passages carefully and choose the best answer to each question out of the four alternatives and mark it in the Answer Sheet.*

PASSAGE-1

Cyber crime is the branded stigma defacing the culture and magnanimity of computer technology. It is up keeping the flag with indomitable triumph against developing computer technology worldwide.

Modern age is striding with marching steps of technology revolution beating the past decade of ancestral belief with ultimate care. Computer invention has unfolded the mystery of quick access with the objective of minimum manpower and cutting the time consumption parameters.

As each coin has dual face of its portrait, likewise computer technology is sick of creeping virus. Synthetic manmade dilemma of site hackers activation is causing setback to the expanding anchor of revolutionary device with great loss of time, economy and data profile as suffered by consumers. A recent report from Internet security firm Websense estimates that 85.6 per cent of all the unwanted e-mails contained links to spam sites. The company's data suggests that the number of malicious sites grew 233 per cent in the last six months and saw 671 per cent growth in the number of malicious sites during the last year. In June alone, the total number of e-mails detected as containing viruses increased by 600 per cent compared to May.

Chat rooms, blogs and message boards where the users post comments have been identified as the top targets of hackers and spammers due to the high traffic these attract. According to Websense, 95 per cent of user-generated comments to blogs, chat rooms and message boards during the first half of 2009 were malicious.

It is advisable not to click on spurious links and stay away from keying in passwords at unknown sites as they are most likely to be spammed. Hackers can steal your passwords and log in to your account and access critical information like account numbers and contact details among other things.

QUESTIONS

1. The above passage is:
A. an advisory for the computer users.
B. an advisory for the Internet users.
C. a warning against possible threat to the Internet users.
D. related to chat rooms, blogs and message boards.

2. People who use chat rooms and blogs,
A. are safe and have no threats from spam.
B. are more prone to malicious e-mails.
C. create virus and hack the accounts of others.
D. are unsafe.

3. According to the writer, it is not safe to:
A. log on to spurious links.
B. access one's own account frequently.
C. have essential information stored in a computer.
D. include data-stealing code.

4. Hackers and spammers, according to the writer, are:
A. a new threat to the Internet users and the economy.
B. only pranksters and not serious threat to the system.
C. trained, professional technocrats who are an asset.
D. not expert professionals.

5. Which word in the passage is synonym of *weblog*?
A. blog B. password
C. site D. e-mail

6. Which agency has assessed the data record with spam sites?

A. Microsoft
B. Internet security from Google
C. Websense
D. Spammers

7. Which month dominates the e-mails detection data record?

A. May B. June
C. Last six months D. Last year

PASSAGE-2

South Asian tropical weather reels valuable geographical aesthetic beauty surrounded by wildlife, mountains, steep elevations with dense forest. Human sapiens has been old and innocent victim of natural calamities branded as flood, hurricane, storm, earthquake and tsunami since ages.

Biological data depicts the loss of valuable men and material suffered by mankind owing to the chain reaction by such fatal natural incidents. Global warming has turned an eyesore to the rapid glory of rising civilsation with great mystery yet to be unfolded. UNO data reveals the rate of mortality owned due to natural disaster with great sway of cruel time factor.

Of the 245 natural disasters in the first 11 months of 2009, 224 or 91.4 per cent were due to weather, a UN study has found.

Of the 58 million people affected, 55 million were affected by weather-related disasters, which accounted for $15 billion (₹ 7,05,000 crore) spent in coping with these disasters.

A study has found that half of these disasters, mainly storms and floods, have taken place in Asia, Debarati Guha Sapir of Brussels-based CRED said.

And this data does not include the loss due to drought because that takes longer to account for. Guha Sapir said, "We have found that this is due to global warming, weak political systems, urbanisation, weak infrastructure, population increase and deforestation."

"We have to cap the emissions of greenhouse gases because they produce greater risk of disasters," WMO head Michel Jerraud said. Greenhouse gases, mainly carbon dioxide, are causing the climate change that is already affecting farm output, making droughts, floods and storms more frequent and more severe, and raising the sea level.

QUESTIONS

1. Mark the correct statement(s).

1. Weather is responsible for most of the natural disasters.
2. There is no need to worry about the climatic changes.
3. All the nations are trying to have a common pact to tackle natural disasters.

A. 1 is correct
B. Only 2 is correct
C. Only 3 is correct
D. 1 and 2 are correct

2. Which one of the following statements is not true?

A. More than 58 million people have been affected by natural disasters.
B. $15 billion have been spent in coping with these disasters.
C. Most of the natural disasters have taken place in Asia.
D. The report does not include the loss caused by droughts.

3. The main cause of natural disasters is :

A. global warming
B. weak political system
C. deforestation
D. all of these

4. The first priority before the nations and the scientists across the world is :

A. to cap the emission of greenhouse gases.
B. to reach an agreement on the nuclear weapons.
C. to help one another when natural disasters occur.
D. to find out the causes of natural disasters.

5. Which word in the passage means the same as *serious*?
   A. Reduce B. Severe
   C. Underlined D. Underscore
6. Which region is mainly affected by these disasters?
   A. United Nation B. Africa
   C. Asia D. Brussels
7. Which statement is true?
   A. Sea level rise is an alarming incident.
   B. Rapid urbanisation is a curse to the global warming.
   C. Deforestation with climatic change is responsible for green house gaseous effect.
   D. All of these.

PASSAGE-3

Time has brought forth different classical and instrumental range of device that serves healing element to the aweful and mentally distressed state of affair. Temperament compatibility matching is a reasonable trend of motion adhered with the concept of body movement termed as dance therapy.

Dance has mobilised different acknowledgement of its noted culture proclaimed by experts and sensational aspirants. Vedas describe the dance origin from aryan culture to the creeping span of modern India. Archaeological Survey of India has claimed the civilsation existence issue owing to excavation of past events traced in the stone idols displayed in dance "mudra".

Dance is an art form that generally refers to movement of the body, usually rhythmic and to music, used as a form of expression, social interaction or presented in a spiritual or performance setting. Gymnastics, figure skating and synchronised swimming are sports that incorporate dance, while martial arts Kata are often compared to dances. Motion in ordinarily inanimate objects may also be described as dances (the leaves dance in the wind). Every dance, no matter what style, has something in common. It not only involves flexibility and body movement, but also physics. If the proper physics is not taken into consideration, injuries may occur. Choreography is the art of creating dances. The person who creates (*i.e.* choreographs) a dance, is known as the choreographer. Dance has certainly been an important part of ceremony, rituals, celebrations and entertainment since the birth of the earliest human civilisations. Archaeology delivers trace of dance from prehistoric times such as the 9,000 years old Rock Shelters of Bhimbetka painting in India and Egyptian tomb painting depicting dancing figures from circa 3300 BC. One of the earliest structured uses of dance may have been in the performance and in the telling of myths. Before the production of written languages, dance was one of the methods of passing these stories down from generation to generation.

QUESTIONS

1. Dance does not necessarily involve:
   A. movement of the body.
   B. face expression.
   C. rhythmic movements.
   D. costumes.
2. According to the passage, which one of the following sports does not incorporate dance?
   A. Figure skating B. Gymnastics
   C. Chess D. Swimming
3. Which one, according to the passage, is not common in all the dances?
   A. Flexibility B. Body movement
   C. Music D. Physics
4. Physics in every dance is an important element to:
   A. master the art of dance.
   B. to perform it scientifically.
   C. to save oneself from injury.
   D. to get an award.
5. In prehistoric times dance was:
   A. a substitute of written language.
   B. a source of entertainment.
   C. a necessary ritual.
   D. not allowed in royal palaces.
6. Choreographer is a term addressed to:
   A. a sports trainer B. a gym coach
   C. a painting teacher D. a dance teacher

7. What does the term 'the telling of myths' refer to?
   A. Telling the beads B. Vedic convention
   C. Spiritual recitation D. Protest march

PASSAGE-4

Personal sentiments exposure portray in sober class of distinct feature with fair and pleasant expression. As the cruelty can be overpowered by the amicable terms likewise, impossible review let with expression can be publically announced by either electronic device or diary writing habit. On line conversation such as chattering, message convey are the rampant tool of the time to manage in communication congestion.

Blogs, online versions of personal diaries, have been a craze for quite some time now. Some of us, before the Internet age, used to maintain a small diary to jot down random thoughts, reflections, sayings, poems and other such stuff. Their online versions, however, are much more than that. The biggest difference between a blog and a personal diary is while the latter was a very private affair accessible not even to family members, a blog is a public account. In fact the whole world connected to the internet gets to read its contents if they come across it.

What a blogger should keep in mind while blogging is that by displaying our thoughts, emotions, opinions and personal life in full public glory, we are revealing a part of our private life. We are giving outsiders, strangers, friends, colleagues and relatives a full view of what's happening inside us and without lives, something we would hesitate to do in real life. Once blogging begins, it's difficult to control, and we end up sharing our personal thoughts and emotions that we would otherwise have kept to ourselves. The blog entices us, and we fall to be bait.

Blogs don't preserve our anonymity. They let us publish our pictures, professional and personal details, physical address and locations, etc. The biggest precaution to be observed therefore is to think twice before publishing anything, and ask oneself if one would like to make such matters public. The blog readers try to judge us, understand us, get information about us and take pleasure while peeping into our private lives without realising it.

QUESTIONS

1. Blogs are __________.
   A. diaries B. personal diaries
   C. online diaries D. official diaries
2. Earlier the personal diaries were not available even to family members but blog can be read by:
   A. family and friends
   B. friends only
   C. anyone who connects to the Internet
   D. relatives
3. Which one of the following statements is not true?
   A. Blogging does not affect our privacy.
   B. Blogging displays our private life in public.
   C. Blogging cannot be controlled easily.
   D. Blogging allows outsiders to peep into our personal life.
4. The writer in the above passage:
   A. favours blogging.
   B. criticises the practices.
   C. does not want the reader to become a victim of blogging.
   D. favours blogging but with some precautions.
5. Which word in the passage stands for *an account from on point of view*?
   A. version B. block
   C. affair D. account
6. The word Anonymity in the passage refers to:
   A. hostility B. friendship
   C. unacknowledged D. differences
7. What precaution is stressed by the narrator while releasing personal information?
   A. Suggest Comprehensive issue only
   B. Reader friendly blog appreciation
   C. Hiding personal facts
   D. Diary maintenance

PASSAGE-5

Pleasure and sorrow being twin face of a coin suffers the sign of commend and condemn since long before the historic ages. Warriors outcry with victory decorated with deep throat laugh has marked the sentimental coverage of battle filed victory. Baffled war victims, war widows, dependents are the oppressed classes. They seek relief against those causing sabotage to their established settlement.

The history of literature really began long before man learned to write. Dancing was the earliest of the arts. Man danced for joy round his primitive camp fire after the defeat and slaughter of his enemy. He yelled and shouted as he danced and gradually the yells and shouts became coherent and caught the measure of the dance and thus the first war song was sung. As the idea of God developed, prayers were framed. The song and prayers became traditional and were repeated from one generation to another, each generation adding something of its own. As man slowly grew more civilsed, he was compelled to invent some method of writing by three urgent necessities. There were certain things that were dangerous to forget and which, therefore, had to be recorded.

It was often necessary to communicate with persons who were some distance away and it was necessary to protect one's property by making tools and so on, in some distinctive manner. So man taught himself to write and having learned to write purely for utilitarian reasons, he used this new method for preserving his songs and his prayers. Of course, among these ancient people, there were only a very few individuals who learned to write, and only a few could read what was written.

QUESTIONS

1. Liguistic comment and condemn refers to:
A. physical grudge against sorrows
B. a temporary verbal communication
C. slip of tongue with praise and denounce
D. a communal fury against the joys

2. Which one of the following statements is true?
A. Study reveals the historic onslaught with cruelty only.
B. Suffers pledge to reform the existing tyranny.
C. A permanent code of sympathetic temper is sought by the suffers.
D. Language dominates with great passion during mental aggression.

3. Before man invented writing, ______.
A. literature was passed on by word of mouth
B. prayres were considered literature
C. literature was just singing and dancing
D. all of the above

4. According to the passage, dance originated from
A. literature
B. yelling and shouting
C. prayers
D. war

5. Writing was invented because
A. there were certain things which had to be remembered.
B. there were certain things which had to be communicated to the people who were away.
C. there were certain rituals which had to be preserved.
D. all of the above

6. Which one of the following statements is not true?
A. Since only a few individuals had learnt to write and a few could read what was written.
B. Prayers were developed after the idea of god developed.
C. People learned writing for utilitarian reasons.
D. Dancing was the earliest form of art.

7. Which one of the following words in the passage stands for *ancient*?
A. primitive B. traditional
C. coherent D. utilitarian

PASSAGE-6

Quality dominates the world ahead of its spherical, classical, racial or any undue discrimination ever exercised by any individual. Physical characteristics of a produce differs its structural attribution in quality from substandard produce with richness of prolong usage features declared by the claimant. Talent Hunt initiated by quality seekers have turned the table of established brand on account of innovative additions presented by their hardships.

The simple message that quality matters because it is cheaper to do things right the first time is yet to sink into the thinking of Indian managers and workers who seem quite content to live in their cloistered world where mediocrity reigns supreme. It is only the ignorant who believe that quality consciousness is a cultural trait. Barely half a century back no one associated Japan with high quality, but today 'Made in Japan' is a symbol of assured quality. The daily drill at school is far more important than the seasonal seminar and an obsession with quality at home is the best way of convincing the world that we value good quality. Indian exports will never be recognised for quality unless Indians are known to insist on good quality at home.

Global appreciation surrounds the exceptional brand by keeping up the physical standard neatly and efficiently. It is designed to meet the international standards' numerous logos and certificates to upkeep the label of quality consciousness. It has prime motto of swaying clean chit observation to the sanctioned produce without any objection. Modern age has been proved a turning point to the old established traditional belief. They are using tiring house hold produce to industrial device responsible to deface the status of rapid development. We breath into the cool and fresh air of healthy surrounding devised by mankind monitored by quality management with rigorous span or struggle tackled with due care.

QUESTIONS

1. The theme of the passage is:
A. quality consciousness
B. export promotion
C. quality management
D. promoting Indian culture

2. According to the passage, the Indian exports will never be recognised for quality:
A. unless there is technical advancement.
B. unless there is competition.
C. unless the Indians are known to insist on good quality.
D. unless government supports the exporters.

3. Which one of the following statements is true?
A. Indians are known for their insistence on quality.
B. Indians are not quality conscious.
C. Japan is not known for its quality product.
D. 'Made in Japan' is not a symbol of assured quality.

4. The best way to convince the world about quality is:
A. to conduct seminars on quality control.
B. to advertise the products.
C. to value for quality products at home.
D. all of the above

5. According to the passage, the main fault with the Indian managers is that:
A. they are not hard-working.
B. they are not quality conscious.
C. they are not well trained in quality control.
D. they lack technical knowledge.

6. How quality consciousness is termed as a cultural trait with the ignorant?
A. The mature opinion of quality.
B. Quality dominates ahead of traditional belief.
C. Cultural trait justifies any quality standard.
D. Quality consciousness leads to management growth.

7. Why 'Made in Japan' is a symbol of assured quality?
A. Traditional belief
B. Quality consciousness
C. Age old negligence suffering
D. High export offer

PASSAGE-7

Creamy outlook with soft speech presentation is a prima facie attraction that brings joy on the withering faces with a mixture of sensational touch. Smile with grace is the ultimate boon to the mankind keeping away any melancholy at bay. Old age is often miscalculated as liability with little attention paid to them. Their talents and learned potential is buried alive with undue care by oblivious approach due to disfigured or deformed physical structure taken over by aged talents of the society.

It happens to us all, however hard we may try to delay the process. We grow old. Cosmetic surgery may remove the wrinkles, skin which has sagged may be tightened by means of a facelift and hair dresser may dye grey hair a more youthful colour, but we cannot remain young forever.

However, what is important is the quality of life. Some people are lucky to be taken care of at home whereas others may have to move to residential homes. The worst part of ageing is that often the mind becomes less alert. As people grow older, they experience short term memory. Later some may suffer from dementia, often in the form of Alzheimer's disease.

By no means all people are in this category. Many senior citizens are in the possession of all their faculties and see retirement as a time of freedom. Not only that if they have a generous retirement pension, they are likely to be quite well off with money to be spent on a holiday and other luxuries. Because of this, both businesses and government have a new respect for what is known as grey power.

It is unfortunate that many people regard old people as geriatrics who have one foot in the grave. Someone should remind them that they too would be old one day!

They are honoured with senior citizen label granted by the authority with due regard paid from distinct possession of living cadres. One should always bear in mind the old saying "Tit for Tat". Which denotes its symbolic regulation of periodical sufferings. The aforesaid misdoings of emotional disparity, done by striding steps is a curse to the mankind.

QUESTIONS

1. Cosmetic surgery :
- A. helps in the retention of youth forever.
- B. cannot stop the natural process of ageing.
- C. is the solution to ageing.
- D. is the fancy of the rich.

2. While ageing man's greatest worry is :
- A. his growing wrinkles.
- B. his short term memory.
- C. his quality of life.
- D. moving to a residential home.

3. The government considers grey power as :
- A. a liability
- B. an asset
- C. neither an asset nor a liability
- D. a spent force

4. Retirement is seen as a time of freedom because people :
- A. no longer have to go to office.
- B. can enjoy their earnings.
- C. can spend time with their families.
- D. finally move into residential homes.

5. *geriatrics* in the passage refers to :
- A. handicapped people
- B. doctors for the aged
- C. a branch of medicine
- D. aged people

6. What is the theme of the passage?
- A. Old is gold
- B. The grey power
- C. Youth domination in the society
- D. Aged suffering

7. What does the phrase 'suffer from dementia' refer to?
- A. Harmful
- B. Short term memory loss
- C. Lunacy
- D. Paralysis

PASSAGE-8

1. The world is teemed with different continents and oceans surrounded with settled and manless island as declared by the geographical experts of the world.
2. Pacific island dominates amongst the oceans escorted with wildlife, ecosphere and manageable resources with identified culture of scientific explorations. Man hunt for unseen spheres remains a landmark occasion yearning for lavish search with instrumental approach. Galapagos Islands remind us of such human efforts noted for spherical search with wildhunt.
3. The Galapagos Islands in the Pacific Ocean are a rocky, lonely spot, but they are also one of the most unusual places in the world. The reason is that they are the home of some of the last giant tortoises left on earth.
4. Weighing hundreds of pounds, these tortoises wander slowly around the rocks and sand of the islands. Each of these islands has its own particular kind of tortoise. There are seven different kinds of tortoises on the eight islands.
5. Hundreds of years ago, thousands of tortoises wandered around these islands. All that changed when people started landing there. When people first arrived, their ships had no refrigerators. This meant that fresh food was always a problem for the sailors on board. The giant tortoises provided a solution to his problem.
6. Ships would anchor off the islands, and crew would seize as many tortoises as they could. Once the animals were aboard the ship, the crew would roll the tortoises onto their backs and use them for soups and stews.
7. Human search never ends with seeking variable resources sustainable to their growth-oriented programme. Man hunt with crew supported by voyage turns the pages of historical map to best transformation regions discovered by his hardcore practice. How long 'wants' arrest his peace of mind with the dream of next destination is yet to know with.

QUESTIONS

1. The author calls the Galapagos Islands an unusual place because :
   A. they are in the Pacific Ocean.
   B. the endangered giant tortoises are found there.
   C. they are rocky and lonely spots.
   D. they are located off the western coast of South America.

2. Which statement is correct?
   A. There is one kind of tortoise found on the seven islands.
   B. There are eight kinds of tortoises found on the eight islands.
   C. There are seven kinds of tortoises found on the eight islands.
   D. All the tortoises are on one island.

3. The giant tortoises provided a solution to the problem of not having refrigerators because :
   A. the sailors went looking for refrigerators as they were starving.
   B. fresh food was available in plenty as the sea was vast.
   C. the fresh giant tortoise could be killed and eaten whenever the sailors were hungry.
   D. the sailors seized the tortoise to store in refrigerators.

4. *Ships would anchor off the islands* means that Ships :
   A. would go off
   B. would be near the shore
   C. would be off to another land
   D. would go to another island

5. In paragraph 6 the word crew means :
   A. the new settlers.
   B. the men arriving on Galapagos Islands.
   C. the men working on the ships.
   D. the men catching the tortoises.

6. Mark the True statement which best suits the passage.
   A. Galapagos is the unusual island due to regular plains.

B. People landed at Island duely in search of tortoises.

C. Lack of refrigerators made crew turn to tortoises.

D. Tortoises numbered more than crews on the Island.

7. Soups and stews refers to :

A. soup apart with flesh.

B. soup extracted out of tortoise cooking.

C. tortoise fat.

D. a synthetic process of vegetation.

PASSAGE-9

The goal of the fair, to be held at the Cervantes Institute in the Indian capital, is to attract the largest number of students in order to present them with information on the educational programmes Spain has to offer, primarily postgraduate. Studying in Spain gives students an added advantage of living and studying in one of the world's most important economies that also aims for an internationalisation of its university system, which plays a decisive role in knowledge-based economy.

In this context, the Spanish universities, both private and public, numbering 77 in total, offer Master degrees and PhD programmes adapted to the European Higher Education Area; a harmonised space between all European countries that have opted to participate in this model. This implies that any student that obtains a postgraduate degree in a Spanish university will automatically have their studies recognised in any participating country and may continue their doctoral studies without needing to validate their degree. In addition, Spanish universities are offering more and more postgraduate degrees in English in order to attract international students. Nevertheless, it is also very common for students to come to Spain intending to complete postgraduate studies in Spanish as well. Students are offered a double advantage from, first, studying in high quality university programmes, and second, studying in a rapidly growing language, that will soon reach 500 million speakers. Spanish is also the official language in more than 20 countries and a second language in important economies such as the United States and Brazil, which gives graduates and edge when entering the workforce.

These are just a few reasons why studying in Spain is such a unique opportunity. On February 19 and 20th, Indian students are invited to visit the Cervantes Institute where they can directly ask the universities any and all questions about studying in Spain as well as get information about programmes that the universities offer.

Another incentive for students to attend will be the prize drawing for six intensive Spanish courses at Spanish universities in summer 2011. The six big winners will have air fare, accommodations, and tuition paid for while attending the month-long course.

QUESTIONS

1. The objective of the fair is __________.

A. to tell about Spain

B. to tell about the courses being started in India

C. to impart information about education in Spain

D. none of the above

2. Decisive role means __________.

A. taking decisions　　B. important role

C. key role　　D. minor role

3. Spanish Universities are offering programmes in English because __________.

A. English is a global language

B. it wants to get students from all over the world

C. English is easy to understand

D. it is easy to get professors to teach in English

4. One of the advantages of studying in Spain is that __________.

A. it is a beautiful country

B. education there is cheap

C. courses are easy

D. Spanish is the second language in some important countries

5. Those who attend the fair ________.
   A. will get to participate in a prize draw
   B. will be given free air ticket to Spain
   C. will get fee waiver for one term
   D. none of the above

PASSAGE-10

An incandescent bulb lights up when electrical power heats a metal filament wire to a high temperature until it glows. You usually get them rated between 15 and 100 watts. Meanwhile, fluorescent lamps (tubes and their newer compact versions, known as CFLs) use inert gases inside to fluoresce and produce light. There are also lamps that use an array of light-emitting diodes (LEDs) working in the way electrons behave, a phenomenon called electro luminescence. Because LED lamps are costly, very few homes use them—and it's best to wait a while before buying for their prices to come down, just as you did with CFLs over the past years.

At about ₹ 20 a piece, incandescent bulbs may look cheap, but they are not. They waste some 90 per cent of the power consumed—as heat. Consumers preferred them to energy-efficient fluorescent tubes not just because they are cheaper, but also because you may place them in choice lamp shades. Or because the bluish-white illumination from tubes can seem harsh and unnatural, and may contribute to glare and eyestrain.

If you don't like the way tube lights look in the hall or bedroom, use them only in passages, verandas and the kitchen.

QUESTIONS

1. Bulbs light up when ______.
   A. metal filament burns
   B. electricity heats up metal filament
   C. electric current is in excess
   D. metal comes in contact with heat
2. CFLs use ______.
   A. gases like Argon, Krypton, etc.
   B. mercury
   C. thin metal strips
   D. any of the above
3. Electro luminescence is the process where ______.
   A. electrons and protons react to emit light
   B. diodes function as electrons and emit light
   C. light is generated by water
   D. light is generated by sun
4. Incandescent bulbs are costly because ______.
   A. they cost ₹ 20 a piece
   B. they break easily
   C. their power consumption is high
   D. none of the above
5. Bulbs are used because they ______.
   A. are cheap
   B. conserve energy
   C. you can place them in choice lamp shades
   D. none of the above

PASSAGE-11

Conservation of water in the agricultural sector is essential since water is necessary for the growth of plants and crops. A depleting watertable and a rise in salinity due to overuse of chemical fertilisers and pesticides have made matters serious. Various methods of water harvesting and recharging have been and are being applied all over the world to tackle the problem. In areas where rainfall is low and water is scarce, the local people have used simple techniques that are suited to their region and reduce the demand for water. In India's arid and semi-arid areas, the 'tank' system is traditionally the backbone of agricultural production. Tanks are constructed either by bunding or by excavating the ground and collecting rainwater.

Rajasthan, located in the Great Indian Desert, receives hardly any rainfall, but people have adapted to the harsh conditions by collecting whatever rain falls. Large bunds to create reservoirs known as khadin, dams called johads, tanks and other methods were applied to check water flow and accumulate run-off. At the end of the monsoon season, water from these structures was used to cultivate crops. Similar systems were developed in other parts of the country. These are known by various local names *jal talais* in Uttar Pradesh, the *haveli* system in Madhya Pradesh, *ahar* in Bihar, and so on.

QUESTIONS

1. There is an increase in water salinity due to ______.

A. conservation of water
B. depletion of water
C. overuse of chemical fertilisers and pesticides
D. water harvesting

2. 'Depleting watertable' means ______.

A. reduction in the groundwater level
B. measurement of water level
C. recharging of water level
D. usage of fertilisers and pesticides

3. In arid and semi-arid regions, rainwater is collected by ______.

A. using industrial methods
B. constructing tanks
C. harvesting of water
D. adapting to the harsh conditions

4. How much rainfall does Rajasthan, the state in the Great Indian Desert, receive?

A. plenty of rainfall B. no rainfall
C. moderate rainfall D. scanty rainfall

5. Where do farmers of Rajasthan get water from to cultivate their crops after the monsoon season?

A. from tanks, bunds, dams and reservoirs
B. from whatever rain that falls
C. from excess rainwater
D. from the rivers

PASSAGE-12

Every family with two or more children often experiences sibling rivalry at one time or the other. Children in general, fight with each other for their parents' attention. They fight among themselves mostly on trivial issues. If it does not get excessive, this kind of rivalry can, in fact, be a healthy competition that trains children to share, respect one another. They will learn to deal with frustration and displeasures in the maturing process.

The firstborns generally feel that they don't have to share their parents' love and attention. But when the next baby or siblings come along, they feel neglected and that changes everything. The first child starts to feel that he/she is no longer the centre of attraction and that he/she is being sidelined because of the new one. Some children might develop negative feelings and emotional imbalance, which may lead to regressive behaviour.

Such problems could be averted if right moves are taken. One way is to explain the firstborns about the arrival of a new child. They need to establish a connection with the new baby before it is born. Older children should be trained to show a positive attitude towards their siblings. They should be involved, along with their parents, in teaching their siblings social and manual skills, which in turn, helps them to accept them. Sometimes personality differences and parental conflicts too have an impact on the children. Parents have to show patience, understand these issues and should openly communicate with their children to resolve them.

QUESTIONS

1. Sibling rivalry means fight between ______.

A. firstborn and second child
B. children of same parents
C. children born to different parents
D. cousins and relatives

2. 'Why do firstborns feel neglected by the arrival of a new child in the family?

A. because they have to share their parents' love and attention
B. because of their negative attitude
C. because they hate their siblings
D. because parents do not love them

3. What does the word 'regressive' in para 2 mean?

A. emotional imbalance

B. withdraw or shy away
C. negative feeling
D. harsh or rude

4. How can older children develop a positive attitude towards their siblings?
A. by developing sibling rivalry
B. by keeping away from their siblings
C. by their involvement in matters related to the young ones
D. by dominating their siblings

5. What should parents do to control sibling rivalry?
A. allow children to fight among themselves
B. do not allow any communication between children
C. punish the children
D. openly communicate with children to resolve issues

PASSAGE-13

Music can have strong consequences on our feelings. One should try to gain benefits from the power of music. Music, in general, helps one to calm down and feel revitalized. It helps to beat a bad mood or to continue a good state of mind. To cheer up or to enhance vitality, one should listen to music with beats, lots of drumming and a fast tempo. When one wants to relax after a busy day, instrumental music with less percussion and a slower rhythm can help. Listening to soothing music before stressful activities has a lot of benefits and so is always advised. A collection of preferred relaxing tunes help to combat stress at work. One can change one's frame of mind by switching from one kind of music to another. To feel refreshed, it is better to start with something tranquil and soothing and to slowly pick up the pace and the beat. But when one prefers to settle down after a busy schedule, follow the reverse style.

Music is an incredible means that people can use to communicate things, especially their feelings and emotions. When added to speech in a song, it becomes a powerful device of communication. Music generally needs special aptitude, inborn talent and rigorous practice. Also, a person needs to have fine muscular strength in order to sing in tune or play a musical instrument. Recollection of the notes demands good memory power. Besides, many people feel that music and love are connected to each other. A person tries to make an impression on his/her love by way of selecting appropriate music.

QUESTIONS

1. Music with fast beats and lots of drumming ________.
A. boosts up one's energy
B. calms down one's mind
C. is less beneficial
D. leads to stress

2. What does 'percussion' mean?
A. stressful condition
B. tranquil mood
C. thumping or fast beat
D. inborn talent

3. What kind of music is preferred when a person wants to settle down?
A. music with lots of percussion
B. first upbeat music and then soothing music
C. music of string instruments
D. first gentle music and then fast music

4. Why is music considered to be a powerful means of communication?
A. because it helps people to express their emotions
B. because it is an incredible tool
C. because it reduces stress at work
D. because it enhances energy in people

5. What qualities are needed for a person to sing or play a musical instrument?
A. love, talent, speech and memory
B. aptitude, emotion, strength and love
C. knowledge, emotion, love and talent
D. aptitude, talent, practice and strength

PASSAGE-14

In order to heal your emotional baggage and prevent it from possibly costing you yet another relationship, you must recognise the roots of your emotional pain or fears and acknolwedge your accountability in them.

According to psychologists, one should review the event or experience that you think caused you to be hurt and identify your role in the experience. "Allow yourself to learn from that and forgive yourself—often misplaced guilt can be the cause for fear. Acknowledge that your past does not have to dictate your future. Release all the emotional hurt and fears that were weighing you down and standing in the way of your seeing each individual relationship for its own merit and potential. It can be difficult to let go of the security blanket of past behaviours but assure yourself that you no longer need them. Sometimes one may require professional help to be able to identify, draw links, acknowledge, accept and forgive themselves. In the end, it all comes down to trust. Want to leave that baggage behind? Allow yourself to trust again," concludes a psychologist.

QUESTIONS

1. It is important to understand __________.
- A. pain
- B. emotions
- C. cause of emotional pain
- D. effect of emotional pain

2. It is advised that we should __________.
- A. stop feeling the pain
- B. review the event
- C. take rest
- D. all of the above

3. We should not allow the past __________.
- A. to guide our future
- B. to bother us
- C. actions to make today's decision
- D. to affect our present

4. We should learn to let go __________.
- A. pain
- B. negative emotion
- C. fear
- D. the security of the past

5. The most important thing in life is __________.
- A. trust
- B. love
- C. compassion
- D. fear

PASSAGE-15

Maintaining work-life balance is necessary because imbalance wreaks chaos in life. Increased pressure on one side will affect the other side too.

After all, the two cannot be completely disconnected! The first step towards this is finding the cause for the imbalance.

Some of the potential causes are—you are genuinely overloaded with work, you are incompetent, your time management skills are poor or you chase conflicting goals.

Once you identify the problem, you should admit it and work towards overcoming it. When you are better organised, your efficiency increases. Make a list of activities and prioritise them. This should be done on daily, weekly and monthly basis.

Plan in advance how you will deal with impending additional responsibilities. If you have to spend extra time at the office, inform your family about it and seek their support. If you have to take leave, inform your boss.

When your organisation is going through a change, there is a crisis or you are vying for a promotion, it can be inevitable to spend more time at work. So explore alternative ways to show your loved ones that you care. When you are with your family and friends, make the most of the time. Do not think about work at least during the 'special' time you allotted for them.

Pay attention to your health. Sleep well. Spend time on activities that can help beat fatigue. Allot time for physical exercises, yoga or sports.

QUESTIONS

1. Chaos here means __________.
- A. disturbance
- B. confusion
- C. happiness
- D. calmness

2. As soon as we identify the problem we should __________.
A. work towards overcoming it
B. forget it
C. overcome it
D. none of the above

3. When there is extra work one should _______.
A. stay up at night B. work from home
C. plan in advance D. all of the above

4. When one is spending time with family __________.
A. one should carry work also
B. one should relax and sleep
C. one should keep thinking about work
D. one should not think about work

5. It is important to take care of one's health because _________.
A. it helps to be positive and chargeable
B. one can do more work
C. work is worship
D. none of the above

PASSAGE-16

You are at a party and want to watch your weight and health. However when the appetisers are served you notice nothing looks healthy. The next thing you know, you go ahead and eat those decorative little morsels and blow your eating plan. Stop!

Those little delicious nuts in that bowl are chock-full of nutrition. They will improve your cardio-vascular health; hold cancer prevention properties and help you lose weight. It's hard to believe but it's true!

The idea that something from nuts may actually help weight control seems a little counter-intuitive at first; bearing in mind the reputation nuts have for being both fatty and fattening. Nuts are nutrient-packed, healthy 'primal' food, and something that experience shows satisfy the appetite and prevent overeating at meal time. High in proteins, unsaturated fats may aid in weight loss and other disease-fighting properties.

What do nuts have that is heart-healthy? Nuts are an intensely fatty food, with about 80 per cent of the calories they offer coming from fat. But bear in mind that the type of oils found in nuts such as almonds, cashews, walnuts is predominantly the healthy monounsaturated and polyunsaturated type.

Researchers found that people who eat nuts regularly have lower risk of heart disease. In 1998, a study conducted by the Harvard School of Public Health found that women who ate nuts less than four times a week were 40 per cent less likely to die of heart disease. Further, potential heart health benefits of nuts were also found among men. In 2002, the Physician's Health Study found that men who consumed nuts two or more times per week had reduced risk of sudden cardiac death.

QUESTIONS

1. Nuts possess __________.
A. nutritive value
B. fattening properties
C. oil
D. all of the above

2. During meal time nuts __________.
A. add taste to the food
B. satisfy appetite
C. should not be consumed
D. create an urge for water

3. Nuts contain __________.
A. unhealthy oils B. cholesterol
C. healthy oils D. none of the above

4. People who consume nuts regularly _______.
A. are not prone to heart attacks
B. are prone to heart attacks
C. are not prone to kidney failure
D. are prone to kidney failure

5. Sudden cardiac death means death due to __________.
A. kidney failure
B. sudden heart failure
C. sudden brain malfunction
D. increase in lung pressure

PASSAGE-17

Acupuncture is an ancient form of healing that dates back to Stone Age. It is a technique of inserting and manipulating fine needles into specific points on the body to relieve pain or for therapeutic purposes. Acupuncture originated in China and is most commonly associated with traditional Chinese medicine. As per the traditional Chinese medical theory, acupuncture points are situated on meridians along which 'Qi' (pronounced as 'chee'), the vital energy, flows. Apparently, there is no known histological basis for the existence of acupuncture meridians. Different types of acupuncture such as Classical Chinese, Japanese, Tibetan, Vietnamese and Korean are practised throughout the world.

The practice of acupuncture is based on the understanding that a vital energy flows along channels or meridians throughout our bodies. When this energy becomes blocked or does not flow freely, it causes disharmony or disease. In order to correct this disharmony, the vital force must be stimulated so that it moves freely again. A set of very fine needles are used to stimulate peculiar points located on the flow of energy and the actions of the various acupuncture points to treat diseases and disharmonies in the body. Quite significantly, acupuncture is not usually painful. Acupuncture needles are tiny and are quickly inserted through the skin, where the nerves that transmit pain are located. The sensation of the insertion is like a "quick pinch". In general, there is an agreement that acupuncture is safe when administered by well-trained practitioners using sterile needles and that further research is appropriate.

QUESTIONS

1. Where does vital energy flow through in human bodies?
A. through muscle cells
B. through blood cells
C. through meridians
D. through sense organs

2. How are acupuncture points stimulated?
A. by inserting find needles into specific points on the body
B. by knowing the histological basis
C. by flow of vital energy
D. by going to China

3. A person specialising in the technique of Acupuncture is called __________.
A. a practitioner B. an acupuncturist
C. a classical Chinese D. a medical doctor

4. How is a disease caused as per the traditional Chinese medical theory?
A. when one feels a quick pinch
B. when blood does not flow through the vessels
C. when needles are inserted into specific points
D. when vital energy does not flow freely through meridians

5. Where are the acupuncture needles inserted?
A. in the nerve cells where vital energy flows
B. on the upper part of the right or left hand
C. in the skin where the nerves transmitting pain are found
D. in the muscular part of the hip region

PASSAGE-18

While many of India's parks have been developed from the hunting preserves of princely India, Keoladeo, popularly known as Bharatpur Wildlife Sanctuary, is perhaps the only case where the habitat has been created by a maharaja. In earlier times, Bharatpur town used to be flooded regularly every monsoon. In 1760, an earthen dam, called the Ajam Dam, was constructed, to save the town from this annual vagary of nature. The depression created by extraction of soil for the dam was cleared and this became the Bharatpur Lake.

At the beginning of this century, this lake was developed and divided into several portions. A system of small dams, dykes, sluice gates, etc., was created to control the water level in different sections. This became the hunting preserve of the Bharatpur royalty and also one of the best duck-shooting wetlands in the world. But hunting was prohibited by mid-60s and the area was then declared a national park on 10 March 1982. This was later accepted as a World Heritage site in December 1985.

The major attractions of tourists visiting this park are the numerous migratory birds, which come from as far away as Siberia and Central Asia to spend their winters in Bharatpur, before returning to their breeding grounds. The migratory birds at this bird sanctuary include several species of Cranes, Pelicans, Geese, Ducks, Eagles, Hawks, Shanks, Stints, Wagtails, Warblers, Wheatears, Fly catchers, Buntings, Larks and Pipits, etc.

QUESTIONS

1. Bharatpur Wildlife Sanctuary was developed ________.
   A. from the hunting preserves of princely India
   B. by constructing Ajam dam
   C. by the Maharaja of Bharatpur Royalty
   D. from the floods of every monsoon
2. What is the reason behind the construction of Ajam dam?
   A. to develop a hunting preserve
   B. to develop a wildlife sanctuary
   C. to bring an end to floods
   D. to save the town from being flooded
3. One of the best duck-shooting wetlands of the world is ________.
   A. Princely India B. Bharatpur lake
   C. Ajam dam D. Bharatpur royalty
4. When was Bharatpur Lake given the status of a national park?
   A. 10 March 1982 B. 10 January 1982
   C. 10 December 1985 D. 10 October 1985
5. What are migratory birds?
   A. birds from Siberia and Central Asia
   B. birds that travel long distances during some seasons
   C. birds from Bharatpur Wildlife Sanctuary
   D. birds from the hunting preserves of India

PASSAGE-19

Lexicographer : a writer of dictionaries, a harmless drudge, that busies himself in tracing the original, and detailing the signification of words. Thus said Samuel Johnson in his Dictionary, with an ironic swipe at his own work. It wasn't the first dictionary of the English language, but it continued to be regarded as an authoritative if quirky icon of language for more than two centuries. In two volumes and 2,300 pages, Johnson tried to tidy up a notoriously untidy and promiscuous language, though he knew at the same time that it was futile to attempt to straitjacket it. We tend to think of dictionaries as "anonymous" productions, but Johnson's personality is all over the work. In his bitter definition of a patron, "commonly a wretch who supports with insolence, and is paid by flattery", Johnson took care of his own patron, Lord Chesterfield, who had promised to help financially but had not delivered till too late. Since Johnson's Dictionary, which has been reprinted, abridged, and is still written about, there have been books too numerous to count on the English language: Melvyn Bragg's The Adventure of English: The Biography of a Language, the most recent (2004), Raymond Williams' Keywords: A Vocabulary of Culture and Society (1985), one of the most respected. But there are hundreds of others.

QUESTIONS

1. Samuel Johnson made an ironic remark at his own work by calling a lexicographer ________.
   A. a harmless drudge
   B. a writer of dictionaries
   C. one who is busy in tracing the original
   D. all the above
2. Johnson's Dictionary ________.
   A. continues to be regarded as an authority on icons
   B. was one of the first dictionaries of English language

C. was regarded a quirky icon of language
D. has been printed for more than two centuries

3. Tick the correct statement.
A. Since Johnson's dictionary many have been reprinted.
B. Johnson's dictionary has been reprinted and abridged.
C. Johnson abridged his dictionary many times.
D. Johnson abridged Melvyn Bragg's 'The Adventure of English'.

4. Which of the following statements are true?
(1) Johnson's dictionary has two volumes.
(2) His dictionary defines 'patron' as commonly a wretch who supports with insolence, and is paid by flattery.
(3) Lord Chesterfield was Johnson's patron.
(4) Lord Chesterfield did not help Johnson financially.
A. (1) and (3) are True, (2) and (4) are False.
B. All are True.
C. (1), (2) and (3) are True and (4) is False.
D. (2), (3) and (4) are True and (1) is False.

5. Find a word in the passage that means the same as 'unsuccessful'.
A. swipe B. insolence
C. straitjacket D. futile

PASSAGE-20

Swaminathan went to school feeling that he was the worst perjurer on earth. His conscience bothered him : he wasn't at all sure if he had been accurate in his description of Samuel. He could not decide how much of what he had said was imagined and how much of it was real. He stopped for a moment on the roadside to make up his mind about Samuel.... His cane skinned people's hands. Swaminathan cast his mind about for an instance on this. There was none within his knowledge. Years and years ago he was reputed to have skinned the knuckles of a boy in the First Standard and made him smear the blood on his face. No one had actualy seen it. But year after year the story persisted among the boys.... Swaminathan's head was dizzy with confusion in regard to Samuel's character—whether he was good or bad, whether he deserved the allegations in the letter or not.... he felt an impulse to run home and beg his father to take back the letter. But Father was an obstinate man.

As he approached the yellow building he realised that he was perjuring himself and was ruining his teacher. Probably the Headmaster would dismiss Samuel and then the police would chain him and put him in jail. For all this disgrace, humiliation and suffering who would be responsible? Swaminathan shuddered. The more he thought of Samuel, the more he grieved for him. As he felt the bulge of the letter in his pocket, he felt like an executioner.

As he entered the school gate an idea occurred to him, a sort of solution. He wouldn't deliver the letter to the Headmaster immediately, but at the end of the day—to that extent he would disobey his father and exercise his independence. There was nothing wrong in it, and Father would not know it anyway. If the letter was given at the end of the day there was a chance that Samuel might do something to justify the letter.

Swaminathan stood at the entrance to his class. Samuel was teaching arithmetic. He looked at Swaminathan for a moment, Swaminathan stood hoping that Samuel would fall on him and tear his skin off. But Samuel merely asked, 'Are you just coming to the class?'

QUESTIONS

1. Swami was not comfortable going to school that day because __________.
A. he was not well
B. he had lied about his teacher Samuel
C. he had not done his home work
D. his friend was not there

2. He was not sure about Samuel's character because __________.
A. what he knew was all hearsay
B. what he knew was his imagination
C. other teachers had told him so
D. none of the above

3. Swami's father was not likely to take back the letter because ________.
   A. he believed that Samuel was a good teacher
   B. his father wanted to help Swami and other children
   C. he was a very stubborn man
   D. all of the above
4. Swami decided to ________.
   A. give the letter to the Headmaster
   B. give the letter directly to Mr. Samuel
   C. tear off the letter
   D. give it to the Headmaster at the end of the school
5. As Swami was late to the school he expected ________.
   A. Mr. Samuel to hit him
   B. Mr. Samuel will allow him into the class
   C. to be shouted at by Mr. Samuel
   D. none of the above

PASSAGE-21

Leadership does not exist without followership. A leader has to be accepted by the group which the former is supposed to lead. To gain acceptability the leader should cause an emotive impact on the group members. The character exhibited by leaders make them dear to their followers. A leader is one who effectively inspires employees to achieve worthwhile goals. What character of the leader motivates the followers? It is not pomp and show or flattery or sanctioning more incentives.

Pomp and show creates a sense of awe and the leader is defied rather than emulated. Flattery is unrealistic and cannot serve as a long-term motivational tool.

A leader's style should be one that can be emulated by all irrespective of cadre, class or calibre. Simplicity in one's day-to-day conduct is the only thing that can be adopted by all. When the leader is simple, he is counted as one belonging to the group of which he is the leader. That's to motivate the people. Motivation is the innate quality that enables an individual or group to contribute unlimitedly with limited means. It is the proud prerogative of enlightened human beings.

QUESTIONS

1. Leadership co-exists with ________.
   A. obedience
   B. followership
   C. discipline
   D. incentives
2. The pre-requisite for the success of a leader is ________.
   A. obedience by the group
   B. simplicity of the leader
   C. acceptability by the group he is supposed to lead
   D. strict discipline of the group
3. The leader should cause an emotive impact on the group members as ________.
   A. to ensure obedience
   B. to enforce discipline
   C. to control the group
   D. to gain acceptability
4. To inspire employees to achieve long term goals, a leader should not use ________.
   A. sanctioning more incentives
   B. flattery
   C. pomp and show
   D. all of the above
5. Find a word having the same meaning as 'emotive' from the words given below:
   A. Prerogative
   B. Enlightened
   C. Sensitive
   D. Proud

PASSAGE-22

We first became aware that something unusual was happening when one of the ship's officers came up to the Chief Engineer, who sat at one table and spoke to him on a low voice. The Chief Engineer at once stood up and with a brief excuse which told us nothing, left the dining room. At first we thought that there had been an accident or that a fire had broken out on board ship, but soon the word went round that a man had been floating in the sea. Then we noticed that the ship had slowed down and was beginning to turn round, with a rather violent motion. Some of the passengers did not wait to finish their meal, but at once rushed upon deck. Others crowded round the portholes, making it impossible for us to eat in comfort. There was such confusion in the dining room that we decided to join those who had come up on deck.

There we learnt that one of the crew had seen a man in the sea some distance from the ship. He had informed the captain who at once ordered the ship to be turned round. We were now only two hundred yards or so from the man and a life boat had already been lowered into the sea. In it there were four sailors, who were sitting ready at the oars, an officer and the ship's doctor. The officer shouted an order and the sailors began to row away the ship. But looking in the same direction as the boat was going, we were able to make out the position of the man in the water. He was clinging to a large piece of wood. At last, after what seemed to us an age the life boat reached the man and two of the sailors pulled him on the boat. This was not at all easy for the sea was rather rough. Then the sailors began to row back to the ship again. The life boat was raised out of the water and the rescued man, wrapped in a blanket was helped out on the deck. Leaning on the arm of the ship's doctor, but still able to walk, in spite of his terrible experience he was led off to the ship's hospital. As he passed along the deck everyone cheered loudly.

QUESTIONS

1. 'We' here refers to ________.
   A. the crew members
   B. the sailors
   C. the passengers of the ship
   D. all of the above

2. The Passengers rushed to the back of the ship because ________.
   A. the ship was drowning
   B. a fire had broken out on board ship
   C. a fight had broken up
   D. the crew was trying to save a drowning man

3. It was tough for the crew to save the drowning man as ________.
   A. the weather was rough
   B. the sea was rough
   C. the man was unwilling to come along with the sailors
   D. the ship had moved ahead

4. Everyone cheered the man loudly as ________.
   A. he had saved the drowning man
   B. he had informed about the drowning man
   C. he had survived a terrible experience
   D. he was the doctor who treated the drowning man

5. The words or the phrase in the passage that means 'it came into knowledge' is ________.
   A. seem to us an age
   B. with a rather violent motion
   C. in comfort
   D. the word went round

PASSAGE-23

In this world there is no worse nuisance than a boy at the age of fourteen. He is neither ornamental nor useful. It is impossible to shower affection on him as a smaller boy; and he is always getting in the way. If he talks with a childish lisp he is called a baby, and if in a grown-up way he is called impertinent. In fact, talk of any kind from him is resented. Then he is at the unattractive, growing age. He grows out of his clothes with indecent haste: His voice grows hoars and breaks and quivers; His face grows suddenly angular and unsightly. It is easy to excuse the shortcomings of early childhood, but it is hard to tolerate even unavoidable lapses in a boy of fourteen. He becomes painfully self-conscious, and when he talks with elderly people is either unduly forward, or else so unduly shy that he appears ashamed of his own existence.

Yet, it is at this age that in his heart of hearts, a young lad most craves recognition and love; and he becomes the devoted slave of any one who shows him consideration. But none dare openly love him, for that would be regarded as undue indulgence and therefore bad for the boy. So, what with scolding and chiding, he becomes very much like a stray dog that has lost its master.

His own name is the only paradise that a boy of fourteen can know. To live in a strange house with strange people is little short of fortune; while it is height of bliss to receive the kind looks of women and never to suffer their slights.

QUESTIONS

1. The expression 'he is always getting in the way' means that he is ________.
   A. found/seen everywhere you go
   B. behaving in a different way from expected/desired
   C. always troubling others with his undesired ways
   D. he goes where he is asked to
2. A lad of fourteen years of age is resented because ________.
   A. he behaves too childishly
   B. he acts like a grown-up
   C. his behaviour becomes neither of a child nor of a grown-up
   D. he looks troublesome
3. A fourteen-year-old boy becomes self-conscious when ________.
   A. when he is regarded neither as a young nor a grown-up
   B. when he is slighted by elders
   C. when he is not appreciated for his good actions
   D. none of the above
4. The great bliss for such a boy is ________.
   A. to be rewarded for his achievements
   B. to receive the kind glances of women
   C. to have the company of jolly friends
   D. to do what he likes to do
5. The writer's own attitude towards the fourteen-year-old boy is ________.
   A. satirical B. sympathetic
   C. indifferent D. none of the above

PASSAGE-24

For years, Fukuoka was widely known as the closest city that Japan had to Venice. It might not have enjoyed the splendid architecture, piazzas or the Basilica San Marco of the Italian city, but the people of the largest metropolis on Kyushu, Japan's most southerly main island, prided themselves on the carefully maintained network of rivers that emptied into the graceful curve of Hakata Bay and gave Fukuoka its blue credentials. Today, however, the capital of Kyushu is forging a new identity for itself as green complements the blue.

Not satisfied with pioneering a method of semi-aerobic landfill known the world over as "The Fukuoka Method", the city has gone on to implement some highly exacting rubbish-segregating standards for both homes and businesses. And it has ambitious plans to turn itself into the world's first city to be powered by hydrogen, a project that is under way and will eventually evolve into a "corridor" of homes and businesses linking Fukuoka with the larger cities of Osaka, Nagoya and eventually, the mammoth Tokyo, some 900 kilometres to the rest.

All that and yet Fukuoka is still regarded as the most pleasant place to live in Japan and among the best in the world. In its annual quality of life survey in July 2010, Britain's *Monocle* magazine ranked Fukuoka the 14th "most liveable" city on the planet, thanks in part to its air connections with the rest of Asia, its low crime rate, sub-tropical climate, excellent public transport services and cultural opportunities.

City authorities also received high marks for subsidising local residents who want to install solar-energy systems in their homes to the tune US$1.2 million. Elsewhere, funds have been invested in the creation of green spaces.

QUESTIONS

1. The city of Fukuoka is considered ________.
   A. closest to Venice
   B. different from Venice
   C. Peaceful city
   D. close to Rome
2. Green complements the blue means ________.
   A. green and blue do not go together
   B. green and blue go well with each other
   C. If we have green in a place, it is auspicious to have blue there
   D. none of these

3. Fukuoka has set very high standards for
   A. cleanliness
   B. keeping city green
   C. separating bash at home as well as work place
   D. maintaining clean air
4. Fukuoka is high on the list of the most liveable cities in the world because __________.
   A. there is less crime
   B. environment is clean
   C. excellent connectivity, within and outside the city
   D. all of the above
5. Residents of Fukuoka who wish to install solar powered system __________.
   A. Know the advantages of the same
   B. will be subsidised by the state
   C. are encouraged by the government
   D. none of these

PASSAGE-25

A tiger relies on stealth to catch its prey. It has excellent eyesight and hearing, which help it track animals in the dark. Tigers hunt large animals such as deer and wild pigs, which will provide food for a few days. They slink up on their prey unseen, only charging when they are within about 20m (65 ft). Tigers kill their prey by biting the back, its neck or throat, then dragging it away into thick cover to feed. When they have eaten enough, they conceal the carcass with leaves so they can return to it later on. Male tigers can eat up to 40 kg (85 lb) of meat in one meal.

Tigers love water and often bathe or cool off in rivers and pools during the heat of the day. They usually hunt at night and rest during the day. Most tigers live alone, although mothers with cubs or young siblings sometimes hunt together. A male tiger roams a territory of up to 100 sq km (60 sq. miles) in area, defining its boundaries with scent markings, droppings and scratch marks on boulders or trees. These signals tell other tigers about its sex and size as well as its territory. Tigers also communicate by roaring and moaning. They defend their territory fiercely against rival males, but will tolerate some overlap with the smaller territories of females.

QUESTIONS

1. Stealth means __________.
   A. by cheating
   B. secret way
   C. attacking from front
   D. jumping at the prey
2. Tigers hunt big animals because __________.
   A. it is easy to hunt them
   B. their meat is tasty
   C. the meat will last them a few days
   D. they are easily available
3. Tigers drag their prey into the bush __________.
   A. so that nobody can disturb them
   B. it is cool under a bush
   C. other animals may snatch their prey
   D. to conceal it
4. During the hot summer season __________.
   A. tigers like to cool by staying in water
   B. tigers go off to sleep
   C. tigers stay under the bush
   D. tigers move to cooler areas
5. Tigers prefer to __________.
   A. stay in small groups
   B. stay alone
   C. stay as a family
   D. take care of their young one

PASSAGE-26

The Kidneys of nearly five per cent of people under the age of 20 are not functioning normally, a study shows. The youngsters have albumin in the urine, which indicates that they could develop a serious kidney disease later in their lives. Doctors say that more youngsters today are at a risk of kidney malfunction due to lifestyle changes, which includes smoking, consumption of junk food and less physical activity from desk-bound jobs. On the eve of World Kidney Day, doctors are stressing on the early detection of Kidney malfunction as the only way to reduce serious complications and chronic kidney disease.

For the pilot study, the institute of nephrology at a hospital used a home detection kit that is dipped in urine to show presence of protein in the sample. During the study, 1,000 people were given the kits. A total of 265 returned them with feedback. Of this, 5% of the young population had urinary protein.

Doctors say that the main issue with kidney disease is the lack of early detection. If detected early, patients can avoid reaching the stage of dialysis, which indicates irreversible and serious kidney damage. "Simple health screening test comprising urine tests, blood test and ultrasounds are important. Early diagonsis and treatment for kidney disease can significantly delay and even prevent kidney failure and need for dialysis." said doctors. One doctor said home detection kits would help in early detection, and added that they were targeting young people in colleges and IT firms to use this kit.

QUESTIONS

1. As many as __________ of youngsters have kidney problem.

A. 20% B. 5%
C. 22% D. 12%

2. This problem is mainly due to __________.

A. obesity in youngsters
B. change in lifestyle
C. poor intake of water
D. none of the above

3. The main problem with kidney related disease is __________.

A. it is fatal
B. it cannot be treated
C. it cannot be detected early
D. it is painful

4. Simple tests will help in __________.

A. preventing and delaying kidney failure
B. giving treatment
C. relieving pain
D. all of the above

5. Hospitals are targeting colleges and IT firms because __________.

A. youngsters need it the most
B. these places have only youngsters
C. they want to bring down kidney issue among youngsters
D. all of the above

PASSAGE-27

Global warming this century could trigger a run away thaw of Greenland's ice sheet and other abrupt shifts such as a dieback of the Amazon rainforest, scientists say.

They urged governments to be more aware of "tripping points" in nature, tiny shifts that can bring big and almost always damaging changes such as a melt of Arctic summer sea ice or a collapse of the Indian monsoon.

"Society may be lulled into a false sense of security by smooth projections of global change," the scientists at British, German and American institutes wrote in a report saying there were many little-understood thresholds in nature.

"The greatest and clearest threat is to the Arctic with summer sea ice loss likely to occur long before, and potentially contribute to, Greenland ice sheet melt", they wrote in the journal "Proceedings" of the National Academy of Sciences. "Tipping elements in the tropics, the boreal zone, and west Antarctica are surrounded by large uncertainty", they wrote, pointing to more potential abrupt shifts than seen in a 2007 report by the UN Climate Panel.

A projected drying of the Amazon basin, linked both to logging and to global warming, could set off a dieback of the rainforest. Many of these tipping points could be closer.

Other sudden changes linked to climate change, stoked by human use of fossil fuels, included a dieback of northern pine forests, or a stronger warming of the Pacific under EI Nino weather events that can disrupt weather world-wide, they wrote.

A possible greening of parts of the Sahel and the Sahara, if monsoon rains in West Africa were disrupted, was one of the few positive abrupt shifts identified by the scientists.

Even a moderate warming could set off a thaw of Greenland's ice sheet that could then vanish in 300 years—raising sea levels by 20ft, or 2 meters a century and threatening coasts, Pacific islands and cities from Bangkok to Buenos Aires. The UN Climate Panel foresees a rise in world sea level ranging up to about 80 cms this century and reckons that a thaw of Greenland would take hundreds of years longer.

The new study said a disappearance of Arctic sea ice in summer time could happen in coming decades—earlier than projected by the UN panel. That could stoke further global warming as dark water soaks up more heat than ice and snow.

QUESTIONS

1. Global warming can cause __________.
   A. thawing of green land
   B. excess rain
   C. severe draught
   D. a green earth

2. Nations should be sensitive to small changes that can cause __________.
   A. famine
   B. melting of Arctic ice
   C. decrease in sea level
   D. chill in polar regions

3. There could be a die-back of the rainforest because of __________.
   A. drying of Amazon Basin
   B. water level
   C. ses level
   D. melting glaciers

4. As a result of rains in West Africa __________.
   A. Sahara will turn into desert
   B. Sahara will turn green
   C. flood will come
   D. none of these

5. According to a UN panel report __________ in this century.
   A. sea level will decrease
   B. sea level will remain same
   C. sea level will rise
   D. none of these

PASSAGE-28

1. Music constitutes mood with variable notes of rhythm transformed from any corner to the destination with a view point of sowing seeds of mental relief with sensational pleasure. It allows generations to bear the pleasure of routing melody of listening lyrics challenging aweful ruckus of mental distress with sweet and melodious voice into individual ears.

   Renowned musicians have earned landmark, attribution to the theme of music therapy, woven with classical and orchestral beat of drum sound shakes beat with thrill and pleasure. Music allotes identity to host and listener with keen interest of sweeping away boring and stranded congestion of monotony.

2. A folk singer from Bengal who sings spiritual Baul songs, on hearing a snatch of Blues music remarked, 'That sounds so much like our kind of singing.' Indeed it is possible to hear Baul, Blues and folk rhythms one after another, without feeling any strangeness. Any kind of good music rejuvenates and moves a person and knows no geographical boundaries.

3. This is also the case with instrumental music. A person listening to a Latin American flute could easily be reminded of a plaintive raga composition. The guitar recital of the Latin American guitarist Paco de Lucia could be just as thrilling as a recital by an Indian sitarist playing in full flow. As for percussion, imagine the dance the gods would break into, if African drums were to play alongside the mridangam, tabla and the dholak!

4. There are scores of music lovers around the world who like Elvis Presley's singing as much as the singing of Subbalakshmi. Even in the

very interior of India it would not be surprising if someone were to talk of the Las Vegas legend with as much feeling, for it is possible to feel comfortable with specific cultures and yet like the music one has been associated with.

5. Since music allows latitude, it encourages an exhilarating exchange of genres and people. In ancient days Muthuswamy Dikshitar introduced many North Indian ragas into Carnatic music. The late John Higgins 'Bhagavatar', an American, was a distinguished scholar of Carnatic music. Similarly, Kadri Gopalan, an exponent of Carnatic music, plays it on the western saxophone. The Beatles produced some wonderfully popular numbers, such as 'Norwegian Wood', and 'Girl', by infusing elements of Hindustani classical music. Suman Kabir uses the tabla to great effect with his trademark solo guitar. Indeed many Indian musicians and groups display comfort in playing a western melodic rhythm in their music. Bollywood has matured in the nineties to mix melodic traditions. A R Rahman pioneered this new trend. In most of his music he uses African beats and the tabla to good effect.

6. Music has promoted the fusion of genres without compromising the identity of any form. Really good musicians around the world like their creative counterparts in other fields to shuttle into each other's traditions while being rooted in their own. That is what the richness of music really means. That is the kind of music that elevates.

QUESTIONS

1. On the basis of your reading of the passage answer the following questions. Write your answers against the correct blank numbers.

(*i*) List two qualities mentioned by the writer about good music.

(*ii*) What is unique about the music of John Higgins and Kadri Gopalan?

(*iii*) What is A R Rahman's contribution to Indian music?

2. Answer the following notes appropriately. Do not add extra information. Write your answers against the correct blank numbers.

(*i*) Folk music of Bengal ________

(*ii*) Las Vegas legend ________

(*iii*) Latin American guitarist ________

(*iv*) Norwegian wood ________

3. On the basis of your reading the passage answer the following. Write your answers against the correct blank numbers.

(*i*) geographical boundaries refer to (Para 2) ________

(*ii*) latitude in this paragraph means (Para 5) ________

(*iii*) a fusion of genres means (Para 6) ________

PASSAGE-29

1. Mind management is a way to control one's mind. To do this, we need to be cautious about our thinking process and also need a high level of understanding and meditation as well. Understanding is wisdom – 80 per cent of people are knowledgeable, while 20 per cent are wise. Knowledgeable men take sides without reason. They feel sad seeing deprived people but jealous when they see happy people. They work in the guidance of others' inspiration, take unnecessary responsibility to keep themselves disturbed.

2. A wise person does not stand for or against any idea without concrete reason. He works according to the situation and capacity. He looks at everything intellectually. To him, failure is a stepping stone for future success. So depression and conflict are not seen. Like the phrase 'Stop, Look, Go', first one should see, and this needs patience. Meditation is necessary to control and manage mind which then becomes an easy task.

3. Unless we control or manage our mind, it is difficult to achieve success and peace. Psychologists say every interest is first born in the mind as a seed. Then it continues to grow. Later it takes its real form which everybody can see. The interest that first appears in the mind remains weak for the first three minutes and it becomes strong within the next five minutes. All the negative aspects should be deleted within the first three minutes. If not taken out, they would become stronger later and you can never throw them out. After taking control over the mind, we can control passion, interest and unrest. Mind management is essential for a peaceful, successful and healthy life.
4. The age of computers has thrown us on the escalator of aspirations but has robbed us of simple charms like falling asleep. The compulsions of hectic schedules burden the mind and cause stress. However, the joys that elude us can be regained by practising power meditation. It creates tranquility, simplifies life and cleanses the mind. It helps control indolence, ego and anger and builds confidence and patience. With power meditation, negative thoughts get dissipated and a sense of happiness is achieved.
5. With happiness and spiritual knowledge, one can relearn the meaning of life. The picture of life's journey also becomes clearer. Osho said, "As science is not based on orthodox and blind beliefs and functions only on the principle of cause and effect, similarly power meditation doesn't function on age-old theories or communal thoughts but originates from rational and divine experience. It strives to make an individual free from the confining pressures of daily life".
6. The beauty of meditation is that it is independent of religion. According to modern medical science, combinations of factors like pollutants, imbalanced diet and high aspirations have rendered the human mind restless, thereby making the body perpetually ill.
7. Here is a meditation method, which will enable you to control stress. Sit in the padmasan or sukhasan, cross-legged and erect. Keep your back, spine and neck straight. Keep your eyes closed. Sit in this position for 10 minutes. The method has two stages: for the first five minutes, breathe in slowly, hold it and then release it very slowly. Again, for the next five minutes, breathe and release your breath slowly.

QUESTIONS

1. Answer the following questions briefly:
(*i*) What is mind management?
(*ii*) What are the character traits of wise person?
(*iii*) Why should all negative aspects be deleted within the first three minutes?
(*iv*) Why do we feel stress in this age of computers?

2. What do the following statement mean :
(*i*) 'Failure is a stepping stone for future success'.
(*ii*) 'Mind management is essential for a peaceful, successful and healthy life.'

3. Find words from the passage whose opposites are given below :
(*i*) to let free [para 1]
(*ii*) peaceful and calm [para 2]
(*iii*) strong [para 3]
(*iv*) complex [para 4]

PASSAGE-30

1. A youngster quit Facebook in December after spending over three years on the social networking site. With that one act, he bid a silent adieu to more than 300 contacts that he had added to his account during the period. Like almost everyone from his "friends' circle," the 20-year-old was a regular on the service; visiting it everyday to post photos and status updates. But last week, a new feature on Facebook called Timeline forced him to reconsider the pros and cons of being on the networking site.

2. 'Everyone has some skeletons in their closet and I am just not comfortable with Facebook digging up and displaying all the facets of my life on a bulletin board,' says this youngster who joined the network in July 2007 while he was in Class11.

3. Facebook, you see, had compressed the time he spent on the site and arranged it in chronological order. And while he initially liked the new, neatly organised scrapbook-like feature, he wasn't happy to reveal posts from the past, those that, until recently, were hidden under layers and layers of recent updates. Just clicking on a date on the timeline could transport his friend back in time and enable them to 'view every embarrassing comment, link or photo he had posted on his profile'.

4. "I think it's a recipe for disaster," he says. "In 2007, I had some wall posts, which seemed appropriate at the time, but now after a lapse of four years, I have moved on and don't want them to be openly displayed for all to see."

5. And he is not alone. Many users, worried about how Facebook activity could possibly affect their offline lives, are choosing to commit 'Facebook suicide'. While some have privacy concerns, others feel that the site that was meant to bring them closer to their friends actually does the opposite – it reduces their friendship to something superficial.

6. "Poking and liking are not enough to keep a friendship going," says a business analyst. Having quit Facebook three years ago, she prefers meeting her 'real' friends face-to-face, instead of reading their trite posts online.

7. "On Facebook, people hype everyday issues including what they ate and where they went on a daily basis," says this analyst who continues to use Twitter.

8. Similarly, an engineering student, quit Facebook last December four years after joining it. One find day, he exported all the data from his account into a little zip file and hit the delete button.

9. "I realised that when it came to my friends who really mattered, I could actually keep in touch with them over the phone or by meeting them in real life," he wrote on his blog.

10. "Facebook had become a time sink and it could not justify the time I spent on it," he says, "I spend more time calling up friends or relatives over the phone now.... I also go out and meet people whenever possible and have a good offline life. I do not regret the change." Today, Facebook has 800 million users of which 37 million are Indian. The site has become an online identity for most, and many of those who decide to quit cannot overcome the withdrawal symptoms and return. Facebook, fully aware of its addictive powers, facilitates this return by allowing users to 'deactivate' their accounts. The option allows members to temporarily disable their accounts, but continues to store their information on its servers so that they can return from their 'break', whenever they wish.

QUESTIONS

1. Answer the following questions briefly.

(*i*) What did this youngster do with his Facebook account and why?

(*ii*) What was this youngster upset about?

(*iii*) Why are people generally not comfortable about their past being revealed?

2. Complete the statements given below.

(*i*) In a period of four years people ________ on.

(*ii*) Facebook suicide means ________.

(*iii*) Instead of bringing friends closer ________.

(*iv*) We generally keep ________ who matter to us.

3. Find words from the passage which mean the same as :

(*i*) the advantages and disadvantages [Para 1]

(*ii*) various aspects of one's life. [Para 2]

(*iii*) complete details of a person [Para 3]

(*iv*) to remove [Pare 4]

III. POETRY

Directions: *Read the following poems carefully and choose the best answer to each question out of the four alternatives and mark it in the Answer Sheet.*

POEM-1

It is an ancient Mariner,
And he stoppeth one of three.
'By thy long grey beard and glittering eye,
Now wherefore stopp'st thou me?
The Bridegroom's doors are opened wide,
And I am next of kin;
The guests are met, the feast is set:
May'st hear the merry din.'

He holds him with his skinny hand,
'There was a ship,' quoth he.
'Hold off! unhand me, grey-beard loon!'
Eftsoons his hand dropt he.

He holds him with his glittering eye —
The Wedding-Guest stood still,
And listens like a three years' child:
The Mariner hath his will.

— ST Coleridge

QUESTIONS

1. What is the most potent factor with the Ancient Mariner that enables him to hold the wedding guest?
   A. His glittering eye
   B. His skinny hand
   C. His long grey-beard
   D. His starting words.
2. What is the significance of comparing the wedding guest to a three years' child?
   A. A three years' child is innocent.
   B. He is afraid of a strange man.
   C. He is fond of listening to stories.
   D. He cannot run away from a grown-up man.
3. Which among the following is not an argument presented by the wedding-guest?
   A. The wedding-guest is a close relative of the Bridegroom.
   B. His participation in some ceremonies is essential.
   C. Merry-making is already going on.
   D. Other guests have already arrived.
4. The Ancient Mariner is:
   A. A young man
   B. A middle-aged man
   C. An old man
   D. It is not clear from the text
5. The Mariner's story is related to:
   A. A ship B. Giants
   C. Fairies D. A forest

POEM-2

Shall I hear the lament of the nightingale, submissively lending my ear?

Am I the rose to suffer its cry in silence year after year?

The fire of verse gives me courage and bids me no more to be faint.

With dust in my mouth, I am abject: to God I make my complaint.

Sometimes You favour our rivals then sometimes with us You are free,

I am sorry to say it so boldly. You are no less fickle than we.

(Iqbal: 'Complaint to God')

QUESTIONS

1. What fault does the poet find in God?
   A. God causes misery to people.
   B. He opposes the poet and his companions and favours their opponents.

C. He is fickle.
D. He does not care for the poor.

2. What gives courage to the poet?
A. The song of the nightingale.
B. The power of poetry.
C. The sweet smell of the rose.
D. God's mercy.

3. What is the present mood of the poet?
A. He is distraught.
B. He is in a happy mood.
C. He is in a contemplating mood.
D. He is talking only frivolously.

4. Why does the poet use the word "lament" for the song of the nightingale?
A. The nightingale is sad at poet's miserable condition.
B. It is only teasing the poet.
C. It seems sad to the poet only.
D. Proverbially, the nightingale is said to sing sweet but sad songs.

5. In what situation is the rose placed in the poem?
A. Very advantageous situation.
B. Helpless situation.
C. Confusing situation.
D. Situation of expectation.

POEM-3

'In vain to me the smiling mornings shine,
And reddening Phoebus lifts his golden fire;
The birds in vain and amorous descant join,
Or cheerful fields resume their green attire.
These ears, alas! for other notes repine;
"A different object do these eyes require;
My lonely anguish melts no heart but mine;
And in my breast the imperfect joys expire;"
Yet morning smiles the busy race to cheer,
And new-born pleasure brings to happier men;
The fields to all their wanted tribute bear;
To warm their little loves the birds complain.
"I fruitless mourn to him that cannot hear,
And weep the more because I weep in vain."

— ***Thomas Gray***

QUESTIONS

1. The poet's object in the given poem cannot hear him because:
A. He has gone deaf.
B. He does not care for him.
C. He is awfully busy.
D. He is dead.

2. What does nature bring to the poet?
A. A sense of loss
B. A feeling of joy
C. A sense of satisfaction
D. A feeling of charm

3. Why does the poet use the phrase "in vain" so many times?
A. To tell about the uselessness of his existence.
B. To tell about the uselessness of beauties of nature and his wails.
C. To tell about the uselessness of birds' love.
D. To tell about waste of morning time.

4. What feeling can a keenly observant reader get from a study of the first twelve lines and the last two lines?
A. A feeling of harmony.
B. A feeling of amplitude.
C. A feeling of dichotomy of sense.
D. A sense of overall satisfaction.

5. What does the morning bring to the "happier men"?
A. A sense of loss.
B. A new joy.
C. A feeling of sorrow.
D. A feeling of sympathy.

POEM-4

'Turn on the prudent Ant thy heedless eyes,
Observe her labours, Sluggard, and be wise;
No stern command, no monitory voice,
Prescribes her duties, or directs her choice;
Yet, timely provident, she hastes away
To snatch the blessings of a plenteous day;
When fruitful Summer loads the teeming plain,

She crops the harvest, and she stores the grain.
How long shall sloth usurp thy useless hours,
Unnerve thy vigour, and enchain thy powers?
While artful shades thy downy couch enclose,
And soft solicitation courts repose,
Amidst the drowsy charms of dull delight,
Year chases year with unremitted flight,
Till Want now following, fraudulent and slow,
Shall spring to seize thee, like an ambush'd foe.

— Dr Samuel Johnson

QUESTIONS

1. What can be said to be the overwhelming quality of an ant?
A. Industriousness
B. Dutifulness
C. Time-consciousness
D. Regular routine

2. What will finally overtake a sluggard?
A. Sloth B. Waste of time
C. Loss of energy D. Want

3. What does the Ant do in summer?
A. It enjoys the beauties of nature.
B. It sits in the shade of trees.
C. It fills its stores with grain.
D. It spends time eating summer fruits.

4. Which among the following is not the characteristic of Want?
A. Fraudulence
B. Ambush
C. Springing over the enemy.
D. Abusing the enemy.

5. What is the main characteristic of summer?
A. It is a very hot season.
B. It is a fruitful season.
C. It expects all to do their duties.
D. It always comes on time.

POEM-5

On their own feet they came, or on shipboard,
Camel-back, horse-back, ass-back, mule-back,
Old civilisations put to the sword.
Then they and their wisdom went to rack;
No handiwork of Callimachus,
Who handled marble as if it were bronze,
Made draperies that seemed to rise
When sea-wind swept the corner stands:
His long lamp-chimney shaped like the stem
Of a slender palm, stood but a day;
All things fall and are built again,
And those that build them again are gay.

— WB Yeats

QUESTIONS

1. Which of the following means of transport was not used by the destroyers of old civilizations?
A. By sea
B. By air
C. On the backs of animals
D. On foot

2. What is the eternal law of life?
A. Destruction and recreation
B. Destruction
C. Creation
D. Failure of art

3. Which of the following could Callimachus do?
A. Make a long thin lamp-chimney last long.
B. Engrave in bronze.
C. Make metallic artefacts.
D. Work with marble without breaking it.

4. Is there no hope for civilizations?
A. Yes, there is.
B. No, there's none.
C. The poet gives no clue to it.
D. There is only a little hope.

5. Who get real happiness from their activity?
A. The destroyers. B. The builders.
C. The observers. D. The sea-creatures.

POEM-6

I lay in sorrow, deep *distressed*:
    My *grief* a proud man heard;

His looks were cold, he gave me gold
    But not a kindly word,
My sorrow passed—I paid him back
    The gold he gave to me;
Then stood *erect* and spoke my thanks
    And blessed his *Charity.*
I *lay* in *want,* in grief and pain:
    A poor man passed my way;
He bound my head, he gave me *bread*
    He watched me night and day.
How shall I pay him back again,
    For all he did to me?
Oh, gold is great, but greater far
    Is *heavenly* Sympathy!

—Charles Mackey

QUESTIONS

1. The proud man heard the poet
A. crying in sorrow B. sing in joy
C. lying in misery D. crying due to pain

2. The proud man helped the poet by
A. giving him comfort
B. assisting him to lie down
C. his cold looks
D. giving him gold

3. The poet thanked the proud man by
A. speaking nicely to him
B. giving him money
C. praising him
D. blessing his large-heartedness

4. The poor man helped the poet by
A. giving him comfort
B. binding his body
C. giving him food
D. serving him like his own

5. The word 'heavenly' means
A. relating to paradise
B. like that of heaven
C. like angels
D. like gods

POEM-7

The earth was green, the sky was blue;
    I saw and heard one sunny *morn*
A *skylark hang* between the two,
    A singing *speck* above the corn.
A stage below in gay *accord*,
    White butterflies danced on wing,
And still the singing skylark *soared*,
    And silent sank and soared to sing.
The *cornfield stretched* a *tender* green
    To right and left beside my walks;
I knew he had a nest unseen
    Somewhere among the million *stalks.*
And as I *paused* to hear his song
    While swift the sunny moments *slid*,
Perhaps his *mate* sat listening long,
    And listened longer than I did.

—Christina Rossetti

QUESTIONS

1. The skylark sang when
A. it rained
B. the sun shone
C. the earth was green and the sky without clouds
D. there were clouds

2. The skylark while singing looked like
A. a star B. an insect
C. an eagle D. a small dot

3. The skylark rose upwards and upwards
A. while flying B. while singing
C. as it sang D. as it flew

4. The nest of the skylark was
A. in the fields below
B. among the numberless stems of corn
C. beside other nests
D. among trees

5. The word 'paused' means
A. stopped B. stood erect
C. flew across D. went straight

POEM-8

The Forst *performs* its secret *ministry*,
Unhelped by any wind. The owlet's cry
Came loud—and *hark*, again! loud as before.
The *inmates* of my cottage, all at rest,
Have left me to that *solitude*, which suits
Abstruser musings : save that at my side
My *cradled infant slumbers* peacefully.
Tis calm indeed! so calm, that it disturbs
And *vexes meditation* with its strange
And extreme silentness ......

—S.T. Coleridge

QUESTIONS

1. The 'secret ministry' of the frost is that
A. it is falling on the ground
B. it ministers the earth
C. it has a secret deal with the nature
D. it deals with the air

2. There is silence all round. This is seen in the phrase
A. and hark, again
B. all at rest
C. that solitude
D. Abstruser musings

3. Who is sleeping in the cradle?
A. the poet's son B. the poet's child
C. the poet's nephew D. a stranger baby

4. What disturb(s) the calm?
A. the surroundings B. nature
C. weather D. calmness

5. The word 'meditation' means
A. prayers B. thought
C. deep thought D. deep ideas

POEM-9

She *dwelt* among the *untrodden* ways
Beside the springs of Dove,
A Maid whom there were none to praise
And very few to love :
A violet by a *mossy* stone
Half hidden from the eye!
—*Fair* as a star, when only one
Is shining in the sky.
She lived unknown, and few could know
When Lucy *ceased* to be;
But she is in *grave,* and, oh,
The difference to me!

—William Wordsworth

QUESTIONS

1. Lucy lived a lonely life because
A. no person loved her
B. no one praised her
C. there was no human population
D. she was born in nature

2. Lucy was like a
A. rose flower B. a star
C. a violet flower D. a daffodil

3. She died on unknown death because
A. no one knew her
B. no one could tell where she died
C. she was never known
D. no one knew when she died

4. That the poet is sad over Lucy's death is clear in the words :
A. she is in grave
B. oh
C. the difference to me
D. Lucy ceased to be

5. The word 'untrodden' means
A. not covered B. unwalkable
C. not walked over D. hard to walk

POEM-10

I wandered lonely as cloud
That *floats* on high o'er *vales* and hills,
When all at once I saw a crowd,
A *host* of golden daffodils ;
Beside the lake, beneath the trees,
Fluttering and dancing in the breeze.
Continuous as the stars that shine

And *twinkle* in the milky way,
They *stretched* in never-ending line
Along the *margin* of a *bay* :
Ten thousasnd saw I at a *glance*,
Tossing their head in *sprightly* dance.
The waves beside them danced; but they
Outdid the *sparkling* waves in *glee* :
A poet could not but be gay,
In such a *jocund* company;
I *gazed*—and gazed—but little thought
What wealth the show to me had brought.
For oft, when on my couch I lie
In vacant or in *pensive* mood,
They *flash* upon that inward eye
Which is the bliss of *solitude*;
And then my heart with pleasure fills
And dances with the daffodils.

—William Wordsworth

QUESTIONS

1. The poet compares himself with
A. a cloud that is rainy
B. a cloud
C. a floating cloud
D. a daffodil

2. The daffodils danced
A. like stars
B. beside the lake
C. like twinkling stars
D. in lake water

3. The daffodils made the waves shy in their
A. dancing B. shining
C. sparkling D. shaking

4. The poet's wealth from daffodils is
A. the bliss of solitude
B. their dancing
C. their bright colour
D. his joyful heart

5. The word 'sprightly' means
A. happy B. blissful
C. joyful D. playing

POEM-11

Is this a holy thing to see
In a rich and fruitful land,
Babes reduc'd to *misery,*
Fed with cold and *usurous* hand?
Is that *trembling* cry a song?
Can it be a song of joy?
And so many children poor?
It is a land of poverty?
And their sun does never shine,
And their fields are *bleak and bare,*
And their ways are fill'd with thorns :
It is *eternal* winter there.
For where'er the sun does shine,
And where'er the rain does fall,
Babes can never hunger there,
Nor poverty the mind *appall*.

—William Blake

QUESTIONS

1. 'Rich and fruitful land' stands for
A. U.S.A. B. England
C. India D. China

2. Babies there sing a song with
A. joy B. trembling hands
C. a trembling cry D. sadness

3. If the babies live a miserable life, that country is indeed a country of
A. sick children B. happy children
C. poor children D. hungry children

4. 'It is eternal winter there' means
A. children's life is not happy
B. children's future is bleak
C. winter is all the year around
D. winter is at the peak

5. The word 'usurous' means
A. of zamindar
B. very cruel
C. of money lender
D. of trader

POEM-12

There was a family of rabbits
who lived near a *pack* of wolves.
The wolves *announced* that they did
not like the way the rabbits were
living. One night several wolves were
killed in an earthquake and this was
blamed on the rabbits, for it
is well known that rabbits *pound*
on the ground with their *hind*
legs and cause earthquakes. On
another night one of the wolves was
killed by a bolt of *lightning*
and this also was blamed on the
rabbits. The wolves *threatened* to *civilise* the
rabbits if they didn't behave, and
the rabbits decided to run away
to a desert island. But the other
animals, who lived at a great distance,
shamed then saying, "You must stay where
you are and be brave. This is no world
for escapists. If the wolves attack you,
we will come to your aid, in all
probability." So the rabbits continued
to live near the wolves. And one day
there was a *terrible* flood which
drowned a great many wolves. This was
blamed on the rabbits, for it is
well known that they with long
ears cause floods. The wolves *descended* on
the rabbits for their own good,
and imprisoned them in a dark *cave,*
for their own protection.
When nothing was heard about
the rabbits for some weeks, the other
animals demanded to know what
had happened to them. The wolves
replied that the rabbits had been
eaten and since they had been
eaten the affair was a purely
internal matter.
"They were trying to escape" said
the wolves, "and, as you know, this
is no world for escapists."

—***James Thurber***

QUESTIONS

1. Rabbits do an activity that is similar to earthquakes. It is
A. moving the soil
B. causing earthquakes
C. shaking their hind legs
D. striking the ground

2. The second time wolves died due to
A. electricity B. lightning
C. floods D. earthquakes

3. The other animals advised the rabbits not to go away because
A. they shouldn't be affraid of wolves
B. there was no fear
C. they must be brave
D. they should oppose the wolves

4. The lesson of the incident is that those who escape
A. can't live
B. can't progress
C. shall be free from danger
D. shall lag behind

5. The word 'announced' means
A. went away B. spoke
C. whistled D. declared

POEM-13

The countryside must *preserved*
(Preferably miles away from me.)
Neat hectares of the *stuff* reserved
For those in need of flower or tree.
I'll make do with *landscape* painting

Film *documentaries* on TV
And when I need to escape, *panting,*
Then open-mouthed I'll head for the sea.
Let others *stroll* and take their *leisure,*
In grasses wade upto their knees.
For I *derive* no earthly pleasure
From the green green *rash* that makes me *sneeze.*

—Roger McGough

QUESTIONS

1. The poet feels that the countryside should look
   A. green
   B. covered with vegetation
   C. full of flowers
   D. good with trees
2. The poet would like to satisfy himself of his desire to see nature from
   A. films B. documentaries
   C. TV D. cable TV
3. The poet gets immense pleasure when he is far from
   A. natural beauty
   B. countryside
   C. villageside
   D. film documentaries
4. The poet hates the greenery because it makes him
   A. sick B. dissatisified
   C. a nature lover D. sneeze
5. The word 'landscape' means
   A. a scene of nature
   B. physical scene of a place
   C. nature beauty
   D. vegetation

POEM-14

One infant grows up and becomes a *jockey;*
Another plays basketball or hockey,
This one the prize ring hates to enter
That one becomes a *tackle or center,*
I am just as glad as glad can be
That I'm not them, that they're not me.
With all my heart do I admire
Athletes who *sweat* for fun or hire,
Who take the field in *gaudy pomp,*
And *maim* each other as they *romp,*
My *limp and bashful spirit* feeds
On other people's *heroic deeds.*
Now A runs ninety yards to score,
B knocks the champion to the floor.
C risking *vertebrae and spine,*
Lashes his steed across the line,
You'd think my *ego* it would please
To *swap* positions with one of these.
Well, ego might be pleased enough,
But zealous athletes play so rough,
They do not ever, in their dealings
Consider one another's feelings.
I'm glad that when my struggle begins
Twixt prudence and ego, prudence wins.
Athletes, I'll drink to you
Or eat with you,
Or anything except compete with you,
Buy tickets worth their weight in *radium,*
To watch you *gambol* in a stadium.
And reassure myself anew
That you're not me and I'm not you.

—Ogden Nash

QUESTIONS

1. The poet admires the sportspersons who
   A. win the game
   B. perspire for goals
   C. beat other participants
   D. enjoy playing
2. The poet's spirit enjoys
   A. the great sport feats of the players
   B. seeing them getting injured

C. knocking one another of sportspersons
D. their fighting for the goal

3. What makes the poet not to be a sportsperson?
A. hatred to be a player
B. wisdom to avoid playing
C. fear of injuries
D. careless playing leading to injuries

4. The poet will do anything
A. to see the players playing
B. to go to the stadium
C. for the sportspersons
D. for the well-being of the players

5. The word 'prudence' means
A. athletics B. wisdom
C. skill D. bravery

POEM-15

The *fair breeze* blew, the white foam flew,
The *furrow* followed free;
We were the first that ever burst
Into that silent sea.
Down dropt the breeze, the sails *dropt* down,
T was sad as sad could be;
And we did speak only to break
The silence of the sea!
All in a hot and copper sky,
The bloody Sun, at noon,
Right up above the mast did stand,
No bigger than the Moon.
Day after day, day after day,
We *struck*, nor breath nor motion;
As *idle* as a painted ship
Upon a painted ocean.

—S.T. Coleridge

QUESTIONS

1. The weather became fine and this is clear from
A. the wind blowing very fast
B. the wind blowing leisurely
C. the furrow being free
D. the white foam

2. But soon the weather became very bad as
A. the ship couldn't move
B. the sails couldn't gather wind
C. they became sad
D. they couldn't speak

3. The sky became
A. very hot
B. bloody
C. hot and copper like
D. very perspiring

4. The ship looked like a painted one because it
A. couldn't run B. couldn't move
C. got fully aground D. got anchored

5. The word 'mast' means
A. a pillar
B. sailing prop
C. upright post in a ship
D. upright post of wood in a ship

POEM-16

The old priest Peter Gilligan
Was *weary* night and day;
For half his *flock* were in their beds,
Or under green *sods* lay.
Once while he *nodded* on a chair,
At the *moth-hour* of *eve*,
Another poor man sent for him,
And he began to *grieve.*
"I have no rest, nor joy, nor peace,
For people die and die";
And after cried he, "God forgive!
My body *spake,* not I!"
He knelt, and *leaning* on the chair
He prayed and fell asleep;
And the moth-hour went from the fields,
And stars began to *peep.*
"*Mavrone,* mavrone! The man has died
While I slept on the chair";

He *roused* his horse out of its sleep,
And rode with little care.
He rode now as he never rode,
By rocky *lane and fern*;
The sick man's wife opened the door :
"Father! You come again!"
"And is the poor man dead?" he cried.
"He died an hour ago."
The old priest Peter Gilligan
In grief *swayed to and fro.*
"When you were gone, he turned and died
As merry as a bird."
The old priest Peter Gilligan
He knelt at that word.

—W.B. Yeats

QUESTIONS

1. Peter Gilligan was very tired because he
A. had not slept for long
B. had been serving the people day and night
C. nursed the sick
D. cared much for his own people

2. He worried much because
A. his people were dying
B. he had had no sleep
C. his own people were sad
D. the poor man came to him

3. He regretted that the man died
A. when he had slept
B. when it was midnight
C. when no one was near him
D. when he slept

4. Father Gilligan found when he visited the poor man's house that
A. God had visited in his place
B. God had excused him
C. he was not wanted
D. he couldn't do anything

5. The word 'moth-hour' means
A. late evening B. midnight
C. morning D. mid-day

POEM-17

It takes much time to kill a tree,
Not a simple *job* of the knife
Will do it. It has grown
Slowly *consuming* the earth,
Rising out of it, feeding
Upon its *crust, absorbing*
Years of sunlight, air, water,
And out of its *leprous hide*
Sprouting leaves.
So *hack and chop*
But this alone won't do it.
Not so much pain will do it.
The bleeding *bark* will heal
And from close to the ground
Will rise *curled green twigs,*
Miniature boughs
Which if unchecked will expand again
To former size.
No,
The root is to be pulled out
Out of the *anchoring* earth;
It is to be roped, tied,
And pulled out—*snapped out*
Or pulled out *entirely,*
Out from the earth-cave,
And the strength of the tree *exposed,*
The source, white and wet,
The most sensitive, hidden
For years inside the earth.
Then the matter
Of *scorching* and *choking*
In sun and air,
Browning, hardening,
Twisting, withering,
And then it is done.

—Gieve Patel

QUESTIONS

1. The tree has come out of the earth after
   A. taking breath in the atmosphere
   B. using the soil
   C. feeling the heat of the sun
   D. absorbing the crust.
2. If the tree is chopped, it will still
   A. live B. wither
   C. stand D. heal
3. If the tree is chopped, its leaves will
   A. glisten
   B. grow to their former size
   C. will rise from the ground
   D. shine beautifully
4. The 'white and wet' part of a tree when uprooted is its
   A. source
   B. sensitive part
   C. life
   D. important part
5. The word 'hidden' means
   A. clear B. obscure
   C. safe D. concealed

POEM-18

The quality of mercy is not *strain'd*;
It droppeth as the gentle rain from heaven
Upon the place beneath. It is twice blest.
It blesseth him that gives and him that takes.
T is *mightiest* in the mightiest; it *becomes*
The *throned monarch* better than his *crown*;
His *sceptre* shows the force of *temporal* power,
The *attribute* to *awe* and *majesty,*
Wherein doth sit the *dread* and fear of kings;
But mercy is above this sceptred *sway,*
It is enthroned in the hearts of kings,
It is an attribute to God himself;
And earthly power doth then show likest God's
When mercy *seasons* justice.

QUESTIONS

1. Mercy is compared with
   A. rain
   B. king
   C. monarch
   D. gentle rain
2. Mercy adds more glory to a
   A. king
   B. monarch
   C. monarch's crown
   D. monarch sitting in his throne
3. When does mercy becoem God-like?
   A. when it enters a king's heart
   B. when it mixes with the king's grace
   C. when it is seasoned with justice
   D. when mercy seasons a king's justice
4. What shows the temporal power of a monarch?
   A. his throne B. his mercy
   C. sceptre D. his crown
5. The word 'attribute' means
   A. quantity B. quality
   C. absolute D. feature

POEM-19

Whose *woods* these are I think I know,
His house is in the village thought,
He will not see me stopping here
To watch his woods fill up with snow.
My little horse must think it *queer*
To stop without a farmhouse near
Between the woods and frozen lake
The darkest evening of the year.
He gives his *harness bells* a shake
To ask if there is some mistake.
The only other sound's the sweep
Of easy wind and *downy flake.*
The woods are lovely; dark and deep,
But I have promises to keep,
And miles to go before I sleep,
And miles to go before I sleep.

QUESTIONS

1. The poet is standing
A. in a village
B. on the bank of a river
C. in a forest
D. by the side of a lake

2. When the poet stands, the horse
A. shakes its harness bells
B. shakes the bells
C. stands silently
D. asks a question

3. What kind of a weather is it?
A. wet and cloudy
B. cold and snowy
C. very cold and windy
D. cold and windy

4. '... before I sleep' means here
A. before I sleep on my bed
B. before I die
C. before I go home and sleep
D. before I 'sleep' at one level and before I 'die' at another

5. The words 'downy flake' mean
A. soft particles of snow
B. soft snow
C. fluffy snow
D. soft and fluffy

POEM-20

The little creature
with a hundred feet
was on its journey
to where
only it knew.
My civilised foot
dressed in polished leather
came down upon it
even so gently
there was only a soft sound
signifying
the end
of a creature of God
my Maker
I looked to see
if my *sole* was *spoiled*
and walked away

QUESTIONS

1. '... with a hundred feet' actually means
A. a hundred feet
B. many feet
C. about a hundred feet
D. near about a hundred feet

2. The poet calls his foot 'civilised' because he
A. means it otherwise
B. is civilised
C. is wearing polished shoes
D. looks civilised

3. This poem can be classified as
A. humorous B. religious
C. satirical D. romantic

4. The poet walked away. It means he
A. didn't bother about the death of the centipede
B. remained indifferent towards the centipede's death
C. regetted the centipede's death
D. felt pity for the insect

5. The word 'signifying' here means
A. displacing
B. indicating
C. making it important
D. proving

POEM-21

I take it you already know
Of tough and bough and cough and dough?
On hiccough, thorough, laugh and through?
Well done! And now you wish perhaps.
To learn of these familiar traps?

Beware of heard, a dreadful word,
That looks like beard and sounds like bird,
And dead : it's said like bed, not bead
For goodness'sake, don't call it deed!
Watch out for meat and great and threat,
They rhyme with suite and straight and debt.
A moth is not a moth in mother
Nor both in bother, broth in brother,
And here is not a match for there,
Now dear and fear for bear and pear,
And then there's does and rose and lose—
Just look them up and goose and choose,...

QUESTIONS

1. Below is a summary of the poem. Complete it by writing the missing word/phrase against the correct blank numbers.

   The poet is talking about the (*i*) __________ of words in English. He concludes that the reader knows how to say certain words and wants to learn the familiar words in the language. He takes up words like 'heard'; 'dead' 'meat'; great; and (*ii*) __________ in the same way. He points out that the word 'moth' is said in the same way in (*iii*) __________ and (*iv*) __________ does not match the sound of there. Finally he asks the reader to look up (*v*) __________.

2. On the basis of your reading the poem, fill in the pronunciations mentioned, against the blank. Write your answers against the correct blank numbers.

   (*i*) __________ is pronounced as in bed broth is not pronunced as in (*ii*) __________. While dear and fear sound as __________.

POEM-22

Will no one tell me what she sings?
Perhaps the plaintive numbers flow
For old, unhappy, far-off things,
And battles long ago:
Or is it some more humble lay,
Familiar matter of to-day?
Some natural sorrow, loss, or pain,
That has been, and may be again?

—William Wordsworth

QUESTIONS

1. Why does the poet seem to be so much puzzled?
2. What type of song is the girl singing according to the poet?
3. About what can the girl's song be?
4. What is the rhyme scheme of the given lines?
5. Do you think the poet really enjoyed the girl's song even if he couldn't understand it?
6. What title would you like to give to poet's such enjoyment of a song without its dialect and theme?

POEM-23

Death be not proud, though some have called thee
Mighty and dreadfull, for, thou art not soe,
For, those, whom thou think'st, thou dost overthrow,
Die not, poore death, nor yet canst thou kill mee;
From rest and sleepe, which but thy pictures bee,
Much pleasure, then from thee, much more must flow,
And soonest our best men with thee doe goe,
Rest of their bones, and soules deliverie.
Thou art slave to Fate, chance, kings, and desperate men,
And dost with poyson, warre, and sicknesse dwell,
And poppie, or charmes can make us sleepe as well,
And better than thy stroake; why swell'st thou then?

One short sleepe past, wee wake enternally,
And death shall be no more, Death thou shalt die.

—*John Donne*

QUESTIONS

1. What have some called death?
2. Why does the poet say that those whom death claims to kill, actually do not die?
3. What are the pictures of death?
4. To whom is death a slave?
5. With whom does death dwell?
6. How does a person seem to die?

POEM-24

I am silver and exact. I have no preconceptions.
Whatever I see I swallow immediately
Just as it is, unmisted by love or dislike.
I am not cruel, only truthful.
The eye of a little god, four-cornered.
Most of the time I meditatie on the opposite wall.
It is pink, with speckles. I have looked at it so long.
I think it is a part of my heart. But it flickers.
Faces and darkness separate us over and over.
Now I am a lake. A woman bends over me,
Searching my reaches for what she really is.
Then she turns to those liars, the candles or the moon.
I see her back, and reflect it faithfully.
She rewards me with tears and an agitation of hands.
I am important to her. She comes and goes.
Each morning it is her face that replaces the darkness.
In me she has drowned a young girl, and in me an old woman
Rises toward her day after day like a terrible fish.

Directions : *Read the given lines of poem in each question-set and answer the questions that follow.*

1

I am silver and exact. I have no preconceptions.
Whatever I see I swallow immediately
Just as it is, unmisted by love or dislike.

Multiple Choice Questions

Q.1. The poetic device used in these lines is
A. Simile
B. Metaphor
C. Irony
D. Personification

Ans. D. Personification

Q.2. 'I am silver and exact' means
A. I stand for truth only
B. I am only truthful
C. I am like a silver
D. I am precious like silver

Ans. B. I am only truthful

Q.3. 'I have no preconceptions' means
A. I have no pre-thoughts
B. I am not biased
C. I stand for nobody
D. I am myself

Ans. A. I have no pre-thoughts

Comprehension Questions

Q.1. Explain : 'I have no preconceptions'.

Ans. It means that the mirror has no pre-thoughts or biased attitude about anything. It is simply exact, truthful and only truthful and nothing else.

Q.2. Which figure of speech is used in 'I swallow'?

Ans. It is 'personification'.

Q.3. Who is the speaker?

Ans. The speaker is the mirror.

2

I am not cruel, only truthful.
The eye of a little god, four-cornered.

Multiple Choice Questions

Q.1. The poetic device used in these lines is
A. Personification B. Metaphor
C. Alliteration D. Simile

Ans. A. Personification

Q.2. 'I am not cruel ......' means
A. I am not mercy
B. I have the capacity to pity
C. I am pitiless
D. I am not indifferent

Ans. B. I have the capacity to pity

Q.3. 'The eye of a little god' means
A. the speaker acts like a god
B. the speaker can be a god
C. the mirror sees things like a little god
D. the god's presence

Ans. C. the mirror sees things like a little god

Comprehension Questions

Q.1. Who does the 'I' refer to?

Ans. 'I' refers to the mirror.

Q.2. Do you think that the mirror is cruel?

Ans. No, the mirror is not cruel but it is only truthful and reflects what it sees.

Q.3. Why has the mirror been called a 'four-cornered god'?

Ans. It has been called so because like a god it watches one fairly. Also it watches one without any preeconceptions.

3

Most of the time I meditate on the opposite wall.
It is pink, with speckles. I have looked at it so long.
I think it is a part of my heart. But it flickers.
Faces and darkness separate us over and over.

Multiple Choice Questions

Q.1. 'It is pink, with speckles' stands for
A. the mirror B. the wall
C. the woman D. the housekeeper

Ans. B. the wall

Q.2. The mirror doesn't meditate actually but
A. is fixed on the wall
B. has become a part of the wall
C. is shown as meditating impliedly
D. looks at things

Ans. C. is shown as meditating impliedly

Q.3. 'Faces and darkness' separate the mirror from
A. the other wall B. the lady
C. the little girl D. the housewife

Ans. A. the other wall

Comprehension Questions

Q.1. How does 'I' meditate on the opposite wall?

Ans. 'I', the mirror, is fixed permanently on the wall. So it rests there day and night and it seems that to be in this state it is involved in deep thinking.

Q.2. How has the wall become a part of the speaker?

Ans. The wall and mirror have become a single thing because the mirror has been fixed permanently on it.

Q.3. Explain : 'But it flickers'.

Ans. By 'it' the mirror means the wall on which the mirror has been fixed. When it moves from this to that side, it shows the wall shaking showing that it flickers it.

4

Now I am a lake. A woman bends over me,
Searching my reaches for what she really is.
Then she turns to those liars, the candles or the moon.
I see her back, and reflect it faithfully.

Multiple Choice Questions

Q.1. The mirror is 'a lake' as it
A. is deep and acts like it
B. reflects the objects and is deep
C. shows the objects
D. reflects the water

Ans. B. reflects the objects and is deep

Q.2. The woman looking at the mirror searches for
A. her beauty that once she had
B. her own identity
C. the reflection of the wall
D. her own body

Ans. A. her beauty that once she had

Q.3. 'The candles or the moon' stand for
A. objects giving out dim light
B. objects showing the beauty of things
C. objects seen by the woman
D. those things that enhance beauty.

Ans. A. objects giving out dim light

Comprehension Questions

Q.1. How is the mirror 'a lake'?

Ans. The mirror is 'a lake' in its action. When the old woman looks at her face into the mirror, she is amazed to look at her old face. She moves this or that way to see her youthful face that she once had. But it has now 'swallowed' or 'drowned' that face.

Q.2. How does the woman behave before the mirror?

Ans. The woman is wonderstruck to see that now she has grown old and she doesn't want to see it. So she searches the mirror to see her young face with the help of the candle or moonlight.

Q.3. How are 'candles or the moon' liars?

Ans. 'Candles and the moon' are liars in the sense that in their misted light the woman can't see her old age. Besides, they help the woman in hiding the wrinkles etc, from her face in the mirror.

5

She rewards me with tears and an agitation of hands.
I am important to her. She comes and goes.
Each morning it is her face that replaces the darkness.

Multiple Choice Questions

Q.1. 'She' here is
A. the woman who looks into the mirror
B. the house owner
C. the young girl
D. the old woman

Ans. A. the woman who looks into the mirror

Q.2. 'She' is in tears over
A. her lost youthfulness
B. her lost youth and her helplessness in it
C. her growing mature
D. her loss of strength

Ans. B. her lost youth and her helplessness in it

Q.3. The mirror is important to her because
A. by it she can look at her face
B. she can see her figure in it
C. she can evaluate her beauty and appearance
D. it can tell how she looks

Ans. C. she can evaluate her beauty and appearance

Comprehension Questions

Q.1. Who is the speaker here and who is 'She'?

Ans. The mirror is the speaker here. 'She' is the woman who looks at her reflection in it.

Q.2. Why does she come there often?

Ans. She comes there often to see her face reflected in the mirror.

Q.3. What is her reaction on seeing her image?

Ans. Her reaction is of showing her sadness at her growing old. Once she was beautiful and young. Now she has grown old and tries to see that reflection of a beautiful woman that once she was.

6

In me she has drowned a young girl, and in me an old woman

Rises toward her day after day like a terrible fish.

Multiple Choice Questions

Q.1. 'In me she has drowned a young girl' means
A. she was once beautiful
B. once she had a girl-like figure
C. once she looked like a girl
D. a young girl in her has become a woman

Ans. D. a young girl in her has become a woman

Q.2. The mirror shows that the young girl has now become
A. an old woman
B. a woman
C. a mature lady
D. the owner of the house

Ans. A. an old woman

Q.3. The old woman looking at the mirror behaves like a terrible fish. It means she is angry at
A. her growing mature
B. her becoming old
C. her losing beauty
D. her becoming wrinkled

Ans. C. her losing beauty

Comprehension Questions

Q.1. Who is 'me' here?

Ans. 'Me' here is the mirror.

Q.2. Who are 'a young girl' and 'an old woman'?

Ans. 'A young girl' and 'an old woman' are the same woman who in her young age was a young girl. But now she has become old.

Q.3. How is she 'a terrible fish'?

Ans. She behaves like 'a terrible fish' because she is now old, always wanted to be 'young'. Now that she is actually old, she agitates her hands in anger and sadness at her age.

Textual Questions

Q.1. On the basis of your understanding of the poem, answer the following questions by ticking the correct choice.

(*i*) When the mirror is being described as being 'unmisted by love or dislike' we understand that the mirror is
A. not misted B. nor prejudiced
C. four angles D. silver in colour

Ans. B. not prejudiced

(*ii*) The other word for 'contemplation' is ......
A. contempt B. meditation
C. mediation D. thoughtful

Ans. B. meditation

(*iii*) When the mirror says 'it has no preconceptions' it means that :
A. it reflects back an image objectively
B. it modifies an image as it reflects it
C. it beautifies an image as it reflects it
D. it gives a biased view of a person/ object

Ans. A. it reflects back an image objectivley

(*iv*) The mirror has been called 'a four-cornered god' because :
A. it is square shaped
B. like God it watches you unbiased and fair from all four angles
C. it reflects back all that it sees
D. it never stops reflecting

Ans. B. like God it watches you unbiased and fair from all four angles

(*v*) The 'speckles' refer to :
A. a pink object
B. the opposite wall which has spots on it
C. a person with pink pimples
D. pink spots in general

Ans. D. pink spots in general

(*vi*) The phrase 'agitation of the hand' suggests that the person is :
A. very ill B. very upset
C. very angry D. very happy

Ans. B. very upset

(*vii*) By saying 'Now I am a lake' the narrator wants to show that

A. the poem is not only about external beauty but also the inside of a person

B. the lake can also reflect surfaces

C. the depth of the lake is important

D. the lake does not show as exact an image as a mirror.

Ans. A. the poem is not only about external beauty but also the inside of a person.

Q.2. Answer the following questions briefly.

(*i*) What is the poetic device used when the mirror says 'I swallow'?

Ans. The poetic device used in it is 'personification'. The mirror is shown as a human being which he is not. 'Swallow' shows the use of 'metaphor' in it.

(*ii*) How does the mirror usually pass its time?

Ans. It passes its time 'meditating', or 'contemplating'.

(*iii*) What distrubs the mirror's contemplation of the opposite wall?

Ans. What disturbs the mirror is the opposite wall that has been painted pink.

(*iv*) Why does the mirror appear to be a lake in the second stanza? What aspect of the mirror do you think is being referred to here?

Ans. The mirror appears to be a lake in the second stanza because like the lake it reflects back the images objectively. The dispassionate and objective reflection of the mirror is intensified in it.

(*v*) What is the woman searching for in the depths of the lake?

Ans. The woman is searching for the beauty of her face in the depths of the lake. Once she was beautiful but now she has grown old and is not what she was earlier. Now she doesn't want to see her old face. So she searches for her old face of her youthful days.

(*vi*) How does the narrator convey the fact that the woman looking at her reflection in the lake is deeply distressed?

Ans. The narrator conveys the fact that the woman looking at her reflection in the lake is deeply distressed by showing her agitating hands. Secondly, she weeps and behaves like 'a terrible fish'.

(*vii*) What makes the woman start crying?

Ans. The wrinkled old face without beauty makes the woman start crying. She wanted to see her face always youthful. But now it is not so as she has grown old.

(*viii*) What do you think the 'terrible fish' in the last line symbolizes? What is the poetic device used here?

Ans. The 'terrible fish' symbolizes the woman agitating at the loss of her youthful beauty. She is now old and behaves like 'a terrible fish' at the loss of her youth. The poetic device used here is 'simile'.

Q.3. Find the various instances of personification used in this poem.

Ans. Various instances of personification :

1. I am silver—as a human being
2. I am the eye of a little god—as a god
3. I am 'a part' of the wall—now a wall
4. 'Now I am a lake'—as a lake.

Brief Answer Type Questions

Q.1. How is the mirror *'exact'* and *'only truthful'*?

Ans. The Mirror is the speaker in this poem and says that it is 'silver and exact' and has no preconceptions. It is just 'truthful' and not less or not more than that. Nor is it affected by love, dislike or any other human emotion. It tells how the woman reacts to her reflection when she looks into it. She searches for what she once was. She has wrinkles and she looks for hiding these truthfully and exactly.

Q.2. Give out the theme of the poem *"Mirror"*.

Ans. The theme of the poem "Mirror" is clear. It is that there is always a change in everything. It is, therefore, the principle of life and every one must understand it. One must not create false ego or illusions as these will never stand permanent. Everything shall change. The woman who looks into the mirror behaves like a terrible fish because she wants to be beautiful always. But it is against the law of nature. Everyone should be like the mirror-exact, truthful and without any previous conceptions.

Q.3. How is the mirror *'the eye of a little god'* and *'a lake'*?

Ans. The mirror is described as 'the eye of a little god' as it is impartial and truthful like a little god. Its judgement is not misled by love or dislike. Like god, it gives a true reflection of the objects that appear before it.

The mirror is also a 'lake' in its action. A woman looks into the mirror. She moves this way or that way to see her face more intently as she wants to see her young face. However, she agitates at her growing old age.

Q.4. Describe the symbolic significance of the comparison between the woman and the terrible fish as given in *'Mirror'*.

Ans. The woman given in the poem was once beautiful. But now she has grown old and her face is getting wrinkled. As the age has grown she had not changed mentally as she still wished to be beautiful as earlier she was. So when she has to face the reality of her fading beauty, she agitates. She cries and cries and hunts for some dim light which might hide her wrinkles. So she looks for the candlelight and the moonlight which may not show her withering face clearly. Thus the symbolic camparison is apt.

Essay Type Questions

1. What do you mean by *'Personification'*? How is *'Mirror'* an example of personification?

Ans. 'Personification' means 'personifying' a thing, an object or some non-living thing with human-like qualities. It makes that thing like a human thing. It also means to make a non-living thing invested with the qualities of living human beings. For this 'Mirror' is a beautiful example of 'personification'. The Mirror assumes the personality of a living human being and becomes itself the speaker. It behaves like a human being and describes itself like him. It tells what it is and where it lives. It also tells what are the reactions of the woman who looks into it. It 'sees', 'swallows', 'meditates', 'thinks', 'is a lake', etc. All these things are had by the human beings. The Mirror relates how it looks at things occuring before it. It doesn't add anything from its side. It beautifully describes the emotions and reactions of the woman who looks into it and behaves like a terrible fish. It doesn't add anything about itself except the truth. It is only truthful.

2. Describe the feeling of the woman as she looks into the mirror.

Ans. The mirror beautifully records the actions and reactions of the woman who looks into it. The woman was once very beautiful. It was in her youth. But now she has grown old. But she has wanted to be beautiful always. She had thought that she would always look young and beautiful. She never thought that time brings a change. Any one born shall degenerate and die one day. Beauty is of the mind and physical beauty shall degenerate one day. However, she is not so now and wants to be beautiful. She turns to 'the candles or the moon'. These dim her face so that the wrinkles are hidden and she looks beautiful. The mirror has shown her grow into an old woman from a young girl as it is truthful only.

3. *"In one she has drowned a young girl"*. Why does the mirror say this?

Ans. The mirror says this because the woman seeing at her face into the mirror was once a pretty young girl. She had thought that she would always look young and beautiful. She never thought that time brings a change. Any one born shall degenerate and die one day. Beauty is of the mind and physical beauty shall degenerate one day. Now this 'girl' is growing into an old woman. She has lost her youthful beauty but she wants to be always beautiful. She turns to candles and the moon. These become 'liars' because they help to hide the wrinkles by adding their lights on her face. The mirror reflects the woman's face truthfully which is growing old. But she behaves like a terrible fish because of her growing old. She in her old age doesn't want to face the reality of life. She has always desired to look young. But the mirror can't help her at all. It shows her what she is at present. It doesn't tell a lie. It is the woman who herself is responsible for this kind of sadness and depression. She must know the truth of life.

POEM-25

Not marble, nor the gilded monuments
Of princes, shall outlive this powerful rhyme;
But you shall shine more bright in these contents
Than unswept stone, besmear'd with sluttish time.
When wasteful was shall statues overturn,
And broils root out the work of masonry,
Nor Mars his sword nor war's quick fire shal burn
The living record of your memory.
'Gainst death and all oblivious enmity
Shall you pace forth; your praise shall still find room,
Even in the eyes of all posterity
That wear this world out to the ending doom.
So, till the judgment that yourself arise,
You live in this, and dwell in lover's eyes.

Directions : *Read the given lines of poem in each question-set and answer the questions that follow.*

1

Not marble, nor the gilded monuments
Of princes, shall outlive this powerful rhyme;
But you shall shine more bright in these contents
Than unswept stone, besmear'd with sluttish time.

Multiple Choice Questions

Q.1. 'This powerful rhyme' here is
A. the rhyme scheme
B. music of the sonnet
C. this very sonnet
D. rhyme having power

Ans. C. this very sonnet

Q.2. 'You shall shine more bright in these contents' means
A. the poet's beloved will shine like a star
B. the poet's beloved shall shine brightly in this sonnet
C. the poet's beloved shall shine more than the monuments
D. the poet's beloved shall be like a star

Ans. B. the poet's beloved shall shine brightly in this sonnet

Q.3. 'Time' here has been personified to
A. give more meaning
B. show its supreme power
C. compare with a slut
D. elaborate the idea of immortality

Ans. B. show its supreme power

Comprehension Questions

Q.1. Why are monuments made?

Ans. Monuments are made by princes, kings etc, to perpetuate their memories till posterity.

Q.2. Who is 'you' in the third line here? How will 'you' shine?

Ans. 'You' here is the poet's beloved or friend. His beloved or friend shall shine more brightly than these monuments.

Q.3. Why has time been called 'sluttish'?

Ans. Time has called 'sluttish' because it spoils these monuments like a slut spoils her virtue.

2

When wasteful was shall statues overturn,
And broils root out the work of masonry,
Nor Mars his sword nor war's quick fire shall burn
The living record of your memory.

Multiple Choice Questions

Q.1. The war has been described as 'wasteful' because it

A. destroys everything
B. destroys the monuments
C. doesn't let anything live
D. spoils everything

Ans. A. destroys everything

Q.2. The work of masonry here is

A. historical buildings
B. old buildings now neglected
C. monuments built in memory of princes etc
D. what is rooted out by wars

Ans. C. monuments built in memory of princes etc

Q.3. The poet's beloved has been immortalised here in the form of

A. art
B. literature
C. this sonnet
D. books

Ans. C. this sonnet

Comprehension Questions

Q.1. What do the wars and fights do to the monuments?

Ans. The wars and fights destroy the monuments.

Q.2. How is Mars recognised? Why has it been referred to here?

Ans. Mars is recognised by his sword. It has been referred to here because of its capacity to destroy everthing.

Q.3. How has the poet's beloved been described here?

Ans. The poet's beloved has been described as a living record in the form of this sonnet.

3

'Gainst death and all oblivious enmity
Shall you pace forth; your praise shall still find room,
Even in the eyes of all posterity
That wear this world out to the ending doom.

Multiple Choice Questions

Q.1. What will pace forth against death and enmity?

A. poet's beloved
B. living memory of poet's beloved
C. this sonnet
D. poet's beloved's memory

Ans. B. living memory of poet's beloved

Q.2. Till when shall the 'praise' live?

A. till next generations
B. till the doomsday
C. till the beloved lives
D. till the edge of ending doom

Ans. D. till the edge of ending doom

Q.3. The poet through this sonnet wants to prove that

A. time is all powerful
B. his beloved is immortal
C. his beloved shall live till the end
D. all has to die soon

Ans. B. his beloved is immortal

Comprehension Questions

Q.1. Which kind of enmity is it?

Ans. The enmity mentioned here is that enmity which forgets everything and seeks to destroy everything.

Q.2. How does the poet immortalise his beloved's memory here?

Ans. The poet immortalizes his beloved's memory by saying that it will find some space even in the eyes of posterity.

Q.3. What will happen to the world when the poet's beloved's praise shall face it?

Ans. The world will be outlived by the beloved's praise even to the edge of doom.

4

So, till the judgment that yourself arise,
You live in this, and dwell in lover's eyes.

Multiple Choice Questions

Q.1. The poet expects that his beloved shall arise

A. till the judgment
B. even after the judgment day
C. when God will command
D. when she will be examined in her actions.

Ans. B. even after the judgment day

Q.2. 'You live in this' means

A. you shall live in this world
B. you shall live in your lover's eyes
C. you shall live for ever
D. you shall never die

Ans. A. you shall live in this world

Q.3. The poet through this sonnet immortalises

A. time
B. wars
C. his friend
D. his beloved

Ans. D. his beloved

Comprehension Questions

Q.1. Till when will the poet's beloved live?

Ans. The poet's beloved will live till the judgement day.

Q.2. Explain '...till the judgment'.

Ans. 'Till the judgment' means the poet's beloved shall live till the judgement day. On the judgement day, it is believed, one's good and bad deeds are examined and one gets reward or punishment from God accordingly.

Q.3. How does the poet look at his beloved when he calls her 'you live in this...'?

Ans. The poet looks at his beloved as a personified being, that is, human being, though till now she has been living in his memory only.

Textual Questions

Q.1. On the basis of your understanding of Shakespeare's sonnet, answer the following questions by ticking the correct options.

(*i*) The rich and powerful get ornate monuments made in order to ______

A. show off their wealth
B. display their power
C. show their artistic talent
D. be remembered till posterity

Ans. D. be remembered till posterity

(*ii*) The poet addresses his sonnet to ______.

A. time
B. war
C. the person he loves
D. powerful rulers

Ans. C. the person he loves

(*iii*) In the line 'The living record of your memory', living record refers to ______

A. the sonnet the poet has written for his friend
B. an existing statue of his friend
C. his friend who lives in the poet's memory
D. the autobiography of the poet's friend

Ans. C. his friend who lives in the poet's memory

(iv) The poet's tone in the poem is ______
A. despairing
B. optimistic
C. loving
D. admiring

Ans. C. loving

(v) The poem is set in ______
A. the place where the poet meets his friend
B. a battlefield where Mars is fighting a battle
C. a city ravaged by war
D. the poet's study where he is writing.

Ans. D. the poet's study where he is writing.

Q.2. Answer the following questions briefly.

(i) Why do you think the rich and powerful people get monuments and statues erected in their memory?

Ans. The rich and powerful people get monuments and statues erected in their memory for being remembered till posterity.

(ii) Describe how the monuments and statues brave the ravages of time.

Ans. The monuments and statues brave the ravages of time. In doing so they get spoiled, disfigured and broken, if they are not taken care of.

(iii) Why does the poet refer to Time as being sluttish?

Ans. The poet refers to Time as being sluttish because Time spoils the marbled or gilded monuments. It discolours them, breaks them or makes them dirty through its agencies. These agencies are like air, rain, natural vegetation etc.

(iv) The poet says that neither forces of nature nor wars can destroy his poetry. In fact, even godly powers of Mars will not have a devastating effect on his rhyme. What quality of the poet is revealed through these lines?

Ans. The quality of the poet is clearly revealed through these lines. It is the immortality of his verse and the permanence of his poetic or literary art. It is true that like Time or Nature, literary art is also permanent and immortal. That's why, we have poets and artists through their works who had lived thousands of years before.

Brief Answer Type Questions

1. How according to the poet, will his beloved outlive monuments and time?

Ans. According to the poet, his beloved being in this sonnet shall outlive the marbled and gilded monuments built by princes etc. These monuments spoiled by time shall not out-live her being in this sonnet.

2. How does the poet call his beloved in the second quatrain? What will not affect her in it? What is her present status?

Ans. The poet calls his beloved 'the living record of your memory'. Wasteful wars, fights, Mars' sword and war's quick fire shall not be able to burn this 'memory' of his beloved. So she is immortal in being in this sonnet.

3. How will the poet's beloved sustain herself against death etc?

Ans. The poet's beloved shall walk forth against death and all oblivious enmity which is forgetful of everything and seeks to destroy everthing. Her praise shall be there in all posterity. She will wear out this world to the ending doom.

4. How does the poet immortalize his beloved?

Ans. The poet immortalizes his beloved by stating that his beloved shall ever live in this sonnet and in the eyes of posterity. Also she will wear out this world till the judgement day and shall outlive it. In this way, she will be immortal.

5. What is the moral of the poem *'Not Marble, nor the Gilded Monuments'*?

Ans. The moral of the poem is that literary art is not affected by time, though marbled and gilded monuments are. They are ravaged by time but it will have no effect on his beloved who is a living record in this sonnet. Time is shown a great leveller and destroyer here.

Essay Type Questions

1. How does the poet describe his beloved in this poem?

Ans. The poet describes his beloved or friend in this poem beautifully. He says that princes, kings etc, build marbled and gilded monnuments to perpetuate their memories. But wars, fights and time destroy them. But his beloved has been immortalized in this sonnet. These monuments shall not outlive 'this powerful rhyme'. On the other hand, his beloved being so will shine more brightly than these monuments spoiled by sluttish time. Wasteful wars, fights and even Mars' sword or war's quick fire shall not destroy her living memory in this sonnet. His beloved shall pace forth agaisnt death and enmity. She will live in the eyes of all posterity and wear out this world to the ending doom. This way she shall always live in this sonnet and dwell in her lover's eyes.

2. As a reader of *'Not Marble, nor the Gilded Monuments'* write out what you learn about the poet's beloved.

Ans. After reading *'Not Marble, nor the Gilded Monuments'* I learn that the poet has immortalized his beloved or friend through this poem. He says that his beloved or friend lies immortalized in 'this powerful rhyme'. She has become a living memory in this literary art. Marbled or gilded monuments of princes etc, shall not outlive her. Nor will these and sluttish time affect her immortality. Wars and fights destroy even the most beautiful works of masonry. But these will not affect her. Mars sword or war's quick fire will not burn this living record in this sonnet. On the other hand, his beloved shall walk against death and enmity. Her praise shall find a place in the eyes of all posterity. This all will wear this world out even to the ending doom. Thus his beloved shall arise even after the judgement day. She shall ever live in this sonnet and consequently in her lover's eyes.

POEM-26

I met a traveller from an antique land
Who said : Two vast and trunkless legs of stone
Stand in the desert. Near them, on the sand,
Half sunk, a shattered visage lies,
whose frown,
And wrinkled lip, and sneer of cold command,
Tell that its sculptor well those passions read
Which yet survive, stamped on these lifeless things,
The hand that mocked them, and the heart that fed ;
And on the pedestal these words appear :
"My name is Ozymandias, king of kings :
Look upon my works, ye Mighty, and despair!"
Nothing beside remains. Round the decay
Of that colossal wreck, boundless and bare
The lone and level sands stretch far away.

Directions : *Read the given lines of poem in each question-set and answer the questions that follow.*

1

I met a traveller from an antique land
Who said : Two vast and trunkless legs of stone
Stand in the desert. Near them, on the sand,
Half sunk, a shattered visage lies,

Multiple Choice Questions

Q.1. When did the narrator meet the traveller?

A. after they had gone to the ancient land

B. after the traveller had visited the ancient land

C. when the traveller was coming from the ancient land

D. when they met in the ancient land

Ans. B. after the traveller had visited the ancient land

Q.2. What had happened to the trunk of the statue?

A. It had fallen down

B. Time had claimed it

C. The wind had swept it

D. The desert had claimed it

Ans. B. Time had claimed it

Q.3. How did the human face look?

A. broken and shattered

B. half sunk

C. in pieces

D. separate from the body

Ans. A. broken and shattered

Comprehension Questions

Q.1. Where has the traveller travelled?

Ans. The traveller has travelled the ancient land.

Q.2. What kind of statue is it that the traveller sees?

Ans. The human statue is vast and big but the trunk of this statue has broken.

Q.3. What has become of the human face?

Ans. The human face is broken and has fallen though the legs still stand.

2

whose frown,
And wrinkled lip, and sneer of cold command,
Tell that its sculptor well those passions read

Multiple Choice Questions

Q.1. '...... whose frown' was it?

A. traveller's | B. narrator's

C. sculptor's | D. Ozymandias's

Ans. D. Ozymandias's

Q.2. What suggested that Ozymandias was a cruel and dictatorial ruler?

A. his wrinkled lip

B. his sneer of cold command

C. his wrinkled visage

D. his shattered face

Ans. B. his sneer of cold command

Q.3. What does the statue of Ozymandias tell about the sculptor?

A. that he was a great sculptor

B. that he was very intelligent

C. that he had beautifully carved Ozymandias's face

D. that he was a real sculptor

Ans. A. that he was a great sculptor

Comprehension Questions

Q.1. What lies in the sands and how?

Ans. A broken human face lies half sunk in the sands.

Q.2. How does the shattered visage look?

Ans. The 'shattered visage' looks very cruel and pitiless with a 'wrinkled lip' and sneer of cold command.

Q.3. What does the face tell of the sculptor?

Ans. The face tells that the sculptor was a great artist and imitated well the real expressions of the king's face in stone.

3

Which yet survive, stamped on these lifeless things,
The hand that mocked them, and the heart that fed ;

Multiple Choice Questions

Q.1. What is 'which' here in the first line?
A. sneer of cold command
B. wrinkled lip
C. passions of the king
D. feelings of Ozymandias

Ans. C. passions of the king

Q.2. The 'hand that mocked ......'. Whose 'hand'?
A. Ozymandias's B. king's
C. sculptor's D. narrator's

Ans. C. sculptor's

Q.3. What did the 'hand' do?
A. It sculpted the expressions of the king.
B. It made fun of Ozymandias by sculpting him as such.
C. It laughed at the king's passions.
D. It ridiculed the king.

Ans. B. It made fun of Ozymandias by sculpting him as such.

Comprehension Questions

Q.1. Which things of the king survive still?

Ans. Two legs and broken human face with its expressions survive still.

Q.2. What are 'these lifeless things'?

Ans. 'These lifeless things' are two vast legs, broken human face with its expression and the sculptor's art.

Q.3. What did the sculptor actually do in sculpting the king's statue?

Ans. The sculptor actually showed his real art in carving the true and genunine feelings of the king in stone.

4

And on the pedestal these words appear :
"My name is Ozymandias, king of kings :
Look upon my works, ye Mighty, and despair!"

Multiple Choice Questions

Q.1. 'My name is Ozymandias, king of kings' shows the
A. despair of the king
B. despair of the king and repentance of his pride
C. uselessness of sneer, frown and hatred
D. futility of life

Ans. B. despair of the king and repentance of his pride

Q.2. The king asks the readers to 'despair' because
A. life is as such
B. pride, arrogance and contempt lead one nowhere
C. time is a great healer
D. time levels all

Ans. B. pride, arrogance and contempt lead one nowhere

Q.3. The poem conveys the moral that
A. pride and sneer are useless emotions
B. one should recognize the power of time
C. pride and cold command take one nowhere
D. pride hath a fall.

Ans. A. pride and sneer are useless emotions

Comprehension Questions

Q.1. What has become of the statue of Ozymandias?

Ans. The statue of Ozymandias was in ruins because of the claim of time on it.

Q.2. What is the underlying thought of the writing on the pedestal?

Ans. The underlying thought of the writing is that time claims everything howsoever powerful it may be. Once Ozymandias was a king of kings but now his statue tells his worth.

Q.3. Why one looking upon Ozymandias's work should despair?

Ans. One should despair that time is all powerful. Even the sneer and cold command are nothing before it. Secondly, these passions are meaningless.

5

Nothing beside remains. Round the decay
Of that colossal wreck, boundless and bare
The lone and level sands stretch far away.

Multiple Choice Questions

Q.1. 'Nothing beside remains'. 'Beside what'?
A. two vast and trunkless legs
B. two vast and trunkless legs and shattered visage
C. sneer of cold command
D. sands

Ans. B. two vast and trunkless legs and shattered visage

Q.2. 'Boundless and bare' symbolise
A. the vastness of sands
B. limitless sand stretches meaning death
C. sands
D. destruction

Ans. B. limitless sand stretches meaning death

Q.3. The last line here refers to
A. nature
B. the capacity of sand to destroy everything
C. the total destruction of things by nature and time
D. the capacity of time to destroy all things.

Ans. C. the total destruction of things by nature and time

Comprehension Questions

Q.1. What does the broken statue symbolise?

Ans. The broken statue symbolises the futility of pride and command and the great power of time.

Q.2. What is the intention of the poet here?

Ans. The poet's intention is clear. He means to say that pride, command and cruelty are nothing before good human values. Time is all powerful.

Q.3. What do the 'colossal wreck' and 'sands' symbolise?

Ans. The 'colossal wreck' and 'sands' symbolise the nature's and time's all pervading power.

Textual Questions

1. Answer the following questions by ticking the correct options.

(*i*) The poem is set in ________
A. the wilderness B. an ancient land
C. a palace D. a desert

Ans. D. a desert

(*ii*) The expression on the face of the statue is one of ________
A. admiration B. anger
C. despair D. contempt

Ans. D. contempt

(*iii*) This poem throws light on the ________ nature of Ozymandias.
A. cruel B. arrogant
C. boastful D. aggressive

Ans. B. arrogant

(*iv*) The sculptor was able to understand Ozymandias' ________
A. words B. expression
C. feelings D. ambition

Ans. C. feelings

(*v*) The tone of the poem is ________
A. mocking B. nostalgic
C. gloomy D. gloating

Ans. A. mocking

2. Answer the following questions briefly.

(*i*) "The hand that mocked them, and the heart that fed." Whose hand and heart has the poet referred to in this line?

Ans. The poet has referred to the hand of the sculptor and the heart of the king Ozymandias.

(*ii*) "My name is Ozymandias, king of kings:" Why does Ozymandias refer to himself as King of Kings? What quality of the king is revealed through this statement?

Ans. Ozymandias refers to himself the king of kings out of sneer, arrogance, haughtiness and contempt for other kings. It is so as he heads them all in these qualities.

(*iii*) "Look on my works, ye Mighty, and despair!" Who is Ozymandias referring to when he speaks of ye Mighty? Why should they despair?

Ans. He is referring to the mighty kings. They should despair at seeing the end of his haughtiness, contempt, pride, arrogance and cruelty.

(*iv*) Bring out the irony in the poem.

Ans. The irony in the poem is that it shows the arrogance, haughtiness, contempt and cruelty of Ozymandias but what is the result. The broken statue and the vastness of the sands symbolise the uselessness of these emotions.

(*v*) 'Nothing beside remains'. What does the narrator mean when he says these words?

Ans. The narrator means that there is no other thing of the king who once was mighty, powerful, ruthless and cruel.

(*vi*) What is your impression of Ozymandias as a king?

Ans. My impression about Ozymandias is that he was a ruthless and contemptible king. He was stupid also and lacked even an iota of wisdom, farsightedness and humility. He was simply a bundle of cruelty and inhumanness.

(*vii*) What message is conveyed through this poem?

Ans. The message conveyed through the poem is the futility of these qualities of arrogance, sneer and cruelty and all the powerfulness of Time and Nature. These qualities meet an end as it comes to this arrogant king.

Brief Answer Type Questions

1. What did the traveller tell the narrator about what he saw in the ancient land?

Ans. The traveller told the narrator that he travelled to an ancient land. There he saw a strange scene in desert. There he saw two vast and trunkless legs of stone standing in the desert. Near them on the sand there lay half sunk a human face.

2. What kind of expression did the human face have? What did it tell of the sculptor and the human being after whom he had carved that statue?

Ans. The human face had the expression of frown and sneer of cold command. The wrinkled lip indicated the feeling of arrogance. These told indirectly that the sculptor who carved this statue had read those passions of the person whose statue he had carved. He had also mocked these.

3. What was written on the pedestal of the statue? What does it indicate?

Ans. On the pedestal of the statue was written: 'My name is Ozymandias, king of kings: Look upon my works, Ye Mighty, and despair'. It indicates that the king wanted to tell the on-lookers that his works, arrogance, pride, cruelty, brutality etc, proved useless against Time.

4. What else remained there beside the broken statue? What does it signify?

Ans. Beside that broken statue there spread sands and sands far away. The desert was limitless, lonely and levelling. This desert indicates vastness of decay and death which claims everything.

5. What is the message given indirectly in the poem?

Ans. The message of 'Ozymandias' is clear. It is that nothing of human emotions like pride, arrogance, sneer, frown, haughtiness etc, guarantee immortality and permanence against all powerful Time or Nature. The broken statue symbolises the destruction caused by Time. The sands, lone, boundless and bare symbolise the power of the elements.

Essay Type Questions

1. What does the traveller tell the narrator of what he saw in a desert?

Ans. The traveller tells the narrator that he saw in an ancient land a strange spectacle. He saw two vast and trunkless legs of stone standing in the desert. Near them there lay a broken human face. It was half sunk in the sand. It had the expressions of frown, scorn and sneer of cold command. The lip was wrinkled. All these suggested that the sculptor had studied these expressions well and had carved them skilfully in the stone. However he had mocked at these in carving on the stone. On the pedestal of his statue were written the words : My name is Ozymandias, king of kings : Look upon my works and despair. Besides this nothing remained there. However, vast, boundless, bare and lonely and level sands stretched away far and wide.

ANSWERS

I. Cloze Test

Passage-1

1	2	3	4	5	6
A	B	A	C	D	A
7	**8**	**9**	**10**	**11**	**12**
A	B	A	B	C	B
13	**14**				
D	B				

Passage-2

1	2	3	4	5	6
B	B	A	D	B	C
7	**8**	**9**	**10**	**11**	
C	B	A	C	A	

Passage-3

1	2	3	4	5	6
C	D	A	A	B	B
7	**8**	**9**	**10**	**11**	**12**
C	D	B	A	B	C

Passage-4

1	2	3	4	5	6
B	C	A	B	D	C
7	**8**	**9**	**10**	**11**	**12**
B	C	A	D	B	A
13					
D					

Passage-5

1	2	3	4	5	6
D	C	A	B	C	B
7	**8**	**9**	**10**	**11**	**12**
C	D	B	A	D	C

Passage-6

1	2	3	4	5	6
A	B	D	B	A	B
7	**8**	**9**	**10**	**11**	**12**
D	C	D	C	B	B

Passage-7

1	2	3	4	5	6
A	B	D	A	B	C
7	**8**	**9**	**10**	**11**	**12**
D	D	C	D	A	B
13					
D					

Passage-8

1	2	3	4	5	6
C	C	B	A	D	B
7	**8**	**9**	**10**	**11**	**12**
D	D	C	D	A	B

Passage-9

1	2	3	4	5	6
B	B	C	B	D	A

7	8	9	10	11	12
D	A	B	C	D	D

Passage-10

1	2	3	4	5	6
A	D	A	D	D	C
7	8	9	10	11	12
B	B	D	A	A	B

Passage-11

1	2	3	4	5	6
C	B	D	A	B	A
7	8	9	10	11	12
A	B	D	C	A	B

Passage-12

1	2	3	4	5	6
A	B	C	A	B	C
7	8	9	10	11	12
B	D	B	D	B	C

Passage-13

1	2	3	4	5	6
D	C	B	C	C	A
7	8	9	10	11	
B	B	C	D	B	

Passage-14

1	2	3	4	5	6
B	C	A	D	C	C
7	8	9	10	11	
D	A	B	A	C	

Passage-15

1	2	3	4	5	6
A	B	D	B	D	B
7	8	9	10	11	
C	A	C	D	B	

Passage-16

1	2	3	4	5	6
C	A	C	B	A	A
7	8	9	10	11	
C	B	D	D	D	

Passage-17

1	2	3	4	5	6
D	B	D	D	D	C
7	8	9	10	11	
A	D	A	A	B	

Passage-18

1	2	3	4	5	6
B	C	B	A	C	C
7	8	9	10	11	12
C	D	D	D	A	D
13	14	15	16	17	
C	A	B	D	C	

Passage-19

1	2	3	4	5	6
B	A	B	C	B	D
7	8	9	10	11	
B	C	D	D	B	

Passage-20

1	2	3	4	5	6
D	C	D	A	A	B
7	8	9	10		
C	C	A	C		

Passage-21

1	2	3	4	5	6
D	B	C	B	C	B
7	8	9	10		
A	D	D	D		

Passage-22

1	2	3	4	5	6
C	A	B	C	B	D
7	8	9	10	11	
A	A	B	D	D	

Passage-23

1	2	3	4	5	6
B	A	C	B	A	A
7	8	9	10	11	12
B	D	C	A	C	B
13	14	15	16	17	18
C	B	C	C	A	C

Passage-24

1	2	3	4	5	6
A	D	C	A	B	D
7	8	9	10	11	12
D	B	B	C	A	A

Passage-25

1	2	3	4	5	6
D	C	B	A	D	C
7	8	9	10	11	12
A	A	C	D	B	D
13	14				
D	A				

Passage-26

1	2	3	4	5	6
A	C	B	C	D	B
7	8	9	10	11	
D	C	B	A	A	

Passage-27

1	2	3	4	5	6
C	B	B	A	A	B
7	8	9	10	11	12
C	A	D	D	B	D
13	14	15	16		
C	C	B	B		

Passage-28

1	2	3	4	5	6
D	D	C	D	B	B
7	8	9	10	11	12
C	C	B	B	C	A
13	14	15			
A	D	C			

Passage-29

1	2	3	4	5	6
B	B	C	D	A	B
7	8	9	10	11	12
A	B	C	D	B	C

Passage-30

1	2	3	4	5	6
B	C	A	A	D	D
7	8	9	10	11	12
D	C	C	B	B	C
13	14	15			
A	B	D			

Passage-31

1	2	3	4	5	6
A	B	D	A	B	C
7	8	9	10	11	12
B	A	B	D	A	B
13	14	15			
D	A	A			

Passage-32

1	2	3	4	5	6
B	C	C	A	D	B
7	8	9	10	11	12
C	A	C	B	D	C
13	14				
B	B				

II. Passages

Passage-1

1	2	3	4	5	6
A	D	A	A	A	C
7					
B					

Passage-2

1	2	3	4	5	6
A	A	D	A	B	C
7					
D					

Passage-3

1	2	3	4	5	6
D	C	D	C	A	D
7					
B					

Passage-4

1	2	3	4	5	6
C	C	A	D	A	D
7					
C					

Passage-5

1	2	3	4	5	6
B	D	D	B	D	C
7					
A					

Passage-6

1	2	3	4	5	6
A	C	B	C	B	C
7					
B					

Passage-7

1	2	3	4	5	6	7
B	C	C	B	D	B	C

Passage-8

1	2	3	4	5	6	7
B	C	C	B	B	C	A

Passage-9

1	2	3	4	5
C	C	B	D	A

Passage-10

1	2	3	4	5
B	A	B	C	C

Passage-11

1	2	3	4	5
C	A	B	D	A

Passage-12

1	2	3	4	5
A	A	B	C	D

Passage-13

1	2	3	4	5
A	C	B	A	D

Passage-14

1	2	3	4	5
C	B	A	D	A

Passage-15

1	2	3	4	5
B	A	C	D	A

Passage-16

1	2	3	4	5
A	B	C	A	B

Passage-17

1	2	3	4	5
C	A	B	D	C

Passage-18

1	2	3	4	5
B	D	B	A	B

Passage-19

1	2	3	4	5
D	C	B	C	D

Passage-20

1	2	3	4	5
B	A	C	D	A

Passage-21

1	2	3	4	5
B	C	D	D	C

Passage-22

1	2	3	4	5
C	D	B	C	D

Passage-23

1	2	3	4	5
A	C	D	B	A

Passage-24

1	2	3	4	5
A	D	A	D	B

Passage-25

1	2	3	4	5
B	C	D	A	B

Passage-26

1	2	3	4	5
B	B	C	A	D

Passage-27

1	2	3	4	5
A	B	A	B	C

Passage-28

1. (i) Good music has mood with variable notes of rhythm and provides mental relief with sensational pleasure.
(ii) Both of them practised Carnatic music.
(iii) He pioneered the use of African beats and tabla in his music.

2. (i) Baul songs (ii) Elvis Presley
(iii) Paco de Lucia (iv) The Beatles

3. (i) limits (ii) freedom
(iii) mixing of styles

Passage-29

1. (i) Mind management is a method to control one's mind.
(ii) A wise person does not accept or oppose any idea without valid reason. He works as per the situation and his capacity. He is always optimistic.
(iii) Because if kept any longer in mind they become stronger and difficult to remove later.

(iv) Because our aspirations are raised. The compulsions of hectic work-schedules burden the mind and cause stress.

2. (i) When one fails, he works hard and strives to achieve success with increased vigour. Hence, his failure acts as stepping stone for future success.

(ii) When we manage our mind, we have patience, peace and calmness which pave the way to success, and a successful and peaceful life is a healthy life.

3. (i) control

(ii) disturbed, unrest

(iii) weak

(iv) easy

Passage-30

1. (i) The youngster closed his facebook account after using it for three years. He did not like the Timeline feature of the facebook that was recently introduced.

(ii) He was upset because his friends will be able to see his old post on facebook easily with the help of the new feature. Until now those were buried under heaps of recent posts.

(iii) Every one commits some mistake or foolishness while posting online comments or photos which are almost forgotten by the time but if the same is easily accessible to all. The situation will be embarrassing and may cause more harm than good.

2. (i) moved

(ii) deactivating it

(iii) separates

(iv) friends

3. (i) pros and cons

(ii) facets of life

(iii) profile

(iv) to delete

III. Poetry

Poem-1

1	2	3	4	5
A	C	B	C	A

Poem-2

1	2	3	4	5
C	B	A	D	B

Poem-3

1	2	3	4	5
D	A	B	C	B

Poem-4

1	2	3	4	5
B	D	C	D	B

Poem-5

1	2	3	4	5
B	A	D	A	B

Poem-6

1	2	3	4	5
C	D	D	D	B

Poem-7

1	2	3	4	5
C	D	B	B	A

Poem-8

1	2	3	4	5
A	B	A	D	C

Poem-9

1	2	3	4	5
A	C	D	B	C

Poem-10

1	2	3	4	5
C	B	A	A	C

Poem-11

1	2	3	4	5
B	C	C	B	C

Poem-12

1	2	3	4	5
D	B	C	B	D

Poem-13

1	2	3	4	5
B	B	A	D	B

Poem-14

1	2	3	4	5
A	A	D	A	B

Poem-15

1	2	3	4	5
B	B	C	C	D

Poem-16

1	2	3	4	5
B	A	D	A	A

Poem-17

1	2	3	4	5
B	A	B	A	D

Poem-18

1	2	3	4	5
D	D	C	C	B

Poem-19

1	2	3	4	5
C	A	C	D	A

Poem-20

1	2	3	4	5
B	A	C	B	B

Poem-21

1. (i) Pronunciation (ii) threat
(iii) mother (iv) here
(v) them

2. (i) dead
(ii) brother
(iii) bear and pear

Poem-22

1. It is because nobody is telling him what a particular girl (the Highland lass) is singing. She seems to be singing in a strange dialect which the poet does not know.

2. The girl is singing a sad song.

3. The poet makes several guesses:

(*i*) His first guess is that the girl is singing about some old and unhappy things which happened in bygone days and, may be, at some distant place.

(*ii*) The poet's second guess is that the girl is singing about some battles which were fought long long ago.

(*iii*) The poet's third guess is that the girl's sad song perhaps pertains to some routine day-to-day matter.

(*iv*) From this, the poet derives the idea that the girl's melancholy song might pertain to some natural sorrow, loss or pain. Such things can happen at any time and to anybody. Once having happened to somebody, they may happen again.

4. It is ab ab cc dd.

5. Yes, it appears he did.

6. It may be titled: "The Power of Music."

Poem-23

1. They have called it mighty and dreadful.

2. It is because they actually wake eternally, and it is, in reality, death itself that dies.

3. Rest and sleep.

4. Death is a slave to fate, chance, kings and desperate men.

5. It dwells with poison, war and sickness.

6. He just sleeps for sometime (after his death) and then he wakes up for ever in heaven.

❑❑❑

Writing Critical Review

Purpose of a Critical Review

The critical review is a writing task that asks you to summarise and evaluate a text. The critical review can be of a book, a chapter, a poem or a journal article. Writing the critical review usually requires you to read the selected text in detail and to also read other related texts so that you can present a fair and reasonable evaluation of the selected text.

What is meant by Critical?

At university, to be critical does not mean to criticise in a negative manner. Rather it requires you to question the information and opinions in a text and present your evaluation or judgement of the text. To do this well, you should attempt to understand the topic from different perspectives (i.e. read related texts) and in relation to the theories, approaches and frameworks in your course.

What is meant by Evaluation or Judgement?

Here you decide the strengths and weaknesses of a text. This is usually based on specific criteria. Evaluating requires an understanding of not just the content of the text, but also an understanding of a text's purpose, the intended audience and why it is structured the way it is.

The determination of the book review is to communicate to the readers mind the ideas and sensations book reviewer experienced while researching the content, in this way explaining the reader what exact meaning the author presumed to transmit, or what did the reviewer experienced while during the reading. The book reviewer, then, stands as reporter, who informs the third party of the events, as an analyst, who makes judgments basing them on own experience, and as the observer from the side, who pretends to act as the reader him/herself should do by expressing own opinion, desires and expectations.

Making book review implies some special skills, as well as obliges with some precise responsibilities. Professional reviewer has not just to read and scrutinize the text, but to realize concealed, implied meaning the author obviously had dropped hints about. Skilled book reviewers' explanations make the reader feel this "that is just what I thought" sensation. The reviewer must also state the main points of the reviewed book. While some aspects are less meaningful, others are have to be marked out as prerogative issues. The task is even more complicated as the writer could unintentionally imply the idea the reviewer of the book can notice.

What is meant by Analysis?

Analysing requires separating the content and concepts of a text into their main components and then understanding how these interrelate, connect and possibly influence each other.

The book review is assigned to develop analytical skills. First, the reviewer has to depict the content, regardless of the type of novel, an historical or critical book. In the subsequent narration the goal of the book reviewer is to discuss the content of the book and provide analysis of what he/she had read, and deduce if the author managed to reveal the core, whether he/she kept to the thesis or properly achieved the purpose of the book. The last thing the reviewer has to do is to speculate on the topic himself/herself. The book reviewer should also undertake through their own research to discuss the theme, assess the authors ability to express and explore this theme, and provide an opinion of the novel.

Summarising and Paraphrasing for the Critical Review

Summarising and paraphrasing are essential skills for academic writing and in particular, the critical review. To summarise means to reduce a text to its main points and its most important ideas. The length of your summary for a critical review should only be about one quarter to one third of the whole critical review. The best way to summarise is to:

1. Scan the text. Look for information that can be deduced from the introduction, conclusion and the title and headings. What do these tell you about the main points of the article?
2. Locate the topic sentences and highlight the main points as you read.
3. Reread the text and make separate notes of the main points. Examples and evidence do not need to be included at this stage. Usually they are used selectively in your critique.

Paraphrasing means putting it into your own words. Paraphrasing offers an alternative to using direct quotations in your summary (and the critique) and can be an efficient way to integrate your summary notes. The best way to paraphrase is to:

1. Review your summary notes
2. Rewrite them in your own words and in complete sentences
3. Use reporting verbs and phrases (*e.g.,* The author describes..., Smith argues that ...).
4. If you include unique or specialist phrases from the text, use quotation marks.

Structure of a Critical Review

Critical reviews, both short (one page) and long (four pages), usually have a similar structure. Check your assignment instructions for formatting and structural specifications. Headings are usually optional for longer reviews and can be helpful for the reader.

Introduction

The length of an introduction is usually one paragraph for a journal article review and two or three paragraphs for a longer book review. Include a few opening sentences that announce the author(s) and the title, and briefly explain the topic of the text. Present the aim of the text and summarise the main finding or key argument. Conclude the introduction with a brief statement of your evaluation of the text. This can be a positive or negative evaluation or, as is usually the case, a mixed response.

Summary

Present a summary of the key points along with a limited number of examples. You can also briefly explain the author's purpose/intentions throughout the text and you may briefly describe how the text is organised. The summary should only make up about a third of the critical review.

Critique

The critique should be a balanced discussion and evaluation of the strengths, weakness and notable features of the text. Remember to base your discussion on specific criteria. Good reviews also include other sources to support your evaluation (remember to reference).

You can choose how to sequence your critique. Here are some examples to get you started:

- Most important to least important conclusions you make about the text.
- If your critique is more positive than negative, then present the negative points first and the positive last.
- If your critique is more negative than positive, then present the positive points first and the negative last.
- If there are both strengths and weakness for each criterion you use, you need to decide overall what your judgement is. For example, you may want to comment on a key idea in the text and have both positive and negative comments. You could begin by stating what

is good about the idea and then concede and explain how it is limited in some way. While this example shows a mixed evaluation, overall you are probably being more negative than positive.

- In long reviews, you can address each criteria you choose in a paragraph, including both negative and positive points. For very short critical reviews (one page or less) where your comments will be briefer, include a paragraph of positive aspects and another of negative.
- You can also include recommendations for how the text can be improved in terms of ideas, research approach; theories or frameworks used can also be included in the critique section.

Conclusion

This is usually a very short paragraph.

- Restate your overall opinion of the text.
- Briefly present recommendations.
- If necessary some further qualification or explanation of your judgement can be included. This can help your critique sound fair and reasonable.

References

If you have used other sources in your review you should also include a list of references at the end of the review.

Critical Review of A Poem or Passage

Critical Analysis of a Poem

With poetry, the author is always very deliberate with his word choice and format to convey meaning. Poems are meant to be read aloud, which is why they have a very lyrical quality or at least have an interesting rhythm that punctuates the elements of the poem. A critical analysis of the poem allows the reader to have a better understanding of the symbols and language used in the piece. This often offers a more intimate appreciation of the work.

Important Steps

1. Find a specific theme in the work that gives the poem larger meaning. Consider the entire piece, including the title. Perhaps the poem is a symbol about growing old or a loss of innocence or maybe the overarching theme is the importance of the environment. If so, the context for the theme is hidden in the words and presentation.
2. Create a critical analysis checklist that you can follow when reviewing the piece. This allows you to dissect the poem into individual pieces that helps you understand the poem as a whole. For example, make a checklist that lists title, setting, point of view, rhyme scheme, meter, genre, conflict or context. Use these elements as a guide for your analysis.
3. Review the plot of the poem. Answer the questions: What is happening? To whom is it happening? Once you have an understanding of what is being described in the poem, you can start to apply its meaning in your analysis.
4. Analyse the rhyme scheme of the poem, if any. Not all poetry has to rhyme. However, poems are often written for the intention of being read, so there should be a rhythm when read aloud. When performing your analysis, be sure to read the poem aloud alone or with a friend to hear the way it sounds, not just to see the words on the page.
5. Consider the format of the poem. It could be free form, without any identifiable pattern, or it can fit into a specific writing scheme. This is often a deliberate act on the part of the author. In your analysis, you should describe what this format could mean and how it helps or hinders communication of the message.
6. Review the figurative language of the poem. Poetry is known for using literary devices, such as simile, metaphor, personification, irony and metonymy in the work. This not only

constitutes the body of the poem, it demonstrates the author's control over language. Evaluation of this language is a crucial part of your analysis.

7. Form a thesis statement based on your understanding of the poem's meaning. When writing any sort of academic work, your paper should have a clear thesis. For example, "The pitfalls of arrogance and power as described in the poem 'Ozymandius.'"
8. Find parts of the poem that support your thesis statement. Throughout the body of your analysis, you should provide clear clues as to where you got your thesis. Use actual lines from the text, as well as a thorough analysis of word choice.

Analysis of Sylvia Plath's Poem—Mirror

Sylvia Plath's poem Mirror is an objectively serious poem which reveals the similarities between poems and the obsessive interest in the truth of reflections and the unhealthy dissatisfaction resulting from dwelling too long on an "exact" image of the present. Plath uses interesting perspective, significant structure, and deep metaphors to also illustrate the similarity between the truthful qualities of poets and mirrors.

The use of first person "I" in the poem Mirror by Sylvia Plath gives an intimate perspective and reveals the mirror's unbiased thoughts. This personified mirror speaking in first person reflects an objective outlook on life from the perspective of a detached observer. Like the mirror's reflection, a poet must also show a clear truth in poetry. The mirror and reflection are metaphors representing the absolute truth of present realities which poets explore and release into the world. The mirror is "unmisted" by prejudice human "preconceptions" and reveals "only" the "truthful" aspects of the world directly in front of it. The mirror's attitudes on life are like a poet's in that they may show a true observation which common people do not wish or are unable to see. Poetry can cut through and unlock social barriers. Though an appearance of a person or situation may be viewed as negative, through a different lens of vision it may then be found to have positive effects. Unlike poetry, mirrors only reflect the present and are unable to predict the future appearance of the area being reflected.

In the second stanza the speaker changes its physical form into a "lake" from a "mirror". The poem is divided by a focus on the mirror itself and the woman who interacts with her reflection in the lake. The division of the poem can also be interpreted as the past and present or present and future of the earth. Just as mirrors reflect images and faces, lakes are giant reflecting pools which claim to show reality, not "cruel" criticism. Reflections are used as a way to measure progress over time. This progress can often become an obsession. The lake is a reference to Narcissus, a youth who fell in love with his image in a lake. The pessimistic woman who visits the lake "each morning" in dedication, like Narcissus, finds herself less young and desirable than the previous days. Though the outcome of aging is inevitable, the woman refuses to accept the laws of nature and continues to be heartbroken by her reflection. The lake is interestingly rewarded with "tears and an agitation of hands", actions which do not hold pleasant appreciation for "truthful" reflections. The woman is so concerned with her appearance compared to her younger days that she is unable to enjoy the present. The woman represents most women's desire to appear young, attractive, and successful all their days. If one lives in the past one will find that each day is a "terrible fish" which holds no hope or happiness. The "terrible fish" is representative of disappointment, unhappiness, and regret stemming from opportunities not seized and an inability to enjoy life as it comes. Instead of embracing and cherishing the time at hand, the woman has "drowned" her youth by disrespecting the truth of the present reflection. This relationship between woman and lake can be translated and applied to many challenges in life. The second stanza is a tragedy because the woman is not "seizing the day" and living out her potential, but is wasting her valuable time. Appearance to the world holds such a great "importance" that it generates an obsession with the worshiped godlike and reflective object.

Mirror by Sylvia Plath has a serious and objective tone to provide an honest interpretation of the people and images which are watched by the square "eye of a little god". The short precise declarative statements create a feeling of detached loneliness. The mirror has grown fond of the familiar and constant "pink" wall "with speckles" and has a slight resentment toward the faces and "dark" nights which force the wall to retreat. Poets will often inform the public about "dark" events in history or everyday life through poetry. Plath creates a dark fateful image by using relatively simple diction. The prominent consonant sounds of the precise word choice create a descriptive scene without a superfluous amount of words. Plath uses figurative language to describe the "mirror" and the woman's reflection in the "lake" to create a similarity of hopeless truth for the future of each object.

Plath's Mirror is a reflection on the way absolute realities of society and the greedy nature of many human's desire for immortality and success can be viewed through objective poems and immediate feedback. The "darkness" of judgment surrounds the young woman and hides the "wall" that has become the "heart" of the "four-cornered" mirror. Poems and Poets can also reflect an accurate or "truthful" picture of present realities. Plath's careful and succinct word choice creates a sparse environment in which the classic situation takes place. The "mirror" knows only truth and is immune from the subliminal judgment which plagues every person's perception of the world. This poem has a distinct correlation between a poet's poem and a mirror's truthful reflection.

Mirror—Summary

In this poem, the mirror is the speaker. It is an autobiographical poem. The mirror talks about itself, its surroundings and the woman who uses it. In this way, it gives its observations in an objective way without any personal bias. The mirror say that its appearance is silver and exact. It does not have any pre-conceptions or anything else about its existence. It is just what it is "Unmisted by love or dislike". It is neither cruel nor biased nor prejudiced, only truthful.

It can be called the eye of a little god, four-cornered, that is, it is framed in a four cornered frame and it remains fixed on the wall and sees the opposite wall and only when someone comes between it and the wall or at night or in darkness, the reflection of the opposite wall goes away.

The mirror is like a lake, it drowns the face of the woman, who tries to see her reflection in it. She searches for her, beauty which she had in her youth. She grows sad to see herself old now. She then turns to "candles" or the moon "which the mirror calls "liars" because these create a misted kind of surrounding around the woman's face due to which she does not see the wrinkles or signs of old age. But the woman's real identity is revealed by the mirror. Seeing her changed face, the woman sheds some tears and moves her hands angrily.

The mirror is very important to the woman. Every morning she sees herself and she is filled with fear at her reflection of having grown old. She feels like a fish out of water, but the mirror can't do anything as it reflects only the truth—that is what one really is. So, in this way, the mirror claims to be a very objective opinion giver or reflector of images.

Summary and Analysis of Wordsworth's Poem—The Solitary Reaper

Behold her, single in the field,
Yon solitary Highland Lass!
Reaping and singing by herself;
Stop here, or gently pass!
Alone she cuts and binds the grain,
And sings a melancholy strain;
O listen! for the Vale profound
Is overflowing with the sound.

No Nightingale did ever chaunt
More welcome notes to weary bands
Of travellers in some shady haunt,
Among Arabian sands:
A voice so thrilling ne'er was heard
In spring-time from the Cuckoo-bird,
Breaking the silence of the seas
Among the farthest Hebrides.

Will no one tell me what she sings?--
Perhaps the plaintive numbers flow
For old, unhappy, far-off things,
And battles long ago:
Or is it some more humble lay,
Familiar matter of to-day?
Some natural sorrow, loss, or pain,
That has been, and may be again?

Whate'er the theme, the Maiden sang
As if her song could have no ending;
I saw her singing at her work,
And o'er the sickle bending;
I listened, motionless and still;
And, as I mounted up the hill
The music in my heart I bore,
Long after it was heard no more.

In the first stanza the speaker comes across a beautiful girl working alone in the fields of Scotland (the Highland). She is "Reaping and singing by herself." He tells the reader not to interrupt her, and then mentions that the valley is full of song.

The second stanza is a list of things that cannot equal the beauty of the girl's singing.

In the third stanza the reader learns that the speaker cannot understand the words being sung. He can only guess at what she might be singing about.

In the fourth and final stanza the speaker tells the reader that even though he did not know what she was singing about, the music stayed in his heart as he continued up the hill.

Analysis

"The Solitary Reaper" was written on November 5, 1805 and published in 1807. The poem is broken into four eight-line stanzas (32 lines total). Most of the poem is in iambic tetrameter. The rhyme scheme for the stanzas is either abcbddee or ababccdd. (In the first and last stanzas the first and third lines don't rhyme, while in the other two stanzas they do.)

This poem is unique in Wordsworth's oeuvre because while most of his work is based closely on his own experiences, "The Solitary Reaper" is based on the experience of someone else: Thomas Wilkinson, as described in his Tours to the British Mountains. The passage that inspired Wordsworth is the following: "Passed a female who was reaping alone: she sung in Erse [the Gaelic language of Scotland] as she bended over her sickle; the sweetest human voice I ever heard: her strains were tenderly melancholy, and felt delicious, long after they were heard no more" (as quoted in The Norton Anthology English Literature).

Part of what makes this poem so intriguing is the fact that the speaker does not understand the words being sung by the beautiful young lady. In the third stanza, he is forced to imagine what she might be singing about. He supposes that she may be singing about history and things that happened long ago, or some sadness that has happened in her own time and will happen again.

As the speaker moves on, he carries the music of the young lady with him in his heart. This is a prevalent theme in much of Wordsworth's poetry. For instance, the same idea is used in "I wandered lonely as a cloud" when the speaker takes the memory of the field of daffodils with him to cheer him up on bad days.

Analysis of John Donne's Poem—Death be not Proud

Death be not proud, though some have called thee
Mighty and dreadfull, for, thou art not soe,
For, those, whom thou think'st, thou dost overthrow,

Die not, poore death, nor yet canst thou kill mee.

From rest and sleepe, which but thy pictures bee,

Much pleasure, then from thee, much more must flow,

And soonest our best men with thee doe goe,

Rest of their bones, and soules deliverie.

Thou art slave to Fate, Chance, kings, and desperate men,

And dost with poyson, warre, and sicknesse dwell,

And poppie, or charmes can make us sleepe as well,

And better then thy stroake; why swell'st thou then?

One short sleepe past, wee wake eternally,

And death shall be no more; death, thou shalt die.

The sonnet "Death Be Not Proud", written by John Donne in England around the year 1618, is one sonnet of nineteen that are part of a collection entitled The Holy Sonnets. Through the use of literary terms and techniques, "Death, Be Not Proud", exemplifies the popular Christian philosophy of the period, that heaven is eternal. John Donne starts the poem "Death Be Not Proud" in utilizing the figurative language of personification, " Death, be not proud, though some have called thee mighty and dreadful, for thou art not so". In using this technique the author is able to apply human qualities which make Death tangible and a being in which the narrator can entertain an argument and eventually win his case based upon Christian philosophy. Additionally, in the personification of treating Death, the embodiment of non-living as a living being, the author has also utilized the literary term irony. It can be seen that through the use of personification and irony John Donne has set the stage for Death to become just as undone as any man. The continued unraveling of Death is illustrated in lines 5 and 6 through the use of metaphor, "... From rest and sleep, which but thy pictures be, much pleasure; then from thee much more must flow". The narrator is claiming that rest and sleep are nothing but pictures of death, an image of what death is, and that they provide much pleasure so when death actually does happen the pleasure will be much greater. This line of conversation brings death who imagines himself to be mighty and feared in line 1 and 2 down to a being who now brings much pleasure instead of fear. Then in lines 9 and 10, "Thou art slave to fate, chance, kings, and desperate men, and dost with poison, war, and sickness dwell," through the use of imagery John Donne hands Death a crushing blow to his fearsome image. Death is presented as a slave to Fate, Chance. Kings, and Desperate men. It is shown that death's home, his dwelling is with poison, war and sickness, and that he must await the outcome and decisions of his masters, the true powers that be fate, chance, kings and desperate men. Finally, in the last two lines of 13 and 14 through the author's further use of irony, Death is told, he "...shall be no more; Death, thou shalt die." . Much of the irony here is that it is only due to Christian philosophy, the belief that there is no death, that the argument is won for the narrator. With the death of ones physical body, man awakens to an eternal spiritual life ad death is over, man wins. It can be seen throughout the poem "Death, Be Not Proud" that the use of literary terms and techniques helped highlight and explore the views of Christian philosophy which during the time of John Donne was eternal life, the only option to believe.

❑❑❑

Styles and Forms of Narration

Narration is an integral part of writing. In some cases it establishes what the protagonist is like, in others it helps to paint the setting. There are many different styles of narration, including first-person, second-person, and the two variations of third-person.

First-person narration is one of the most popular narration styles. This type of narration uses the words "I", "me" and "my", unlike most other narration styles. It is designed to make the story sound as if it is being told by the protagonist by portraying the story's world through their eyes alone. Although this style was very popular in older literature such as *"To Kill a Mockingbird"* by Harper Lee ("It was times like this when I thought my father, who hated guns and had never been to any wars, was the bravest man who ever lived."), it is still fairly prominent today and is a common narration choice for young writers.

Writing first-person narration well usually depends on the author's ability to see the story through the eyes of their character. If the character and author are extremely different in terms of personality, then writing an accurate transcription of the character's views will be substantially more difficult than an author writing a character who is very much like them. However, it is important to note that an author who can write a dissimilar character well is a skilled writer, while an author writing a character with many similarities runs the risk of creating a Self Insert. Another problem is that "first-person narrators usually intrude on readers with their thoughts." Thought intrusion often causes subtlety problems. To write first person narration, one must honestly *understand* their character, which is easy for some and difficult for others.

Second-person narration is rarely used, and its usages are normally for advertising purposes or for wish fulfillment in fanfiction. Wikipedia defines it as "a narrative mode in which the protagonist...is referred to by....second-person personal pronouns." It is characterized by words like "you" and "your". It treats the reader as the protagonist and was common on websites such as prior to its banning. Although virtually nonexistent in modern writing, the Choose Your Own Adventure series is a good example of second-person narration.

Writing second-person narration is relatively simple, but advised against. It is most common in the fanfiction world as a simple wish fulfillment device, and should most likely not be attempted in original work. Effectively, second-person narration is a gimmick and should be avoided.

There are two distinct subtypes of third-person narration: third-person limited and third-person omniscient.

Third-person limited narration is an extremely popular style, eclipsing first-person in use. It uses the views of one character, focusing only on their thoughts and actions. However, it is different from first-person narration in the fact that it narrates as if invisibly watching the character from afar, instead of the character literally telling their story. A good example of third-person narration is in the Harry Potter series by J. K. Rowling ("Hermione looked ready to fling her arms around him again, but Harry was glad she held herself in as his head was still very sore.").

Writing third-person limited narration is usually more difficult than writing first person, although authors who are unable to accurately capture the thoughts of their characters in first-person might have an easier time writing third-person limited. Like with first-person narration, the author must be able to understand who their characters are in order to write third-person limited narration well. Overall, third-person limited is one of the most reliable forms of narration, merely by being relatively easy for an author to create.

The other type of third-person narration is commonly called third-person omniscient. Like third-person limited, its narrator figure acts like a watcher. What sets third-person omniscient apart from its counterparts is the way that it focuses on the viewpoints of all of the characters in the novel, as opposed to one. Novels using third-person omniscient will often switch between characters. Some of Jane Austen's works use third-person omniscient in order to convey the thoughts of mulitple characters.

The third-person omniscient narration style is difficult for most young authors, and is extremely confusing if not written well. Superhero Nation describes it as "flitty" and "disorienting" when done incorrectly. It is advised that an author becomes skilled at other forms of narration before attempting it. Third-person omniscient is also hard to pull off in most works, as too many point of view characters will confuse the reader, especially if two characters are extremely similar. In short, third-person omniscient narration should mainly be used by veteran authors possessing the skill to pull the style off.

The above styles are the oldest and most popular styles of narration, although a few new types have surfaced in modern works.

Journal or diary style narration is relatively recent, although it is still found in some older works. It is similar to first-person narration in that it focuses on one character. True to its name, the story is written like the protagonist's diary. This style is common in female-oriented teen literature and more rarely in historical fiction, although it shows up in other genres from time to time.

Blog or chat style narration is journal narration's modern counterpart. It is effectively the same as its older relative, and gaining popularity. It is also common in female-oriented teen fiction.

Finally, some narration breaks the fourth wall. Within this narration the characters are aware that they do not exist or exist only within the books. This style treats the narrator as another character who the protagonists interact with. It is extremely rare and found only in works with a comedic tone.

Narration is an invaluable part of writing, and mastering the variations is the sign of a skilled writer. Some authors have an affinity for one type of narration and fail at writing others, while others can write the different types of narration indiscriminately. It's up to the author to find their narration niche and make the most of it.

Here are some Stylish Excerpts from...

Late 19th Century Fiction

She did so. He washed the pots, straightened, and then took her boots. They were quite clean. Mrs. Morel was one of those naturally exquiste people who can walk mud without dirtying their shoes. But Paul had to clean them for her. They were kid boots at eight shillings a pair. He, however, thought them the most dainty boots in the world, and he cleaned them with as much reverence as if they had been flowers.

Sons and Lovers
(by D.H. Lawrence)

'The aristocracy' he continued,' is a really military institution. Take Germany, now, She's got thousands of aristocrats whose only means of existence is the army. They're deadly poor, and life's deadly slow. So they hope for war. They look for war as a chance of getting on. Till there's a war, they are leaders and Commanders. There you are then—they want war!

Sons and Lovers
(by D.H. Lawrence)

(***Style:*** Realistic, poetical; philosphical; a peep into the life of the poor; Author known for his consummate employment of the "Oedipus Complex".)

20th Century Poetry

April is the cruellest month, breeding
Lilacs out of the dead land, mixing
Memory and Desire, stirring
Dull roots with spring rain.
Winter kept us warm, covering
Earth in forgetful snow, feeding.
A little life with dried tubers.

The Waste Land
(by T.S. Eliot)

I think we are in rats' alley
Where the dead men lost their bones.
'What is that noise?
The wind under the door.
'What is that noise now?
What is the wind doing?
Nothing again nothing.
'Do you know nothing? Do you see nothing?
Do you remember 'nothing'.
I remember
There are pearls that were his eyes.
'Are you alive, or not? Is there nothing in your head?
But
OOOO that Shakespeherian Rag -
It's so elegant
So intelligent
'What shall I do now? What shall I do?

The Waste Land
(by T.S. Eliot)

(***Style:*** Realistic, rational, musical, inventive, partly obscure, mythical, philosophical, pessimistic).

Early 20th Century Prose

I have borne your hard words because I knew you would be sorry for them when you found out the truth.

Man and Superman
(by G.B. Shaw)

Common sense is good enough for him; and in our business affairs common sense is good enough for me.

Man and Superman
(by G.B. Shaw)

(***Style:*** Full of ideas, philosophy, irony, repartee; touching; anti-romantic)

Early 20th Century Fiction

How fresh, how calm, stiller than this of course, the air was in the early morning; like the flap of a wave; the kiss of a wave; chill and sharp and yet (for a girl of eighteen as she then was) solemn, feeling as she did, standing there at the open window, that something awful was about to happen; looking until Peter Walsh said; 'Musing among the vegetables?' — was that it? I prefer men to cauliflowers' — was that it? He must have said it at breakfast one morning when she had gone out on to the terrace — Peter Walsh. He would be back from India one of these day, June or July, she forgot which, for his letters were awfully dull; it was his sayings one remembered; his eyes; his pocket-knife, his smile, his grumpiness and, when millions of things have utterly vanished — how strange it was! — a few sayings like this about Cabbages."

Mrs. Dalloway
(by Virginia Woolf)

"But proportion has a sister, less smilling, nor formidable, a Goddess.... Conversion is her name and she feasts on the wills of the weakly, loving to impress, to impose, adoring her own features stamped on the face of the populace.... offers help, but desires power.... concealed as she mostly is under some plausible disguise; some venerable name; love duty, selfsacrifice."

Mrs. Dalloway
(by Virginia Woolf)

(***Style:*** Poetical; annihilation of time, psychological)

Late 20th Century Fiction

The Certainty that his day was assigned gave him a mysterious immunity, an immortaity for a fixed period that made him invulnerable to the risks of war and in the end permitted him to win a defeat that was much more difficult, much more bloody and costly than victory.

One Hundred Years of Solitude
(by Marquez)

It was a delirious prosperity that even made him laugh, and he could not help doing crazy things to release his good humor.

One Hundred Years of Solitude
(by Marquez)

(***Style:*** Romantic; musical, imaginative; mixture of history, romance and realism; ***Language:*** Sweet, charming, paradoxical ironial, humorous.)

American Fiction

Then he began to pity the great fish that he had hooked. He is wonderful and strange and who knows how old he is, he thought. Never have I had such a strong fish nor one who acted so strangely. Perhaps he is too wise to jump. He could ruin me by jumping or by a wild rush. But perhaps he has been hooked many times before and he knows that this is how he should make his fight. He cannot know that it is only one man against him, nor that it is an old man. But what a great fish he is and what he will bring in the market if the flesh is good. He took the bait like a male and he pulls like a male and his fight has no panic in it. I wonder if he he has any plans or if he is just as desperate as I am?

The Old Man and the Sea
(by Hemingway)

I must not think nonsense, he thought. Luck is a thing that comes in many forms and who can recognize her? I would take some though in any form and pay what they asked. I wish I could see the glow from the lights, he thought, I wish too many things. But that is the thing I wish for now. He tried to settle more confortably to steer and from his pain he knew he was not dead.

The Old Man and the Sea
(by Hemingway)

(***Style:*** Simple; touching; precise; focussing; contemplative; psychological; humanistic).

American Fiction
Late 20th Century Fiction

Yes, I had met this old gentleman in the hot chemical bath at the club, the circular bubbling whirlpool where people sat sweating, gossping about sports, taxes, television programmes, best sellers, or chatting about Acapulco and numbered bank accounts in the Cayman Islands. I didn't know but what this old fence had one of those infamous cafanas near the swimming pool to which young chicks were invited for the siesta. There had been some scandal and protest over this. What was done behind drawn drapes in the Cabanas was no one's business, of course, but some of the old guys, demostrative and exhibitionistic, had been seen fonding their little dolls on the sun-terrace. One had removed his false teeth in public to give a girl soul kisses.

Humboldt's Gift
(by Saul Bellow)

(***Style:*** idiomatic; minute details; highly intellectual, realistic, ironical, paradoxical, a mixture of the worldly and the philosophical).

Indian English Novel

Kartik has come to Kanthapura, sisters — Kartik has comme with the glow of lights and the unpressed footsteps of the wandering gods: white lights from claytrays and red lights from copper-stands and diamond lights that glow from the bowers of entrance-leaves; lights that glow from banana-trunks and mango twigs, yellow light behind green leaves; and night curls through the shadowed streets, and hissing over belied boulders and hurrying through dallying drains, night curls through the Brahmin

Street and the Pariah street and the Potters street and the Weavers' Street and flapping through the mango grove, hangs clawed for one moment to the giant pipal, and then shooting across the broken fields, dies quitly into the river — and gods walk by lighted streets, blue gods and quiet gods and bright-eyed gods, and even as they walk in transparent flesh the dust gently sinks back to the earth, and many a child in Kanthapura sits late into the night to see the crown of this god and that god, and how many a god has chariots with steads white as foam and queens so bright that the eyes shut themselves in fear lest they be blinded.

Kanthapura
(by Raja Rao)

(***Style:*** Realistic Indian places, pictures and characters; soft-flowing language.)

Indian English Fictional Prose

When I put her out of my mind I put aside my self-pity too. It would not do to dream of a different kind of life. My life had been planned and its course charted by my parents and relatives. I was to be the victim of a young man's carnal hunger and perhaps, out of our union, there would be born a few children. I would be a middle-class housewife and walk along the vegetable shop carrying a string bag and wearing faded chappals on my feet. I would beat my thin children when they asked for expensive toys, and make them scream out for mercy. I would wash my husband's cheap underwear and hang it out to dry in the balcony like some kind of a national flag, with wifely pride..........

My Story
(by Kamla Das)

(***Style:*** Confidential, autobiographical; realistic; simple and impressive.)

Indian English Fiction

'Oh, you think these engineers know more? A man like me who has to kick and prod a car to keep it on the road has, you may be sure' — I was safe; I had turned his mind from Rosie. I sat in suspense. I was in an abnormal state of mind. Even this did not escape Gaffur's attention. He mumbled often as he was driving me downhill, 'you are becoming rather stuck-up now-a-days, Raju. You are not the old friend you used to be.' It was a fact. I was losing a great deal of my mental relaxation. I was obsessed with thoughts of Rosie. I revelled in memories of the hours I spent with her last or in anticipation of what I'd be doing next.

The Guide
(by R.K. Narayan)

(***Style:*** Conversational; popular, impressive, sweet and revealing).

Munoo yawned and stretched his arms. Then he rubbed his eyes with his fists and looked around. The shades of the night enveloped the white-sheeted humanity which lay spread on charpais on the flat roofs of nearby houses. But the dawn was approaching. The horizons of the high rocks about his village came back before his eyes; also the herd of cows, walking under a sky which was dotted by swarms of birds veering out in an anguished flight towards the slopes of the moutains. He had seldom remembered home at Sham Nagar, because there he had got up comparatively late, when the sun was already up. But he did not want to remember home, he said to himself. Nor did he want to think of the Babu's house. 'They must be missing me now,' he reflected. 'I wonder what they will do. My uncle must be angry. I shall write to him and tell him I am safe and sound, but that I don't want to come back.'

Coolie
(by Mulk Raj Anand)

(***Style:*** Descriptive; typically Indian; progressive; picaresque; psychological; realistic; philosophical)

Late 20th Century Indian English Fiction

In the heat of that silent night (I was silent; outside me, the sea rustled like distant paper; crows squawked in the throes of their feathery nightmares; the puttering noises of tardy taxi-cabs wafted up from Warden Road; the Brass Monkey, before she fell asleep with her face frozen into a mask of curiosity begged, 'come on, Saleem; nobody's listening; what did you do? Tell tell tell!" .... while, inside me, the voices rebounded against the walls of my skull) I was gripped by hot fingers of excitement — the agitated insects of excitement danced in my stomach because finally, in some way I did not then fully understand, the door which Toxy Catrack had once nudged in my head had been forced open; and through it I could glimpse — shadowy still, undefined, enigmatic — my reason for having been born.

Midnight's Children
(by Salman Rushdie)

(***Style:*** Poetical; picturesque; highly descriptive and narrative, realistic)

Indian English Fiction of 1990's

Ammu gathered up her heavy hair, wrapped in around her face, and peered down the road to Age and Death through its parted strands. Like a medieval executioner peering through the tilted eye-slits of his peaked black hood at the executionee. A slender, naked executioner with dark nipples and deep dimples when she smiled. With seven silver stretchmarks from her two-egg twins, born to her by candlelight amidst news of a last war.

The God of Small Things
(by Arundhati Roy)

Once again Velutha heard himself say something which made no difference to the man he spoke to. His own voice coiled around him like a snake.

The God of Small Things
(by Arundhati Roy)

(***Style:*** Inventive in language; full of minute details; poetic; musical; picturesque; paradoxical; grotesque, frank and candid).

Some examples of works of good writers of English—both Indian and foreign—are given below for understanding their style of narration for the readers :

1

How then was this spiritual training to be given? I made the children memorize and recite hymns, and read to them from books on moral training. But that was far from satisfying to me. As I came into closer contact with them I saw that it was not through books that one could impart training of the spirit. Just as physical training was to be imparted through physical and intellectual exercise even so the training of the spirit was possible only through the exercise of the spirit. And the exercise of the spirit entirely depended on the life and character of the teacher. The teacher had always to be mindful of his p's and q's whether he was in the midst of his boys or not.

It is possible for a teacher situated miles away to affect the spirit of the pupils by his way of living. It would be idle for me, if I were a liar, to teach boys to tell the truth. A cowardly teacher would never succeed in making his boys valiant, and a stranger to self-restraint could never teach his pupils the value of self-restraint. I saw, therefore, that I must be an eternal object lesson to the boys and girls living with me. They thus became my teachers, and I learnt I must be good and live straight, if only for their sakes. I may say that the increasing discipline and restraint I imposed on myself at Tolstoy Farm was mostly due to those wards of mine.

—M. K. Gandhi

2

These then, are the antecedents which make the emphasis on my mother's honesty not insulting but necessary. The padlock and the key are in some ways the symbol of our existence. Wherever I go I find home life in the rigorous custody of padlocks and keys. You go on to the balcony and padlock your sitting-room, you go into the lavatory and padlock your bedroom, you go up to the roof for air and padlock your staircase door. In recent times I have also heard of highly educated modern young ladies counting every potato in the house before going out and re-counting them on return as a precaution against their theft by servants. I have heard too of mistresses who do not possess the courage to dismiss their thievish servants, but quietly search their belongings and salvage the stolen articles and thus win the battle of wits. It was the example of Father Prior of the Oxford Mission which first taught me that mankind could live without the protection and guarantee of padlocks. Since I saw him leaving everything about in open drawers in an open room, I too gave up padlocks, and I have not been a loser.

—Nirad C. Chaudhuri

3

1. CASTING a preparatory glance at the bottom of this article–as the wary connoisseur in prints, with cursory eye (which, while it reads, seems as though it read not), never fails to consult the *quis sculpsit* in the corner, before he pronounces some rare piece to be a Vivares, or a Woollet methinks I hear you exclaim, Reader, *Who is Elia?*
2. Because in my last I tried to divert thee with some half forgotten humours of some old clerks defunct, in an old house of business, long since gone to decay, doubtless you have already set me down in your mind as one of the self-same college–a votary of the desk–a notched and cropt scrivener–one that sucks his sustenance, as certain sick people are said to do, through a quill.
3. Well, I do agonise something of the sort. I confess that it is my humour, my fancy–in the fore-part of the day, when the mind of your man of letters requires some relaxation (and none better than such as at first sight seems most abhorrent from his beloved studies)–to while away some good hours of my time in the contemplation of indigos, cottons, raw silks, piece-goods, flowered or otherwise. In the first place * * and then it sends you home with such increased appetite to your books * * * * * not to say, that your outside sheets, and waste wrappers of foolscap, do receive into them, most kindly and naturally, the impression of sonnets, epigrams, *essays*–so that the very parings of a counting-house are, in some sort, the settings up of an author. The enfranchised quill, that has plodded all the morning among the cart-rucks of figures and ciphers, frisks and curvets so at its ease over the flowery carpet-ground of a midnight dissertation.–It feels its promotion.

—From "Oxford in the Vacation" by Charles Lamb

4

"The old enchantment seems to be breaking today and she is looking around and waking up to the present. But however she changes, as change she must, that old witchery will continue and hold the hearts of her people. Though her attire may change, she will continue as of old, and her store of wisdom will help her to hold on to what is true and beautiful and good in this harsh, vindictive, and grasping world.....

"My generation has been a troubled one in India and the world. We may carry on for a little while longer, but our day will be over and we shall give place to others, and they will live their lives and carry their burdens to the next stage of the journey. How have we played our part in this brief interlude that draws to a close? I do not know. Others of a later age will judge. By what standards do we measure success or failure? That too I do not know. We can make no complaint that life has treated us harshly, for ours has been a willing choice, and perhaps life has not been so bad to us after all. For only they can sense life who stand often on the verge of it, only they whose lives are not governed by the fear of death. In spite of all the mistakes that we may have made, we have saved ourselves from triviality and an inner shame and cowardice. That, for our individual selves, has been some achievement. Man's dearest possession is life, and since it is given to him to live but once, he must so live as not to be seared with the shame of a cowardly and trivial past,"

—J. L. Nehru

5

She could never have been pretty; but she was always beautiful. She hobbled about the house in spotless white with one hand resting on her waist to balance her stoop and the other telling the beads of her rosary. Her silver locks were scattered untidily over her pale, puckered face, and her lips constantly moved in inaudible prayer. Yes, she was beautiful. She was like the winter landscape in the mountains, an expanse of pure white serenity, breathing peace and contentment.

—Khushwant Singh

6

The question whether the possession of a good memory is altogether desirable has often been discussed, and men with fallible memories have sometimes tried to make out a case for their superiority. A man, they say, who is a perfect remembering machine is seldom a man of the first intelligence, and they quote various cases of children or men who had marvellous memories and who yet had no intellect to speak of. I imagine, however, that on the whole the great writers and the great composers of music have been men with exceptional powers of memory. The poets I have known have had better memories than the stock-brokers I have known. Memory, indeed, is half the substance of their art. On the other hand, statesmen seem to have extraordinarily bad memories. Let two statesmen attempt to recall the same event-what happened, for example, at some cabinet meeting-and each of them will tell you that other's story is so like a sieve or is an audacious perverter of truth.

—Robert Lynd

7

"Sudie, some day I hope to paint the Bay of Naples."

The doctor came in the afternoon, and Sue had an excuse to go into the hallway as he left.

"Even chances," said the doctor, taking Sue's thin, shaking hand in his. "With good nursing you'll win. And now I must see another case I have downstairs. Behrman, his name is–some kind of an artist, I believe. Pneumonia, too. He is an old, weak man, and the attack is acute. There is no hope for him; but he goes to the hospital today to be made more comfortable."

The next day the doctor said to Sue, "She's out of danger. You've won. Nutrition and care now–that's all."

And that afternoon Sue came to the bed where Johnsy lay, contentedly knitting a very blue and very useless woollen shoulder scarf, and put one arm around her, pillows and all.

"I have something to tell you, white mouse," she said, "Mr. Behrman died of pneumonia today in hospital. He was ill only two days. The janitor found him on the morning of the first day in his room downstairs helpless with pain. His shoes and clothing were wet through and icy cold. They couldn't imagine where he had been on such a dreadful night. And then they found a lantern, still lighted, and a ladder that had been dragged from its place, and some scattered brushes, and a palette with green and yellow colours mixed on it, and–look out the window, dear, at the last ivy leaf on the wall. Didn't you wonder why it never fluttered or moved when the wind blew? Ah, darling, it's Behrman's masterpiece–he painted it there the night that the last leaf fell."

—From "The Last Leaf" by O. Henry

8

"Believe me, my dear Miss Elizabeth, that your modesty, so far from doing you any disservice, rather adds to your other perfections. You would have been less amiable in my eyes had there *not* been this little unwillingness; but allow me to assure you, that I have your respected mother's permission for this address. You can hardly doubt the purpose of my discourse, however your natural delicacy may lead you to dissemble; my attentions have been too marked to be mistaken. Almost as soon as I entered the house, I singled you out as the companion of my future life. But before I am run away with by my feelings on this subject, perhaps it would be advisable for me to state my reasons for marrying– and, moreover, for coming into Herdfordshne with the design of selecting a wife, as I certainly did."

The idea of Mr. Collins, with all his solemn composure, being run away with by his feelings, made Elizabeth so near laughing, that she could not use the short pause he allowed in any attempt to stop him farther, and he continued:

"My reasons for marrying are, first, that I think it a right thing for every clergyman in easy circumstances (like myself) to set the example of matrimony in his parish; secondly, that I am convinced it will add very greatly to my happiness; and thirdly–which perhaps I ought to have mentioned earlier, that it is the particular advice and recommendation of the very noble lady whom I have the honour of calling patroness. Twice has she condescended to give me her opinion (unasked too!) on this subject; and it was but the very Saturday night before I left Hunsford–between our pools at quadrille, while Mrs. Jenkinson was arranging Miss de Bourgh's footstool, that she said, 'Mr. Collins, you must marry. A clergyman like you must marry. Choose properly, choose a gentlewoman for my sake; and for your *own*, let her be an active, useful sort of person, not brought up high, but able to make a small income go a good way. This is my advice. Find such a woman as soon as you can, bring her to Hunsford, and I will visit her."

—Jane Austen

9

If today I have a quarrel with another man, I do not get beaten merely bacause I am physically weaker and he can knock me down. I go to law, and the law will decide as fairly as it can between two of us. Thus in disputes between man and man right has taken the place of might. Moreover, the law protects me from robbery and violence. Nobody may come and break into my house, steal my goods, or run off with my children. Of course, there are burglars, but they are very rare and the law punishes them whenever it catches them.

It is difficult for us to realize how much this safety means. Without safety those higher activities of mankind which make up civilization could not go on. The inventor could not invent, the scientist find out or the artist make beautiful things. Hence order and safety, although they are not themselves civilization, are things without which civilization would be impossible. They are as necessary to our civilization as the air we breathe is to us; and we have grown so used to them that we do not notice them any more than we notice the air.

—C. E. M. Joad

10

All of us desire a better state of society. But society cannot become better before two great tasks are performed. Unless peace can be firmly established and the prevailing obsession with money and power modified, there is no hope of any desirable change being made. Governments are not willing to undertake these tasks; indeed, in many countries they actively persecute those who even express opinion that such tasks are worth-performing. Private individuals are prepared to undertake them in the ordinary way of business. If the work is to be done at all and it is clear that, unless it is done, the state of the world is likely to become progressively worse it must be done by associations of devoted individuals. To tend the sick, to relieve the poor, to teach without charge these are all intrinsically excellent tasks. But for associations of devoted individuals to perform such tasks is now a work of supererogation and, in a certain sense, an anachronism. It was right that they should undertake them when nobody else was prepared to do so. If they undertake them now, when such tasks are being performed, very efficiently, by other agencies, they are wasting the energy of their devotion. They should use this energy to do what nobody else will do, to break the new ground that nobody else will break.

—Aldous Huxley

11

"Why in the name of *Davy Jones*," said he, "is Dr. Livesey mad?"

"I take it," I replied, "the doctor has his idea; and if I am right, he's going to see Ben Gunn."

In the meantime, I began to get another thought in my head, which by not by any means so right. I began to envy the doctor. As no one was observing me, I took the first step towards my escapade, and filled both pockets of my coat with biscuits. These biscuits, should anything *befall* me, would keep me, at least, from starving till far on in the next day. The next thing I laid hold of was a *brace* of pistols. Thus with a powder-horn, bullets and pistols I felt myself well supplied with arms.

As for the scheme I had in my head, it was not a bad one in itself. I was to go down the sandy *spit* that divides the anchorage on the east from the open sea, find the white rock, I had observed last evening, and *ascertain* whether it was there or not that Ben Gunn had hidden his boat. My plan was to slip out when nobody was watching. I was only a boy, and I had my mind made up. Soon I found an opportunity. I made a *bolt* for it over the stockade and into the thicket of trees, and before my absence was observed I was out of cry of my companions. This was my second folly, but like the first, it was a help towards saving all of us.

It was already late in the afternoons. I have never seen the sea so quite round the Treasure Island. When I thought that I was far enough to the south, I took the cover of some bushes, and crept *warily* up to the ridge of the spit. Behind me was the sea, in front the anchorage. The *Hispaniola* was exactly *portrayed* from the truck to the water line, the Jolly Roger hanging from the peak. Alongside lay one of the gigs, Silver in the *sternsheets*.

A couple of men were leaning over the *stern bulwarks,* one of them with a red cap. Apparently they were langhing and talking. All at once, there began the most horrid, unearthly screaming, which at first startled me badly. Soon after the jolly-boat *shoved off* and pulled for shore, and the man with the red cap and his comrade went below. Just about the same time the sun had gone down behind the Spy-glass, and it began to grow dark in *earnest*. I saw I must lose no time if I were to find the boat that evening.

The white rock, visible enough above the brush, was still some eighth of a mile further down the spit. Night had almost come. Right below it there was an *exceedingly* small hollow of green *turf* and in the centre of the *dell*, sure enough, a little tent of goat-skins. I dropped into the hollow, lifted the side of the tent and there was Ben Gunn's boat, a rude, *lop-sided* framework of tough wood. The thing was extremely small, and I can hardly imagine that it could have floated with a full-sized man. There was one *thwart* set as low as possible, a kind of stretcher in the bows and a double *paddle* for *propulsion*. The great advantage it certainly possessed was that it was exceedingly light and portable.

Well, now that I had found the boat, I had taken another *notion*. This was to slip out under cover of the night, cut the *Hispaniola adrift* and let her go where she *fancied*. I had quite made up my mind that the mutineers, after their *repulse* of the morning, had nothing nearer their hearts than to up anchor and away to sea; this, I thought, it would be a fine thing to prevent.

Down I sat to wait for darkness, and made a hearty meal of biscuit. At last the rays of daylight *dwindled* and disappeared, absolute blackness settled down on the Treasure Island. And when, at last, I *shouldered* the boad and *groped* my way out of the hollow, there were but two points visible on the whole anchorage.

—From "Treasure Island" by R. L. Stevenson

12

"Rules," I said, "are necessary things, but there are rules and rules. Some are hard and fast, rules like the rules of the road, which cannot be broken without danger to life and limb. But some are only rules for our guidance, which you can apply or wink at as common sense dictates—like that rule about the dogs. They are meant to be observed in the spirit, not in the letter for the comfort and not the discomfort of the passenger. You have kept the rule and broken the spirit. You want to mix your rules with a little good-will and good temper."

—A. G. Gardiner

13

I got up. The Burmans were already racing past me across the mud. It was obvious that the elephant would never rise again, but he was not dead. He was breathing very rhythmically with long, rattling gasps, his great mound of a side painfully rising and falling. His mouth was wide open–I could see far down into caverns of pale pink throat. I waited a long time for him to die, but his breathing did not weaken. Finally I fired my two remaining shots into the spot where I thought his heart must be. The thick blood welled out of him like red velvet, but still he did not die. His body did not even jerk when the shots hit him, the tortured breathing continued without a pause. He was dying, very slowly and in great agony, but in some world remote from me where not even a bullet could damage him further. I felt that I had got to put an end to that dreadful noise. It seemed dreadful to see the great beast lying there, powerless to move and yet powerless to die and not even to be able to finish him. I sent back for my small rifle and poured shot after shot into his heart and down his throat. They seemed to make no impression. The tortured gasps continued as steadily as the ticking of a clock.

In the end I could not stand it any longer and went away. I heard later that it took him half an hour to die. Burmans were arriving with baskets even before I left, and I was told they had stripped his body almost to the bones by the afternoon.

Afterwards of course, there were endless discussions about the shooting of the elephant. I was very glad that the *coolie* had been killed; it put me legally in the right and it gave me a sufficient pretext for shooting the elephant. I often wondered whether any of the others grasped that I had done it solely to avoid looking a fool.

—George Orwell

VARIOUS FORMS OF WRITING

Drama and Its Major Forms

The following are the Major Forms of Drama :

1. Morality, Miracle and Mystery Plays and Interludes
2. The Tragedy
3. The Melodrama
4. The Tragi-Comedy
5. The Romantic Comedy
6. The Comedy of Humours
7. The Comedy of Manners
8. The Farce
9. The Masque
10. The Poetic Play
11. The Dramatic Monologue
12. The Problem Play
13. The One-Act Play

Prose and Its Major Forms

The following are the Major Forms of Prose :

1. Long Prose-Works
2. The Essay
3. The Periodical Journals
4. The Biography
5. The Autobiography
6. The Memoirs

Poetry and Its Major Forms

Poetry and its Major Forms are these :

1. The Epic
2. The Mock Epic
3. The Sonnet
4. The Ode
5. The Lyric
6. The Idyll
7. The Pastoral
8. The Elegy
9. The Pastoral Elegy
10. The Ballad
11. The Satire

Novel and Its Major Forms

The following are the Major Forms of the Novel :

1. The Prose Romances
2. The Travelogues
3. The Gothic Novel
4. The Picaresque Novel
5. The Epistolary Novel
6. The Domestic Novel
7. The Historical Novel
8. The Regional Novel
9. The Prophetic Novel
10. The Psychological Novel
11. The Short Story

❑❑❑

Essay Writing

IMPORTANT TIPS

An essay is generally speaking, a written composition containing an expression of one's personal opinions or ideas on a subject. A good essay must hold its readers' attention from the beginning to the end. For this, it must possess certain qualities, which make a piece of writing readable and enjoyable.

Every essay depends on two things: (*a*) its subject matter, and (*b*) its language.

To write an essay you require 'material'—clear ideas based on experience, reading and observation. These ideas have to be put into words and these words must convey what you wish to say. For this you should know the right words and the most appropriate ways to put them together.

An essay is generally divided into three parts:

1. The Introduction. **2.** The Body. **3.** The Conclusion. And each of these requires careful attention.

(*i*) **The Introduction Paragraph:** It is the first paragraph of your essay. It introduces the main idea of your essay. A good opening paragraph captures the interest of your reader and tells why your topic is important. The introduction should be designed to attract the reader's attention and give the reader an idea of the essay's focus. Begin with an attention grabber.

(*ii*) **Supporting Paragraphs (Body):** Supporting paragraphs make up the main body of your essay. They develop the main idea of your essay.

To form a perfect body of your essay, you should:

1. List the points that develop the main idea of your essay. 2. Place each supporting point in its own paragraph. 3. Develop each supporting point with facts, details and examples. To connect your supporting paragraphs, you should use special transition words. Transition words link your paragraphs together and make your essay easier to read. Use them at the beginning and end of your paragraphs.

(*iii*) **Summary Paragraph (Conclusion):** The summary paragraph comes at the end of your essay after you have finished developing your ideas. The summary paragraph is often called a "conclusion". It summarises or restates the main idea of the essay. You want to leave the reader with a sense that your essay is complete. Restate the strongest points of your essay that support your main idea. Conclude your essay by restating the main idea in different words. Give your personal opinion or suggest a plan for action. Use a summary statement rather than phrases like the following: "In summary...," "To conclude...," "To summarise...," or "In closing...." These are too obvious and vague to be effective. Use a transitional phrase, which summarises a point in your essay instead.

In a short essay, you can deal with a very few points only. It is of no use to write down a lot of things that have nothing to do with the subject. Write down facts that will help you in your essay. Write down your own ideas. Find the main idea of your essay. Choose the most important point you are going to present. Organise your facts and ideas in a way that develops your main idea. Once you have chosen the most important point of your essay, you must find the best way to tell your reader about it. Develop each supporting paragraph and make sure to follow the correct paragraph format. Write simple sentences to express your meaning. Use simple words; be clear as well as brief. Focus on the main idea of your essay. Check your essay for mistakes and correct them. Make sure that your handwriting is clear and legible. The examiner may not have enough time to take pains to read each and every word carefully. An illegible handwriting might only put off his interest in reading your essay even though it might be good. An essay can be written just about anything, even a poem. Hence it will be difficult to predict which essay you may be asked to write about in your exam. Here are a few selected essays for your study.

SELECTED ESSAYS

EXAMINATIONS : RIGHT OR WRONG

Life is all along an examination and all of us have to face one or the other tough task daily, wherever and in whatever position we may be.

Most of the students are virtually in a state of depression near the examinations, though strictly in medical terms, this state may not be technically admitted to be such a state. But, we can say with jubilation "The examination blues !" And jubilation not at the poor fellows who suffer these blues but at the finding out of a term even like Galileo who exclaimed, "Eureka! Eureka! Eureka!" on a new astronomical discovery.

We learn from the counsellors about the students' common complaints like lack of appetite, insomnia, fear of failure, fear of being rebuked by parents, fear of loss of status among the student community in particular and society in general, etc. Sometimes, even suicidal tendencies are noticed by these counsellors. In certain cases, students who have shown remarkable performance in the previous classes are afraid that they may not be able to repeat the performance and be taken to task by their parents. In certain cities, helplines are available round the clock. Even the CBSE has been running such helplines for students.

Some of such helplines for students in blues to make some queries to get rid of them are Disha, Snehi, Sarthak, CBSE, etc. It deserves to be noted that not always calls are made by the students themselves, sometimes, even parents make a fervent call about their ward and at times even express their anger over the phone at the defective examination system, which reduces the students to robots and automatons, snatching all the emotions, charm and joy from their life.

Since many of us will be inclined to say that after a lot of experimentation in several ways, the net decision for the present seems to be that examinations in one form or the other are unavoidable. They may be called a necessary evil. In whatever form they may be, they are, after all examinations and there is hardly a student who does not shudder at the sheer mention of the word "Examination."

A great bane of the modern examination system is that we have too many examinations. Even to get admission in the nursery or pre-nursery class, the child has to take a test. Not only the child but also its parents have to appear for an interview. Then throughout the career of the poor child, there are tests and examinations galore such as daily, weekly, monthly, bimonthly, semester-related, annual, etc.

If a student has to seek admission in any other institution for any reason, he has to take a test. Even after getting a certificate, diploma or degree, one has to appear in a test, examination and/or interview or viva voce, group discussion and what not in order to join a vocational, technical or professional course or a job.

We have a pertinent saying: "Excess of everything is bad." This should and does equally apply to the examinations. The examinations always keep the students on tenterhooks. They are often a worried lot. It is hard to find a ray of cheerfulness on the faces of most of the students. Then in this world of hard competition and pressing demands on the students from their parents and teachers, many students fall a prey to such unethical practices as copying. Gone are the days when students like Gandhiji refused to copy the spelling of a word from another student's exercise book even when he was urged by his teacher to do so. Now, not only the students themselves but also many times even their parents and the so-called all well-wishers try to exhort the student to indulge in the unhealthy practice of copying.

Another great menace, perhaps the greatest of all other menaces, is the menace of leakage of papers of various examinations. There have been reports about the leakage of PMT papers right from the beginning. Similarly, leakage of papers of many other examinations has sporadically taken place in the past. During the recent few years, however, the leakage of papers pertaining to various examinations has taken the shape of an epidemic.

The leakage of All India Pre-Medical Test (AIPMT) was detected in Delhi. It is a different matter that two students were arrested. And, now we hear a well-organised racket has been caught in Chandigarh engaged in facilitating copying in post-graduate medical course admissions tests through high-tech devices such as bluetooth and pen-scanners. They are even said to place dummy candidates for this job.

Such a state of affairs can make the students lethargic. They can seriously and sincerely think that if they can get through an examination just by buying a question paper a few hours or a day before the examination, why should they lick the books the whole year? What they now actually need is a few lakhs of rupees for which their parents may be willing even more. Let the nation, society and the world go to hell! So this is what the present examination system makes them and from what. How raw they were and how crude, rude and rough now they are!

Let some methods be devised to uplift the moral standard of not only the students but also the parents, teachers, government functionaries and all others concerned.

India's education and examination systems are now being lauded all over the world for being of quite-high quality, though we still find several deficiancies in them. A positive factor in this context is the will for constant rethinking and making changes where necessary. An example can be given in the matter of rethinking about the examinations pertaining to Class X. One of the proposals mooted mainly by the CBSE was concerning making class X examinations optional. The boards, however, did not find favour with this proposal. Instead, the council, allowing flexibility to students, agreed to implement the grading system by 2008 and also made a case for including internal assessment in schools. It allowed students. The new idea emerged in that the annual examinations should be spread over a couple of months so that a student can take a few papers in one month and the rest in the subsequent months, instead of appearing in the examinations in one go. However, it was agreed that the results should be declared in one go. It was believed that the system would prevent the students from neglecting their school education.

RESERVATION A CURSE IN TODAY'S SOCIETY

Again after a decade and more Indian government has added new fuel to the fire of discontent of the youth and students by modifying the existing policy of reservation and has decided to implement a hike in reservation from 22.5% to 50% at one blow especially in higher studies and professional courses like medical, engineering and management courses in April'06 in accordance with the 93rd amendment of the Indian constitution, adopted in December 2005.

Obviously this has inflamed the anger of the would be workers (Students and youth who quite rightly consider themselves to be the immediate victims of this policy) and this wrath and anger against the system led them to streets against the new policy of reservation. On the other hand, the 'Other Backward Castes (OBC)' –category of students for whom the recent hike in reservation is applicable, have also mobilized themselves in favour of the decision of the government, though the anti-reservation movement has been very widespread in almost all parts of India.

The movement has been started by the medicos in Delhi. They have asked the government for the clarification of the 'parameter' used to define 'OBC', wanted to know other 'affirmative actions' of the government for the real development of the social strata for which the government seems to be very much eager(!). The engineering faculty students have also joined them.

However, finally the Supreme Court has intervened, directed the government to submit to it the rationality of the recent hike in reservation for the other backward castes and the definition of the other backward castes.

In spite of all this, root causes of the movement are still there with the same form and content and any day there may be a more forceful burst out with more anger in a more consolidated way!

SEEING CHALLENGES AS OPPORTUNITIES

Most of us know that great rewards require great sacrifice and effort. In a sense that's true. If everything we wanted was handed to us, we probably wouldn't have a lot of appreciation for it. On the other hand, when we work hard for something and then see it manifest before our eyes, we get such a powerful sense of pride and accomplishment. We can point to it and say, "I did that. It was tough, but I did it anyway."

Challenges are truly opportunities. Opportunities to grow and learn, to strengthen ourselves, to test ourselves and our faith. They reveal how badly we want to create the dreams in our hearts, and how hard we're willing to work for them. This is such a blessing. It may not seem that way at first, but with a tiny shift in attitude, we can see that we have been handed an incredible opportunity.

When challenges rise up before us, we may not know how to get around them, or through them. It might seem hopeless at first. Challenges can seem so overwhelming when we don't have a solution. However, life itself is very much like this too. Sometimes life is akin to bumping around in a dark room, trying to find the light switch. It is possible to get through the room without finding the light switch immediately, we just need to step slowly and carefully. Moment to moment, we find our way.

Once we begin to change our attitude about obstacles and challenges, they can actually become fun. Our competitive human nature rises up and gets ready to win, no matter what. We develop a steely determination to not be beaten.

WHY TODAY'S YOUTH CULTURE HAS GONE INSANE?

Today's youth culture indeed seems to have gone insane. The signs and reasons are many. First of all, there's sex. Very simply, there seem to be neither boundaries nor taboos any more when it comes to sex. Anything goes — from heterosexual to homosexual to bi-, trans-, poly-, and not to mention sexual experiences.

Moreover, with the evolution of online pornography, every type of sexual experience has literally been shoved under the noses of millions of peoples against their will, who find their e-mail in-boxes filled with hard-core sexual images.

And body piercing! It has progressed from traditional earrings for females, to earrings for males (eager to display their "feminine side" which the '60 cultural revolution sold them), to multiple piercings for both males and females in literally every part of the body – the tongue, nose, eyebrow, lip, cheek, navel, breasts and even genitals.

It's the same progression to extremes with tattooing. But why stop with "conventional" piercing and tattooing? Ritual scarification and 3D-art implants are big. So are genital beading, stretching and cutting, transdermal implants, scrotal implants, tooth art and facial sculpture.

Strangest of all is the fact that any behavior, any belief – no matter how obviously insane – is rationalized so it sounds reasonable, even spiritual. Satanism itself, and especially its variant, the worship of Lucifer (literally, "Angel of Light") can be made to sound almost enlightened – of course, only in a perverse way. But if one is sufficiently confused, rebellious and full of rage – if one had been set up by cruelty or hypocrisy (or both) to rebel against everything "good" – the forbidden starts to be mysteriously attractive.

No wonder our youth are rebelling. And today's insane culture, which we have allowed and in many ways created, stands waiting in the wings to welcome them with open arms.

Each of us must awaken. Otherwise, the marketers of evil will lead us all down to ever darker and lower levels of hell on earth.

E-BANKING/INTERNET BANKING

Computers and internet have brought revolution in our lives in many ways. Our banks and banking system are also revolutionized by these. Now a days you may do all bank-related work without even entering the bank premises, sitting at home or in the office. You do not have to bother about the bank distance, timings, holidays and negligent staff and long queues. This type of banking is known as internet banking or electronic banking. Even to withdraw or deposit cash you do not have to visit your bank's branch. All you have to do is to visit the nearby ATM and use your ATM card to do this. Even if your branch is located in another city. You can do all type of banking transactions sitting in a remote place or city. Thanks to e-banking!

Banks are trying to make your life easier. Not just bill payment, you can make investments, shop or buy tickets and plan a holiday at your fingertips.

Each bank has tie-ups with various utility companies, service providers and insurance companies across the country. You can facilitate payment of electricity and telephone bills, mobile phone, credit card and insurance premium bills.

All you need is a computer with a modem or other dial-up device, a checking account with a bank that offers online service.

You can transfer any amount from one account to another of the same or any other bank. You can now open an FD online through funds transfer.

Now you no longer need to rush to the vendor to recharge your prepaid phone. Just top-up your prepaid mobile cards by logging in to Internet banking.

Leading banks have tie ups with various shopping websites. With a range of all kind of products, you can shop online and the payment is also made conveniently through your account. You can also buy railway and air tickets through Internet banking.

Through Internet banking, you can check your transactions at any time of the day, and as many times as you want to.

There are many advantages of online banking. It is convenient, it isn't bound by operational timings, there are no geographical barriers and the services can be offered at a minimal cost.

Customers should never share personal information like PIN numbers, passwords etc with anyone, including employees of the bank.

WI FI : A NEW TOOL OF INTERNET TECHNOLOGY

WiFi stands for Wireless Fidelity. It is a new technology that helps the mobile Internet users take the advantage of Wireless Technology in a building, office or home. The user can connect his laptop PC to the Net through this technology. He has to insert a special card in his PC. This card can receive signals from a transmission tower that is installed in the building in which, he arrives. This building could be an office, airport, residential complex, shopping mall etc. The transmission tower would send Internet signals to the PC through this special card. The user can connect his PC to the Net and exchange E-mail, V-mail, and data. He can also surf through various websites of the Net. Finally, he can also download data from such web sites. Hence, WiFi is a wireless connection that makes a PC Internet-enabled. It is different from Blue Tooth, which is another wireless technology.

Nowadays, laptops are quite costly viz-a-viz their desktop cousins. With the passage of time, the cost of the gadgets of WiFi is likely to come down. Hence, laptops as well as WiFi would be affordable. WiFi can be used in desktop systems as well. Hence, persons working in a large building can use a single Internet connection to use the information superhighway. Thus, ideal use of WiFi in desktops is not a distant reality in India.

We should welcome this new technology, which has yet to make deep inroads into the industries, Net cafes and business houses of our country. Its future is bright because it is a wireless technology.

MERCY KILLING

Mercy Killing or Euthanasia refers to the practice of ending a life in a manner which relieves pain and suffering. It is a deliberate intervention undertaken with the express intention of ending a life, to relieve intractable suffering.

Euthanasia may be classified according to whether a person gives informed consent into three types: voluntary, non-voluntary and involuntary.

There is a debate within the medical and bioethics literature about whether or not the non-voluntary (and by extension, involuntary) killing of patients can be regarded as euthanasia, irrespective of intent or the patient's circumstances. According to few experts, consent on the part of the patient is not considered necessary. However, others see consent as essential. Medicalized killing of a person without the person's consent, whether non-voluntary (where the person is unable to give consent) or involuntary (against the person's will) is not euthanasia: it is murder. Hence, euthanasia can be voluntary only.

Euthanasia conducted with the consent of the patient is termed voluntary euthanasia. Euthanasia conducted where the consent of the patient is unavailable is termed non-voluntary euthanasia. Examples include child euthanasia, which is illegal worldwide but decriminalised under certain specific circumstances in the Netherlands under the Groningen Protocol. Euthanasia conducted against the will of the patient is termed involuntary euthanasia.

In a country like ours, the religious aspects also have to be considered before taking such decisions. The Bible says, "Thou shalt not kill" And even Islam does not allow anyone to take away life. Is our society mature enough to understand the implications of this? We have cases, where doctors are often beaten up if the patient was not treated properly, what would happen to a doctor if he merely suggested euthanasia to the relatives? Will the relatives be able to understand the suffering of the patient?

Life is a gift, and even a life of pain is a life at least. Some people feel we don't choose when to be born and we should not be given the right to choose when to die. On the contrary, others feel that a life of pain is not a life but an imposition and we should be at least allowed to end it in a dignified peaceful manner. Euthanasia could be legalized, but the laws would have to be very stringent. Every case will have to be carefully monitored taking into consideration the point of views of the patient, the relatives and the doctors. But whether Indian society is mature enough to face this, is yet to be seen, after all it's a matter of life and death.

WOMEN EMPOWERMENT

Women account for more than fifty per cent of population and are the main drivers behind the economy of India. The government of India ushered in the new millennium by developing the year 2001 as 'women's empowerment year'.

Notwithstanding steps taken by the Government for women empowerment in the last two decade, much needs to be done. The pillars of women's empowerment essentially consist of literacy, education, better health facilities and nutrition for the mother and child, political representation and financial security including opportunities for self-employment options to become self-reliant. All this is dependent on making women aware about their rights, making them feel proud of being women, creating a conducive atmosphere and giving them opportunities to live the life of dignity. It is often being seen that women are given jobs with lesser wages and that they are not given the same opportunity as men for advancement. Whenever, Indian women have been given a conducive environment and appropriate facilities they have been successful and have become engineers, doctors, administrators, industrialists, members of the police force and armed forces and even astronauts.

Government policies and programmes should be designed with a focus on women's needs and concerns. Women should be supported to set up their own business with the support of self-help groups and the availability of microcredit facilities. These steps will help women achieve economic independence and contribute to their empowerment.

It should be the objective to give women opportunities to work, and to create a social environment in which women can live with respect and dignity and can play a role in nation building.

Full potential as a nation will only be realized when women, who constitute about half of our population, can fully realize their potential. As long as that does not happen, half the talent, half the progress, half the development, would be lost. So to move the chariot of our country forward, both the wheels-men and women have to be strong and to move ahead jointly.

END CHILD LABOUR : PROTECT CHILDREN'S RIGHTS

Child labour usually refers to children up to the age of 14. If we consider the age group 5-14, and the definition of worker as in the Census of India, then, in 2001, there were 12.6 million child workers in the country.

There is no doubt that bonded labour and other extremely exploitative forms of child labour should be ended at once, and require priority attention. All forms of labour are hazardous to the well being of children.

Children work long hours for low wages in dangerous work environments. Literacy among child workers is very low, they suffer ailments at an early age, and their life expectancy is unlikely to be high.

In a country like India where 28 per cent of the population is living in conditions of extreme poverty, child labour is a complex issue. The social scientists say that the main cause of child labour is poverty. The children either supplement their parents' income or are the only wage earners in the family. In these circumstances, the alternative to work may be idleness, destitution, or worse, crime.

Undoubtedly, poverty is the seed-bed for child labour. It is the children of the poor, and the socially and economically deprived sections of the population, who work. However, the persistence of child labour depends critically on the demand for it.

It is commonly argued that child labour cannot be stopped till such time as poverty is reduced, and, therefore, the main policy thrust should be towards the eradication of poverty.

It is time to end all forms of child labour, and to recognize that all children have a right to education and leisure and other means to develop their physical and mental capabilities during childhood.

JUDICIAL ACTIVISM IN INDIA

Judicial activism has introduced a new dimension regarding judiciary's involvement in public administration. Judicial activism was made possible in India, thanks to PIL (Public Interest Litigation).

After the Constitution (Twenty fifth Amendment) Act, 1971, by which primacy was accorded to a limited extent to the Directive Principles vis-a-vis the Fundamental Rights making the former enforceable rights, the expectations of the public soared high and the demands on the courts to improve the administration by giving appropriate directions for ensuring compliance with statutory and constitutional prescriptions have increased.

The judicial power under our Constitution is vested in the Supreme Court and the High Courts which are empowered to exercise the power of judicial review both in regard to legislative and executive actions. Judges cannot shirk their responsibilities as adjudicators of legal and constitutional matters.

A common criticism we hear about judicial activism is that in the name of interpreting the provisions of the Constitution and legislative enactments, the judiciary often rewrites them undermining the authority of the legislature and the executive by encroaching upon the spheres reserved for them.

Judicial creativity even when it takes the form of judicial activism should not result in rewriting of the Constitution or any legislative enactments. In the name of doing justice and taking shelter under institutional self-righteousness, the judiciary cannot act in a manner disturbing the delicate balance between the three wings of the State.

Judicial activist fervour should not flood the fields constitutionally earmarked for the legislature and the executive. That would spell disaster. Governmental machinery cannot be run by judges. Any populist views aired by judges would undermine their authority and disturb the institutional balance.

Judicial activism characterised by moderation and self-restraint is bound to restore the faith of the people in the efficacy of the democratic institutions which alone, in turn, will activate the executive and the legislature to function effectively under the vigilant eye of the judiciary as ordained by the Constitution.

ENVIRONMENT POLLUTION

Important elements constituting the earth are air, soil and water. These together comprise the environment. The earth has a cover of air around it which is called atmosphere. More than two–thirds of the area of the earth comprises oceans and seas which contain water.

All the elements together form climate. All the living beings can live only in a particular type of climate. We are living on the earth because a climate suitable for our living is available on this planet. Our earth took more than 400 crore years to evolve the present climate.

It is quite clear that if the climate at present available on the earth is disturbed excessively, life on this planet may be in danger. Unfortunately, this is what man is doing at present. His actions are causing the depletion of ozone and oxygen and increasing the production of harmful gases such as carbon dioxide, carbon monoxide, sulphur dioxide, etc. These gases are produced by the smoke released by chimneys of factories, automobiles, burning of wood, etc. Such gases also cause greenhouse effect. They cause increase in temperature all over the earth. This undue increase in temperature is melting the snow on mountain-tops. This can lead to increase in the volume of water in oceans. The result of this can be the merger of many islands and coastal areas in many countries under the water.

Man is at present cutting down forests recklessly. Forests cause rain and maintain a balance of oxygen in the atmosphere.

The excessive use of pesticides and insecticides and the use of spurious fertilizers is polluting the soil. The water channels are being polluted due to the toxic matter released by factories. Non-disposal or improper disposal of medical and domestic waste is also polluting the soil and water.

Another kind of pollution is the noise pollution. We have so much noise in cities and towns. We hear sounds of factory hooters and generators, noises made by hawkers and customers in markets and loudspeakers used at religious places and functions of all types, including religious and political functions and social gatherings such as marriages, etc. Loud noises have an adverse effect on human nerves and they affect the brain and the hearing system of the body.

If man wants to continue living on this planet, he will have to mend his ways. Otherwise, there is no certainty that mankind will live for more than a century on it.

DRUG-ADDICTION

When the Hippies came to India, they brought not only strange dresses but also drugs. It is common knowledge that the young people are greatly influenced by anything strange and new.

At present, our country is under the grip of drug-addiction. Most of the drug-addicts live in cities. They include both boys and girls. University, college and school hostels are particularly full of drug-addicts.

Drug-addiction is, however, not restricted to urban areas only. Even in the rural areas there are so many drug-addicts. There are not only men but also women in large numbers who take drugs. This vice has invaded all sections of society. Many rickshaw-pullers, factory workers, government employees and even businessmen can be seen who are given to the habit of drug-taking.

Most often it so happens that a person takes a drug just for the thrill of it. Then he takes it the second or third time to repeat the experience. When he takes it a number of times, he forms the habit. Then a time comes when he wants to get rid of it. But he cannot do so because he feels restlessness if he does not take the drug.

Most of the young people start this habit in the company of their friends in hostels. One reason for this wide-spread practice is that drugs are easily available everywhere. There are so many peddlers who sell drugs. Drugs are of many kinds such as heroin, smack, LSD, opium, ganja, charas, etc. All drugs are habit-forming.

A drug-addict gets his health spoiled. He also wastes his precious money on drugs. Some of these drugs such as heroin are very costly. But those who are addicted to drugs cannot get rid of them easily. If they do not have money to buy a drug, they steal money from home or from wherever they can. They can even commit some more serious crime to get money for drugs.

Drug-taking makes a person lazy. It can cause even death. Young people should be taught in schools and colleges to avoid this bad habit. If a youth falls a prey to this habit, he should be taken to the drug-deaddiction centre as early as possible. Strict action should be taken against drug-peddlers and chemists and others who sell drugs.

One reason for this menace is that the young people feel frustrated. They find the education system worthless. They do not get proper love from parents. They are unemployed and have no hope of getting a job. The parents, teachers, NGO's, social workers, government agencies and media should join hands to save the youth of our country from this menace.

SEX EDUCATION

It is a hot topic in India and some other countries of the world whether sex education should be imparted to children in schools and colleges or not.

As far as the Indian society is concerned, we generally do not talk about sex. This is also one of the reasons why AIDS is spreading so fast in our country.

All of us know that sex is an integral part of all life, including human life on earth. If there is no sex, there can be no life. Without sex, all life, including mankind will come to an end.

It is quite clear that sex education is unavoidable. If children are not taught about sex in an educational institution, they try to know about it from other sources such as Internet, friends or books which they read secretly. Some of the books are misleading as they are written to arouse passions and make money.

A very systematic and comprehensive syllabic plan should be drawn out to impart sex education to children. They should be told very tactfully about male and female anatomy. They should be told how child is conceived in the mother's womb.

If children are not given sex education properly, they get wrong information about it from here and there and develop habits of premature and unnatural sex.

In order to impart sex education to children, very competent and tactful teachers should be employed. Such teachers should have high knowledge of human anatomy, physiology, biology and child psychology.

In educational institutions, already we teach the students about the sexual parts of plants and to some extent of animals. Heavens will not fall if we teach them something of this about human beings. As it is, when sex education is started in a systematic way, it will become routine with children. As their curiosity is over, the danger of harmful side-effects in the form of delinquency will be no more there.

It is, therefore, advisable that sex education should be given to students in educational institutions, but that in a very cautious, planned and systematic way.

FEMALE FOETICIDE

Of all the crimes and immoral acts, perhaps female foeticide is the most heinous. Female foeticide means killing the girl child in the womb. It is no different from killing a girl who is born, as a girl in the womb is as much a living being. She is only at a developing stage.

The main reason for female foeticide is that the girls are not a desirable thing in our city. It is mainly because of our faulty social customs. A girl is considered a burden on the parents. It is because, as per the common social practice in our country, the girl's parents have to give a very rich dowry on her marriage. In fact, they have to continue giving money and material to the girl's inlaws all her life. Therefore, if the problem of female foeticide is to be solved in right earnest, the problem of dowry system must also be solved on equal footing along with it.

Indians are fond of having a male child to continue the lineage. Those who have one or more girl children go in for female foeticide till they get a male child. In this respect, the use of ultrasonic machines has played a negative role. As a matter of fact, these machines are very useful for scanning purposes to determine the presence of any abnormality in the body. But they are being used unscrupulously for knowing the sex of the infant in the womb. No doubt, there is an Anti–prenatal sex determination law, but the unhealthy practice of knowing the sex of the unborn child is going on secretly. For this, the greedy practitioners charge a hefty amount which the parents of the unborn child gladly pay.

The sex ratio against girls has been declining during the last few decades. It is particularly the condition in some of the northern states, Punjab and Haryana in particular. The situation has become alarming after the arrival of ultrasound scanning machines.

If this trend continues, a stage may come when girls will be a rare breed. Already there are so many crimes against women in society such as rapes, murders, bride-burning, immoral trafficking, etc. We will certainly shudder to think of final stage, and that is the world without women! If there are no women, there will be no mankind. So, if we do not take any drastic steps right from now, we may be heading towards a womanless world which means the end of mankind. Hence all the educationsts, students, teachers, parents, government, NGO's and the media should strain every nerve to enlighten the people and put an end to this unhealthy practice.

POPULATION EXPLOSION

The rapidly increasing population may be a matter which can cause scare in the minds of all thinking people. It is a kind of explosion no less horrible than the explosion of an atom bomb!

At the time India got Independence in 1947, it had the population of about 35 crore. Now, it is inhabited by more than 120 crore people. The world-over population has greatly increased. It is around 700 crore mark at present. It also means that every 7th person in the world is an Indian. Population is increasing more rapidly in developing countries than in developed countries. It means industrialisation or development is an answer to the rising trend in population.

India is second only to China in the matter of population. But in India population is increasing much more rapidly than in China. It is estimated by the demographers that within the next two decades India may overtake China in the matter of population.

There are several reasons for this rapid increase of population. One of the reasons is the improved health facilities. These facilities have reduced the number of infant mortality and increased the life span. Another reason is illiteracy. Many people, mostly in slum and rural areas do not have much knowledge of means of family planning.

Still, another reason is poverty. Many poor people want more and more children to increase the earning capacity of their family as they put their children to some sort of work at a very early age. Child marriages and early marriages are other reasons.

It is very important that awareness should be brought about among the people to adopt the means of family planning especially, the traditionally and religiously minded people of poor families should be brought around to adopt these methods.

PRICE RISE

India is a land of problems. One of the most serious problem is the problem of price rise. Whenever we go to market, we often find that the prices of all the essential articles have risen. Now, the situation has become more serious because of unprecedented rise in the prices of food items.

It is very difficult for a common man to make both ends meet. The income of the common people does not rise so much as the prices of goods. The salaried people and those who live on pensions are hit the most as they have only a fixed income. The condition of those who live on daily wages is even worse.

One great reason for the rise in prices is the rapid increase in population. Another reason is that most of the people are trying to raise their standards of living. Now people are giving more attention to food, clothing, health, housing, entertainment, education of children, etc. Many people have ACs, cars, desert coolers, geysers, mixers, refrigerators, television sets, telephones, etc. in their homes which previously they did not have. All this increases their expenditure and ultimately, prices.

Goods are not produced at the same rate as the population and demand rise. Many people waste money on luxuries and functions and marriages. The government does not care to control its expenditure. Taxation system is also defective in our country. Then, there are so many ministers and legislators and government employees who have to be paid from treasury. Not much money is left with the government for development purposes.

India has to import a lot of petroleum products and gas to meet her energy requirements. There is much wastage of petrol on running luxury cars. Black money and corruption also lead to price rise. Some traders hoard essential items and raise prices to earn more profits. Famines, floods and strikes also cause price rise.

To check prices, population should be controlled. Strikes should be avoided. Taxation system should be overhauled. Wastage should be avoided. Black money and corruption should be dealt with strictly. Unnecessary imports should be avoided, particularly the imports of luxury items. More attention should be given to exports. Production should be increased. More attention should be given to energy resources.

Much expenditure has to be done on defence. This cannot be helped. However, it should be avoided wherever the security of the country is not compromised. Good relations with neighbouring countries should be established to minimise expenditure on wars and encounters.

With the coming of the VAT system of taxation, people hoped that the prices of goods would by and large go down to a considerable extent. But this has not happend. Let the government and people cooperate with each other to solve all problems, including the problem of price rise.

A NEED TO CHECK ON REALITY SHOWS

These days there is a growing trend towards reality TV shows that are based on external shallow values. But while reality TV may seem like a harmless form of entertainment, the damage is very powerful and therefore it deserves a closer look.

The popularity of reality TV shouldn't come as a surprise considering the fact that we live in a culture that worships vanity, rather than virtue, and lives by the mantra of "He with the most toys lives", rathar than "He with the most joys lives."

Reality TV, which is in the business of making us feel good rather than be good, actually contributes to the growing problems in our society by celebrating human weakness rather than human excellence. Reality TV doesn't empower us, but rather overpowers us by taking our innate power and inner knowing and spirituality away from us, leaving us feeling insecure, inadequate, less fulfilled, isolated and confused by virtue of the promotion of anti-social behaviour, excessive self-indulgence, self-entitlement, greed, compromised integrity, obsession with winning at all costs, and erosion in morality.

Reality TV today makes a lot of unpleasant things acceptable. Abusive language is the least of the grimacing middle-class concern. It's the disrespect for a fellow human being, the emphasis on success at any cost and judgement based on little or no evidence. It is this that a society perhaps should guard against. The debate around reality TV isn't about freedom or the right to expression. It's a debate about the society we want to build.

No court judgement can curb this. Our schadenfreude is our weakness. It's also only our cross to bear. It's easy to blame the channels and the advertisers that support them, but their world revolves around us, the viewers. We're at the centre of it all. It's free market. Stop watching and it'll stop airing.

ARE SPORTS JUST A MONEY-SPINNING BIZ?

There is lot of talk in the air that big money and big business are killing sports. Recently, Michelle Wie announced she was turning pro and received commercial endorsements worth RM38mil, making her the richest 16-year-old in sports. She even made it to the cover of Fortune magazine. Sports are now big business worth hundreds of billions of dollars and provide jobs to millions of people.

However, it is generally believed that big money and big business pose a danger to the future of sports. An example of this can be seen in football. We are concerned with immensely-rich individuals with little or no history of interest in the game buying up football clubs; of players abetted by greedy agents demanding (and getting) huge sums of money to join clubs and play; of clubs that are more interested in the players' performance on the pitch rather than their welfare; and of the huge disparity between earnings of "star" players and the rest of the team, not to mention the many thousands of players in other teams and clubs around the world who earn a pittance. Thus, sports today are nothing more than money spinning biz.

Ninety percent of Sharapova's earnings are from endorsements. Sachin Tendulkar, who signed a three-year deal for reportedly 40 million dollars with Iconix, earns a miniscule fraction of it in match fees. The rapid strides made by M. S. Dhoni in becoming a top brand in India are revealing. First his performances on the field endeared him to the advertisers. He has single-handedly won games for India. Then there is the fact that he is from a small town, he gives people a reason to dream.

So, making moral judgments on the role of money in sports is at once very easy and yet very difficult.

CORRUPTION IS AN ACCEPTED NORM

The standard definition of corruption is — the use of public office for private gain. Its roots and seductions lie much deeper in the quality of human relationships that characterize a society.

Corruption and Indian society are inter-woven closely. Each and every office whether it comes under Central or State administration is no exception. Corruption is simply a consequence of the fact that the state has wide discretionary powers.

The motivations that produce and sustain corruption are of course complex. Avarice and ambition doubtless play an important part.

The experience of both state and society in India is profoundly alienating in more ways than one can list and many forms of corruption stem directly from this experience. Indian society is profoundly inegalitarian. Vast disparities of income and power exist almost everywhere, but the depth, to which in India inequality has subjected individuals to a million humiliations, small and large, is almost unprecedented.

Generally, all this corruption goes on under a cloak, although one can almost see it happening before one's eyes, Bureaucracy is also moulded and influenced to take decisions favourable to vested interest due to corruption. In case of large contracts rules are relaxed and then negotiated without transparency. Not a new phenomenon in India or in many other countries.

If the senior bureaucrat or officer disassociates himself/herself from wrong decisions and does so on the files, wrongdoing or corruption would diminish greatly.

But India is considered especially as a case of its own *i.e.* it is only when the higher bureaucracy or officer becomes compliant and suitably "Cooks the case", then corrupt practice could occur. But any one with even a mild conscience will hesitate to do so.

It has been rightly pointed that in a society in which honesty and patriotism are laughed at and poked fun of; corruption is going to be all pervading because there is no moral barrier to it at any level. And also an honest officer is always looked down upon as incapable person who is not suiting to the present environment.

TERRORISM

It is the law of nature that as we solve one problem, new problems appear before us. At one time, the world wanted to get rid of war. When there was hope that the world might somehow get rid of the problem of war in the near future, a new problem arose. It was the problem of terrorism. 'Terrorism' means the process of terrorising others to do or not to do something. A terrorist is one who indulges in such a practice.

A terrorist may prefer to belong to a particular religion or country, but actually he has no religion nor he is a real citizen of any country. No religion preaches terrorism and patriotism also does not mean terrorising the people of any country for the sake of one's own country.

Terrorists are heartless people. They kill or maim unarmed, innocent men, women and children. They are highly immoral and irreligious people as they rape and molest girls and women of all religions and castes whomever they can capture. They can never be regarded as patriotic or religious people. They are enemies of mankind and destroyers of peace. Their only creed is violence. One thing, however, is to be noted. It is that after all, terrorists are also human beings. Then why do they indulge in such activities when others don't do so?

Most of the terrorists are immature young people who can easily be misled. Unemployment is also one of the major causes. Such young people can easily be incited in the name of religion. This is what Pakistan is doing. Then the question of human rights arises. Sometimes, excesses are committed by the security forces. This causes resentment on a large scale and new terrorists are born.

Let the world community join hands to root out this menace which is a danger to mankind. It is because the terrorists the world over are trying to procure nuclear, chemical and biological weapons. If they succeed in their aim, it can lead to the doom of mankind on this planet.

MNCS : SAVIOURS OR SABOTEURS

Multinational Corporations (MNCs) are those private companies that work in more than one country. They produce or provide goods or services of highest quality and according to the latest global norms. They also employ the best human resource in a country and thus build brand images that are unique, stable and, above all, saleable.

In India, MNCs had arrived in the mid-sixties of the last century. Colgate, Palmolive and Coca-Cola were the most trusted names of those times. The sixties also saw the presence of the drug giants. Glaxo, Nicolas and other drug majors gradually made deep forays into the Indian markets as the population demanded more medicines. But our economy remained a mixed one and our governments always looked at the MNCs with suspicion. During those times, the concept of MNCs was not born. The Japanese had just started their marathon run in the field of consumer electronics. They were disliked by most of the Indian consumers because of nil credibility.

However, Indians could not give full support to Coca-Cola due to political reasons. The company was sent packing during the seventies; those were the times when relations between India and the USA were at their lowest ebb. Glaxo, Biological Evans, Smith Kline & French and Pfizer were other drug majors, which firmly established themselves in India during the mid-seventies. And, then came the Japanese—highly efficient, cheap, determined and techno-savvy. They introduced products of the silicon age, which we fondly know as semiconductor revolution. Radio, television, wireless, electronics, telex systems, etc., were in vogue. Music got a new meaning when the Japanese majors like Sony,

Matsushita and Sharp introduced hi-fidelity stereo system. The revolution had begun!

During the dying years of the seventies, the stage was set in India. During the last years of eighties, this stage was re-set by Integrated Circuits, CNC machines, drugs for fighting heart attacks and the like. So, the Indians had to rely on MNCs, which had become synonymous with technology, comfortable products and cheap rates. Most of MNCs entered India during the late eighties or early nineties. The government favoured their entry because of its changed (and liberal) policies related to economic reforms. Several MNCs established their offices and factories in urban centres of India. Some even went to villages and signed deals in collaboration (partnership) with the Indian firms. Sales soared and FMCGs became the hot goodies on the television shows and in advertisements. Cable TV networks, satellite connections and Internet connections did the rest of the job. Western culture brought the concept of consumerism or "fast eaters". Naturally, a nation that had a population of above one billion had to be given these new products, services and gizmos. And MNCs filled the void that was left by local manufacturers. It is surprising to note that not a single firm has been able to compete with Colgate Palmolive in the toothpaste market; it is the undisputed leader in this segment even today, despite the fact that there are nearly one dozen competitors.

This credibility did not sneak in the minds of the Indian consumer in a day. It took several years and billions of dollars to make these products and services instant success. And there were fiascos too. The cases of Enron and Cogentrix are the two glaring examples, which bluntly tell us that we may not have any collaboration in the power generation sector. Although, Enron has displayed several flaws (like high price of power kwh at Dabbol Power Corporation), yet we cannot deny the fact that we also made a mess of the issue and moved in an unplanned fashion.

The free market economy of India has made the task of MNCs quite easier. Many of us may contend that we are not "completely free", if they keep scandals, scams, corruption and the PSUs in their view. But this ultimate change is inevitable. If ours is not a fully free economy today, it shall be one after fifty years. The MNCs realise this fact and so they have started establishing themselves in India—physically and psychologically. Several MNCs align their advertisements with local festivals, religions, beliefs and political sentiments. They have become a part of our culture quietly and in a stealthy manner. Thus, saviours may be deemed saboteurs by many a political outfit. We agree that the opponents of these global economic giants are not totally wrong. They are saviours on many fronts—medicines, heavy engineering, information technologies, medical diagnostic equipment, aircraft, chemicals, rubber products and electronic gadgets. New technologies and devices have put Indians on the path of ultimate progress. No wonder, we may become a developed nation soon due to inflow of capital, technologies, consultancy and manpower into this land. Thus, MNCs have contributed a lot to our economy and will do so in the future too.

MNCs are also being allowed to enter those sections which were hitherto deemed the exclusive areas reserved for the Indian firm. Ironically, we must state that the MNCs would do much better in those areas, thus putting out our own coin under shade. Banking, insurance, car production and telecommunication services are some of the areas in which they would outperform Indian firms. Thus, Indian firms would either be required to meet the challenge or fade into oblivion.

Finally, every MNC comes to India to earn money. In a free market system, any amount of money can be transferred by an MNC to its parent country. This would lead to drain on our precious foreign exchange reserves. We cannot check the flight of this capital. Had our own enterprises been efficient, productive and innovative, we would not have threats of this kind. It is a pity that we import shirts, jeans and electronics gadgets, whereas we can manufacture them at much cheaper rates in India. Our quality control norms are poor and so, customers get swayed by the quality of products and services of MNCs. Our own firms (like NIIT, Reliance and RITES) are multinationals. So, we can easily emulate them.

We can conclude by stating that we need MNCs as we are a part of the global treading culture. We must allow them to operate in those high-technology areas in which, we lack the expertise. We should also import technologies through them but we should manufacture products (or services) in India. MNCs should not be viewed as saboteurs. But, at the same time, they must not be allowed to control the destiny of our nation.

ELEPHANT VS. DRAGON : WHO WILL SURGE AHEAD?

In the race between Asia's two major developing nations, China's dragon is, by most indicators, beating India's elephant, hands down. Its gross domestic product (GDP) is growing at a rate almost double that of India's, and the aisles of Wal-Mart are cluttered with products made in China. But the United States and the rest of the world had better keep an eye on the elephant and resist temptation to declare the dragon the victor quite yet, says a Harvard Business School (HBS) professor.

However, it is remembered that while China has successfully leveraged its governmental structure to attract the foreign companies fueling its manufacturing boom, India's indigenous entrepreneurship is thriving in a way that cannot be ignored. Despite—or perhaps because of—the fact that its government lacks the economic savvy of China's, India has bred homegrown entrepreneurial ventures that are thriving. So-called "knowledge" industries like software, pharmaceuticals and biotechnology, advertising, and even the film industry are giving India an edge over its neighbour.

India is far ahead of China. For bringing home the point, measures like the Forbes magazine list of medium-sized fast-growing companies, which boasts far more Indian than Chinese companies, and international banks' ratings of many Indian firms as far better managed than other Asian companies, including several better-known firms from Japan and Korea can be easily cited. China, on many dimensions, is just the exact opposite of India. While authoritarian China has aggressively courted foreign investment, democratic India is "allergic" to it. Here you have two large, populous, ancient civilizations that formed modern nation states in geographically proximate locations at roughly the same time, yet have chosen radically different development paths, and have no interconnection with each other whatsoever. Their historic hostility has accentuated the independence of their development paths.

The economic differences arise partly out of the different governmental structures in the two countries. In China, where there is little distinction between the bureaucracy and the government, rising through the ranks of the party has been based, since 1978, on how much one contributes to the local GDP. You have an incentive to promote not just local enterprise but any enterprise. So you open your arms and lay out the red carpet for foreign multinationals. India, on the other hand, is the home of "rampant bureaucratic incompetence." There, bureaucrats' incentives are unrelated to economic outcomes. "You have to work to attract investments, so why bother?"

Yet while China's government provides incentives to the state-supported commerce that has fed its economic success, indigenous enterprise has flourished in India as the government has turned its back. Increasingly, these enterprises are gaining ground in the international economy as in the case of Indian software giants Infosys and Wipro, the pharmaceutical company Ranbaxy, the biotechnology firm Biocon, and the manufacturing firm Moser Bayer. These companies have thrived despite the failure of the government to provide appropriate infrastructure.

Whether India overtakes China or not, frankly, it's immaterial. Much more important is the fact that the United States and the rest of the world learn from China, India, and other developing nations like Brazil or Russia. There's a lot of competition that's going to come out of left field.

Using markedly different strategies and policy reforms, China and India have sustained high growth rates over a number of years. This has had and will continue to have profound effects on their social, economic, cultural and political structures. The rapid growth in China and India has brought about tremendous opportunities and challenges for other countries as well.

The question of whether the dragon or the elephant would dominate the global market is a question that raises passionate debates between millions of Chinese and Indians, all filled with pride over their nation's own ascendancy. Since it is impossible to make a judgment call based on every factor, conclusion can be based on two current indicators which will be the key hallmarks of a potential economic superpower—a strong knowledge based industry, and the existence of a highly entrepreneurial high tech environment. On these two counts, India score higher than China.

India is more likely to take over the role of America as the leading player in the knowledge economy. The current edge obviously goes to India, where marquee names have sprung up over the last few years. Tata Consultancy, Infosys, iflex Solutions, Ranbaxy have become powerhouses in their own fields. Besides having stellar homegrown IT enterprises, the solid infrastructure and a huge base of college graduates in the key cities have allowed it to become the first choice for IT outsourcing.

China, on the other hand, lacks the same kind of luster in its IT sector. This problem goes deep. The lack of IP protection and massive piracy has served as a lesson to a whole generation of Chinese that producing software is pointless. After all, if goods can be pirated, and patents bypassed, where is the incentive for Chinese entrepreneurs to innovate and produce software and drugs of their own? Also, as shown by a recent MGI research, China produces massive number of IT graduates, but a large number of them are technicians, as opposed to highly skilled engineers able to take up managerial and senior engineering roles. With competition for these capable graduates becoming fierce, the labour shortage might become a real issue impeding growth of the IT sector.

Changes in mindset around IP protection, as well as huge investments in education to meet the higher end needs of industry are needed to ignite the knowledge industry in China. One thing China has going for it though, is its strong manufacturing base, which would generate internal demand for advanced technology to help in automation and supply chain management. With its better reputation for IP, and established base of IT companies and colleges, India is definitely looking to be the next key knowledge based economy.

ECONOMIC REFORMS IN INDIA

In the center of India's flag sits a spinning wheel, a symbol used by Gandhi to protest English textile imports under colonial rule and to demonstrate the nobility of a society of small-scale agriculture and industry. For much of its independence, India's economy was governed by the principle of the spinning wheel – with disastrous economic and social effects. Just as the United States, in industrializing, had to overcome the belief in the nobility of agriculture that shaped its founding fathers, India is still struggling to move beyond Gandhi-era economics and raise its standard of living.

While the U.S. media has focused on India's increasing competitiveness in software development and information technology, software and IT constitute only a small part of the Indian economy: more than 50% of India's output comes from its manufacturing and agricultural sectors, and 70% of its labour force is employed in agricultural. India needs policies to improve these sectors' long-term competitiveness in order to sustain and enhance its current growth rate. The reform process of the last 15 years is far from complete.

Fiscal And Administrative Reforms

India's fiscal policy is a key part of its overall economic history and central to its growth prospects. It was a major contributor to the 1991 BOP crisis, and in the future, persistent budget deficits may hinder the country's economic growth. The shortfalls of India's public services and infrastructure are quite obvious, and a miserable fiscal policy is a major reason for this gross underinvestment. While inadequate public revenues and low rates of public savings have contributed to India's fiscal shortcomings, the heart of the problem lies in India's public expenditures and management systems. Major administrative reform is required.

What's Been Done and The Way Forward

India's fiscal reforms focused on generating revenue through rationalizing the tax structure and increasing compliance. Specifically, the reforms: Lowered taxes (individual, corporate, excise and custom); Broadened the tax base; Removed exemptions and concessions to reduce distortions; Simplified laws and procedures to close loopholes and increase compliance, including using technology to better track tax payments.

"If India's government is going to make a difference, it needs to raise more taxes," The Economist wrote recently, which, considering the source, indicates the severity of the problem. To improve its tax system, India should: Increase taxes on services and implement a tax on e-commerce; Modernize tax administration through better utilizing technology; Restructure tax collection and allocation system to increase revenues at local and state levels; Complete the replacement of complex sales taxes with a more coordinated, coherent VAT system; Use technology to better enforce property and agricultural income taxes; Remove distortionary tax exemptions; Reduce the mean and variance of import tariffs; Repeal the corporate tax.

On the expenditure side, the various levels of government should: Reduce subsidies (which are generally poorly targeted); Downsize overstaffed public institutions, particularly at state and local levels; Separate policy and implementation functions through administrative reforms; Reduce bureaucratic controls and set performance targets; Institute mechanisms like greater public transparency to increase accountability.

Financial Sector Reforms

Because the BOP crisis prompted reforms of the financial system, this sector has experienced some of the most extensive improvements. India must continue to deepen its financial sector in order to guarantee adequate access to capital for its most dynamic industries. This can be achieved through the involvement of venture capital funds, the expansion of corporate debt markets, and the modernization of public bank management.

What's Been Done and The Way Forward

India has implemented reforms that have led to relatively well-functioning capital markets. These reforms: Liberalized interest rates; Abolished cumbersome approval requirements for financial transactions; Liberalized capital markets through the abolition of the Controller of Capital Issues, which controlled all funding activities of large manufacturing corporations; Allowed companies to more easily sell stock.

In order to continue supporting the most dynamic sectors of the economy, India should: Design strategies to increase venture capital; Allow investment in securities as an alternative to domestic saving in order to reduce reliance on foreign inflows in capital markets; Allow pension funds to invest in stocks; Improve and deepen debt markets for larger corporations; Increase competition from commercial and foreign banks in the financial sector.

International Trade and Investment Reforms

Having moved from barring foreign ownership in a wide swath of industries to encouraging foreign investment, India has made significant progress in opening its economy. Yet, while its foreign investment inflows increased from 0.5% of GDP in 1991 to 4.1% in 2000, these figures are dwarfed by other emerging Asian markets, particularly China.

What's Been Done and the Way Forward

Recent trade and investment policy reforms: Eliminated import licenses and reduced import duties from rates that had been the world's highest; Reduced tariffs; Liberalized trade in service and technology industries; Improved recognition of international intellectual property rights; Allowed 100% ownership in firms in a large majority of industries (excluding banks, insurance, telecommunications, and airlines).

To improve its trade and investment environment, India should: Further reduce import duties and restrictions; Reduce costly procedures for exporting finished or intermediate goods; Attract foreign investment to meet demand for infrastructure projects; Reduce foreign investment barriers within the retail sector; Invest in infrastructure and education, as a recent survey of global CEOs cited infrastructure and poor skill level as the two leading deterrents; Pursue free trade agreements in the spirit of creating a greater global balance and to advance India's economic interests.

Industrial Sector Reforms

While the chairman of Ittiam, a Bangalore commericial electronics design firm, attributes the success of the Indian IT industry in part to the absence of government regulations, government policy continues to limit manufacturing growth and hinder the ability of business to take advantage of the country's pool of cheap labour.

What's Been Done and the Way Forward

Opened up the economy broadly to competition; and Reduced reservations for some small-scale industries. To build on its success in industrial policy reform, India should: Further reduce reservations for small businesses; and Formalize special economic zones (SEZs), where normal investment and trade restrictions do not apply, to help leverage further reform.

Though small in comparison to China's vaunted SEZs, such efforts may hail a more drastic sea change in industrial policy as new ideas for further reforms become more prevalent in Delhi's circles of power. Milind Deora, a young and rising member of India's parliament, sees such a shift occurring today, suggesting that "the old guard is leaving."

Infrastructural Reforms

Infrastructure remains perhaps the greatest drag on India's current growth prospects. Major public work projects, however, present implementation challenges, particularly due to corruption.

What's Been Done and the Way Forward

Previous infrastructure reforms: Invested, with limited success, in improving airports and road networks; Privatized successfully a small number of ports and roads; Improved the reach of the telecom sector.

India's growth will be severely jeopardized without substantial improvements in infrastructure. India needs to: Implement major public works projects, taking advantage of public-private partnerships where possible; Privatize the energy sector and base user-charges on economic cost (some states have already taken lead in this effort); Continue to increase tele-density among its population, as India remains way behind countries like China and Thailand; Increase transparency in implementing infrastructure projects; Invest in a variety of renewable sources like ethanol and wind energy.

Labour Reform

Although India's restrictive labour laws are not a problem during times of expansion and do not affect high-skilled workers in the software and R&D sectors, they discourage further private investments, particularly in the manufacturing sector.

What's Been Done and the Way Forward

Labour markets remain one of the most regulated sectors of the Indian economy as labour reform was not addressed in the early 1990s. A more flexible labour policy will support business development and enhance India's growth. In particular, policies should be designed to: Remove restrictions on laying-off workers; Moderate benefits obtained by unions; Deregulate wage practices. Labour reforms should be coupled with the creation of a stronger social safety net to support affected employees.

FDI IN RETAIL

The persistent slow down in Indian economy and rising pressure on fiscal deficit forced Manmohan Singh government to initiate the strategy of reducing subsidy burden on the exchequer and introducing a few well-awaited economic reforms. Besides raising the diesel prices and restricting supply of subsidised LPG, government allowed FDI in multibrand retailing, civil aviation and the broadcasting sector.

Government allowed 51% FDI in multi-brand retails but subject to state government's permission. Government opened the doors to global super market chains like Walmart, Carrefour and Tesco, which have been in waiting for several years but their entry has been capped at 51 per cent ceiling on the one hand and getting state government's approval before opening their business on the other.

In another step on economic reforms, government approved 49% FDI in country's airlines. In other words, domestic airline companies, in screaming need for funds, have been allowed up to 49% FDI from foreign airlines. Also, broadcasting services such as direct to home (DTH) can attract up to 74 per cent foreign investment and power exchanges have been opened up to 49 per cent FDI. Single brand retail policy, too, has been diluted to make way for the likes of IKEA to set up shop and invest freely in India.

Manmohan Singh's decision on FDI got appreciation from the industrial sector. Country's capital market too showed an upward bounce showing revived and improved health. As per government's declaration, a few more decisions will be announced shortly to speed up the chain of economic reforms in the country.

We should first analyse the reach and nature of retailing in the country, before we try to analyse the views regarding the granting of permission to global retailers to carry out full-fledged business in the country. Retailing is one of the pillars of the Indian economy, as it accounts for 15% of the nation's Gross Domestic Product. From the global market share point of view, India is considered one of the five largest retail markets in economic output. Indian retail sector is divided into two sectors—organised and unorganised. Organised retailing is, however, absent in most rural and small towns in India. It is referred to as trading activities undertaken by licensed retailers. Licensed retailers are registered for sales tax, income tax, etc. These retailers are, in fact, publicity-traded supermarkets, corporate-backed hypermarkets and retail chains. Organised retailers also include privately-owned large retail businesses. Unorganised retailing, however, encompasses all the traditional formats of low-cost retailing *i.e.* local kirana shops, owner-manned general stores, betel/beedi/cigarette shops, convenience stores, handcart and pavement vendors of vegetables, fruits, etc.

If we look closely at the shares of organised and unorganised retailing in India, we find that most Indian shopping takes place in open markets or in millions of small, independent grocery and other retail shops. Generally, the product does not have any price label in these shops, though some branded products do have a manufacturer-suggested retail price (MRP) on them. The shopkeeper, as is in practice, fixes arbitrarily the prices of most of the products to be sold. The result is that two customers buying the same item at two different stores pay two different prices on the same day. It is because of the fact that given the margin of profit, the shopper and the shopkeeper negotiate the price between themselves. In most of the cases, the customers do not have time to examine the product label and do not have any choice to make any informed decision between competitive products. Compared to these open markets and retail shops, supermarkets and similar organised retail account for only a few percent India's retail and logistics industry, both organised and unorganised, employs about 40 million Indians.

Generally, typical Indian retail shops are very small. More than 14 million outlets operate in India and only 4 percent of them are larger than 500 sq. feet in size. India has about 11 shops/outlets for every 1,000 people. Vast majority of the unorganised retail shops in India do not employ people from outside their families and lack the resources to procure or transport products at wholesale scale. Small retailers have, as it has been experienced for long, limited or no quality control or mechanism to check the authenticity of products. They also lack training on safe and hygienic storage, packaging or logistics. The unorganised retail shops source their products from a chain of middlemen who mark up the product as it moves from farmer or producer to the consumer. The unorganised retail shops typically offer no after-sales support or service. In other words, most transactions at unorganised retail shops are done in cash with all sales being final.

When we analyse the employment scenario in India, we are at once acquainted with the novel trend that has gained momentum. An ever-increasing number of people in India are turning to the services sector for employment. They are doing so because of the relatively low compensation offered by the traditional agriculture and manufacturing sectors. The organised retail market is growing at a very high speed, while traditional retail sector is growing at a snail's pace. According to the ICRIER Report (2007), the retail business in India was estimated to grow at 13 percent from $322 billion in 2006-2007 to $590 billion in 2011-12. But organized retail, or large chains, making up less than 10 percent of the market, is expanding at 20 percent a year. This is driven by the emergence of shopping centres and malls, and a middle class of close to 300 million people that is growing at nearly 2 percent a year. The fact, however, is that the retail sector in India is estimated to have annual sales of $500 billion with nearly 90 per cent of the market still controlled by family-run shops.

As far as opening the retail industry inside India is concerned, debates and discussions both on the risks and prudence have taken place for years. Numerous economists have, however, repeatedly recommended to the Indian Government that legal restrictions on organised retail must be removed.

CRIME AGAINST WOMEN

Since time immemorial women have been the worst victims of male-dominated world whether it is war or riot or general law and order disturbance or robbery or domestic clashes, the fair sex has to bear the burnt of barbarism. Human history is full of atrocities committed on women in the form of forced abduction and marriage as in medieval period, as revenge killing and rapes in Bosnia, or as war prize in countless conflicts worldwide. "War" said Virginia Woolf, " is not women history".

Women bear a disproportionate burden of the consequences of war from beginning to end. First, women are not involved in the decisions that lead to war, not engaged in the appropriation of funds that make weapons and war possible, but they are tortured, kidnapped and raped as revenge tactic. Women as victims of war and women's role in peace building has been an important topic of discussion in several forums, most notably the United Nations.

Women have been labelled as 'sub-ordinates', 'homely', 'weak', and 'trouble-inviting' and in India as well in other nations they have been granted low status in society, being considered as a commodity, and birth of a girl child is still lamented.

Crime against women (CAW) traditionally includes rape, kidnapping and abduction, dowry death, torture, molestation, sexual harassment, importation of girls, cases under the Immoral Traffic (Prevention) Act, Sati Prevention Act, Dowry Prohibition Act, Indecent Representation of Women (Prevention) Act. Crime against women is usually classified as marital and sexual crime. However, one that victimises women is robbery and dacoity. Women are prime targets of robbery because of the jewellery they keep at home.

Like most offences, CAW is steadily on the rise in India. Of the total crimes reported in the country, 7% constitute CAW. The all-India rate, number of crimes per 100, 000 population reported to the police, was 13.8 during 1999 with a total 1,35,771 cases were reported.

Women comprise some 80 per cent of internally displaced persons and refugees when there is a war. Women as well as little girls are also victims of rape, domestic violence, sexual exploitation, trafficking, sexual humiliation and mutilation. However, their voice is seldom heard when "the important men" talk peace and war.

Women and girls are vulnerable both in times of peace and war, due to profound gender inequalities that still characterize societies. Reversing this situation requires political will and determination to fulfil all commitments concerning the protection and promotion of the women's rights. In the words of the President of the Security Council, "women are half of every community, are they therefore not half of every solution?" How can we, in good conscience, bring warlords to the negotiating table and not women, the representative of the UN's agency for women, UNIFEM asked.

Among the Indian cities safest for women, Chennai accounted for 21.2 per cent followed by Delhi at 12 per cent. Among the six metros, Kolkata is the safest for women. As much as 31.2 per cent of dowry deaths were from Uttar Pradesh alone, followed by Bihar with 15.2 per cent. But incidence of torture (under section 498 A IPC) accounted for 12.3 per cent in UP and only 3.2 per cent of cases reported in Bihar. Harassment for dowry is noticed only when the authorities are confronted with bodies of the helpless women.

Though the sex ratio in the country was 946 females for 1,000 males in 1951 it has worsened to 933 females for 1,000 males in 2001. What, then, has happened to our pre-natal, post-natal, nutritional support, health care and education programmes for the girl child? The deep-seated bias in India against the girl child with the availability of the most modern scientific technique to determine the sex of the foetus has resulted in large-scale female foeticide.

Sadly, this is not reflected in the crime records of the country. Only 87 cases of infanticide and 61 cases of foeticide were reported in 1999 and in 2004 the number of cases rose to 256 only. Infanticide and foeticide are a way of life in both urban and rural India and, therefore, the provisions of a progressive law like the Pre-natal Diagnostic Techniques (Registration and Prevention of Misuse) Act, 1994 remains a worthless scrap of paper.

In cases of rape, victims knew the offenders in 84 of every 100 cases. A conviction of an errant husband under Section 498 A IPC does not give the woman divorce. She has to approach a civil court and also pursue the criminal case filed in a police station. If she is economically dependent on the husband and if he is imprisoned, the question of maintenance may not arise. So, women use Section 498 A IPC to redress all marital grievances for a quicker and advantageous settlement.

Acquittal/discharge in cases of cruelty by husbands and relatives is high at 81 per cent of cases. The crime rate of cases of cruelty by husband or relatives is as high as 4.4 while the crime rate for dowry death is 0.7 and sexual harassment is 0.9 in every 100, 000 population. Similarly, the arrest rate for cases of cruelty by husband or relatives is 10.3 per cent.

Thus there is no single way by which a woman can obtain relief on an emergency basis beginning from basic protection from violence; being turned out from the husband's home; restraining the husband from disposing of property, emptying bank lockers and accounts and depriving her of custody of her children and the right to be with them.

Consequently, the harassed woman is forced to agree to what is far less than her due. Most harassed women can file a criminal case under Section 498 A IPC on the charge of mental and physical cruelty and a divorce on the same grounds. But, deterred by the long time that it takes to secure the court order, she is forced to seek closure under Section 498 A IPC and settle for divorce on grounds of mutual consent. The Domestic Violence (Prevention) Bill is a significant step forward in recognising the problems of women, children and other family members living in an atmosphere of violence.

The failure of the investigating agency can be seen from the fact that 36 per cent of the cases remain under investigation, without finalisation.

These are cases in which victims remained untraced or the investigation was under way to establish the charge. The police closed as many as 4,229 cases of kidnapping and abduction as false, mistake of fact or law. This signifies the shifting stand taken by the victim or her family towards the crime and the criminal in view of the existing social environment.

The number of sexual harassment cases, referred to as eveteasing in the past, rose by 10 per cent. More than 25 per cent of these cases were reported from Uttar Pradesh, followed by Tamil Nadu and Andhra Pradesh contributing 20 per cent each. It is natural to expect a significant co-relation in the pattern of rape, molestation and sexual harassment cases reported from a state. But, this pattern is not reflected in the statistics. Madhya Pradesh recorded the largest number of rape and molestation cases but ranks much lower in the reporting of sexual harassment cases. The reason for Uttar Pradesh recording far lesser number of rapes and molestation cases than other states but recording the highest number of sexual harassment cases is an issue for serious study.

Both, the Immoral Traffic (Prevention) Act and the Indecent Representation of Women Act, are comprehensive laws. But, these were made without repealing provisions in existing laws in the state and that of the Indian Penal Code. Consequently, investigating officers take advantage of the more lenient provisions of old laws to register the case or book the culprits. It is possible to herd a dozen women accused of prostitution and get them fined Rs.25 each under an existing law. This is a cakewalk in comparison to the elaborate investigation required under the Immoral Traffic (Prevention) Act to book financiers, brokers, building owners and the clients of prostitutes.

Another area of focus is suicides. Housewives accounted for 52 per cent of the total female suicide cases. Married women account for 66.6 per cent. The complex way in which bad marriages drive women to suicide is still to be fully understood. Further, 46.8 per cent of the victims had less than middle school education. Women preferred to drown, hang or immolate themselves.

However, this temporary relief should be followed up by setting up more family courts to deal with divorce, maintenance, child custody and division of property and reverting to the spirit that led to the formation of the family courts providing early, easy solutions to domestic problems.

Delhi Police advertised 'Dos and Don'ts for Women' in leading newspapers and opened 'women helpline' with every DTC bus bearing the telephone numbers for immediate contact. Not only this, women can take the shelter of various NGOs working for this purpose like the Navjyoti Centre. This is a healthy trend as far as women safety is concerned.

RIGHT TO EDUCATION

The April, 1st 2010, was marked in history as India joined groups of few countries in the world, with a significant law, making education a fundamental right of every child coming into force.

The Right to Education bill was passed by the Parliament on 4th August, 2009. Six years after an amendment was made in the Indian Constitution, the Union Cabinet cleared the Right to education bill, which premises free and compulsory education to every child.

The Government of India by Constitutional (86th Amendment) Act, 2002 had added a new Article 21A, which provides that the state shall provide free and compulsory education to all children of the age 6 to 14 years as the state may by law determine." And further strengthened this Article 21A by adding clause (K) to Article 51-A which provides—"who is a parent or guardian to provide opportunities for education to his child or ward between the age 6 and 14 years." On the basis of constitutional mandate provided in Article 41, 45, 46, 21A and various judgments of Supreme Court, the Government of India has taken several steps to eradicate illiteracy, improve the quality of education and make children back to school who left the school for one or the other reasons. The government schools shall provide free education to all the children and the schools will be managed by school management committees. Private schools shall admit at least 25% of the children in their school without any fee. The National commission for elementary education shall be constituted to monitor all aspects of elementary education including quality.

Soon after gaining independence in 1947, make education available to all had become a priority of the government. As discrimination on the basis of caste and gender has been a major impediment in the healthy development of the Indian society they have been made unlawful by the Indian Constitution.

While the right to education, is a fundamental right now, the government have yet to acknowledge its proper implementation. The National Commission for Protection of Child Rights (NCPCR) has been designated as the agency to monitor provisions of the Right to Free and Compulsory Education (RTE) Act. To ensure that the RTE Act is implemented successfully in letter and spirit, the NCPCR has taken the initiatives to build a consensus among institutions, government departments, civil society and other state holders. It had instituted an expert committee comprising officials from various government departments, persons of eminence and experience in field of education, to focus on roadmap for proper implementation of RTE.

In view of this, the Prime Minister of India Dr. Manmohan Singh, emphasized that it is important for the country that if we nurture our children and young people with the right education, India's future as a strong and prosperous country is scene. He also said, that to realise the right to education, the Government at the centre, in the states and union territories and at the district and village level must work together as a part of common endeavour. He called upon all the state Governments to join hands in this national effort with full resolve and determination. He also ensured that in this partnership of the government with state Governments financial constraints would not hamper the implementation of the Right to Act. Any cost that prevents a child from accessing school will be borne by the state which shall have the responsibility of enrolling the child as well as ensuring attendance and competition of eight years of schooling. No child shall be denied admission for want of documents; no child shall be turned away if the admission cycle in the school is over and no child shall be asked to take an admission test. Children with disabilities will also be educated in the mainstream schools.

There are various issues which need to be considered for the actualisation of the act. The bill had earlier faced resistance from the law and finance ministries on issues involving the states financial contribution. The law ministry expected problems to arise from the 25% reservation, while human resource development ministry estimates put the total cost at Rs 55,000 crore every year.

The draft bill aim to provide elementary schools in every neighbourhood within three years–though the word 'school' encompasses a whole spectrum of structures.

A set of minimum norms have been worked out as there's the usual barrier of paperwork in remote rural and poor urban areas. The state in also obliged to tide over any financial compulsions that may keep child out of school.

However, for better implementation and monitoring of the Act, there needs to be greater awareness in the country so that its provisions are understood and incorporated by all institutions. In order to do so, a massive campaign will have to be undertaken, including translation of the act into different languages, perhaps jointly with Ministry of Human Resource and Development and other agencies. NCPCR has begun the process by preparing materials that can be used in this campaign including a simplified version of the Act, posters, primers and pamphlates describing the basic provisions and rights. It will also design special materials for children so that they also understand the Act.

This is a fact that mere laws and bills will solve the problem of education. Everyone has to understand their own social responsibility, that every children get access to education.

The government of India has been working tremendously on the education system over the past few decade. Even with such laudable efforts, drop outs from school is in continuation. It has been also noted that they do not acquire the basic of literacy and numeracy as the additional knowledge and skills necessary for their all-round development as specified under RTE.

The RTE act provides a right platform to reach the unreached, with specific provisions for disadvantaged groups, such as child labourers, migrant children, children with special needs, or those who have a disadvantage owing to social, cultural, economical, geographical, linguistic, gender or other such factor.

But for the complete pursual of the act, is dependent on so many factors. The success of any educational endeavour in based on the ability and motivation of teachers. Parents, guardians, families and communities have a large role to play to ensure child-friendly education for each and every one of the estimated 190 million girls and boys in India who should be in elementary school today.

With RTE, India can emerge as a global leader in achieving the millennium development goal of ensuring that all children complete their primary schooling by 2015. Though a challenge, but with the resources and political support, it is not an impossible task. The world is waiting far India to have rightful leadership role in education on the global stage. RTE will help in propelling this great nation to reach great heights of prosperity and productivity, when every Indian child, girl or a boy, will be touched by the light of education.

PRIVATE COACHING INSTITUTIONS

Since the establishment of first university in 1875 in Calcutta, Delhi and Madras, modern education has come a long way with more than 250 universities and more than one thousand colleges all over the country. Yet private coaching intitutes boom has been on the rise.

The universities, colleges and schools have been controlled by the government. Till 70's there were no coaching institutes in India and all qualified professionals had been the direct products of government owned institutions and universities. Then education sector witnessed severe degradation and teachers of schools and colleges fell down from competence to incompetence and classes became boring as these teachers considered government jobs as sacred marriage that will never be broken. The decline of education in government schools and colleges have been pathetic.

Private coaching institutes are the direct products of glaring incompetency of government institutions and their men in control. A private coaching institute is a parallel classroom education by the same set of teachers who fail to perform in the schools and colleges they belong to. However in comparison to government schools and colleges where education is free, the private coaching institutes extract huge sums of money. Ironically, the syllabus remains the same, the teachers are the similar faces but the standard of teaching and class environment dramatically change to be labelled as the highest professional education.

The more the government schools and colleges became apathetic to the educational competence and professional responsibility, the more the private coaching institutes mushroomed in various parts of the country. However, it all started with public school trend which came as an alternative to raise the standard of education for more and more guardians and parents preferred their wards to study in these schools.

The private coaching institutes have reasons to set the trend of parallel educational institutions where professionalism and educational responsibility vis-a-vis the whopping charges.

Now every city, big or small, in India has more private coaching institutes than the government academic institutions where in money is being minted in the name of 'novel ways', 'excellent teachers', 'nurture talent' and 'sure success' from the students who are passionate more to learn the short cuts than the real study. Privatisation gets impetus from the fact that only the change of label from government to private makes all the difference, however, it initiated the filthiest trend in our education system by frequent paper leaks which is being carried out by those teachers who are associated with the coaching institutes and who are also the government employees. Corruption crept in via these teachers and academicians who prepare the question papers and who have the access to get the examination papers before it is commenced. In recent years many prestigious examinations including the CAT and CBSE medical examinations, were in news due to paper leaks.

In order to be the top in the race of the best coaching institutes, the associated professionals come out with huge advertisements showing hundred per cent success results.

Education is becoming imperialistic in nature in this country. For the rich it is easy to get enrolled and admitted into the prestigious institutes with the power of money. And those poor masses who have no money, face double discrimination : they are not taught properly in the government owned schools or colleges and they have no access to famous private coaching institutes. Thus many a bright talents are being denied the standard of education which is their birth right by the same academicians and teachers who change their professional competence like the colour of a chameleon. The law must ban either the private coaching institutes or privatise the whole education system in India else this trend of double standard shall result in an educational chaos. At least government teachers should be punished for running private coaching institutes or for being a part of it or should even be barred from advisory role. Private coaching institute exposes the hypocrisy of our schools and colleges, our teachers and academicians and educational experts. The rise of private coaching institute will create a class of Indian who shall initiate a powerful educational revolution for their immediate end.

PREPARATION FOR COMPETITIVE EXAMINATIONS

This is the age of stiff competition. And to be a successful fighter followed by a smiling winner is not a child's play. Competitive examinations are the basis for selection of suitable candidates for jobs in government as well as in private sectors. In addition, interviews and psychological tests are part of preparation to reach the final stage.

Competitive examinations are the tests other than the traditional system of examinations which are conducted by the universities and colleges. In colleges and universities, question papers are based on prescribed syllabus with likely chances of matching questions, but in competitive examinations though the syllabus are fixed, the range of question selection is very wide and varied. This is because the number of candidates appearing in these examinations far exceeds the total number of vacancies to be filled.

Preparation is the action or process of getting ready to face the challange; the intellectual, physical and psychological strength are the bases of firm preparation. It is an all-round endeavour to get ready for a event or undertaking as 'fortunes favour those who are prepared'. This is not an easy task.

Preparation is a complete effort, a decoration or accomplishment, or to be fully equipped with required knowledge, skills and stamina.

A competitive examination is a wall or barrier between a success in professional career or utter failure. Those who cross this barrier or scale the wall are the successful winners. As in sports, out of the ten competitors in the 100m race in Olympics, only top three get the medal and the topper receives gold medal. The remaining seven go without any citation and the world forgets them very soon.

As any competition examination is a tough fight, the preparation should also be matching. For a successful fighter in competitive examination, a few necessary pre-requisites are to be followed :

* Selection of the career field based on natural inclination, subject knowledge and the amount of energy to be exhausted.
* Research skill and wide range of studies.
* Fixed schedule for preparation.
* Materials, notes and books accarding to the syllabus.

* Daily assessment report of the prepared skills.
* Current affairs updates.
* Language proficiency.
* Planned study and self-examination.
* Group discussion
* Knowledge of theoretical part.
* Previous years questions to be solved and Knowledge of questions trend.
* Problem solving skills.

However, for sure success in any competitive examinations, three basic fundamentals are the key :

* Preparation as per the fixed schedule
* Preparation as per the syllabus
* Preparation must be regular

A detailed exploration of the above concepts is mandatory. A fixed schedule generates discipline among youth which is the most difficult part of the preparation. This is based on a well-planned strategy. Naturally any fixed schedule may clash with other engagements, and it is the priority, which determines one's preference. For example, friend's birthday clashes with your fixed schedule and you prefer the former over latter, the tempo of discipline will be broken. It has long term implications that can be exploited by the competitors.

Following the fixed time table—no less no more—on a daily basis for a planned period of time is a Herculean task. And those who maintain this are ultimate winners. Regularity makes things easy, even the junk mind can be enlighten towards a firm base of knowledge.

'Stick to syllabus' or topic is another area of concern for chances of derailment are very high among youths. Prescribed syllabus may be boring and all laborious students would switch over to the books or topics of their interest. They might provide knowledge but they fail to get them through in the competitive examinations. So 'keep revising your dreams'—always taking of your syllabus will keep you nearer the topics and it helps giving firm commitment. For example, many a competitors rush for too much newspaper reading or magazine collections spending time on useless gossips over a topic they have no basic knowledge at all. You can take of 'Indian Politics' without knowing the political system and philosophies of India, or you can indulge in endless talk of Nehru being a staunch socialist without knowing the socialism, the great socialist thinkers and their contributions.

Preparation is not only knowing of the subject or topics but using them in proper context. Fundamental knowledge of the syllabus-covered topics is a must. And to drink deep one has to step down into the ocean of information. One point here is important : information can mislead, as human interests would follow the mind-boggling events forgetting the 'fixed' path of 'stick to syllabus' motive.

Also, fixed timing clash with entertainment, serials, marriage, festivals, cermonies etc. A competitor is at war, and in war your only concern is to fight till victory, and all other sundry thing are useless.

Physical health is also important along with good habits like early rising, walk, timely diet and sound sleep. One thing is to be remembered : only tested and tried are the successful people, so regular tests are necessary to weigh the weight of your knowledge and skills.

WHISTLE BLOWING : A BOLD CONCEPT

Whistle blowing is an act of providing secret information on an illicit or illegal transaction or corrupt practices in an office. This is a very old practice and came to limelight when False claim Act-1863 enacted—a watchdog law to restrict illegal practices in USA. There were widespread abuses in Government contracts during Civil War in which higher officials were exposed of malpractices. Since then American history has been full of whistle blowing that helped expose companies especially, Pharmaceutical industries involved in illegal practices. In 1987, 33 whistle blowing cases were filed which rose to 320 in 2002. However, the most popular was the Big Tobacco Scandal. Jeffrey

Weigand—a famous whistle blower gained wide publicity for his role in exposing the Big Tobacco Scandal wherein the company had been involved in mixing carcinogenic ingredients in the cigarettes, a poisonous element.

A whistle blower is a person in a government office or in an institution who spies on the unofficial or illegal or corrupt practices and deals with the officials and then report the matter to the authority for action. In some cases, a whistle blower helps to expose the corrupt or to catch them red-handed. The practices is very healthy to keep the corrupt officials in check. But at the same time, known whistle-blower faces risk or danger to his life. To help whistle-blowers, US government enacted whistle-blower Protection Act-1989 furthering the provisions of erstwhile false claim Act 1863. The reports of whistle-blower being intimidated came as a shock to the world. However, the trend continues in spite of risk involved in it. To provide new impetus to the whistle-blowing, 'Time' magazine in 2002 selected three whistle-blowers as 'Time's People of the Year Award 2002'. They were—Cynthia Cooper of world com, Sharon Watkins of Enron and Colleen Ronley of FBI. These three whistle blowers were given the front page coverage.

India is perhaps the best playground for whistle-blowing as corruption has made inroads in every department, office, institution and establishment. Laws are many, departments are also enough and officials are in abundance to check corrupt practices, yet due to lack of evidence against the wrong-doers they are let off. And because not all officials in any department are corrupt, those who are fair must venture out to expose the wrong-doers or illegal transaction. This will be a great service to the nation.

Indian political history is full of scams and scandals whereby hundreds of thousands of crores have been siphoned off yet on the level of prosecution hardly any one is executed as trails linger too long. So one process of checking corruption is to generate an environment of unknown fear that some one is watching or a pair of hidden eyes are keeping surveillance. Bringing the culprits to book is a legal process but holding back the wrong doers before he does anything corrupt is a moral trend. This can not only create a wave of fear among officials but would help increase the efficiency level as well.

Our country does not lack the daring souls who could go out to expose the unofficial deals and illegal transactions, even if there are big fishes in the pond. The government agencies give reward to such people who help nab the culprits. This trend needs to be followed at war footing if India has to survive the onslaught of corruption. In US the reward is very handsome, and at one occasion a whopping sum of 100 million is paid to a whistle blower or they can get a share of 15-30% stake in company's profit. What is needed in India is whistle-blower Act that can help whistle-blower morally, legally and financially. This would certainly provide legal basis for exposing the corrupt colleagues who are sucking the life-blood of the nation. A cash reward would generate general awareness and would encourage the honest professionals or citizens to go all out in exposing the system, the deals and those who are involved in such murky affairs.

Remember, speeches, discussions and research papers won't help root out the corruption but the beginning from the fellow honest employees will do the trick. As Lanka was won over with the help of a genuine fellow in the court of the Ravana leading to the end of unjust rule and the ruler, same can be accomplished in today's environment if masses come out and recognize their moral duty of reporting the corrupt or illegal practice/person.

BENEFITS OF READING

"Reading maketh a full man; conference a ready man; and writing an exact man," said Francis Bacon, while highlighting the after effects of reading. Human race took a giant leap forward once he held a book in his hand or followed it or wrote it for the general benefits.

Habits and tastes vary from man to man, but more men are familiar with the book as the start of education down with a bunch of books in the satchel. Among the habits and tastes, book reading can be considered as one of the best as the set "serves for delight, for ornament and for ability."

Books open the gates of knowledge if properly studied which, in turn, leads to wisdom—the highest form of human intellect. A man can never feel loneliness if he has book as his companion, even in desert or on a lonely Island for the enjoyment created out of reading is matchless. A world full of aesthetic delight always engulf the reader which ultimately generates creativity. Besides, a strong feeling of weight from within heralds upon the intellectual realm of book reader.

The next benefit of reading is : the sure success in the professional field which provide status and recognition among the social classes, and monetary gains follow like an obedient lover. Hence, economic prosperity has its roots in the steady habit of book readings.

Book reading enhances intellectual ability, which is a jewel of men and women that will never get old or rusty. In the debates and discourses, a reader who has the wide-range of knowledge on various subjects and topics will ultimately prevail. Certainly reading gives a sense of judgment which is the utmost requirement in today's competitive world.

Reading can have electrifying effects : many a lives have been entirely transformed and the works of great men don't leave without instilling the forceful impacts. Therefore selection of books for reading is of primary importance for "some books are to be tasted, others to be swallowed, and some few to be chewed and digested." For students, the first and foremost reading materials are the prescribed syllabus and those books which are relevant to the syllabus. To gain excellence on a subject most liked, the students can go for related books from libraries or via Internet, but reading irrelevant magazines and books could mislead them totally from the pursued path. The selection of books to be read must be done judiciously as it keeps concentration on the height. To explore the events and deeds of the past History reading is a wise decision.

Philosophy is for serious men and political science and management are for the leadership. Fiction is common for all particularly for students who wish to command the language skills, and stories generate curiosity among the young minds which is a sign of creative development. In this genre, classics from every language is a must reading for apart from language skills, they open up a whole new world of human events, experiences, relationships and judgements.

Reading for part time can also be fruitful. If reading is carried consistently for gaining knowledge in the name of fun it will not remain so as the effect of a book is far reaching.

Knowing one's own country via books is the best way to be familiar with the process of nation building, and serious study of Georgaphy upto a level is a pre-requisite for all.

And those young aspirants trying for coveted posts in the professional fields must have a wide and varied reading habits as factual statements are more relevant than the lengthy discourses. Magazines, newspapers and journals for specific information can be gathered to create a multi-dimensional realm of knowledge.

However, the first priority for students and learners is to read their subjects which can lead them to enter the professional world easily, and for teachers, broad reading of the same topic to raise the level of teaching skills is indispensible. Researchers delve into the content like a navigator. But it is advisable not to read controversies as they trouble the mind which could derail from the path chosen for one's success.

STUDENTS & POLITICS

Our nation is growing democracy with complete political independence and are likely to attain economic independence by the year 2050 AD. Indian students are allowed to form students unions. As they are the future managers of the nation (and they have to steer our nation towards political, socio-economic and industrial prosperity, they must know the art and science of governance of this nation.

This necessitates the growth of student unions in colleges and universities as the real training of a student starts from the educational institute itself.

The political parties support (or create) one student union and try to influence the students. Political machinations take evil turns and manifest themselves in the forms of phoney elections, arson, violence on campuses and even murders. Therefore, valuable property worth millions is destoyed; state transport buses or local buses are the worst hit due to rampage and violence of students. All types of guns and other arsenal are freely available in a free market economy. Therefore, in order to rule the college or university campus, the power of the gun is used quite often. Political parties initiate wicked election campaigns and cook their own recipes for ensuring their presence in the educational institute. The ordinary student suffers on account of loss of freedom and disruption in academic sessions. A few hooligans rule the roost and the majority of students remains neglected.

Academic schedules, sports and the intellectual development of the students suffer. The useful time of the yount students is wasted in political campaigns, strikes and protests. The student suffers, his or her family suffers and the nation suffers in the long run. Politics on campus may have benefited a few but most of the students remain untouched by and large. What is the use of politics on campus if it cannot affect the lives of atleast 80 per cent of students?

Politics and educational institutes must be separate. This would eliminate wastage of time and precious human resources ad public property. The idea of involvement of those students in politics who are really keen to take up politics as a career in their later lives will be a welcome trend. They could form organisations, clubs and unions in order to hone their political skills. But why bother the ordinary student whose parents await the completion of his or her graduation so that he or she could become a wage earner for the family? Political parties must keep their hands off the educational institutes. They develop students as their pawns and exploit them to achieve their bare political ends. The State must pass strict legislations (at the centre and state levels) to this effect. The temples of learning should never be allowed to operate as hotbeds of politics. The nation has already suffered on account of marriage of politics with hooliganism and our youth have paid heavy price due to this unholy alliance.

The youth of today would not study on account of a strike call issued by their unions. But they would not miss the nearest fast food joint either (as strikes and bandhs bring holidays with them). These double standards would have to be shunned. We would suggest that instead of participating in campus politics, our students should take up part-time jobs so that they could become financially independent and earn enough money for meeting their educational expenses. This would help their parents in meeting other financial obligations and the students would also be pleased to earn. Part-time assignments could include jobs in factories, computer operations, home coaching etc. Constructive and result oriented activities like painting, multimedia, AUTOCAD, fashion technology and Internet operations would also develop their vocational skills. Moreover, they would be able to get better jobs when they pass out from their institutes. Strikes, bandhs and petty student politics would not be able to develop their faculties, which could enable them to be independent after the completion of their academic tenures.

The political affiliations of students should be allowed only for those students who are studying political science or who are keen to accept politics as a career. Our college and university campuses should be able to grow sans political affiliations. The State would have to take far-reaching decisions for ensuring their a political operations.

❑❑❑

GENERAL AWARENESS

NATIONAL SYMBOLS

STATE EMBLEM

State Emblem of India is an adaptation from the Sarnath Lion Capital of Ashoka. It was adopted by the Government of India on January 26, 1950. In the adapted form, only three lions are visible, the fourth being hidden from the view. The wheel (Dharma Chakra) appears in relief in the centre of the abacus with a bull on the right and a horse on the left.

The bell-shaped lotus has been omitted. The words ''Satyameva Jayate'' meaning ''Truth alone triumphs'' are inscribed below the Emblem in Devanagari script.

NATIONAL FLAG

The National Flag of India is a horizontal tricolour of deep saffron (Kesari), white and dark green in equal proportion. In the centre of the white band there is a wheel in navy blue colour. It has 24 spokes. The ratio of the length and the breadth of the flag is 3 : 2. Its design was adopted by the Constituent Assembly of India on July 22, 1947.

NATIONAL ANTHEM

Rabindranath Tagore's song 'Jana-gana-mana' was adopted by the Constituent Assembly as the National Anthem of India on January 24, 1950.

Jana-gan-mana-adhinayaka jaya he, Bharata-bhagya-vidhata
Punjab-Sindh-Gujarat-Maratha-Dravida-Utkala-Banga
Vindhya-Himachala-Yamuna-Ganga Uchhala-jaladhi-taranga.
Tava subha name jage, Tava subha asisa mange, Gahe tava jaya gatha,
Jana-gana-mangala-dayak, jaya he Bharata bhagya vidhata,
Jaya he, jaya he, jaya he, Jaya jaya jaya, jaya he.

NATIONAL SONG

Bankim Chandra Chatterji's 'Vande Mataram' which was a source of inspiration to the people in their struggle for freedom, has been adopted as National Song. It has an equal status with the National Anthem.

Vande Mataram
Sujalam, suphalam, malayaja-shitalam,
Shasya shyamalam, Mataram
Shubhrajyotsna,pulkita yaminim,
Phulla kusumita drumadalashobhinim,
Subhasinim sumadhura—bhashinim,
Sukhadam, Varadam, Mataram.

NATIONAL CALENDAR

It is based on the Saka era with Chaitra as its first month and a normal year of 365 days. It was adopted from March 22, 1957. Dates of the national calendar have a permanent correspondence with dates of Gregorian calendar as Chaitra I falls on March 22 in a normal year and March 21 in a leap year. In official communications, both Saka and Gregorian calendar dates are written. Months of the national calendar are Chaitra, Vaishakha, Jaishtha, Ashada, Shravan, Bhadra, Ashvina, Kartika, Margashirsha, Pausha, Magha and Phalguna.

NATIONAL ANIMAL

The magnificent tiger — Panthera tigris (Linnaeus) is the national animal of India. Tiger is found in several parts of the country and is known for its grace, strength, agility and enormous power. 'Project Tiger' was launched in 1973 to check their dwindling population in India.

NATIONAL BIRD

The Indian Peacock — Pavo Christatus (Linnaeus) is the national bird of India. It is a colourful, swan-sized bird with a fan-shaped crest of feathers on its head and a long-slander neck. The male species is more colourful with blue breast and a spectacular bronze-green train of around 200 elongated feathers.

National Flower—Lotus

National Tree—Banyan

National Fruit—Mango

National Currency—Rupee '₹'

(One Rupee = 100 Paise)

National Aquatic Animal—Dolphin

BOOKS AND AUTHORS

Name of Book	Author	Name of Book	Author
Ain-e-Akbari	Abul Fazal	Mother (Maa)	Maxim Gorky
Anand Math	Bankim Chandra Chatterjee	Mother India	Katherine Mayo
An Unknown Indian	Nirad C. Chaudhuri	My Experiments with Truth	Mahatma Gandhi
Arthshastra	Kautilya	My Presidential Years	R. Venkataraman
Coolie	Mulk Raj Anand	Neeti Shatak	Bhartrihari
Das Kapital	Karl Marx	Nehru and His Vision	Dr. K.R. Narayanan
Discovery of India	Jawaharlal Nehru	Old Man and the Sea	Ernest Hemingway
Eternal India	Mrs. Indira Gandhi	One World	Wendell Wilkie
Godan	Prem Chand	Panchtantra	Vishnu Sharma
Gitanjali	Rabindranath Tagore	Paradise Lost	John Milton
Gora	Rabindranath Tagore	Ramayana	Valmiki (in Sanskrit)
Geet Govinda	Jayadeva	Raghuvansham	Kalidas
Harsha Charit	Bana Bhatta	Rajtarangini	Kalhan
Hindu View of Life	Dr. S. Radhakrishnan	Ram Charit Manas	Tulsi Das
India Wins Freedom	Maulana Abul Kalam Azad	Abhijnan Shakuntalam	Kalidas
Jobs of Millions	V.V. Giri	Satanic Verses	Salman Rushdie
Jungle Book	Rudyard Kipling	Saket	Maithili Sharan Gupta
Kamayani	Jai Shankar Prasad	Speed Post	Shobha De
Kadambari	Bana Bhatta	The God of Small Things	Arundhati Roy
Life Divine	Sri Aurobindo	Treasure Island	R.L. Stevenson
Last days of Netaji	G.D. Khosla	Twelfth Night	William Shakespeare
Les Miserables	Victor Hugo	Train to Pakistan	Khuswant Singh
Mahabharat	Veda Vyas	Uttara Ram Charitra	Bhava Bhuti
Macbeth	William Shakespeare	Vanity Fair	W.M. Thackeray
Mein Kempf	Hitler	War and Peace	Leo Tolstoy
Meghduta	Kalidas	Wealth of Nations	Adam Smith
		Wake up India	Annie Besant

INVENTIONS AND DISCOVERIES

Geographical Discoveries

Discovery	Discoverer
America	Columbus
Brazil	Cabral
North Pole	Robert Peary
Everest (Conquered)	Tabie Junko
Planetary Motion	Kepler
Hawaiian Islands	Captain Cook
South Pole	Amundsen
Solar System	Copernicus

Chemistry and Physics

Discovery	Discoverer
Atom Bomb	Otto Hahn
Atomic Theory	Dalton
Atomic Numbers	Moseley
Cosmic Rays	R.S. Millikan
Dynamite	Alfred Nobel
Electrons Theory	Bohr
Electricity (current)	Volta
Electric Telegraphy (Code)	S. Morse

Discovery	Discoverer
Gravitation	Newton
Gas Light	Murdock
Oxygen	J. Priestly
Photography	L. Daguerre
Printing for the blind	Louis Braille
Radium	Madame Curie
Telegraph	Samuel Morse
Television	J.L. Baird
Telephone	Graham Bell
Wireless	G. Marconi
X-rays	W.K. Roentgen
Mechanical	
Aeroplane	Wright Brothers
Bicycle	Macmillan
Computer	Charles Babbage
Dynamo	Michal Faraday
Diesel Engine	Rudolf Diesel
Engine (Railway)	Stephenson
Fountain Pen	Waterman
Gramophone	Edison
Locomotive Power of Steam	James Watt
Helicopter	Brequet
Life Boat	Henry Greathead

Discovery	Discoverer
Microscope	Z. Jansen
Printing Press	Gutenberg
Revolver	Colt
Sewing Machine	Elias Howe
Thermometer	Fahrenheit
Transistor	W. Shockley
Typewriter	Sholes
Telescope	Hans Lippershey
Tank (Military)	Swinton
Medical	
Antiseptic Surgery	Lord Joseph Lister
Bacteria	Leeuwenhock
Circulation of Blood	William Harvey
Homoeopathy (Discovered)	Hahnemann
Insulin	F. Banting
Penicillin	Alexander Flemming
Malaria Parasite	Dr. Ronald Ross
Stethoscope	Laennec
Vitamins	Funk
Anti-Rabies Treatment	Pasteur
General	
Nylon	Carouthers
Science of Geometry	Euclids

WORLD'S GEOGRAPHICAL SURNAMES

• City of Sky-scrapers—New York • City of Seven Hills—Rome • City of Dreaming Spires—Oxford • City of Golden Gate—San Francisco • City of Magnificent Buildings—Washington D.C. • City of Eternal Springs—Quito (S. America) • China's Sorrow—Hwang Ho • Cockpit of Europe—Belgium • Dark Continent—Africa • Emerald Isle—Ireland • Eternal City—Rome • Empire City—New York • Forbidden City—Lhasa (Tibet) • Garden City—Chicago • Gate of Tears—Strait of Bab-el-Mandeb • Gift of the Nile—Egypt • Granite City—Aberdeen (Scotland) • Hermit Kingdom—Korea • Herring Pond—Atlantic Ocean • Holy Land—Jerusalem • Island Continent—Australia • Islands of Cloves—Zanzibar • Isle of Pearls—Bahrein (Persian Gulf) • Key to the Mediterranean—Gibralter • Land of Cakes—Scotland • Land of Golden Fleece—Australia • Land of Maple Leaf—Canada • Land of Morning Calm—Korea • Land of Midnight Sun—Norway • Land of the Thousand Lakes—Finland • Land of the Thunderbolt—Bhutan • Land of White Elephant—Thailand • Land of Thousand Elephants—Laos • Land of Rising Sun—Japan • Loneliest Island—Tristan De Gunha (Mid-Atlantic) • Manchester of Japan—Osaka • Pillars of Hercules—Strait of Gibraltar • Pearl of the Antilles—Cuba • Playground of Europe—Switzerland • Quaker City—Philadelphia • Queen of the Adriatic—Venice • Roof of the World—The Pamirs, Central Asia • Sugar bowl of the world—Cuba • Venice of the North—Stockholm • Windy City—Chicago • Whiteman's grave—Guinea Coast of Africa • Yellow River—Huang Ho (China) • Sickman of Europe—Turkiye

CAPITALS AND CURRENCIES OF COUNTRIES

Country	Capital	Currency	Country	Capital	Currency
Afghanistan	Kabul	Afghani	Indonesia	Jakarta	Rupiah
Algeria	Algiers	Dinar	Iran	Teheran	Rial
Angola	Luanda	New Kwanza	Iraq	Baghdad	Dinar
Argentina	Buenos Aires	Peso	Ireland	Dublin	Euro
Armenia	Yeravan	Dram	Israel	Jerusalem	Shekel
Australia	Canberra	Dollar	Italy	Rome	Euro
Austria	Vienna	Euro	Jamaica	Kingston	Dollar
Azerbaijan	Baku	Monat	Japan	Tokyo	Yen
Bahrain	Manama	Dinar	Jordan	Amman	Dinar
Bangladesh	Dhaka	Taka	Kazakhstan	Akmola	Tenge
Barbados	Bridgetown	Dollar	Kenya	Nairobi	Shilling
Belgium	Brussels	Euro	Korea (S)	Seoul	Won
Bhutan	Thimphu	Ngultrum	Korea (N)	Pyongyang	Won
Bolivia	La paz	Boliviano	Kyrgyzstan	Bishkek	Som
Brazil	Brasilia	Cruzeiro	Kuwait	Kuwait City	Dinar
Bulgaria	Sofia	Lev	Laos	Vientiane	Kip
Byelorussia	Minsk	Zaichik	Latvia	Riga	Lat
Cambodia	Phnom-Penh	Riel	Lebanon	Beirut	Pound
Canada	Ottawa	Dollar	Libya	Tripoli	Dinar
Chile	Santiago	Peso	Lithuania	Vilnius	Litas
China	Beijing	Yuan	Malaysia	Kuala Lumpur	Ringgit
Colombia	Bogota	Peso	Maldives	Male	Rufiyya
Congo	Brazzaville	Franc	Mauritius	Port Louis	Rupee
Croatia	Zagreb	Kuna	Moldavia	Chisinau	Leu
Cuba	Havana	Peso	Mexico	Mexico City	Peso
Cyprus	Nicosia	Euro	Morocco	Rabat	Dirham
Czech Republic	Prague	Crown	Mozambique	Maputo	Metical
Denmark	Copenhagen	Krone	Myanmar (Burma)	Nay Pyi Taw	Kyat
Egypt	Cairo	Pound			
Estonia	Tallinn	Kroon	Nepal	Kathmandu	Rupee
Ethiopia	Addis Ababa	Birr	Netherlands	Amsterdam	Euro
Fiji	Suva	Dollar	New Zealand	Wellington	Dollar
Finland	Helsinki	Euro	Nigeria	Abuja	Naira
France	Paris	Euro	Norway	Oslo	Krone
Georgia	Tbilisi	Lari	Oman	Muscat	Rial
Germany	Berlin	Euro	Pakistan	Islamabad	Rupee
Ghana	Accra	Cedi	Philippines	Manila	Peso
Greece	Athens	Euro	Poland	Warsaw	Zloty
Guatemala	Guatemala City	Quetzal	Portugal	Lisbon	Euro
Hong Kong	Victoria	Dollar	Qatar	Doha	Riyal
Hungary	Budapest	Forints	Romania	Bucharest	Leu
Iceland	Reykjavik	Krona	Russia	Moscow	Ruble
India	New Delhi	Rupee	Saudi Arabia	Riyadh	Rial

Country	Capital	Currency
Slovakia	Bratislava	Euro
Spain	Madrid	Euro
Sri Lanka	Colombo	Rupee
Sudan	Khartoum	Dinar
Sweden	Stockholm	Krona
Switzerland	Berne	Swiss Francs
Syria	Damascus	Pound
South Africa	Capetown (Legislative) Pretoria (Administrative)	Rand
Tajikistan	Dushanbe	Somoni
Taiwan	Taipei	Dollar
Tanzania	Dodoma	Shilling
Thailand	Bangkok	Baht
Turkiye	Ankara	Turkish Lira
Turkmania	Ashikabad	Manat
Uganda	Kampala	Shilling
Ukraine	Kiev	Hyrvna
United Arab Emirates	Abu Dhabi	Dirham
U.K.	London	Pound Sterling
U.S.A.	Washington	Dollar
Uzbekistan	Tashkent	Som
Vietnam	Hanoi	Dong
Yemen	Sana'a	Rial/Dinar
Zimbabwe	Harare	Dollar
Congo (Democratic Republic)	Kinshasa	Franc
Zambia	Lusaka	Kwacha

INDIAN CITIES AND THEIR RIVERS

City	State	River
Agra	U.P.	Yamuna
Ahmedabad	Gujarat	Sabarmati
Alwaye	Kerala	Periyar
Kolkata	West Bengal	Hooghly
Cuttack	Odisha	Mahanadi
Delhi	Delhi	Yamuna
Haridwar	Uttarakhand	Ganga
Kanpur	Uttar Pradesh	Ganga
Ludhiana	Punjab	Sutlej
Lucknow	Uttar Pradesh	Gomati
Nasik	Maharashtra	Godavari
Patna	Bihar	Ganga
Prayagraj	U.P.	Confluence of the Ganga, Yamuna and invisible Saraswati
Srinagar	J & K	Jhelum
Surat	Gujarat	Tapti
Tiruchirapally	Tamil Nadu	Kaveri
Ujjain	Madhya Pradesh	Shipra
Vijayawada	Andhra Pradesh	Krishna
Varanasi	Uttar Pradesh	Ganga

WONDERS OF THE WORLD

Seven Wonders of the Ancient World: (1) the Pyramids of Egypt, built in approximately 2700 BC; (2) the Hanging Gardens at Babylon; (3) the temple of Artemis at Emphesus; (4) the statue of Zeus at Olympia; (5) the tomb of Mausolus at Halicarnassus, built in nearly 350 BC; (6) the Colossus of Rhodes, built in nearly 280 BC; (7) the Pharos Lighthouse at Alexandria.

Seven Wonders of the Medieval World: (1) the Colosseum of Rome; (2) the Great Wall of China; (3) the Porcelain Tower of Nanking; (4) the Mosque at St. Sophia (Constantinople); (5) Stonehenge; (6) the Catacombs of Rome; (7) the Leaning Tower of Pisa.

Seven New Wonders of the World: (1) Taj Mahal of Agra (India); (2) Pyramid at Chichen Itza (Mexico); (3) Machu Picchu (Peru); (4) Statue of Christ The Redeemer (Brazil); (5) Great Wall of China; (6) Roman Colosseum, Italy; (7) Ruins of Petra, Jordan.

STATES & UNION TERRITORIES OF INDIA (CAPITALS, PRINCIPAL LANGUAGES)

States & Union Territories	*Capitals*	*Principal Languages*
■ Andhra Pradesh	Amravati	*Telgu and Urdu*
■ Arunachal Pradesh	Itanagar	*Monpa, Adi, Nissi etc.*
■ Assam	Dispur	*Assamese and Bengali*
■ Bihar	Patna	*Hindi and Maithili*
■ Chhattishgarh	Raipur	*Hindi*
■ Goa	Panaji	*Konkani*
■ Gujarat	GandhiNagar	*Gujarati*
■ Haryana	Chandigarh	*Hindi*
■ Himachal Pradesh	Shimla	*Hindi and Pahari*
■ Jharkhand	Ranchi	*Hindi*
■ Kerala	Thiruvananthpuram	*Malyalam*
■ Karnataka	Bengluru	*Kannada*
■ Madhya Pradesh	Bhopal	*Hindi*
■ Maharashtra	Mumbai	*Marathi*
■ Meghalaya	Shillong	*Khashi, Jayantia and Garo*
■ Manipur	Imphal	*Manipuri*
■ Mizoram	Aizawl	*Mizo and English*
■ Nagaland	Kohima	*Naga, Assamese and English*
■ Odisha	Bhubaneshwar	*Odiya*
■ Punjab	Chandigarh	*Punjabi*
■ Rajasthan	Jaipur	*Hindi, Rajasthani*
■ Sikkim	Gangtok	*Sikkimese and Gorkhali*
■ Tamil Nadu	Chennai	*Tamil*
■ Tripura	Agartala	*Bengali, Tripuri*
■ Uttar Pradesh	Lucknow	*Hindi*
■ Uttarakhand	Dehradun	*Hindi*
■ West Bengal	Kolkata	*Bengali*
■ Telangana	Hyderabad	*Telgu and Urdu*
■ Jammu & Kashmir	Srinagar/Jammu	*Kashmiri, Dongri, Urdu, Dardi and Pahari*
■ Andaman and Nicobar Islands	Port Blair	*Hindi, Nicobarese, Bengali, Malayalam, Tamil, Telugu*
■ Chandigarh	Chandigarh	*Hindi, Punjabi, English*
■ Dadar and Nagar Haveli and Daman and Diu	Daman	*Gujarati, Hindi*
■ Delhi	Delhi	*Hindi, Punjabi*
■ Lakshadweep	Kavaratti	*Malayalam*
■ Puducherry	Puducherry	*Tamil, Telugu, Malayalam, English and French*
■ Ladakh	Leh	*Ladakhi*

HIGH COURTS IN INDIA

Name	*Territorial Jurisdiction*	*Seat*
Allahabad	Uttar Pradesh	Prayagraj (Bench at Lucknow)
Andhra Pradesh	Andhra Pradesh	Amaravati
Bombay	Maharashtra, Goa Dadar and Nagar Haveli and Daman and Diu	Mumbai (Benches at Nagpur, Panaji, and Aurangabad)
Calcutta	West Bengal and Andaman & Nicobar Islands	Kolkata (Circuit Benches at Port Blair and Jalpaiguri)
Chhattisgarh	Chhattisgarh	Bilaspur
Delhi	New Delhi	NCT of Delhi
Gauhati	Assam, Nagaland, Mizoram and Arunachal Pradesh	Guwahati (Benches at Kohima, Aizawl and Itanagar)
Gujarat	Gujarat	Ahmedabad
Himachal Pradesh	Himachal Pradesh	Shimla
Jammu & Kashmir and Ladakh	Jammu & Kashmir/Ladakh	Srinagar and Jammu
Jharkhand	Jharkhand	Ranchi
Karnataka	Karnataka	Bengaluru (Circuit Benches at Dharwar and Gulbarga)
Kerala	Kerala & Lakshadweep	Ernakulam
Madhya Pradesh	Madhya Pradesh	Jabalpur (Benches at Gwalior and Indore)
Madras	Tamil Nadu & Puducherry	Chennai (Bench at Madurai)
Orissa	Odisha	Cuttack
Patna	Bihar	Patna
Punjab and Haryana	Punjab, Haryana and Chandigarh	Chandigarh
Rajasthan	Rajasthan	Jodhpur (Bench at Jaipur)
Sikkim	Sikkim	Gangtok
Uttarakhand	Uttarakhand	Nainital
Tripura	Tripura	Agartala
Meghalaya	Meghalaya	Shillong
Manipur	Manipur	Imphal
Telangana	Telangana	Hyderabad

FAMOUS HILL STATIONS

Hill Station	**State/UT**
1. Almora, Mussoorie Nainital	Uttarakhand
2. Cherrapunji (Shillong), Khasi Hills (Shillong)	Meghalaya
3. Ooty, Kodaikanal Yereaud	Tamil Nadu
4. Dalhousie, Kassauli	Himachal Pradesh
5. Darjeeling	West Bengal
6. Gulmarg, Srinagar	Jammu and Kashmir
7. Mahabaleshwar	Maharashtra
8. Mt. Abu	Rajasthan
9. Panchmarhi	Madhya Pradesh

FAMOUS NATIONAL PARKS

1. Corbett National Park : Nainital, Uttarakhand
2. Dudhwa National Park : Lakhimpur Kheri, Uttar Pradesh
3. Kaziranga National Park : Jorhat, Assam
4. Kanha National Park : Jabalpur, Bhedaghat
5. Gir National Park : Rajkot, Junagarh, Gujarat
6. Guindy National Park : Guindy, Chennai, Tamil Nadu
7. Nagairhole National Park : Coorg, Karnataka
8. Bandipur National Park : Mysore, Karnataka

FAMOUS NATIONAL WILDLIFE SANCTUARIES

1. Dachigam Wildlife Sanctuary : Srinagar, Jammu and Kashmir
2. Sariska : Alwar, Rajasthan
3. Hazaribagh Wildlife Sanctuary : Hazaribagh, Jharkhand
4. Tiger Project : Sawai Madhopur, Rajasthan
5. Mudhumali Wildlife Sanctuary : Mudhumalia, Nilgiri, Tamil Nadu
6. Periyar Wildlife Sanctuary : Idukki, Kottayam, Kerala

HOLY PLACES IN INDIA

1. Amarnath	Jammu and Kashmir
2. Ayodhya	Uttar Pradesh
3. Badrinath	Uttarakhand
4. Dwarka	Gujarat
5. Haridwar	Uttarakhand
6. Kancheepuram	Tamil Nadu
7. Kedarnath	Uttarakhand
8. Mathura	Uttar Pradesh
9. Puri	Odisha
10. Rameswaram	Tamil Nadu
11. Tirupati	Andhra Pradesh
12. Ujjain	Madhya Pradesh
13. Varanasi	Uttar Pradesh
14. Bodh Gaya	Bihar

SPORTS

Terms Associated With Sports :

Cricket : Ashes, Bye, Bodyline, Bowling, Break, Cover-point, Creases, Chinaman, Chucker, Drive, Duck, Follow on, Googly, Hit-Wicket, Hat-trick, Leg-before-wicket, Leg break, Leg-bye, Maiden over, No ball, Night-watchman, Runner, Run-out, Stumped, Silly-point, Slip.

Football : Handball, Corner kick, Dribble, Free Kick, Hat-trick, Off-side, Penalty Kick, Try, Throw in, Wembley.

Hockey : Bully, Carry, Corner kick, Corner, Penalty stroke, Off-side, Penalty, Roll in scoop, Sticks, Sudden death, Striking circle, Short Corner, Scoop, Tie-breaker, Under-cutting, Hat-trick.

Tennis : Backhand drive, Deuce, Fault, Half-volley, Net, Let, Volley, Smash, Service.

Billiards : Break; Cannons, Cue, Pot, Jigger, Scratch, In Bauk, In, Off.

Bridge : Dummy, Finesse, Grand-slam, Little Slam, Revoke, Ruff slam, Trump, Tricks, Vulnerable.

Volley Ball : Booster, Love, Service, Volley, Smasher.

Badminton : Smash, Drop, Let.

Chess : Check, Checkmate, Gambit, State-mate.

Golf : Bogy, Caddie, Hole, Links, Stymie, Tee, Put.

Polo : Chukker, Mallet, Bunder.

Baseball : Bunting, Diamond, Pitcher, Put-out, Strike, Home.

Boxing : Knockout, Punch, Upper-cut, Jab, Hook.

FAMOUS TROPHIES

Agha Khan Cup	Hockey
Beighton Cup	Hockey
Corbillion Cup	World Table Tennis (Women)
Davis Cup	Lawn Tennis
Duleep Trophy	Cricket
Durand Cup	Football
Ezra Cup	Polo
I.F.A. Shield	Football
Irani Cup	Cricket (India)
Jayalaxmi Cup	Table Tennis (Women)
Lady Rattan Tata Trophy	Hockey (Women)
Nehru Cup	Hockey (India)
Obaidullah Cup	Hockey
Ranji Trophy	Cricket (India)
Rangaswamy Cup	Hockey (India)
Rovers Cup	Football (India)
Santosh Trophy	Football (India)
Subroto Cup	Football
Thomas Cup	Badminton
Uber Cup	Badminton (Women)
Wellington Trophy	Rowing (India)

BIGGEST, LARGEST, TALLEST OF THE WORLD

Airport, *Largest*—King Fahd International Airport, Dammon (Saudi Arabia)

Animal, *Tallest*—Giraffe (Average height 6.09 m); *Largest and Heaviest*—Blue Whale (190 tonnes)

Longest recorded Animal—Boot lace Worm (55 m); *Fastest*—Cheetah (Approximately 100 km/hr)

Bay, *Largest*—Bay of Bengal

Continent, *biggest*—Asia (31,845,872 km^2); *Smallest*—Australia Mainland (Area 76,17,930 km^2)

Desert, *Largest*—Sahara (N. Africa; maximum length 5,150 km EW; maximum width 3,200 km NS)

Dome, *Largest*—Singapore National Stadium (310 m)

Fish, *Largest fresh water*—Plabeuk (China, Laos and Thailand); *Most abundant*—Bristle mouth; *Most venomous*—Stone Fish (Indo-Pacific Waters)

Fountain, *Tallest*—King Fahd's Fountain (Jeddah, Saudi Arabia)

Gulf, *Largest*—Gulf of Mexico (1,544,000 sq. km)

Island, *Biggest*—Greenland (Kalaatdlit Nunaat-2,175,000 sq km)

Lake, *Largest*--Caspian Sea (Azerbaijan, Russia, Iran border: 37.18 lakh km^2); *Deepest*—Baikal (Siberia); *Largest (fresh water)*—Superior Lake (USA---Canada border: 82,350 km^2)

Mountain, *Highest peak*—Mt. Everest (8848 m; Nepal); *Highest range*—Himalayas, Asia (upto 4200 m); *Greatest mountain range*—Himalaya-Karakoram (96 out of 109 peaks over 7315 m are here)

Museum, *Largest*—American Museum of Natural History, New York

Ocean, *Largest and Deepest*—The Pacific (Area: 166,240,000 km^2; Depth: 10,924 m)

Platform, *Longest (rail)*—Shri Siddharoodha Swamiji Railway Station, Hubballi (Karnataka; India, 1507 m. long)

Railway Station, *Largest*—Grand Central Terminal (New York City; 19 hc)

Rivers, *Longest*—(i) Nile (6650 km) (ii) Amazon (6437 km)

Sea, *Largest*—Philippine Sea (5,695,000 sq. km)

Star, *Brightest*—Sirius A (also called Dog Star)

Temple, *Largest*—Angkor Vat (Cambodia: 402 acres)

Tunnel, *Longest (railway)*—Gotthard Base Rail Tunnel (Switzerland; 57.1 km); *Largest (road)*—Laerdal, Norway (24.51 km)

FIRST IN INDIA

Governor General of Independent India — Lord Mountbatten

Cosmonaut — Sq. Ldr. Rakesh Sharma

Field Marshal — S.H.F.J. Manekshaw

Indian Governor General of Indian Union — C. Rajagopalachari

Indian I.C.S. Officer — Satyendra Nath Tagore

Indian to swim across English Channel — Mihir Sen

Indian Women to swim across English Channel — Miss Arti Saha

Man to climb Mount Everest — Tenzing Norgay

Man to climb Mount Everest without Oxygen — Phu Dorjee

Man to climb Mount Everest twice — Nwang Gombu

Nobel Prize Winner — Rabindra Nath Tagore

President of Indian National Congress — W.C. Banerjee

President of Indian Republic — Dr. Rajendra Prasad

Talkie Film — Alam Ara (1931)

Test Tube Baby (Documented) — Indira

Viceroy of India — Lord Canning

Woman Minister of Indian Union — Rajkumari Amrit Kaur

Woman Governor — Mrs. Sarojini Naidu

Woman President of Indian National Congress — Dr. Annie Besant

Woman Prime Minister — Mrs. Indira Gandhi

Woman Speaker of a State Assembly — Mrs. Shanno Devi

Prime Minister of India — Pt. Jawaharlal Nehru

Muslim President of Indian Union — Dr. Zakir Hussain

Speaker of Lok Sabha — G.V. Mavlankar

Women to Climb Mount Everest — Bachhendri Pal

Woman Judge in Supreme Court — Mrs. Meera Sahib Fatima Biwi

Women Chief Justice of a High Court — Smt. Leela Seth

The First Indian Weightlifter to Win bronze medal in Olympics — Karnam Malleshwari (Sydney, in 2000)

Chief of Defence Staff (CDS) —General Bipin Rawat

World Chess Champion — Vishwanathan Anand

India's First Woman Merchant Navy Officer — Sonali Banerjee

The First Woman Air Vice-Marshal — P. Bandopadhyaya

The First Indian to be appointed as United Nations Civilian Police Advisor — Ms. Kiran Bedi

The First Women to be appointed Deputy Governor of Reserve Bank of India — K.J. Udeshi

The First Indian Lady to win a medal in World Athletic Championship — Anju Bobby George

The First Sikh Prime Minister of India — Dr. Manmohan Singh

IMPORTANT DAYS

15th January	—	Army Day
26th January	—	Republic Day
30th January	—	Leprosy Eradication Day/ Martyr's Day
28th February	—	National Science Day
8th march	—	International Women's Day
15th March	—	World Consumer's Day
21st March	—	World Disabled Day
5th April	—	National Marine Day
7th April	—	World Health Day
18th April	—	World Heritage Day
22nd April	—	International Earth Day
Ist May	—	Worker's Day
3rd May	—	International Sun Day
21st May	—	Anti-Terrorism Day
24th May	—	Commonwealth Day
31st May	—	World No Tobacco Day
5th June	—	World Environment Day
21st June	—	World Yoga Day
26th June	—	International Day against Drug Abuse
11th July	—	World Population Day
15th August	—	Independence Day
24th August	—	Sanskrit Day
5th September	—	Teacher's Day
8th September	—	World Literacy Day
27th September	—	World Tourism Day
1st October	—	World Elder's Day
4th October	—	World Animal Day
8th October	—	Air Force Day
10th October	—	National Solidarity Day
16th October	—	World Food Day
24th October	—	U.N. Day
14th November	—	World Diabetes Day
14th November	—	Children's Day
19th November	—	National Integration Day
26th November	—	Law Day
1st December	—	World AIDS Day
4th December	—	Navy Day
7th December	—	Flag Day
10th December	—	Human Rights Day

PARLIAMENTS OF IMPORTANT COUNTRIES

Afghanistan	—	Shora
Britain	—	Parliament House of Commons, House of Lords
Denmark	—	Folketing
The Netherlands	—	States General
India	—	Sansad
Israel	—	Knesset
Iran	—	Majlis
Ireland	—	Airetann
Iceland	—	Althing
Japan	—	Diet
Norway	—	Storting
Russia	—	Supreme Soviet
Spain	—	Cortes
Sweden	—	Riksdag
U.S.A.	—	Congress Senate
Germany	—	Bundestag

MINERAL RESOURCES OF THE WORLD

Mineral	Largest Producers
Iron Ore	China, Japan, Russia
Tin	China, Indonesia, Peru
Lead	China, Australia, U.S.A.
Zinc	China, Australia, Peru
Manganese	South Africa, Brazil, Australia
Aluminium	China, Russia, Canada
Petroleum	Saudi Arabia, Russia, USA
Silver	Peru, Mexico, China
Coal	China, USA, India

WORLD'S LARGEST PRODUCERS

Articles	Producers	Articles	Producers
Carpets	Iran	Cheese	USA
Cocoa	Cote d'Ivoire	Coffee	Brazil
Copper	Chile	Cotton	China
Diamonds	Russia	Jute	India
Rice	China	Rubber	Thailand
Silk	China	Steel	China
Sugar	Brazil	Tea	China
Tin	China	Wheat	China
Wool	Australia		

TEN LARGEST COUNTRIES BY AREAS

Rank by Area	Country	Area (sq. km.)
1.	Russia	17,075,400
2.	Canada	9,976,139
3.	China	9,561,000
4.	U.S.A.	9,363,123
5.	Brazil	8,511,965
6.	Australia	7,686,848
7.	India	3,287,263
8.	Argentina	2,776,889
9.	Kazakhstan	2,724,900
10.	Algeria	2,381,741

PRESIDENT OF INDIA

He is the constitutional head of the Republic but not the real executive.

Qualifications: (1) Indian citizen; (2) age not less than 35 years; (3) should have qualifications for election to Lok Sabha; (4) should not hold any office of profit; (5) should not be a Member of Parliament or State Legislature.

Election: He is elected by the elected Members of Parliament and State Legislative Assemblies in accordance with the system of proportional representation by means of single transferable vote.

Powers: He makes appointment to all the Constitutional posts. He can address either House of Parliament and send message to them. He can summon and prorogue either House of Parliament and dissolve Lok Sabha. All Bills passed by Parliament must receive his assent to become an Act. He issues Ordinance when Parliament is not in session. No money Bill can be introduced in Lok Sabha without his recommendation. He can grant pardon, reprieve or remit punishment and he can commute death sentences. He can declare national emergency, state emergency and financial emergency.

VICE-PRESIDENT OF INDIA

The Vice-President acts as the ex-officio Chairman of Rajya Sabha and acts as the President when the latter is unable to discharge his functions due to illness, absence or any other reason, or till the election of a new President when a vacancy is caused by the death, resignation or removal of the President.

The Vice-President is elected by an electoral college consisting of the members of both Houses of Parliament in accordance with the system of proportional representation by means of the single transferable vote. He must be a citizen of India, not less than 35 years of age, and should be eligible for election as a member of the Council of States.

PRIME MINISTER OF INDIA

The Prime Minister is the leader of the majority party in the Parliament and the President cannot exercise his discretion in the appointment of the Prime Minister. He stays in office till the majority of the members of Lok Sabha has confidence in him. He occupies an important posi-tion in relation to the council of Ministers. He recommends the names of the persons to be included in the Council of Ministers. He allocates portfolios among them and can ask any minister to tender resignation. He can drop a minister while reshuffling the ministry. He coordinates the administration of various departments. He is the chief link between the President and the Council. He is the leader of the majority party and so, he has a great influence on the Parliament and the party. The Prime Minister enjoys such extensive powers as have been described as the virtual ruler of the country.

THE SOLAR SYSTEM: SOME FACTS

Number of Planets: 8—Mercury, Venus, Earth, Mars, Jupiter, Saturn, Uranus and Neptune.

Largest most

Massive planet .... Jupiter
Brightest planet .... Venus
Brightest star .... Sirius
Fastest orbiting planet .... Mercury
Longest (Synodic) day .... Mercury
Planet with largest moon .... Jupiter
Greatest average density .... Jupiter
Tallest mountain .... Earth
Strongest magnetic fields .... Jupiter
Most circular orbit .... Venus
Shortest (synodic) day .... Jupiter
Hottest planet .... Venus
No moons .... Mercury, Venus
Planet with moon with most eccentric orbit .... Neptune
Lowest average density .... Saturn
Deepest Oceans .... Jupiter
Greatest amount of liquid on the surface .... Earth

THE EARTH: FACTS AND DATA

Composition of the Earth: Aluminium (0.4%), Sulphur (2.7%), Silicon (13%), Oxygen (28%), Calcium (1.2%), Nickel (2.7%), Magnesium (17%), Iron (35%)

Surface area	: 510100500 sq km
Land Surface (29.1%)	: 148950800 sq km
Ocean Surface (70.9%)	: 361149700 sq km
Type of water	: 97% salt, 3% fresh
Total area of water	: 382672000 sq km
Equatorial diameter	: 12753 km
Equatorial Circumference	: 40066 km
Polar Circumference	: 39992 km
Polar diameter	: 12710 km
Equatorial radius	: 6376 km
Polar radius	: 6335 km
Mass (estimated weight)	: 594×10^{19} metric tons
Mean distance from the Sun	: 149407000 km

Earth's orbit speed (around sun)	: 107320 kmph	Time of Rotation (on its axis)	: 23 hrs 56 min 4.09 seconds
Period of Revolution (round the sun)	: 365 days 5 hrs 48 min. 45.51 seconds	Inclination of the axis (to the plane of the ecliptic)	: 23°27'

PRINCIPAL MOUNTAIN PEAKS OF THE WORLD

Mountains	Height in Metres	Range	Date of First Ascent
1. Mount Everest	8,848	Himalayas	May 29, 1953
2. K-2 (Godwin Austen)	8,611	Karakoram	July 31, 1954
3. Kanchenjunga	8,597	Himalayas	May 25, 1955
4. Lhotse	8,511	Himalayas	May 18, 1956
5. Makalu I	8,481	Himalayas	May 15, 1955
6. Dhaulagiri I	8,167	Himalayas	May 13, 1960
7. Mansalu I	8,156	Himalayas	May 9, 1956
8. Chollyo	8,153	Himalayas	Oct. 19, 1954
9. Nanga Parbat	8,124	Himalayas	July 3, 1953
10. Annapurna I	8,091	Himalayas	June 3, 1950
11. Gasherbrum I	8,068	Karakoram	July 5, 1958
12. Broad Peak I	8,047	Karakoram	June 9, 1957
13. Gasherbrum II	8,034	Karakoram	July 7, 1956
14. Shisha Pangma (Gosainthan)	8,014	Himalayas	May 2, 1964
15. Gasherbrum III	7,952	Karakoram	Aug. 11, 1975

POPULAR NICK NAMES OF SOME FAMOUS PERSONALITIES

Andhra Kesari	T. Prakasam	Lal, Bal, Pal	Lala Lajpat Rai, Bal Gangadhar Tilak, Bipin Chandra Pal
Anna	C.N. Anna Durai	Little Corporal	Napoleon Bonaparte
Bang Bandhu	Sheikh Mujibur Rehman	Lokmanya	Bal Gangadhar Tilak
Bapu	Mahatma Gandhi	Mahamana	Pt. Madan Mohan Malaviya
Bard of Avon	William Shakespeare	Maid of Orleans	Joan of Arc
Chachaji	Jawaharlal Nehru	Maiden Queen	Queen Elizabeth I
Desh Bandhu	C.R. Das	Missile Man	A.P.J. Abdul Kalam
Frontier Gandhi	Khan Abdul Gaffar Khan	Man of Destiny	Napoleon Bonaparte
Fuhrer	Adolf Hitler	Netaji	Subhash Chandra Bose
G.B.S.	George Bernard Shaw	Nightingale of India	Sarojini Naidu
Grand Old Man of India	Dadabhai Naoroji	Panditji	Jawaharlal Nehru
Grand Old Man of Britain	Gladstone	Punjab Kesari	Lala Lajpat Rai
Guru Dev	Rabindra Nath Tagore	Shastriji	Lal Bahadur Shastri
Guruji	M.S. Golwalkar	Uncle Ho	Ho Chi Minh
Iron Man of India	Sardar Patel	Wizard of the North	Walter Scott
Lok Nayak	Jayaprakash Narayan		
Lady with the Lamp	Florence Nightingale		

FAMOUS INTERNATIONAL ORGANISATIONS, HEADQUARTERS

International Organisations	*Headquarters*
United Nations Organisations (U.N.O.)	New York
International Monetary Fund (I.M.F.)	Washington D.C.
World Health Organisation (W.H.O.)	Geneva
Food & Agricultural Organisation (FAO)	Rome
International Labour Organisation (ILO)	Geneva
UNESCO	Paris
International Court of Justice	The Hague
Universal Postal Union (UPU)	Berne
International Civil Aviation Organisation (ICAO)	Montreal
UNIDO	Vienna
International Atomic Energy Agency (IAEA)	Vienna
International Finance Corporation (IFC)	Washington
United Nations Development Programme (UNDP)	New York
UNICEF	New York
International Maritime Organisation (IMO)	London
World Meteorological Organisation (WMO)	Geneva
International Telecommunication Union (ITU)	Geneva
Arab League	Cairo
Commonwealth of Nations	London
World Trade Organisation (WTO)	Geneva
International Development Association (IDA)	Washington D.C.
International Bank for Reconstruction and Development (IBRD)	Washington D.C.
World Intellectual Property Organisation (WIPO)	Geneva
Organisation of Islamic Conference (OIC)	Jeddah (Saudi Arabia)
European Union	Brussels
Red Cross	Geneva
Interpol	Lyons (France)
Asian Development Bank (ADB)	Manila
North Atlantic Treaty Organisation (NATO)	Brussels
Association of South East Asian Nations (ASEAN)	Jakarta

AWARDS

NOBEL PRIZES

- These Prizes were instituted in 1901 by a Swedish scientist, Dr. Alfred Nobel; the discoverer of Dynamite.
- Six prizes are awarded annually for (*i*) Chemistry, (*ii*) Physics, (*iii*) Medicine, (*iv*) Literature, (*v*) Peace and (*vi*) Economics —started since 1969.
- The following Indians so far have been awarded these prizes: (*i*) Dr. Rabindra Nath Tagore (1913) for his "Geetanjali". (*ii*) Dr. C.V. Raman for Physics in 1930, (*iii*) Mother Teresa for Peace in 1979, (*iv*) Prof. Amartya Sen in 1998 for Economics and (*v*) Kailash Satyarthi in 2014 for Peace.
- In addition, four non-resident Indians have also been awarded the Nobel Prize. They are: (*i*) Hargobind Khurana for Medicine in 1968, (*ii*) Subramanian Chandrasekhar for Physics in 1983, (*iii*) Venkatraman Ramkrishnan for Chemistry in 2009, (*iv*) Abhijit Vinayak Banerjee for Economics in 2019.

BHARAT RATNA

- Bharat Ratna is India's highest Civilian Award. It was first awarded in 1954.
- The actual award is designed in the shape of a *peepal* leaf with Bharat Ratna inscribed in Devanagri script in the Sun Figure.
- This is India's highest civilian award. It is given for exceptional work on art, literature, science and recognition of public service of the highest order.
- The emblem, the Sun and the rim are of platinum. The inscriptions are in burnished bronze.
- Government servants are not eligible for it

ART AND CULTURE

☞ Classical Dances

Dance	*State*	*Famous Artists*
Bharat Natyam	Tamil Nadu	Yamini Krishnamurthy, Rukmini Devi Arundale, Swapna Sundari, Sonal Mansingh, Vaijanti Mala, Mrinalini Sarabhai, Chandralekha, Indrani, Ram Gopal, Bal Saraswati
Kathakali	Kerala	Gopinath, K.K. Nayar, Kunju-Kurup, T.K. Chandu
Kuchipudi	Andhra Pradesh/ Telangana	Sapna Sundari, Raja Reddy, Shobha Nayar, Radha Reddy, Vedantam Satyanarayan, Vimpanti Chinna Satyam.
Kathak	North India	Birju Maharaj, Gopi Krishna, Shambhu Maharaj, Sitara Devi, Vishnu Sharma, Durga Lal, Shobhana Narayan
Odissi	Odisha	Kelucharan Mahapatra, Indrani Rehman, Madhavi Mudgal, Pratima Bedi, Samyukta Panigrahi, Sonal Mansingh, Debudas
Manipuri	Manipur	Uday Shankar, Bipin Singh, Suryamukhi, Darohra Jhaveri

☞ Famous Folk Dances

State/UT	*Folk Dance*	*State/UT*	*Folk Dance*
Andhra Pradesh/ Telangana	Dandari, Banjara	Kerala	Mohini Attam, Padayuni
Assam	Bihu, Keli Gopal, Sataria	Madhya Pradesh	Lota Nritya, Jawara
Bihar	Chhau, Magahi, Durga dance	Maharashtra	Tamasha, Dahi Handi, Gof Deepak Dindi
W. Bengal	Kirtan, Kalatri, Asweabadh, Brita, Kalidance	Manipur	Dhol Cholam
Chhattisgarh	Saila, Karama, Bhagoria	Meghalaya	Nongakarem
Gujarat	Garba, Rasalila, Tippani, Dandia,	Nagaland	Bamboo dance
Haryana	Damyal, Lahoor	Odisha	Chhau, Maya Shabari, Dalachai
Himachal Pradesh	Dussehra dance, Hikat, Notio	Punjab	Gidda, Bhangra, Panihari
Jammu & Kashmir	Dumhal	Rajasthan	Thumar, Kathaputali, Tera Tali
Jharkhand	Jhau, Ghumakudia, Jadur, Sarhul, Soharai, Karama, Vaima, Loojhari, Jat-Jatin, Vidayat	Tamil Nadu	Terukalathu, Kabalatam, Kargam, Pulivesham
Karnataka	Yakshagan, Dolu Kunitha	Tripura	Hazagiri
		Uttar Pradesh	Rasalila, Nautanki, Thali, Dhurang, Jhumela, Huraka, Bol.
		Uttarakhand	Kajari, Karan
		Goa	Dhode Modini

MUSIC

Main Schools of Classical Music

- There are two main schools of classical music, namely, the Hindustani and the Carnatic. The Hindustani school of classical music is in vogue in north-western India, eastern India and northern parts of the South India.

Musical Instruments

- ***They are:*** Tabla, Mridangam, Pakhawaj, Chandai, Dholak, Veena, Sitar, Sarod, Gootuvadhyam, Sarangi, Flute, Nadaswaram, Shehnai, Shringi and Turahi.

FAMOUS INTERNATIONAL AIR SERVICES

Air Service	*Name of Country*	*Air Service*	*Name of Country*
Air India	India	Lufthansa Airlines	Germany
British Overseas Airways Corporation	Britain	Iraqi Airways	Iraq
Trans World Airlines	America	National Airlines	Iran
Russian Airlines	Russia	Quantas Airlines	Australia
Japan Airlines	Japan	Hong-Kong Airlines	Hong-Kong
Pakistan International Airlines	Pakistan	Egypt Airlines	Egypt
Malaysia Airlines	Malaysia	Slovak Airlines	Slovakia
Royal Nepal Airlines	Nepal	S.I.A.	Singapore
Swiss Airways	Switzerland	Garuda Airways	Indonesia
Air France	France	Bangladesh Viman Sewa	Bangladesh
Kuwait Airways	Kuwait	Air Lanka	Sri Lanka
Pan American World Airways	America	Elitalia Airlines	Italy
K.L.M. Royal Airlines	The Netherlands (Holland)	Air Canada	Canada

FAMOUS RELIGIONS, FOUNDERS, HOLY BOOKS & PLACES OF WORSHIP

Religion	*Founder*	*Holy Books*	*Place of Worship*
Hinduism	Hinduism has no one Founder. (This religion is based upon the religion of original Aryan Settlers)	Ramayan, Vedas, Puranas and Geeta	Temple
Sikh	Guru Nanak Dev	Guru Grantha Sahib	Gurdwara
Christianity	Jesus Christ	Bible	Church
Islam	Prophet Mohammed	Koran (Quran)	Mosque
Parsi	Zoroaster	Zend Avesta	Fire Temple
Jainism	Adinath Rishavdev	Jain Granth	Jain Temple
Buddhism	Gautam Buddha	Tripitaka	Buddha Temple
Jew	Moosa	Torah	Synagogue

INTELLIGENCE AGENCIES OF SOME PROMINENT COUNTRIES

Country	*Intelligence Agency*
India	Research & Analysis Wing (RAW), Intelligence Bureau (I.B.), Central Bureau of Investigation (C.B.I.)
Pakistan	Inter Service Intelligence (I.S.I.)
U.S.A.	Central Intelligence Agency, Federal Bureau of Investigation
Britain	Military Intelligence (M.I.)-5 and 6, Special Branch, Ultra, Joint Intelligence Organisation
Israel	Mosad
Egypt	Mukhabarat
Japan	Nicho

Country	*Intelligence Agency*
Russia	K.G.B. (Komitel Gosudarstvennoy Bezopasnosty) (Committee for State Security)
Canada	Security Intelligence Service
S. Africa	Bureau of State Security
Iran	Sabak
Iraq	Al-Mukhabarat
Australia	Australian Security and Intelligence Organisation
France	S.D.E.C.E.
Spain	C.E.S.I.D.
Cuba	D.G.I.

SOME PROMINENT RACES OF THE WORLD

Races	Country/Area	Races	Country/Area	Races	Country/Area	Races	Country/Area
Veddas	Sri Lanka	Pygmy	Congo Basin	Eskimo	Canada, Tundra Region	Bushman	Kalahari Desert
Somaid	West Siberia	Bantu	Central and South Africa	Lapps	European Tundra	Red Indian	North America
Masai	East Africa	Tartars	Siberia	Hausa	Nigeria		
Muree	New Zealand	Baddu	Arab's Desert	Kirghiz	Steppes (Russia)		
Yakoot	Russian Tundra	Semang	Malaysia				
Papuans	New Guyana						

FAMOUS STRAITS OF THE WORLD

Strait	Between	Country
Malacca Strait	Andaman Sea and South China Sea	Indonesia
Palk Strait	Mannar and Bay of Bengal	India-Sri Lanka
Magellan Strait	Pacific and South Atlantic Ocean	Chile
Dover Strait	English Channel and North Sea	England-France
Berring Strait	Berring Sea and Chukasi Sea	Alaska-Russia
Sugaroo Strait	Japan Sea and Pacific Ocean	Japan
Sunda Strait	Java and Indian Ocean	Indonesia
Gibralter Strait	Mediterranean Sea and Atlantic Ocean	Spain
Harmuj Strait	Persia and Bay of Oman	Oman-Iran
Hudson Strait	Bay of Hudson and Atlantic Ocean	Canada

FAMOUS NEWSPAPERS OF THE WORLD

Newspaper	Place of Publishing	Language
Daily News	New York (America)	English
Guardian	London (Britain)	English
Pravada	Moscow (Russia)	Russian
Al-Ahram	Cairo (Egypt)	Arabic
Merdeca	Jakarta (Indonesia)	Indonesian
Times	London (Britain)	English
People's Daily	Beijing (China)	Chinese
New Statesman	Britain	English
Daily Mirror	Britain	English
Hindu, Hindustan, Times of India, Tribune, Statesman, Indian Express, Economic Times	India	English
Hindustan, Nav Bharat Times, Dainik Bhaskar, Dainik Jagaran, Punjab Kesari	India	Hindi

IMPORTANT BOUNDARY LINES

Boundary Line	Countries
Durand Line	Pakistan and Afghanistan
Hindenberg Line	Germany-Poland
Maginot Line	France and Germany
Mannerhein Line	Russia-Finland
Mc Mahon Line	India-China
Order Niesse Line	Germany-Poland
Radcliff Line	India-Pakistan
Seigfrid Line	Germany-France
24th Parallel	India-Pakistan
17th Parallel	The line which defined the boundary between North Vietnam and South Vietnam before the two were united.
38th Parallel	North Korea and South Korea
49th Parallel	U.S.A. and Canada

SIGNALS/SIGNS AND MEANING

Signal/Sign	*Meaning*	*Signal/Sign*	*Meaning*
Red Triangle	Family Planning	White Flag	Treaty or Surrender
Red Cross	Medical Help	Yellow Flag	Vehicles with patients of contagious diseases
Red Light	Danger, 'Stop' for the movement of vehicles	Two Bones across with a Skull	Danger of electricity
Green Light	Go	Half mast flown Flag	National mourning
Olive Branch	Peace	Lotus and culture	Sign of civilization
White Pigeon or Dove	Peace	Wheel (Chakra)	Sign of Progress
Black Strip on Arm	(i) Opposition (ii) Sorrow	A blind folded woman with scale in hand	Sign of Justice
Black Flag	Opposition	Reversed flown	National calamity flag
Red Flag	(i) Danger (ii) Revolution		

NATIONAL EMBLEMS OF IMPORTANT COUNTRIES

Country	*National Emblem*	*Country*	*National Emblem*
America	Golden Rod	New Zealand	Kiwi, Fern Southern Cross
Australia	Kangaroo	Norway	Lion
Ireland	Shamrock	Nepal	Kukri
Italy	White Lily	Pakistan	Crescent
Israel	Candelabrum	Poland	Eagle
Iran	Rose	France	Lily
Canada	White Lily	Belgium	Lion
Great Britain	Rose	Bangladesh	Water Lily
Chile	Candor and Huemul	Mongolia	The Soyombo
Germany	Corn Flower	Russia	Double headed eagle
Japan	Chrysanthemum	Lebanon	Cedar Tree
Zimbabwe	Zimbabwe Bird	Sudan	Secretary Bird
Denmark	Beach	Syria	Eagle
Turkiye	Crescent and Star	India	Lioned Capital
The Netherlands	Lion		

THE CONTINENTS OF THE WORLD

Name	*Population (2021) (In million)*	*Per cent of the world's population*
Asia	4,584	59.1
Africa	1,375	17.4
Europe	747	9.8
North America	373	4.8
South America	651	8.4
Australia	41.66	0.5
Antarctica	NA	NA

COMPUTER

The computer is the system of that electronic device through which various informations are processed on the basis of a definite set of instructions called program and mathematical (numerical) and non-mathematical both types of informations are processed.

The first mechanical computer was composed or fabricated by Blaise Pascal in 1642 and it is called Pascalene. But in 1833, Charles Babbage first time conceived an automatic calculator or computer. Charles Babbage is called the father of modern computer. Herman made an electronic tabulating machine based on punch cards which operates automatically.

In 1937, first mechanical computer mark-I was fabricated by Howard Akeen. The most outstanding contribution in the development of modern computer goes to John Wan Newmaan who brought the 2nd revolution in the area of computer in 1951. He discovered EDVAC (Electronic Discrete Variable Automatic Computer) and utilised the stored program and the binary number system in the computer.

FUNCTIONS OF COMPUTER

1. Collection and composition (input) of datas;
2. Storage of datas.
3. Processing of datas.
4. Retrieval or output of the proccessed informations and datas.

UNITS OF COMPUTER

1. Input unit.
2. Central processing unit–CPU.
3. External Memory unit.
4. Output unit.

The CPU of the computer is called brain of the computer and sometimes CPU is also called Micro Processor of the computer. The data is entered through the input unit in the computer and through the central processing unit with the help of External Memory Unit datas are arranged and processed. Ultimately by the output unit these datas or informations are issued or released.

PARTS OF COMPUTER

- **Monitor :** The monitor of the computer is like a television in which the picture appears in the form of doted points on the screen and these are called pixcels.
- **Hard Disc and Floppy Disc :** The Hard Disc is the permanent disc in the computers while the Floppy Disc is the disc utilised when datas or informations are to be transferred from one computer to another.
- **Mouse :** The mouse of the computer is like the remote control of TV through which computer is directly regulated or controlled without utilising the key-board.
- **Printer :** The printer is a device which prints any documents or processed informations of the computer.

SOME HIGH LEVEL LANGUAGES

1. **FORTRAN :** This language was developed for solving the mathematical formulae very quickly and conveniently.
2. **COBOL :** This language was developed for the commerical purposes. For the processing of this language a group of sentences is selected called paragraph and all paragraphs composed are called a section, while all sections composed are called a division.
3. **BASIC :** In basic a definite part of the prescribed instruction is only inserted in the computer.
4. **ALGOL :** This was basically fabricated and designed for the complex algebraic calculations.
5. **PASCAL :** It is an amplified and modified form of ALGOL.
6. **COMAL :** This computer language is used for the students of secondary level.
7. **LOGO :** This language is used for children and kids for drawing Graphic line diagrams.
8. **PROLOG :** This language is developed in 1973 in France and this language is used for Artificial Intelligence which is capable and equivalent to the logical program.

9. **FORTH :** This language was invented by Charles Mure which is frequently used in all types of the works in the computer.

COMPUTER VIRUS

The computer virus is an electronic code which is used to abolish or erradicate the inclusive informations or programs of the computer. Some important computer viruses are Micheleanjalo, Dork Avangor, kilo, filip, Macmug, Scores, Casecade, Jeruslem, Date crime, Coloumbs crime, Internet virus, Pachcom, Pach EXE, COM-EXE, Marizuana, C-brain, bloody, Chenge Mungu and Desi etc.

COMPUTER NETWORKING

There are two types of networkings which are usually occur—Local Area Networking (LAN) and Wide Area Networking (WAN). By LAN all the computers of the same buildings are connected like the computers of university premises, computers of offices etc.

By WAN all the comptuers of a large area are connected like the computers of all the offices of a city or town etc. In India a very large computer network namely INDONET has been installing through which all the main towns and cities has to be interlinked.

COMPUTER TERMINOLOGY

- **Bit :** The bit is a unit of measurement of the electronic data. One bit is either 0 or 1 but not both. On composing 8 bits, 1 byte is formed.
- **Bug :** The Bug is the error in the computer program or system and its eradication is called Debug.
- **Byte :** Total eight bits compose a byte. Thus 8 bits = 1 byte.
- **CD-ROM :** A CD like of music CD in which data can be stored substantially called CD-ROM. In a CD with comparison to floppy extremely more datas can be stored but one problem in it is that one time recorded data can not be deleted or modified.
- **Chip :** It is a thin slice on which by a special mechanism a circuit is designed which is normally made from Silicon.
- **Memory System :** The place where computer data and program are temporarily kept is called Memory system. Usually memory is implied from RAM.
- **Modem :** The device which converts digital signals into analogue signals and vice-versa is called Modem.
- **RAM :** It is Random Access Memory (a place) where datas to be processed are kept temporarily and it is unstable memory.
- **ROM :** It is Read Only Memory and it is stable or Non-valatile memory which doesn't ended after power off.
- **Scanner :** It is a device through which graphic image is transformed to digital image and the scanners are of usually two types one desktop and another hand operating.

PROGRAMING

Computers perform phenomenal feats of calculation, but they do not do so in a complicated way. They actually carry out very simple operations, such as addition and subtraction. They achieve their fantastic computing power by carrying out these operations at incredible speed.

The programme, or set of instructions for operating the computer, is therefore written as a sequence of very simple steps. (See box below) Several computer languages have been developed for different applications, including BASIC, COBOL, FORTRAN and PASCAL. Writing programmes is very skilled and time-consuming work. But for most typical computer applications ready-written programmes are available, called "packages".

☞ How A Programme Works

Without a programme to tell it what to do and how to do it, a computer is unable to function. If, for example, you wanted to know how many times the word 'the' appears in this paragraph, or in the whole book, it would not be enough merely to put the text into a computer and then ask it how many times the word appears. For the computer to accomplish the calculations it has to be told what to do in simple steps. The instructions might be:

1. Scan the text until a space followed by 'T' or 't' is found.
2. If the next letter is not 'h', go back to step 1.
3. If the letter is 'h', is the next letter 'e'?
4. If not, go back to step 1. If it is, go to step 5.
5. If 'e' is followed by a space, add 1 to the total.
6. Go back to step 1.

A full computer programme for this operation would need to be broken down into even more simple steps, but a series of such programmes could enable a computer to analyse any amount of text in great detail.

DEFENCE

The Supreme Command of the Armed Forces is vested in the hands of the President of the Country. The responsibility for national defence, however, rests with the Cabinet. All important questions having a bearing on defence are decided by the Cabinet Committee on Political Affairs, which is presided over by the Prime Minister. The Defence Minister is responsible to Parliament for all matters concerning the Defence Services. All the administrative and operational control of Armed Forces are exercised by the Ministry of Defence. The three services – Army, Navy and Air Force function through their respective service headquarters headed by the chief of Staff.

COMMISSIONED RANKS IN DEFENCE SERVICES

Army	Navy	Air Force
General	Admiral	Air Chief Marshal
Lieutenant-General	Vice-Admiral	Air Marshal
Major-General	Rear-Admiral	Air Vice-Marshal
Brigadier	Commodor	Air Commodor
Colonel	Captain	Group Captain
Lieutenant-Colonel	Commander	Wing Commander
Major	Lt.Commander	Squadron Leader
Captain	Lieutenant	Flight Lieutenant
Lieutenant	Sub-Lieutenant	Flying Officer

INTERNAL SECURITY ORGANISATIONS OF INDIA

S. No	Name of Organisation	Year of Creation	Headquarters
1.	Assam Rifles (A.R.)	1835	Shillong
2.	Central Reserve Police Force (C.R.P.F.)	1939	New Delhi
3.	National Cadet Corps (N.C.C.)	1948	New Delhi
4.	Territorial Army	1948	In different States
5.	Indo-Tibetan Border Police	1962	New Delhi
6.	Home Guard	1962	In different States
7.	Coast Guard	1978	New Delhi
8.	Border Security Force (B.S.F.)	1965	New Delhi
9.	Central Industrial Security Force (C.I.S.F.)	1969	New Delhi
10.	National Security Guard	1984	New Delhi
11.	Police	—	In different States

COMMANDER-IN-CHIEFS OF INDIA

1. General Sir Rob Lockhart	Aug. 15, 1947 — Dec. 31, 1947
2. General Sir Roy Bucher	Jan. 1, 1948 — Jan. 14, 1949
3. General K. M. Kariappa	Jan. 15, 1949 — Jan. 14, 1953
4. General Maharaj Rajendra Sinhji	Jan. 15, 1953 — March 31, 1955

FIRST INDIAN CHIEFS OF STAFF OF INDIAN FORCES

1. General Maharaj Rajendra Sinhji (Army Staff)	April 1, 1955 — May 14, 1955
2. Vice Admiral R.D. Katari (Naval Staff)	April 22, 1958 — June 4, 1962
3. Air Marshal S. Mukherjee (Air Staff)	April 1, 1954 — Nov. 8, 1960

ARMY INSTITUTES

1. Sainik Schools upto +2 Level	33 places in India
2. Rashtriya Indian Military College (prepare for entrance to N.D.A)	Dehradun
3. National Defence Academy (three services)	Khadakwasla, Pune
4. Indian Military Academy (Army)	Dehradun
5. Officers Training Academy (3 services) Short Courses	Chennai
6. National Defence College	New Delhi
7. The College of Combat	Mhow
8. The College of Military Engineering	Kirkee
9. Military College of Telecommunication Engineering	Mhow
10. The armoured Corps Centre and School	Ahmed Nagar
11. The School Artillery	Deolali
12. The Infantry School	Mhow and Belgaum
13. College of Material Management	Jabalpur

AIR FORCE INSTITUTIONS

Air Force Academy	Hyderabad
Helicopter Training School	Hakimpet
Flying Instructors School	Tambaram, Chennai
The College of Air Warfare	Secunderabad
Air Force Administrative College	Coimbatore
Air Force Technical College	Jalahalli

DEFENCE PRODUCTION UNITS

1. Bharat Dynamites Ltd.	Hyderabad
2. Praga Tools	Hyderabad
3. Mishra Dattu Nigam	Hyderabad
4. Bharat Electronics Ltd.	Bangalore
5. Bharath Earthmovers Ltd.	Bangalore
6. Heavy Vehicles Ltd.	Avadi, Chennai
7. Garden Reach Ship Builders and Engineers Ltd.	Kolkata
8. Mazagaon Dock	Mumbai
9. Goa Shipyard	Marmugao
10. Hindustan Shipyard Ltd.	Vishakhapatnam
11. Hindustan Aeronautics Ltd.	Bangalore, Hyderabad, Nasik, Koraput, Kanpur, Lucknow

☞ Indian Army Commands

Command	HQ Location	Command	HQ Location
Eastern Command	Kolkata	Western Command	Chandigarh
Northern Command	Udhampur	Southern Command	Pune
Central Command	Lucknow	Training Command	Shimla
South-Western Command	Jaipur		

☞ Indian Air Force Commands

Command	HQ Location	Command	HQ Location
Western Air Command	New Delhi	South-Western Air Command	Gandhinagar
Central Air Command	Prayagraj	Eastern Air Command	Shillong
Southern Air Command	Thiruvananthapuram	Training Command	Bengaluru

☞ Indian Navy Commands

Command	HQ Location	Command	HQ Location
Eastern Naval Command	Vishakhapatnam	Western Naval Command	Mumbai
Southern Naval Command	Kochi		

☞ Missile and Other Weapons

Name	Class	Range
✶ Agni I	SRBM	850 km
✶ Agni II	MRBM	2500 km
✶ Agni III	IRBM	3500 km-5500 km
✶ Agni IV *or* Agni II Prime	IRBM	4000 km
✶ Agni V	ICBM	5000 km-6000 km
✶ Agni VI	ICBM	8000 km-10000 km
✶ Agni 3SL	ICBM	5200 km-11600 km
✶ Dhanush	SRBM	350 km
✶ Nirbhay	Subsonic Cruise Missile	1000 km

Name	Class	Range
✶ Brahmos	Supersonic Cruise Missile	290 km
✶ Brahmos 2	Hypersonic Cruise Missile	290 km
✶ Prithvi I	SRBM	150 km
✶ Prithvi III	SRBM	350 km
✶ Sagarika	SLBM	700 km-2200 km
✶ Shaurya	TBM	700 km-2200 km
✶ Astra	Air to Air Missile	80 km-100 km
✶ Barak-I	SRSAM	12 km
✶ Barak-8	SRSAM	90 km

☞ Chief of Defence Staff (CDS)

To bring in reform in higher defence management in the country, the post of Chief of Defence Staff (CDS) was created in the rank of a four-star General with salary and prerequisites equivalent to a Service Chief. The Chief of Defence Staff will also head the Department of Military Affairs (DMA), to be created within the Ministry of Defence and functions as its Secretary. Gen. Bipin Rawat was the first CDS of the country from January 1, 2020 to December 08, 2021. Gen. Anil Chauhan assumed the charge of the second CDS on September 30, 2022.

MULTIPLE CHOICE QUESTIONS

1. Match List-I with List-II and select the correct answer from the codes given below the lists:

List-I

(*a*) Napoleon Bonaparte
(*b*) Jean Jacques Rousseau
(*c*) Croce
(*d*) Madame Roland

List-II

1. 'A history is contemporary history'
2. 'Liberty what crimes are committed in thy name'
3. 'Man is born free but everywhere he is in chains.'
4. 'I am the Child of Revolution'

Codes :

	(*a*)	(*b*)	(*c*)	(*d*)
A.	1	2	3	4
B.	4	3	1	2
C.	3	4	2	1
D.	3	4	1	2

2. Abraham Lincon was elected the President of United States in:
A. 1862 B. 1860
C. 1875 D. 1855

3. Who was known as the 'Prince of Humanists'?
A. Francisco Petrarch B. Dante
C. Boccacio D. Erasmus

4. D-Day is the day when:
A. Germany declared war on Britain
B. US dropped the atom bomb on Hiroshima.
C. Allied Troops landed in Normandy
D. Germany surrendered to the allies

5. Whose teachings inspired the French Revolution?
A. Locke
B. Rousseau
C. Hegel
D. Plato

6. At a time when empires in Europe were crumbling before the might of Napoleon which one of the following Governor-Generals kept the British flag flying high in India?
A. Warren Hastings B. Lord Cornwallis
C. Lord Wellesley D. Lord Hastings

7. Which one of the following statements regarding Fascism in Italy is *not* true?
A. The Fascists came to power as a result of popular uprising
B. In 1926, all political parties except Mussolini's party were banned
C. The Fascists suppressed the Socialist movement
D. The Fascists were hostile to the Communists

8. The fall of Czar Nicholas-II is known as:
A. Bloody Sunday
B. Bolshevik Revolution
C. February Revolution
D. October Revolution

9. Industrial Revolution took place first in:
A. France B. Germany
C. United Kingdom D. Japan

10. The British Prime Minister at the outbreak of World War II was :
A. Churchill B. Baldwin
C. Attlee D. Chemberlain

11. The 'Great Depression' (1929) economic crisis was met by adopting the policy of
A. Stimulus B. Marshall Plan
C. New Deal D. Open Door

12. The slogan "No taxation without representation" was raised during the:
A. American War of Independence
B. Russian Revolution
C. French Revolution
D. Indian Freedom struggle

13. In the nineteenth century the people of Europe started moving from the villages to the cities due to the impact of :
A. Epidemics
B. War
C. Industrialisation
D. Population explosion in villages

14. The important cause of the Civil War in America was:
A. Abolition of slavery
B. Quest for freedom
C. Industrialisation
D. Rebellion by the native Americans

15. Industrial Revolution could not have come about without:
A. Merchant capitalism
B. The Enclosure Movement
C. The services of the proletariat class
D. An agricultural revolution

16. Consider the following statements :
The French Revolution came about mainly due to the :
1. Extreme poverty of the people
2. Impact of the works of great writers
3. Cruelty of the rulers
4. Impact of impulsive reaction
Which of the above statements are correct?
A. 1, 2 and 4 B. 2 and 3
C. 1, 3 and 4 D. 1, 2, 3 and 4

17. Asia's oldest and largest Buddhist monastery is situated in :
A. Tawang (Arunachal Pardesh)
B. Lhasa (Tibet)
C. Trincomallee (Sri Lanka)
D. Ulan Bator (Mongolia)

18. Who was the main architect of the Russian Revolution?
A. Karl Marx B. Lenin
C. Stalin D. Tolstoy

19. V.I. Lenin is associated with :
A. Russian Revolution of 1917
B. Chinese Revolution of 1949
C. German Revolution
D. French Revolution of 1789

20. Which one of the following statements is *not* correct?
A. Voltaire believed in Natural Religion
B. Rousseau wrote *Social Contract*
C. Montesquieu authored *The Spirit of Laws*
D. Necker believed in 'General Will'

21. 6th April, 1930 is well known in the history of India because this date is associated with..........
A. Dandi March by Mahatma Gandhi
B. Quit India Movement
C. Partition of Bengal
D. Partition of India

22. Which ruler enforced the system of 'Price Control' in India?
A. Mohammad Tughlak
B. Razia Begum
C. Alauddin Khilji
D. Sher Shah Suri

23. The concept of 'Din-e-Elahi' was founded by which king?
A. Dara Shikoh B. Akbar
C. Sher Shah Suri D. Shahjahan

24. Who are supposed to be the earliest inhabitants of India? Where did they come from?
A. Aryans from Central Asia
B. Dravidians from Mediterranean
C. Negroids from Africa
D. Bhils and the Santhals from West Asia

25. The one chief characteristic of temple architecture of the Gupta Age was :
A. Absence of dome
B. Huge size
C. Beautiful carvings
D. absence of a covered courtyard for the gathering of worshippers

26. The Rigveda consists of :
A. 1000 hymns B. 2028 hymns
C. 1028 hymns D. 1038 hymns

27. The central point in Ashoka's dharma was :
A. royalty to kings
B. peace and non-violence
C. respect to elders
D. religious tolerance

28. The social evil which was conspicuously absent during ancient India was :

A. *Sati*-System B. *Devadasi*-System

C. Polygamy D. *Purdah*-System

29. Which, among the following, can be accepted as a novelty introduced by Mughal emperors to their buildings?

A. Domes B. Minarets

C. Arches D. Attached gardens

30. The first ruler of India who defeated Muhammud of Ghur was :

A. Mularaja II of Gujarat

B. Prithviraja Chauhan of Delhi

C. Jayachand of Kannauj

D. Parmaldeva of Bundelkhand

31. What important event happened in India in 1911?

A. Bengal was partitioned

B. Non-Cooperation movement was launched

C. India's capital was shifted from Calcutta to Delhi

D. Mahatma Gandhi presided over the Congress session

32. The first phase of the Congress Party (1885-1905) was characterized by its efforts to secure:

A. limited independence

B. complete freedom

C. Indianization of services

D. constitutional reforms

33. The Muslim League demanded a separate homeland for the Indian Muslims openly for the first time at its annual session held in Lahore in the year :

A. 1931 A.D. B. 1936 A.D.

C. 1940 A.D. D. 1941 A.D.

34. Under whose governorship did the East India Company secure the Diwani Rights in Bengal, Bihar and Odisha from Emperor Shah Alam?

A. Lord Cornwallis

B. Lord William Bentinck

C. Lord Clive

D. Lord Wellesley

35. The Simon Commission was generally boycotted by the Indian political parties. What was the reason for this general non-cooperation?

A. the Commission aimed at dividing the people

B. it was an 'all white' Commission

C. it came after the Jallianwala Bagh carnage

D. it was an eye wash

36. Aligarh Muslim University was founded by :

A. Dr. Saifuddin Kitchlu

B. Mohammad Ali Jinnah

C. Sir Syed Ahmed Khan

D. Maulana Mohammad Ali

37. Ibn Batutah was an African traveller visiting India during the time of :

A. Alivardi Khan

B. Ala-ud-din Khalji

C. Iltutmish

D. Mohammad-bin-Tughlaq

38. The battle of Wandiawash was fought in :

A. 1726 B. 1760

C. 1818 D. 1857

39. The abolition of *Sati* by government regulation was at the time of :

A. Warren Hastings B. Lord Wellesley

C. Lord Bentinck D. Lord Ahmerst

40. Pick out the wrong combination :

A. Dilwara Temple : Mt. Abu

B. Pashupati Temple : Kathmandu

C. Padmanabh Temple : Bangalore

D. Minakshi Temple : Madurai

41. Match the following:

(*a*) Chanhudaro (*b*) Kalibangan

(*c*) Lothal (*d*) Surkotada

1. Alleged discovery of the skeleton of horse.
2. Bead making.
3. Traces of a dock and ship on seal.
4. Evidence of ploughing the fields.

The Correct code is :

	(*a*)	(*b*)	(*c*)	(*d*)
A.	2	4	3	1
B.	2	1	3	4
C.	1	2	3	4
D.	2	1	4	3

42. Match the Harappan settlements with the banks of rivers on which they were located :

(*a*) Harappa	1. Ravi
(*b*) Mohenjodaro	2. Indus
(*c*) Ropar	3. Sutlej
(*d*) Kalibangan	4. Ghaggar
(*e*) Lothal	5. Bhogava

Codes :

	(*a*)	(*b*)	(*c*)	(*d*)	(*e*)
A.	1	2	3	4	5
B.	1	2	3	5	4
C.	2	1	3	5	4
D.	2	1	4	3	5

43. The Goddess 'Kannagi' whose many temples were erected during the 'Sangam Age' was the goddess of :

A. Chastity B. Love
C. Prowess D. Wisdom

44. The Jain goal of life is to attain deliverance from the fetters of mudane existence, the way to which lies through three jewels. Which one of the following was not included among the 'three jewels' of Jainism?

A. Right faith B. Right action
C. Right knowledge D. Right conduct

45. The most striking feature of the Ashokan pillar is polish. Name the Ashokan pillar which is considered to be the most graceful of all Ashokan pillars.

A. Sarnath
B. Rampurva
C. Laurya-Nandangarh
D. Rummindei

46. Which are the correct statements?

1. The land grants, started in Satavahana period, paved the way for feudal developments in India.
2. Silk and spices were the Chief Indian export articles of Indo-Roman trade.
3. The Guptas issued the largest number of gold coins in ancient India.
4. The first memorial of a 'SATI' dated 510 A.D. is found at Eran in Madhya Pradesh.

A. 1 and 2 B. 1, 3, and 4
C. 1 and 4 D. 1, 2, 3 and 4

47. Who among the following patronised the 'Gandhara' (Indo-Greek style) School of Art?

A. Ashoka, the Great
B. Harsha Vardhana
C. Kanishka
D. Chandragupta Vikramaditya

48. The Sultanate of Delhi had five ruling dynasties. The dynasty having longest and shortest period were :

A. Ilbari and Khalji
B. Tughlaq and Khalji
C. Tughlaq and Sayyid
D. Ilbari and Lodis

49. Which one of the following events took place at the last during reign of Muhammad-bin-Tughlaq?

A. Introduction of token currency
B. Increase of land-revenue in Doab
C. Transfer of Capital from Delhi to Devagiri.
D. Conquest of Khurasan and Iraq

50. The most learned medieval Muslim ruler who was well versed in various branches of learning including astronomy, mathematics and medicine was :

A. Jalaluddin Khilji
B. Sikander Lodi
C. Ghiyasuddin Tughlaq
D. Muhammad-bin-Tughlaq

51. The 'Sufis' had 12 silsilas. They propounded the idea of Union with God through:

A. Love B. Rituals
C. Fasts D. Prayers

52. Match the following:

(*a*) Peshwa	1. Foreign affairs
(*b*) Panditrao	2. Audit and accounts
(*c*) Amatya	3. Providing grants to scholars
(*d*) Sumant	4. General supervision
	5. Military affairs

Select the correct code :

	(*a*)	(*b*)	(*c*)	(*d*)
A.	2	3	4	5
B.	4	1	2	3
C.	4	3	2	1
D.	3	1	4	2

53. The Regulating Act of 1773 can be regarded as the first measure to :
A. assert the right of British Parliament to legislate for India
B. separate the legislature from the executive
C. separate the judiciary from the executive
D. centralise law-making

54. What was the exact constitutional status of the Indian Republic on 26th January, 1950?
A. A Democratic Republic
B. A Sovereign, Democratic Republic
C. A Sovereign, Secular, Democratic Republic
D. A Sovereign, Socialist, Secular, Democratic Republic

55. When the British obtained the grant of Diwani of Bengal, Bihar and Odisha they acquired the right to :
A. maintain law and order in these territories
B. administer civil justice and collect revenue in these territories
C. collect revenue and establish revenue administration in these territories
D. militarily defend these territories

56. Which of the following were responsible for the growth of nationalism in India during the British rule?
1. Economic exploitation of India.
2. Impact of western education.
3. Role of the Press.
Select the correct answer using the codes given below :
Codes:
A. 1, 2 and 3 B. 1 and 2
C. 2 and 3 D. 1 and 3

57. Which one of the following nationalist leaders has been described as being radical in politics but conservative on social issues?
A. G.K. Gokhale
B. B.G. Tilak
C. Lala Lajpat Rai
D. Madan Mohan Malviya

58. Provincial Autonomy in British India was envisaged by the :
A. Act of 1909 B. Act of 1919
C. Act of 1935 D. Act of 1947

59. Dyarchy means :
A. double government
B. a government in which the centre is very powerful
C. a government based on division of power between centre and provinces
D. None of the above

60. The Indian National Congress observed 'Independence Day' for the first time on 26th January in :
A. 1920 B. 1925
C. 1930 D. 1947

61. ....is situated near the banks of Sabarmati River
A. Bhavnagar B. Aurangabad
C. Ahmedabad D. Rajkot

62. Sericulture is:
A. science of the various kinds of serum
B. artificial rearing of fish
C. art of silkworm breeding
D. study of various cultures of a community

63. The most abundant constituents of earth's crust are:
A. Igneous rocks
B. Sedimentary rocks
C. Metamorphic rocks
D. Granite

64. Indian Standard Time is based on:
A. 80°E longitude B. 82½°E longitude
C. 110°E longitude D. 25°E longitude

65. Tides in the oceans are caused by :
A. Gravitational pull of the moon on the earth's surface including sea water
B. Gravitational pull of the sun on the earth's surface only and not on the sea water
C. Gravitational pull of the moon and the sun on the earth's surface including the sea water
D. None of these

66. Nagarjunasagar Project is situated on the river:
A. Tungabhadra
B. Cauvery
C. Krishna
D. Godavari

67. The difference between the Indian Standard Time and the Greenwich Mean Time is:
A. – 3½ hours B. + 3½ hours
C. – 5½ hours D. + 5½ hours

68. Which of the following dams is not on Narmada river?
A. Indira-Sagar Project
B. Maheshwar Hydel Power Project
C. Jobat Project
D. Koyna Power Project

69. Which of the following statements is **not true** about the availability of water on the earth, the crisis for which is going to increase in the years to come?
A. About 97.5 per cent of the total volume of water available on the earth is salty
B. 80 per cent of the water available to us for use comes in bursts as monsoons
C. About 2.5 per cent of the total water available on the earth is polluted water and cannot be used for human activities
D. Possibility is that some big glaciers will melt in the coming ten-fifteen years and sea level will rise by 3-4 metres all over the earth

70. Which of the following is **not** a cash crop?
A. Jute B. Paddy
C. Cashewnut D. Sugarcane

71. Through which States does Cauvery River flow?
A. Gujarat, M.P., Tamil Nadu
B. Karnataka, Kerala, Tamil Nadu
C. Karnataka, Kerala, Andhra Pradesh
D. M.P., Maharashtra, Tamil Nadu

72. Indian Standard Time is the local time of 82½°E which passes through :
A. Guntur B. Delhi
C. Allahabad D. Kolkata

73. The 17th parallel defines the boundary between:
A. North and South Korea
B. USA and Canada
C. North and South Vietnam
D. China and Russia

74. During the period of south-west monsoon, Tamil Nadu remains dry because:
A. the winds do not reach this area
B. there are no mountains in this area
C. it lies in the rain shadow area
D. the temperature is too high to let the winds cool down

75. Which country does top in producing cocoa?
A. Cote d'Ivoire B. Brazil
C. Croatia D. Nigeria

76. The biggest reserves of thorium are in :
A. India B. China
C. The Soviet Union D. U.S.A.

77. The Girnar Hills are situated in which of the following states?
A. Gujarat B. Karnataka
C. Madhya Pradesh D. Maharashtra

78. During December 22nd the sun is vertically over:
A. Tropic of Cancer
B. Tropic of Capricorn
C. The Equator
D. None of the above

79. Photosphere is described as the :
A. Lower layer of atmosphere
B. Visible surface of the sun from which radiation emanates
C. Wavelength of solar spectrum
D. None of the above

80. Broadly, there are three layers of the earth of the crust, the mantle and the core. The crust forms what percentage of the volume of the earth?
A. 0.5% B. 2.5%
C. 7.5% D. 12.5%

81. The grassland of Argentina is known as :
A. Pampas B. Campos
C. Savanna D. None of the above

82. Different seasons are formed because :
A. Sun is moving around the earth
B. of revolution of the earth around the Sun on its orbit
C. of rotation of the earth around its axis
D. All of the above

83. Eskers and Drumlins are features formed by:
A. underground water
B. running water
C. the action of wind
D. glacial action

84. Match List-I and List-II and select the correct answer using the codes given below the Lists :

List-I *(Rivers)*	**List-II** *(Towns)*
(*a*) Ghaghara	1. Lucknow
(*b*) Brahmaputra	2. Hoshangabad
(*c*) Narmada	3. Ahmedabad
(*d*) Sabarmati	4. Guwahati
	5. Ayodhya

	(*a*)	(*b*)	(*c*)	(*d*)
A.	4	5	1	2
B.	5	4	2	3
C.	5	4	3	1
D.	3	5	2	1

85. Which of the statements as regards the consequences of the movement of the earth is not correct?
A. Revolution of the earth is the cause of the change of seasons.
B. Rotation of the earth is the cause of days and nights.
C. Rotation of the earth causes variation in the duration of days and nights.
D. Rotation of the earth effects the movement of winds and ocean currents.

86. The world is divided into :
A. 12 time zones
B. 20 time zones
C. 24 time zones
D. 36 time zones

87. The 'Kiel' canal links the :
A. Pacific and Atlantic Oceans
B. Mediterranean Sea and Red Sea
C. Mediterranean Sea and Black Sea
D. North Sea and Baltic Sea

88. Match the following :

List-I	**List-II**
(*a*) Himadri	1. Outer Himalayas
(*b*) Shivalik	2. Inner Himalayas
(*c*) Himanchal	3. Middle Himalayas
(*d*) Sahyadri	4. Western Ghats

Codes:

	(*a*)	(*b*)	(*c*)	(*d*)
A.	1	2	3	4
B.	4	2	3	1
C.	2	1	3	4
D.	1	2	3	4

89. The term 'Regur' refers to:
A. Laterite soils
B. Black Cotton soils
C. Red Soils
D. Deltaic Alluvial Soils

90. Location of sugar industry in India is shifting from north to south because of:
A. cheap labour
B. expanding regional market
C. cheap and abundant supply of power
D. high yield and high sugar content in sugarcane

91. Consider the following statements :
1. Ozone is found mostly in the Stratosphere.
2. Ozone layer lies 55-75 km above the surface of the earth.
3. Ozone absorbs ultraviolet radiation from the Sun.
4. Ozone layer has no significance for life on the earth.

Which of the above statements are correct?
A. 1 and 3 B. 2 and 4
C. 2 and 3 D. 1 and 4

92. Match List-I with List-II and select the correct answer using the codes given below the Lists :

List-I *(Crops)*	**List-II** *(Producer)*
(*a*) Banana	1. Brazil
(*b*) Cocoa	2. Cote d'Ivoire
(*c*) Coffee	3. India
(*d*) Tea	4. China

Codes :

	(*a*)	(*b*)	(*c*)	(*d*)
A.	2	3	1	4
B.	3	2	1	4
C.	3	2	4	1
D.	2	3	4	1

93. Darjeeling and Dharamsala would be the right places to visit if one wanted to get a clear view respectively of :
A. Kanchanjunga and Dhauladhar ranges
B. Nandadevi and Dhauladhar ranges
C. Kanchanjunga and Nandadevi ranges
D. Nandadevi and Nanga Parvat

94. Atmosphere exists because:
A. The Gravitational force of the Earth
B. Revolution of the Earth
C. Rotation of the Earth
D. Weight of the gases of atmosphere

95. Victoria lake is located in the continent:
A. Africa
B. Asia
C. North America
D. South America

96. The famous Lagoon Lake of India is :
A. Dal Lake B. Chilka Lake
C. Pulicat Lake D. Mansarover

97. Where are most of the earth's active volcanoes concentrated?
A. Indian Ocean B. Pacific Ocean
C. Aral Sea D. Atlantic Ocean

98. Through which of the following states does the river Chambal flow?
A. U.P., M.P., Rajasthan
B. M.P., Gujarat, U.P.
C. Rajasthan, M.P., Bihar
D. Gujarat, M.P., U.P.

99. Which country is called the sugar bowl of the world?
A. Cuba B. India
C. Argentina D. USA

100. The area covered by forest in India is about:
A. 46% B. 33%
C. 23% D. 21.76%

101. A closed economy is the one which :
A. does not permit emigration or immigration
B. permits emigration but no immigration
C. engages in no foreign trade
D. engages in no foreign and domestic trade or transit

102. In a developed economy the major share of employment originates in the :
A. primary sector B. tertiary sector
C. secondary sector D. any of the above

103. The Economic and Social Commission for Asia and Pacific (ESCAP) is located at :
A. Bangkok B. Kuala Lumpur
C. Manila D. Singapore

104. Commercial vehicles are not produced by which of the following companies in India?
A. TELCO B. Ashok Leyland
C. DCM Daewoo D. Birla Yamaha

105. In India, the Public Sector is most dominant in:
A. transport
B. steel production
C. commercial banking
D. organised term-lending financial institutions

106. The main argument advanced in favour of small scale and cottage industries in India is that:
A. cost of production is low
B. they require small capital investment
C. they advance the goal of equitable distribution of wealth
D. they generate a large volume of employment

107. The most serious economic problems of India are:
A. Poverty and unemployment
B. Stagnation, not poverty
C. Unemployment, not poverty
D. Underdevelopment, not poverty

108. Which of the following is not one of the three central problems of an economy?
A. What to produce
B. How to produce
C. When to produce
D. For whom to produce

109. If saving exceeds investment, the national income will:
A. fall B. rise
C. fluctuate D. remain constant

110. In which of the following industries in India are the maximum number of workers employed?
A. Sugar B. Jute
C. Textiles D. Iron and Steel

111. Terrace Cultivation is practiced mostly:
A. in urban areas
B. on slopes of mountains
C. on tops of hills
D. in undulating tracts

112. Which of the following is a Selective Credit Control method?
A. Bank Rate
B. RBI directives
C. Cash Reserve Ratio
D. Open market operations

113. Which of the following taxes is not shared by the Central Government with the States?
A. Union excise duties
B. Customs duty
C. Income tax
D. Estate duty

114. ICICI is the name of a:
A. Financial Institution
B. Chemical Industry
C. Cotton Industry
D. Chamber of Commerce and Industry

115. Structural Unemployment arises due to
A. Deflationary conditions
B. Heavy industry bias
C. Shortage of raw material
D. Inadequate productive capacity

116. Which Commission replaced the Planning Commission in 2015?
A. NIYAM Aayog
B. NAGRIK Aayog
C. NITI Aayog
D. Jan Aayog

117. The largest public sector bank in India is:
A. Central Bank of India
B. Punjab National Bank
C. State Bank of India
D. Indian Overseas Bank

118. Which of the following statements best explains the term contraband goods?
A. Goods produced only for exports
B. Goods produced in joint sector only
C. Goods for the trading of which licence is not required
D. Goods that are forbidden, from export, import or even possession, by law

119. Price in the market is fixed by:
A. Stock exchange rates
B. The demand and supply ruling in the market at a particular time
C. The Finance Minister
D. None of the above

120. Devaluation of currency helps to promote:
A. National Income
B. Savings
C. Imports at lower cost
D. Exports

121. Balanced economic growth can be achieved only if:
A. All the sectors of economy grow at the same rate
B. Population growth is arrested
C. All the inter dependent sectors grow in harmony
D. Basic and heavy industries are assigned highest priority

122. P.V. Sindhu is associated with which of the following sports?
A. Badminton
B. Weightlifting
C. Swimming
D. Tennis

123. 'MODVAT' stands for:
A. Modified Value Added Tax
B. Deduction of cost of inputs from the value of output
C. Reduction in import duties
D. Imposition of tax on professions

124. Who among the following is the first to receive 'Dada Saheb Phalke' award?
A. Shivaji Ganeson B. Devika Rani
C. Dr. Raj Kumar D. None of the above

125. The term 'devaluation' means:
A. Reducing the value of a currency in terms of another currency
B. Increasing the value of a currency
C. Revising the value of a currency
D. None of the above

126. Per capita net availability of pulses has shown a tendency of:
A. Increase over time
B. Decrease over time
C. Constant over time
D. First increase then decrease

127. National Income is the same as:
A. Net national product at market price
B. Net domestic product at market price
C. Net national product at factor cost
D. Net domestic product at factor cost

128. Which one of the following is not an example of indirect tax?
A. Sales tax B. Excise duty
C. Customs duty D. Expenditure tax

129. The major aim of devaluation is to:
A. encourage imports
B. encourage exports
C. encourage both exports and imports
D. discourage both exports and imports

130. Structural unemployment arises due to:
A. deflationary conditions
B. heavy industry bias
C. shortage of raw materials
D. inadequate productive capacity

131. When was the Family Planning Programme officially started in India?
A. 1950 B. 1952
C. 1956 D. 1962

132. When was the Reserve Bank of India nationalised?
A. 1947 B. 1949
C. 1950 D. 1951

133. Which of the following is *not* a feature of the Indian economy?
A. High rate of population growth
B. Disguised unemployment
C. Lowest rate of adult literacy
D. High rate of exports

134. The 'Relative Deprivation' approach for measuring poverty has been adopted by:
A. developing countries
B. developed countries
C. under-developed countries
D. None of the above

135. One of the main factors that led to rapid expansion of Indian exports is:
A. Imposition of import duties
B. Liberalisation of the economy
C. Recession in other countries
D. Diversification of exports

136. Sustainable economic development means an increase in the rate of growth of real:
A. total and per capita product
B. total and per capita product and level of literacy rate
C. total and per capita product and life expectancy at birth
D. total and per capita product, taking into account the cost of degradation of the quality of environment in this process

137. Functional unemployment occurs when:
A. unemployed have no qualification for job
B. people frequently change their job
C. people were thrown out from job due to recession
D. None of these

138. Which among the following does **not** have a 'free trade zone'?
A. Kandla B. Mumbai
C. Visakhapatnam D. Thiruvanantpuram

139. Sun Belt of USA is important for which one of the following industries?
A. Cotton textile
B. Petrochemicals
C. Hi-tech electronics
D. Food Processing

140. Commercial banking system in India is
A. unit banking B. branch banking
C. mixed banking D. None of the above

141. Who gives recognition to political parties in India?
A. Parliament

B. President
C. Supreme Court
D. Election Commission

142. The Quorum of the Legislative Council is :
A. one-fourth of its total membership
B. one-third of its membership
C. one-tenth of its membership
D. 25

143. The Indian Constitution is:
A. federal
B. unitary
C. a happy mixture of the federal and unitary
D. federal in normal times and unitary in times of emergency

144. Universal adult franchise implies a right to vote to all:
A. adult residents of the State
B. adult male citizens of the State
C. residents of the State
D. adult citizens of the State

145. When a resolution prefering a charge against the President has been passed by a specified majority in the House, it is sent to the other House for investigation. If, as a result of such an investigation, a resolution is passed through a specified majority by the other House, declaring that the charge has been sustained, the President shall leave his office. The specified special majority must not be less than :
A. two-third of the members present and voting
B. one-third of the members present and voting
C. three-fourth of the members present and voting and two-third of the total membership
D. two-third of the total membership

146. Which one of the following judicial powers of the President of India has been *wrongly* listed?
A. he appoints the Chief Justice and other judges of the Supreme Court
B. he can remove the judges of the Supreme Court on grounds of misconduct
C. he can consult the Supreme Court on any question of law or fact which is of public importance
D. he can grant pardon, reprieves and respites to persons punished under Union Law

147. The Vice-president of India can be removed from his office before the expiry of his term if :
A. the Rajya Sabha passes a resolution by a majority of its members and the Lok Sabha agrees with the resolution
B. if the Supreme Court of India recommends his removal
C. the President so desires
D. None of the above

148. The Chief Justice of a High Court in India is appointed by the :
A. Governor of the State
B. Prime Minister of India
C. Chief Justice of the Supreme Court
D. President of India

149. Which of the following statements is constitutionally not true about the passing of the Union Budgets, Railway Budgets and Finance Bill in India?
1. Under the law, Finance Bill should be adopted by both the Houses of the Parliament within 45 days of its introduction.
2. If the Finance Bill is not adopted within specified period, the government loses its authority to levy the taxes proposed in the budgets.
3. In the absence of full budget, a vote-on-account gives the power to the government to spend.
4. Government cannot raise revenues without a proper approval of the Finance Bill

A. Only 2　　B. Only 3
C. Only 4　　D. Only 1, 2 and 3

150. Normally, on whose advice the President's Rule is imposed in a State?
A. Chief Minister
B. Legislative Assembly
C. Governor
D. Chief Justice of High Court

151. Which Article of the Indian Constitution deals with Amendment procedure?
A. Article 368 B. Article 358
C. Article 367 D. All of these

152. Government is the agency through which the will of :
A. the state is expressed
B. the people is expressed
C. the head of the state is expressed
D. the majority is expressed

153. In a unitary system of government :
A. The centre is all powerful
B. The centre is weaker than the states
C. The centre and states stand at par
D. The states and centre are supreme in their respective spheres

154. In Cabinet System of Government the real executive authority rests with :
A. The Council of Ministers
B. The Prime Minister
C. The Constitution
D. The Parliament

155. The Head of the State under a parliamentary government:
A. is an elected representative
B. is a hereditary person
C. is a nominated person
D. may be any one of the above

156. In the event of a ministerial proposal being defeated on the floor of the legislature, under the parliamentary system :
A. the government waits for a general no-confidence motion
B. the minister concerned is taken to task by the Prime Minister
C. the minister is forced to resign
D. the whole Council of Ministers resign

157. The "due process of law" is an essential characteristic of the judicial system of:
A. UK B. France
C. USA D. India

158. Under the Constitution it is :
A. obligatory for the President to accept the advice of the Council of Ministers but is not obliged to follow it
B. obligatory for the President to accept the advice of the Council of Ministers
C. not obligatory for the President to seek or accept the advice of the Council of Ministers
D. obligatory for the President to seek the advice of the Council of Ministers if his own party is in power

159. Which one of the following statements is correct?
A. the Presiding Officer of Rajya Sabha is elected every year
B. the Presiding Officer of Rajya Sabha is elected for a term of two years at a time
C. the Presiding Officer of Rajya Sabha is elected for a term of six years
D. the Vice-President of India is the ex-officio Presiding Officer of Rajya Sabha

160. The introduction of "no confidence" motion in the Lok Sabha requires the support of at least:
A. 50 members B. 70 members
C. 60 members D. 80 members

161. The High Court comes under :
A. State List B. Union List
C. Concurrent List D. None of the above

162. Which one of the following has been wrongly listed as a Fundamental Duty of the Indian citizens?
A. to develop scientific temper, humanism and spirit of inquiry and reform
B. to work for raising the prestige of the country in the international sphere
C. to protect and improve the natural environment
D. to strive towards excellence in all spheres of individual and collective activity

163. Which one of the following is not a Fundamental Duty as outlined in Article 51A of the Constitution?
A. to abide by the Constitution and respect its ideals
B. to defend the country and render national service when called upon to do so

C. to work for the moral upliftment of the weaker sections of society
D. to preserve the rich heritage

164. The main characteristics of the Directive Principles of State Policy given in the Indian Constitution are :
A. not enforceable by any court
B. fundamental in the governance of the country
C. 'Like instruments, instructions, political manifesto and a code of moral precepts which have to guide governors of the country'
D. no law can be passed, which is opposed to these principles

165. Of the following which are true?
A. In a State, the Legislative Council is dominant with regard to non-financial bills and the Legislative Assembly with regard to financial (money) bills
B. Vidhan Parishad can virtually block legisla-tion even if the same is passed by the Vidhan Sabha
C. In case of a tie between the two Houses, the Governor is duty-bound to call a joint session of the two Houses to have the issue settled on a majority verdict
D. If a Bill is twice approved by the Vidhan Sabha, it becomes law even if rejected by the Vidhan Parishad

166. Which one of the following types of emergency can be declared by the President?
A. Emergency due to threat of war and external aggresion
B. Emergency due to break-down of constitu-tional machinery in a State
C. Financial emergency on account of threat to the financial credit of India
D. all the three emergencies

167. The chairman of which of the following parliamentary committees is invariably from the members of ruling party?
A. Committee on public undertakings
B. Public accounts committee
C. Estimates committee
D. Committee on delegated legislation

168. Which of the following is not a formally prescribed device available to the members of parliament?
A. Question hour
B. Zero hour
C. Half-an-hour discussion
D. Short duration discussion

169. Which of the following is not a tool of executive control over public administration?
A. Power of appointment and removal
B. Line agencies
C. Appeal to public opinion
D. Civil services code

170. If the Speaker of the State Legislative Assembly decides to resign, he should submit his resignation to the:
A. Judges of the High Court
B. Deputy Speaker
C. Chief Minister
D. Finance Minister

171. Who was the first Home Minister of Independent India?
A. Rajendra Prasad
B. Jawahar Lal Nehru
C. B.R. Ambedkar
D. Sardar Vallabh Bhai Patel

172. India is a Federal State because of:
A. dual judiciary
B. dual citizenship prevalent here
C. share of power between the Centre and the States
D. rigid Constitution

173. Residuary Subjects are those subjects which are:
A. contained in the State list
B. contained in the Union list
C. contained in the Concurrent list
D. not covered by any of the three lists

174. Which of the following writs can be issued, by the Supreme Court, to enforce Fundamental Rights?
A. Writ of Habeas Corpus
B. Writ of Mandamus
C. Writ of Quo Warranto
D. All of these

175. When the offices of both the President and the Vice-President of India are vacant, who will discharge their functions?
A. Prime Minister
B. Home Minister
C. Chief Justice of India
D. The Speaker

176. The Supreme Court tenders advice to the President of India on a matter of law or fact:
A. on its own
B. only when such advice is sought
C. only if the matter relates to some basic issue
D. only if the issue poses a threat to the unity and integrity of the country

177. Six months shall **not** intervene between two sessions of the Indian Parliament because :
A. it is the customary practice
B. it is the British convention followed in India
C. it is an obligation under the Constitution of India
D. None of the above

178. The States of the Indian Union can be recognised or their boundaries altered by:
A. the Union Parliament by a simple majority in the ordinary process of legislation
B. two-thirds majority of both the Houses of Parliament
C. two-thirds majority of both the Houses of Parliament and the consent of the legislatures of concerned States
D. an executive order of the Union government with the consent of the concerned State governments

179. The Basic Feature theory of the Constitution of India was propounded by the Supreme Court in the case of :
A. Minerva Mills Vs. Union of India
B. Golaknath Vs. State of Punjab
C. Maneka Gandhi Vs. Union of India
D. Keshavananda Vs. State of Kerala

180. Which one of the following writs is issued by a court in case of illegal detention of a person?
A. Habeas corpus B. Mandamus
C. Certiorari D. Quo-warranto

181. Name the instrument with the help of which a sailor in a submarine can see the objects on the surface of the sea.
A. Telescope B. Periscope
C. Gycroscope D. Stereoscope

182. 'HEMOPHILLIA' is the disease of ....
A. liver B. blood
C. brain D. bones

183. Vitamin A is abundantly found in ....
A. Brinjal B. Tomato
C. Carrot D. Cabbage

184. .... is not soluble in water.
A. Vitamin A B. Vitamin B
C. Vitamin C D. None of these

185. The blood vessels with the smallest diameter are called ....
A. capillaries B. arterioles
C. venules D. lymphatics

186. Out of the following .... has the greatest elasticity.
A. steel B. rubber
C. aluminium D. annealed copper

187. Cooking gas is a mixture of which of the following two gases?
A. Carbon Dioxide and Oxygen
B. Butane and Propane
C. Carbon Monoxide and Carbon Dioxide
D. Methane and Ethylene

188. The substance most commonly used as a food preservative is:
A. sodium carbonate B. tartaric acid
C. acetic acid D. benzoic acid

189. Normally, the substances that fight against diseases in human systems are known as:
A. dioxyribonucleic acids
B. carbohydrates
C. enzymes
D. antibodies

190. The SI unit of temperature is ....
A. Kelvin B. Celsius
C. Fahrenheit D. None of the above

191. One of the common fungal diseases of man is :
A. plague B. ringworm
C. cholera D. typhoid

192. A clear sky is blue because:
A. red light is scattered more than blue
B. ultraviolet light has been absorbed
C. blue light is scattered more than red
D. blue light has been absorbed

193. Jenner introduced the method of making people immune to :
A. small pox B. rabies
C. cholera D. polio

194. The largest cell in the human body is :
A. Nerve cell B. Live cell
C. Muscle cell D. Kidney cell

195. What is the device that steps up or steps down the voltage?
A. Dynamo B. Conductor
C. Inductor D. Transformer

196. The protein deficiency disease is known as :
A. Kwashiorker B. Cirrhosis
C. Eczema D. Clycoses

197. Iron deficiency causes :
A. rickets B. anaemia
C. cirrhosis D. goitre

198. Blood group of an individual is controlled by :
A. Haemoglobin B. Shape of RBC
C. Shape of WBC D. Genes

199. In a normal man the amount of blood pumped out by the heart per minute is about :
A. 1 litre B. 3 litres
C. 4 litres D. 5 litres

200. Red/green colour blindness in man is known as :
A. Protanopia
B. Deutetanopia
C. Both A and B above
D. Marfan's syndrome

201. The blue colour of the water in the sea is due to :
A. Reflection of the blue light by the impurities in sea water
B. Reflection of the blue sky by sea water and scattering of blue light by water molecules
C. Absorption of other colours by water molecules
D. None of the above

202. The image formed on the retina of the eye is:
A. upright and real
B. larger than the object
C. small and inverted
D. enlarged and real

203. Unit of loudness of sound is:
A. bel B. decibel
C. phon D. none of these

204. Oil rises up the wick in a lamp :
A. because oil is volatile
B. due to the capillary action phenomenon
C. due to the surface tension phenomenon
D. because oil is very light

205. The 'stones' formed in human kidney consist mostly of :
A. calcium oxalate
B. sodium acetate
C. magnesium sulphate
D. calcium

206. We hear the sound later, while the light is seen earlier:
A. because light's speed is more than that of sound
B. because lights travel in a straight direction while sound in a zigzag direction
C. because sound's frequency is lower than light
D. All of the above

207. Which part of an eye is transplanted?
A. Cornea B. Retina
C. Iris D. Sciera

208. The Universal donor group of blood is:
A. O B. A
C. B D. AB

209. The green colour of the leaf is due to :
A. Presence of Chloroplast
B. Presence of Chromium
C. Presence of Nicoplast
D. Presence of excess of oxygen

210. Voice of a child is more shrill than that of an elderly person because:
A. the pitch of the child's voice is higher than that of the person
B. the pitch is lower
C. the child is more energetic
D. None of the above

ANSWERS

1	2	3	4	5	6	7	8	9	10
B	C	D	C	B	C	A	C	C	D
11	12	13	14	15	16	17	18	19	20
C	A	C	A	A	D	A	B	A	D
21	22	23	24	25	26	27	28	29	30
A	C	B	C	D	C	B	D	D	B
31	32	33	34	35	36	37	38	39	40
C	D	C	C	B	C	D	B	C	C
41	42	43	44	45	46	47	48	49	50
A	A	A	B	C	D	C	B	B	D
51	52	53	54	55	56	57	58	59	60
A	C	A	B	B	A	B	C	A	C
61	62	63	64	65	66	67	68	69	70
C	C	B	B	C	C	D	D	D	B
71	72	73	74	75	76	77	78	79	80
B	C	C	C	A	A	A	B	B	A
81	82	83	84	85	86	87	88	89	90
A	B	D	B	C	C	D	C	B	D
91	92	93	94	95	96	97	98	99	100
A	B	A	A	A	B	B	A	A	D
101	102	103	104	105	106	107	108	109	110
C	B	A	D	D	D	A	C	D	C
111	112	113	114	115	116	117	118	119	120
B	B	B	A	D	C	C	D	B	D
121	122	123	124	125	126	127	128	129	130
C	A	A	B	A	D	C	D	B	D
131	132	133	134	135	136	137	138	139	140
B	B	D	A	B	D	B	D	D	C
141	142	143	144	145	146	147	148	149	150
D	C	D	D	D	B	A	D	C	C
151	152	153	154	155	156	157	158	159	160
A	B	A	A	A	D	C	B	D	A
161	162	163	164	165	166	167	168	169	170
B	B	C	B	D	D	C	B	B	B
171	172	173	174	175	176	177	178	179	180
D	C	D	D	C	B	C	A	D	A
181	182	183	184	185	186	187	188	189	190
B	B	C	A	A	A	B	D	D	A
191	192	193	194	195	196	197	198	199	200
B	C	A	A	D	A	B	D	D	A
201	202	203	204	205	206	207	208	209	210
B	B	B	B	A	A	A	A	A	A